Richenda Miers

SCOTLAND

'...fast-flowing rivers slice through
steep mountain glens, with
sudden glimpses of snow-capped peaks
massing on the horizon...'

CADOGANguides

Contents

About the author

Richenda Miers is a novelist, freelance journalist and travel writer. Part English and part Scottish, she divides her time between the two countries, and has spent many years living north of the border. She has many ties to the country she loves: her husband served in a Highland regiment; her son was born in Inverness; two of her daughters went to school in Aberdeen; and two of her children studied at Scottish universities. The Miers family shares a home in the Outer Hebrides.

This book is for my husband, Douglas, with love. It is also for Monty Alexander Charles who, like a perfect gentleman, allowed his mother Catherine to finish editing before making his entrance into the world. May he prosper.

Cadogan Guides
Network House, 1 Ariel Way, London W12 7SL
cadoganguides@morrispub.co.uk
www.cadoganguides.com

The Globe Pequot Press
246 Goose Lane, PO Box 480, Guilford,
Connecticut 06437–0480

Copyright © Richenda Miers 1987, 1989, 1991,
1994, 1998, 2002

Cover and photo essay design by Kicca Tommasi
Book design by Andrew Barker
Cover photographs: Olivia Rutherford
Maps © Cadogan Guides, drawn by Map Creation
Ltd. This product includes mapping data
licensed from Ordnance Survey® with the
permission of the Controller of Her Majesty's
Stationery Office. © Crown copyright 2002. All
rights reserved. Licence number 100037865.
Editorial Director: Vicki Ingle
Series Editor: Christine Stroyan
Editors: Catherine Charles and Georgina Palffy
Art direction: Jodi Louw
Proofreading: Susannah Wight
Indexing: Judith Wardman
Production: Book Production Services

Printed in Italy by Legoprint
A catalogue record for this book is available
from the British Library
ISBN 1-86011-866-6

The author and publishers have made every effort to ensure the accuracy of the information in this book at the time of going to press. However, they cannot accept any responsibility for any loss, injury or inconvenience resulting from the use of information contained in this guide.

Please help us to keep this guide up to date. We have done our best to ensure that the information in this guide is correct at the time of going to press. But places and facilities are constantly changing, and standards and prices in hotels and restaurants fluctuate. We would be delighted to receive any comments concerning existing entries or omissions. Authors of the best letters will receive a copy of the Cadogan Guide of their choice.

Scotland
a photo essay

by Olivia Rutherford

01

Old Man of Storr, Skye

Machrie Standing Stones, Arran

Celtic cross cathedral, St Andrews

Blackwaterfoot, Arran

fishing boats lobster creels

ruined church, Skye

Tobermory, Mull

seals

Aberdeen harbour

'Chariots of Fire' sands, St Andrews

Clyde River, Glasgow

Glenfinnan Viaduct

Plockton bridge

Rosslyn Chapel

Scott Monument, Edinburgh

Urquhart Castle

Introduction

O Caledonia! stern and wild,
Meet nurse for a poetic child!
Land of brown heath and shaggy wood,
Land of the mountain and the flood,
Land of my sires! what mortal hand
Can e'er untie the filial band
That knits me to thy rugged strand!

Sir Walter Scott

Even Scotland's most ardent advocate failed to capture the essence of his native land. No poem can perfectly evoke the evening sun, dipping below the horizon beyond islands that stand out in dark relief against a blazing sky, nor the heart-stopping sound of a lone piper playing a graveside lament in a remote Highland glen. And no artist, not even 19th-century Scottish landscape painter Horatio McCulloch, has yet done full justice to the scenery: smoke-grey hills; stark mountain ranges; wild moorland carpeted with mulberry-red heather; mossy glens shaded by rowans and gnarled oaks; rivers and burns swirling over slabs of granite, and slicing through steep-sided gorges into lochs where fragments of mist overlay peat-coloured water.

Ceud Mìle Fàilte! You'll see this poster all over Scotland; it means 'A Hundred Thousand Welcomes!' But don't expect the Scots to gush over you; their hospitality comes from the heart, with quiet dignity tempered by shrewd wit. To find their true nature, you must peel away layers of tartan, haggis, monsters and whimsical blether. The Romans called them Caledonians, failed to subdue them, and went away. Brave, proud and fiercely independent, they have been fighting for freedom from England since their earliest history; yet when Bonnie Prince Charlie swept through Scotland, rallying the clans to his father's standard and offering them an alternative to Hanoverian rule, far more fought against him or remained neutral than fought with him.

Although it is possible to enjoy a holiday in Scotland for its versatile beauty and its generous hospitality alone, a superficial knowledge of its history is a tremendous bonus and well worth a little study. The whole country is peppered with grand houses, castles and ruins, some no more than turf-covered earthworks, and they hold far more fascination if something is known of their origins. Even a brief perusal of the History and Topics sections in this book should be enough to transform a tumbled pile of stones into a poignant memorial to a persecuted community; or a stark cairn beside a loch into the reminder of a year of romantic folly that cost the Highlands the best of its men and the death of *Gaidhealtachd* – Gaeldom.

The Scots defy classification – they are canny, yet generous; taciturn, yet eloquent; dour, yet witty; realistic, yet unashamedly romantic. A piper, decked out in kilt and plaid, will serenade a captive audience in a loch-side lay-by, and expect a tip; but if you break down and a Highlander comes to your rescue with a tractor, petrol or makeshift fan-belt, reward him with a dram or a bottle, don't insult him with a fiver. A Gaelic-speaking bard will sit on a bench outside his cottage surrounded by picture-postcard scenery, beguiling you with Celtic tales, while round the back there's a tangle of rusting machinery, and empty cans and bottles lie strewn like confetti in the heather.

Whatever sort of holiday you want, you'll find it in Scotland. You can climb in the Cuillins with crampons and ropes, reel in a salmon as it thrashes about in the Spey, or play golf at St Andrews. You can sail among the islands on the west coast at the helm of a sturdy ketch, anchor for the night in a sheltered sea loch, and fall asleep to the eerie wailing of seals. You can explore the blanket bog of the Flow Country, spotting rare birds and insects and carnivorous plants. You can sit in a croft-house kitchen, pungent with acrid peat-smoke, and listen to Gaelic songs and stories of the past that have been passed down by word of mouth over many generations. You can gaze at paintings in Edinburgh's 'finest small gallery in the world', or marvel at priceless tapestries in Glasgow's Burrell Collection. If you are a gourmet you can dine on smoked salmon or local oysters, followed by a succulent lobster, fresh from the Minch, or an inch-thick Aberdeen Angus steak, and finish off with raspberries from the Carse of Gowrie. And for your picnic lunch, you can buy scampi off one of the fishing boats, boil them up in a billycan over your camp fire, and eat them still warm with wholemeal bread. You can go north and look for that elusive cosmic stunt, the Aurora Borealis (Northern Lights), when shafts of coloured lights, mostly green and red, flash across the sky like a pageant of searchlights. If none of these attractions are to your taste, you can rent a bothy on a remote island and curl up in front of a peat fire with a glass of whisky and your favourite companion (or, failing that, the complete works of Sir Walter Scott). *Ùine gu leòir* is Gaelic for 'time enough', and the word 'whisky' comes from *uisge-beatha* – water of life.

Choosing Your Holiday

Each of Scotland's regions has its own unique character and attractions to captivate the visitor. Whether you dip into just one of the regions or you have the leisure to explore the whole country, careful planning should ensure that you get the best from your trip. Where you choose to go is, of course, up to you, but these brief sketches of the regions may help you to decide which places are most likely to suit you.

Borders

The region was fought over time and again as control switched back and forth between the Scots and the English, and the Border reivers quarrelled amongst themselves, their exploits recalled today in the many Common Riding Festivals that are a feature of this part of the country. Ruins dotted across the landscape give mute testimony to the violence of the times. The Borders are rich in salmon and trout rivers, and offer excellent walking over the Southern Uplands.

Dumfries and Galloway

This is a major centre for Robert Burns enthusiasts; after spending some time as a farmer near the town, he became an exciseman in Dumfries itself. The mild climate of

Chapter Divisions

21 NORTHERN ISLES

Foula

Lerwick

Shetland

Fair Isle

N

20 km
10 miles

40 km
20 miles

N

Kirkwall

Orkney

Pentland Firth

North Sea

Outer Hebrides

The Minch

Lewis

Western Isles

20 WESTERN ISLES

North Uist

Benbecula

South Uist

Isle of Skye

Barra

Rum

Eigg

Muck

Coll

Tiree

Mull

Inner Hebrides

HIGHLANDS

Inverness

Moray Firth

MORAY

19 HIGHLANDS

18 ABERDEEN

ABERDEENSHIRE

Aberdeen

ANGUS

17 KINROSS

PERTHSHIRE AND KINROSS

Dundee

Perth

St Andrews

FIFE

16 FIFE

Oban

ARGYLL

15 CENTRAL SCOTLAND

STIRLING

Stirling

14 LOCH LOMOND

Colonsay

Jura

Islay

Bute

12 GLASGOW

WEST LOTHIAN

10 EDINBURGH

11 LOTHIAN

Isle of Arran

NORTH AYRSHIRE

Firth of Clyde

13 CLYDE

SOUTH LANARKSHIRE

8 BORDERS

SCOTTISH BORDERS

Ayr

EAST AYRSHIRE

SOUTH AYRSHIRE

9 DUMFRIES

DUMFRIES AND GALLOWAY

Dumfries

Atlantic Ocean

NORTHERN IRELAND

Belfast

Stranraer

Solway Firth

ENGLAND

the region makes it a magnet for a number of rare bird species, and for the people who want to see them. If you are not amongst them, you may simply enjoy walking over the hills of the Galloway Forest Park or along the coast of the Solway Firth.

Edinburgh

Edinburgh is a city that is difficult to tire of, with its medieval Old Town high on a crag, its skyline seen from the grandeur of the Georgian New Town. The ancient castle is steeped in history; the art galleries are world famous; the International Festival has something for everyone; the Museum of Scotland and the Royal Museum hold a lifetime's exhibits, while Gladstone's Land and The Georgian House take you back to tenement life in the 17th century and fashionable upper class life in the 18th century.

The Lothians

Lothian's jewel is Edinburgh, capital city of Scotland, flanked by the Lammermuir and Pentland Hills and washed by a varied coastline, all of which offer much to the walker. The Royal Burgh of Linlithgow, birthplace of Mary, Queen of Scots, is well worth a visit.

Glasgow

Glasgow is a modern, sprawling city full of canny, rumbustious, generous people, who don't give a damn for pretension. This super-modern phoenix has arisen from a post-depression dump and competes favourably with its genteel neighbour a stone's throw away to the east. The Art Gallery and Museum and the Hunterian Museum satisfy both fine art and dinosaur buffs, while the Burrell Collection and Pollok House are packed with art treasures; the medieval cathedral and adjacent necropolis capture the spirit of the old city and the Merchant City, once prosperous, then virtually derelict, has been regenerated into an area of fine buildings and renowned shops; gourmets are spoilt for choice; Scottish Opera and Scottish Ballet, in the Theatre Royal and the City Hall cater for music lovers; Citizens Theatre and Kings Theatre offer drama, and The Arches offers everything in the way of popular culture.

The Clyde Valley and Ayrshire

At the heart of this area is Glasgow, but much of the region is far from being urban, with fertile farmland, moorland, small villages and peaceful islands. Ayr lies at the other end of the Burns axis.

Loch Lomond, Cowal, Kintyre, Argyll and Islands

Although parts of this region are very much on the tourist map – Loch Lomond and most of Cowal, for instance – a lot of Argyll is unspoilt and beautiful with several easy-to-get-to but not yet exploited islands, and a seaboard that compares well with the northwest coast of Wester Ross. Even in the popular beauty spots it is possible to drive or walk only a short distance to leave the crowds behind and find peace and solitude.

Central Scotland, Stirling, Trossachs, Breadalbane

Central Scotland is the physical heart of the country. Much of it is urbanized, but it is easy to find your way to the country, particularly to the wooded Trossachs. Stirling, rich in history, is the ideal centre from which to explore further.

Fife and St Andrews

Fife, across the Firth of Forth from Lothian, juts out into the North Sea yet enjoys a surprising amount of sunshine. Once known as the Kingdom of Fife, it has rich pickings for the historian, particularly in Dunfermline and St Andrews. The Royal and Ancient Golf Club at St Andrews will require no introduction for sporting readers.

Perthshire

Across the Firth of Tay, Perthshire is the ancient home of the Picts, that mysterious vanished race whose hill forts and stone circles abound. Festivals at Perth and Pitlochry, and Highland Games at places such as Blair Atholl, entice the tourist. Perthshire offers several challenges for the walker, including the imposing Ben Lawers and Schiehallion.

Aberdeen and the Grampians

This is an attractive region, with the North Sea on one side and magnificent mountains on the other. Speyside malt whiskies are justly famous and a happy time may be had wandering the Whisky trail. Aberdeen, the Granite City, is worth a visit and makes a good starting point for your explorations.

The Highlands

The remoter parts of the Highlands seem untouched by time. It is here, particularly in the islands, that you will find the majority of Scotland's Gaelic speakers. It is said, with some truth, that Scotland divides into two nations across the Highland Line. This is walking country that is unexcelled anywhere in the world. Delights are everywhere.

Western Isles

The Western Isles have a character all their own. There are literally hundreds of them, although not all are inhabited. Skye, Mull, Uist, Harris and Lewis all command attention, together with the smaller islands around them, and a warm welcome is practically guaranteed. If you have access to a boat this is idyllic sailing territory.

Northern Isles: Orkney and Shetland

Far to the north, these island outposts are scarcely 'Scottish' at all. These were the bastions of the Vikings and still retain much in the way of Norse character. A birdwatchers' paradise, where sea birds throng the cliffs and islands.

History

Scotland, wild and fiercely independent, was always a thorn in England's flesh. No one wants hostile neighbours and Scotland has struggled continually to remain independent. The Romans tried to occupy it for a few years, found it invincible and slunk away. The English spent centuries trying to annex it until eventually they had to accept a Scottish king on their throne. Intrepid younger sons, black sheep, political exiles and the dispossessed sailed from Scotland to leave their mark on the world.

The first edition of the *Encyclopaedia Britannica* was published in instalments in Edinburgh in 1768. John Logie Baird invented television; Alexander Bell invented the telephone; Alexander Fleming discovered penicillin; James Watt invented the steam engine. James Clerk Maxwell demonstrated the existence of radio waves in 1873, before Marconi pioneered their use for communication; Lord Reith of Stonehaven greatly influenced the early development of the BBC and was its first general manager. John Paul Jones founded the American Navy. David Hume, the 18th-century philosopher and historian, influenced thought up to the 20th century. Patrick Gordon was a general to Tsar Peter the Great; James Keith was a field marshal to Frederick the Great. 'Adam' is a household word used to describe the style of architecture designed by brothers Robert and James Adam. Thomas Telford's bridges, roads and canals, Robert Stevenson's lighthouses, Carnegie's benevolent institutions, are all renowned. Gladstone, Ramsay MacDonald, Harold Macmillan and Alec Douglas-Home each served as prime minister of Britain. Eleven of America's presidents were of Scottish descent, as were 25 of the 73 Americans honoured in their Hall of Fame, a third of their secretaries of state and half their secretaries to the Treasury. John McDouall Stuart was the first man to cross Australia, through the central desert, in 1866; John Macarthur laid the foundations of Australia's agricultural system; Lachlan MacQuarie was responsible for turning the penal colony of Botany Bay into Sydney. These are but a few of the Scots who spread their talents across the world.

Prehistory

The Ice Age eradicated evidence of any previous habitation in Scotland. **Stone Age** settlers, at least 7,000 years ago, were the first to leave clues to their existence. Burial sites and middens (rubbish heaps) from those times have thrown up enough to tantalize archaeologists, but not enough to leave more than a shadow of the identity of those nomadic tribes. They came from Asia and Europe, through England and Ireland, wave after wave of them, creeping up the coast in dug-out canoes, settling for long enough to leave traces of their culture and way of life, before vanishing into obscurity. They lived off deer and wild boar, fish and crustaceans. Some only stayed a short time, living in caves. An excavated stone building in Grampian dates from 7000 BC. Later, farmers came from the Continent and introduced agriculture. People settled for longer periods, burning forests and enriching the land with potash.

After the hunters and gatherers came the **Beaker People**, who laid beakers in the tombs of their dead. They were skilful engineers, and historians puzzle over their mysterious stone circles and monoliths, and over the true purpose of their brochs (massive stone towers built near the sea in the far north, about 2,000 years ago). Metal was introduced about a thousand years before Christ, and with it the sword and shield. Scotland, on the trade route between Ireland and Scandinavia, was able to barter food and hides for bronze and copper. During this millennium the Celtic-speaking Britons arrived, a sturdy, fair-haired race, quick to attack in order to acquire precious land. The local people built defensive forts, with ditches and ramparts, such as the ones on Barry Hill and Finavon, and skirmishing became part of life.

The Romans: AD 82–4th century

The Romans arrived in AD 82 and with them came the first record of Scottish history, written by the historian **Tacitus**, who describes how his father-in-law, **Agricola**, defeated an army of tall, red-haired men on an unidentified hillside in the northeast, in the **Battle of Mons Graupius**. The exact location of this battle is debatable, but it was somewhere in today's Grampian, so called from a misprint of 'Graupius' by a 16th-century chronicler. Roman remains were found as far north as the Moray Firth, and Tacitus recorded that they 'discovered and subdued' Orkney.

The Romans called their victims *picti*, the painted ones, from which the name 'Picts' is thought to derive, and failed to subdue them. Highly trained legionnaires could not compete with hostile tribes who faded into the mountains, forests and marshes, laying cunning ambushes for their aggressors. The Romans fell back, and evidence unearthed recently shows they were posted elsewhere.

In 121 **Hadrian** built a wall between the Solway and the Tyne, hoping to contain the barbarians in the north, but the wall was so frequently attacked that another was constructed between the Forth and the Clyde in 141–2 – the **Antonine Wall**. This proved to be no more effective and was soon abandoned. Exasperated, the Romans withdrew to Hadrian's Wall. In 208 **Emperor Severus** sailed into the Firth of Forth and laid waste Fife and the land around the Tay. In spite of the devastation he caused, the barbarians refused to be conquered. The old emperor died, the Romans withdrew again, and an uneasy peace existed between the north and south until the middle of the 4th century. The Picts then resumed their ferocious attacks while Saxons began to invade from the northeast. The Roman Empire was in decline: more and more legions were being recalled to fight nearer home. By the end of the 4th century the Romans abandoned Scotland completely, leaving the untamed Picts to defend themselves against new invaders. They not only failed to subdue their foes, but also failed to impose any of their sophisticated culture on them. The only evidence of their occupa-tion is a few straight roads, a number of forts and the remains of the Antonine Wall.

The Coming of Christianity: 397–7th century

Four races dominated Scotland, then called Alba, or Alban. The **Celtic Picts** were the most powerful, occupying the land from Caithness to the Forth; the **Teutonic Angles**, or **Anglo-Saxons**, occupied Bernicia, south of the Forth; the **Britons**, another Celtic race, occupied the western lands south of the Clyde. Finally there were the **Scots**: Celts who had come over from Ireland during the 3rd and 4th centuries and settled north of the Clyde, establishing the **Kingdom of Dalriada** and eventually giving their name to all Scotland. **St Ninian** founded the first Christian centre at Whithorn, near the Solway Firth, in 397, and started the daunting task of converting the pagans. Then came **Columba**, a clever man of royal birth, who was exiled from Ireland and arrived in Scotland in 563. He established himself on the island of Iona, continuing St Ninian's work, and sent missionaries to the mainland and to the other islands. They penetrated further and further into Pictland. Columba's influence was political as well as religious and he did much to consolidate the strength of the Scots.

For those who believe there is some historic truth in the Arthurian legends, King Arthur led his army north at some time in the 5th or 6th century and had a crack at the Picts and Scots. Geoffrey of Monmouth, in his *History of the Kings of Britain*, describes the **Battle of Loch Lomond** in graphic detail. The loch, with its islands, streams and crags provided sanctuary for the barbarians. They fled to the islands, where Arthur besieged them for 15 days until he had reduced them to such a state of famine that they died in their thousands. The Irish arrived with a fleet and a 'huge horde of pagans' to help the Scots, but Arthur cut them to pieces mercilessly and forced them to return home. He then continued to massacre the barbarians until they 'fell on their knees and besought him to have mercy'. The king was moved to tears and pardoned them. True or false, it is stirring stuff and well worth a read.

By the end of the 7th century the four kingdoms of Alban were nominally converted to Christianity – a Celtic Christianity, not yet in line with that dictated by Rome.

Norse Invasion: 8th century

At the end of the 8th century Norsemen began to attack from the north, conquering the Northern and Western Isles, Caithness and Sutherland, while the four kingdoms continued to fight amongst themselves, weakening their resistance to outside attack.

The Birth of Scotland: 843–1034

In 843 **Kenneth Macalpine**, King of the Scots, achieved some sort of union between Scots and Picts, making himself king over all the territory north of the Forth and Clyde, which then became Scotia. The Picts, who had been dominant for more than 1000 years, vanished for ever. They remain an enigmatic people whose history is unrecorded and unknown. It was not until 1018, however, that **Malcolm II** defeated the Angles and brought Bernicia (Lothian) into the kingdom. He was succeeded in 1034 by his grandson, **Duncan I**, who already ruled the Britons, and the four kingdoms were finally united into one Scotland, except for those parts occupied by the Norsemen. The country was divided into seven main kingdoms, of which Fife was the strongest, plus a few smaller ones, each ruled by a *mormaer*. The *Ard Righ* or High King was their overlord – King of the Scots, but not of Scotland, for each *mormaer* owned his land (*see* **Topics**, 'The Stone of Destiny', p.66). In those days, under a remarkable clan system in which no one was subservient, Scotland was truly democratic.

The Norman Influence: 11th century

Duncan I was killed in 1040 by **Macbeth**, the last Celtic king. Shakespeare portrayed Macbeth as a weak man, but in fact he ruled for 17 years and his reign was chronicled as a time of plenty. He was killed by Duncan's son, **Malcolm Canmore**, with the help of the English, in 1057.

It was Malcolm Canmore's second wife, **Margaret**, who made his 36-year reign memorable. She was an English princess, sister of Edgar Atheling – Edward the Confessor's heir, usurped by William the Conqueror. She and her brother had taken refuge in Scotland after the Norman Conquest in 1066. Margaret, who was extremely pious and later canonized, set about anglicizing the Celtic church. She brought in English clergy and established an English court, and it was her influence that civilized Scotland and transformed it into a kingdom similar to Norman England. It was now that in the Lowlands *mormaers* became earls and established a feudal system, while the Highlands and Islands retained the old, patriarchal clans.

Inspired by the presence in his court of his English brother-in-law, Malcolm coveted the English throne. He made several border raids into Northumberland and Cumbria, forcing William the Conqueror to invade Scotland to subdue him. In order to prevent the subsequent destruction of Scotland, Malcolm was then forced to pay homage to William at Abernethy in 1071. He continued to harass the English until he was treacherously killed while laying siege to Alnwick Castle in 1093. Queen Margaret, already mortally ill, survived him by only three days.

David I: 1124–53

David I, ninth son of Malcolm Canmore, inherited the throne in 1124 from a succession of unremarkable monarchs, and ruled for nearly 30 years, bringing many beneficial changes to Scotland. He had been brought up in England and most of his friends were Norman. His wife was a Norman heiress; his sister, Maud, was married to King Henry I of England. He gave large Scottish estates to his Anglo-Norman friends, including the ancestors of the Balliols, Robert the Bruce and the Stewarts. The old Celtic families merged with French-speaking incomers, establishing families in the Lowlands and the northeast whose names are common throughout Scotland today: Frasers, Maxwells, Gordons and Crichtons. However, the Highlanders retained their traditional clan system and took little notice of these southern interlopers.

David led an army against England in 1138. Although the outcome of the **Battle of the Standard** was inconclusive, subsequent negotiation won him Northumberland and Cumbria. He encouraged Flemish weavers to settle along the east coast, granting them special privileges. These ancestors of the Flemings and the Taylors introduced new fabrics and new skills, and their ways were absorbed by their new neighbours.

David had little time for vows of poverty: he founded a number of lavish cathedrals, churches and monasteries, including the Border abbeys, importing religious communities from Europe and urging the monks to establish commercial interests to the glory of God. He granted royal charters to towns, permitting markets and fairs; he tried to establish a national judiciary; he encouraged foreign trade. He died in 1153, heartbroken from the death of his son and heir the year before.

The Treaty of Falaise: 1174

Malcolm IV was 13 when he inherited the throne from his grandfather, David I. Known as Malcolm the Maiden, he was nevertheless a brave young man, whose courage inspired many of his followers. Gentle and religious, he ruled for only 12 years before he died, to be succeeded by his brother, **William the Lion**. William was ambitious and ruthless in his desire to recover parts of his kingdom annexed by England. An ill-conceived expedition into Northumberland in 1174 failed and William was taken prisoner. He was sent to Normandy, where he was forced to sign the humiliating **Treaty of Falaise**. This placed Scotland under feudal subjection to England. Fifteen years later, when the English king Richard Coeur de Lion needed money for a Crusade, he agreed to annul the Treaty of Falaise in return for 10,000 marks.

The End of the Norse Occupation: 13th century

England and Scotland were at peace, then, for over 100 years. **Alexander II** succeeded to the throne in 1214, and directed his attention to the Western Isles, whose lords gave their allegiance to Norway. It was his son, **Alexander III**, however, who managed to expel the Norsemen from the Hebrides. He did this by defeating old **King Haakon IV of Norway** in the **Battle of Largs** in 1263. The Hebrides became part of Scotland again, though the Lords of the Isles paid little heed to any outside authority

Alexander continued to enrich Scotland, emulating his great-great-grandfather, David I. He married the English Princess Margaret, daughter of Henry III. Their daughter, also Margaret, married King Eric of Norway. Alexander had a long and successful reign. He outlived his first wife and three children and married again, desperate for an heir. He was, however, killed six months later, in 1286, when thrown from his horse, leaving his grand-daughter **Margaret of Norway** to succeed him, under the regency of John Balliol, a powerful Norman-Scot.

The Auld Alliance: 1295

Edward I of England, determined to unite Scotland to England, proposed a marriage between his son Edward and the eight-year-old **Maid of Norway**. The little queen died of seasickness on her way to Scotland, and Edward declared himself to be overlord of Scotland. There were several claimants to the throne, the strongest being **John Balliol**, son of the regent, and **Robert the Bruce**. Both were Anglo-Norman nobles with estates in England and Scotland, given to their ancestors by David I. They were descended from David's youngest son and had both fought in Edward's army. In 1292 Edward gave the crown to John Balliol in Berwick Castle, believing him to be more easily manipulated than Robert the Bruce. He ordered Balliol to pay homage to the English throne and accept himself as Scotland's overlord. He also insisted that Scotland should contribute to English defence costs and join with them in an invasion of France. Rather than do this the Scots instead formed the **Auld Alliance**, as it became known, with France in October 1295. Edward saw it as a declaration of war.

In 1296 Edward's army laid waste to Berwick, slaughtering almost every male inhabitant. The Scots army that advanced against him was heavily defeated at Dunbar and King John was captured a few months later and humiliated by Edward at Montrose Castle, being ritually stripped of his royal trappings. This episode earned King John the epithet 'Toom Tabard', or 'Empty Coat'. Edward, 'The Hammer of the Scots', progressed through Scotland, compelling nobles and lairds to sign the **Ragman Roll** acknowledging him to be their king. He then returned to England, taking with him what he thought to be the Stone of Destiny, which had always been used in the coronation of Scottish kings (*see* **Topics**, p.66). He was convinced he had finally conquered Scotland.

William Wallace: 1274(?)–1305

William Wallace was a young Scot from the southwest, outlawed in 1297 for killing the Sheriff of Lanark in revenge for the murder of his wife. In exile Wallace became the leader of a fast-expanding resistance movement against English repression. In September 1297 he defeated the English at the **Battle of Stirling Bridge**, kindling new hope in Scottish hearts, and paving the way to freedom. Wallace was made Guardian of the Realm, but the following year he was defeated by Edward at the **Battle of Falkirk** and had to go into hiding. Wallace evaded capture for seven unhappy years before he was betrayed. He was paraded through the streets of London, tried on a series of trumped-up charges and condemned to death. He was hanged, drawn and emasculated, his entrails being burnt before his eyes as he died. Quarters of his body and his head were subsequently displayed throughout Britain.

Robert the Bruce: 1306–29

Robert the Bruce, grandson of John Balliol's rival, replaced Wallace as Guardian of Scotland, alongside Balliol's nephew, **Red John Comyn**. In 1302 Bruce resigned the guardianship and went over to Edward's side. In 1306 Bruce and Red Comyn met at Greyfriars Kirk, in Dumfries. They quarrelled and Bruce killed Comyn, possibly because of his refusal to help Bruce in a campaign for the Scottish throne. Bruce was excommunicated for this sacrilege and hounded by the powerful Comyns. Seizing the initiative, he went to Scone and had himself crowned King of Scotland in March 1306.

Edward hurried north and defeated Bruce, a month later, at Methven. Outlawed, his friends and allies dead, Bruce went into hiding. During this time of exile, probably on the island of Rathlin off the Irish coast, he encountered the legendary spider, whose persistence enabled it to swing from one rafter to another on its frail homespun web. If the spider could succeed, then so could he.

Bruce returned to Scotland in 1307, overcame all other claimants to the throne and defeated Edward I's successor, Edward II, at **Bannockburn** in 1314. Excommunicated by the Pope, Bruce's sovereignty was not recognized by Europe. In 1320 his Council decided to send a petition to the Pope, asking him to tell Edward to lay off Scotland and acknowledge Bruce as the rightful king. Bernard, Abbot of Arbroath, composed a defiant letter to the Pope, a passionate plea for freedom from English harassment, emphasizing the ancient Celtic line of the Scots and upholding Robert I, 'Yet even the same Robert, should he turn aside from the task and yield Scotland or us to the English king or people, him we should cast out as the enemy of us all, and choose another king to defend our freedom; for so long as one hundred of us shall remain alive, we shall never under any conditions submit to the domination of the English. For we fight, not for glory nor for riches nor for honours that we fight, but only and alone for freedom, which no good man surrenders but with his life.'

The Pope was sufficiently impressed by the spirit of the appeal and advised Edward to leave Scotland alone.

On the day of Edward III's coronation in 1327, the Scots launched a raid into England and Edward was almost captured by the Scots when he led a retaliatory expedition the following year. A peace treaty was concluded in 1328, in which Scotland's independence was acknowledged. Bruce's four-year-old son, David, was married to Joan, Edward III's seven-year-old sister. Bruce died at Cardross Castle on the Clyde in 1329.

Struggle for Power: 1331–71

Bruce was succeeded by his young son, **David II**, with **Thomas Randolph, Earl of Moray**, as regent. The 42 years of David's reign were troubled times for Scotland. Encouraged by Edward III of England, who declared the peace treaty void, the Scottish nobles tried to put Toom Tabard's son, **Edward Balliol**, on the throne. Moray was killed, as was his cousin the Earl of Mar who succeeded him as regent, and Balliol was crowned King of Scotland at Scone in 1332. David was sent to France for safety with his child-wife Joan. By 1337 Andrew Murray, Guardian of David's kingdom, had practically driven out Balliol's supporters. David and Joan returned to Scotland in 1341 and made a series of raids into England. He was captured by the English at the **Battle of Neville's Cross** in 1346, however, and spent the next 11 years as a captive. Following his ransom and release in 1357, David was offered easier terms if he would name Edward III or one of his sons as his successor. Not surprisingly, the Scottish parliament rejected this notion. David reigned until his death in 1371, to be succeeded by his steward, Robert.

The Stewarts: 14th–15th century

The Stewarts took their name from their hereditary position as stewards to the kings of Scotland. Robert, the first Stewart king, was better as regent than monarch. Anarchy, rebellion and internal squabbles disturbed the peace he strove for. Border raiding was rife, and the whole country seethed in a turmoil of lawlessness. Robert II died in 1390 and was succeeded by his son, **Robert III**. Crippled by a kick from a horse, Robert was in poor health and much of the responsibility of government passed to his brother, the **Duke of Albany**, as Guardian of the Realm. In 1399 Albany gave way to Robert's son, **David, Duke of Rothesay**, but three years later had him arrested and imprisoned. Within two months Rothesay was dead and Albany once again took over. The ailing Robert III sent his son and heir, **James I**, to France in 1406, fearing Albany had plans to remove him from the succession, but the young prince was captured by pirates and handed over to the English. Too shocked to go on living, Robert died a month later, leaving Albany in full power for 18 years while James was held hostage. Powerful nobles seized the opportunity to consolidate their strength. They expanded their estates and built up private armies. Most notable among them was the **Douglas** family, whose lands and subjects rivalled those of the king. Meanwhile, in the north-west, the Lords of the Isles allied themselves with the English and continued to live their own lives with little regard for central government.

James I: Anarchy, 1406–37

James I returned to his throne in 1424, aged 29, with an English bride, Joan Beaufort, cousin of Henry VI. Reared and educated in England, he had a good grounding in statesmanship and military strategy. He found his country in turmoil. His nobles were too powerful, and anarchy, poverty and lawlessness were rampant. His first step was the execution of the Albany family in 1425 and the seizure of their considerable estates. In 1427 he summoned the Highland chiefs and arrested 40: Alexander of the Isles retaliated by burning Inverness. Further rebellion from the west was subdued, and James redressed the balance of power in the Lowlands by annexing many of the earldoms that had threatened his supremacy. James achieved much for Scotland, restoring order and introducing reforms, but his decisive methods made enemies, and in 1437 he was stabbed to death, leaving his six-year-old son **James II** as his heir.

The Douglases: 15th century

Scotland was once again ruled by regency, and once again the nobles, in particular the Douglas family, became too powerful. In 1440 Sir William Crichton, who had custody of the young king, invited the 14-year-old Earl of Douglas and his younger brother to dine with the eight-year-old king at Edinburgh Castle. This became known as the '**Black Dinner**' – the two Douglas youths were seized and summarily executed. For a while, the Douglas family was subdued.

James II came to his throne in 1449 at the age of 19. He continued the reforms so dear to his father, but was threatened by an alliance between the Douglases, Crawfords and John of the Isles. The king summoned the Earl of Douglas to Stirling Castle and stabbed him to death. With English help the Douglases attempted revenge, and James defeated them at the **Battle of Arkinholm**, killing three of the murdered earl's four brothers. The power of the Douglas family was squashed. James was killed in 1460 when a cannon exploded during the siege of Roxburghe.

James III: 1460–88

James III was nine when his father died so Scotland was once more ruled by regents, until his accession at the age of 19. He married the King of Norway's daughter, whose dowry included Orkney and Shetland. James was an intellectual, better fitted for academic life than a crown. He antagonized his nobles, who rose against him. They hanged his favourites and imprisoned him in Edinburgh Castle. James survived this attempt to dethrone him, but six years later his son led a successful coup against him, becoming James IV in his place. James III was killed in mysterious circumstances at the decisive Battle of Sauchieburn.

James IV: Renaissance, 1488–1513

James IV, most popular of the Stewart kings, was 15 when he came to the throne. He was clever and charming, a good leader, pious and energetic, generous, flamboyant and sensual. His mistresses bore him a number of bastards. His reign brought the Renaissance to Scotland: the arts and education blossomed and James led the way. He authorized the building of palaces and churches. His court was elegant and cultured and the country was peaceful and prosperous. But on the doorstep the Lords of the Isles continued to live as they always had, their loyalties rooted in their clans. James, who had learnt Gaelic, decided to visit the Western Highlands and Islands, hoping to win the friendship of the clans. His attempts were viewed with suspicion, so he desisted and appointed overlords to rule them. This resulted in an uprising of the Macdonalds and Macleans who stormed and burned Inverness in 1503.

In that same year James married 12-year-old Margaret Tudor and signed a Treaty of Perpetual Peace with England. But in 1511 his brother-in-law, Henry VIII of England, joined the Pope, the King of Spain and the Doge of Venice in a Holy League against France. James passionately desired a united Europe. Determined to maintain a balance of power, therefore, he renewed the Auld Alliance with France and tried, in vain, to mediate. In 1513, threatened from all directions, France appealed to Scotland for help. James in turn appealed to Henry, who replied with insults. Against advice, in August 1513 James led a Scottish army across the Tweed to **Flodden Field**, where they were massacred by the superior forces of the English. The King, his nobles and most of Scotland's best men were killed in a battle as pointless as it was valiant. The country was left leaderless, its army slain, its new king James V, a toddler, and its regent, Margaret Tudor, with divided loyalties.

James V: 1513–42

There followed a period of more turmoil until the King was old enough to take office and try to restore order. Ignoring several offers of brides, he chose French Madeleine, who only lived two months after their marriage. The following year he took a second French wife, **Marie de Guise-Lorraine**, who bore him two sons, both of whom died. James was an ingenuous man. He liked to disguise himself as a commoner and mingle with his subjects, fooling no one but himself, and getting into several unfortunate escapades. He squabbled with the English, aggravated his nobles, and tried to invade England. His pathetic, mutinous army, quarrelling amongst itself, was defeated by Henry VIII's army at **Solway Moss** in 1542. Sick and despairing, James returned to Falkland Palace to hear that his wife had just given birth to a daughter. The news was too much for him and he died, leaving as his heir the newborn Mary, Queen of Scots.

Mary, Queen of Scots: 1542–67 (d. 1587)

Henry VIII, determined to absorb Scotland, proposed a marriage between Mary and his delicate son, Edward. A marriage treaty was arranged, but the Scottish parliament rejected such a treaty with England and renewed instead the Auld Alliance with France. Furious to be thus snubbed, Henry began what Sir Walter Scott later named the **Rough Wooing**. He devastated the south of Scotland and earned the bitter hatred of the Scots. Mary, aged five, was sent to France for safety, where she stayed for 15 years, marrying the French dauphin.

While she was away, learning French ways, Protestantism was gaining power in Scotland. In 1554 Marie de Guise-Lorraine became regent. The presence of a great many French officials in the regent's government greatly upset a number of the Scottish nobility. Several of them, calling themselves 'The Lords of the Congregation', declared their support for the Protestant religion. Fear of French domination increased when Mary's husband became King Francis II of France on his father's death. In 1559, with the support of much of the nobility, **John Knox**, a powerful

Reformer, delivered a fiery sermon in Perth, denouncing the Church of Rome. A series of armed conflicts between the Lords of the Congregation and the regent's French and Scottish forces ensued, which led to her being deposed. In 1560 she died, and shortly afterwards the Treaty of Edinburgh was concluded between England and France, bringing about the removal of all foreign troops from Scotland.

Mary's French husband died at the end of 1560 and she returned to her country as queen in 1561 – now Mary Stuart, the French form of her name which was adopted in England. French in education and attitude, a devout Catholic, high-spirited, passionate, sensual and beautiful, she had the best intentions. She had no desire to tangle with the Protestants; she merely wished to be allowed to practise her own religion in peace.

In 1565 she married her cousin, **Henry Stewart**, **Lord Darnley**, a dissipated Catholic youth, four years her junior, and mistrusted by all. Within a year, when Mary was six months pregnant, Darnley became jealous of her Italian secretary, Rizzio, and helped to murder him, in Mary's presence. She never forgave him. When he himself was murdered, in 1567, some hinted that Mary may have known of the plot.

Eight weeks later, Mary married **James Hepburn, Earl of Bothwell**, a buccaneering Protestant of great charm and little honour. Bothwell had been heavily implicated in the murder of Darnley and this ill-advised marriage sparked off an inferno of protest from both Catholics and Protestants. Bothwell was forced into exile and Mary imprisoned and forced to abdicate in favour of her baby son, **James VI**. Her half-brother, **James Stewart, Earl of Moray**, bastard son of James V, was proclaimed Regent.

Mary escaped from her imprisonment the following year, 1568, and Scotland was torn by civil war for the next five years as her supporters fought the Reformers. Mary fled to England and threw herself on the mercy of her cousin, Elizabeth I. But they never met. Elizabeth, without an heir, could not forget Mary's claims to the English throne. Mary was imprisoned for 20 years, and then beheaded.

James VI/I: 1567–1625

After another spell of regency, James proclaimed himself king in 1585 and found himself to be head of a country divided between Catholics and Protestants. He aspired to impartiality, incurring the animosity of both factions. A Protestant in name, if not belief, James had no wish to antagonize his Protestant cousin Elizabeth of England and spoil his chances of inheriting her throne. He concluded an alliance with England and made no more than a formal protest when Elizabeth agreed to the execution of his mother in 1587.

Protestantism in Scotland now presented problems. It was divided between the extreme Presbyterians, who wanted a religion with equality of ministers and no bishops or elaborate ritual, and James' English form, with bishops appointed by the Crown and a formal liturgy. He tried to impose his will on the Kirk, but failed. Presbyterians grew more and more averse to Episcopacy and their religion became less and less formal, with extempore prayers replacing those in the prayer book.

In 1603 Elizabeth I died, appointing James her heir. Thus, he became James VI of Scotland and I of England. He hurried to London and only returned to Scotland once, preferring the magnificence of the English court, and the ritual of the Church of England. He died in 1625 and his son, **Charles I**, succeeded him.

The Last of the Stewarts: 1625–88

Charles, reared in England, a devout Anglican and Episcopalian, had no love for the Kirk. When he went north for his Scottish coronation, his subjects were scandalized by the 'Popish' practices he brought with him. He authorized the revision of the English prayer book in an attempt to produce one for Scotland that might replace extempore prayer. This produced violent opposition, riots and protest. In February 1638 thousands flocked to Greyfriars Kirk in Edinburgh to sign the **National Covenant**, condemning all Catholic doctrines and upholding the 'True Religion'. Copies of the Covenant were carried all over the Lowlands and signed amidst strong national feeling. The Covenant, however, was somewhat ambivalent: its signatories swore, not only to uphold the True Religion, but also to be loyal to a king who demanded the Episcopacy they shunned.

When civil war broke out in England, the Covenanting Scots agreed to help the English Parliamentarians, on condition that Presbyterianism was adopted throughout England and Ireland, as well as Scotland. In 1649 Charles I was defeated by Cromwell and executed. The Scots grasped this opportunity to invite his exiled son, **Charles II**, to Scotland as king, on condition that he supported the Covenant. Furious, Cromwell invaded Scotland. Charles went back into exile and Cromwell ruled both countries until he died in 1658. The **Restoration** in 1660 brought Charles II back to the throne. He ignored the promises he had made, and sought to reintroduce Episcopacy. This rekindled the fervour of the Covenanters, who fled to the hills and worshipped in secret 'Conventicles'. In 1670 these conventicles were declared treasonable, and there followed the **Killing Times**, when thousands of Covenanters were slaughtered.

Charles II died of apoplexy in 1685 and was succeeded by his brother, **James VII/II**, Scotland's first Catholic sovereign for 120 years, who tried unsuccessfully to introduce religious tolerance. He was deposed in 1688 by his Protestant daughter, Mary, and her Dutch husband, William of Orange. He fled to France and **William and Mary** were crowned king and queen. Some Scots, mostly Highlanders, remained true to James. The **Jacobites**, as they were called, rose under **Graham of Claverhouse** and almost annihilated William's army at the battle of **Killiecrankie** in 1689. But Claverhouse was killed, leaving them leaderless, and they lost heart and returned to their Highlands.

The Massacre of Glencoe: 1692

The government, uneasy about the rebellious Highlanders, issued a proclamation ordering all clans to take an oath of allegiance to the Crown by the first day of 1692. Circumstances prevented **Alisdair Maclain of Clan Donald** from taking the oath until after the deadline. This provided the government with a chance to intimidate the Highland clans. A company of Campbell soldiers, commanded by a relation of Maclain's, **Captain Robert Campbell of Glenlyon**, billeted themselves on the MacDonalds in Glencoe. Under orders from higher authority, they rose at dawn and slaughtered their hosts. The barbarity of the massacre produced public outcry, not so much because of the number killed – 38 out of about 150 – but because of the abuse of hospitality.

The Union of Parliaments: 1707

Between 1698 and 1700 Scotland's economy was shattered by an unsuccessful attempt to colonize the Darien coast on the isthmus of Panama. The **Darien Scheme** failed as a result of deaths from fever and inhospitable natives, Spanish hostility and the withdrawal of English investment in what was seen as a rival to the East India Company. Scotland, bankrupt and plunged into political crisis, was forced to accept the **Treaty of Union** in 1707 uniting the parliaments of England and Scotland. This gave Scotland a badly needed boost to her economy and the right to Presbyterianism, and removed the threat of further war between the two countries. It did little, however, to foster love for England in Scottish hearts.

The Jacobite Rebellions: 1708–46

The signing of the Treaty of Union forced the Scots to accept a Hanoverian succession, but Jacobite loyalties still prevailed in the Highlands. **James Edward Stuart**, son of the deposed James VII/II, was regarded by many as Scotland's king. The Old Pretender, as he called by the Hanoverians, made three unsuccessful attempts to regain his throne. His expedition from France in 1708 only got as far as the Firth of Forth. In 1715 the Earl of Mar, upset by his treatment at the hands of the Hanoverian George I, raised the Pretender's banner and proclaimed James king. The rising looked promising, but following the inconclusive battle at **Sheriffmuir** support for it fell away. The Old Pretender put in a brief appearance in Scotland but soon returned to France. In 1719 a final attempt was made, backed by the Spanish; but the supporting fleet was lost in a storm and the Highlanders dispersed.

Stringent measures were taken to quell the clans. Between 1726 and 1737 **General Wade** built military roads and forts, opening up the Highlands and linking strategic strong points, at Fort William, Fort Augustus and Fort George. He raised a regiment of clansmen loyal to the Whig government, the **Black Watch**, whose duty was to keep order among the resentful clans.

George I was an unattractive German who disliked the British as much as they disliked him. His son, **George II**, was equally Germanic and unsuitable to rule over Highlanders who still clung to their Jacobite dreams. Exiled in Rome, the Old Pretender's son, **Prince Charles Edward Stuart**, was a brave young man with charisma and magnetism. He pawned his mother's rubies, set sail for Scotland and landed in Eriskay on 23 July 1745, determined to win the crown for his father. At first his reception was daunting: Macdonald of Boisdale told him to go home. 'I am come home,' he retorted. MacLeod, and Macdonald of Sleat, refused to help, but Macdonald of Clanranald stood by him. Cameron of Lochiel was reluctant to encourage what he believed to be romantic folly, but he was won over and on 19 August the standard was raised in **Glenfinnan** and the Old Pretender proclaimed King James VIII/III, with Prince Charles as his regent. The prince picked up support as he advanced on Edinburgh, but his army probably never exceeded 8,000 men. Capturing Perth on the way, he held glorious court at Holyrood, defeated General Cope's soldiers at **Prestonpans** (inspiring the song 'Hey Johnny Cope, are you wauking yet') and gathered enthusiastic support.

On 1 November Prince Charles led his motley army of 5,000 men south, with the intention of taking London. Meeting little resistance, but picking up little support, they reached Derby, only 127 miles from their target, on 4 December. At this point Charles' prudent advisers insisted that to go further was madness. On 6 December the Highlanders turned round to march in an orderly retreat back to Scotland.

On 17 January 1746 the Jacobites won their last battle, defeating Cope's successor, General Hawley, at Falkirk. Hearing news of the advance of the Duke of Cumberland's army from England, the Prince took his army back into the Highlands, capturing Inverness on 21 February. On 16 April Cumberland marched towards Inverness, his forces meeting the Jacobite army on Drummossie Moor, south of **Culloden**. Out-numbered and out-gunned, the Jacobites were soon defeated. Defeat turned into a rout in which Cumberland's men showed no mercy to their opponents.

The Prince escaped, with a price of £30,000 on his head, and spent the next five months in hiding in the Western Highlands and Islands. Aided by brave **Flora Macdonald**, he escaped eventually to Europe, where he lived in squalid exile for the rest of his life, dying in Rome in 1788.

The Aftermath of Culloden: 1746–1860

The English and the Lowland Scots were determined to squash the rebellious Highlanders for ever. They enforced the **Act of Proscription** in 1747, banning Highland dress and the bearing of arms. Jacobites who had not died at Culloden were either executed or transported. The old way of life was dead. The act was repealed in 1782, but by this time it was no longer relevant: the **Highland Clearances** had begun (*see* **Topics**, p.52). Between 1780 and 1860 thousands of crofters were evicted from their homes in the Highlands and Islands to make way for sheep. Many others emigrated voluntarily, to escape persecution, to Canada, America, New Zealand and Australia. In the mid-19th century Ireland's potato famine reached the Highlands, resulting in appalling hardship and causing further emigration. By the end of the 19th century the rural Highlands and Islands were almost deserted.

The Scottish Enlightenment: 18th–19th centuries

Meanwhile, the Lowland aristocracy drifted south, seduced by London, leaving room for a burgeoning middle class, and a new intelligentsia emerged in a surge of genius to dazzle the world. Egalitarian social clubs became centres for debate and the free exchange of views. Philosophy and literature flourished. David Hume, Adam Smith and Thomas Carlyle were but a few of the great names that contributed to the Enlightenment. Sydney Smith, though not a Scot, taught in Edinburgh and helped to found the *Edinburgh Review*. The poet Allan Ramsay lived long enough to see the birth of the Enlightenment. Robert Burns was a product of the period; Sir Walter Scott was a leading influence. Others were: James Thomson the poet, Tobias Smollett the writer, James Boswell, biographer of Dr Johnson, James Watt the engineer who invented the steam engine. These remarkable men, and many more, achieved an astonishing record of success in all fields of human accomplishment. Scottish physicians, engineers and inventors led the world. The Enlightenment spanned about a century, until Queen Victoria discovered Scotland in the mid-19th century and herds of nobility stampeded north to smother the blasts of innovation with cosy convention.

A flourishing cotton industry collapsed in the 1860s, when the American Civil War cut off supplies of raw cotton, and heavy industry developed instead. Glasgow, once the biggest tobacco importer in Britain, led the world in shipbuilding. Expanding industries meant expanding labour forces; there were concentrations of population in industrial areas, fed by refugee Highlanders and Irish.

20th-century Scotland

Shipbuilding and engineering developed rapidly from the mid-19th century until, by the beginning of the 20th century, some 100,000 jobs were related to Clydeside shipbuilding alone, and the entire economy of west and mid-Scotland depended on Glasgow's heavy industry. The First World War took its toll, but it needed a constant supply of arms and ships and machinery. It was the Great Depression in the 1920s and 1930s that dealt Scotland a mortal blow. After the Wall Street Crash in 1929 the global wave of economic disaster washed over Clydeside, and by 1936 the output from the shipyards had fallen from three-quarters of a million tons to less than 60,000, with at least two-thirds of the workforce unemployed. In order to try to increase efficiency and generate more trade, firms merged and pruned their labour forces still further, resulting in more job losses. Not surprisingly, socialism flourished, passionately fuelled by leaders like James Maxton and Emmanuel Shinwell. Public opinion favoured the plight of the workers, and by the end of the 1930s things were beginning to look up. The Second World War brought with it a fresh demand for armaments and ships: Clydeside boomed and Scotland grew prosperous again. But after the war competition from abroad began to steal trade. Instead of seeing the need to modernize, the Scots, led by militant unions, grumbled and groaned and went on strike, refusing to accept innovations which could have kept them in the forefront of the world's industry. Strikes led to failure to meet deadlines, and buyers went elsewhere. Shipyards, steelworks and factories closed. Less coal was needed so coalmines closed. Sullen Scots queued for their dole cheques and blamed their employers. The oil boom in the 1970s brought new prosperity for a while, but this was short-lived.

A new generation of enterprising minds, particularly from Glasgow, is turning the tide of apathy. Diversification has spread a rash of light industry throughout the country. The Scottish education system is more democratic and more effective than that of England. The legal system is also different: rooted in Roman and Germanic customary law, it is more logical than English law and is based on common law. Politically, Scotland leans to the left and juggles with nationalism. Those in favour of autonomy hold that they are the poor relations of politicians at Westminster, whose survival-of-the-fittest policies make no allowance for Scotland's circumstances. But when, in 1979, they were invited to vote for devolution, over 36 per cent didn't bother to vote. There were further stirrings of nationalist feeling prior to the general election of 1992, when it seemed likely that the Conservative Party's 13-year grip on government would be loosened. The opposition parties were united in offering greater or lesser degrees of autonomy to the Scottish people, but these promises came to nothing when the Conservatives, although winning a mere 11 of Scotland's 72 seats in Parliament, were once again returned to power in the south.

In the 1997 general election the New Labour Party led by Tony Blair won a landslide victory in Britain, wiping out all Tory constituencies north of the border. Scotland's most able MPs won seats in England, leaving no obvious National leader. A referendum was held in September and the Scots voted by 74 per cent for a Scottish Parliament and by 63.5 per cent for that parliament to have tax-raising powers. The outcome was greeted with jubilation, but there remain a number of questions to be answered. There is, for example, the 'West Lothian Question': why should Scottish MPs continue to vote on English matters at Westminster, while English MPs are denied reciprocal rights in Edinburgh? The new Scottish Parliament is in its infancy, with all the teething problems to be expected. The first First Minister, Donald Dewar, died in office. His successor was forced to resign after allegations of misuse of public funds. Time alone will reveal its strengths and weaknesses, its successes and failures.

Scottish Nationalists hail devolution as the first, irrevocable step on the road to independence. They believe that an alliance with Europe would be better for their country than union with England. Meanwhile, the true Stone of Destiny still waits... (*see* **Topics**, p.66).

Topics

04

Religious Differences

In the Highlands and Islands, where communities tend to be slow to change, there are predominantly Catholic areas, where some of the people rejected the Reformation, while others, following the laird, became Protestant. On the whole, Catholics and Protestants live together perfectly happily with few of the sectarian problems experienced in Ireland. The football field proves an occasional exception, particularly when fans of the two Glasgow teams, traditionally Catholic Celtic and Protestant Rangers, meet. Sometimes, too, an innovation conflicts with the strict Sabbatarian beliefs and practices of a small proportion of Presbyterians, and invariably members of the media will manage to stir up an 'incident'.

In the Outer Hebrides, South Uist, Eriskay and Barra are almost entirely Catholic. In their belief God belongs to every day and Sunday is for celebration, both in church and out. North Uist, Harris and Lewis are Presbyterian and the most rigid Protestants in Britain. Their interpretation of the Fourth Commandment is stringently enforced by the Lord's Day Observance Society, who exert moral, social and political pressure. Sunday is for long sermons in church, full of the threat of damnation; for reading the Bible and holy tracts; for dark clothes and solemn faces. No work must be done, not even cooking; the washing must come in off the line; the fishing boats must lie at anchor. In some places, they say, swings are padlocked and cocks are separated from hens.

Not so long ago, no ferries ran to the islands on Sundays. Then Caledonian MacBrayne announced a changed schedule including some Sunday sailings. The uproar was clamorous. There were huffings and puffings and threats of barricades. Running in tandem with this dispute, there was friction over a new £12 million school, built at tax-payers' expense, on the island of Benbecula, midway between the Catholic south and Protestant north and serving both. The predominantly Protestant Western Isles Council would not employ supervisory staff on Sundays, so no one could use the school's leisure facilities – swimming pool, cafeteria, games hall, library, etc. Catholics protested that their beliefs allowed them to have fun on Sundays and they saw no reason why Sabbatarian rules should prevent them from doing so. The situation was satisfactorily resolved in the end, but not without lasting damage to the hitherto dignified, *laissez-faire* attitudes that enabled such extreme creeds to live side by side in harmony.

The majority of Scots belong to the Established Church of Scotland, or Presbyterian Church, and its many breakaway sects. The Episcopal Church, with its bishops, is the equivalent of the Church of England. The Free Presbyterian Church of Scotland (Wee Frees) is a tiny, fundamentalist sect who believe that the Pope is 'Antichrist' and the Mass ... 'the most blasphemous form of religious worship that Satan ever invented; an offence unto God and destructive of the souls of men.' In 1989 Britain's Lord Chancellor, Lord Mackay of Clashfern, a member of this strict sect, was castigated by fellow members of his congregation because he attended requiem masses for two of his Catholic friends. The Free Church Synod suspended him from his position as a senior Elder of the Kirk, and from Communion. Lord Mackay, who once said his Church gave 'the most tender love that has ever been described', was forced to resign from it.

Clans and Tartans

The Scottish clan system was once an integral part of the Highlands and Islands. Every member of the clan bore the name of the chief, whether related by blood or by allegiance, and each was an equal member of the clan family (Mac means son of). The chief was the father, ruler and judge, and the strength of the clan lay in his justice, kindness and wisdom, and in the loyalty of the members of the clan to him and to one another. Rents were mostly paid in kind or man-rent and, in return for his patronage and protection, the chief could call on his people at any time to form an army and fight for him.

It is known that Highlanders wore some sort of brightly coloured, striped and checked material as far back as the 13th century, though whether the designs, or 'setts', were related to clans or to territories is not known for certain. The Suppression of the Highlands after Culloden in 1746 broke up clans, forbade tartan and Highland dress to all civilians, and led to the death of the clan system. During the 36 years Highland dress was banned, many of the old setts were lost or forgotten.

The Highland regiments were exempt from the ban, so it is through them that the kilt survived. The early regiments all wore the Government, or Black Watch, tartan, sometimes introducing coloured overstripes to differentiate one regiment from another. It was not until Hanoverian George IV appeared at Holyrood in 1822, in an astonishing Highland outfit, that the fashion for tartan was revived. In a wave of enthusiasm, a large number of tartans were hastily designed, and adopted by clans who had for many years been kindred in name only. They were also keenly worn by Lowlanders whose ancestors would have died rather than be seen in Highland dress. It is these relatively modern patterns that make up most of today's enormous range of tartans, which can be seen all over the world, not only in cloth but also adorning luggage, footwear and a staggering range of knick-knacks. The average Scotsman doesn't stride over his native hills swathed in tartan. On the whole, kilts are kept for ceremonial or formal occasions, or for 'Sunday best', and a great many Scotsmen don't even own one.

Clan feelings still run strong, especially in the veins of expatriates, but the clan name is now no more than an umbrella for museums, annual gatherings and ceremonial, with the chief as a figurehead, in a tartan costume redolent of mothballs. The mystique that has grown up round clan tartans is put into perspective by the apocryphal story of the irate chieftain, towering over one of a coach party, visiting his ancestral castle:

'By what right are you wearing my tartan, my man?'
'By the ri' o' purrchis, at fifteen pounds a yard, my lord.'

The Highland Clearances

The Clearances are an emotive subject and it has to be remembered that the first emigration ship sailed out of Fort William as early as 1773, almost 20 years before *Bliadhna nan Caorachd* – the year of the sheep. There were several reasons for the depopulation of the Highlands after Culloden. Some Jacobites who had escaped execution found it expedient to go abroad for a few years; others were transported. Many Catholics, unable to practise their religion publicly at home, sought liberty across the ocean. The suppression of the Highlands and the breaking up of the clan system deprived chiefs of their hereditary status as patriarchs, and many drifted south to become London Scots. Away from the womb of the clan and the benefits of feudality, however, they felt the pinch financially. Vast, infertile estates in the north, overpopulated by impoverished peasants, brought in little or no revenue. Rents paid in kind were of little use to those trying to keep up with society in fashionable assembly rooms or pay off gambling debts in gentlemen's clubs. Sheep farmers from the south offered good rent for sheep-runs in the north, but they wanted land free of people. Highland landowners, desperate for money, began to evict their tenants. Some built resettlement towns and villages for them and established new livelihoods such as fishing; some merely served eviction notices and employed agents to enforce them; some offered to assist with fares to new countries. Hundreds of crofting communities – those which relied entirely on their smallholdings for a living – broke up and scattered. Those who didn't emigrate flocked to the cities in the hope of finding work, or to settlements, mainly on the coast, where the land was unsuitable for sheep.

Meanwhile, in the islands landlords basked in a false prosperity from the kelp industry. Seaweed, of which there was a seemingly inexhaustible supply, was collected after each tide, burned in kilns, processed into valuable fertilizer and exported. All that was needed was a huge labour force to cut, carry and burn it. Island proprietors with an eye to the main chance offered tiny plots of land to dispossessed crofters from the mainland. They charged high rent and deliberately ensured each tenant did not have enough land for self-sufficiency, forcing them to work at the kelp. By 1812 the islands were crammed with people entirely dependent on kelp for their living. After the Napoleonic Wars, import duty was abolished and cheap foreign kelp flooded the market: prices plummeted; people starved. Proprietors and politicians, faced with the problem of destitute multitudes, offered inducements to encourage emigration, and many people went. The final blow came in 1846. The potato blight, responsible for the famine which had already decimated Ireland, drifted across the sea in wind-borne spores and descended on Scotland, half of whose population lived on potatoes. For the already starving Highlanders and Islanders, the effect was catastrophic. Many of those who had managed to stay on, often surviving several evictions, were now forced to join their compatriots in Canada, America, Australia and New Zealand. By the end of the 19th century, the rural Highlands and Islands were almost deserted.

Gaelic

Gaelic is still the first language in the Outer Hebrides but, even there, with an influx of non-Gaelic speakers and television, the children are growing up speaking English among themselves. Elsewhere it is no longer a living language, though many people are trying to revive it and there are many great Gaelic scholars. Sabhal Mor Ostaig, in Skye, is a popular and very successful Gaelic college; television and radio have a lot of Gaelic slots. It is taught in schools and in adult classes, and there are a large number of Gaelic publications. It is an almost impossible language to 'pick up' by ear and eye because the spoken word bears little resemblance to the written. More and more notices are appearing now in the Highlands and Islands, proclaiming place names in Gaelic. They must cost a fortune: local people don't need them, and visitors can neither understand nor pronounce them.

Gaelic, which is much older than English, stems from the Goidelic branch of Celtic languages, which were an offshoot from the earlier Indo-European language. Scottish Gaelic became a distinct dialect separate from Irish around the 13th century, and there are still many similarities. With the revival of Gaelic has come a revival of Gaelic culture. Groups like Runrig and Capercaillie, who perform modern-style Gaelic music, are enormously popular and an important part of the Scottish music scene.

Crofting

Since the Highland Clearances, croftland tenure has been strictly controlled to protect the rights of the tenant. A croft is a smallholding with a few acres, as many sheep as the land will support, and sometimes cows and poultry. If there is arable land it will be tilled. In the old days, *feannagan*, or inappropriately named lazy-beds, were dug for potatoes, involving much hard work, deep digging and the carting of heavy creels of seaweed for fertilizer. Some of the work on the croft is still done communally – sheep-dipping and shearing for instance, and cutting the peat and haymaking. Peat is still used as fuel in some areas. Composed of partially rotted vegetation, compressed in waterlogged conditions in temperate or cold climates, it takes 3,000 years to form a depth of one foot, so peat bogs are getting scarce. It is cut in the spring in oblong slabs with a special digger and stacked *in situ*, on end like miniature wigwams, until dry. In a wet summer the peat can still be lying late into the year. Once dry, it is built into neat beehives. As recently as the 1970s hay was cut by hand, with scythes, and it is still turned with pitchforks until dry. The crofter is the owner or tenant of the croft. Most crofters have a subsidiary job as well: fishing, building or public works.

The family dwelling is the croft-house – often mistakenly called the croft. Less than 50 years ago many Highlanders still lived in a *tigh dubh* or black house, now almost extinct except as a folk museum or byre. It had thick, double walls, about 6ft high, made of local stone and packed with earth and rubble. Unlined on the inside, it had rounded corners, no gables, and a reed- or heather-thatched roof anchored by boulders tied to ropes of plaited heather. Inside, the furniture was functional: a dresser, box-beds, a bench, stools, rat-proof meal chests, coffers and a spinning wheel. A peat fire was laid on a stone slab on the earthen floor in the middle of the room, the smoke escaping out of a hole in the thatch. In earlier times, light came from a *crùis-gean* – a lamp fuelled with fish liver oil burning on a wick of plaited rushes. Even within the 20th century, in some island communities the beasts shared the family house, penned at one end with the floor sloping down towards them and the effluent running out through holes in the wall.

Open rebellion by some communities (*see* p.514) against Draconian landlords, at the climax of the Clearances, attracted the attention of 'the media'. Unwelcome publicity, coupled with unrest over the demand for Irish Home Rule, forced Gladstone's government to set up a Royal Commission of inquiry in 1883, with Lord Napier in the chair. The Commission comprised two landowners who were sympathetic to the crofters' problems, two Gaelic scholars and an MP who was also a member of the Highland Land Law Reform Association. These men toured the Highlands and Islands during 1883–4 (once getting shipwrecked off Stornoway), collecting overwhelming evidence in favour of reform. With the extension of the parliamentary franchise in 1885, entitling crofters to vote, the crofter question was a dominant issue in the general elections of 1885 and 1886, with a new political party emerging. As always, Scottish affairs seldom received priority at Westminster, but public opinion was by now so strong that the Crofters' Holdings (Scotland) Act was passed, in which crofters were granted security of tenure and a Crofters Commission was appointed to fix fair rents. There were teething problems but by the end of the century crofters' rights were secure and peace prevailed.

Recent legislation has made it possible for crofters to buy their crofts. This has not been an attractive proposition for many, except in a few cases such as Assynt where a community 'buy out' has taken place aided by Government funding. There are controversial proposals in a current bill before the Scottish Parliament to allow the 'Community' in crofting areas to buy fishing and mineral rights. The complications and ramifications are endless and stretch into the future across a morass of invective.

Ceilidh

Céilidh (pronounced kayly) is a Gaelic word meaning visit. In winter, when nights were long, crofters used to gather in one of the houses when darkness fell, packed in round the central fire. One of the older members, often a bard or musician, acted as the master of ceremonies, and everyone was expected to contribute to the entertainment. The women knitted or spun, men repaired fishing nets or whittled wood; everyone listened. Stories, songs, poems, proverbs and legends were recited, passing their history, folklore and tradition from one generation to the next. Their music stirred the soul: mouth-music, straight from the heart; Gaelic songs; pipe, harp and fiddle music. Children grew up steeped in the past and could tell you who their great-great-great-grand-uncle was and whose sweetheart he had run off with. The practice is dying now, thanks to television, and ceilidhs tend to be commercial shows, staged in halls and hotels.

Piping

with thanks to David Murray

Two kinds of bagpipes are played in Scotland these days, the 'warm wind' and the 'cold wind'. The Highland bagpipe, being mouth blown, is 'warm wind'; the Lowland or Border bagpipe is blown by a bellows operated by the piper's right elbow, hence 'the cold wind pipes'. The Highland bagpipe is designed to be played out of doors; the Lowland is essentially an indoor instrument. Recent improvements in the manufacture of the Highland bagpipe, along with the higher standards now being demanded by audiences, have altered the tone of the instrument until it can be listened to with pleasure indoors, where the most prestigious piping events are held. The Highland bagpipe no longer 'skirls'. The 'Small Music' of the Highland bagpipe includes marches and dance tunes in differing tempi; the *ceòl mor*, the 'Great Music' (usually anglicized as 'pibroch' from *pìobaireachd*, meaning piping) comprises tunes constructed on a theme followed by up to ten variations.

Pibroch pieces date from the late 15th century and their names commemorate great events in Highland history. Pibroch is listened to in silence. It is unwise for the visitor to interrupt, even by a whisper. The Lowland pipes are intended to accompany social events indoors, and fit in well with the folk music groups now popular in Scotland and beyond. Their tone is sweet and mellow and the repertoire includes the ancient Border ballads from the days of the cross-border raids and feuds, as well as a wide range of dance music and song airs. Both instruments are taken seriously in Scotland, for their own sake as well as for their traditional connotations. Derogatory comment is not appreciated, especially if voiced in the accents of south Britain. The pipes were never specifically proscribed by the Disarming Act of 1747, but it would have been a brave piper who played within earshot of a Government post. The oldest thesis on pipe music was written during the proscription, and there are several pibroch pieces that were composed while the Act was still in force.

Seers

The second sight, *taibhsearachd* in Gaelic, goes hand in hand with sorcery, and among the many seers who emerged from the Celtic mists were Thomas the Rhymer and the Brahan Seer. Thomas, born in 1220, lived for nearly 80 years, and earned himself the title 'True Thomas'. He predicted the death of Alexander III and the Battle of Bannockburn. Traditionally, he had a passionate affair with the Fairy Queen and went off to live with her for three years in Elfland, deep in the Eildon Hills.

The Brahan Seer, Còinneach Odhar, is an enigmatic figure of unauthenticated provenance, known for the uncanny accuracy of many of his prophecies about the

Highlands, some of which are still to be fulfilled. He fell asleep, so it is said, on an enchanted hillside: when he awoke he was clutching a stone with a hole in it, through which he could see the truth and the future. Among the events he foretold that have already happened are the depopulation of the Highlands, the demise of crofting, the arrival of rich landowners, and the making of the Caledonian Canal. He said that when it was possible to cross the River Ness in Inverness dryshod in five places, a terrible disaster would strike the world. There were four bridges over the Ness until a fifth was erected to replace one about to be demolished. This was opened at the end of August 1939: on 1 September Hitler marched into Poland.

The Brahan Seer met his death by antagonizing his patroness, the Countess of Seaforth. The Earl visited France, soon after the Restoration of Charles II in 1660, and had not returned. The Countess sent for the Brahan Seer and asked what her husband was doing. When he was reluctant to say, she pressed him until he revealed that the Earl was in a sumptuous gilded room, grandly decked out in velvet, silk and cloth of gold, with a voluptuous lady on his lap. The Countess was furious, accused him of malice and ordered him to be burnt in a barrel of tar at Fortrose. Before he died he predicted the downfall of the Seaforth MacKenzies, whose line came to an end after a dramatic chain of events, precisely following the prophecy, in 1815.

Bonnie Prince Charlie

Charles Edward Louis John Casimir Silvester Severino Maria Stuart, better known as Bonnie Prince Charlie and as the Young Pretender (from the French 'prétendre', to claim), was born in Rome on 31 December 1720. He was brought up to believe that his father, James, the Old Pretender, was the rightful heir to the British throne and that he himself was the heir apparent.

James, born in 1688, was the only son of James VII/II by his second wife, Mary of Modena. Both England and Scotland wanted a Protestant king and James VII/II was staunchly Catholic, so he was removed from the throne in 1689 and replaced by Mary, his eldest daughter by his first marriage to Anne Hyde, and her unattractive husband, William of Orange. They were succeeded by Mary's sister, Anne, in 1702, and on her death in 1714 the throne passed to George I, great-grandson of James VI/I through his daughter Elizabeth, to preserve the Protestant line. He was an unpleasant man who disliked the English as much as they disliked him. He was succeeded by his son, George II, in 1727.

The Old Pretender, recognized and funded by the Pope as the legal King of Britain, made several abortive attempts to claim his throne. He married Clementine Sobieska who bore him two sons, Charles and Henry (born 1725). He believed that his sons should mix with Protestants as well as Catholics and saw to it that they did so. Charles grew up in an atmosphere of intrigue, finding himself courted as Prince of Wales and heir apparent to the throne of Great Britain. He had a natural charm that would win support in the future.

In 1743 the French decided that an invasion of Scotland, with Prince Charles Edward Stuart as leader, would confound the English and install a pro-French Jacobite on the throne. Having instigated the plot, the French were not over-generous in their support, but Charles raised the necessary funds and in July 1745 set sail for Scotland in the *Du Teillay*.

Off the Lizard the Prince's escort ship *Elisabeth* was involved in an engagement with HMS *Lion*. Both ships were badly damaged and *Elisabeth* was forced to retreat to France, carrying with her most of the invading force's arms and stores. The Prince continued north to Scotland. Eighteen days after leaving France he went ashore on the tiny island of Eriskay in the Outer Hebrides. Legend has it that seeds of a pink convolvulus carried on his shoes from France fell and germinated where he walked. True or not, the flower still grows on Eriskay and nowhere else in the Hebrides.

His reception was not wholehearted. Macdonald of Boisdale advised him to return home. 'I am come home, sir,' retorted the Prince. Landing on the mainland at Loch nan Uamh in Arisaig, he was faced by the reluctance of the clan chiefs to support him. Eventually, however, he won the grudging support of the Macdonalds and Cameron of Lochiel, and on 19 August 1745 he raised his father's standard at Glenfinnan. The Old Pretender was proclaimed King James VIII of Scotland and Charles appointed his regent. His supporters numbered just 1,200 ill-equipped clansmen, mostly Macdonalds and Camerons.

The Highlanders marched first to Invergarry, collecting support on the way, and on to Blair Atholl, by which time their number had reached 2,000. From Blair Atholl they carried on to Perth where the Prince heard that General Cope was planning to take the Government army from Inverness to Edinburgh to defend the capital. The Prince arrived at Edinburgh on 16 September and the Government troops stationed there fled in disarray. The Highlanders took control of the city in the name of King James VIII.

General Cope arrived at the outskirts of Edinburgh and was famously beaten by the Highlanders in the 15-minute Battle of Prestonpans on 21 September. With the benefit of local knowledge of the terrain, the Prince's men were able to overwhelm the enemy with the sheer speed and ferocity of their attack.

The outcome of this battle so boosted the Prince's morale that he came to believe he and his army were invincible, in spite of the fact that many of the Highlanders deserted after the battle. A recruiting campaign brought his army up to about 5,500 and in November they set off for London, believing that the Prince's brother, Henry, was to come to their aid with a considerable French army.

By 4 December the Highlanders had reached Derby, just 127 miles from London. Charles was confident of going on to take the capital but his staff thought otherwise. They had found little support for their cause in England and had no way of knowing that almost nothing lay between them and the capital, nor that the French were close to launching their invasion of the south coast. Reluctantly, the Prince agreed to retreat to Scotland.

The Highlanders' retreat was an orderly one and by 20 December, just six weeks after his campaign had begun, Charles was back in Scotland. On 17 January 1746 the

Highlanders won their last battle, defeating Cope's successor, General Hawley, at Falkirk. Lack of firepower prevented the Highlanders from taking Stirling Castle and, knowing the Duke of Cumberland's army to be heading north, they carried on to Inverness.

On 16 April 1746 Charles' army of 6,000 faced the 9,000-strong army of the Duke of Cumberland on Drummossie Moor near Culloden, 5 miles from Inverness. Within an hour the Jacobite rebellion was finally over. Over 1,000 Highlanders were slaughtered by the better disciplined and equipped English army; on Cumberland's orders many more were butchered as they lay wounded and helpless.

Charles escaped to begin five months of hiding in the Highlands and Islands with a price of £30,000 on his head. During all that time no one betrayed him. Famous among his exploits was his trip 'over the sea to Skye' from South Uist, disguised as Flora Macdonald's serving woman 'Betty Burke'. On 19 September Prince Charles Edward Stuart sailed from Borrodale, never to return. He spent the rest of his life in France and Italy, drowning his bitterness in habitual drunkenness. He died in January 1788 of a stroke, leaving his legend behind him.

Dr Samuel Johnson (1709–84) and James Boswell (1740–95)

When Dr Samuel Johnson, English critic, poet and lexicographer, aged 63, and his companion 32-year-old James Boswell, Scottish writer and Johnson's biographer, set off on their journey to the Hebrides in 1773, the first emigrant ships had already sailed and the Highlands were rapidly losing the character Dr Johnson wished to observe. The Act of Proscription imposed after the 1745 Jacobite Rising had virtually wiped out the clan system and everything that went with it.

What they found was a wild land, totally foreign to Johnson's experience. A fierce supporter of the underdog, whether slave or victim of the Clearances, Johnson's account of their journey, read in parallel with Boswell's, gives a graphic picture of the Highlands in the latter part of the 18th century.

Boswell was a well-born snob who 'collected' Johnson some 10 years before they set out on their journey. Whether he actually liked Johnson or not is disputable. After their first meeting in 1763, he described him thus: 'Mr Johnson is a man of most dreadful appearance. He is a very big man, is troubled with sore eyes, the palsy and the King's evil [scrofula]. He is very slovenly in his dress and speaks with a most uncouth voice. Yet his great knowledge and strength of expression command vast respect and render him very excellent company.'

The unlikely pair set off on their journey – the frighteningly literate Johnson, dogmatic and irascible, susceptible to female charms and careful of his health, accompanied by Boswell, intelligent but largely self-taught, sensitive to the opinions of others, punctilious, and randy as a goat. They left Edinburgh on 18 August 1773 and travelled via St Andrews and Montrose up the east coast to Aberdeen. From here they visited Slains Castle. Johnson was intrigued by the architecture and by the local features. Boswell was more concerned with the discomfort of his room and the smell of his pillow.

As they continued through Forres they both record a mention of Macbeth. Johnson noted that they were approaching 'a prelude to the Highlands, leaving fertility and culture behind with nothing ahead but a great length of road, nothing but heath'. At Nairn they saw their first peat fires and first heard the Gaelic language.

In Inverness Boswell was embarrassed by Johnson's espousal of the benefits gained by Scotland following the Act of Union in 1707, and worried about what people who didn't know him might think. From Inverness they took to horses and rode down Loch Ness. Passing a druid's temple Johnson commented, 'To go and see one druidical temple is only to see that it is nothing, for there is neither art nor power in it; and seeing one is quite enough.'

They visited an old woman in a bothy, where Johnson first discovered the primitive conditions in which the peasants lived. He was interested to know where the old crone slept, but she suspected his motives and he withdrew. Boswell was less tactful and inspected her humble sleeping area by the light of a taper.

From Fort Augustus they travelled west. On this part of their journey Johnson noted that the country was 'totally denuded of its wood, but the stumps both of oak and firs, which are still found, shew that it has been once a forest of large timber'. They passed a party of soldiers to whom they gave 'two shillings to drink'. The soldiers turned up at the pub in Glenmoriston where Boswell and Johnson had put up for the night. The travellers clearly sat up with them and their hangovers the following morning were attributed to the poor quality of the whisky. Their host during this visit bemoaned the fact that the rent for his farm had gone up to 20 pounds from 5 pounds in 20 years.

As they progressed into the 'bosom of the Highlands' Johnson recorded that they now had 'full leisure to contemplate the appearance and properties of mountainous regions, such as have been, in many countries, the last shelters of national distress, and are everywhere the scenes of adventures, stratagems, surprises and escapes'. He was amazed to see snow on the peaks and to learn that it might stay there until added to by the following winter's snows.

As they passed Bernera Barracks near Glenelg, Boswell thought wistfully of the hospitality they might have had from such a place, but the barracks was manned by only a sergeant and a few soldiers and they passed on to an inn at Glenelg. Here they were shown to a room that was 'damp and dirty, with bare walls, a variety of bad smells, a coarse black greasy fir table, and forms of the same kind'. Johnson slept in his clothes on a bundle of hay. Boswell 'being more delicate, laid himself sheets with hay over and under him and lay in linen like a gentleman'.

They then crossed to Armadale in Skye where they were welcomed by Sir Alexander Macdonald and entertained by bagpipes. They encountered the beginnings of the island winter of wind and rain, in contrast to the Highland winter of snow and ice. On the island of Raasay they were lavishly entertained by the laird, Mr Macleod, and his family of three sons and ten daughters. They dined and danced and listened to Gaelic songs. While exploring the island Boswell discovered the ruins of Castle

Brochel, complete with inside lavatory, a facility rarely found in the houses of Scotland at the time. 'Sir,' he said to his host, 'you take very good care of one end of a man, but not the other.'

From Raasay they made their way anticlockwise around Skye and called on Macdonald of Kingsborough and his wife, Flora. She, renowned for her part in the escape of Bonnie Prince Charlie after the failure of the '45, so impressed Johnson that he wrote of her: 'Flora Macdonald, a name that will be mentioned in history and if courage and fidelity be virtues, mentioned with honour.'

On they went to Dunvegan where they found 'Lady Macleod, who had lived many years in England, who knew all the arts of southern elegance and all the modes of English economy'. Johnson found Dunvegan so comfortable that Boswell had to prod him into continuing their journey.

As they travelled on Johnson noted details of the agriculture and the Highlands generally, while Boswell noted the hangovers that resulted from over-indulgence in bowls of punch. A storm during their crossing to Coll frightened Boswell more than Johnson, who retired to his berth and ignored it. Bad weather kept them on Coll longer than either of them found amusing.

They sailed for Mull on 14 October. Travelling across the island put Johnson in a bad humour, partly because his horse was too small for him and could hardly bear his weight and partly because he lost the oak stick he had brought from London. They crossed to Iona by moonlight. Johnson said, 'If this be not roving among the Hebrides, nothing is.' Both men were deeply moved by 'treading that illustrious island which was once the luminary of the Caledonian regions whence savage clans and roving barbarians derived the benefits of knowledge and the blessings of religion'. They spent the night in a barn and the next day explored the monastery, abbey and other buildings. Boswell was disappointed to find it all so broken down, and was unimpressed by the uninscribed gravestones of the kings. He had expected marble monuments such as those found in Westminster Abbey.

They returned to Mull where they were entertained by the Laird of Lochbuy, described by Boswell as a 'bluff, comely, noisy old gentleman, proud of his hereditary consequence and a very hearty and hospitable landlord'. Johnson was not pleased to be offered cold sheep's head for breakfast. They inspected the castle and Johnson recorded a general description of castles in the Highlands and Islands.

From Mull they crossed to Oban on the mainland, somewhat relieved to be not so much at the mercy of the elements. They were amused to read in a newspaper that they were thought to be still weather-bound on Skye. At Inverary they were entertained by the Duke of Argyll, whom Boswell knew, and were well pleased with his hospitality. Continuing on horses supplied by the Duke they crossed the Rest and Be Thankful and descended to Loch Lomond.

The remainder of their journey took them out of the Highlands, south to Ayrshire and so back to Edinburgh. Boswell recorded that Johnson had told him that the time he had spent on his journey was the pleasantest part of his life.

Two Enlightened Men

Walter Scott (1771–1832)

A woman who knew Walter Scott as a child described him as sweet and intelligent and 'the most extraordinary genius of a boy'. One of his tutors described him as an incorrigibly idle imp but never a dunce. In maturity he was worldly, genial, magnanimous, never jealous or petty, patriotic and loyal. He was a combination of romantic and practical and his integrity was much admired. Scott was one of 12 children, son of a Writer to the Signet in Edinburgh and a physician's daughter. A childhood illness affected his right leg. From the age of three he spent much of his youth at his grandparents' farm, Sandyknowe, in the Tweed valley, where his grandparents tried every sort of cure for his lameness, such as wrapping his leg in the fleece of a newly killed sheep, but without success. He sat for hours listening to the Border shepherds and country people, and to the songs his grandmother sang for him and her endless fund of legends. The essence of the land seeped into his soul to become his inspiration.

When stronger, he was sent to Edinburgh High School, where, though lazy, he excelled at Latin. In spite of his deformity, he was physically brave and was renowned for climbing on the dangerous crags of the Castle Rock. He was also quick to square up to the 'town boys' who used to taunt their more privileged peers. Growing too fast in adolescence, he became weak and was sent to Kelso for six months' convalescence. Here he read Percy's *Reliques*, a collection of ancient ballads, songs, sonnets and romances discovered, restored and edited by Percy, and these, together with the romances of 16th-century Torquato Tasso, and Spenser's *Faerie Queene*, fired his imagination. He also studied the old romantic poetry of France and Italy, and modern German poetry. Even in his teens he had the gift of spinning a good yarn, and he would ramble over Arthur's Seat in Edinburgh, swapping stories with a friend.

He went to Edinburgh University, where he was no less idle but continued to collect material to feed his passion for romantic ballads and songs. By the time he was a law clerk in his father's office, he was tall and strong, with a graceful figure and 'the chest and arms of Hercules'. His features were 'not handsome but singularly varied and pleasing', with bright eyes and a 'brilliant complexion'. He fell deeply in love with a girl of 16 called Williamina Belsches, but because of her age her father forbade their friendship. His friends believed this was the strongest passion of his life and that Williamina appears in several of his novels.

He was called to the Bar in 1792 and travelled the country, always listening, observing, absorbing. His first visit to the Highlands, second only to the Borders as background for his stories, was while he was on a case, directing one of the evictions of the Clearances. In 1796 he published, anonymously, a collection of translations of German ballads. On holiday in Cumbria, he met Margaret Charlotte Carpenter, daughter of a Royalist émigré from the French Revolution, who was taking the waters at Gilsland Spa. She was high-spirited and beautiful with an entrancing French accent, dark brown eyes, masses of black hair and a 'fairy-like figure'. They fell in love and were married in Carlisle Cathedral on Christmas Eve 1797.

Two years later he was appointed Sheriff of Selkirkshire, a position he held for 27 years, during which time he wrote the majority of his books. To begin with he stuck to ballads and romantic poems. His first publication was *Border Minstrelsy*, three volumes of ballads he had collected and edited, and this was followed by his first original work, the romantic poem 'The Lay of the Last Minstrel'. He became a partner in James Ballantyne's printing business. In 1811, with the money rolling in from his prolific (but still anonymous) output and his post of Sheriff, he bought land on the Tweed and built himself a fanciful baronial castle, described by Ruskin as an incongruous pile. The place was originally called Clarty Hole – *clarty* being the Scots word for dirty or muddy – so he changed it to the more dignified Abbotsford, in memory of the days when it was just that.

About this time, Byron hit the headlines with 'Childe Harold' and Scott, recognizing without rancour a greater talent than his own, decided to turn his pen to prose. He was self-deprecating about his poetry: when someone asked his daughter if she had read 'The Lay of the Last Minstrel', she shook her head and answered demurely: 'Oh no, Papa says there is nothing so injurious for young people as reading bad poetry.' Indeed, when he was offered the laureateship in 1813, he turned it down, suggesting Southey as an alternative, although many would argue that his loose, flowing verse was preferable to Southey's rather stilted, plodding style. *Waverley* was Scott's first novel, published in 1814, a stirring Jacobite tale in which the turncoat hero is rescued from reprisals after Culloden by an English colonel whose life he had saved. In the following 16 years he published 29 stories. When he had milked Scottish history dry, he turned to England in the Middle Ages, and rattled off *Ivanhoe*. Among the many places and periods he wrote about was 15th-century France, in *Quentin Durward*, and he frequently returned to his beloved Scotland, as in *Redgauntlet*, the imaginative story of Prince Charlie's abortive return, some years after 1745, to have another crack at the throne. Scott entwined his extensive knowledge of the minutiae of history with romance and adventure, and he brought the past vividly to life by endowing it with the present. He was not always strong on character, though some of his simple country people were brilliant, and his plots were a bit shaky, but his sense of place was outstanding and his passion for history gave him a limitless supply of stories. His books were good clean fun, and as such were loved by the reading public. As well as novels, he wrote and edited a number of learned publications including histories, essays, biography and the delightful children's history: *Tales of a Grandfather*.

Scott's influence as a novelist was unquestionable. He established the form of the historical novel and was a model to such other novelists as Mrs Gaskell, George Eliot and the Brontës. 'The Two Drovers' and 'The Highland Widow' were, in themselves, a new form of short story. Abbotsford became a popular meeting place for all the learned men of the day. Scott was liked and admired and had many friends. In maturity he was described as a straightforward man who got on equally well with dukes and peasants, a delightful companion, not only to his contemporaries but also to his children. Growing up as he had during the Scottish Enlightenment, his circle included many of the great men who created Scotland's Golden Age. He contributed to the *Edinburgh Review* until its Whiggish leanings outraged his Tory heart, when he promoted the rival *Quarterly Review*. In 1818 he instigated a successful search for the 'Honours of Scotland', as the crown jewels were called. Tucked away in a chest at the Union of Parliaments in 1707, they had been forgotten. Scott's passion for history embraced a passion for the trappings of the past and the Scottish regalia were the oldest in Europe. In 1820 he was created a baronet and in 1822 he had an enthusiastic hand in George IV's flamboyant visit to Edinburgh. He was always surrounded by a crowd of dogs and thoroughly enjoyed gentlemanly sport. It was a period of prosperity and happiness until 1826, when disaster struck.

Due partly to the inefficiency of James Ballantyne, the printer, and partly to rash borrowing, the firm went bankrupt, together with Scott's publisher, Constable. As a partner, Scott himself was liable for some £114,000. Determined to repay every penny to his creditors, he threw himself into an even greater frenzy of work, breaking his health and shortening his life. In 1827, no longer Sheriff of Selkirkshire, he emerged from the anonymity he had previously sheltered behind and poured a torrent of words into several more books, some of which reflect the rapid decline in his health. Scott's own pathetic *Journal* shows how anguished his last few years were. He died in 1832 at the age of 61, within sight and sound of the River Tweed, surrounded by his family. All his debts were paid as a result of his labours, and Abbotsford, which had been restored to him by his creditors, was preserved as a monument. It is an apt memorial to a man whose passion for Scotland was unrivalled and who himself epitomized the things he admired most about his beloved country.

Perhaps the most informative biography of Scott is *Memoirs of the Life of Sir Walter Scott* by his son-in-law, John Gibson Lockhart, a comprehensive account full of personal anecdotes, but perhaps a little too tender in some details.

Robert Burns (1759–96)

Immortal Robert Burns of Ayr,
There's but few poets can with you compare;
Some of your poems and songs are very fine:
'To Mary in Heaven' is most sublime;
And then again in your 'Cottar's Saturday Night',
Your genius there does shine most bright,
As pure as the dewdrops of night...
tribute from 'Scotland's worst poet', William McGonagall

Burns, the ploughman-poet, came from a very different background from that of Walter Scott, but he was no less remarkable a product of the Scottish Enlightenment. He was a genius. He cut through elegant devices and rhetoric and went straight to the heart of mankind. No subject was sacrosanct: 'Holy Willie's Prayer' is a blueprint for satire. Nothing could be more tender than his 'To a Mouse', that 'Wee, sleekit, cowrin', tim'rous beastie' he turned up in her nest with his plough, nor more romantic than his love who was 'like a red, red rose, that's newly sprung in June'. Nationalism blazes in 'Scots, wha hae wi' Wallace bled', and the revolutionary spirit was so strong in 'A man's a man for a' that' that it had to be published anonymously.

Burns' admirers shroud him with an almost mawkish sentimentality, personified in the statue in Dumfries High Street of a languishing beau clutching a posy of flowers. In fact he was an earthy man with a wicked sense of humour, contemptuous of the hypocrisy of Kirk and officialdom, as his satirical poems show. He was sensitive and perceptive and his heart frequently ruled his head, but he was not sentimental. On the contrary, he was extremely down to earth. He was fiercely humanitarian; loathed oppression; despised privilege through birth and wealth; hated cruelty. His easy wit and natural charm endeared him to peasant and noble alike. He was convivial and thoroughly enjoyed tavern life and a night out with the boys, but was by no means a reeling drunkard. James Currie, three years his senior, was a reformed alcoholic, and his biography of Burns was strongly influenced by his vehement abhorrence for the Demon Drink. Burns liked his dram, but most of the time poverty and a weak heart kept him fairly abstemious. He was extremely good-looking with dark hair, large dreamy eyes, a straight nose and a quirky, sensual mouth. Sir Walter Scott said of him: 'There was a strong expression of sense and shrewdness in all his lineaments: the eye alone, I think, indicated the poetical character and temperament. It was large and of a dark cast, which glowed, I say literally glowed, when he spoke with feeling or interest. I never saw such another eye in a human head, though I have seen the most distinguished men of my time.' Women found him irresistible and fell like skittles. He fathered 15 children, six of whom were bastards, but he made no distinction and was a good father to them all. He had an easy morality, believing that 'the light that led astray was light from Heaven'. But in spite of his many infidelities and the rough passage of their early years together, he loved Jean Armour more than any of his mistresses and their marriage was happy. He farmed for all but the last five years of his life, and was far more at home on the end of a plough than in an Edinburgh drawing room. Tough work on the land when he was undernourished and still growing led to recurring bouts of rheumatic fever which strained his heart.

Oldest of the seven children of an impoverished market gardener, he grew up hungry, always labouring, barely subsisting at times. He went to the village school when he was six and his retentive memory impressed his teachers. He learnt some Latin and French, and devoured any book he could lay his hands on. *The History of Sir William Wallace*, borrowed from the blacksmith, 'poured a Scottish prejudice into my veins which will boil along there till the floodgates of life shut in eternal rest.'

He wrote his first song, 'Handsome Nell', to Nelly Kirkpatrick, a 'bewitching creature' who worked in the fields with him and probably initiated him into that 'delicious passion which I hold to be the first of human joys'. In 1775 he went to Kirkoswald to study surveying, but 'a charming Fillette who lived next door to the school overset my Trigonometry and set me off on a tangent from the sphere of my studies'. It was here he developed a liking for tavern life and learned 'to look unconcerned on a large tavern bill'. His cronies in the inn were Douglas Graham of Shanter Farm – model for Tam o' Shanter – and John Davidson the cobbler – Souter Johnie .

When he was 18 he joined a dancing class at Tarbolton, against his father's wishes, 'to give my manners a brush'. A year later he helped found the Tarbolton Bachelors' Club, and he and his friends sat debating long into the night. These were exciting times to be growing up in and his sharp mind was uncluttered by received opinions and prejudices. The French Revolution was ten years ahead, but its labour pains were starting. Poverty made him sympathetic towards any movement against oppression. The Scottish Enlightenment was in full bloom: new ideas were burgeoning. Men were arguing, inventing, abandoning moribund conventions. Burns was ripe for rebellion. When he was 26 he met Jean, one of 11 children of stonemason James Armour, and declared her his common-law wife. At the beginning of the following year, however, desperate for money, he made plans to emigrate to Jamaica to work on a plantation. Before departing, he arranged for some of his poems to be published in Kilmarnock. James Armour renounced him as a son-in-law, and issued a writ against him, although Jean was by now pregnant. Robert in his turn renounced Jean and went into hiding. In July 1786 *The Kilmarnock Poems* was published. Six days later he was hauled up before the Kirk in Mauchline and ordered to sit on the penitential stool in chastisement for his irregular marriage. (He stood, defiantly, beside it and such was his magnetism that no one insisted on the full humiliation.) For all his failings, he was a religious man, but his clear, revolutionary mind despised the hypocrisy of strict Calvinistic discipline.

Three weeks later he exchanged a pledge of marriage with Mary Campbell of Auchnamore, near Dunoon. A wistful apotheosis has left the impression that Highland Mary was a pure, virginal maiden whose tragic death, five months later, left him heartbroken. In fact, if rumour is to be believed, she was little more than a local floozie, and a number of writs and claims for paternity settlements soon after her death indicate that he was not slow to seek solace in other arms. In September Jean Armour gave birth to twins, Robert and Jean, who did not survive long.

The Kilmarnock Poems was an instant success. Burns cancelled his plans for Jamaica and went to Edinburgh where he was lionized by society and the *literati*. After a second edition of his poems appeared, he was asked if he would help collect old Scottish songs for the Scots Musical Museum. He threw himself into this venture and during the last ten years of his life collected, edited and wrote over 200 songs. He travelled in the Highlands and the Borders to find material and accepted no payment, saying it was his patriotic duty. In January 1787 the Grand Lodge of Scotland (Masonic) hailed him as 'Caledonia's Bard'. That same year he met Mrs Agnes McLehose and started a passionate correspondence of high-flown letters, addressing her as Clarinda and signing himself as Sylvander. In February 1788 he left Edinburgh, bought Jean Armour a mahogany bed, and set up house with her in an upper room in Mauchline, publicly declaring them to be married (again). Just over a week later, Jean gave birth to another set of twins, neither of whom survived the month. The couple moved to Ellisland and, while trying his hand at experimental farming, Burns trained as an excise officer. The Kirk Session finally acknowledged the authenticity of the marriage but, eight months after the birth of the twins, a Jenny Clow bore him a son and claimed paternity settlement.

In 1790 Burns was posted to Dumfries as Excise Officer. He moved his family to the town and for the last six years of his life continued to write, procreate, and pay up for his indiscretions. An inquiry was launched at the end of 1793 to investigate his revolutionary leanings. He was acquitted, and when the French declared war on Britain in 1795 he was the first to join the Dumfries Volunteers and wrote several patriotic songs. He died in July 1796 at the age of 37, from a heart defect contracted after rheumatic fever. On the day of his funeral Jean, with not a shilling in the world, gave birth to his son Maxwell.

The Stone of Destiny (Stone of Scone)

Traditionally, the Stone of Destiny was the pillow on which Jacob laid his head when he dreamt about the ladder of angels reaching from earth to heaven. Its subsequent history is shadowy. It floated around the world carrying mystical powers of sovereignty until it arrived in Ireland, whence it was brought to Dunadd by early missionaries and used as a throne in the coronation of Scottish kings. In those days, *mormaers* owned their kingdoms and the High King was their overlord, King of the Scots but not of Scotland. At the coronation, each *mormaer* filled a shoe with earth from his kingdom and poured a little into a footprint carved into a rock. The King sat on the Stone of Destiny and put his foot over this cocktail of Scottish soil.

From here the Stone was moved to Dunstaffnage. In the 9th century Kenneth Macalpine took it to Scone, where it continued to be a coronation throne for the united Scots and Picts. Edward I, believing firmly in its mystical powers, pinched what he thought to be the Stone of Destiny during one of his ravages of the north, and whisked it off to become part of the Coronation Chair in Westminster Abbey. There it remained, apart from a brief hiatus in 1950 when some daring students from Glasgow University kidnapped it on Christmas morning and hid it for a couple of weeks in Arbroath Abbey. In 1996, thanks to John Major, the then Prime Minister, the stone was ceremoniously returned and installed in Edinburgh Castle. However, as is well known, the Scots were far too canny to allow King Edward to walk off with one of their most sacred possessions. The stolen stone was almost certainly substituted for the real, intricately carved Stone of Destiny which is safely hidden in a secret cavern, possibly on the Isle of Iona. It will be brought out by its hereditary guardians when the time is right, its whereabouts having been passed down orally from father to son over the centuries.

> *Oh flower of Scotland when will we see your like again*
> *That fought and died for your wee bit hill and glen*
> *And stood against him proud Edward's army*
> *And sent him homeward tae think again*
>
> *The hills are bare now and autumn leaves lie thick and still*
> *O're land that is lost now which those so dearly held*
> *Those days are past now and in the past they must remain*
> *But we can still rise now and be the nation again*
>
> Corries Music Ltd

Food and Drink

National Dishes

Fair fa' your honest, sonsie face,
Great chieftain o'the puddin'-race!
Aboon them a' ye tak your place,
Painch, tripe, or thairm:
Weel are ye wordy o' a grace,
As lang's my arm.

from 'Address to a Haggis', by Robert Burns

Everyone should try haggis – if only once. It is made of the heart, liver and lungs of a sheep, mixed with suet, oatmeal and onion, highly seasoned and sewn into the sheep's stomach. Traditionally it is eaten with 'bashed neeps' (mashed turnip; turnip, in Scotland, is what the English call swede) and washed down with neat whisky. Try black pudding, too: its unusual flavour is strangely addictive.

Scotland has an unmatched reputation for salmon, both fresh and smoked. The development of fish farming has increased the availability, but it has to be said that 'wild' salmon is usually nicer than that which has been reared in a farm. Apart from salmon, national dishes include trout, sea fish, shellfish, game, beef, lamb and venison. Almost without exception you should go for these served simply in the traditional ways. Poached salmon with mayonnaise, new potatoes and cucumber; a freshly caught mackerel, fried so that its skin is crisp and curling, with wedges of lemon and watercress; an Aberdeen Angus fillet steak, medium-rare, an inch thick, with a green salad of lettuce, chives and a hint of garlic; well-hung roast grouse with game chips, fresh petit pois, fried breadcrumbs, bread sauce, and gravy. These will linger on the taste buds as well as in the memory long after any dish wrapped up in an exotic sauce and given a pretentious name.

Arbroath smokies are fresh haddock, dry salted and smoked in pairs; a delicate, mild flavour makes them particularly delicious and the best way to eat them is cold, with brown wholemeal bread and butter, a generous squeeze of lemon juice and plenty of freshly ground black pepper.

Porridge is no longer a national habit, but you can usually get it in hotels. The popular myth that Scotsmen eat their porridge with salt, standing up or walking about, is quickly disproved when you discover how many of them sit down and tuck into it heaped with sugar and cream, and sometimes even syrup.

Scottish cheeses are worth pursuing. Crowdie is unique to Scotland, a creamed cottage cheese made from skimmed milk. Dunlop cheese, originally made in an Ayrshire village of the same name, is now also made in Orkney, Arran and Islay. Caboc is a rich double-cream cheese rolled in pinhead oatmeal. Galic and Hramsa are both soft cream cheeses flavoured with wild garlic and herbs.

Oatcakes are unsweetened biscuits made with oatmeal, best eaten with cheese, honey or marmalade. Brand-named oatcakes can be dull compared with delicious local and home-made varieties that crumble and melt in the mouth. Shortbread originated in Scotland and is known all over the world. You will find many local variations.

Soups include cock-a-leekie, made with chicken and leeks; Scotch broth, made with mutton stock and barley; Cullen skink – delicious – made with smoked haddock; and partan bree, made with crab.

Scotch pies are to be found all over the country: small round pies made of hot-water pastry filled with minced meat, eaten hot. Bridies are pies made with a round of pastry folded over, filled with meat, sometimes padded with potatoes and vegetables.

Cranachan, if properly made, is memorable: double cream, and sometimes crowdie, is mixed with toasted oatmeal, sweetened and eaten with fresh soft fruit, preferably raspberries – another of Scotland's specialities.

The Scottish Tourist Board brings out a 'Taste of Scotland' booklet every year offering details of over 200 hotels and restaurants specializing in good Scottish cooking.

Drink

Inspiring, bold John Barleycorn!
What dangers thou canst make us scorn!
Wi' tippenny [ale], we fear nae evil;
Wi' usquabae [whisky], we'll face the devil!
                from 'Tam o' Shanter', by Robert Burns

Among the myths that need to be taken with a pinch of salt is the whisky myth. The average canny Scot will go for the two bottles of cut-price blended whisky that he can get from the supermarket, for the price of one bottle of vintage malt. On the whole, except among the rich, malt whisky is kept for special occasions, bought as presents for other people – or exported. There are over a hundred malts and every connoisseur will swear to the unquestionable superiority of his particular fancy. However, experiments involving the transfer of a 'favourite' malt into a bottle with a rival label will often prove that it is the eye rather than the taste buds that dictate preference. Most of the distilleries are on Speyside, northeast of Aviemore, in the north, or on the islands of Islay and Jura, and a large number of them run guided tours lasting about an hour, complete with a free dram, showing the process of whisky making. The Malt Whisky Trail, on Speyside, is a 70-mile voyage of discovery, taking in eight distilleries. Tourist information centres will provide details.

Traditionally malt whisky should be drunk neat or with a little water. Purists will tell you that any other additions spoil the flavour. No other country in the world has the essential ingredients for that unique taste that makes Scotland's whisky so special: a blend of snow melt, peaty water and carefully malted barley. A Scotsman will never ask for 'Scotch' – unless, perhaps, he is abroad and in danger of being served with a foreign impostor.

Drambuie is a whisky liqueur, very drinkable for those who enjoy 'stickies'. Gingermac or whisky-mac is a mixture of whisky and ginger wine which slips down easily on cold days.

Scotsmen prefer to drink seriously, in bars, though wine bars and English-type pubs are mushrooming. You may hear someone ordering 'a pint of heavy and a chaser'. This will be a pint of bitter and a dram of whisky – the accepted way to spin out the precious *uisge-beatha* – the 'water of life'. Often the dram is not sipped and savoured, but tossed down in a single reviving gulp. In the old days, when the licensing laws were restrictive, there was no time for leisurely drinking. Now licensing laws in Scotland permit public houses to stay open for 12 hours a day, or longer with special extensions, but not all of them choose to do so. Generally, a bar will be open from 11am to 2.30pm, and from 5pm to about 11pm, with reduced hours on Sunday. Most city centre bars will stay open till at least midnight, and residents in licensed hotels can buy drinks at any time. Children under 18 may not be served drink in a public house or restaurant, nor may they be sold alcohol in a shop. Some establishments provide special family rooms where children can join their parents, but they must not drink alcohol here. Landlords risk losing their licences if they break the law in this respect.

Slàinte (pronounced slahn-tchuh) is Gaelic for 'health', and is often heard as a toast.

Travel

06

Getting There

By Air

Scotland has a reasonable choice of direct
air links with cities in the UK and Europe. Since
11 September 2001 the only US airline flying
direct to Scotland (Glasgow) is Continental,
from New York. It is hoped that American
Airlines will soon resume their service from
Chicago, and Air Canada, Air Transit and Air
Tours from Toronto. Tourists from other countries must fly via one of the international
airports in England, see *www.visitbritain.com.*

From England
British Airways fly from Heathrow and
Gatwick to Edinburgh, Glasgow and Aberdeen;
and from Gatwick to Inverness. **British
Midland** fly from Heathrow to Edinburgh and
Glasgow. **easyJet** fly from Luton to Edinburgh,
Glasgow, Inverness and Aberdeen. **Ryanair** fly
from Stansted to Prestwick. **British European**
fly from London City to Edinburgh and
Aberdeen; and from Birmingham to Glasgow.
go fly from Stansted to Edinburgh. **Scot
Airways** fly from London City, Norwich and
Cambridge to Edinburgh; and from London
City to Glasgow and Dundee.

Transport from the Airports
Edinburgh: t (0131) 333 1000,
   www.baa.co.uk/edinburgh. Eight miles to
   city centre. Coaches run every 6 to 20
minutes; taxi costs *c.* £15. Car hire, banking
and tourist information available.
Glasgow: t (0141) 887 1111,
   www.baa.co.uk/glasgow. Eight miles to city
   centre. Coaches run every 15 to 30 minutes;
   taxi costs *c.* £12. Car hire, banking and tourist
   information available.
Prestwick: t (01292) 479 822, *www.gpia.co.uk.*
   30 miles to Glasgow. Trains run every 30
   minutes, coaches every hour; taxi costs
   c. £45. Car hire and banking available.
Aberdeen: t (01224) 722 331,
   www.baa.co.uk/aberdeen. Seven miles to city
   centre. Coaches run at peak times; taxi to
   Dyce Station *c.* £5, then fast and frequent
   trains to Aberdeen and Inverness; taxi direct
   to city centre *c.* £10. Car hire and banking
   available.
Inverness: t (01667) 464 000. Eight miles to
   city centre. Regular coach service (*exc Sun*);
   taxi costs *c.* £9. Car hire available.
Dundee: t (01382) 643 242,
   www.dundeeairport.co.uk. Two miles to
   town centre. Taxi costs *c.* £2.50.

By Ferry

Frequent ferry services run from the continent to the north of England, within easy
reach of Scotland. **P&O North Sea Ferries** run
services from Zeebrugge and Rotterdam to
Hull. **DFDS Seaways** run services from Esbjerg
and Hamburg to Harwich; Amsterdam and
Gothenburg to Newcastle; Bergen to Lerwick.

Airlines
British Airways, t 0845 773 3377,
   www.britishairways.com.
British Midland, t 0870 607 0555,
   www.britishmidland.com.
easyJet, t 0870 600 000,
   www.easyjet.com.
Ryanair, t 0870 156 9569,
   www.ryanair.com.
British European, t 0870 567 6676,
   www.britisheuropean.com.
go, t 0845 605 4321, *www.go-fly.com.*
Scot Airways, t 0870 606 0707,
   www.scotairways.co.uk.
Continental Airlines, t 1 800 231 0856,
   www.continental.com.

Ferry Companies
P&O North Sea Ferries, t 0870 129 6002,
   www.ponsf.com.
DFDS Seaways, t 0870 533 3000,
   www.dfdsseaways.co.uk.

Rail Companies
Eurostar, t 0870 518 6186, *www.eurostar.com.*
Eurotunnel, t 0870 5353 535,
   www.eurotunnel.com.

Coach Companies
Eurolines, t (01582) 404 511,
   www.eurolines.com.
National Express, t 0870 5808 080,
   www.nationalexpress.co.uk.

By Train

Eurostar is the high-speed passenger rail service operating between Paris, Brussels, Lille, Calais and London Waterloo. Journey time from Paris is 3 hours; from Brussels 2 hours 40 minutes. In London, transfer to King's Cross or Euston stations for trains to Scotland.

Eurotunnel operates non-stop throughout the year, taking 35 minutes between Calais/Coquelles and Folkestone. Terminals have shops and services. Trains carry cars, motorbikes, campervans and coaches.

By Bus or Coach

Express coach network, **Eurolines**, link over 500 places in 25 countries. They connect with National Express, in London, for Scotland.

The journey from London to Edinburgh takes about 8 hours, and to Glasgow about 7½ hours, including 'comfort stops'. The coaches are reasonably comfortable, with toilets. Some have a snack service and show a film.

By Car

An excellent network of motorways means that you can drive comfortably from London to Edinburgh or Glasgow in about 7 hours, sticking to the 70 mph limit. The M1, A1(M) and A68 is the quickest route to Edinburgh; the M1, M6 and A74 to Glasgow.

Getting Around

By Air

There is an excellent air network within the country, with daily flights connecting the islands and most of the regional airports with Edinburgh, Glasgow, Aberdeen and Inverness. Most internal flights are operated by British Regional Airlines (part of British Airways).

Discounts and Passes

Book well in advance for special offers, and ask for details of **discount fares** and **airpasses**, for example, **Apex** and **SuperApex**, which must be booked by a certain date prior to departure.

Using the Internet

The internet can be one of the best places to start looking for cheap flights, rail and coach fares, car rentals and holiday package deals. It is often easier to compare ticket prices on the web. Most low-cost airlines offer discounts of £5–10 for bookings made via the internet, and frequently offer special deals, such as London to Glasgow return flights for £10.

There are countless internet-only travel agencies. A good starting point for flights is *www.cheapflights.co.uk*.

For short breaks, special-interest or activity holidays, try *www.visitscotland.com/os*.

---

easyJet, go and Ryanair offer good 'no frills' prices.

British Airways and British Midland both offer airpasses. British Regional Airlines has a **Highland Rover Pass** which includes 5 flights within the Highlands and Islands (including the Western and Northern Isles) for about £169. This must be bought at least 7 days in advance, and **before you arrive** in Scotland.

Several companies offer flight packages within Scotland; contact the Scottish Tourist Board's Information Service, **t** (0131) 332 2433, *www.visitscotland.com/os*.

By Ferry

Caledonian MacBrayne ferries sail to 22 islands off the west coast and in the Firth of Clyde; most of them carry vehicles as well as passengers. Summer timetables operate from Easter to mid-October, with reduced services in winter. Reservations for vehicles are advised and often obligatory.

Caledonian MacBrayne offer **Island Hopscotch** and **Island Rover** discount tickets.

Cruises

Hebridean Princess, **t** (01756) 704 704, *www.hebridean.co.uk*. A floating luxury hotel with a crew of 30 serving 40 passengers making 6- or 7-day cruises around the Highlands and Islands off the west coast. Plenty of opportunities to go ashore, but you need to be lucky with the weather.

P&O Scottish Ferries run mini-cruises off the Orkney and Shetland islands.

Ferry Information

Caledonian MacBrayne, t (01475) 650 100, *www.calmac.co.uk.*

Western Ferries, t (01369) 704 452, *www.western-ferries.co.uk*; in Firth of Clyde.

Serco Denim, t (01496) 840 691; Islay to Jura.

Corran Ferry, t (01397) 703 701; between Ardgour and Nether Lochaber (no reservations necessary).

Glenelg-Kylerhea Ferry, t (01599) 511 302, *www.skyeferry.co.uk.*

P&O Scottish Ferries, t (01224) 572 615, *www.poscottishferries.co.uk*; to Orkney and Shetland.

NorthLink Orkney and Shetland Ferries, *info@northlinkferries.co.uk, www.northlinkferries.co.uk*; due to take over services between Aberdeen and Scrabster, Orkney and Shetland from October 2002.

John O'Groats Ferries, t (01955) 611 353, *www.jogferry.co.uk*; to Orkney.

Orkney Ferries, t (01856) 872 044, *www.orkneyislands.com*; inter-island ferries.

Shetland, Shetland tourist board, **t** (01595) 693 434, *www.shetland-tourism.co.uk*; inter-island ferries.

Rail Information

National Rail Enquiries, t 0845 748 4950, *www.scotrail.co.uk.*

Scotrail, t 0845 755 0033.

GNER, t 0845 722 5225, *www.gner.co.uk*; for east coast services.

Virgin, t 0845 722 2333, *www.virgintrains.co.uk*; for west coast services.

The Trainline, *www.thetrainline.com*; to book all rail tickets online.

Royal Scotsman, t (0131) 555 1021, *www.royalscotsman.com.*

Bus and Coach Information

Scottish Citylink, t 0870 550 5050, *www.citylink.co.uk.*

Stagecoach, t (01463) 239 292 (Inverness); **t** (01862) 892 683 (Tain).

Postbus, t (0131) 228 7404; for timetables.

Caledonian MacBrayne run afternoon and evening cruises around the west coast.

By Train

The British railway services are in a state of flux, with promises of improvement, modernisation and innovation. All information and details should be checked.

There are frequent high-speed trains from all parts of England to Edinburgh, Glasgow, Aberdeen and Inverness, with connections to regional stations. London to Edinburgh takes about 4½ hours, to Glasgow about 5 hours. There are frequent trains throughout the day, with air-conditioned carriages (1st and 2nd class), dining facilities and a buffet service.

ScotRail's **Caledonian Sleeper** is the overnight service between London Euston and Edinburgh, Glasgow, Aberdeen, Inverness and Fort William (*every night exc Sat; single and twin berths*). Reservations can be made at any mainline station in the UK, or through travel agents or BritRail offices.

The **Royal Scotsman** is a delightful luxury train offering 2- and 4-night rail tours of Scotland from Edinburgh (*April–Oct*).

The **West Highland Line**, from Glasgow to Fort William and then on up to Mallaig, on the *Jacobite*, a restored steam train, is worth doing just for the beauty of the journey (*see* p.456).

Arriving in Edinburgh and Glasgow

Edinburgh has two stations, Waverley and Haymarket. Waverley is the main station, in the city centre, and the airport bus terminates here. All facilities, including tourist information, are available.

Glasgow has two stations, Queen Street and Central. Queen Street is near the bus station, and the airport bus terminates here. Both stations have full facilities.

Passes and Railcards

BritRail Pass: unlimited access to the entire rail network in Britain with a Consecutive Pass or a Flexipass. You **must** buy your BritRail pass before you arrive: it **cannot** be bought in Britain. *www.britrail.co.uk*

Freedom of Scotland Travelpass: unlimited travel on all scheduled train services within Scotland, all Caledonian MacBrayne scheduled ferry services, and various Scottish Citylink coach services.

Highland Rover: available in the UK for rail travel between Glasgow and Oban, Fort William and Mallaig; Scottish Citylink coach travel between Oban, Fort William and Inverness; and rail travel between Inverness and Wick, Thurso, Kyle of Lochalsh, Aberdeen and Aviemore. Also reduced rate ferry travel between Oban and Mull, Mallaig and Skye.

Central Scotland Rover: includes rail travel between Edinburgh, Glasgow and various other towns in central Scotland.

Young Person's Railcard: for people aged between 16 and 25, and mature students in full-time education. Valid for a year, offering 1/3 discount on most fares for leisure travel in Britain. *www.youngpersons-railcard.co.uk*

Senior Railcard: available to anyone aged 60 and over. Valid for a year, offering 1/3 discount on most fares for leisure travel in Britain. *www.senior-railcard.co.uk*

Family Railcard: Valid for a year, offering 1/3 discount on most fares for adults and a 60% discount for children for leisure travel in Britain. Minimum group must include one adult and one child.

By Bus or Coach

There is a good network of coach services in Scotland. **Scottish Citylink** is the main operator, travelling to 190 destinations. Stagecoach also offer good bargains and special tickets.

There are many local bus companies throughout the country, and a number of saver tickets. The **Postbus** carries fare-paying passengers in the more remote areas where there is no other form of public transport, but space is limited.

Special summer bus services operate in 'scenic' areas, with names like The Trundler, The Heather Hopper, The Speyside Rambler, The Border Harrier. Local tourist information centres will have details.

There are numerous coach touring companies offering scheduled itineraries, ranging from luxury with first-class accommodation to budget tours with basic accommodation.

Passes and Discount Cards

Citylink Smart Card: discounts of around 30%, valid for a year.

Citylink Explorer Pass: unlimited travel, plus 50% discount on some ferries and hostels.

By Car

Good main roads will take you north from Edinburgh to Inverness (and on to John O'Groats) – M90/A9; and from Glasgow to Inverness via Loch Ness – A82. There are no toll roads in Scotland, but there are four toll bridges: Forth, Tay, Erskine and Skye. There are 12 signed National Tourist Routes (white writing on a brown background with a blue thistle): scenic routes along quieter roads. A car is almost essential for anyone wishing to explore remoter areas.

Overseas driving licences are valid for a year in Britain. Green card insurance and car registration documents are necessary if you bring your own car.

You drive on the left in Scotland, as in the rest of the British Isles, and it is law for drivers and all passengers to wear seat belts. Road signs are similar to those in Europe. Unless otherwise specified, there is a mandatory speed limit of 70mph on motorways and dual carriageways, 60mph on single carriageways, and 30mph in built-up areas.

Parking in towns is usually restricted to parking meters and car parks. A single yellow line by the kerb means you can't park by day; a double yellow line, and zigzag lines by pedestrian crossings, mean no parking at any time. The police are very hot on drink-driving.

Main roads are generally good, although many are not dual carriageways. In rural areas there are many single-track roads with passing bays. These are also for slow cars to pull into, to allow faster ones to overtake. When touring in the far north and the islands, remember that there aren't many petrol stations and that some close on Sundays.

Car Hire

Car hire firms operate from airports and stations, and there are always local firms: usually the more rural, the better the bargain. Most companies require the driver to be between 23 and 75 years old with a current driving licence that has been held for at least one year.

Hitchhiking

It is neither more nor less chancy to thumb a lift in Scotland than anywhere else.

In populated areas, be extremely wary. In the islands, however, locals will invariably stop and offer a lift without being thumbed; it is part of their instinctive hospitality.

Specialist Tour Operators

If you like to build your holiday around a theme or particular activity, the Scottish Tourist Board publishes an excellent free brochure, 'Adventure and Special Interest Holidays in Scotland', with details of dozens of ideas for different holidays, and addresses to contact. Write for a copy to the Scottish Tourist Board, 23 Ravelston Terrace, Edinburgh EH4 3TP, *info@stb.gov.uk*, who also publish a free brochure with details of over 300 good-value holidays; or consult *www.visitscotland.com/os*.

The following are a random selection of tour operators in the UK and the USA. Also check out *www.visitscotland.com*.

In the USA

Abercrombie and Kent, Oak Brook, IL, **t** (630) 954 2944, **f** 954 3324. Up-market customized tours. UK contact number: **t** (020) 7559 8500.

Atlantic Golf, Westport, CT, **t** (203) 454 1086, **f** 454 8840, *atlanticgolf@atlanticgolf.com*. Golf holidays.

Backroads, Berkeley, CA, **t** (510) 537 1889 ext 117, **f** 527 1444, *kathleend@backroads.com*, *www.backroads.com*. Bicycling holidays.

BCT Scenic Walking, Carlsbad, CA, **t** (760) 431 7306, **f** 431 7782, **t** 800 473 1210, *info@bctwalk.com*, *www.bctwalk.com*. Walking holidays.

Extraordinary Places, Seattle, WA, **t** (425) 775 3660, **f** 775 3661, *adrianc@eplaces.com*, *www.eplaces.com*. General holidays and touring.

Skipper Travel Services, Capitola, CA, **t** (831) 462 5333, **f** 462 5178, *skipperltd@earthlink.net*, *www.skippercruises.com*. Cruises.

In the UK

Alternatively, there are package tours arranged from all over Britain, ranging from luxury coach tours with scheduled itineraries and first-class accommodation, to cheaper tours with less ritzy accommodation.

ALBA Clan and Theme Tours, Glasgow, **t** (0141) 427 0588, **f** 427 7776, *muklum@netscapeon-line.co.uk*. Clan tours.

Amethyst Travel, Comrie, **t** (01764) 670 509, **f** 670 584, *info@amethyst-travel.com*, *www.amethyst-travel.com*. Golf, sightseeing, heritage and themed holidays.

Bobsport (Scotland) Ltd, Edinburgh, **t/f** (0131) 332 6607, *bbrownless@aol.com*, *www.bobsport.co.uk*. Salmon fishing, skiing, golf and shooting holidays.

Braemar House, Fochabers, **t** (01343) 821 525, **f** 821 018, *mrtoo9@yahoo.com*. De luxe holidays: shooting, stalking, fishing and golf.

Celtic Trails, Edinburgh, **t/f** (0131) 664 1980, *jac@celtictrails.co.uk*, *www.celtictrails.co.uk*. Short residential courses and day tours exploring ancient sacred sites.

The Golf Experience, Park Lane House, 47 Broad Street, Glasgow G40 2QW, **t** (0141) 572 4611, *info@thegolfexperience.co.uk*, *www.thegolfexperience.co.uk*. For a hassle-free golfing holiday, if you have a penny or so to spare. They will design your individual golfing itinerary on the best championship courses, with luxury travel, 5-star restaurants, de luxe accommodation, and activities for the non-golfing partner.

Lomond Walking Holidays, Stirling, **t/f** (01786) 447 752, *paul@milligan.force9.co.uk*, *www.biggar-net.co.uk/lomond*. Guided walking holidays staying in budget accommodation.

Scotsell Ltd, Glasgow, **t** (0141) 762 0838, **f** 762 0297, **t** 772 5928, *holidays@scotsell.com*, *www.scotsell.com*. Island holidays, ferries included; hotels or self-catering.

Timberbush Tours, 555 Castlehill, Edinburgh, **t** (0131) 555 4689, *www.timberbush-tours.co.uk*. One-to two-day tailormade coach tours of Scotland.

Three minibus companies run tours from Edinburgh for independent travellers:
Go Blue Bananas: **t** (0131) 220 6868.
The Haggis Backpackers: **t** (0131) 557 9393.
Rabbie's Trail Burner Tours: **t** (0131) 554 2612.

Practical A–Z

07

Climate

A popular postcard shows someone sitting in a deck chair under an umbrella in pouring rain, with the caption 'Having plenty of weather here in Scotland'. In fact, with a bit of luck, you can return from a holiday in Scotland with a tan not entirely inflicted by wind, and memories of blue sky and brilliant sunshine. Unpredictability is the main drawback, often with wide contrasts in one place in a day. When the weather is good, no other country compares. When the weather is bad and people struggle against piercing wind and relentless rain, and a damp chill pervades to the marrow, Siberia would be preferable. It is worth remembering that places in the north of the country have an average of 18 to 20 hours of daylight in the summer, and resorts on the east coast are noted for their hours of sunshine. In the far north, in the middle of summer, it is never completely dark. In spite of the Gulf Stream, whose warm waters are alleged to lick the west coast, the sea is gelid.

In general, the west is wettish, and mild enough in some coastal regions to support palm trees and tropical vegetation. The east is drier with a more bracing climate and colder winds. Winter in the Highlands, when the precipitation is mainly snow, can be very beautiful, with clear skies and sun, though temperatures may seldom rise above freezing.

An unfortunate side-product of the moist, mild weather in the west is the 'midge', a particularly virulent breed of gnat unequalled in persistence anywhere else in the British Isles. They are at their worst in warm, humid conditions; they hide when it is windy and sometimes, though not always, in very bright sunshine. Anyone contemplating camping or picnicking during the midge season should have lots of the strongest possible repellent. In truth, midges can completely ruin an outdoor holiday. The only good thing about them is they won't follow a boat offshore.

Eating Out

You can choose between *haute cuisine*, good plain cooking, bar meals, and fast food. In the cities, meals are served at fairly flexible hours, but in smaller places you should aim to have

Restaurant Price Ranges

Expensive	£30 and above
Moderate	£15–30
Cheap	£15 and below

Prices are per person, not including drinks. For further information, including local specialities, *see* **Food and Drink**, pp.67–70.

lunch between 12.30 and 2pm, and dinner between about 7 and 9pm. If you know you will be late it is wise to make arrangements in advance. Some of the country's best restaurants are to be found tucked away in out-of-the-way places.

Historic Scotland

Historic Scotland (HS) is a division of the Scottish Education Department (**t** (0131) 668 8800, *www.historic-scotland.gov.uk*), responsible for the care and upkeep of many of the country's historic ruins, buildings and sites. Some castles and historic houses open to the public are privately owned and each has its own opening times and admission charges.

There is an explorer ticket which entitles you to free entrance to 563 places of historic interest: castles, abbeys, stately homes, famous gardens, etc., in Scotland, England, Wales and Northern Ireland. These can be bought from major tourist information centres. Prices range from £12 for 3 days for adults (OAPs £9, family ticket £25), £17 for a week (£12.50/£33), and £22 for 14 days (£16.50/£42). Many castles, historic houses and smaller museums close for the winter.

Doors Open Day is Scotland's contribution to 'Heritage Days', two weekends every September when Europe's finest buildings are open free to the public. You can explore historic churches, towers, country houses, breweries, power stations and many more. Details from local tourist information centres.

Maps

Good maps are essential. Bartholomew's half-inch maps are good, but you may need several of them and they are expensive. There is a very adequate Ordnance Survey Motoring Atlas, 3 miles: 1 inch (Scottish Highlands and Islands, 7 miles: 1 inch), available from most garages and bookshops. A 'tourist map' of the whole of Scotland, marking special attractions, is useful. Maps of each region are obtainable from the relevant tourist information centre. If you plan to walk or climb then you should get the appropriate Ordnance Survey sheets, scale 1:50,000. One of the best places to get maps and travel books is Stanford's, 12–14 Long Acre, London WC2E 9LP, t (020) 7836 1321, *www.stanfords.co.uk*.

National Trust for Scotland

Many of Scotland's historic buildings, and much of its conserved land, are under the care of the National Trust for Scotland (NTS), a charity formed in 1931 to promote the preservation of the country's heritage (28 Charlotte Square, Edinburgh EH2 4ET, t (0131) 243 9300, *information@nts.org.uk, www.nts.org.uk*). Over a hundred properties, including castles, small houses, islands, mountains, coastline and gardens come under its protection. Most are open from April to October; admission charges vary. Annual membership admits one person free to all NTS properties, and to all National Trust properties in the rest of the UK.

Packing

Because of the unpredictability of the weather, sweaters and waterproof clothing are essential all year round. Remember Scotland is famous for its woollen industry, so you can buy Fair Isle, Shetland, cashmere and tweed locally. Rubber boots are useful, but uncomfortable for walking long distances – they are cheap to buy if wet weather sets in. Go prepared for rain and cold; the chances are you will have hot sunshine and drought. Scottish waters are cold, but if the sun shines you might regret not bringing bathing things.

Shopping

Food and Drink
Try and squeeze a side of smoked salmon into your suitcase, but make sure it is well wrapped. Buy shortbread, oatcakes and

> **Public Holidays**
> New Year's Day is the only statutory public holiday in Scotland. Most towns and districts have local public trades' and other holidays which vary from place to place and from year to year (check with local tourist offices).
> Bank Holidays are mainly for banks only, and include:
> **New Year** 1 and 2 January
> **Good Friday** Friday before Easter
> **May Day** First Monday in May
> **Spring Bank Holiday** Last Monday in May
> **August Holiday** First Monday in August
> **St Andrew's Day** 30 November
> **Christmas Day** 25 December
> **Boxing Day** 26 December.

Dundee cake, in tins. Choose between the malt whisky you have adopted as your 'special' (if in doubt, go for Glenmorangie) and Drambuie, Scotland's whisky liqueur.

Glass and Pottery
Some Scottish glass is beautiful. At Caithness Glass in Perth, Oban and Wick, factory tours show all the processes of glass-blowing, moulding and engraving, and there are good shops. Potters' workshops can be found all over Scotland.

Hoots Memorabilia
Traditional accessories to Highland dress, set with cairngorms and amethysts, in wrought silver and gold, can be bought from most jewellers. Jewellery made from local stones can be found in workshops and craft shops throughout the country. With such a large deer population, both decorative and functional objects carved from horn are made all over Scotland. Take home a shepherd's crook, called a crommach, with a handle carved from ramshorn or, if you don't have room, go for a horn salt spoon or drinking bowl.

Tweed and Wool
As well as the tourist-traps, there are still a few sheds and cottage parlours where weaving is done on hand looms, mostly in the islands and parts of the Highlands. They are invariably signposted from the road. Hardwearing Harris tweed is acclaimed all over the world, *see p.528.*

Sports and Activities

For information on the net on all available activities, try *www.activity-Scotland.co.uk*.

Scottish Sports Council, Caledonia House, South Gyle, Edinburgh EH12 9DQ, **t** (0131) 317 7200, *www.sportscotland.org.uk*. Information on any recognized sport.

Canoeing

This is possible all around the coast and on many of the rivers, where the fast flow is often ideal for 'white-water' canoeing. There are many water-sport centres.

Scottish Canoe Assoc., Caledonia House, South Gyle, Edinburgh EH12 9DQ, **t** (0131) 317 7314. Organises tours, and caters for beginners.

Climbing and Walking

From the gentlest stroll to the toughest climb, Scotland, small as it is, has as much to offer as any country and a lot more than most. The scenery is unbeatable, the terrain everything from easy to challenging. The choice is endless. The one drawback is the capricious weather. A day that begins in brilliant sunshine can end in freezing rain.

Unfortunately there are still a number of people who don't take the dangers of climbing and hill walking in the Highlands and Islands seriously. They set out ill-equipped and with insufficient skills and knowledge of the terrain. Frequently it falls to the brave men and women of the mountain rescue services to extricate these foolhardy people, often at the risk of their own lives.

There are a few **simple rules** that, if observed, can save lives, money and tempers:

Get a weather forecast for the area in which you intend to walk or climb. Watch the weather the whole time you are out and be prepared to turn back if conditions become dangerous: if visibility decreases, the wind gets up, or the temperature falls dramatically.

Plan your route carefully, remembering that rivers and burns can fill quickly after a rainstorm and cut you off, and peat bogs and rocks can be exhausting to walk over.

Tell someone where you are going, when you expect to return, and how many are in your party. Leave a clearly visible note in your car with this information. And don't forget to tell your informant that you've come back! It's not unknown for such forgetfulness to send rescue services out on a wild goose chase for someone who is happily propping up a bar.

Take appropriate clothing and equipment: even in summer a sweater and waterproofs are essential. On any serious hill walk or climb take gloves, hat, waterproof and windproof jacket and trousers. Wear proper walking boots with good ankle support and a good grip. Take enough food and drink to see you through a crisis (high-energy rations such as chocolate and dried fruit are useful), a torch, first-aid kit, whistle and survival bag. These precautions could save your life.

Always carry a map – Ordnance Survey maps are ideal – and a good compass, ideally with a protractor, and be sure you know how to use them. It is easy enough to find your way when you can see where you have been and where you are going, but if the mist or a blizzard closes in, it's a different story. For serious mountain climbing, take an ice axe and crampons, and know how to use them.

It would be impossible to list the literally thousands of walks and climbs in the Highlands and Islands. There are 279 peaks over 3,000ft in height (seven over 4,000ft) in Scotland. These are called **Munros** after the mountaineer Sir Hugh Munro who first listed them. 'Munro bagging' is a popular pastime, and most of them are reasonably accessible, often within easy reach of public roads.

The Cuillins in Skye have provided a testing training ground for some of the world's top mountaineers. The Arrochar Alps, the peaks northwest of Loch Lomond, particularly the Cobbler (2,891ft/867m), and the Trossachs are both popular and accessible, as is Ben Vorlich (3,231ft/969m), near Lochearnhead. North of Loch Tay, Ben Lawers (3,984ft/1,195m), with its exceptional alpine flowers, is another Munro, looked after by the National Trust for Scotland. Perthshire has a number of hills, including Schiehallion (3,554ft/1,066m), near Loch Rannoch. The hills around Glen Lyon are also good and Glencoe has a variety of challenging peaks. Further north, Ben Nevis (4,406ft/1,322m) is Scotland's highest mountain, with several routes up, including a well-marked tourist route. To the northwest, the highest peaks of the Grampians are truly arctic in winter, but splendid for experienced climbers. The eastern edge of the Grampians, around

Glen Clova, and the Lochnagar area, accessible from Deeside, are also popular. North of the Great Glen, Torridon, in the west, offers spectacular rock scenery, equalled only by the peaks of the Inverpolly Nature Reserve north of Ullapool, including the distinctive Stac Pollaidh (2,009ft/603m), Canisp (2,779ft/834m) and Suilven (2,399ft/720m). Ben Hope (3,042ft/913m), southwest of Tongue, is Scotland's most northerly Munro.

There are coastal footpaths, nature and woodland trails, and long-distance footpaths, including the **West Highland Way**, which runs 95 miles from Milngavie on the outskirts of Glasgow to Fort William. It includes a marvellous range of Lowland and Highland scenery, on old drove roads, forestry tracks, an old military road and a railway track bed.

The **Speyside Way** runs 30 miles from Tugnet to Ballindalloch, then a further 15 miles to Tomintoul, with splendid and very varied scenery along the route.

The 212-mile **Southern Upland Way** runs from Portpatrick in Dumfries and Galloway, east to Cockburnspath in the Borders. It is signposted and well marked all the way.

Ski lifts for walkers are available at **Cairngorm**, **Glencoe** and **Glenshee** (out of season only), for easy access to higher terrain.

Useful Addresses
Mountaineering Council of Scotland, 4a St Catherine's Road, Perth, PH1 5SE, **t** (01738) 638 227.
Ramblers' Association Scotland, 23 Crusader House, Haig Business Park, Markinch, Fife KY7 6AQ, **t** (01592) 611 177.
Scottish Rights of Way Society, 10 Sunnyside, Edinburgh EH7 5RA, **t** (0131) 652 2937.
Travel-lite at 'McFarlanes', 5 Mugdock Road, Milngavie, **t** (0141) 956 7890, *www.travel-lite-uk.com*. Daily baggage transfer for walkers on the West Highland Way.
Winter Road Check: Highland, **t** (01898) 654 610; Grampian, **t** (01898) 654 620.

Curling
Scotland's traditional winter game is usually played on indoor rinks these days. It has been played for over 450 years and is described as 'a sort of bowls on ice'. For information on where you can go to watch or participate contact the Scottish Sports Council, *see* p.80.

Diving
The wonderful clarity of the sea around the coast, full of highly coloured sea animals and plants, makes Scottish waters among the best in the world for diving. There is a wide choice of good places where you can dive. The following are outstanding.

In the north there is **Scapa**, in Orkney. Four ships of the sunken German fleet, scuttled at the end of the First World War, lie untouched below the clear waters of this huge anchorage and offer marvellous scope for wreck diving.

On the west coast the waters around **Oban** are excellent. The **Sound of Mull** is littered with wrecks, and there is sub-aqua cliff scenery. **Ailsa Craig** and the **Firth of Clyde** are also good diving sites. The **Summer Isles**, in the northwest, are also ideal for diving.
Scottish Sub-Aqua Club, 40 Bogmoor Place, Glasgow G51 47Q, **t** (0141) 425 1021.

Fishing
With thanks to Michael Wigan.
In the first half of the 19th century southern fishermen began making the stagecoach trek to Scotland to ply for **salmon** with rod and line. The industrial revolution had begun to pollute England's great salmon rivers, and was to wipe the salmon out in many of them by the turn of the century. The Scottish lairds had been accustomed to sending forth their 'seal-gairs' (hunters) to procure fish and game for them. They were amazed and delighted to be paid by these newcomers for the right to dangle their baits in the water.

Much has changed since Scotland made its name as the world's best fishing venue. The night-time revellers who hunted spawning salmon in their breeding places with lamps and pronged spears have been replaced by fishermen and women throwing out high-tech fishing lines with rods made of supremely light, flexible and strong new materials. Where once the huge bulk of Scottish salmon was caught by estuary nets, now salmon nets (challenged by the low price of farmed salmon) are becoming uneconomic. The silver king of the river is chiefly valuable as a game fish, and the value of fishing rentals to Scotland, apart from the knock-on benefits, is enormous. The capital value of salmon fishing in Scotland has been calculated at close to £1 billion. It is no exaggeration to say that in the valleys of some of the great rivers like the Spey and Tay, the way of life is chiefly determined by the fishery. Fishing hotels and lodges occupy strategic positions above the precious waters, and ghillies' and water bailiffs' houses are never far away. For many villages on rivers the focal point is the tackle shop, trading not only in fishing paraphernalia, but also in gossip about pools in which fish have been caught and the flies that have caught them.

The sources of many of Scotland's great rivers are swampy spring-fed patches in hanging valleys high in the mountains, or even springs in the floors of lochs. Many Scottish rivers can be fished from the mountain burns near the headwaters right through to the wide sleepy stretches flowing through farmland nearer the coast. In some places fishermen use rod and line to spin for migratory fish in the sea off the river mouths, usually for sea trout. **Sea trout** are the members of the native brown trout family which choose to migrate to sea, but, unlike the Atlantic salmon which forage as far as the Greenland shelf to feed, sea trout winter offshore, generally returning in spring and early summer.

The water surface to all fishermen is a hypnotic thing, always moving, always changing with the shifting light. Cunliffe Pearce has written evocatively of 'the top of the water, that magic looking-glass through which trout and man mysteriously make acquaintance with each other'. In Scotland there is the extra factor of supreme scenery. The Highland lochs – Loch Lomond, Loch Awe – are famed for beauty, yet also loved in a different way by the connoisseurs for the fishing they offer. Some of the far north rivers – Helmsdale, Brora, Naver, Dionard – open out through heather moorland, and become faster as they drop through rocky passages before entering the sea. The outer isles have magnificent salmon and seatrout fishing, and it is on the magical Grimersta, where running fish can stream by in a seemingly endless flow, that the British record catch by one man in a day was recorded – 52 salmon. Some of the most exciting trout lochs are those gem-like bodies of water in the far north, famous for being dour and uncooperative in one mood, then

exploding into action the next. A hundred fish in a day to two rods is not unimaginable.

Scottish salmon fishing is not, as is sometimes said, the preserve of rich tenants on famous water. There are thousands of miles of fishing in Scotland, and many opportunities for those who seek them out. The game fishing magazines, *Trout and Salmon* and *Salmon Trout and Seatrout*, advertise plenty of rentable fishing, and once embarked on the salmon fishing circuit, chances spring up for keen fishermen through contacts made along the way. Some local councils own water, and many rivers are open to day-ticket fishermen through angling associations, fishing hotels, local river boards, or private riparian owners. Salmon fishing permits start at around £10 per day. Trout fishing is available in greater supply than is ever utilized, particularly in the far north and west of Scotland, and some of the famous fishing hotels have access to numerous remote lochs which never see a fisherman year-round. A boat on a loch costs around £10 a day, bank fishing around £8. Tourist information centres circulate fishing information, and details of self-catering accommodation which is accompanied by trout fishing. The more expensive salmon fishing possibilities are marketed through the main sporting agencies, and often sold in exclusive packages based in neighbouring fishing lodges.

The salmon fishing season varies from river to river, starting from January in some places and as late as March in others. Trout fishing is from 15 March to 6 October. Sea fishing is extensive, with such a length of coastline. Porbeagle shark, halibut, cod, bass, hake, ling, skate and turbot are but a few of the many species of fish you can expect to find. There is never a shortage of charter boats or, in most places, of experienced locals to take you out. There is no closed season: weather and availability are the only limitations. Ask at your hotel, or in the tourist information centre.

Useful Addresses for Fishermen
Central Scotland Anglers Association, 53 Fernieside Crescent, Edinburgh, **t** (0131) 664 4685.

Scottish Anglers National Association, Admin Office, Caledonia House, South Gyle, Edinburgh EH12 9DQ, **t** (0131) 339 8808.

Scottish Federation for Coarse Angling,
TighnaFleurs, Hill o' Gryfe Road, Bridge of
Weir, Renfrewshire, **t** (01505) 612 580.
The Scottish Federation of Sea Anglers,
Flat 2, 16 Bellevue Road, Ayr KA7 2SA,
t (01292) 264 735.

Golf

The Borders and Lothian

The countryside between Edinburgh and the
border is not to the forefront of Scotland's
golfing heritage, but there are one or two
gems, none more so than **Hawick** where the
views from the higher parts of the course are
breathtaking. **Minto** and **St Boswells** are also
worth taking in should you be in the vicinity.

Lothian positively teems with courses, and
East Lothian in particular contains some of the
finest links courses to be found anywhere.
Furthest to the east is **Dunbar**, whose 14 holes
that run along the seashore are on a par with
the best. While at Dunbar, and if looking to
play 9 holes after tea, pop inland to **Gifford**
and sample one of the least-known delights in
this part of the world. Moving north and east
to **North Berwick**, a collector's item for any
acquisitive golfer is West Links, probably little
changed from when it came into being in
1832. Shots over ancient walls and across bays
confirm that courses, then, materialized rather
than were designed.

Five miles closer to Edinburgh lies **Muirfield**,
the home of the Honourable Company of
Edinburgh Golfers and for many the best
seaside course of all. The Open Championship
has been coming here regularly since the
course was founded towards the end of the
19th century. For those wishing to play, a letter
to the secretary beforehand is a must, preferably endorsed by the applicant's own club
secretary. Muirfield lies on the eastern edge of
the town of Gullane, which has three courses
of its own. **Gullane No 1** is a fine test and, like
North Berwick, is used as one of the qualifying
courses when the Open is at Muirfield. **Nos 2
and 3** get progressively shorter and easier, but
all are a stiff test when the wind blows. The
Bruntsfield Links Golf Society and the **Royal
Burgess Golfing Society** have adjacent parkland courses in the western suburbs of the
city. To the west of Edinburgh are a number of
mostly parkland courses, undoubtedly the

best of which is **Dalmahoy**. The scene of
several national and international tournaments, Dalmahoy has 36 holes and is the
centre of a fine hotel and leisure complex.

Fife and Tayside

Fife is as blessed as East Lothian both in the
quality and the quantity of its golf courses.
If golf did start in Scotland, then it probably
began somewhere along the shores of Fife
or Tayside.

St Andrews is the golfing capital of the
world. It is from their clubhouse overlooking
the first and last holes of the Old Course that
the **Royal & Ancient Golf Club** look after the
customs of the game and mastermind the
world's premier golf event, the Open
Championship.

The **Old Course** is unique. There are huge
double greens; the 17th, the Road Hole, is probably the most famous hole in golf; and the
massive shared fairway of the opening and
closing holes is seemingly in the middle of the
'Old Grey Toun'. The other courses of
St Andrews – the **Jubilee**, the **Eden** and the
New – lie deep in the shadow of their famous
sister, but are all well worth a game.

A few miles to the south are a number of
fine links courses, some whose origins go back
over 200 years. The nearest is the **Crail Golfing
Society** who play over the Balcomie Links, a
course built over sloping terrain, looking out
over the Firth of Forth. Perhaps best known
after St Andrews is **Elie**, where the members of
the Golf House Club play.

Further up the coast, **Montrose** is a must.
One of the oldest of the lot, the current layout
is largely unchanged since the middle of the
19th century. Of inland character, the
Downfield Club at Dundee is a fine, relatively
modern course and is a most pleasant change
from the staple diet of links golf. To the north,
Forfar has an excellent 18 holes, not very long,
but full of interest. While on the subject of
inland courses, it is vital to take a swift drive to
the west and visit the glorious rolling hills of
Perthshire. **Rosemount** at Blairgowrie is
ranked amongst the most beautiful courses in
the world, set amongst heather and pine.
Another in a stunning setting is **Pitlochry** and,
while not very long, its hill-top situation gives
panoramic views.

Strathclyde, Dumfries and Galloway

In the west, the Ayrshire coast is as blessed as Fife and East Lothian both in terms of quality and quantity. Once again, standards are measured in terms of the Open Championship. The top of the heap are those that host the Open, followed by the courses that are used for the final qualifying rounds. This great golfing stretch begins just south of the town of Irvine, with **Western Gailes** and **Glasgow Gailes**. Of the two, Western Gailes just has the edge, perched as it is on a narrow strip of land between the Glasgow to Ayr railway line and the sea. Glasgow Gailes is flatter, but both have served with distinction in the qualifying stages when the Open is held at Troon. Immediately south is **Barassie**, also a 'qualifier' but perhaps a little gentler than the Gailes courses. Barassie is just north of Troon, a town ringed with courses. **Royal Troon** is the Championship course, and typical of many old links courses in that it runs straight out and back along the seashore, with the 9th at the farthest point. Flattish at start and finish, the best holes are through the dunes around the turn. It also has the distinction of having the longest and shortest holes in British Championship golf, the 6th measuring nearly 600 yards and the 8th, the 'Postage Stamp', just 126 yards.

The Highlands

The monarch in these parts is **Gleneagles**, in the lee of the Ochils. The **Kings** and the **Queens** are a fine a pair of courses, and the combination of great golf and good living is hard to beat, if you can afford it.

Golf in the Highlands is concentrated around the east coast. Aberdeen boasts 11 courses of which **Royal Aberdeen** and **Murcar** stand out, both classic links and right next door to one another. **Cruden Bay** is a splendid seaside course and, were it a little longer and more accessible, could be a great test for a full-blown professional tournament. **Fraserburgh** is a pure links and great fun. Banff sports a couple of titled courses in **Royal Tarlair** and **Duff House Royal**. Neither are really links courses, but are nonetheless one of the delights of Highland golf.

In Morayshire, **Moray** (**Lossiemouth**) and **Forres**, both next to the sea, are the pick,

together with **Elgin** some 12 miles inland. Still moving west, at **Nairn** there is a highly regarded links course, which on more than one occasion has played host to the Scottish Championships. **Boat of Garten**, in the Spey Valley, is a relatively short course, but a joy to play. James Braid designed it, and there are superb views – making it a must!

North of Inverness, **Fortrose** and **Rosemarkie**, **Muir of Ord** and **Strathpeffer Spa** all offer a pleasant 18 holes, but **Tain** is the choice if time is short. A new bridge at Tain has cut an hour from the journey north to **Royal Dornoch** and made this magnificent links more accessible. But for its location, Dornoch would be the choice for the most important championships, and indeed the Amateur Championships were played there for the first time in 1985.

The Islands

Arran has seven courses of which **Blackwaterfoot**, **Lamlash** and **Brodick** are the pick. **Machrie** on Islay is the only course amid eight distilleries, so care is needed with your priorities!

Pony Trekking

This is a pleasant way of seeing the country, and you don't have to be an experienced rider. There are lots of pony-trekking centres, offering a choice of day trekking or trekking and camping. Tourist information centres will give you addresses: most tourist maps mark them with a horseshoe. The Scottish Tourist Board publishes a leaflet called 'Pony Trekking and Riding Centres in Scotland'.

Sailing

Sailing off the west coast of Scotland and among the western and northern islands is so beautiful that it makes cruising among the admittedly warmer and more glamorous locations further south, such as the Greek Islands, something of an anti climax. The weather can be tricky, of course, but this should not deter experienced sailors, and there will be many fine days to enjoy. Experience is also necessary to navigate the rocks, currents and whirlpools that make these waters such a challenge. Proper maritime charts are essential. Less experienced sailors should stick to the lochs and inshore waters.

Once you are afloat with a good skipper and navigator there could be no better way of exploring this incomparable coastline. Seen from the sea the scenery is somehow even more magnificent than it appears from the land, and you will be able to explore sea lochs that are virtually inaccessible by overland routes. As well as dozens of harbours and official moorings, there are innumerable sheltered anchorages far from any human habitation. Here you can drop anchor and swim in the cold waters with only sea birds and sheep to see you, before going ashore to enjoy a supper of freshly caught mackerel cooked on an open fire as you listen to the eerie sound of seals calling to each other.

There are marinas and sailing centres around the coast from the Clyde to Ullapool, and on many of the larger lochs. You can charter a boat from a variety of places, either fully-manned or one to crew yourself. 'On the Water in Scotland' is a directory of water sports facilities. It lists names and addresses of firms that hire boats of all categories, for all uses, together with information about slipways, chandlers, moorings, canals, and so on. It is available from the Scottish Tourist Board.

Useful Addresses

Royal Yachting Association (Scotland), Caledonia House, South Gyle, Edinburgh EH12 9DQ, **t** (0131) 317 7388.
North of Scotland Yachting Association, **t** (01343) 850 334.

Shinty or Shinny

Scotland's version of Irish hurling is said to derive from cries used in the game: shin ye, shin t'ye. It's like hockey, with a leather ball and curved sticks.

Shooting and Stalking

The terrain is ideal, with farmland, mixed woodland and moorland, and Scotland has a long tradition of good game management. The estuaries and marshes provide excellent scope for wildfowlers, and there are plenty of deer. Stalking, for the uninitiated, involves spending all day wriggling through wet undergrowth until your prey is within range and then, at a signal from the keeper, missing it, or wounding it and spending the night following it to administer the *coup de grâce*.

Stalking with a camera instead of a rifle can be infinitely more rewarding. Game-shooting species include pheasant, snipe, grey partridge, woodcock, grouse, capercaillie and ptarmigan. Permitted wildfowl species include many varieties of duck and geese. Rough shooting is for wood pigeon, rabbit and hare. Deer species include red deer, roe, fallow and sika. All other species of wildlife, both bird and mammal, are strictly protected in Scotland by the Wildlife and Countryside Act. No game shooting is allowed on Sundays, and a certificate is required by anyone owning or using either a rifle or a shotgun. Before you shoot game you must get a game licence, available in all main and branch post offices throughout the country. Some hotels will arrange shooting and stalking, and local tourist boards will advise on contacting estates and on shooting seasons.

Skiing

There are five ski centres in the Highlands: Glencoe, the Nevis Range (Aonach Mhor), Cairngorm, Glenshee and the Lecht. All have excellent runs and lift networks, as well as equipment hire and ski schools. First timers should note that the picture-postcard conditions often found in the Alps are not so common in Scotland. At times only the most enthusiastic of skiers will enjoy their sport here, when the slopes are icy, balding and pitted with rocks and tree stumps and a piercing wind cuts through even the best thermal clothing. But on the many good days, skiing in Scotland is good fun amongst some of the most beautiful scenery in the world.

Ski Hotline Scotland gives information on road and snow conditions and weather forecasts in the five ski centres. For all areas, **t** 09001 654 654, *www.skiscotland.net* (updated daily during the season).

Glencoe is situated on the A82, 25 miles from Fort William. There are 15 runs (including a particularly easy one called Mugs' Alley), and six lifts. There is a log cabin restaurant and a Museum of Scottish Skiing and Mountaineering. *Open Thurs–Mon during the season; Easter daily.* **Ski Hotline: t** 09001 654 658.

The **Nevis Range** is 5 miles north of Fort William off the A82. The access road, signposted Aonach Mhor, is seldom affected by snow. There are 18 runs of all standards and nine lifts. There is also a 250ft dry ski slope. The Snowgoose Restaurant and Bar seats over 200 and there is a snack hut. *Open throughout the season (as early as Oct–as late as May). Crêche for three- to seven-year-olds open 9–12 and 1–4.* **Ski Hotline: t** 09001 654 660.

Cairngorm is situated off the A9, 28 miles from Inverness and 9 miles from Aviemore. There are plans for a £15 million redevelopment, but there are already plenty of good runs of all categories. There is a day-lodge with licensed restaurant, shop and ski hire, and snack bars on the slopes. **Ski Hotline: t** 09001 654 655.

Glenshee is 12 miles from Braemar on the A93. Spread over three valleys, it has the widest selection of runs in Britain, 38 in all ranging over all categories. There are 26 lifts, a licensed restaurant and cafés, ski schools, shop and a crêche in high season. **Ski Hotline: t** 09001 654 656.

The Lecht is 7 miles from Tomintoul on the A939. It has 12 lifts and 17 runs of varying degrees of difficulty. There is a summer ski slope, and night skiing on three of the runs. Facilities include a licensed day lodge, shop and ski hire, and a crêche. **Glenmulliach**, 4 miles north of the Lecht, is the centre for Nordic Cross Country Skiing. **Ski Hotline: t** 09001 654 657. **Cross Country Ski Hotline: t** 09001 654 659.

Surfing

Surfing in Scotland hardly conjures up images of Hawaiian shores and hot weather, but the north of Scotland can lay claim to some of the best surfing waves in Europe; the European Amateur Surfing Championships were held in Thurso in 1981. The northernmost section of the long coastline, from Bettyhill almost to John O'Groats, has a reputation for the most consistent swells and variety of breaks. There are waves to suit everyone, from gentle beachbreaks to massive reefs, point breaks and river mouths. This is wild-frontier surfing against stunning backdrops of mountains and castles. The water is a slightly off-putting brown, but don't be alarmed because it's only coloured by peat washed down from the hills.

Water Sports

Water sports are available all over the country, including sailing, windsurfing, water-skiing and swimming. Coastal resorts invariably have sailing clubs where you can get tuition and hire boats and equipment. There are a large number of inland water sport centres on the lochs. For full details get the booklet 'Scotland Holiday Afloat' from the Scottish Tourist Board.

Tourist Offices

For tourism purposes, Scotland is divided into regions covered by Area Tourist Boards; each has its own Tourist Information Centre and publishes its own free brochure with local information and a fully comprehensive accommodation guide. Readers are strongly advised to use these brochures to supplement the recommendations made in this book. Information centres will also advise on routes, sporting permits and local events, and will book accommodation.

The **Scottish Tourist Board's Scottish Travel Centre**, 19 Cockspur Street, London SW1 5BL, **t** (020) 7930 8661 (*open Mon–Fri*), provides a full range of information, advice and literature. It also helps with route planning, and has a travel agency where you can make reservations for accommodation and book for events such as the Edinburgh Military Tattoo.

Also in London is the **British Travel Centre**, 12 Regent Street, Piccadilly Circus, W1, **t** (020) 7730 3400 (*open daily; no telephone service on Sundays*), with a comprehensive booking service covering rail, air and sea travel, sightseeing tours, theatre tickets and accommodation. They also change currency.

For drivers using the M6 route north, **Southwaite Tourist Information Centre**, in the Southwaite Service Station, a few minutes south of the border near Carlisle, offers full information on all areas in Scotland, and accommodation services.

The main Tourist Information Centre for the whole of Scotland is **Edinburgh Marketing** in Waverley Market, 3 Princes Street, Edinburgh (*open Oct–May Mon–Sat; personal callers only*). Run in partnership with American Express and Europcar, it offers advice to

Area Tourist Boards

Dumfries and Galloway: 64 Whitesands, Dumfries DG1 2RS, **t** (01387) 253 862, **f** 245 555, www.dumfriesandgalloway.co.uk.

Scottish Borders: Tourist Information Centre, Murray's Green, Jedburgh TD8 6BE, **t** (01835) 863 435/688/170, **f** 864 099, www.scot-borders.co.uk.

Ayrshire and Arran: Block 2, 15 Skye Road, Prestwick KA9 2TA, **t** (01292) 288 688/673 743, **f** 288 686, www.ayrshire-arran.com.

Argyll, the Isles, Loch Lomond, Stirling and the Trossachs: Dept SOS, 7 Alexandra Parade, Dunoon PA23 8AB, **t** (01369) 703 785, **f** 706 085, www.scottish.heartlands.org.

Kingdom of Fife: 70 Market Street, St Andrews KY16 9NU, **t** (01334) 472 021, **f** 478 422, or **t** (01592) 260 270, www.standrews.co.uk.

Perthshire: Lower City Mills, West Mill Street, Perth PH1 5QP, **t** (01738) 627 958/450 600, **f** 630 416, www.perthshire.co.uk.

Angus and Dundee: 21 Castle Street, Dundee DD1 3AA, **t** (01382) 527 527/535, **f** 527 551, www.angusanddundee.co.uk.

Highlands of Scotland: Peffery House, Strathpeffer IV14 9HA, **t** (01997) 421 160, **f** 421 168, www.host.co.uk.

Aberdeen and Grampian: 27 Albyn Place, Aberdeen AB10 1YL, **t** (01224) 632 727/288 825, **f** 620 415, www.agtb.org.

Western Isles: 26 Cromwell Street, Stornoway, Isle of Lewis HS1 2DD, **t** (01851) 703 088, **f** 705 244, www.witb.co.uk.

Orkney: 6 Broad Street, Kirkwall KW15 1NX, **t** (01856) 872 856, **f** 875 056, www.orkney.com.

Shetland: Market Cross, Lerwick ZE1 0LU, **t** (01595) 693 434, **f** 695 807, www.shetland-tourism.co.uk.

Greater Glasgow and Clyde Valley: 11 George Square, Glasgow G2 1DY, **t** (0141) 204 4400/221 0049, **f** 204 4772, www.seeglasgow.com.

Edinburgh and Lothians: Edinburgh and Scotland Information Centre, 3 Princes Street, Edinburgh EH2 2QP, **t** (0131) 473 3800, **f** 473 3881, www.edinburgh.org.

tourists in all areas, accommodation and travel booking, route planning, a Scottish bookshop, currency exchange and car hire.

The **Scottish Tourist Board** is at 23 Ravelston Terrace, Edinburgh EH4 3EU, **t** (0131) 332 2433, www.visitscotland.com.

Another useful website is www.aboutscotland.com.

Tracing Your Ancestors

For many reasons, not least the Highland Clearances, a large number of exiled Scots, and descendants of exiled Scots, return to the land of their origins hoping to trace their family history. Many clans have their own clan historian or library and will give advice.

Scottish Record Office, Her Majesty's General Register House, Princes Street, Edinburgh EH1 3YY, **t** (0131) 557 1022. Send all the information you have on your ancestors.

Scottish Genealogy Society Library and Family History Centre, 15 Victoria Terrace, Edinburgh EH1, **t** (0131) 220 3677, www.scotsgenealogy.com.

Scottish Roots Ancestral Research Service, Edinburgh, **t** (0131) 477 8214, **f** 550 3701 www.scottish-roots.co.uk.

Mark Kennedy Windover, Williamstown, MA, USA, **t** 800 634 5399, www.windover.com. American genealogist.

Where to Stay

The choice of accommodation in Scotland is enormous, ranging from superb, luxury hotels to simple bed and breakfasts (B&Bs), or self-catering. The price is not always a reliable guide. The STB accommodation guides give full details of price and facilities; this book gives only a very small selection.

As little as £15 a night can buy bed and breakfast in a clean house, with a warm welcome and a thumping good breakfast. £120 can buy a night in a four-poster bed or over £200 a suite with a jacuzzi. You can rent a whole house or cottage from as little as £60 a week to over £1,000. Prices often vary seasonally; single rooms are usually more expensive, per head, than double. Many hotels and guest houses do special breaks for longer stays or off-peak times – it's always worth asking.

A static caravan costs from £50 a week upwards, and campsites charge from about £5 a night for visiting caravans. Campsite facilities vary enormously, but often the scenery makes up for primitive plumbing. The one at Braemar is excellent.

Many B&Bs serve an evening meal, and all hotels provide full service. In the more rural areas, and indeed in the towns, don't be put off by the lack of en-suite bathrooms in the smaller hotels. What they lack in modern facilities is invariably made up for in friendly hospitality. Very often you will have sole use of a bathroom across the passage.

Scottish Tourist Board Accommodation Gradings

An impartial team of inspectors visits hotels, guesthouses, bed and breakfast and self-catering establishments, to assess their quality. They award classifications ranging from 'Listed' to five crowns, and gradings from 'Approved' to 'Highly Commended', depending on the standard and facilities. Full details can be obtained from the Scottish Tourist Board. Visitors should be aware that these awards are based on a set range of standards and facilities such as: TV, shoe-cleaning kit, full-length mirror, trouser press, luggage stand, hospitality tray, etc., as well as the more obvious requirements such as heating and towels. They do not necessarily apply to soul or character. It is therefore possible to opt for a Highly Commended, five-crown hotel only to find yourself in a sweltering, double-glazed bedroom crammed with gadgets and electric goodies, totally lacking in atmosphere. Equally, an old-fashioned, slightly shabby ex-shooting lodge, as full of Highland character and hospitality as you could ever wish for, with blazing log fires instead of central heating, pure cotton sheets, early-morning tea brought to you, and delicious home cooking, may be excluded from the Scottish Tourist Board's list because of its lack of tangible 'facilities'.

Wolsey Lodges are a consortium of privately owned homes where guests are welcomed as friends, entertained as family, and often dine with their hosts. The houses range from grand country houses with antiques and family heirlooms, to farmhouses, former manses and modest family homes. Because you are treated as a family friend, you are expected to behave like one. You may ask to borrow an iron, or the shoe-cleaning kit – but don't put

Accommodation Price Ranges

Prices change frequently. In this guide accommodation is loosely graded into three categories, based on the price of bed and breakfast (B&B) for one person in a single room – double rooms are almost always cheaper per person. Many hotels do special bargain breaks.

Expensive	over £70
Moderate	£30–70
Cheap	£15–30

your dirty shoes outside your door or hand your hostess your crumpled skirt. If there is no licence you can take your own drink; many of the houses have an 'honesty bar' where you help yourself and write it in a book. The standard of Wolsey Lodges is always high and they are usually extremely reasonable in price. They are so called after Cardinal Wolsey who, when touring the kingdom during his ascendancy, expected to be entertained like royalty wherever he chose to stop.

Youth Hostels

There are more than 80 youth hostels in Scotland, marked on most maps by a triangle. They fall into five grades: Superior, Standard, Simple, Standard with Limited Access, and Unclassified/adopted. The one on Loch Lomond was once a stately home; the one near Bonar Bridge is Carbisdale Castle; while Garenin, in Lewis, is a converted black house. Some have central heating, hot showers, carpets, etc.; some include continental breakfast in the price; many serve substantial budget meals; and all offer dormitory accommodation and self-catering facilities. Quite a few have 'family rooms', which should be booked well in advance, and there are even 'family cottages'. Anyone over the age of five may use a youth hostel, and younger children are allowed to use the cottages. It is a membership organization and you can join on arrival at the hostel – children are included in adult membership. The membership card lets you stay in 5,000 hostels throughout the world and entitles you to some excellent travel discounts.

SYHA (Scottish Youth Hostel Association), 7 Glebe Crescent, Stirling FK8 2JA, t (01786) 891 400. Central Reservations Service, t 08701 553 255, www.syha.org.uk.

The Scottish Borders

08

The Scottish Borders

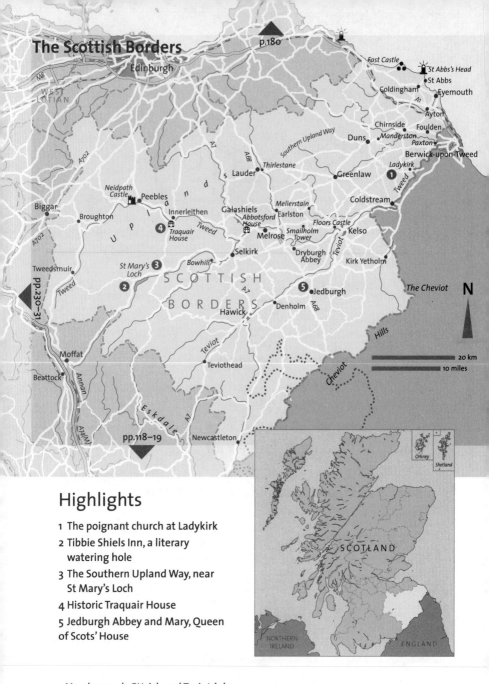

p.180

Edinburgh

WEST LOTHIAN

Fast Castle
St Abb's Head
St Abbs
Coldingham
Eyemouth
Aytor
Chirnside
Foulden
Manderston
Paxton
Duns
Berwick-upon-Tweed
Southern Upland Way
Thirlestane
Lauder
Greenlaw
Ladykirk **1**
Coldstream
Neidpath Castle
Peebles
Innerleithen
Galashiels
Abbotsford House
Mellerstain
Earlston
Floors Castle
Kelso
Biggar
Broughton
4 Traquair House
Melrose
Smailholm Tower
Dryburgh Abbey
Kirk Yetholm
St Mary's Loch **3**
Bowhill
Selkirk
2
SCOTTISH
BORDERS
5 Jedburgh
The Cheviot
Tweedsmuir
Denholm
Hawick
pp.230–31
Hills
Moffat
Teviot
Cheviot
Beattock
Teviothead
20 km
10 miles
Eskdale
pp.118–19
Newcastleton

N

Orkney
Shetland

SCOTLAND

NORTHERN IRELAND

ENGLAND

Highlights

1 The poignant church at Ladykirk
2 Tibbie Shiels Inn, a literary watering hole
3 The Southern Upland Way, near St Mary's Loch
4 Historic Traquair House
5 Jedburgh Abbey and Mary, Queen of Scots' House

March, march, Ettrick and Teviotdale,
Why the deil dinna ye march forward in order?
March, march, Eskdale and Liddesdale,
All the Blue Bonnets are bound for the Border.
from *Blue Bonnets Over the Border*, by Sir Walter Scott

Most routes into Scotland top a summit from which you look across a chequer-board of fertile farmland, laced with wooded river valleys within a rim of undulating hills. In contrast is the savage, rocky coastline with cliff-hung fishing towns and villages. This borderland was bitterly fought over from prehistoric times until the middle of the 17th century: many ruins bear witness to those violent times. Buildings and towns were sacked and hastily rebuilt; most settlements were fortified. The four abbeys, at Melrose, Jedburgh, Kelso and Dryburgh, built by David I in the 12th century within a few miles of each other in the fertile river valleys, were destroyed and repaired often before the Reformation led to their final decay. It was not just the invading English who caused havoc: the Border Reivers, powerful border families, warred amongst themselves, raiding each other's territory and stealing cattle. Ballads and folk tales romanticize them; in reality they were savage and barbaric. The fast-flowing rivers, internationally famous for salmon and trout, were harnessed in the old days to drive woollen mills; today, the Borders are still famous for their textiles. Farming and horse-breeding also play an important part in the economy of this fertile land, and the annual agricultural shows provide robust local colour. Much has been written in prose, poetry and song, trying to capture the elusive spirit of the Borders. Perhaps Sir Walter Scott, who made the Borders his domain, wrote most.

In several towns the turbulent days of the Border Reivers are revived with **Common Riding Festivals**, remembering the days when the men rode out to check the boundaries. These celebrations provide light-hearted entertainment and pageantry and take place throughout the summer months. You also get a good taste of Border atmosphere at the many agricultural shows, games and horse sales that proliferate.

The Coast and Northeast Corner

Fishing and smuggling played an important part in forming the characters of those whose descendants live along the coastal fringe of the Borders. Some of the towns and villages are little changed since the days when smugglers teemed in the warrens of twisting wynds and closes, evading the excisemen in underground hideaways.

St Abbs

St Abbs, on the northeast corner, is a pretty village, almost Cornish in character, clinging to the cliffs, with narrow zigzag streets running steeply down to the harbour, lined with brightly painted terraced fisher cottages, some of which still have quaint 'doll's house' sheds in front. St Abbs is a holiday village now, with just a few lobster boats replacing the trawlers that used to go out for haddock, cod and turbot. Boats still come in during bad weather for shelter. Down in the harbour there are upturned boats, piles of nets, tottering stacks of creels and fish boxes, backed by old stone tackle-sheds. St Abbs has one of the few sandy beaches on this coast.

St Abbs Head is a rugged promontory north of the village – a towering headland of black volcanic rock, pounded by the sea, with a lighthouse at its tip. Only cars for disabled, old or infirm people can go all the way to the lighthouse, but it is an invigorating half-mile walk, across sheep-cropped turf dotted with whins and wind-stunted trees, the restless sea in the background. You can tour the lighthouse at the keeper's discretion. This desolate headland is a wildlife reserve owned by the NTS, and there are many species of sea bird: guillemots, razorbills, shags, and many more. The air is vibrant with their noise. There is a visitors' centre at Northfield Farm Steading, with information about the reserve, and a coffee shop (*see* below). The Rangers for the wildlife and marine reserve are based here, **t** (01890) 771 443.

Fast Castle, on Wheat Stack to the west, attached to the mainland by a terrifying gangway, is a lovely walk along the cliffs, but take care – the path approach is hazardous. All you can see now are the tattered remains of what was once a notorious fortress, used by wreckers and robbers, perched halfway up the cliff. It is easy to see why Scott used Fast Castle as the model for 'Wolf's Crag' in *The Bride of Lammermoor*. Like many of the Border castles, it was fought over by the Scots and English, frequently destroyed and rebuilt over the centuries. It was owned by some of the most important of the Border families, the Lumsdens and the Logans and the powerful Homes, whose stronghold it was by the end of the 14th century. It was during Sir Patrick Home's ownership in 1503 that Margaret Tudor, Henry VIII's sister, stayed here on her way to marry James IV, leaving her entourage of 1,500 attendants at Coldingham Priory. She was 14 years old. In just 10 years' time in an upstairs room in Linlithgow, she was to weep for her faithless husband, one of the many flowers of the forest that were 'a' wede awae' on Flodden Field.

Coldingham

Inland, Coldingham is an attractive, twisting village with the remains of a 13th-century priory; the choir is now the parish church. A soaring arch rises from the ruined foundations, ancient gravestones and fragments of carved masonry scattered at its feet. **Coldingham Priory**, originally founded by Ebba in about 660, makes an impressive foreground to a distant seascape. It has been sacked, burnt, plundered and rebuilt over the centuries, and was finally destroyed by Cromwell in 1650. Renovations in 1854 and 1954 produced what you see today. It once offered the right of sanctuary for lawbreakers, the boundary within which they were safe being marked by crosses.

Eyemouth

Just down the coast, Eyemouth is a small seaside town with a busy commercial fishing industry that includes the export of shellfish. When James VI (James I of England) created it a burgh of barony in 1566 with the status of a free port, it became a thriving centre for smugglers. The intricate design of the older part of the town provided a maze of hiding places and escape routes; many of the houses still have hidden chambers and secret passages. The cliffs around are honeycombed with caves.

Stand on the harbour wall, looking out to sea and think back to Friday 14 October 1881. The fishing fleet sailed on a day that dawned too bright and too still, with the barometer reading too low. At noon there was a dark stillness, followed by a sudden storm – a tornado that devastated the fleet. Many drowned at once; others, struggling home, were smashed on the rocks outside the harbour in sight of their helpless families. Only six boats got back safely: 23 were lost and 129 men were drowned, leaving 107 widows. Other fleets up and down the coast suffered in the same way.

The **Eyemouth Museum** (*open Easter–June and Sept Mon–Sat 10–5, Sun 1–3; July and Aug Mon–Sat 10–6, Sun 11–4.30; Oct Mon–Sat 10–12.30 and 1.30–4.30; adm*), in the converted Georgian Auld Kirk in the Market Place near the harbour, was opened in 1981 as a centenary memorial to the fishing disaster. The tapestry, a most striking piece of contemporary work, has pictures of the storm, sea scenes and the names of all the boats that were lost and of the men aboard them. There is also the wheelhouse of a modern fishing boat as well as local fishing and farming history.

Eyemouth Harbour, recently improved and enlarged, is long and narrow and teeming with maritime life. Fish boxes are stacked in open-sided sheds surrounded by all the clutter of the sea: nets and derricks and craft of all sizes, and great ribbed skeletons of hulls propped in cradles. **Gunsgreen House**, opposite the harbour, is alleged to have secret passages leading to the water.

Ayton

Ayton is a crossroads village, southwest of Eyemouth. Prominent here is **Ayton Castle** (*open May–Sept Sun 2–5, or by appointment t (01890) 781 212*), a vast red Victorian pile, clearly seen from the road and the railway. This architectural extravaganza is so ostentatious it is easy to believe the local legend that it developed from its foundations without plans or architect, its creator crossing the river each day to order the erection of yet another turret or crow-stepped gable according to his mood. A splendid example of Scottish Baronial at its most fanciful, it was in fact designed by Gillespie Graham in 1851 for William Mitchell Innes, Governor of the Bank of Scotland. Later additions were made on the site of an ancient fortalice destroyed by the English in the 15th century and finally burnt down in 1834. It is now a family home.

Beyond the church, near the imposing entrance to the castle, are the ruins of a pre-Reformation church. Among these ivy-covered stones, emissaries of Scots and English kings often met to arrange short-lived truces during the years of the Border wars. Many ancient bones lie buried far below the present layer of graves in this tranquil resting place, and the ugly castle intrudes like a brash newcomer on the ancient ruin.

Foulden

Foulden, to the south, is little more than a row of cottages on a cobbled terrace on one side of the road, facing a green beyond which the land falls gently away to the Cheviot Hills on the southern horizon. The Flemish-style cottages gaze out over the

Chirnside

Chirnside, west of Foulden, is where the racing driver Jim Clark is buried. The church has a 12th-century Norman doorway on the south wall. In 1674 the Chirnside minister's wife was buried in this churchyard, wearing a valuable ring. The sexton, returning at night to rob the grave, tried to hack off the ring with a knife. The corpse sprang up, screamed and rushed to the manse, yelling: 'Open the door, open the door, for I'm fair clemmed wi' the cauld.'

Tourist Information

Eyemouth: Auld Kirk, Manse Road, **t** (01890) 750 678, *eyemouth@scot-borders.co.uk*; *open April–Oct.*

Festivals

May: Horse Show, Duns.
July: Children's Picnic and Herring Queen Festival, Eyemouth; a week of endless fun and activities for children of all ages. **Summer Festival**, Duns; Common Riding Celebration.
August: Lifeboat Weekend, Eyemouth. Berwickshire Agricultural Show, Duns.

Sports and Activities

The coast here is ideal for divers. Boats can be chartered from **D&J Charters**, **t** (01890) 771 377, or **St Abbs Boat Charter**, **t** (01890) 771 681.

Where to Stay and Eat

Chirnside Hall Country House Hotel, **t** (01890) 818 219, *www.chirnsidehallhotel.com* (*expensive–moderate*). Modernized Victorian mansion house in secluded gardens and woodland.

Bridgend Guest House, West High Street, Greenlaw, **t** (01361) 810 270, *aproposdes@FSBDial.co.uk* (*moderate*). Built in 1861, this place sits by the river and has trout fishing.
The Castle Inn Hotel, Greenlaw, **t** (01361) 810 217 (*moderate*). Greenlaw has several hotels of which this, a family-run 'A' listed Georgian coaching inn, is friendly and comfortable.
Churches Hotel, Albert Road, Eyemouth, **t** (01890) 750 401, **f** 750 747, *www.churcheshotel.co.uk* (*moderate*). A newly done-up house upgraded to 4 stars, with a restaurant specialising in seafood.
Cul-Na-Sithe ('corner of peace'), Coldingham Bay, **t** (01890) 771 355, *culnasithe@clara.co.uk* (*moderate*). Overlooking Coldingham Sands and the coast. B&B; dinner on request.
Dolphin Hotel, North Street, Eyemouth, **t** (01890) 750 280 (*moderate*). Small hotel offering live entertainment.
Press Castle, Coldingham, **t** (01890) 771 257, *www.presscastle.co.uk* (*moderate*). 17th-century mansion house in woodland, offering B&B, dinner B&B, or self-catering in lodges, suites or a cottage. Its **restaurant**, on the ground floor, has a Victorian conservatory (*open Tues–Sun 6.30–9*).
Wellfield House, Preston Road, Duns, **t** (01361) 883 189, *www.wellfield.com* (*moderate*). Elegant Georgian country house with log fires and a billiard room. Dinner on request.

magnificent view, their gabled eyebrows forever raised in surprise. To the left of the row, in the old schoolhouse, the door to the post office is set back behind four delightfully incongruous fluted columns.

By the church is a restored 18th–19th-century two-storey **tithe barn** (*no access*), with an outside stair and crow-stepped gables, where the minister stored the grain given him by his parishioners as a stipend.

Duns

Heading inland towards the heart of the Borders you come to the small county town of Duns, straggling uphill from a solid-looking church on a green mound with narrow streets behind, where buildings seem to jostle each other, all set at odd angles in no apparent order. Duns was designed as the capital of Berwickshire and has some very fine buildings. The town hall was intended to be the county hall.

Duns Nature Reserve, reached by a path from the top of Castle Street, has pleasant walks and a short, steep climb up **Duns Law**. The town clung to the southwest slope of this hill until it was completely destroyed in 1545 during Henry VIII's Rough Wooing. It was rebuilt in its present position within 50 years. On top of the law is a stone with

Barniken House Hotel, 18 Murray Street, Duns, t (01361) 882 466 (*cheap*). Family-run Georgian house in its own grounds, with a few rooms, a putting green and bar food.

The Black Bull, Black Bull Street, Duns, t (01361) 883 379 (*cheap*). A few bedrooms and a beer garden, in the centre of things.

Castle Rock Guest House, Murrayfield, St Abbs, t (01890) 771 715 (*cheap*). On the cliffs above the harbour, with fabulous sea views from the bedrooms.

Cockburn Mill, Duns, t (01361) 882 811, *amp@co-mill.freeserve.co.uk* (*cheap*). Riverside farmhouse with trout fishing. B&B; dinner by arrangement.

Kirkside House, Bonkyl, nr Duns, t (01361) 884 340 (*cheap*). A charming old manse in a pretty garden. Nice hosts, children over 12 and pets welcome. No smoking. B&B, with dinner by arrangement.

St Vedas House, Coldingham Bay, t (01890) 771 478, *www.stvedas.com* (*cheap*). B&B; dinner on request.

The Ship Hotel, on the harbour, Eyemouth, t (01890) 750 224 (*cheap*). Small family-run hotel with fresh local fish and bar meals (*meals daily 12–2.30 and 6.30–9.30*).

Springbank Cottage, The Harbour, St Abbs, t (01890) 771 477, *davemac55@hotmail.com* (*cheap*). Cosy fisherman's cottage on the edge of the harbour for B&B.

Waterloo Arms Hotel, Chirnside, t (01890) 818 520 (*cheap*). Reasonable village inn.

Wheatsheaf Hotel, Main Street, Reston, t (01890) 761 219 (*cheap*). Small inn for B&B and golf breaks. *Open for meals Mon–Sat 12–2 and 6–9, Sun 12.30–2 and 6–9.*

The Contented Sole, Harbour Road, Eyemouth, t (01890) 750 268. Bar meals. Try Eyemouth pale, a lighter, more delicate version of smoked haddock, and Eyemouth tart, made with walnuts, currants and coconut. *Open Mon–Sat 11–8, Sun 12.30–2.30.*

The Flemington Inn, Burnmouth, t (01890) 781 277. Cosy pub with bar meals, shellfish and salmon. *Open daily 12.30–9.*

Giacopazzi's, 18 Harbour Road, Eyemouth, t (01890) 750 317. Restaurant and takeaway with good fish and chips and home-made ice cream. Since 1900. *Open daily 11–9.*

The Headstart Coffee Shop. Home-baked goodies. A good fuel stop after the walk at St Abb's Head. *Open April–Oct daily 10.30–5.*

The Old Bakehouse, 4 Manse Road, Eyemouth, t (01890) 750 265. Licensed coffee shop–restaurant with a patio and walled garden. *Open Mon–Sat 9–5, Sun 10–5.*

The Riverside, Abbey St Bathans, t (01361) 840 312. Friendly café–restaurant by a trout farm.

The Craw Inn, Auchencrow, t (01890) 761 253. Good seafood and steaks. *Open 12–2.30 and 6–9.30.*

a hole in it, from which a Covenanter army flew its standard in 1639, awaiting a battle that never took place. Their general, Leslie, is thought to have had his headquarters in **Duns Castle**, at the foot of the hill. The stone at the castle gate was erected by Franciscans, claiming Duns to be the birthplace of Johannes Duns Scotus (or Scotyus), a great medieval scholar who questioned the teachings of Thomas Aquinas. After his death his radical beliefs were scorned as stupid and thus evolved the word 'dunce'.

The **Jim Clark Memorial** (*44 Newton Street; open April–Sep Mon–Sat 10.30–1 and 2–4.30, Sun 2–4; Oct Mon–Sat 1–4; adm*) is clearly signposted on the west side of the town. Trophies, photographs and memorabilia celebrate the motor racing career of Jim Clark, twice world champion in the 1960s before his death in 1968. Clark was born in Fife in 1936 and moved to the Chirnside area when he was six.

Edin Hall Broch

Edin Hall Broch, north of Duns on the northeast shoulder of Cockburn Law, is the sturdy remains of one of the Iron Age towers that are unique to Scotland and rare so far south. The 20–30-minute climb from a pine wood by the road is clearly marked. It crosses a bridge over Whiteadder Water, which cascades down over gleaming slabs of granite below, the sound of its turmoil carrying far across the bleak moorland. Scattered piles of stones on the grassy slopes are relics of those settlers who roamed the desolate hillside with their beasts, huddling for refuge within the tall, double-walled tower, honeycombed with chambers and galleries. The massive walls were the base of a tapering tower about 40ft high, its one passage-entrance easily defended.

Manderston

Open bank holidays and mid-May–Sept, Thurs and Sun 2–5; group visits by appointment all year, t (01361) 883 450; adm; www.manderston.co.uk.

Manderston, east of Duns, is one of the finest Edwardian stately homes in Scotland, with 56 acres of formal gardens. The rhododendrons are especially worth seeing. In the house is what is believed to be the only silver staircase balustrade in the world – actually silver plated. To judge by the 56 bells in the servants' quarters, there were plenty of silver cleaners when the house was built. The stables are lavish and there is a marble dairy, a Biscuit Tin Museum, cream teas and a gift shop.

Greenlaw

Greenlaw, a little town southwest of Duns on the Blackadder, has a remarkable **church** whose spire actually contained the prison. Known locally as **Hell's Hole**, it has a sinister gridiron gate, or yett, and barred windows. Originally the courthouse was also joined to the church.

The Tweed Valley

The River Tweed is one of Scotland's most famous salmon-fishing rivers, and also one of its most delightful. It rises in the hills above Moffat, quickly gathering strength to flow through a wide, mostly wooded valley until it reaches the sea at Berwick-upon-Tweed, across the border in England.

Berwick to Coldstream

Paxton House

Open Good Friday–Oct daily, tours of house 11.15–4.15; adm; tearoom 10–5; www.paxtonhouse.com.

Paxton House, just outside Berwick, is a perfect example of an 18th-century neo-Palladian mansion. Built in 1758 to designs by John and James Adam, and later embellished by Robert Adam, it was intended as the home of Patrick Home of Billie, later 13th Laird of Wedderburn, in anticipation of his marriage to the natural daughter of Frederick the Great of Prussia. The marriage never took place. The house contains

Chippendale furniture and important paintings from the National Galleries of Scotland. There are gardens, riverside walks, a tearoom and an adventure playground.

Ladykirk

Ladykirk, a few miles southwest of the mouth of the Tweed, is just a handful of houses surrounding a pale rose-coloured cruciform **church** that is worth travelling a long way to see. Built in 1500, its solid buttresses, topped by carved finials, support the tremendous weight of an overlapping slabbed-stone roof. The curiously oriental tower was added in 1743 by William Adam. James IV was almost drowned crossing the Tweed here, and he vowed to build a shrine to Our Lady in gratitude for his survival; Ladykirk was the fulfilment of his promise. Inside this well-restored gem, a spiral stair leads up to the original living quarters of the priest, with a small window from which he could watch the altar. James often visited Ladykirk, and he knelt at prayer here before the Battle of Flodden in 1513. Sit in one of the pews for a moment and catch an echo of that poignant lament, composed by Jean Eliot over 200 years after Flodden, that enshrines the whole tragedy of the battle:

I've heard the lilting at our yowe-milking,
Lasses a-lilting before the dawn o' day;
But now they are moaning on ilka green loaning;
'The Flowers of the Forest are a' wede awae.'

Coldstream

Literally a border town, Coldstream clings to the banks of the Tweed a few miles southwest of Ladykirk, seeming to ignore the rumble and grind of the traffic that thunders up its narrow main street. The Tweed, winding through its broad valley, casts a spell over this area. The fast, dark currents whirl seawards carrying memories of the past when the mingled blood of Scots and English so often stained the water. Coldstream was the first place where it was easy to cross the river: many armies passed this way and camped on the banks. In the middle of the bridge that spans the Tweed, a plaque marks the spot where Robert Burns first put a foot across the border into England in 1787. On the north side of the bridge is a tiny 'marriage house', used by fugitive lovers from England in the 18th century. The figure in a frock-coat, just beyond, who stands Nelson-like on a fluted column, dispatch papers in hand, was a Victorian MP – Charles Marjoriebanks.

Henderson Park is a formal garden overlooking the river off Main Street. The engraved stone, erected by the Coldstream Guards, records how, in 1660, their predecessors crossed the Tweed nearby, following their beloved General Monk, to crush Cromwell and establish Charles II on the throne. Although they were not raised here, they adopted their title of Coldstream Guards in honour of this historic event.

The **Coldstream Museum** (*open April–Sept Mon–Sat 10–4, Sun 2–4; Oct Mon–Sat 1–4; adm*) is in General Monk's Headquarters in the town's asymmetrical Market Square. This simple building houses regimental (Coldstream Guards) and local history exhibits. Abbey Road leads down from Main Street to where a Cistercian priory stood

Tourist Information

Coldstream: Town Hall, High Street, **t** (01890) 882 607, *coldstream@scot-borders.co.uk*; *open April–Oct.*

Festivals

August: Common Riding Celebrations, Coldstream; during Civic Week at the beginning of August.

Where to Stay and Eat

With one exception, the best hotels around Coldstream are across the river – in England. Sneak back over that bridge to Cornhill-on-Tweed in Northumberland.

Coldstream t (01890–)

Elizabeth and Francis Gradidge, Ruthven House, **t** 840 771, *www.bordersovernight. co.uk* (*moderate*). Special B&B with uninterrupted views of the hills for 20 miles around,

and a warm friendly welcome. Dinner by prior arrangement. Francis offers computer lessons to his guests, specialising in jargon-free language for the over 50s.

Tillmouth Park Hotel, Cornhill-on-Tweed, **t** 882 255, *www.tillmouthpark.co.uk* (*moderate*). An imposing Victorian baronial pile in 15 acres of grounds, with antique furniture, a galleried drawing room and a library dining room. Special fishing breaks and good food.

Wheatsheaf Hotel, Swinton, **t** 860 257, *www.wheatsheaf- swinton.co.uk* (*moderate*). The exception (*see* above) is a traditional country inn overlooking the village green near the Tweed, with only six bedrooms (en suite) and exceptionally good food.

The Coach House, Crookham, just outside Cornhill, **t** 820 293, *www.coachhouse-crookham.com* (*cheap*). Very comfortable hotel built around a sunny courtyard, with good home cooking.

There's not much in the way of gourmet restaurants around here, apart from the **Wheatsheaf Hotel** (*see* above).

for four centuries until it was destroyed by the English in 1545. Human bones were excavated in 1834, which may have been the remains of the bodies that arrived here, piled on waggons, in 1513: Flodden's dead, brought to the Lady Abbess for burial.

The Hirsel, on the western edge of town (*house not open to the public; park open all year; small charge for car park*), is the seat of the Douglas-Home family. The late Lord Home (pronounced Hume) of the Hirsel was Prime Minister when President Kennedy was assassinated in 1963. He made history by renouncing his peerage and fighting a by-election at Kinross, during which, although Prime Minister, he was technically not a member of either the House of Lords or the House of Commons. A picturesque stableyard has been converted into a **Homestead Museum** (*open daily 10–5*) with a craft centre and workshops, each stall containing domestic displays: wash house, joiner's shop, forestry, archaeology. Maps and guides are sold and there's a coffee shop.

Kelso and Around

Two famous Border rivers, the Teviot and the Tweed, meet under the walls of **Kelso**, a compact market town facing south across green plains towards the Cheviots. Originally called Calkou (Chalk-hill), Kelso was never strongly fortified, relying on its status as an abbey town for immunity from attack. However, being on the threshold of Scotland, it was frequently sacked by the English; it was also the last staging post for Scottish armies on their way south. The Old Pretender was proclaimed king in the market place in 1715, and his son, retreating north in 1745, stayed here.

In spite of shocking architectural vandalism in the 19th century, when the town hall's piazza was filled in and a monstrous bank was built, the elegant Georgian square is still very fine, almost Flemish in style, its spaciousness a contrast to the narrow streets of most Border towns, crammed behind defensive walls. It was the first central square in any Border town.

By **29 Roxburgh Street** a horseshoe set into the road marks the spot where Prince Charles' horse cast a shoe in 1745, during his progress south to Derby. The graceful five-arched bridge over the Tweed was built by John Rennie in 1803 as a model for the now-demolished Waterloo Bridge, two of whose lamps adorn it.

Kelso Abbey

Open April–Dec Mon–Sat 9–5, Sun 2–5;
Jan–Mar ask for key from tourist office.

Kelso Abbey was founded by David I in 1128. All that can be seen today is the façade of the northwest transept, the tower and a small part of the nave. This was once the most powerful ecclesiastical establishment in the land, and one of the most wealthy, collecting revenue from dozens of parishes, manors, granges, mills and fisheries. The infant James III was crowned here in 1460. In 1523 the English began their attacks on the abbey, tearing off the roofs and firing the monastic buildings. In 1545 they finished it off, slaughtering a hundred brave defendants, including twelve monks.

Floors Castle

Open mid-April–Oct daily 10–4.30, last adm 4;
closed 1 May; adm; www.floorscastle.com.

Two miles northwest of Kelso, Floors Castle is the home of the Duke of Roxburghe, the largest inhabited castle in Scotland. Built by William Adam (1718–1740), and added to by William Playfair in 1840, this immense, eastern-looking, castellated mansion, flanked by vast pavilions, with minarets and cupolas, is best appreciated from a distance. A tree in the grounds marks the spot where James II was killed by an exploding cannon in 1460. Inside are fine tapestries, porcelain and paintings. There is an excellent garden centre (*open all year*) with a separate entrance, in walled enclosures with wonderful old greenhouses and a spectacular herbaceous border. There is a coffee shop in the walled garden, a licensed restaurant, and a gift shop.

Roxburgh

Roxburgh was once a mighty walled royal burgh, built round the fortress of Marchmount, about a mile southwest of Kelso, so large that in the 12th century some of its inhabitants had to be rehoused outside the town. This metropolis was so bitterly fought over and so frequently annexed by the English that in 1460 the Scots decided the only way to keep it permanently from their enemies was to remove it from the map. They made a pretty good job of it: all that remains are the earthworks of the castle, and you have to search for them. (The present village of Roxburgh, further southwest, dates from more recent times.)

Tourist Information

Kelso: Town House, The Square, **t** (01573) 223 464, *kelso@scot-borders.co.uk*; *open April–Oct.*

Festivals

February: Berwickshire Hunt Point-to-point, Kelso.
April: Buccleuch and Jed Forest Point-to-point, Kelso.
June: Kelso Dog Show.
July: Kelso Civic Week; Common Riding Festival and Border Union Agricultural Show.
September: Kelso Horse Sales. Kelso Ram Sales.
October–May: Kelso Races.

Where to Stay

Kelso t (01573–)

The Roxburghe Hotel, Heiton, **t** 450 331, *www.roxburghe.net* (*expensive*). If you're after luxury, then it has to be here. Owned by the Duke of Roxburghe, the hotel is 18th-century baronial, in 200 acres on the banks of the Teviot. Conversion to an hotel has not spoiled its atmosphere, with antique furniture and excellent food and wine. There is fishing on the Tweed and the Teviot, shooting, tennis, croquet, an 18-hole championship golf course and a beauty clinic.
Black Swan Hotel, 7 Horsemarket, **t** 224 563. Small, friendly hotel (*moderate*).

Belford-on-Bowmont, Yetholm, **t** 420 362 (*moderate*). Friendly and welcoming Georgian farmhouse. Well worth booking ahead. 24 hours' notice needed for dinner.
Border Hotel, The Green, Kirk Yetholm, **t** 420 237, *www.theborderhotel.co.uk* (*moderate*). 17th-century coaching inn, ideal for Pennine Way walkers.
Cross Keys Hotel, The Square, **t** 223 303, *www.cross-keys-hotel.co.uk* (*moderate*). One of Scotland's oldest coaching inns, completely modernized, in the middle of town. It has won awards for its food.
Ednam House Hotel, Bridge Street, **t** 224 168, *www.ednamhouse.com* (*moderate*). A comfortable 18th-century mansion over-looking the Tweed. Modern extensions haven't spoiled the original ceilings, fireplaces and woodwork.
White Swan Inn, Abbey Row, **t** 225 800 (*moderate*). 300-year-old town house which claims Bonnie Prince Charlie was a guest.

Eating Out

Floors Castle, overlooking the Tweed, **t** 223 333. Try the restaurant in the old stable courtyard for lunch: Floors kitchen pheasant pâté, or fresh or smoked local salmon. Good home baking comes from the castle kitchen, too, none of it expensive. A local speciality to look out for is *Yetholm bannock*, a very rich shortbread with crystallized ginger.

Otherwise try the **Roxburghe**, **Cross Keys** and **Ednam House** hotels, *see* above.

Mellerstain House

Open Easter weekend and May–Sept daily exc Sat 12.30–5; adm; **t** *(01573) 410 225.*

Mellerstain, northwest of Kelso, is the home of Lord Haddington, partly built by William Adam in 1725 and finished by his son Robert in 1778. It is one of Scotland's finest Georgian mansions, approached down a mile-long avenue of giant beeches, oaks and firs, with formal Italian terraced gardens at the back sloping down to an ornamental lake. Inside are original Robert Adam ceilings and plasterwork, fine furniture, and paintings by Gainsborough, Allan Ramsay, Constable and Veronese.

In the recent past, a brief liaison between a son of the house, Robbie, and Pippin, a lady of easy virtue who lived in one of the estate cottages, resulted in the birth of a jaunty, wolfish Borderer known as Tam o' Shanter. Picaresque tales of his life as a charismatic, maverick hunter became legend, even in his lifetime.

Smailholm Tower

Open April–Sept Mon–Sat 9.30–6.30, Sun 2–6.30; Oct–Mar Sat 9.30–4.30, Sun 2–4.30; adm; **t** *(01573) 460 365.*

Smailholm Tower, south of Mellerstain off the B6404, is a fine example of a 16th-century Border peel tower. Well restored, it stands, gaunt and forbidding, 57ft high on a turf-carpeted crag above a small, weed-choked loch, overlooking flat arable land 636ft above sea level. To the south, Great Cheviot, guardian of the border, dominates the horizon. Monks from Dryburgh Abbey were given these lands in 1160 and grazed their sheep here. In 1799 the tower was a ruin. Walter Scott, who had spent many holidays with his grandparents at Sandyknowe Farm just to the east, made a deal with the owner, Scott of Harden, who agreed to save the tower if Sir Walter would write a ballad about it. *The Eve of St John* was the result, and Smailholm also got a mention in *Marmion*. With piped 'atmospheric' music to fuel the imagination, it isn't difficult to picture the five storeys as they were, with store rooms below and living quarters above, despite the present museum of dolls and tapestries. When the wind is howling outside one almost hears the war cries of marauding clans and the clash of broadsword and pike.

Kirk Yetholm

Kirk Yetholm, southeast of Kelso on the B6352, is the northern terminus of the Pennine Way, a 250-mile hike down into Yorkshire. This was the gypsy capital of Scotland, where all gypsy queens were crowned until 1883, when the last one, Esther Faa Blythe, died. You can still see the Gypsy Palace, a tiny cottage in the village. Many of Flodden's dead were buried in the churchyard here around an earlier church.

Down the Tweed to Galashiels

Dryburgh Abbey

Open April–Sept Mon–Sat 9.30–6.30, Sun 2–4.30;
Oct–Mar Mon–Sat 9.30–4.30, Sun 2–4.30; adm.

Ten miles west of Kelso is one of the quartet of 12th-century Border abbeys founded in the reign of David I, all within a few miles of each other. Built in 1150, it is a beautiful ruin, standing in a loop of the Tweed. Its cloister buildings are more complete than those of other Scottish monasteries, though little remains of the church itself, built with the pinkish, warm-coloured local stone. In common with the other abbeys, Dryburgh was continually ravaged by the English until 1545 when Hertford, acting for Henry VIII, left it a smoking ruin. It was robbed of its usefulness, but not of its tranquil beauty and atmosphere of sanctity. Look for Walter Scott's tomb, behind a railing: his great-grandfather owned the abbey lands at the beginning of the 18th century. Earl

Tourist Information

Melrose: Abbey House, **t** (01896) 822 555, *melrose@scot-borders.co.uk, www.melrose@bordernet.co.uk*; open April–Oct.
Galashiels: 3 St John's Street, **t** (01896) 755 551, *galashiels@scot-borders.co.uk, www.galashiels.bordernet.co.uk*; open April–Oct.

Festivals

June: Summer Festival, Earlston. **Summer Festival**, Melrose; some of the ceremonies, re-enacting history, take place among the ruins of the abbey. **Common Riding**, Galashiels; the Braw Lads Gathering.
August: Common Riding, Lauder.

Where to Stay and Eat

Abbotsford Arms Hotel, Stirling Street, Galashiels, **t** (01896) 752 517, *abb2517@aol.com* (*moderate*). Cosy family-run hotel.
Birkhill, Earlston, **t** (01896) 849 307, *birkhill@btinternet.com* (*moderate*). A delightful Georgian house overlooking Leadervale and rolling hills; a Wolsey Lodge with nice furniture, a daughter running a training and livery yard beside the house, and excellent food. A great place to stay.
The Buccleuch Arms, St Boswells, **t** (01835) 822 243, *www.buccleuch armshotel.co.uk* (*moderate*). A restored 16th-century coaching inn, very traditional and cosy, overlooking the village green. Excellent food – try the trout mousse with lemon and dill mayonnaise. They will arrange fishing, golfing, shooting and pony trekking.
Burts Hotel, Market Square, Melrose, **t** (01896) 822 285, *www.burtshotel.co.uk* (*moderate*). A more imposing, traditional hotel. Well run

and comfortable, with warm hospitality. Good bar food and an excellent restaurant.
Clint Lodge, St Boswells, **t** (01835) 822 027 (*moderate*). Small guesthouse with a cosy country-house atmosphere and good food. Very reasonable
Clovenfords Hotel, 1 Vine Street, Clovenfords, **t** (01896) 850 203 (*moderate*). An old coaching inn 3 miles from Galashiels.
Dryburgh Abbey Hotel, St Boswells, **t** (01835) 822 261, *www.dryburgh.co.uk* (*moderate*). An imposing pile in wooded grounds on the Tweed, next to the abbey.
The George and Abbotsford Hotel, High Street, Melrose, **t** (01896) 822 308, *www.georgeand-abbotsford.co.uk* (*moderate*). A former coaching inn in the town centre.
Hoebridge Inn, Gattonside, Melrose, **t** (01896) 823 082 (*moderate*). Modern Scottish–Mediterranean cuisine. *Open Tues–Sun eves.*
Kingsknowes Hotel, Selkirk Road, Galashiels, **t** (01896) 758 375, *www.kingsknowes.co.uk* (*moderate*). A 19th-century mansion house full of Victorian character, overlooking the Tweed and Abbotsford.
Millars, Market Square, Melrose, **t** (01896) 822 645 (*moderate*). Melrose's best value hotel.
Waverley Castle Hotel, Skirmish Hill, Waverley Road, Melrose, **t** (01896) 822 244 (*moderate*). Reasonable hotel with entertainment.
Woodlands House Hotel and Restaurant, Windyknowe Road, Galashiels, **t** (01896) 754 722, *woodlands.uk@virgin.net* (*moderate*). A Victorian Gothic mansion on the outskirts of town. Comfortable, and reasonable food.
Overlangshaw Farm, Galashiels, **t** (01896) 860 244 (*cheap*). A working farm where children are encouraged to participate. Very comfortable and cosy. Family room and double room.
Marmions Brasserie, Buccleuch Street, Melrose, **t** (01896) 822 245. Excellent bistro-style restaurant with unusual oak-panelled walls and lively atmosphere. *Closed Sun.*

Haig, the First World War leader, is also buried here. The stately cedars of Lebanon that throw their shade across the grass were brought back from the Holy Land during one of the Crusades.

Scott's View

A detour from Dryburgh, 5 miles north up the B6356, to Earlston, takes in Scott's View from below the crest of Bemersyde Hill. This typical Borders' panorama, across a chequerboard of woods and fields to distant hills, with the Tweed sparkling below, was such a favourite of Sir Walter's that when his mile-long funeral cortège passed by on the way to Dryburgh Abbey, his horses paused here of their own accord. For the history of the Eildon Hills, the three nearest hills to the southwest, *see* pp.114–16. Legend has King Arthur and his knights sleeping below the Eildons, awaiting summons back to the world.

Earlston

Earlston was the home of Thomas the Rhymer, the 13th-century seer whose gift of prophecy, given by the Fairy Queen, was so effective that he was known as True Thomas. A stone, worn almost bare, in the east wall of the church is carved with his name, and the chunk of ruined wall behind the café to the south of the village is said to be all that remains of his tower. **Sorrowlessfield** in Earlston was so called because it was the only farm in the Borders to which all the men returned safely after the tragic battle of Flodden in 1513.

Lauder

Go on up the valley of Leader Water, 6 miles or so northwest to Lauder – a one-street town with a marketplace in the middle, once an important staging post. The pink stuccoed church, built in 1673, is in the form of a Greek cross with each arm equal and the pulpit in the middle under the tower.

Thirlestane Castle

Open April–Oct daily exc Sat 10.30–4.15 (last adm); adm; www.thirlestanecastle.co.uk.

Thirlestane Castle, home of the Maitland family for 400 years, is on the outskirts of Lauder. This huge pile, built on to in many different styles over the centuries, was originally a 13th-century fortress, Lauder Fort, though most of what you see today is late Tudor and early Victorian. William Maitland, Secretary of State to Mary, Queen of Scots, converted the original fortress into a home; John Maitland was Secretary and Chancellor to her son, James VI. A lot of the rich decoration inside was the work of the architect Sir William Bruce in the 17th century, commissioned by John Maitland's grandson, the Duke of Lauderdale, who was Secretary of State for Scotland to King Charles II. Among the treasures in the magnificent staterooms are paintings by Gainsborough, Lawrence, Hoppner and Romney. The nurseries are a delight, with old toys on display. There is a Border Country Life Museum in the grounds, a tearoom and gift shop. They say that a Duke of Lauderdale haunts the castle.

Melrose

Melrose is an unpretentious town best known for its ruined abbey, fragments of which are incorporated into a few of the older houses. The Southern Upland Way passes close to the north of the town – a delightful walk along the Tweed.

> ## Heart of the Bruce
> Robert the Bruce's heart is believed to be buried in Melrose Abbey in a casket. In fulfilment of a vow, Sir James Douglas cut out the king's heart and set off to the Holy Land, where it was to be buried. But Douglas was killed on the way, fighting the Moors in Spain, and the heart was returned to Scotland and buried in the abbey. An embalmed heart, excavated in the 20th century and hastily reburied, is claimed to be the royal organ.

Melrose Abbey (*open April–Sept daily 9.30–6.30; Oct–Mar Mon–Sat 9.30–4.30, Sun 2–4.30; adm*) was the most beautiful and richest of the four abbeys founded by David I in the 12th century. Established in 1136 to replace a Celtic monastery at Old Melrose nearby, it was, like its sisters, sacked frequently by the English and as frequently rebuilt by its monks. Much of its mellow stone remains, soaring upwards, a harmony of arches, towers and windows, splendidly decorated. Don't miss the carving of a pig playing the bagpipes. The abbey has a **museum**, in the Commendator's House, with local history and a room devoted to excavations from the Roman fort at Trimontium.

The **Trimontium Exhibition**, in the Market Square (*open April–Oct daily 10.30–4.30, Sat and Sun closed for lunch 1–2; adm; t (01896) 822 651; www.trimontium. freeserve.co.uk*), is 'a celebration of Romans and Celts at Newstead'. Here are Roman artefacts from Trimontium, which was the headquarters of the Roman army in Scotland. There are models of forts, an audiovisual room, photographs and other displays including a children's corner.

Horticulturalists should slip across to **Priorwood Gardens**, also by the abbey (*open April–Sept Mon–Sat 10–5.30, Sun 1.30–5.30; Oct–Dec Mon–Sat 10–4, Sun 1.30–4; adm*), owned by the NTS. The flowers are all suitable for drying. For anyone who has tried to grow everlasting flowers and then tried to tease them into chic, fashionable arrangements, there is inspiration in these gardens. If you feel daunted, there is a shop where you can buy them. There is also a NTS Visitor Centre, an orchard walk and picnic area.

Abbotsford House

Open mid-Mar–Oct Mon–Sat 10–5; June–Aug also Sun 10–5; Mar–May and Sept also Sun 2–5; adm; t (01896) 752 043.

Abbotsford House, less than 2 miles west of Melrose, was Sir Walter Scott's home for the last 20 years of his life. He bought a farm here in 1811 but wasn't happy with its name, Cartley Hall ('clarty' being a Scots word meaning dirty), and decided on Abbotsford in memory of the monks from Melrose who used to cross the river nearby. He demolished the farmhouse and, bit by bit, as the money came in from his books, built the house. When financial disaster struck, his creditors made him a present of the house. Scots Baronial, it is Sir Walter's monument to himself, with ideas borrowed from many sources: a cloister from Melrose; a porch from Linlithgow; a ceiling from Roslin. Now a museum, it is a must for Scott enthusiasts. Visitors can see his personal possessions, the rooms just as they were, and the extraordinary range of things he collected: a lock of Bonnie Prince Charlie's hair, for instance, and one of Robert Burns' drinking tumblers. The most romantic names in history seem to be represented. When you've had enough nostalgia, inspect the 9,000-volume library. There is also a tearoom and gift shop.

Galashiels

On another tributary of the Tweed, the Gala, 6 miles or so north of Selkirk, Galashiels (**Shieling-on-the-Gala**) is a busy town concentrating on the manufacture of textiles. Plain and unpretentious, it lies among hills and fast rivers. Flemish weavers came here in 1570 and what had previously been cottage weaving then flourished until the first Weavers' Guild was founded in 1660. Galashiels built the first Scottish carding machine in 1790 and is famous for its tweed and woollen hosiery.

The Galashiels **War Memorial** is a reconstruction of a peel tower with a death-roll engraved on a bronze tablet in the wall, serving as a backdrop to a statue of one of the Border Reivers sitting on his horse, proud and vigilant. The town crest, on a wall of the municipal buildings, consists of a fox reaching up for some plums, with the motto 'Soor Plooms'. It commemorates an incident in 1337 when men of Galashiels disposed of a band of English soldiers who were looking for wild plums in the woods.

Old Gala House and Scott Gallery (*open April–Sept Tues–Sat 10–4; July and Aug also Mon 10–4 and Sun 2–4; Oct Tues–Sat 1–4*) dates from 1583 and was the home of the lairds of Gala. It contains an interpretation centre showing the history of the burgh and three art galleries – the Christopher Boyd, the Pringle and the Scott – with changing exhibitions and programmes. There is a fine painted ceiling.

Lochcarron Cashmere and Wool Centre is at Waverley Mill, Huddersfield Street (*open Mon–Sat 9–5; June–Sept also Sun 12–5; mill tours all year Mon–Thurs 10.30, 11.30, 1.30 and 2.30, Fri 10.30 and 11.30; adm; t (01896) 752 091, www.lochcarron.com*). As well as guided tours of the mill, there are displays tracing the history of Galashiels' textile industry and a very tempting shop. It takes three goats a year to produce enough cashmere for a smallish sweater, and 24 for an overcoat!

Selkirk and the Yarrow and Ettrick Valleys

Selkirk

Selkirk means 'kirk-of-the-shieling', a peaceful, rural connotation that no longer applies to this town on the hillside above the valleys of the Ettrick and Yarrow, its spires and gables visible for miles, its textile mills tucked away along the river banks. These valleys were once extensive forests, hunting ground for kings and refuge for fugitives. Selkirk men are still called 'Souters' (shoemakers) from the days when cobbling was the main occupation: Prince Charles ordered 4,000 shoes from Selkirk for his barefooted army in 1745.

Of the 80 Selkirk men who rode out to fight at Flodden in 1513, only one returned, throwing down a captured English standard at the feet of the waiting families in

Tourist Information

Selkirk: Halliwell's House, **t** (01750) 20054, www.selkirk.bordernet.co.uk; open April–Oct.

Festivals

June: Common Riding, Selkirk; culminates in a re-enacting of the 'casting of the colours'.

Where to Stay and Eat

Selkirk t (01750–)

Ettrickshaws Hotel, Ettrickbridge, **t** 52229, www.ettrickshaws.co.uk (*moderate*). Family-run Victorian mansion 6 miles southwest of Selkirk in 10 acres of the Ettrick Valley beside the river. Fishing and riding available.

Philipburn House Hotel, a mile out of Selkirk on the A708 to Peebles, **t** 720 747, www.philipburnhousehotel.co.uk (*moderate*).

Built in 1751 as a dower house, it overlooks the site of the battle of Philiphaugh in 1645. Attractive, homely country house in 5 acres of grounds with some of its rooms around the outdoor swimming pool. Splendidly family-orientated, with award-winning cooking: saddle of roe deer in port and bilberry sauce. Packages include riding, mountain biking, walking, fishing and excursions.

Cross Keys Inn, Ettrickbridge, **t** 52224 (*cheap*). Very cosy 17th-century inn in a peaceful village, with B&B and self-catering cottages.

Tibbie Shiels Inn, St Mary's Loch, **t** 42231 (*cheap*). Historic inn on St Mary's Loch, *see* p.107, with B&B, camping, bar and food.

Tushielaw Inn, Tushielaw, **t** 62205, www.tushie.co.uk (*cheap*). An 18th-century coaching inn on the banks of Ettrick Water. Very good value and excellent food if you don't mind 'inventions' like smoked haddock crumble. Very friendly staff.

silent tribute to his fallen friends. The Standard is preserved in the library, ceremoniously folded up by the Burgh committee. Most of the mills around Selkirk have mill shops, selling tweed and woollen goods.

The triangular **Market Place** has a statue of Sir Walter Scott on a 20ft pedestal in front of the town hall. Scott was county sheriff here for 33 years. In **Sir Walter Scott's Courtroom** (*open April–Sept Mon–Sat 10–4; June–Aug also Sun 2–4; Oct Mon–Sat 1–4; t (01750) 20096*), where court sessions were heard in the days of Sir Walter's jurisdiction, there are mementos of him and of other famous 'Souters'.

Halliwell's House Museum and Robson Gallery (*open Easter–Oct Mon–Sat 10–5, Sun 2–4; June–Aug daily 10–6*) is off the main square. This row of 18th-century houses has been renovated to re-create Selkirk's history, the history of the buildings and an ironmonger's shop. The Robson Gallery holds art exhibitions. The statue at the east end of the High Street is of **Mungo Park**, the 18th-century explorer. He was born 4 miles away at Foulshiels and gave up medical practice to devote himself to exploring the River Niger in Africa, in which he was drowned while escaping in a canoe from hostile natives. **The Flodden Monument**, just beyond Mungo Park's statue, depicts a standard bearer, with the inscription 'O Flodden Field'.

A plaque over a shop doorway in West Port marks where Montrose lodged in 1645 before his defeat at the battle of Philiphaugh, a couple of miles to the west. After the battle, General Leslie and his Covenanters butchered the remains of Montrose's army, including hundreds of women and children, in the name of their God.

Selkirk Glass (*open Mon–Sat 9–5, Sun 11–5*), on the A7 just north of Selkirk, has a visitors' centre and gives demonstrations of making glass paperweights.

Bowhill

Grounds open April–Aug Mon–Thurs and Sat 12–5;
July daily 12–5; house open April–Aug daily exc Fri 12–5;
adm; t (01750) 22204.

Three miles west of Selkirk, this Georgian mansion, built in 1812, is the home of the Scotts of Buccleuch, surrounded by wooded hills that dazzle the eye in autumn. The renowned art collection includes paintings by Leonardo da Vinci, Gainsborough, Reynolds, Claude, Canaletto, Guardi and Raeburn. There are also proof copies of books by Walter Scott, relics of the Duke of Monmouth, and a good deal more. Look out for the clock that plays tunes except on the Sabbath. More philistine delights include an adventure playground, nature trails, a riding centre, an audiovisual show, mountain-bike hire, a gift shop and a licensed tearoom. Just off the courtyard below the house, **Bowhill Little Theatre** has intermittent programmes, varied and always good (*ring first, and if possible book supper afterwards, t (01750) 20732*).

Find time to walk in the grounds and visit the ruins of **Newark Castle**, where one hundred of General Leslie's luckless victims were shot after the battle of Philiphaugh. Even without its grim history – you may find yourself looking for bloodstains on the walls, and listening out for screams – it is an impressive ruin. It stands five storeys tall, a tower house within a curtain wall on a green mound above the river, once a royal hunting seat for the Forest of Ettrick, with the 15th-century arms of James I on the west gable. This was the setting for Walter Scott's *Lay of the Last Minstrel*.

St Mary's Loch

Follow the Yarrow Valley to St Mary's Loch, 14 miles southwest of Selkirk. This 3-mile stretch of reed-fringed water set among hills is a popular spot for sailors and fish-ermen. Stop for refreshment at **Tibbie Shiel's Inn**, on the southeast shore of the loch, called after the innkeeper who served Walter Scott, Thomas Carlyle, Robert Louis Stevenson and James Hogg. These literary giants came here for convivial gatherings. Hogg lived nearby, and his statue overlooks the inn from the other side of the loch. An annual service is held in the churchyard of **St Mary's of the Lowes**, overlooking the loch on the northwest, celebrating the Blanket Preaching, when the preacher deliv-ered his message from a tent made from a blanket. The church has now gone .

One of the most beautiful stretches of the Southern Upland Way skirts the eastern shore of the loch, and the walk north from here, about 8 miles, to Traquair House (*see below*) is not stiff and worth the effort. There is also a route from Cappercleuch, on the west side of the loch, about 9 miles to Tweedsmuir, steep, twisting and remote, with panoramic views. This goes past **Megget Reservoir**, long and wide, cradled below hills, and winner of a major design award. This valley was once part of the Forest of Ettrick, a favourite hunting ground in the days of David I.

In the Ettrick Valley, to the southwest of Selkirk, **Alkwood Tower** (*open May–Sept Tues, Thurs and Sun 2–5; adm*) is a restored 16th-century Border tower with a James Hogg exhibition. This former home of fierce Border Reivers was also said to be the home of the wizard Michael Scott.

Peebles and Around

Flanked by wide greens, the River Tweed hurries through Peebles, a peaceful old town with narrow streets leading to quaint yards and buildings with carved lintels. The name is derived from *pebylls*, meaning tents, which refers to the tents of the nomadic Gadeni, the first inhabitants of the town. St Mungo came in the 6th century, baptizing converts in the well that bears his name. Traces remain of the wall built to protect the town from the destructive English. Cromwell garrisoned troops here.

Peebles

The **Tweed Bridge**, with five elegant stone arches decorated with ornate lamp standards, dates from the 15th century. **The Chambers Institute** (*open Mon–Fri 10–12 and 2–5; Easter–Oct also Sat 10–1 and 2–4*), once the town house of the Queensberrys, was given to the town by William Chambers, the publisher, in 1859. With the help of a grant from Andrew Carnegie, it was enlarged to house reading rooms, libraries, two museums and an art gallery. **The Cornice**, Innerleithen Road, is a museum of ornamental plasterwork, with a re-creation of a plasterer's casting shop, cornices, corbels, mouldings, gargoyles, statues, and all the tools of the craft.

Cross Kirk (*open daily; key from the custodian next door*) is the 13th-century ruined nave and west tower of a Trinitarian friary, with the foundations of the cloister buildings. When the English burnt down the collegiate church of St Andrew, Cross Kirk was used as the parish church.

Innerleithen

When Walter Scott's *St Ronan's Well* was published in 1824, his readers identified the spa in the novel as the mineral spring above Innerleithen and flocked there to take the waters. The contemporary Earl of Traquair who owned the land, a canny Scot, built a pump room to exploit his natural resources and you can buy a gulp of the water, and see the well. One of the earls, perhaps an urbanite at heart, named the streets: Bond Street, The Strand, Princes Street, etc.

Robert Smaïl's Printing Works (*open May–Sept Mon–Sat 10–1 and 2–5, Sun 2–5; Oct Sat 10–1 and 2–5, Sun 2–5; adm*) in Innerleithen, restored by the NTS, is a working printing museum with vintage machinery including a 100-year-old press once driven by water, and an NTS Visitor Centre. It has been imaginatively restored and is well worth a visit.

Traquair House

Open Easter–Oct daily 12.30–5.30; June–Aug from 10.30; adm;
t (01896) 830 323, www.traquair.co.uk.

Traquair House is 3 miles southwest of Walkerburn. The name comes from *Tra* – a dwelling or hamlet – and *quair* – a winding stream. Originally a royal hunting lodge built on to 10th-century remains, Traquair is said to be the oldest mansion in Scotland

The Bear Gates

Prince Charles Edward Stuart was the last person to leave through the 'Bear Gates', which bar the entrance to the avenue, on his march to Derby in 1745. They were then clanged shut by the Jacobite Fifth Earl of Traquair, who vowed they would never be reopened until a Stuart ruled Scotland again. Another version of this story is that in the days when Catholics were not allowed to own carriages, but continued to do so clandestinely, an unfriendly neighbour of the Catholic Earl told the authorities. His carriage and horses were confiscated and he slammed his gates in protest. Whichever story is true, the gates remain closed.

continuously inhabited by the same family: Alexander I signed a charter here in the 12th century, William the Lion held court here in 1175, and the 'modern' wings were added in 1680. The house hums with domesticity, unlike most stately homes. The grey harled walls rise to four storeys, with corbelled turrets and a steeply pitched roof like a French château. Twenty-seven monarchs visited Traquair, notably Mary, Queen of Scots, with Darnley and their infant son, whose cradle you can see. Mary's rosary, crucifix and purse are also displayed. The staunchly Catholic Stuarts of Traquair gave shelter to persecuted priests and were imprisoned, fined and ostracized for their faith. One of them fell at Flodden in 1513, fighting for James IV.

At one time the Tweed ran so close to the house that its owner could fish from his windows. Finding that unfortunately he could also swim in his cellars, James Stuart, the 17th-century laird, diverted the river's course so it now flows a quarter of a mile away. His descendants, the Maxwell Stuarts, have turned Traquair into a splendid tourist attraction. The grounds offer woodland walks, a maze, craft workshops and exhibitions. Ale is produced in the 18th-century brewhouse and the Traquair Fair is in August. The Southern Upland Way passes close to Traquair. You can have lunches and teas in a 1745 cottage.

Glentress Forest

Glentress Forest is about 3 miles northwest of Traquair on the way to Peebles, with signposted walks, one of which leads to **Cardie Hill Fort**, with grass-covered ramparts, and another to **Shielgreen Tower**, of which little now remains. At the entrance to the park a trio of tall wooden figures stand, unornamented and graceful in their simplicity, carved from local wood.

Neidpath Castle

Open July–Sept daily 11–6, Sun 1–5; adm;
group bookings, t (01721) 702 333.

L-shaped, 13th-century Neidpath Castle, west of the town, stands on a green mound overlooking the Tweed. Continuously inhabited for almost 700 years, its ochre walls, nearly 12 foot thick in places, withstood the bombardment of Cromwell's troops in the mid-17th century for longer than any other castle south of the Forth. You can see the pit prison hewn out of the rock and some of the original vaults, and climb on to

Tourist Information

Peebles: Scottish Borders Tourist Board Office, High Street, **t** (01721) 720 138, *peebles@scotborders.co.uk*; *open all year.*

Festivals

June: **Beltane Festival**, Peebles; with pagan roots and incorporates Peebles' celebration of the Common Riding of the Marches. **Sheepdog Trials**, Peebles.
August: **Agricultural Show**, Peebles.
September: **Highland Games**, Peebles. **Arts Festival**, Peebles.

Shopping

The Olive Tree, 7 High Street, Peebles. An outstanding deli, with excellent cheeses and other local goodies.

Where to Stay and Eat

Peebles t (01721–)
Cringletie House Hotel, at Eddleston, **t** 730 233, *www.cringletie.com* (*expensive*). Privately owned, baronial mansion, 2 miles outside Peebles. In 28 acres with wonderful views, imaginative food and an open-air theatre.
Stobo Castle, Stobo, nr Peebles, **t** 760 249, *www.stobocastle.co.uk* (*expensive*). Early 19th-century castle with luxurious health spa, gourmet food and enough activities for anyone wanting to combine a self-indulgent holiday with a fitness regime.
Traquair House, Innerleithen, *see* p.108, **t** (01896) 830 323, *www.traquair.co.uk* (*expensive*). Two double rooms, use of the lower drawing room and gardens, and a free tour of the house, with meals in the 1745 cottage and dinner by arrangement.
Peebles Hotel Hydro, Innerleithen Road, **t** 720 602, *www.peebleshotelhydro.co.uk* (*expensive–moderate*). Huge and château-like, in 30

the roof and look out over wooded hills and valleys. Along the grassy path to the castle are a few yew trees. These are all that remain of a once famous avenue (the Neidpath Yews) from which bows were made for the crusaders. The majority of the yews were cut down to pay the gambling debts of that debauched reprobate 'Old Q', William Douglas, Duke of Queensberry, in 1795. Wordsworth was so shocked by this vandalism that, during his tour of Scotland in 1803, he wrote the sonnet 'Composed at Neidpath Castle', starting:

> Degenerate Douglas! oh, the unworthy Lord!
> Whom mere despite of heart could so far please,
> And love of havoc (for with such disease
> Fame taxes him) that he could send forth word
> To level with the dust a noble horde
> A brotherhood of venerable Trees.

Neidpath stages one of the ceremonies of the annual Beltane Festival, when the Warden of Neidpath – someone in high office – is proclaimed from the castle steps. There are nice walks along the river here, and an excellent spot below the castle for experienced swimmers.

Kailzie Gardens (*open April–Oct daily 11–5.30; Nov–Mar daily 11–5; adm; restaurant open daily 11–5.30 and 7–9*), 2 miles east of Peebles, include a rose garden with lovely old-fashioned roses, herbaceous border, shrubs, a 19th-century walled garden with greenhouses, a 'laburnum alley', an art gallery, gift shop and an excellent licensed tea room in the courtyard – try the apple cake. Woods surround the gardens, along a acres with a backdrop of rolling hills. It has a swimming pool, jacuzzi, saunas, solaria, gym, games room for badminton, tennis and squash, golf, riding and pitch-and-putt. Also theme holidays, such as golfing and walking.

Castle Venlaw Hotel, t 720 384, *www.venlaw.co.uk (moderate)*. Castle built in 1782 in the Venlaw Hills, with magnificent views. A completely refurbished and upgraded family-run baronial pile. Very comfortable, with good food.

The Crook Inn, Tweedsmuir, **t** (01899) 880 272, *thecrookinn@btinternet.com (moderate)*. Dates from 1604 and claims (with several others) to be the oldest coaching inn in Scotland. Robert Burns wrote *Willie Wastle* in the bar. The food is 'imaginative', and fine if you like slightly unusual sauces.

Green Tree Hotel, 41 Eastgate, **t** 720 582, *green-tree-hotel@compuserve.com (moderate)*. A comfortable hotel with ground-floor rooms.

Lyne Farmhouse, Lyne Farm, **t** 740 255, *awad-dell@farming.co.uk (cheap)*. A splendid family holiday base with lots for children to do, on the farm and beyond.

The Park Hotel, Innerleithen Road, **t** 720 451, *reserve@parkpeebles.co.uk (moderate)*. Views of peaceful gardens and the Cademuir Hills.

Traquair Arms Hotel, Innerleithen, **t** (01896) 830 229, *www.trad-inns.co.uk/traquair (moderate)*. A comfortable, 19th-century family-run hotel, very traditional and cosy with excellent food and friendly people.

Tweed Valley Hotel, Walkerburn, **t** (01896) 870 636, *www.tweed-valley.com (moderate)*. Edwardian country house overlooking the Tweed, with sauna and gym, and offering fishing, walking, cycling, golf, bird-watching and wildlife, as well as courses in fly fishing.

Horse Shoe Inn, Eddleston, **t** 730 225 *(cheap)*. A village pub in the old blacksmith's forge. Very good food, cosy and friendly.

Sunflower Restaurant, Bridgegate, **t** 722 420. A deli in the front and cosy bistro-type rooms beyond.

sparkling burn, where the ground is golden with daffodils in spring, and waterfowl are abundant.

Dawyck Botanic Gardens *(open Mar–mid-Nov 9.30–6; adm; www.rbge.org.uk)*, 8 miles southwest of Peebles, were created by Sir James Nasmyth in 1720, under the influence of his mentor Linnaeus, the great Swedish botanist. The woods are particularly magnificent: the first larches introduced into Scotland were planted here in 1725. Carpets of scented narcissi lie among rare trees and shrubs from all over the world, twisting and climbing to a Dutch bridge over a waterfall. The chapel in the woods was designed by William Burn.

Broughton

Broughton, 10 miles southwest of Peebles, is a village in the valley of Biggar Water, below layers of rounded hills. **Broughton Gallery** *(open April–Dec daily exc Wed 10.30–6; ring* **t** *(01899) 830 234, for details of special exhibitions)* is a treasure which could be missed – look out for the signs, up a steep drive. It is a 20th-century castle, designed by Sir Basil Spence in the 1930s, in the style of the Border fortresses. It looks startlingly authentic against its background of blue-grey hills. Inside is a first-class art gallery, opened in the '70s. Many contemporary artists and craftsmen show their work here, including the proprietor Graham Buchanan-Dunlop.

The **John Buchan Centre** *(open Easter and May–mid-Oct daily 2–5; adm)* is also in Broughton, in a converted chapel, with biographical information for devotees of the remarkable 1st Baron Tweedsmuir, writer and creator of Richard Hannay. He not only wrote more than 50 books but was also a barrister, statesman and Governor General of Canada. Buchan grew up here and, looking around at the wild hills, it becomes

> ## Merlin's Grave
>
> Merlindale, in Drumelzier, 9 miles southwest of Peebles, is one of the legendary sites of the grave of Merlin, Britain's elusive magician. Thomas the Rhymer, 13th-century seer, said: 'When Tweed and Powsayl meet at Merlin's grave, England and Scotland shall one monarch have.' The day Elizabeth I died, when James VI of Scotland inherited the English throne, the River Tweed burst its banks and flooded across Drumelzier into the neighbouring Powsayl.

clear where he got many of the settings for his Scottish novels. You will leave determined to reread his books. Six miles to the south, to the west of the A702, **The Crook Inn** is one of the oldest pubs in the Borders. John Buchan was a frequent customer, as were Walter Scott and his circle. In the bar, cast your mind back to the 18th century when this was the kitchen: Robert Burns sat here, drawn in no doubt by the charms of one of the kitchen staff, and dashed off one of his poems at the table! Another mile south is the village of **Tweedsmuir**, from which John Buchan took his title.

Further south, to the east of the A702, is **Tweed's Well**, the source of the Tweed. It is hard to believe this small beginning will so quickly develop into that torrent that swirls through the Borders to the sea.

The Teviot Valley

The River Teviot rises in the hills south of Teviothead, on the border of Dumfries and Galloway, descending rapidly to cut a beautiful valley northeastwards to Kelso, where it joins the Tweed.

Jedburgh

Jedburgh lies in the valley of Jed Water, a tributary of the Teviot, surrounded by fields and woods whose vivid autumn colours are a delight. Its proximity to the border made it the target of many raids, and its position on one of the main routes north brought a succession of armies through its streets. Built round its abbey, Jedburgh is packed with history. The men of Jedburgh were renowned for their resistance to invasion, defending their town with gruesome tenacity. 'Jethart Handba', a local game played with a hay-stuffed leather ball, is said to originate from when Jedburgh (or Jethart) men returned from routing the English and played ball with the heads of their victims.

Jedburgh Abbey

*Open April–Sept daily 9.30–6.30; Oct–Mar Mon–Sat 9.30–4.30,
Sun 2–4.30; last adm half an hour before closing; adm.*

Jedburgh Abbey has a history spanning several centuries. Fragments of carved Celtic stonework, found during the restoration of the abbey, suggest that it was built on the site of a 9th-century church that appears in the records of Lindisfarne. Founded as a priory in 1138 by David I, and raised to abbey status in 1147, it was frequently sacked by the English, the most devasting attack being by Hertford in 1544 during his ruthless execution of the orders of Henry VIII. It stands on a green sward, its mellow stone supporting graceful arches and windows, including a rose window, called St Catherine's Wheel. The **visitors centre** gives an interpretation of the abbey's history, with displays of how the monks lived and recordings of their music and chanting.

Jedburgh Castle Jail Museum (*open Easter–Oct Mon–Sat 10–4.30, Sun 1–4; adm; t (01835) 863 254*) was built at the top of Castlegate in 1820 as the county prison, on the site of Jedburgh Castle, built around the same time as the abbey. The castle was a popular royal residence; Alexander III chose it for his wedding feast when, desperate for an heir, he married his second wife, Jolande, in the abbey in 1285. The spectre of Death is said to have appeared at this feast, prophesying the death of the king – which happened six months later when he fell from his horse. Frequently occupied by the English, and in fact ceded to them under the Treaty of Falaise in 1174, it was destroyed by order of the Scottish Parliament to keep it from the enemy. The museum contains reconstructed rooms showing the 'reformed' system of imprisonment in the early 19th century – a gruelling insight into the penal and social history of those days.

Mary, Queen of Scots' House

Open Mar–Nov Mon–Sat 10–4.30, Sun 12–4.30;
April–Oct Sun 12–4; June–Aug Sun 10–4.30; adm; t (01835) 863 331.

Queen Mary's House in Queen Street is haunted with memories of Scotland's tragic queen. Mary came here in 1566, still married to Darnley, to preside over the Court of Justice at the Assizes. She stayed in this house, reputedly because it was the only one with indoor sanitation. During her stay she heard that James Bothwell had been wounded and was ill at Hermitage Castle, 20 miles away. Perhaps already in love, she rode over to Hermitage and back again, in the same day, to visit him. As a result she became critically ill of a fever from which she nearly died. Her attendants opened the window at the crisis of her illness, to let her soul fly free. Years later she was to say: 'Would that I had died, that time in Jedburgh.' Darnley came to visit her while she was ill and when she was better she rode back to Edinburgh with Bothwell, now also recovered, in her entourage. The ochre-coloured house has high crow-stepped gables and a turret stair; the steep roof was once thatched. It has been restored and is much as it was when Mary was there: you can see the great hall, withdrawing room and fireplace and the stuffy little room where she lay so ill for a month, near the chamber occupied by her four Marys: Mary Beaton, Mary Seton, Mary Livingston and Mary Fleming. The **visitor centre** was upgraded to mark the 400th anniversary of her death in 1987, and presents an interpretation of her life and times. Among the exhibits are one of the rare portraits of Bothwell, done in 1565; a facsimile of Mary's death-warrant, signed by her cousin Elizabeth, and her watch, apparently found in the marshy land near Hermitage Castle 200 years after she lost it on her impulsive visit to Bothwell. There is also a gift shop.

Harestanes Countryside Visitor Centre (*open April–Oct daily 10–5*) is 3 miles north of Jedburgh off the A68. A discovery room in converted farm buildings describes the flora and fauna on the signed walks on the estate. There is also a play area, tearoom, shop, exhibitions, audiovisual display and games room. **Jedforest Deer and Farm Park** (*open May–Aug daily 10–5.30; Sept–Oct daily 11–4.30; adm*), 4 miles south of Jedburgh, is a working upland farm with deer, many breeds of animals, an adventure playground, walks, information centre, café and shop.

Hermitage Castle

Open April–Sept Mon–Sat 9.30–6.30, Sun 2–6.30; adm.

Although closer to Hawick than Jedburgh, it is really from Jedburgh you should visit Hermitage Castle, so you can appreciate Mary's frantic ride (*see* Mary, Queen of Scots' House above). Twenty miles southwest, it stands stark and indestructible, on a grassy platform surrounded by earthworks; an angular fortress with frowning arches. On all sides, moorland rises in peaks whence watch could be kept in every direction, including across the border. Even in sunshine, with the sparkling Hermitage Water at its feet, it has a grim aura. The 14th-century tower, built round a small courtyard, has later additions of massive square towers and walls, set with holes and corbels that once supported a continuous walkway, high on the exterior walls, reached through rectangular doorways. Close by are the ruins of St Mary's Chapel and traces of the medieval village that grew up round the castle.

Legends of such horror and cruelty surround this melancholy lump of history that locals believed the weight of its iniquities would eventually cause it to sink into Hades, though it shows no sign of doing so yet. The first man to build on the site was Nicholas de Soulis, in the 13th century. He was so cruel and evil that his neighbours and servants carted him off to Ninestone Rig, a mile to the northeast, wrapped him in a sheet of lead, and boiled him to death. The 11-foot-long grave outside the walls of the kirkyard beyond the castle is believed to contain the remains of the Cout of Kielder, a giant baron who came over the hills from Kielder Castle across the border to Hermitage to slay de Soulis. He was drowned by his intended victim, in a deep pool in the river still known as Cout of Kielder Pool. A 'gallant Scottish patriot', Alexander Ramsay of Dalhousie, was lowered into the pit-prison still visible in the castle. He existed for many days on a trickle of grain that fell from the granary above, before he starved to death.

Denholm

Denholm, 5 miles southwest of Jedburgh, is a conservation village, its 18th-century houses built close together around a green in the style of earlier settlements when the beasts were herded on to the green against raiders, the narrow alleyways making defence easier. The elaborate monument on the green is to **Dr John Leyden**, who was born in the thatched cottage just off the north side of the square in 1775. This remarkable scholar, physician and poet, who died at the age of 36, was almost entirely self-taught, astounding his contemporaries, including Sir Walter Scott, with the range and scope of his knowledge.

Tourist Information

Jedburgh: Scottish Borders Tourist Board, Murray's Green, **t** (01835) 863 435/863 688, *www.injedburgh.freeserve.co.uk; open all year.*
Hawick: Drumlanrig's Tower, Tower Knowe, **t** (01450) 372 547, *hawick@scot-borders.co.uk, www.hawick.org.uk; open all year.*

Festivals

April: **Rugby Sevens**, Hawick.
June: **Common Ridings**, Hawick.
July: **Jedburgh Festival**; two weeks of pageantry dominated by the Jeddart Callants – the young men of Jedburgh – who re-enact the Common Ridings of the past. **Jedburgh Border Games. Traditional Music Festival**, Newcastleton.
August: **Summer Festival**, Hawick.

Where to Stay and Eat

Glenfriars, Jedburgh, **t** (01835) 862 000, *book-ings@edenroad.demon.co.uk* (*moderate*). An attractive Georgian house, with a few four-posters and exceptional service.
Hobsburn, Bonchester Bridge, Hawick, **t** (01450) 860 720, *www.mcleanmay.com* (*moderate*). Excellent B&B in an early 17th-century laird's house in 60 acres. Cosy and comfortable, with dinner by arrangement.
Jedforest Hotel, Camptown, Jedburgh, **t** (01835) 840 222, *www.jedforesthotel. freeserve.co.uk* (*moderate*). A country house hotel in a 35-acre private estate, with free fishing and excellent food.
Kirklands Hotel, West Stewart Place, Hawick, **t** (01450) 372 263 (*moderate*). Comfortable Victorian town house with croquet, snooker room, library, and a babysitting service.
Mansfield House Hotel, Hawick, **t** (01450) 373 988, *www.mansfield-house.com* (*moderate*).

Comfortable and relaxed Victorian house. Good home cooking.
Willow Court, the Friars, Jedburgh, **t** (01835) 863 702, *mike@willowct77.freeserve.co.uk* (*moderate*). Good views over the town from a large, quiet garden. Very reasonable, and mostly en suite, ground-floor rooms.
Ancrum Craig, Ancrum, by Jedburgh, **t** (01835) 830 280, *www.ancrumcraig.clara.net* (*cheap*). A special B&B in a part 18th-century part Victorian house. Excellent breakfast, and good walking country. Supper on request.
Bridgehouse, Jedburgh, **t** 01835 863405 (*cheap*). Very good B&B in a former toll house (1817). The owners are extremely accommodating. Supper on request.
Glenbank Country House Hotel, Castlegate, Jedburgh, **t** (01835) 862 258, *www. glenbankhotel.co.uk* (*cheap*). Georgian house set in attractive gardens, 5 minutes' walk from the town centre. Bar meals all day.
Newmill Country Inn, Newmill-on-Teviot, **t** (01450) 850 266 (*cheap*). On the River Teviot, with lots of character. Good value.
The Auld Bakery Bistro, Westside, Denholm, **t** (01450) 870 530. A licensed bistro, with antiques and an art gallery.
Auld Cross Keys Inn, Main Street, Denholm, **t** (01450) 870 305. The best eating place in the area, on the Green, with an excellent, varied choice. *No food on Mon.*
Castlegate Restaurant, 1 Abbey Close, Jedburgh, **t** (01835) 862 552. Specializes in Scottish meals with local produce.
Forresters Restaurant, 23 Castlegate, Jedburgh, **t** (01835) 862 380. Good value restaurant, with separate non-smoking area.
The Fox and Hounds, Main Street, Denholm, **t** (01450) 870 247. Pub with reasonable food, cask ales, log fires, a courtyard and beer garden with play area.
The Pheasant Lounge Bar, High Street, Jedburgh, **t** (01835) 862 708. For a good, very reasonably priced meal.

The village is dominated by **Rubers Law** to the southeast, accessible from all sides and easily scaled to see the remains of an Iron Age hill fort at the top. This was a Roman signal station, within sight of a similar one on nearby Bonchester Hill. There is a rock on the law, known as Peden's Pulpit, from which Alexander Peden preached to huge congregations of Covenanters during the Killing Times.

It is said that the Devil used to get so irritated at being woken every morning by the chanting of the monks in Melrose Abbey that he decided to move three of the Cheviot Hills and plant them between Melrose and the rising sun. Unfortunately, during the move, he dropped the top half of the last one. This was Rubers Law, and explains why it would fit exactly on to the flat top of one of the Eildon Hills.

Hawick

In a fold of the hills on the banks of the Teviot, Hawick (pronounced Hoyk) owes its prosperity to the textile mills along the river, many with their own shops, and to the well-stocked timberyards in the area. The hub of the town is a bronze statue in the High Street, an armoured youth on a charger, holding a standard above his head. In 1514 a band of English troops, looting their way through the Borders, were camped at nearby Hornshole, secure in the knowledge that the death-toll from the Battle of Flodden the previous year had reduced the fighting strength of the Border towns to old men and boys. The Callants – teenaged youths – of Hawick rode out in a brave, ragged band, routed the English and returned with the enemy standard.

Drumlanrig's Tower Visitor Centre (*1 Tower Knowe, High Street; open late Mar–Oct Mon–Sat 10–5, Sun 12–5; June and Sept daily 10–5.30; July and Aug daily 10–6; ring for winter hours; adm; t (01450) 377 615*) tells the history of Hawick's turbulent life since medieval times, displayed with modern technology.

Hawick Museum and Scott Art Gallery (*open April–Sept Mon–Fri 10–12 and 1–5, Sat and Sun 2–4.45; Oct–Mar Mon–Fri 1–4, Sun 2–4; adm*), in Wilton Lodge Park on the western outskirts of the town, covers the textile industry, Border history, archaeology and local natural history. The Scott Art Gallery has a 19th-and 20th-century Scottish art collection, and holds temporary exhibitions. William Wallace visited here in 1297 and you can see the tree where he is supposed to have tethered his horse. The park has walks, gardens and sports facilities.

The **Teviotdale Leisure Centre**, north of the town on the A7, has a swimming pool, restaurant and entertainments such as puppet shows.

Teviothead

In the village of Teviothead, southwest of Hawick, is a poignant memorial. A stone set into the wall of the graveyard opposite the kirk is dedicated to the 16th-century freebooter Johnnie Armstrong and his followers. Armstrong rode to this lonely place from Langholm, further south, hoping to win the favour of his teenaged sovereign, James V. He offered the service and allegiance of his men and himself, but the young king, intent on cleaning up the lawless Borders, was not won over. Armstrong and his band were hanged from a makeshift gallows at Carlenrig to the southwest.

Newcastleton

Newcastleton, by Liddel Water, about 5 miles south of Hermitage Castle, was founded in 1793 by the Duke of Buccleuch and has an unusual symmetrical layout.

Dumfries and Galloway

09

Dumfries and Galloway

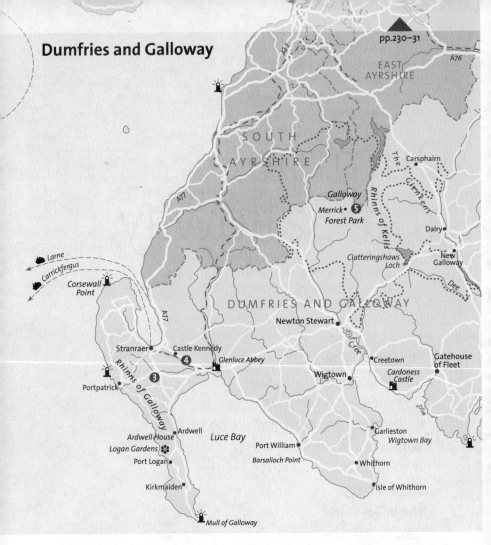

pp.230–31

EAST AYRSHIRE

SOUTH AYRSHIRE

A77

A76

A77

Carsphairn

The Glenkens

Galloway
Forest Park

Merrick • **5**

Rhinns of Kells

Dalry

New Galloway

Clatteringshaws Loch

Dee

Larne
Carrickfergus

Corsewall Point

DUMFRIES AND GALLOWAY

Newton Stewart

Cree

Creetown

Gatehouse of Fleet

Stranraer • Castle Kennedy
4   Glenluce Abbey

Rhinns of Galloway

3

Portpatrick

Wigtown

Cardoness Castle

Ardwell House
Logan Gardens
Port Logan •

Ardwell

Luce Bay

Port William

Barsalioch Point

Garlieston
Wigtown Bay

Whithorn

Kirkmaiden

Isle of Whithorn

Mull of Galloway

Dumfries and Galloway borders the northern shore of the Solway Firth, with the dramatic hammerhead of the Rhinns of Galloway at its western tip. Apart from the extreme east, this is an isolated corner, off the main route to anywhere except Ireland, to which it is closer than to much of the rest of Scotland.

The name Galloway derives from the Gaelic *gallgaidhel* – land of the stranger. It was here, early in the 6th century, that Celtic Christian Scots from Ireland landed, drove out the Picts and moved north to establish the Kingdom of Dalriada. Earlier still, St Ninian brought the first message of Christianity to Whithorn in AD 397. Many churches and abbeys were built in the area, becoming places of pilgrimage for Scottish monarchs and people from distant lands. Frequent wars, the Reformation and Henry VIII's 'Rough Wooing' in the 16th century reduced most of these to ruins, but the shells of their splendour remain. Towns near the border suffered their share of hammering from the English, and settlements on the coast were well fortified against invasion.

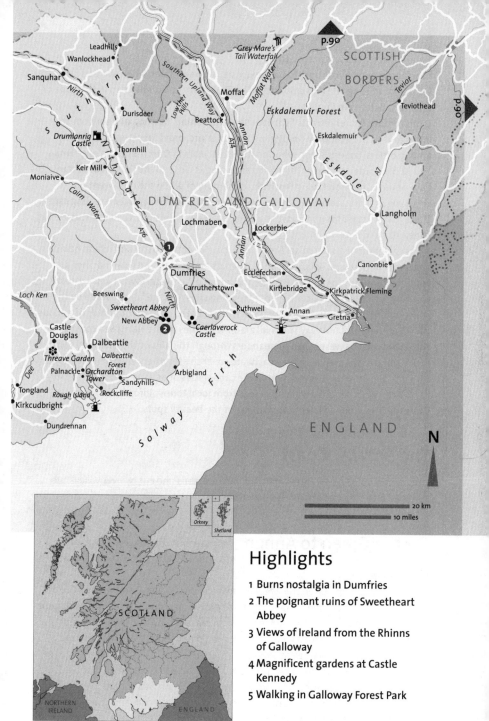

Highlights

1 Burns nostalgia in Dumfries

2 The poignant ruins of Sweetheart Abbey

3 Views of Ireland from the Rhinns of Galloway

4 Magnificent gardens at Castle Kennedy

5 Walking in Galloway Forest Park

Mary, Queen of Scots passed through in 1563, escorted by a train of nobles: a light-hearted progress in contrast to her next visit, five years later, when she fled here after her defeat at Langside and embarked from Port Mary at Dundrennan in the hope of finding sanctuary in England.

This remote corner attracts little industry, and fishing, farming and tourism are important to the economy. Smuggling was once rife, providing employment for, among others, Robert Burns, who spent his last years in Dumfries as an exciseman.

As in the Borders, some of the towns and villages close to the English boundary have annual **Common Riding Festivals**, in memory of when the men went out to check the marches, to make sure Border Reivers hadn't been at work, stealing cattle. These festivals last for up to a week and incorporate events in local history, as well as pageantry and entertainment.

This is a naturalist's paradise. The mild climate of both coastal and inland habitats attracts countless rare species of birds, animals and plants. The tidal marshes are wintering grounds for barnacle geese and lots of other waterfowl. If you are lucky you may see peregrine falcons, whose breeding sites are carefully guarded by the police against avaricious crooks who sell the incubated eggs for hundreds of pounds.

The **Southern Upland Way** starts its 212-mile journey to the North Sea coast at Portpatrick on the west coast. It meanders through the hills of the Galloway Forest Park – some of them quite high – eastwards over the Lowthers and then the Moffat Hills into the Borders. It is well within the capabilities of anyone who is reasonably fit. You can get a series of walking guides from local tourist information centres. There are also guided walks around many of the beauty spots.

The Solway Coast

Tidal mud flats and sandy beaches, fringed by woods and cut by river valleys, are bordered by a string of towns.

Gretna Green to Annan

Gretna Green

Coming from England, on the A74, you cross the border into Dumfries and Galloway at Gretna Green. From the romance that has grown up around this famous village, it is difficult to untangle the squalid reality of an era when a great many innocent females were duped by men whose motives could not stand the test of a formal betrothal with parental consent. Runaway lovers, cheated of 'irregular marriages' in England by the 1754 Hardwicke Marriage Act, were able to cross the border until 1856 and be married by declaration before a witness. The union was 'forged' over an anvil by the blacksmith. Even in the 20th century couples came north because, until the age of consent in England was altered in 1969, Scotland was the only place where parental consent was not required after the age of 16. The Border villages of Gretna and Springfield vied with each other for the considerable profit that could be made from these often disastrous unions. One blacksmith, Rennison, is said to have performed 5,147 ceremonies. Springfield lost its trade to Gretna in 1830, when the building of the Sark Bridge caused it to be bypassed by the main north–south route. At the height of the marriage industry, rivalry between the 'priests' in the area was ferocious and each had his agent, promoting his superiority in hotels in Carlisle. Because of the modern trend towards unusual marriage locations, several thousand couples apply to tie the matrimonial knot in Gretna Green even today. There are two 'Blacksmith shops'. The first one you come to from the M74 is the **Original Old Blacksmith Shop Centre** (*open Jan–Mar and Nov–Dec daily 9–5; April, May and Oct daily 9–6; June and Sept daily 9–7; July and Aug daily 9–8; adm; www.gretnagreen. com*). Within this complex is 'the original marriage room' with displays of suitable artefacts and memorabilia. There is also a shop, restaurant, wine bar and open-air sculpture park.

Gretna Hall Blacksmith Shop (*open April–Oct daily 9–8; Nov–Mar daily 9–5; adm*), about half a mile further on, is a smithy behind Gretna Hall Hotel, set back off a cobbled yard through a 'kissing gate'. Dating from 1710, it contains a 'marriage room', anvil, and many photographs and documents. A kilted piper may welcome you, and the nearby shop has predictable souvenirs.

The **Lochmaben Stone**, on the shore of the Solway Firth not far south of Gretna, weighs at least 10 tonnes and is thought to be the remains of a stone circle, possibly connected with a shrine to Maponos, god of youth and music: an appropriate trysting place for runaway lovers. Fairs were held here in the Middle Ages and it was the site where Border disputes were discussed and settled, under daylight truce.

King Robert the Bruce's Cave (*open summer daily 9–9; winter daily 9–5; adm*), signposted off the A74 northwest of Gretna, is a local beauty spot beside the River Kirtle at Kirkpatrick Fleming.

At Eastriggs, 4 miles west of Gretna, look into the **Devil's Porridge** in St John's Church (*open mid-May–Oct Wed–Sun 10–4; adm*) and see the poignant tribute to the 30,000 people who worked in the explosives factory at Gretna during the Second World War. There is also a Children at War exhibition, with the story of evacuations and Barnard Boys in local stately homes.

Annan

Annan is on the northern shore of the Solway Firth. Once a busy main-road town, it is now bypassed by the A75. Although its history goes back a long way, the town was too frequently torn apart in Border disputes to show much sign of antiquity now. In 1317 it was recorded that 'the Vale of Annan lay so wasted and burned that neither man nor beast was left'. You may see haaf-net fishermen (from the Norse 'haf' – the open sea) standing up to their chests in the water, holding out their awkward nets, framed like soccer goalposts. This ancient tradition, dating from Viking days and protected by Royal Charter, is restricted by licence to the men of Annan only.

Shrimp-canning was once a valuable industry, and in the 19th century tea-clippers were made here. The blind poet Dr Thomas Blacklock lived here; a man who did much

Tourist Information

Gretna Green: t (01461) 337 834; *open Easter to mid-Oct.*

Southwaite M6 Service Area, near Carlisle: t (01697) 473 445/6; *open all year.*

Festivals

July: **The Riding of the Marches**, Annan.

Shopping

Gretna Gateway Outlet Village, Glasgow Road (signed off the M74). Designer Outlet Centre selling designer gear at up to 50% off normal shop prices. *Open daily 10–6.*

Pinneys, at Brydhill, Annan. High-class fish-smokers with very good smoked fish pâtés, smoked salmon, trout, mackerel, etc.

Sports and Activities

Broom Fisheries, Newbie, off the A724 south of Annan, t (01461) 700 209, *www.broomsfish-eries.co.uk.* Four trout waters stocked with rainbow, brown, golden and brook trout. Coarse fishing, tuition, tackle shop, hire, etc. *Open April–Oct daily 9–dark; Nov–Mar Mon and Wed–Sun 9–dark.*

Where to Stay and Eat

Annan t (01461–)

Comlongon Castle, Clarencefield, t (01387) 870 283, *www.comlongon.com* (*expensive*). Family-run hotel, in a 14th-century castle adjoining a mansion. Popular for weddings.

Blacketlees, nr Annan, t 205 706, *blacketlees@ukgateway.net* (*moderate*). Georgian farm-house overlooking the River Annan. Run as a Wolsey Lodge, with their high standards of comfort, hospitality and good food.

The Gables Hotel, Gretna, t 338 300 (*moderate*). A listed building with some of its original features.

Gretna Chase Hotel, t 337 517, *www.gretnachase.co.uk* (*moderate*). Creeper-clad hotel built in 1856 for eloping couples, but modernised since.

Hunters Lodge Hotel, Annan Road, Gretna, t 338 214, *www.hunterslodgehotel.co.uk* (*moderate*). A listed building near the centre of Gretna, with four-poster beds.

Queensberry Arms Hotel, High Street, Annan, t 202 024 (*moderate*). 18th-century coaching inn in the town centre, recently done up, old-fashioned and reliable with good food and an 'Annan Suite' for special occasions.

Warmanbie Hotel and Restaurant, Annan, t 204 015, *www.warmanbie.co.uk* (*moderate*). An elegant Georgian country house in 40 acres of secluded woodland overlooking the River Annan, with free fishing. The rooms are comfortable with private bathrooms and colour TV. Good food and wine. Special rates for weekend breaks and off-season holidays.

Kirkland Country House Hotel, Ruthwell, t (01387) 870 284 (*moderate–cheap*). The Manse and home of Henry Duncan (*see below*), next to the Ruthwell Cross. Cosy and welcoming. Children welcome.

Hurkledale Farm, Cummertrees, by Annan, t 700 228 (*cheap*). Very cosy, friendly, working dairy farm, with good home cooking.

Kinmouth House, nr Annan, t 700 486 (*cheap*). 8 self-catering cottages (sleeping 2–6). Well renovated, attached to the main (rather baronial) house, with good views. Salmon and trout fishing, tuition, swimming pool, gym, games room. 2 miles from the beach and golf club, and 4 miles from local shops.

to promote the genius of Robert Burns and who prevented him from emigrating when times were hard. The **Historic Resources Centre** in Bank Street (*open Wed–Sat and hols 11–4*) is a museum of local history, arts and crafts.

The **Brus Stone**, built into the wall of the town hall, is a carved tablet from a castle built by the Brus lords. It is inscribed with the name Robert de Brus, thought to be King Robert the Bruce. This relic was stolen in the 19th century and lost for 100 years before someone found it in North Devon in 1916.

Ruthwell Cross

*Always open; get the key from Mrs Coulthard, t (01387) 870 249;
www.dumfriesmuseum.demon.co.uk.*

Ruthwell is the start of the Solway Coast Heritage Trail to Stranraer. In a specially
built apse in the church is the 7th-century Ruthwell Cross, one of Scotland's greatest
treasures, with incredibly clear sculpted figures, vine scrolls, birds and animals. The
runic inscriptions, the longest and perhaps oldest known in Britain, have been deci-
phered by scholars and are extracts from a devotional poem, 'The Dream of the Rood',
the oldest poem in the English language, written by 7th-century Northumbrian
poets. The arms of the 18ft-high cross are modern, but they don't detract from the
grace of this ancient relic. The reason why it is so well preserved is that it was buried
in the 17th century by the minister, to protect it from the iconoclasm of Presbyterian
reformers. The man who subsequently unearthed and re-erected it was the Rev.
Henry Duncan, who also established Scotland's first savings bank, in Ruthwell, in 1810.
The cottage where this first bank was founded is now the **Savings Bank Museum**
(*open Easter–Sept daily 10–1 and 2–5; Oct–Easter Tues–Sat 10–1 and 2–5*), with bank,
family and social history, and details of the restoration of the Cross.

Comlongon Castle, at Clarencefield just northwest of Ruthwell, has been restored
and turned into an expensive hotel (*see above*). The 14th-century keep has spooky
dungeons, atmospheric panelled rooms, a great hall, a ghost and heraldic devices. It is
privately owned, so it might be politic to patronize the hotel first.

Caerlaverock Nature Reserve (*open daily 9–5; www.wwt.org*), west of Ruthwell,
between Lochar Water and the mouth of the Nith, is a great tract of wild salt marsh
and mud flats, belonging to the Wildfowl Trust. It is the most northerly breeding
ground of the natterjack toad.

Caerlaverock Castle

*Open April–Sept daily 9.30–6.30; Oct–Mar Mon–Sat
9.30–4.30, Sun 2–4.30; adm.*

Caerlaverock is a massive triangular-shaped ruin on the western part of the nature
reserve, its moat still full, so you cross a footbridge to reach it. Its shape was governed
by that of the rock on which it was built, just above the high-tide level at the mouth
of the Nith. Aptly described by a medieval monk as 'shield-shaped', in 1300 the castle
held off 3,000 English troops under Edward I for two days, defended by only 60 men.
It is surrounded by treacherous sinking-mud and swampland, adding to its impreg-
nability. Built in 1290, the castle was a Maxwell stronghold, and it has an elegant
Renaissance interior designed by the first Earl of Nithsdale in the 17th century. There
is something very French about its three-storey façade, surrounding the triangular
courtyard, decorated with sculpted doors and windows. Covenanters destroyed it not
long after the first Earl's improvements. The Maxwell crest and motto are above the
door. There is a children's adventure park, a model siege engine and a nature trail.

Dumfries and Around

Dumfries, on the banks of the Nith, is surrounded by farmland, woods and beautiful gardens. Its history is as bloodstained as that of any Border town, its inhabitants known for their brave opposition to invasion. William the Lion made it a Royal Burgh in 1186, and it was granted a charter in 1395 by Robert III. Bronze- and Iron Age relics have been excavated nearby, and it is almost certain that there was a Roman settlement with a Roman road up Nithsdale. Edward I captured the now-vanished castle; Robert the Bruce murdered Red Comyn here in 1306; Prince Charles Edward Stuart passed through in 1745. Robert Burns lived and died in Dumfries, and described it as 'Maggie by the banks of Nith, a dame wi' pride eneuch'. The name Dumfries comes from *dun*, or *drum*, *phreas* – the fort, or ridge, in the brushwood.

Dumfries Museum (*open April–Sept Mon–Sat 10–5, Sun 2–5; Oct–Mar Tues–Sat 10–1 and 2–5*) adjoins a water mill – a round whitewashed tower, built about 1730. 'Period' rooms contain local exhibits: archaeology, natural history, Roman altars, early-Christian monuments and costumes and, of course, Burns memorabilia. A **camera obscura** in the old mill (*adm*) gives an ingeniously reflected view of the town and surrounding countryside.

Devorguilla Bridge, a six-arched footbridge above a tumbling caul (weir) created in the 18th century to provide power for grain mills, replaced a wooden bridge built by Devorguilla Balliol in the 14th century (*see* Sweetheart Abbey, below). The present bridge dates from 1432 but was considerably restored after the 17th century when floodwater reduced it from nine, or even 13, arches, to the present six. This was once the gateway into Galloway. The quaint **Old Bridge House** (*open April–Sept Mon–Sat 10–5, Sun 2–5*), dating from 1662, is a folk museum with Victorian and Edwardian rooms, displaying everyday life in the town.

Burns House (*open April–Sept Mon–Sat 10–5, Sun 2–5; Oct–Mar Tues–Sat 10–1 and 2–5*) is a red-brick workman's cottage in what is now Burns Street, but which was called Mill Vennel when he lived and died there. He called it 'Stinking Vennel' because of an open drain running down the alley, carrying effluent from the meat market to the river. An elaborate **Mausoleum** in the grounds of St Michael's Church contains the bodies of Burns, his wife Jean Armour and five of their children. Like the statue in the High Street, this Grecian temple, sculpted by Turnerelli, with the muse of poetry encountering Burns at the plough, is too mawkish for the man. It was erected early in the 19th century, costing £1,450. The **Robert Burns Centre**, in Mill Road (*open April–Sept Mon–Sat 10–8, Sun 2–5; Oct–Mar Tues–Sat 10–1 and 2–5*), is the latest tribute to the poet. In an 18th-century red sandstone mill on the banks of the Nith, it has a 70-seat theatre with audiovisual shows (*adm*). A model shows 18th-century Dumfries as Burns would have known it, and there are displays of his life, a bookshop and a café.

The **Crichton Museum** in Easterbrook Hall, Bankend Road (*open Easter–Sept Thurs–Sat 1.30–4.30, Mon, Wed and Sun by appointment; Oct–Easter Thurs and Fri 1.30–4.30, otherwise by appointment; t (01387) 244 228*), in landscaped grounds and gardens, has displays of hospital-type artefacts and patients' art from 1839.

Robert Burns

Dumfries glows with Burns nostalgia. Listen for the echo of an ironic chuckle from that most earthy of romantic poets in the High Street, in front of Greyfriars Church where several roads meet, and look up at the splendidly sentimental statue of him. A white marble Adonis lounges against a tree-stump, hand on heart, clutching a posy of flowers, his dog resting its head on his rustic boot. He stares out over the town wearing a rather vapid expression that does not quite square with his colourful life. Two of the poet's favourite inns in the High Street, The Globe Tavern, where the barmaid bore one of his many children, and the Hole in the Wa', are both crammed with Burns memorabilia. It's hard to believe he died nearly 200 years ago, so alive is his memory. Burns lived in Dumfries for the last 4½ years of his life, working as an exciseman and writing nearly 100 of his works, including 'Auld Lang Syne'.

The **Dumfries and Galloway Aviation Museum** at Heathhall (*open April–Oct Sat and Sun 10–5; Nov–Mar Sun 11–4; adm*) features aviation history from the First World War, with artefacts and aircraft. You can see restoration work in action, including a Spitfire and Chipmunk.

A plaque in Castle Street is all that remains of the **Monastery of Greyfriars**. It commemorates a turning point in Scottish history, when Robert the Bruce stabbed to death Red Comyn, his rival claimant to the Crown, in 1306 in a quarrel. Having disposed of opposition with the double crime of murder and sacrilege, Bruce was then able to seize the throne. The early 18th-century **Midsteeple** in the town centre was the tolbooth. A plan on the wall shows Dumfries in Burns' day. This was also the prison and ammunition store.

Lincluden Collegiate Church (*open April–Sept daily 9–5*) stands on the northern outskirts of the town on a grassy plateau within a bend of Cluden Water. It was founded for Benedictine nuns in the 12th century: in 1339 the nuns were thrown out by Archibald the Grim and the church became collegiate. Archibald's son, the fourth Earl of Douglas, son-in-law of Robert III, was killed fighting for France against England. His wife, Princess Margaret, endowed a chapel in the south transept in memory of her husband, and was herself buried in the richly decorated, canopied tomb in the ruins. There are plenty of Douglas signatures on the walls in the form of coats of arms, shields, and so on, and carvings on the rood screen showing scenes from the life of Christ.

About 6 miles southwest of Dumfries on the A711, **Beeswing** village is named after a 19th-century racehorse who won a fortune for a gambling butler. He used his winnings to buy an inn and called it Beeswing; the village grew up round it. The inn is now a private house, identifiable by the large yellow butterfly by the front door.

Drumcoltran Tower (*always open*), 8 miles southwest of Dumfries just off the A711, is a 16th-century tower house among farm buildings, three storeys high with a wheel-stair in a projecting turret. A hoard of Bronze Age rapiers was found in a ditch nearby.

Signposted off the A710 at Kirkbean, **John Paul Jones Cottage** (*open April–Sept Tues–Sun 10–5; July and Aug and hols daily 10–5; adm*) has been excellently adapted to tell the story of this flamboyant character who was born here in 1747, son of a

Tourist Information

Dumfries, 64 Whitesands: **t** (01387) 253 862 (24-hour answering service), *info@dgtb. ossian.net, www.dumfriesandgalloway.co.uk; open all year*. For Burns sights, try *www.dumfriesmuseum.demon.co.uk*.

Festivals

June: **Guid Nychburris Festival** (Good Neighbours), Dumfries; week-long festival, incorporating many historic events including the granting of the charter and the Riding of the Marches.

Where to Stay and Eat

Dumfries **t** (01387–)

Cairndale Hotel and Leisure Club, English Street, **t** 254 111, *www.cairndalehotel.co.uk* (*expensive*). Reasonably priced, with heated pool, sauna, steam room, spa, gymnasium, health/beauty salon, toning tables, etc. Leisure and golf breaks available. Jolly entertainment thrown in: not for the recluse.

Abbey Arms Hotel, next door to the Criffel Inn, **t** 850 489, *john.owens@virgin.net* (*moderate*). Much the same as its neighbour.

The Auldgirth Inn, Auldgirth, **t** 740 250, *www.auldgirth-inn.co.uk* (*moderate*). 8 miles northeast of Dumfries, this inn dates back to the 1500s when it was a pilgrims' rest. It was frequented by Burns.

Cowans Farm Guest House, Kirkgunzeon, **t** 760 284, *www.cowansfarmguesthouse.co.uk* (*moderate*). Friendly and comfortable, with all rooms on the ground floor, and free coarse fishing on the lochs. Very tranquil.

Criffel Inn, The Square, New Abbey, **t** 850 244 (*moderate*). Small 19th-century country inn, very friendly and cosy, with delicious food and high teas. Close to the abbey, sandy beaches and golf.

Embassy Hotel, Newbridge, **t** 720 233, *www.embassyhotel.co.uk* (*moderate*). Neoclassical country house in 17 acres of parkland.

Hetland Hall Hotel, Carrutherstown, 7 miles southeast of Dumfries along the A75, **t** 840 201 (*moderate*). Georgian mansion with panoramic views of the Solway coast and lots of facilities for 'Sporting Breaks' and fitness fanatics.

Mabie House Hotel, Mabie, near Dumfries, **t** 263 188, *www.mabiehouse.co.uk* (*moderate*). Elegant country house hotel, 4 miles from Dumfries in Mabie Forest.

Station Hotel, Lovers Walk, **t** 254 316, *www.stationhotel.co.uk* (*moderate*). A listed building, and not as prosaic as it sounds. A comfortable hotel, and the food is good.

Balmoral Fish and Chip Shop, Balmoral Road. Especially good fish and chips.

Bruno's, 3 Balmoral Road, **t** 255 757. Another good Italian.

The Old Bank, 95 Irish Street. Splendid coffee shop with good snacks.

Pierre's, 117 Queensbury Street, **t** 265 888. Reasonable bistro food.

Pizzeria Il Fiume, in Dock Park by St Michael's Bridge, **t** 265 154. Good Italian atmosphere. *Evenings only*.

Speddoch, **t** 820 342. A rambling house in large grounds, lived in by the same family for about 300 years. It is a Wolsey Lodge, with excellent food and hospitality. No dogs in the house, and no smoking.

Wisharts, Mill Road, **t** 259 679. Good food, but not cheap. *Closed Sun and Mon.*

gardener at Arbigland. He served part of a prison sentence for a murder he did not commit, and then made his home in America. A brave, dashing sailor, he fought for the Americans in the War of Independence, helping to establish their navy, and led several raids on English and Scottish territory in command of an American brig. A true mercenary, he fought for France and for Russia and died in Paris. There are many stories of his exploits, including one in which he returned some treasure, plundered by his crew, to its owner – a lady who lived on the Solway Firth. His body was later exhumed and shipped to America for reburial amidst great public acclamation.

Sweetheart Abbey

Open April–Sept daily 9.30–6.30; Oct–Mar Mon–Wed
and Sat 9.30–4.30, Thurs 9.30–12.30, Sun 2–4.30; adm.

Sweetheart Abbey, at New Abbey south of Dumfries, is one of Scotland's most poignant monastic ruins. Roofless, its grass-carpeted nave is enclosed within red sandstone arches. It was founded in 1273 by Devorguilla Balliol – mother of King John Balliol, the luckless 'Toom Tabard' – who also founded Balliol College in Oxford. Devorguilla was buried here with her husband's embalmed heart, which she had carried around with her in an ivory and silver casket since his death, and the abbey became known as Dulce Cor, or Sweet Heart. Devorguilla's tomb, marked by a raised platform of turf with a cross cut in it, lies in front of the high altar.

The shell of the abbey dominates the village of **New Abbey**, with its main street lined by single-storey whitewashed cottages curving up to the gates of what were the precincts. Part of the enormous boulder wall that once encircled the grounds remains. Criffel, the highest of the coastal hills (1,868ft), can be climbed from here. **New Abbey Cornmill** (*demonstrations April–Sept daily 9.30–6.30; Oct–Mar Mon–Wed and Sat 9.30–4.30, Thurs 9.30–12.30, Sun 2–4.30; adm*) is a renovated 18th-century water-powered oatmeal mill in full working order. **Shambellie House Museum of Costume** (*open April–Oct daily 11–5; winter by appointment; adm; t (01387) 850 375*), in a Victorian house with nice gardens, displays period costumes in appropriate settings.

Dalbeattie to Newton Stewart

Dalbeattie

Dalbeattie, 14 miles southwest of Dumfries, is in the Stewartry, so called from the time when Balliol lands were confiscated and placed under a royal 'steward' – hence also the origins of the Stewart/Stuart dynasty. Much of the town is built with glittering granite, acclaimed for beauty and durability and used to strengthen buildings all over the world: the Eddystone Lighthouse, the Thames Embankment, lighthouses in Ceylon, and paving stones in Russia and South America.

The **Old Buittle Tower** (*t (01556) 612 607*) is a 16th-century tower house, where they stage a variety of period events, including mounted Border Reivers and hussars, displays of arms and domestic artefacts, cooking, and an archaeological dig.

Moonstone Miniatures, at Kirkpatrick Durham (*open May–mid-Sept Thurs and Fri 10–5, Sat and Sun 2–5; adm; t (01556) 650 313*), has a display of miniature houses and shops which is intriguing for all ages.

Sulwath Brewery, in Castle Douglas (*open April–Oct Mon–Sat 10–4; Nov–Mar Mon–Fri 10–4, Sat 10–1; adm*), has brewing demonstrations including free sampling.

The **Motte of Mark** at Rockcliffe, on the Urr Water, is a 5th or 6th-century hillfort commanding such a spectacular view of the coast that few invaders could have slipped past unnoticed. The **Motte of Urr**, nearly 3 miles north of Dalbeattie, just off the B794, is another fortified hill – the most extensive motte and bailey earthwork castle in Scotland. It is an almost circular mound, rising in three tiers on a platform surrounded by a deep trench; a relic of Saxon-Norman occupation.

Colvend Coast

The attractive coast south of Dalbeattie, around Colvend, Rockcliffe and Sandyhills Bay, has good walks, a bird sanctuary at Rough Island, and a picturesque harbour at Kippford. This was smugglers' territory in the old days. A good 5-mile walk is from Kippford, southeast along the coast to Castlehill Point, passing the Motte of Mark and back past Dalbeattie Forest.

West along the coast, **Palnackie**'s silted-up harbour hosts the World Flounder-tramping Championships in summer. Competitors find the flounders in the mud with their bare feet and spear them, at considerable risk to their toes. Alternatively you can watch glass-blowing, welding and sculpting at the **North Glen Gallery** (*open daily*).

Less than 2 miles south, just off the A711, **Orchardton Tower** (*open daily; key from the custodian who lives in a cottage nearby*) is a 15th-century cylindrical tower built by John Cairns in a wooded dip. This is the only tower of its kind in Scotland, modelled on a style common in Ireland. **Screel Hill**, on the other side of the A711 from Orchardton, has a signed trail up through the forest to the craggy summit, with panoramic views.

Dundrennan Abbey

Open April–Sept daily 9.30–6.30; Oct–Mar Sat 9.30–4.30, Sun 2–4.30; adm.

About 6 miles down the coast, Dundrennan Abbey is a must for anyone with romance in their veins. There is little left of its former splendour, but its roofless aisles and transepts, its pointed arches and blind arcades reverberate with echoes of Mary, Queen of Scots. Founded for Cistercians in 1142, and falling into ruin after the Reformation, the abbey provided the queen with her final resting place before she embarked for England from Port Mary. She arrived in tattered clothes, her head shorn for disguise, and sat somewhere in these ruins to write a final letter to her cousin Elizabeth of England, begging for sanctuary. It is heartbreaking to picture her tall, slender figure passing through the 13th-century pointed doorway between two arched windows into the chapterhouse, to the care of the abbot and his monks.

Kirkcudbright

Gaily painted houses and old streets beside the mouth of the Dee make Kirkcudbright (pronounced Kir-coo-bry) one of Scotland's most enchanting towns. It was a medieval port and a royal burgh, named after the Kirk of St Cuthbert, when the saint's bones rested there on the way to interment in Durham. With its mild, almost Mediterranean climate and sea views, the town is a thriving artists' colony.

MacLellan's Castle (*open April–Sept daily 9.30–6.30; adm*) is an impressive turreted ruin off the High Street, dating from 1582, built by Thomas MacLellan with stones from a ruined friary which once stood here. The jagged fangs of this castellated mansion draw you from across the town. In the great hall, look for the single stone lintel that spans the 10ft aperture, and also for the small closet behind the fireplace with a peephole, hinting at intrigue in the past. MacLellan's elaborate tomb is in the 16th-century aisle of Greyfriars Church.

Broughton House and Garden, in the High Street (*open April–Oct daily 1–5.30; ring for winter times; adm; t (01557) 330 437*), was built in the 18th century. It was the home of E. A. Hornel, one of the first settlers of the Kirkcudbright artists' colony and a renowned artist himself. Hornel died in 1933 and left this house to the town with a collection of books and manuscripts on Galloway. The **Tolbooth** (1627), also in the High Street (*open June–Sept Mon–Sat 11–4, Sun 2–5; adm; t (01557) 331 556*), features an outside stone stair. Several witches were imprisoned here, as was John Paul Jones, wrongly convicted for causing the death of a seaman, but later freed. Don't miss the 'jougs' with which miscreants were tethered by the neck for public humiliation. There is also an arts centre, with an audiovisual show and paintings.

The **Stewartry Museum**, in St Mary Street (*open June–Sept Mon–Sat 11–4, Sun 2–5; adm*), tells of the buccaneering life of John Paul Jones, and has displays of social history going back to prehistoric times, as well as works by local artists.

In **St Cuthbert's Churchyard**, on the edge of town, is a tombstone marking the grave of 'William Marshall, Tinker', who died in 1792, aged 120. He is alleged to have fathered four of his many children after the age of 100, which may account for the ram's horns engraved on the reverse side of the headstone.

Tongland

Tongland Power Station and **Galloway Hydro Visitor Centre** (*open late May–end June and first half Sept Mon–Fri 9.30–5; July and Aug also Sat 9.30–5; adm*) have guided tours and a fish ladder. Try to spot salmon leaping up the man-made ladder, and think back to the colourful history of Tongland Abbey, which once stood here. One of its abbots was murdered as he knelt at the altar in 1235, and its most famous abbot was John Damian, an alchemist. Damian enjoyed the patronage of James IV, the king who would undoubtedly have been a leading entrepreneur today and whose enquiring mind encouraged many experiments. In an attempt to show the king that it was possible for man to fly, Damian leapt off the walls of Stirling Castle in his presence. He broke his thigh.

Gatehouse of Fleet

The **Mill on the Fleet Visitor Centre** (*open Easter to late September daily 10.30–4.30; adm; t (01557) 814 099*) is a restored 18th-century cotton mill, with water wheels and a video presentation. There is also a model of the town 200 years ago, and displays of local history. The shop and café are by the river, and you may see a kingfisher if you are lucky. The **Fleet Forest Centre** has a log cabin shelter with an information board showing the various walks with flora and fauna.

The **Cream O'Galloway Visitor Centre** at Rainton, 1½ miles south of Gatehouse of Fleet, is a farm dairy (*open April–Aug daily 11–6; Sept and Oct daily 11–5*). There is excellent ice cream in the making, observed from a viewing gallery, as well as nature trails, play areas, a shop and a tearoom.

Tourist Information

Kirkcudbright: Harbour Square, t (01557) 330 494; *open Easter to mid-Oct.*

Gatehouse of Fleet: car park, t (01557) 814 212; *open Easter to mid-Oct.*

Newton Stewart: Dashwood Square, t (01671) 402 431; *open Easter to mid-Oct.*

Festivals

July: **Civic Week**, Dalbeattie.

July–mid-August: **Summer Festivities**, Kirkcudbright; Scottish Nights, a raft race, a puppet festival, sports, walks and a floodlit Tattoo in front of MacLellan's Castle.

Where to Stay and Eat

Cally Palace Hotel, Gatehouse of Fleet, t (01557) 814 341, *www.callypalace.co.uk* (*expensive*). Unfortunately named, vast and sumptuous Georgian mansion with original moulded ceilings, in 100 acres of parkland, with a heated swimming pool, leisure facilities and its own 18-hole golf course.

Creebridge House Hotel, Newton Stewart, t (01671) 402 121, *www.creebridge.co.uk*

(*expensive*). Built in 1760 for the Earl of Galloway close to the town centre, this has a real country-pub atmosphere with comfortable rooms and two restaurants, both serving above-average, award-winning food. Weekend and short-break rates available.

Kirroughtree Hotel, Newton Stewart, t (01671) 402 141, *www.kirroughtreehouse.co.uk* (*expensive*). Luxury Georgian mansion in 8 acres, with free golf on five local courses, nice gardens and good food.

Auchenskeoch Lodge, near Dalbeattie, t (01387) 780 277 (*moderate*). Splendidly welcoming family house 7 miles southeast of Dalbeattie, with 20 acres of wooded grounds and excellent food (on request).

Balcary Bay Hotel, Auchencairn, t (01556) 640 217, *www.balcary-bay-hotel.co.uk* (*moderate*). Imposing, family-run country house hotel, literally on the beach. The seafood is excellent. *Closed Dec–Feb.*

Barons Craig Hotel, Rockcliffe, south of Dalbeattie, t (01556) 630 225, *www.baronscraighotel.co.uk* (*moderate*). Imposing, comfortable Victorian country house in 12 acres overlooking the Solway Firth. Good food and efficient staff. *Open April–Oct.*

Cardoness Castle (*open April–Sept Mon–Sat 9.30–6.30, Sun 2–6.30; Oct–Mar weekends only; adm*), a mile southwest of Gatehouse of Fleet, is a roofless, 15th-century tower house, four storeys high above a turf mound, with a vaulted basement, original stairway, stone benches and fireplaces. It is said that at one time the owners got so carried away celebrating the birth of an heir that they all went skating on the loch before the ice was firm, and that was the end of them.

Dirk Hatteraick's Cave, on the shore just east of the mouth of Kirkdale Burn, is tricky to get at, crossed by the A75 about 7 miles west of Gatehouse of Fleet. It is the largest of several caves in this area. Hatteraick was a notorious smuggler.

Barholm Castle, a 16th-century ruin in a glen to the northeast, was one of John Knox's refuges when he was a fugitive.

Cairnholy

Half a mile up the glen of Kirkdale Burn are two Neolithic **burial tombs** at Carsluith. The first is a stone cist with standing stones; the second has a double burial chamber. These ancient stones, silhouetted against an evening sky, have a primal mystery that stirs the imagination. What were they like, those mourners, 4,000 years ago?

Carsluith Castle (*open April–Sept*) is a well-preserved four-storey 16th-century tower house with 18th-century outbuildings. The last abbot of Sweetheart Abbey lived here.

Clonyard House Hotel, Colvend, **t** (01556) 630 372 (*moderate*). Serves excellent food, is comfortable and caters for disabled guests.

Mains of Collin, Auchencairn, **t** (01556) 640 211, *fionawallace@mainsofcollin.freeserve.co.uk* (*moderate*). A splendid working farm B&B. Comfortable and friendly.

Murray Arms Hotel, on the corner of Ann Street and High Street, Gatehouse of Fleet, **t** (01557) 814 207 (*moderate*). One of the haunts of that discerning pub-crawler, R. Burns. It was here that he composed *Scots, Wha Hae*, inspired, no doubt, by their fine wine and excellent cuisine. Try the local beef.

Old Smugglers Inn, Auchencairn, **t** (01556) 640 331 (*moderate*). Small, cosy, 17th-century inn.

The Selkirk Arms, High Street, Kirkcudbright, **t** (01557) 330 402, *www.selkirkarmshotel.co.uk* (*moderate*). Excellent food and a friendly atmosphere. Burns wrote the *Selkirk Grace* here:
Some hae meat and canna eat,
And some wad eat that want it:
But we hae meat and we can eat
And sae the Lord be thankit.

Flowerbank Guest House, Newton Stewart, **t** (01671) 402 629 (*moderate–cheap*). 18th-century house on the River Cree, with good food and a friendly welcome.

Rowallan House, Corsbie Road, Newton Stewart, **t** (01671) 402 520, *www.rowallan.co.uk* (*moderate–cheap*). Attractive Victorian country house, 5 minutes' walk from the town centre. Deserved winner of a 'good room' award.

Anchor Hotel, Kippford, **t** (01556) 620 605 (*cheap*). Delightful old inn overlooking the Urr estuary. Great character and good food.

Baytree Guest House, 110 High Street, Kirkcudbright, **t** (01557) 330 824 (*cheap*). Elegant Georgian town house with very good food.

Gladstone House, 48 High Street, Kirkcudbright, **t** (01557) 331 734 (*cheap*). Georgian guesthouse, with hospitable atmosphere and good food.

Gordon House Hotel, 116 High Street, Kirkcudbright, **t** (01557) 330 670 (*cheap*). In the same vein as Gladstone House.

Low Cordorcan Cottage, in the RSPB reserve at Woods of Cree (*cheap*). Good conversion of 18th-century barn (sleeping 4).

The Royal Hotel, Kirkcudbright, **t** (01557) 331 213, *www.pheasanthotel.co.uk* (*cheap*). Traditional hotel, bustling and friendly. The Pheasant Carvery and Grill has excellent meals with unusual dishes like 'hot mozzarella melt' and 'deep-fried ice cream'.

Creetown

Following the coast on round for about 6 miles, you come to Creetown on the eastern shore of the Cree estuary, the granite gateway to Wigtownshire, a village whose public image has recently had a facelift. With hills, forests, lochs and sandy beaches all within easy reach, this is a good holiday base. Town and country walks are signposted from Adamson Square. Gemmologists should see the **Gem Rock Museum and Crystal Cave** (*open Easter–Sept daily 9.30–6; Oct–Dec daily 10–4; Jan and Feb weekends 10–4; Mar–Easter daily 10–4 or by appointment; adm; t (01671) 820 357, www.gemrock.net*), up the road opposite the clock tower. This collection of gems and rocks from all over the world took 50 years to gather: it is awe-inspiring to see a rock that contains water two million years old. There is a gem-cutting workshop, a tearoom, a gift shop and internet café. The **Creetown Exhibition Centre** in St Johns Street (*open Easter–mid-Oct Mon, Tues, Thurs Fri and Sun 11–4; July and Aug Wed–Sat 11–4; adm*) has displays of local interest, including village life, local history and wartime memorabilia.

Barholm Mains Open Farm (*open April–Sept Sun–Fri 10.30–4; adm; t (01671) 820 346*) has a variety of farm and other animals.

Newton Stewart

Another 5 or so miles along the A75, on the banks of the River Cree, Newton Stewart grew around the first easy place to ford the river. It is a holiday centre and market town, surrounded by moors and farmland on the reclaimed mud flats of the estuary. From here you can enjoy walking, fishing, boating, bird-watching, sightseeing or just relaxing in the mild, often hot, sunshine. It is a good base from which to explore the enormous Galloway Forest Park, to the north. **Sophie's Puppenstube and Dolls House Museum**, in Queen Street (*open Easter–Oct Mon–Sat 10–4; phone for winter times; adm; t (01671) 403 344*), has over 50 dolls' houses and interiors, and a shop.

The **Marbury Smokehouse** (*open Feb and Mar Tues–Fri 11–4, Sat 10–2; April–Oct Mon 11.30–4, Tues–Fri 11–4, Sat 10–2; Nov and Dec Tues–Sat 11–2*) at Bargrennan, north of Newton Stewart, has smoking demonstrations and cookery days.

Wigtown and the Machars

Seven miles south of Newton Stewart on the western shore of Wigtown Bay, **Wigtown** is another holiday resort. It has two mercat crosses, the second rather ostentatious, having been erected to celebrate the victory at Waterloo in 1816. The railed enclosure in the large town square was for penning up cattle at night, a practice necessary not only to stop them straying, but also to protect them from reivers.

Torhouse Stone Circle

The Torhouse Stone Circle, dating from about 2000 BC, some 5 miles west of Wigtown, is one of the best of this type in Britain. There are 19 roundish boulders forming a complete circle 60ft in diameter, with three more in the centre. As with all other standing-stone circles, historians can only guess at their original purpose.

Bladnoch Distillery and Visitor Centre (*open mid-Mar–early Nov shop Mon–Fri 9.30–5.30, tours 10–4.30; early Nov–mid-Dec Mon–Fri 11–3.30; adm*), half a mile south of Wigtown (1817) also has fishing, canoeing, walks and a campsite.

Galloway House Gardens (*open Mar–Oct daily 9–5; adm*) at Garlieston, about 6 miles south of Wigtown on the coast, is a woodland garden. Informal walks among

The Wigtown Martyrs

Wigtown will always be remembered for its two martyrs, Margaret McLachlan, aged 62, and Margaret Wilson, aged 18. In 1685 they were convicted of having attended 20 conventicles – illegal Covenanter prayer meetings. They were tied to stakes in the estuary and drowned by the rising tide, watched by an avid crowd. Margaret Wilson was placed so that she could witness the final throes of her older companion, and was given the chance to 'repent'. She refused. Their graves, with those of six other Covenanter martyrs, are in the churchyard beside the present parish church. There is a monument on the hill above the town, and you can see a simple pillar on the shore where the drownings took place, and watch the tide rising over the estuary mud flats – emphasizing the full horror of the appalling event.

Shopping

Wigtown is known for its large number of antiquarian and secondhand bookshops, *www.wigtown-booktown.co.uk*.

Where to Stay and Eat

Corsemalzie House Hotel, Port William, **t** (01988) 860 254 (*moderate*). Highly recommended for dependability and comfort in 40 acres of wooded gardens. Good food, free golf, private fishing and rough shooting. Try the smoked fish. *Open Mar–mid-Jan*.

Castlewigg Hotel, 2 miles from Whithorn, **t** (01988) 500 213 (*cheap*). Cosy and relaxed hotel overlooking the Galloway Hills, with log fires in the bar.

The Steampacket Hotel, overlooks the harbour in Isle of Whithorn, **t** (01988) 500 334 (*cheap*). Busy, friendly, informal waterside inn with an emphasis on good-value food and good company. The bar is much frequented by sailers and fishermen.

shrubs, borders, wild flowers, fine trees and exotica lead down to a sandy bay, and there is a walled garden with a camellia house. The house is not open to the public.

Whithorn

About 10 miles south of Wigtown, Whithorn (from the Anglo-Saxon *huit aern* – white house) was the birthplace of Christianity in Scotland. Born nearby, some time in the middle of the 4th century, and of royal descent, St Ninian went to Rome on a pilgrimage and returned here in 397, a consecrated bishop. He built a white stone church which became known as *Candida Casa*, and set about converting the Britons and southern Picts to Christianity. Whithorn is the oldest Royal Burgh in Scotland, its first charter having been granted by Robert the Bruce in 1329.

To get to **Whithorn Priory**, go through the Pend, a deep 17th-century arch flanked by 15th-century pillars with a stone panel above carved with the Scottish coat of arms, as it was before the Union in 1707. **Whithorn Museum** (*open April–Oct daily 10.30–5; adm*), also through the Pend, is worth visiting first because it describes Whithorn and the vital part it played in the birth of Christianity in Britain. There are also early Christian crosses and stones.

A ticket includes entry to the Priory on the site of *Candida Casa*: you can see the 13th-century nave and a doorway in the south wall, built by Fergus of Galloway who founded the priory in 1126. It was a place of pilgrimage for more than 400 years, until 'idolatry' was made illegal in 1581 by the Reformers. Many of Scotland's monarchs paid visits to the shrine: James IV walked from Edinburgh on one occasion. Mary, Queen of Scots was the last, in 1563, during her tour of the west. Part of the tour covers extensive archaeological **excavations** (most now protected by perspex) of the original Christian community, with buildings and graves going back to the 5th century, the remains of a Viking settlement, medieval burials and even a medieval herb garden.

A mile west of Whithorn, **Rispain Camp** is a rectangular settlement defended by a bank and ditch, dating from the 1st century AD.

Isle of Whithorn

Isle of Whithorn, 3 miles southeast of Whithorn village on the southeast tip of the peninsula, is a port built on what was once an island and is still a fishing centre, with boats working out of the harbour. The ruin of a 12th-century chapel, dedicated to

Pre-Christian Settlers

The coast road northwest along Luce Bay from the Isle of Whithorn to Glenluce links up several sites of early settlements on or near the shore. **The Wren's Egg Stone Circle** is on the left after Craiglemine, another of those ancient remains whose purpose remains a mystery. **Barsalloch Fort**, an Iron Age fort surrounded by a horseshoe ditch, on a cliff 6oft above the sea, is by Barsalloch Point. It's quite a steep climb up a track, but worth it for an example of how the ancient Britons defended themselves. Archaeologists found remains of Mesolithic fishermen here, over 6,000 years old. In summer the foreshore is a glorious blue carpet of saxifrage.
Drumtrodden Stones, less than 3 miles inland from Barsalloch, have Bronze Age cup-and-ring markings carved in the rock. These symbols, a foot in diameter, are found on stones scattered throughout the north as well as on the Continent.
Druchtag Motehill, to the north beyond Mochrum village, is a typical early medieval earthwork mound, steep, with traces of stone buildings.

St Ninian, stands on the site of one probably built for the use of foreign pilgrims for whom special safe-conducts were granted.

St Ninian's Cave, 3 miles southwest of Whithorn, is believed to have been the saint's private oratory, with early Christian crosses carved on the rock, on your left as you look in, small and quite hard to spot. There is something moving about this corner of Galloway: you cannot fail to wonder at the strength of the faith of those first missionaries, working among barbaric pagans, sowing seeds that grew into the Christian Church as we know it. You reach the cave by the minor road south off the A747, a mile east of its junction with the A746. There's a car park at Kidsdale Farm and the cave is signposted from there, 3 miles the round trip – a nice walk through Physgill Woods. Be cautious approaching the cave as there have been rockfalls.

The **Gavin Maxwell Memorial** is a life-like sculpted otter on a cliff top overlooking Monreith Bay. Maxwell, author of *Ring of Bright Water* and many other books, grew up in this area. **Chapel Finian**, little more than a few stones now, beside the A747, 5 miles northwest of Port William, was a 10th-century chapel dedicated to St Finbarr. It was built for pilgrims landing from the sea on their way either to Whithorn or Glenluce.

Glenluce Abbey

Open April–Sept daily 9.30–6.30; Oct–Mar Sat 9.30–4.30,
Sun 2–4.30; adm.

Glenluce Abbey at the head of Luce Bay, restored during the 20th century, was founded in 1192 by Roland, Lord of Galloway. The 15th-century vaulted chapterhouse is almost intact, entered by a round, carved doorway. Inside, a single octagonal pillar supports the stone vaulting-ribs on carved corbels, each arch decorated with twined foliage, grotesques and emblems. Of even greater interest are the excavated baked-clay water pipes and drains, laid by those monks so long ago and still sound today. These traces of early plumbing are expertly put together, and possibly a great deal more durable than modern plastic drains. A 13th-century wizard, Michael Scott, is said to have lived here and saved the community from extinction by luring a plague that attacked them into the abbey, shutting it up in a vault and starving it to death. He is also said to have commissioned witches who helped him at his work to spin the ropes of sand, revealed when the tide goes out as broken strands of sand south of the abbey at Ringdoo Point. Robert the Bruce, James IV and Mary, Queen of Scots all stayed here.

Glenluce Motor Museum (*open April–Oct daily 10–7; Nov–Mar Wed–Sun 11–4; adm*) has a collection of vintage and classic cars and motorbikes. **Castle of Park** (1590), west of Glenluce, is a well-preserved castellated tower house (*private, but worth a look*).

The Rhinns of Galloway

The Rhinns of Galloway, the hammerhead butt on the western extremity of Dumfries and Galloway, gives many panoramic views from the rugged cliffs. Sometimes Ireland looks so close you feel it would make an easy swim. Seldom more than spitting distance from the sea, you can experience fierce storms here, as well as the mild gentle climate of the rest of the region. Try to catch a sunset from the Mull of Galloway.

Stranraer

Stranraer, a busy port and market centre, is also a popular holiday resort. Very sheltered, at the head of Loch Ryan, it is the gateway to the Rhinns of Galloway. Although not a beautiful town, it has numerous hotels and guesthouses, golf courses, good beaches, excellent trout and sea fishing, boating and exploring. Frequent car-ferries make the two-hour crossing to Larne in Northern Ireland. High-speed catamarans also cross from Stranraer to Belfast, several times a day, in just one hour.

It is odd to think, as you walk about the modern town, that below your feet lie oystershells that were thrown out by Mesolithic settlers 6,000 years ago. Look across Loch Ryan and picture it in Roman times when they used the sheltered anchorage for their galleys in their expeditions against the Gallovidians, calling it *Rericonius Sinus*.

Old Castle of St John, in Castle Street, is a 16th-century tower house, occupied by Claverhouse during his persecution of the Covenanters in 1682. His victims were imprisoned in the dungeons, where many perished. This was also the police station and prison in the 19th century. There are exhibitions on the castle, Covenanters and the jail, in the **visitors' centre** (*open mid-April–mid-Sept Mon–Sat 10–1 and 2–5; adm*).

Stranraer Museum (*open Mon–Sat 10–5*) in George Street gives information about Sir John Ross (*see below*), and local history, with the emphasis on dairy farming.

North West Castle Hotel, opposite the pier in Stranraer, was the home of Sir John Ross, the 18th-century Arctic explorer who sailed in search of the Northwest Passage and discovered the magnetic North Pole. A passionate seaman, Ross built his house as much like a ship as possible: a flamboyant, castellated mansion with the dining room modelled like a ship's cabin with rounded stern (*see* 'Where to Stay', p.136).

Tourist Information

Stranraer: Bridge Street, **t** (01776) 702 595; *open Easter to mid-Oct.* To find out about good beaches go to *www.south-rhinns.co.uk.*

Where to Stay and Eat

Stranraer **t** (01776–)

Knockinaam Lodge Hotel, Portpatrick, **t** 810 471 (*expensive*). One of the best hotels in this area: a proper country-house hotel in a secluded glen, with a private beach and glorious sea views across to Ireland. The grounds are lovely and include a croquet lawn. All the rooms are elegantly decorated and comfortable, and the food is excellent.

North West Castle Hotel, Stranraer, **t** 704 413, *www.northwestcastle.co.uk* (*expensive*), *see above.* Recommended if you like comfort combined with something out of the ordinary. On the seafront, it has a swimming pool, games room, saunas, sunbeds and even a curling rink. There is a splendid bar–restaurant overlooking the curling rink, with a nice old-fashioned atmosphere.

Chlenry Farmhouse, Castle Kennedy, nr Stranraer, **t** 705 316, *wolseleybrinton@*

aol.com (*moderate*). Comfortable, hospitable family home where you feel like a special guest. Delicious dinners on request. Book in advance.

Corsewall Lighthouse, Kirkcolm, **t** 853 220, *corsewall_lighthouse@msn.com* (*moderate*). Without doubt the nicest place to stay. It has everything you could want, from comfort, views, activities and value to good food. You can wave-watch from your room.

The Fernhill Hotel, Portpatrick, **t** 810 220, *www.fernhillhotel.co.uk* (*moderate*). Above the harbour overlooking the Irish Sea, 400 yards from the golf course. Every dish is cooked to order.

Kildrochet House, by Stranraer, **t** 820 216, *www.kildrochet.co.uk* (*moderate*). Attractive 18th-century Adam dowerhouse in 6 acres overlooking the Rhinns of Galloway. Dinner on request. Marvellous family atmosphere.

Portpatrick Hotel, Portpatrick, **t** 824 824, *www.shearingsholidays.com* (*moderate*). Overlooking the harbour, and good value. Welcomes families. *Open Feb–Nov.*

Mount Stewart Hotel, Portpatrick, **t** 810 291 (*cheap*). Overlooking the harbour.

Rickwood Private Hotel, Portpatrick, **t** 810 270 (*cheap*). Overlooking the sea.

Castle Kennedy Gardens

Open Easter–Sept daily 10–5; adm.

Three miles east of Stranraer just off the A75, Castle Kennedy Gardens were laid out by the second Earl of Stair, who was inspired by the gardens of Versailles while he was Ambassador in France. Not slow off the mark, the Earl used soldiers of the Royal Scots Greys and Inniskilling Fusiliers (who were in the area to quell Covenanters) to build his garden around Castle Kennedy, now a ruin softened by swathes of ivy, on an isthmus between two lochs. The castle was burned down in 1715 and the gardens were neglected until 1847, when they were rescued and restored to their original design, with a sunken garden. The rhododendrons, azaleas, magnolias and embothriums are remarkable, and the pinetum was the first to be grown in Scotland. The monkey puzzle avenue is one of the longest in Scotland. The present Scots–French mansion, Lochinch Castle, home of Lord Stair, was built in 1867 to replace Castle Kennedy. There is a tearoom and you can buy plants. **Meadowsweet Herb Garden**, also at Castle Kennedy, has over one hundred herbs with instructive tours. **Glenwhan Gardens** (*open April–Sept daily 10–5; adm; nursery open all year*), near Castle Kennedy, include a hilltop garden with good views over Luce Bay and the Mull of Galloway, and a delightful water garden with two lochans created by damming up bogland.

Corsewall Point and its lighthouse are along a rough track on the northwest tip of the Rhinns. The dominating cone of Ailsa Craig rises from the sea to the north. Robert Louis Stevenson's grandfather built the lighthouse.

Portpatrick

Portpatrick, on the west coast of the peninsula, is a holiday resort and fishing village. Only 22 miles northeast of Donaghadee in Ireland, this was once the port for the main route west, but southwesterly gales frequently made docking hazardous, so the port was moved to sheltered Stranraer. Portpatrick is an idyllic holiday centre with sandy bays, a golf course and a picturesque harbour. When the sun shines you could easily be in a Mediterranean resort. The landscape is bright with flowers, the air deliciously scented. It is said that St Patrick landed here on a visit from Ireland.

The **Southern Upland Way** (*see* p.120) starts here, and the least taxing stretch is the first 6 or 7 miles to Castle Kennedy.

Dunskey Castle, a jagged ruin dating back to the 16th century, stands on a cliff less than a mile to the south. It is one of those ruins that fire your imagination with pirates and wreckers and damsels in distress. Take care walking on the cliff paths.

The 5th or 6th-century **Kirkmadrine Stones**, 8 miles south of Stranraer off the A716, are against the church wall, with a description board. Some bear Latin inscriptions and the 'ChiRho' symbol, formed by a combination of the first two letters of Christ's name in Greek. These stones prove St Ninian established Christianity in this area; they are the earliest Christian memorials in Scotland after those at Whithorn.

Ardwell House Gardens (*open April–Oct daily 10–5: adm*) are 2 miles south of the stones off the A716. Go not only for the almost tropical gardens around the 18th-century house, but also for the sea views. At **Ardwell Bay**, on the west coast, there is a narrow rock spit, cut off by a wall, with one of the few brochs in the southwest, unusual in that it had two entrances, one to seaward and one to landward.

About a mile south of Ardwell on the A716, turn right on to the B7065 to **Port Logan**, a sheltered harbour with a stone jetty, lighthouse and small beach. **Logan Botanic Garden** (*open Mar–Oct daily 9.30–6; adm; www.rbge.org.uk; excellent licensed salad-bar restaurant*) is just over a mile to the north. A branch of the Royal Botanic Garden in Edinburgh, this is a riot of subtropical plants, tree-ferns, cabbage palms and the Brazilian *Gunnera manicata*, the largest-leafed outdoor plant in Britain. Plants from all over the world flourish in the mild climate.

The Mull of Galloway

The Mull of Galloway, the most southerly point in Scotland, less than 25 miles from Ireland and the Isle of Man, is a dramatic headland on the southern tip of the Rhinns with cliffs 200ft high. Stand here, buffeted by wind and salt spray, and watch a boiling cauldron far below, at certain times and conditions, when seven currents meet. The lighthouse is unmanned and there is no public access. **Double Dykes** is the name of the trench across the western end of the point – said to have been the last defence of the Picts, retreating from the Scots who had driven them down the peninsula early in the 6th century.

The Valleys

Dumfries and Galloway is cut by a number of valleys bringing rivers cascading into the Solway Firth from the hills and moorland in the north. If you have time, you won't regret pausing to trace some of these rivers up to their source.

Eskdale

Many streams rise in the hills of Eskdalemuir Forest to the north, joining above Langholm to form the River Esk, which chatters and tumbles south through gorges and ravines until it steadies its pace and flows into the Solway Firth by Gretna.

On the English border, **Scotsdyke** has a 16th-century trench and dyke dug to mark the border in the days when the 'Debatable Lands' were hotly contested.

16th-century **Gilnockie Tower** (*open April–Oct daily 10–12.30, or by appointment; adm; t (01387) 371 876*), south of Langholm, was one of Johnnie Armstrong of Gilnockie's strongholds – that hero of Border ballads (*see* p.116). Ruffian he may have been, but he was reputed never to do harm to any of his countrymen. It is easy to feel a twinge of affection for him, looking up at this romantic tower, with crow-stepped gables and a carved parapet-walkway round the top, standing high above the Esk Valley. His descendant, Neil Armstrong, was the first man on the moon in 1969.

Langholm

Langholm, about 10 miles north of the border, is a mill-town where the Esk gathers up the waters of the Wauchope and Ewes. Narrow and twisting, with market place and town house, the old town is quite different from the spacious, stately looking quarter across the river that developed in the 18th century when Langholm became a flourishing textile centre. The **Armstrong Clan Museum**, Lodge Walk, Castleholm Langholm (*open mid-April–Oct Tues–Sun and hols 2–5; winter by appointment only; adm; t (01387) 380 610*), has displays on clan history with archives and a library.

A memorial to the poet **Hugh MacDiarmid**, one of the founding fathers of the 'Scottish Renaissance' in literature and politics, is 2 miles to the northeast on the Newcastleton road. A two-fold panel stands like a great open book overlooking Eskdale with carvings of wildlife and countryside, dramatic in their simplicity. Local feeling ran high when this memorial was first commissioned after the poet's death in 1978. Although he had referred to his home town as 'my touchstone in all creative matters', he was not loved by many Langholmites. Stuffy locals objected to some of his bawdy anecdotes and his veiled references to the sexual habits of a local citizen in his autobiography *Lucky Poet*. When the sculpture was finished, it was initially refused by a six to five vote from the Dumfries and Galloway Planning Committee.

There is a good walk from Langholm up to the **Malcolm Monument** – the obelisk that dominates the hill to the east. Start from the car park beside the A7, just north of the town, and go up past the golf course. The round trip is 5 miles, and the view from the monument makes the final steepish climb well worth it. (Malcolm was Sir John

Festivals

July: Common Riding, Langholm; a charge of riders through a narrow bend and up the hill from the square – a dramatic stampede.

Where to Stay and Eat

Cross Keys Hotel, Canonbie, **t** (01387) 371 382/371 205, *www.gretnaweddings.com/ crosskeys.html* (*moderate*). 17th-century coaching inn in the village, overlooking the Border Esk. Fishing can be arranged.

Kirklands, Canonbie, **t** (01387) 371 769, *irvineho@aol.com* (*moderate*). Charming, sunny Georgian house on the banks of the Border Esk. Elegant, south-facing rooms and hospitable hosts. A Wolsey Lodge.

The Reivers Rest, Langholm, **t** (01387) 381 343, *www.reivers-rest.demon.co.uk* (*moderate*). Small, family-run inn in the middle of town.

Bush of Ewes Farmhouse, near Langholm, **t** (01387) 381 241 (*cheap*). Cosy farmhouse–B&B on a mixed working farm. *Open Mar–Dec.*

Crown Hotel, Langholm, **t** (01387) 380 247 (*cheap*). More attractive 18th-century former coaching inn in the middle of town. Slightly more expensive and less hushed than the Cross Keys.

Eskdale Hotel, Langholm, **t** (01387) 380 357 (*cheap*). Family-run former coaching inn in the middle of town, whose stern exterior conceals respectability and good plain cooking. Shooting and fishing available.

North Lodge, Canonbie, **t** (01387) 371 409, *jeanette@north-lodge.fsnet.co.uk* (*cheap*). Late 19th-century lodge on the edge of the village, with disabled facilities.

Burnfoot House, Westerkirk, **t** (01387) 370 611, *www.burnft.co.uk* (*moderate*). Nice house with panoramic views of the Eskdale Valley.

Malcolm who, in 1782, aged 13, was commissioned into the East India Company, and 45 years later became Governor of Bombay.)

Westerkirk

In 1757 Thomas Telford was born at Westerkirk, further northwest on the B709. Here, overlooking his beloved Esk, is a memorial to this giant of the Industrial Revolution, who built roads and bridges all over the country, serving his apprenticeship locally.

There is something inspiring about **Kagyu Samye Ling Tibetan Monastery** (*open daily 9–6;* **t** *(01387) 373 232; www.samyeling.org; café and shops*), the largest Buddhist temple in Western Europe, just north of Eskdalemuir on the B709. Founded in 1967 and completed in the mid-80s, in this tranquil setting near the source of the Esk, it is a far cry from the persecution and atrocities of Communist Tibet. Whatever your creed, you won't regret taking a conducted tour around the temple and monastery.

Annandale

Follow the River Annan north along the back roads to its source just north of Moffat: the scenery gets progressively wilder and more impressive.

Kirkpatrick Fleming, 3 miles northeast of Annan off the A74, has a cave where Robert the Bruce hid for three months. Accessible now by a path, it was then reached by swinging down the cliff on a rope. The cave was originally cut from rock by Stone Age people whose tools were found near the river. Locals will tell you that it was here that Bruce took courage from the persevering spider.

For antiquities, go to **Kirtlebridge**, 3 miles further on off the A74, where the 15th-century Merkland Cross, 9ft high with intricate carvings, was erected in memory of a

Maxwell who was killed in battle. People alive today remember the shock of the train crash near here in the First World War, when over 200 people were killed.

Ecclefechan, about 5 miles north of Annan off the A74, was Thomas Carlyle's birthplace in 1795. He was born in the white **Arched House**, now a museum (*open April–Sept Fri–Mon 1.30–5.30; adm*), so called because of its arched gateway. The house was built by his father and uncle. His parents were unpretentious, god-fearing people. His mother learnt to write so she could answer his letters. They sent him to Edinburgh University to train for the Church in 1809. His inherited intelligence, fed by education, flowered: he developed a critical awareness and knowledge of books and men that set him apart from his peers. Among the things he wrote was *Sartor Resartus* (Tailor Repatched) in which he describes a village, 'Entepfuhl', recognizable as Ecclefechan.

A mass of memorabilia is packed into the cottage. The kitchen would have been the heart of the household and you can almost see the family, seated at the table, listening to dissertations from the young student, surrounded by the domestic clutter of country life. Upstairs, the box-bed, although not original, is a contemporary of that in which Carlyle was born, in this bedroom. Other furniture and items come from Cheyne Row, Chelsea, where the Carlyles lived for more than 30 years. The museum is of interest for its social history as well as being a memorial to a complex man.

Carlyle refused burial in Westminster Abbey and is buried below a simple sandstone slab in the churchyard behind the cottage, an unfussy monument to a brilliant man who loathed ostentation. He was a temperamental husband to intellectual Jane Baillie Welsh, with whom he shared a stormy relationship reflected in her caustic, witty letters. Although they were devoted to each other (Jane's death in 1866 'shattered my whole existence into immeasurable ruin'), she left instructions that she was not to be buried with him, but with her father in Haddington, Lothian.

Hoddam Castle, 2 miles to the southwest, was built in the 16th century by John Maxwell, 4th Lord Herries, with a watchtower on Repentance Hill to the south. (Repentance, they say, because the noble lord threw his prisoners into the sea during a storm after a piratical raid on England.) Some of the castle has been demolished and the rest of it is at risk, though there are plans to develop it into a leisure complex.

Lockerbie

At 6pm on Wednesday 21 December 1988, a Pan-Am Boeing 747, en route from Frankfurt to New York, took off from London Heathrow. It carried in its hold a transistor radio packed with explosives, planted by terrorists. The device exploded over Lockerbie at 7.19pm, killing all the crew and passengers in the plane. The wreckage fell on and around the town and on the adjacent motorway, flattening houses in a quiet crescent, killing the residents and a number of people driving up the motorway. In all, nearly 280 people died. The town lives on, with Scottish guts and stoicism.

By the end of the 18th century, Lockerbie, 10 miles north of Annan, was a substantial town, with lamb sales held annually on Lamb Hill. These sales were great occasions for the whole of Annandale: colourful fairs, with sideshows and noisy, jostling crowds.

Spedlins Tower

Ruined Spedlins Tower, 3 miles north of Lochmaben, was once haunted by a gruesome ghost. In the 17th century the local miller, Porteous, was locked in the dungeon by the laird who then rode off to Edinburgh, forgetting his prisoner. Porteous starved to death, eating his own flesh in an attempt to survive, and his ghost haunted the tower until they confined it to the dungeon by laying a black-letter Cranmer Bible on the cellar steps.

Birrenswark (or Burnswark) has a distinctive outline which can't be missed. It is a steep, flat-topped hill southeast of Lockerbie, visible for miles. This commanding position was the site of a large fort, many centuries BC, with circular huts inside sturdy ramparts. Along came the Romans, besieged the inhabitants and moved in, leaving the present foundations. It is worth the 940ft climb, not just for the view from the top, but for the feeling of ancient history among those ancient ramparts and ditches. In AD 937 the ferocious Battle of Brunanburh took place here between the Saxon English and the united Scots and Norse armies, victory going to the English.

Lochmaben

The history of Lochmaben, west of Lockerbie, goes back to the 12th century when Robert the Bruce's forebears were powerful. It is one of the places claimed as his birthplace – his statue glowers down the main road. Many of the buildings were built with stone from 13th-century **Lochmaben Castle**, whose scant remains are on a promontory signposted down a track south of Castle Loch. The massive, ivy-clad walls and humpy arches, gap-toothed among saplings on a grassy mound with traces of a moat, are the only vestiges of what was once a 16-acre concourse with four moats. It was one of James IV's favourite places in the 16th century, though his preferences were often influenced by female charms available in the area. Mary, Queen of Scots came here with Darnley and it is said she introduced vendace to the lochs – small rare fish, considered a great delicacy; they have to be netted because they won't take bait.

Moffat

Moffat has a wide High Street, dissected by a double avenue of lime trees. The Colvin Fountain, at the end, a cairn of boulders with a huge bronze ram on top, underlines the town's importance as a sheep-farming centre.

In 1633 Rachel Whitford, a bishop's daughter, tasted the water from a spring to the east and recognized the tang as that of sulphur. Within 100 years, peaceful Moffat, deep in its valley among the hills, became one of the most fashionable spas in Europe, attracting the ailing rich from far afield.

It was here in 1759 that James Macpherson produced his first 'Ossianic' Fragments, poems he swore he had 'translated from the Gaelic of Ossian, the son of Fingal'. The authenticity of these poems was hotly debated by Dr Samuel Johnson, among others, and, although many scholars were convinced they were genuinely collected from oral

Tourist Information

Moffat: Churchgate, **t** (01683) 220 620;
www.moffattown.com; open Easter–mid-Oct.

Shopping

Moffat Toffee Shop, Moffat. First-class 'sweetie shop', renowned for its Moffat toffee.

Where to Stay and Eat

Beechwood Country House Hotel, Moffat
t (01683) 220 210 (*expensive–moderate*).
Friendly hotel overlooking the Annan Valley, with good food and wine. It was built as 'an adventure boarding school for young ladies' in Victorian times. *Open Feb–Dec.*

Applegarth House, Lockerbie, **t** (01387) 810 270, *jane@applegarthtown.demon.co.uk* (*moderate*). Former manse overlooking the River Annan, partly dating from 1727. Frank and Jane Pearson run it as a comfortable country house and look after you well. Jane is an excellent cook. Bring your own wine.

Auchen Castle Hotel and Restaurant, Beattock, near Moffat, **t** (01683) 300 407, *www.auchen-castle-hotel.co.uk* (*moderate*). 19th-century baronial mansion with a modern extension in 50 acres with a trout loch. Gracious living, with excellent food. There is also a separate lodge overlooking the trout loch.

Kirkside of Middlebie, Lockerbie, **t** (01576) 300 204 (*moderate*). A former manse, and an idyllic base for a family holiday. Two double rooms and one single, with shared bathroom and drawing room.

Knockhill, Lockerbie, **t** (01576) 300 232 (*moderate*). Delightful house once patronized by Robert Burns. Warm family home with great hospitality, tennis court and croquet.

Moffat House Hotel, Moffat, **t** (01683) 220 039, *www.moffathouse.co.uk* (*moderate*). In an Adam mansion in the town centre in over 2 acres. Very comfortable, with bargain breaks.

The Black Bull Hotel, Churchgate, Moffat, **t** (01683) 220 206, *www.blackbullmoffat. co.uk* (*cheap*). Dates from the 16th century; the oldest part, in the main building, was used by Graham of Claverhouse as his headquarters. Robert Burns was an enthusiastic customer. An interesting menu includes such dishes as 'Moffat Ram Pie' and 'Devil's Beef Tub Pie'. Good value and friendly.

Corehead Farm, Annanwater, Moffat, **t** (01683) 220 182 (*cheap*). Guesthouse on a 2,500-acre hill farm at the base of the Devil's Beef Tub. Marvellous home cooking justifies its Farmhouse Award. Children and pets are positively welcomed – if you have children you could forget them all day among the farm animals. *Open April–Oct.*

Hartfell House, Moffat, **t** (01683) 220 153, *www.freespace.virgin.net/robert.white/* (*cheap*). Listed Victorian manor house overlooking hills. Friendly guesthouse with good dinners by prior arrangement.

tradition, others believed that Macpherson composed them when he was a student. The truth seems immaterial: they are excellent in their own right.

Moffat Museum (*open Easter and Whitsun–Sept Mon, Tues, Thurs–Sat 10.30–1 and 2.30–5, Sun 2.30–5; adm*), in a converted bakery, presents local history, from sheep to spa. The **Moffat Woollen Mill**, at Ladyknowe (*open Mar–Oct daily 9–5.30; Nov–Feb daily 9.30–5*), has weaving demonstrations, a Clan Tartan Centre and a mill shop.

The Devil's Beef Tub, 6 miles north of Moffat off the A701, is a natural corral where cattle thieves hid their stolen beasts. An electric fence borders the edge, but there is a gate. As you peer down the steep grassy walls into the black abyss where swirling mist rises from a stream at the bottom, you can almost hear the thudding hoofs and the harsh calls of the Johnstone men, rounding up their Maxwell neighbours' cattle. Many stories are told: when prisoners from Culloden were being marched up here in 1746, one broke away and rolled down the almost sheer sides and escaped in a thick mist. Walter Scott met this man and used his story in *Redgauntlet*:

It looks as if four hills were laying their heads together to shut out daylight from the dark hollow space between them. A d – d dark black blackguard looking abyss of a hole it is and goes down straight from the roadside as perpendicular as it can do.

This is the watershed between the sources of the Annan and the Tweed – high, wild country, cut off in winter. Covenanters used to seek shelter in these hills, and a memorial grave to one, who was shot opposite, stands on the lip of the Tub.

Grey Mare's Tail

Grey Mare's Tail, one of the highest waterfalls in the country, is 10 miles northeast of Moffat on the A708. The corrie was gouged out by a retreating glacier in the Ice Age. Tail Burn pours in a single cascade, 200ft from Loch Skeen into Moffat Water. The part you see from the road seems to hang motionless in the air but, when you approach, spray fills the air like mist and the sound of water becomes a roar. In winter it can freeze solid and climbers test their skills on it with crampons and ice-axes. The National Trust for Scotland owns the land around the falls – rich in wild flowers and supporting a rare herd of wild goats. There is a 7-mile walk from Birkhill on the A708. You can go just to the foot of the waterfall, or continue up its right side to Loch Skeen, a mist-shrouded loch surrounded by hills. Be cautious walking here; there are precipitous edges and there have been several serious accidents, some fatal. (Sir Walter Scott and his horse fell into a bog-hole round here and had the devil of a job 'to get extricated'.) On the way back to Birkhill, go left up the narrow rocky gorge of Dob' Lin.

Nithsdale

The River Nith rises across the Strathclyde border, rushes through the upper moors fed by many streams and descends at a more leisurely pace into Dumfries and on out into the Solway mud flats. It is hugged by the A76, but try to stick to the back roads where you can. At Newbridge, northwest of Dumfries off the A76, **Twelve Apostles Stone Circle** is Scotland's widest stone circle: the 11 stones are clearly visible from the gate, or are about a 100m walk from the road. Follow the road along the Cairn Water from here to **Routin Brig**, where the river cascades down through the woods in a series of waterfalls.

Six miles north of Dumfries off the A76, **Ellisland Farm** (*open daily 10–4; adm*) is another Robert Burns landmark, recently upgraded into a good museum crammed with memorabilia. Burns took over the farm in 1788, built the house and made his last, abortive attempt to make a living from the soil with new farming methods. Alas, his mind was too absorbed by poetry and the ladies, and it was a dismal failure. He auctioned the stock in 1791 and moved to Dumfries to be an exciseman. He wrote some of his most famous poems here, including 'Tam O' Shanter'. In the granary you can see Burns portrayed as a farmer. There is a walk along the river, said to be where he went for inspiration.

Moniaive, 5 miles to the west on the A702, is an attractive village with brightly painted houses, narrow streets and wynds. The **James Paterson Museum** (*open* *mid-April–Sept Fri–Sun and hols 10–6; Tues–Thurs by appointment, **t** (01848) 200 583)* is on North Street. Paterson was one of the founder members of the Glasgow Boys, an influential group of artists in the late 19th century who eschewed picturesque paintings and favoured ordinary life and realism. The museum has memorabilia, a library, photographs and archive material.

A 10th-century, Anglian cross-shaft 9ft high can be seen at Nith Bridge, half a mile west of **Thornhill** along the A702.

Keir Mill, 3 miles southwest of Thornhill, signposted off the A702, is where the world's first pedal bicycle was built at Courthill Smithy in 1839. Kirkpatrick Macmillan, the inventor, rode his 'Dandy Horse' to Glasgow – where he was fined for 'dangerous behaviour, furious driving and knocking down a girl...' Macmillan, who never bothered to patent his invention, is buried in the churchyard. There is a signed bicycle trail from Keir Mill to Dumfries.

Morton Castle (*always accessible*), 3½ miles north of Thornhill, is a splendid ruin on a tongue of steep, rocky ground washed on three sides by a loch that was artificially formed by a dam across the glen. The approach would have had a deep ditch across it with a drawbridge, to separate the castle from the mainland. Thought to have been built in the first half of the 15th century, on the site of an older castle, Morton has almost no recorded history. Dunegal, the Lord of Nithsdale, is thought to have had a stronghold here in the 12th century.

Drumlanrig Castle

Grounds open mid-April–Sept; castle opening hours
vary to fit in with family arrangements; adm;
t (01848) 330 248; www.drumlanrigcastle.org.uk;
there's a wheelchair lift. Nature trails, adventure play area,
visitor centre, craft centre, working forge, gift shop and tearoom
open all year. You can hire bicycles.

Drumlanrig Castle, about 18 miles northwest of Dumfries off the A76, is a pink sandstone Renaissance palace on a grassy dais beside the Nith among the Lowther Hills. Owned by the Duke of Buccleuch, this pile, with its mass of turrets and windows, was built in 1689 for his ancestor, the first Duke of Queensberry. The Duke moved in, spent one night, didn't like it and moved out, having virtually ruined himself paying for this folly. When the fourth Duke, the notorious 'Old Q', inherited the castle in 1778, he sold the beautiful avenue of lime trees to help pay his gambling debts. There are state rooms panelled with carved oak, French furniture, paintings by Leonardo da Vinci, Rembrandt, Holbein, Murillo, Ruysdael and Rowlandson, and portraits by Kneller, Reynolds and Ramsay.

Durisdeer

At Durisdeer, a hamlet tucked away at the entrance to the Dalveen Pass less than 5 miles to the northeast of Drumlanrig, off the A702, don't miss the delightfully 'Baroque-Arcadian' Queensberry Aisle in the 17th-century church (*key from the cottage*

Sports and Activities

There are several **open farms** in this area, demonstrating farming methods both modern and extinct. One is **The Barony**, 8 miles northeast of Dumfries off the A701, which includes farm walks with a woodland bird hide, a fishery and nature reserve.

Where to Stay and Eat

Blackaddie House Hotel, Sanquhar, t (01659) 50270 (*moderate*). 16th-century farmhouse specialising in organic food.
Buccleuch and Queensberry Hotel, Thornhill, t (01848) 330 215, *www.buccleuchhotel.co.uk*

(*moderate*). Built in 1856 as a coaching inn in the middle of the village. Friendly service. A good base for fishermen.
George Hotel, Thornhill, t (01848) 330 326 (*moderate*). An old coaching inn in the middle of the village, cosy and welcoming.
Trigony House Hotel, Closeburn, Thornhill, t (01848) 331 211, *www.trigonyhotel.co.uk* (*moderate*). Cosy, family-run Edwardian country house in secluded grounds with good food. Salmon and sea trout fishing can be arranged.
Woodlea Hotel, Moniaive, t (01848) 200 209, *www.woodleahotel.co.uk* (*moderate*). Good for family holidays, with an indoor swimming pool, tennis, play area, clays, golf and pony riding.

nearby). This mausoleum contains a white marble monument, designed by Van Nost, in memory of the second Duke and Duchess of Queensberry who died in 1711 and 1709 respectively. Surrounded by twisted columns, garlands and cherubs, the duchess lies supine, with her husband propped on an elbow beside her, like lovers in a pastoral tryst. Above the romantic-looking couple there is a scroll, extolling their virtues: it doesn't mention their heir, Lord Drumlanrig, who, in 1707, murdered and tried to eat a spit-boy, in Queensberry House, Edinburgh. There are 29 lead coffins in the vault containing dead Douglases.

The A702 continues north through the dramatic scenery of the **Dalveen Pass**, towards the A74, and can be linked with a visit to Wanlockhead.

Wanlockhead

Wanlockhead is the highest village in Scotland, 1,380ft up in the moors, off the A76 on the B797, which climbs a narrow valley beside Mennock Water, through unreal-looking, mottled green and brown hills. The village is a wedge-shaped cluster of houses built on turf mounds, in a bowl of moorland.

The **Museum of Lead Mining** (*open April–Oct daily 11–4.30; Nov–Mar for groups by arrangement; adm; t (01659) 74387; www.leadminingmuseum.co.uk*) has been revamped and is now an excellent museum with a new visitor centre and a good restaurant. If you don't suffer from claustrophobia, part of the tour takes you into the Loch Nell Mine. There are well-reconstructed miners' cottages, mining artefacts and a beam-pumping engine. Gold was once panned from the streams here; a piece weighing 4 to 5 oz is in the British Museum, and you can have a go yourself. The heather-covered moorland was a haunt of Covenanters. They held their illegal Conventicles up here during the Killing Times in the 17th century, with lookouts on guard on surrounding peaks to warn of approaching soldiers.

The **Southern Upland Way** passes through Wanlockhead, one of its more lonely stretches with panoramic views. (For Leadhills, Scotland's second-highest village, just a short distance on up the road across the regional boundary, *see p.250*.)

Sanquhar

A small town about 27 miles up the A76 from Dumfries, Sanquhar's chief interest is historic. Two Covenanters' declarations were pinned to the mercat cross: the first, by Richard Cameron in 1680, the second, by James Renwick in 1685, both protesting against the Episcopalian leanings of Charles II during the Killing Times. An obelisk marks the site of the cross. Richard Cameron was killed, but his followers were granted an amnesty by William III, and it was from them that the regiment of the Cameronians was founded – now disbanded. Renwick was also killed, and there is a memorial to him near Moniaive. There is a Sanquhar Town Trail, with a map and plaques marking places of historic interest.

The **Sanquhar Tolbooth Museum** (*open April–Sept Tues–Sat 10–1 and 2–5, Sun 2–5*) is in the building designed by William Adam in 1735, with clock tower and double external steps. It has displays of Sanquhar knitting, mines and miners, local literature, the jail, archaeology and social history. Post a letter in the **Sanquhar Post Office** – the oldest in Britain, founded in 1712, many years before the introduction of the mailcoach service, and still in use. The 19th-century **Sanquhar Church** (*call t (01659) 50596, to get the key*) has historic displays, including medieval artefacts.

The **Admirable Crichton**, 16th-century genius and child prodigy, was born at Elicock Castle, 2 miles to the south. He was killed in a brawl in Mantua when he was 22.

The Glenkens and Galloway Forest Park

Bordering the eastern flank of the Rhinns of Kells and the Galloway Forest Park, the Glenkens is a string of rivers and lochs, descending through windswept moorland to Loch Ken, which narrows to become the River Dee, flowing into the Solway Firth at Kirkcudbright. Loch Ken offers fishing, bird-watching and water sports.

Castle Douglas

Nine miles northeast of Kirkcudbright, Castle Douglas' history goes back to when Iron Age builders created two crannogs on Carlingwark Loch below the town. These islets, built on wooden platforms submerged in shallow water, provided protection for the inhabitants of the huts on top. Horseshoes, excavated from the shore of the loch, which the Civic Park now covers, are thought to originate from a shoeing-forge that served the horses of Edward I's army when he was hammering the Scots. The town was once the village of Carlingwark, changing its name in honour of a pedlar, William Douglas, who made his fortune in Virginia and returned to his homeland in 1789, buying up the village and developing it into a prosperous cattle market.

Threave Castle (*open April–Sept daily 9.30–6.30; adm; ring bell for custodian to ferry you across; t (01316) 688 800*), 1½ miles west of Castle Douglas on an island in the Dee, was a Black Douglas stronghold dating from the 14th century. It was the last of their fortresses to surrender to James II in 1455 during his struggle to throw off their powerful grip on his kingdom. James won his victory with the help of Mons Meg, that mighty cannon now in Edinburgh. The 70ft tower had five storeys, each with a single

Tourist Information

Castle Douglas: Markethill, **t** (01556) 502 611; *open Easter to mid-Oct.*

Where to Stay and Eat

Castle Douglas **t** (01556–)
Chipperkyle, Kirkpatrick Durham, **t** 650 223, *dickson@chipperkyle.freeserve.co.uk* (*moderate*). Very nice Georgian B&B with dinner on request. Attractive rooms and family atmosphere.
The Crown Hotel, **t** 502 031, *www.thecrownhotel.co.uk* (*moderate*). Comfortable 19th-century coaching house. Winter breaks available.
Douglas Arms Hotel, **t** 502 231, *doughot@aol.com* (*moderate*). Also serves reasonable food.
Imperial Hotel, **t** 502 086, *www.the-golfhotel.co.uk* (*moderate*). A golfers' hotel, with itineraries organised by the golfing

proprietor. Pool room and bargain breaks available. Reasonable food.
Longacre Manor, **t** 503 576, *ball.longacre@btinternet.com* (*moderate*). Delightful country house with oak panelling, antiques and cordon bleu food. Specialises in family house parties (4 double rooms).
Urr Valley Country House Hotel, **t** 502 188, *www.urrvalleyhotel.co.uk* (*moderate*). In 14 acres, with good food.

New Galloway **t** (01644–)
Cross Keys Hotel, **t** 420 494 (*moderate*). 18th-century hotel, with an 'olde worlde bar'.
Ken Bridge Hotel, **t** 420 211 (*moderate*). Georgian coaching house on the river bank (and the main road), with free fishing.
Kenmure Arms Hotel, **t** 420 240 (*moderate*). Has recently been refurbished, and has good bar meals.
Leamington Hotel, High Street, **t** 420 327, *www.leamington-hotel.com* (*moderate*). Offers sporting packages.

room linked by a spiral stair, surrounded by a curtain wall and four drum towers. The stone projecting above the doorway was 'The Gallows Knob', and Archibald the Grim, the aptly named 14th-century Earl of Douglas, boasted that it 'never lacked a tassel'. Covenanters stormed the castle in 1640 and demolished the interior.

The National Trust for Scotland's **Threave Gardens** (*open all year daily 9.30–sunset, walled garden and glasshouses 9.30–5; visitor centre open April–Oct daily 9.30–5.30; adm*), a mile south of the castle, provide a school of practical gardening. Students get a two-year training in skills that might once have been learnt at the knee of that almost extinct breed, the head gardener. They live in the Victorian house in the grounds, and between them and their instructors maintain a garden that is a joy to walk in. There is a visitor centre, exhibitions, a shop and a licensed restaurant. The **Threave Wildfowl Refuge** (*access limited in the breeding season; adm*) has many species of wild geese and ducks.

New Galloway

Although it was only a village, New Galloway, 18 miles north of Kirkcudbright, was created a Royal Burgh in 1633, the smallest in Scotland, so that the Gordon Laird of nearby Kenmure Castle (private) could have easy access to a market. It is an attractive place, its steep main street flanked by freshly painted stone cottages. Surrounded by moorland and forest, the landscape was transformed in 1929 by Scotland's first hydroelectric development, with reservoirs where rivers and burns once ran.

Dalry is a well-kept village a couple of miles north of New Galloway. In **Carsphairn**, 10 miles to the north, there is a heritage centre (*open June–Sept Mon, Tues, Thurs–Sat, 10.30–5, Sun 2–5; mid-April–May weekends only*) with exhibitions on local history.

Kenmure Castle is off the A762, just south of New Galloway, a shell on a hill, topped by tall chimneys, visible through trees and accessible only on foot. With 15th-century origins, this ruin is cloaked in history. The owners, staunchly Jacobite Gordons of Lochinvar, welcomed Mary, Queen of Scots during her state tour in 1563, and later sheltered her when she was escaping to England, providing her with the disguise she was wearing when she arrived at Dundrennan.

Lochinvar

If you had to learn 'Young Lochinvar' in your youth, you might feel compensatory delight in finding traces of Lochinvar's birthplace – bringing reality to what may have seemed legend. Go 3 miles northeast of Dalry, off the A702 and along a track to the left. When, in Scott's 'Marmion', brave Lochinvar came out of the west to rescue fair Ellen from having to marry a 'laggard in love and a dastard in war', it could have been from the fragment of castle on the islet that he set out.

Galloway Forest Park

Formerly Glen Trool Forest, the Galloway Forest Park, owned by the Forestry Commission, covers 250 square miles. There are many walks in lovely scenery, with wildlife that includes roe deer, red deer and wild goats. Moorland, peat bog, hills, lochs and fast-flowing rivers and burns, dominated by the great bulk of Merrick, 2,765ft high, make a visit here unforgettable. In autumn the range of colour is staggering. Guide books, sold locally, give details of the many walks as well as campsites, picnic areas and special view points. **Queensway** is the scenic drive between New Galloway and Newton Stewart on the A712, with diverting attractions along the way.

Clatteringshaws Loch

One of these attractions is Clatteringshaws Loch, about 5 miles west of New Galloway. Here, the **Clatteringshaws Forest Wildlife Centre** (*open April–Sept daily 10–5; Oct daily 10.30–4.30; car park £1*) provides information about deer and other wildlife in the area, along with geology and history. There is a **Red Deer Range** (*open late June–mid-Sept Tues and Thurs 11 and 2, Sun 2.30; adm; t (07771) 748 401*). **Bruce's Stone** in the Forest Park commemorates Bruce's victory over the English at the Battle of Rapploch Moss in 1307. It is reached either by following the National Trust for Scotland signs up into the moor northwest from Clatteringshaws Loch – quite a long haul – or from the A714, through Glentrool village. Another **Bruce's Stone** is a massive engraved boulder overlooking Loch Trool, marking the site where Robert the Bruce defeated the English in 1307 by rolling boulders down on them. If the stones were anything like this, you can see why. This particular stone is where Bruce is said to have leant after the battle.

Edinburgh

10

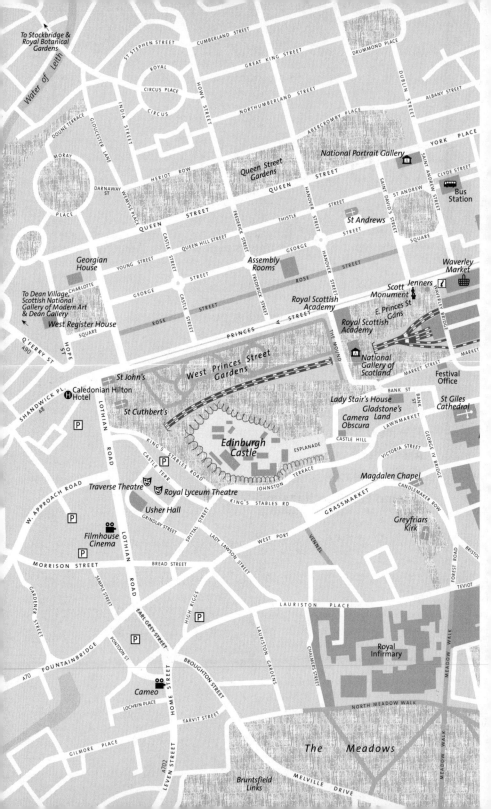

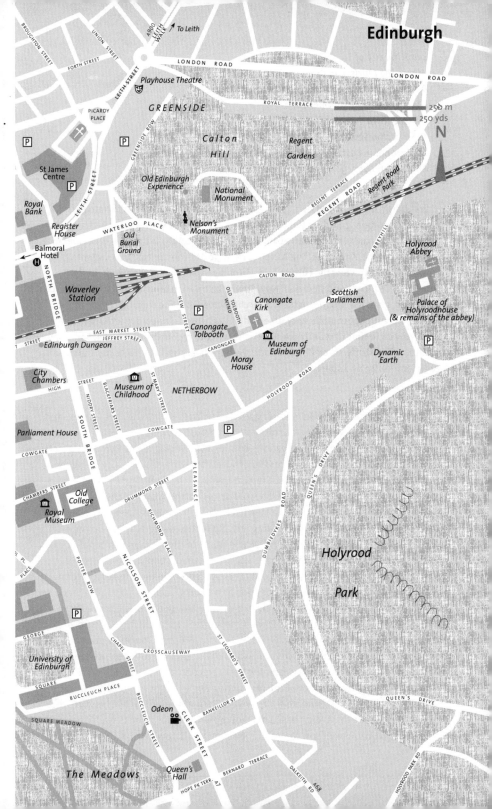

Edinburgh

To Leith

A900 LEITH WALK

LONDON ROAD

LONDON ROAD

UNION STREET

BROUGHTON STREET

FORTH STREET

Playhouse Theatre

ROYAL TERRACE

PICARDY PLACE

LEITH STREET

GREENSIDE

Calton Hill

Regent Gardens

REGENT TERRACE

250 m

250 yds

N

St James Centre

Old Edinburgh Experience

National Monument

Nelson's Monument

REGENT TERRACE

REGENT ROAD

Regent Road Park

Royal Bank

Register House

Balmoral Hotel

WATERLOO PLACE

Old Burial Ground

ABBEYHILL

Holyrood Abbey

NORTH BRIDGE

Waverley Station

CALTON ROAD

NEW STREET

OLD TOLBOOTH WYND

Canongate Kirk

Scottish Parliament

Palace of Holyroodhouse (& remains of the abbey)

EAST MARKET STREET

JEFFREY STREET

Canongate Tolbooth

CANONGATE

Museum of Edinburgh

Dynamic Earth

Edinburgh Dungeon

Moray House

HOLYROOD ROAD

City Chambers

HIGH STREET

Museum of Childhood

NETHERBOW

ST MARY'S STREET

BLACKFRIARS STREET

NIDDRY STREET

SOUTH BRIDGE

Parliament House

COWGATE

COWGATE

CHAMBERS STREET

Old College

Royal Museum

DRUMMOND STREET

RICHMOND PLACE

PLEASANCE

DUMBIEDYKES ROAD

QUEEN'S DRIVE

Holyrood Park

POTTER ROW

NICOLSON STREET

GEORGE SQUARE

CHAPEL STREET

CROSSCAUSEWAY

ST LEONARD'S STREET

University of Edinburgh

BUCCLEUCH PLACE

SQUARE MEADOW

BUCCLEUCH STREET

Odeon

CLERK STREET

RANKEILLOR ST

QUEEN'S DRIVE

The Meadows

Queen's Hall

HOPE PK TERR. A7

BERNARD TERRACE

DALKEITH RD A68

HOLYROOD PARK RD

Beautiful city of Edinburgh!
Where the tourist can drown his sorrow
By viewing your monuments and statues fine
During the lovely summer-time.
I'm sure it will his spirits cheer
As Sir Walter Scott's monument he draws near,
That stands in East Prince's Street
Amongst flowery gardens, fine and neat...
                    William McGonagall

Edinburgh is dominated by a castle built high on a craggy ridge. Its strategic, elevated position, guarding the route to the north, with the river at its feet and easy access to the south, made it an obvious choice for a capital in the days when defence was paramount. Known as 'The Athens of the North', the capital has a violent, romantic history, versatile culture and a proud people. The juxtaposition of its medieval Old Town and Georgian New Town, facing each other across what used to be a loch, gives it a unique architectural character. Once the cultural capital of the north, a century of complacency lulled Edinburgh into a dangerous lethargy. Recently, Glasgow stole that title and Edinburgh is striving to regain its reputation. Some say Edinburgh is 'stuffy, stuck-up, pompous'. Perhaps it is: but it is a lively city, bursting with enterprise and spirit.

History

The unwritten history of Edinburgh goes back to ancient British tribes who existed in clusters of wooden huts on the rocky slopes of the Castle crag, choosing the windy heights for greater security. Excavations on the Castle Rock revealed Roman artefacts dating from the first centuries after Christ, when the Romans were busy trying to conquer Britain. They built a fort at Cramond, west of the town, and a naval harbour from which the Emperor Severus embarked on his northern campaigns.

When the Angles of Northumbria invaded Lothian in the Dark Ages, they built a fortress on the rock, Din Eidyn, meaning literally 'Fortress-on-a-hill'. This became Edwin's Burgh and more excavation revealed traces of their occupation. Small communities settled around the Castle walls, tradesmen supplying the needs of those in the garrison, but it was not until the 11th century, in the reign of Malcolm Canmore, that Edinburgh began to develop as a town. Queen Margaret persuaded her husband to move into the Castle, and from then on building flourished.

Queen Margaret's youngest son, David I, moved the capital to Edinburgh from Dunfermline in 1124, founding Holyrood Abbey in 1128. Robert the Bruce granted the town a Royal Charter in 1329. A city wall was built in 1436. The 16th century saw the building of a palace at Holyrood, and the hasty erection of the Flodden Wall, in 1513, to stem the anticipated advance of the conquering English. Shortly after, the city suffered a dreadful battering from Henry VIII's 'Rough Wooing'. Mary, Queen of Scots spent most of her short reign based in Edinburgh, riding out from its walls on frequent excursions. Her son, James VI, moved his court down to London in 1603.

Tourist Information

Edinburgh t (0131–)
**Edinburgh and Lothians Tourist Information
Centre**, 3 Princes Street, **t** 473 3800,
www.edinburgh.org.
Tourist Desk, Edinburgh Airport, **t** 333 2167.
Edinburgh International Festival Box Office,
The Hub, 348 Castle Hill, **t** 473 2000,
www.eif.co.uk.
Fringe Office and Society, 180 High Street,
t 226 5257, *www.edfringe.com*.
Tattoo Office, 32 Market Street, **t** 225 1188,
www.edintattoo.co.uk.
www.cac.org.uk is the official website for
Edinburgh's museums and galleries.

Getting There

By Air

A frequent service operates between
Edinburgh and London and Europe. Special
offers are frequently available. Booking on-line
usually offers large discounts and last-minute
deals. *See* 'Getting There', p.72.

By Train

Waverley Station, in the middle of the city, is
linked by frequent inter-city trains to London
King's Cross in as little as 4 hours, as well as all
other main towns and cities in Britain. There is
a range of tickets which vary depending on
when you travel. *See* 'Getting Around', p.74.

By Coach

A number of coach companies operate
between Edinburgh and London, taking about
6 hours, with an hour's stop on the way. This is
the cheapest way to travel and not uncomfortable. *See* 'Getting Around', p.73.

Getting Around

Edinburgh t (0131–)
Edinburgh is notorious for its abundance of
traffic wardens, and feet are unquestionably
the best form of transport in the compact city
centre. There are plenty of **taxi-cabs** (at the
end of the journey, pay the driver from inside
the vehicle) and a good public **bus service**,
with buses to all areas, and maps displayed so
you can plot your route. There are also several
conducted **tours**, *see* below – an excellent way
to orientate yourself before a more detailed
exploration. The **walking tours** of the city are
better than you might expect.

Tours

Arkon Awaydays, 2 Braehead Loan, **t** 476
4210/2138. Special tours for couples or small
groups.
Celtic Trails, 299b Gilmerton Road, **t** 664 1980,
www.celtictrails.co.uk. Day tours from
Edinburgh to Celtic and prehistoric sites.
Dunedin Guided Tours, 195 Pleasance, **t** 662
9497, *www.visitweb.com/dunedin*. Half- and
full-day tours of city and environs.
Edinburgh Tour – City Sightseeing, Waverley
Bridge, **t** 555 6363, *www.edinburghtour.com*.
Open-top bus tours of the city, with all-day
open ticket so you can get on and off as
much as you like. Bus departs every 15mins
from Waverley Bridge.
Guide Friday, 133–5 Canongate, **t** 556 2244,
www.hoponhopoff.com. Same as above.
Mac Tours, Waverley Bridge, **t** 220 0770.
Vintage open-top bus from Waverley Bridge.
**The McEwan's 80/- Edinburgh Literary Pub
Tour**, **t** 226 6665/7, *www.scot-lit-tour.co.uk*.
Call for details.
Ossian Archaeology Tours, Flat 2/1 335 Easter
Road, **t** 553 7574, *www.ossian.fsnet.co.uk*.
Ancient monuments in the Lothians.
Rent A Local, 15a India Street, **t** 538 8341,
www.rentalocal.net. Guides for walks, drives
and cycling in the city and all over Scotland.
Volcano Tours, Geowalks, 23 Summerfield Pl,
t 555 5488, *www.geowalks.demon.co.uk*.
400 million years of geological history.
Walkabout Scotland, 2 Rossie Place, **t** 661 7168,
www.walkaboutscotland.com. Guided daily
hill walking tours from Edinburgh.

Spooky Walking Tours

Auld Reekie Tours, 45 Niddry Street, **t** 557 4700,
www.auldreekietours.co.uk. Tours of the
underground city, a haunted vault, a pagan
temple, a medieval torture exhibition...
Black Hart Storytellers and Walking Tours,
t 447 2230, *www.blackhart.uk.com*. Tours of
the Old Town featuring a graveyard and a
poltergeist.

The Cadies – Witchery Tours, 352 Castlehill,
t 225 6745, *www.witcherytours.com*. Plague
and disaster. Light-hearted spookery.
Mercat Walking Tours, Niddry Street South,
t 557 6464, *www.mercattours.com*. History
and vaults.

Festivals

April: Edinburgh International Science Festival.
End May–beginning June: Scottish
International Children's Festival.
August–September: Edinburgh Festival,
featuring the International Festival, the
Fringe, the Military Tattoo, the International
Film Festival, the Book Festival and the
International Jazz and Blues Festival,
see p.160.
New Year's Eve: Hogmanay.

Shopping

Princes Street and the rather more up-
market George Street, with lots of new
designer shops and trendy café-bars, are the
main shopping areas in the city centre.
Jenners, in Princes Street, is the 'Harrods' of
Edinburgh: if you can't get what you want
anywhere else they usually have it. Coming
soon is Harvey Nichols in St Andrew Square
(due to open Autumn 2002). There are any
number of tweed, tartan and wool shops.
Rose Street and its lanes – running parallel
to Princes Street and George Street – are lively,
buzzing with bars, restaurants, hot-food take-
aways and boutiques. Rose Street used to be
the 'red light' district and had more pubs than
any other street in Britain. Many of the shops
sell gimmicky knick-knacks and craft work.
The St James Centre, at the east end of
Princes Street, is an ugly but useful indoor
shopping complex. Princes Mall, above
Waverley Station, is attractive, with lots of
specialist shops and representatives of larger
stores located elsewhere.
There are plenty of gift shops for tartans,
woollens, whisky, etc. in and just off the Royal
Mile, as well as antique shops, bars and
restaurants.
The Grassmarket and the area around it is
good shopping territory: there are second-

hand bookshops and several antique shops.
There are also clothes and accessory shops,
gift shops and smart interior decorating
shops. The Grassmarket is also renowned for
its good eating and drinking places. Victoria
Street has an excellent cheesemonger and
antique, clothes and bric-a-brac shops.
St Stephen Street, at the bottom of
Northwest Circus Place, is lined with antique
and junk shops. Some are smart and expensive, some a delightful clutter of cast-offs –
clothes, boxes of old 78-rpm records, glass jars
full of buttons, stuffed birds.
Stockbridge, down by the Water of Leith on
the edge of the New Town, has a village
community atmosphere and several good
shops, particularly for food, and restaurants.
Les Cadeaux, 121 George Street. Good range of
china, crystal and gifts. Tax-free mailing
service to the USA.
Hamilton and Inches, 87 George Street. Old-
established shop selling antique and
modern silver and jewellery, Highland accessories, watches, clocks, crystal and china.
Droopy and Brown, 37–39 Frederick Street.
Have a reputation for their own design of
clothes.
Galloways, St Stephen Street. Antique shop
that also does high-class interior decoration.
Herbys, 66 Raeburn Place, Stockbridge.
Licensed delicatessen and take-away with
everything anyone could want for an
impromptu picnic: mouth watering cheeses,
pâtés, cold-cuts, home-made bread, etc.

Where to Stay

Edinburgh t (0131–)
The choice is enormous and you should
consult the Edinburgh and Scotland
Information Centre, t 473 3800, *www.
edinburgh.org(accommodation)*. Book well
ahead during the summer and especially
during the Festival and at New Year.

Expensive
The Balmoral, at the east end of Princes Street,
t 556 2414, *www.rfhotels.com*. Better known
to many as the North British Hotel, from the
days when it was the doyen of Edinburgh's
hotels, the stage for elegant balls and smart

receptions attended by Scotland's aristocracy. It suffered a grim decline but a facelift a few years ago restored it to the top rank.

The Bonham, 35 Drumsheugh Gardens, t 226 6050, *reserve@thebonham.com*. Ultra-contemporary interior design, blending with Victorian features. Very luxurious.

Bruntsfield Hotel, 69 Bruntsfield Place, t 229 1393, *www.thebruntsfield.co.uk*. Victorian town house overlooking Bruntsfield Links.

Caledonian Hilton Hotel, at the west end of Princes Street, t 459 9988, *ednchirm@hilton.com*. Has a long-established reputation for comfort and impeccable standards; there are several bars and restaurants, including the elegant Pompadour Restaurant.

Channings, S. Learmonth Gardens, t 315 2226, *reserve@channings.co.uk*. Tasteful and well run, with less of the city-centre bustle.

Edinburgh Sheraton Grand, on Lothian Road, t 229 9131, *www.sheraton.com*. Recently refurbished. Looking down on fountains and a paved garden in Festival Square, at the heart of Edinburgh's new financial district, it is well up to the standard of all Sheraton hotels. It is launching a new state-of-the-art health spa: 6 storeys of pure self-indulgence.

The George Inter-Continental Hotel, at the east end of George Street, t 225 1251, *edinburgh@interconti.com*. Has long been one of Edinburgh's top traditional hotels.

Holiday Inn Crowne Plaza, 80 High Street, t 557 9797, *www.crowneplazaed.co.uk*. Built as a mock medieval tower amidst some controversy. It is very comfortable.

The Howard, 32–36 Great King Street, t 557 3500, *www.thehoward.com*. A completely refurbished hotel in the Georgian New Town which has been voted the Most Excellent City Hotel in Great Britain and Ireland.

Prestonfield House Hotel, Priestfield Rd, t 668 3346, *prestonfield_house@compuserve.com*. A unique 17th-century country house in lovely grounds. Go for one of the five rooms in the main building, which have a delightful quirky charm, are not too expensive and all have en-suite facilities. Also *see* 'Eating Out', below.

Royal Terrace, 18 Royal Terrace, t 557 3222, *reservations&royalterrace@principalhotels.co.uk*.

Central Georgian town house with sports facilities.

Scotsman Hotel, North Bridge, t 557 0584. Brand new luxury hotel with health club.

Moderate

17 Abercrombie Place, t 557 8036, *www.abercrombyhouse.com*. The former home of the Georgian architect William Playfair, now a Wolsey Lodge run by its advocate/barrister owner as a very comfortable family home overlooking large private gardens. Extremely reasonable. No smoking.

Albany Hotel, 39–43 Albany Street, t 556 0397, *www.albanyhoteledinburgh.co.uk*. Classical town house near the centre.

Braid Hills Hotel, 134 Braid Road, t 447 8888, *bookings@braidhillshotel.co.uk*. A Gothic building with good views of the Castle and surrounding countryside, golf and tennis.

The Carlton Hotel, North Bridge, t 472 3000, *carlton@paramount-hotels.co.uk*. A turreted baronial pile, very much at the hub of the city, with a sports and leisure centre underneath and very un-baronial decor inside.

Ellersly Country House Hotel, 4 Ellersly Road, t 313 2543. An Edwardian house in a walled garden with excellent food.

Holyrood Hotel, Holyrood Road, t 550 4500, *info@holyrood.macdonald-hotels.co.uk*. Fairly newly opened, with impressive leisure facilities.

Melvin House Hotel, 3 Rothesay Terrace, t 225 5084, *reservations@melvinhouse.demon.co.uk*. Elegant Victorian house in city centre, with grand public rooms.

The Point, 34 Bread Street, t 221 5555, *www.point-hotel.co.uk*. Stylish modern designer hotel, near the Castle.

Thistle Hotel, 59 Manor Place, t 225 6144. A friendly establishment in the West End, not far from the centre.

Cheap

The Addison Hotel, 2 Murrayfield Avenue, t 337 4060, *booking@addisonhotel.freeserve.co.uk*. Victorian house in quiet avenue only minutes from the centre.

The Bridge Inn, Ratho, t 333 1320/333 1251. Near the airport. Excellent value, built in 1750 to serve travellers on the Union Canal – the current landlord was instrumental in getting the canal reopened in 1970s. Excellent hearty meals, casseroles, roasts and haggis – all very jolly.

Herald House Hotel, 70 Grove Street, **t** 228 2323, *www.heraldhousehotel.co.uk*. Convenient for Princes Street and the Royal Mile.

Maitland Hotel, 33 Shandwick Place, **t** 229 1467. A Georgian house in the West End, once owned by the Earl of Maitland. It offers a variety of package holidays which include dinner, B&B, and tours of the city.

Osbourne Hotel, 53/9 York Place, **t** 556 5577, *reservations@osbourne-hotel.com*. A comfortable town-house hotel within a few minutes' walk of Princes Street.

Simpsons, 79 Lauriston Place, **t** 622 7979, *www.simpsons-hotel.com*. Quiet and comfortable hotel with good disabled facilities.

B&Bs

A and S Hamilton, 16 Lynedoch Place, **t** 225 5507, *susie.lynedoch@btinternet.com*. Attractive Georgian house near the city centre. Great hospitality.

E and H Clouston, 41 Heriot Row, **t** 225 3113. Prime address in the New Town.

Gillian Charlton-Meyrick, 2 Fingal Place, The Meadows, **t** 667 4436, *bleish1936@aol.com*. Friendly hostess and nice atmosphere.

Hillcroft, 2 Riselaw Rd, **t** 447 2825, *hillcroft@zoom.co.uk*. Without doubt, one of the nicest B&Bs in town. Mike and Anne White will help to make your stay memorable and you will leave their comfortable house with regret, having added their names to your address book, as friends.

Sarah Nicholson, 44 Inverleith Row, **t** 552 8595, *inverleithbandb@yahoo.com*. Nice friendly atmosphere.

Serviced Apartments

Glenfinlas Street, 10 Glenfinlas Street, **t** 225 8695, *www.edinburgh-holidays.com*. Ground floor of an A-listed Georgian town house.

Holyrood Aparthotel, 1 Netherbakehouse, Holyrood, **t** 524 3200, *www.holyroodaparthotel.com*. Luxury 2-bedroom apartments.

Eating Out

There are masses of restaurants, cafés and wine bars, tucked away down steps, in narrow wynds and courtyards or on the main streets, where you can eat very well and with tremendous variety. It is said that there are more restaurants per head of population in Edinburgh than in any other city in Britain. When the sun shines you can even sit at tables in the street. The following are a few suggestions – and it is always wise to book.

A useful website for eating and drinking is *www.list.co.uk*.

Expensive

'36', in the Howard Hotel, **t** 557 3500. Basement restaurant in splendid contrast to the rather conventional ambience above, with a contemporary, minimalist atmosphere. Classical Scottish dishes are served in its original Georgian dining room: try the kipper and whisky mousse, poacher's broth, and flummery Drambuie.

The Atrium, in the Traverse Theatre, Cambridge Street, **t** 228 8882. Excellent food. Upstairs is **Blue** (*see* below).

Chambertin, in the George Hotel, **t** 225 1251. Smart restaurant.

Keepers Restaurant, 13b Dundas Street, **t** 556 5707. Provides candlelit pre-theatre dinners in a friendly 'bistro' atmosphere.

Lemongrass Bar and Brasserie, 56 St Mary Street, **t** 556 5888. Elegant, stylish restaurant serving the best Scottish produce, imaginatively and skilfully Frenchified. Try the terrine of venison.

Merchants Restaurant, Merchant Street, **t** 225 4009. Small with a friendly atmosphere, in a converted tartan warehouse.

Number One Princes Street, in the Balmoral Hotel, **t** 556 2414. Smart and cosmopolitan atmosphere.

Pompadour Restaurant, in the Caledonian Hotel, **t** 225 2433. Decorated in the style of Louis XV's famous mistress, Mme de Pompadour, this restaurant commemorates Scotland's Auld Alliance with France. Somehow, the Pompadour embodies Edinburgh's golden age, with subtle colours and delicate murals to soothe the digestion;

its bar overlooks the Castle. Jacket and tie required. Music while you eat.

Prestonfield House, Priestfield Road, t 668 3346. A 17th-century house in attractive grounds, where peacocks strut and Highland cattle graze. Excellent food in a country-house atmosphere. You can also stay here (*see* above).

The Tower, in the Museum of Scotland, Chambers Street, t 225 3003. Rooftop restaurant in the corner tower – great views. Emphasis on good Scottish food.

The Witchery, 352 Castlehill, t 225 5613. Not for the timid, The Witchery's eerie decor emphasizes its original purpose as a haunt for witches – but it does serve good food. For those who like organized spookery, walking tours set out from here at various times, with costumed guides and simulated ghoulery. There are two rooms and an apartment upstairs; an unusual place to stay.

Moderate

Black Bo's, 57–61 Blackfriars Street, just off the Royal Mile, t 557 6136. Unpretentious and imaginative, with good vegetarian food.

Café Royal Oyster Bar, 17a West Register Street, t 556 4124. If you saw the film *Chariots of Fire*, you will recognize this 1830s restaurant with its dark gleaming wood and reflecting glass.

City Café, 19 Blair Street, t 220 0125. Trendy US-style soda bar. Stark but stylish.

Creelers, 3 Hunter Square, Royal Mile, t 220 4447. Very good seafood bistro and restaurant. Scottish paintings on the walls.

The Doric, 15 Market Street, t 225 1084. Upstairs bistro opposite the Fruitmarket Gallery. Good bistro food.

Duck's, at Le Marché Noir, Eyre Place, t 558 1608. Malcolm Duck is the proprietor, serving splendid French provincial food and atmosphere: nouvelle cuisine, but not precious. Excellent set menus, limited à la carte.

Favorit, 20 Teviot Place, t 220 6880, and 30 Leven Street, t (0131) 221 1800. Meals served from 8am–3am.

Hadrian's, 2 North Bridge, t 557 5000. Attached to the Balmoral Hotel, this restaurant has the advantage of the services of Martin Wishart, an international chef with a special interest in Scottish food served as it should be, with no pretensions.

Igg's, 15 Jeffrey Street, t 557 8184. First-class Mediterranean food, with an all-day tapas bar.

Kalpna, 2–3 St Patrick's Square, t 667 9890. Excellent vegetarian Indian food.

Le Sept, Old Fishmarket Close, t 225 5428. Cheerful bistro serving good-value French food.

Martin's Restaurant, 72 Rose Street North Lane, t 225 3106. Personally run, intimate, and aptly described as 'a country restaurant in the city', this is among the best in Edinburgh and serves first-class food. No smoking in the dining room, and a cheese board that defies description for freshness and imagination; Martin will give the history of each cheese. Highly recommended.

Negociants, 45 Lothian Street, t 225 6313. Predominantly Far Eastern menu.

Patisserie Florentin, 8–10 Giles Street, t 225 6267. Serves the best croissants in town.

Tinelli Ristorante, 139 Easter Road (opposite the entrance to Hibernian FC's stadium), t 652 1932. Straight out of Italy. Highly recommended for food, bistro décor, service and atmosphere. Follow the advice of Paolo when choosing from the menu.

Cheap

The Apartment, 7 Barclay Place, t 228 6456. Good cheap meals near the Kings Theatre.

Bannermans, 55 Niddry Street, off Cowgate, t 556 3254. Built in the 1770s as a shellfish warehouse, then a dwelling, and later a tavern called 'The Bucket of Blood', Bannermans has managed to retain its original pub atmosphere, with plenty of bare, wooden surfaces: you almost expect to see rushes on the floor. It has traditional Scottish folk music, live, on Sundays, Tuesdays and Wednesdays, and serves excellent soup and homely food. Highly recommended for its lively atmosphere.

Blue, Cambridge Street, t 221 1222. Upstairs from the Atrium (*see* above) in the Traverse Theatre. Informal, lively and good.

Bouzy Rouge, 1 Alva Street, t 225 9594. Very good bistro food.

Café Hub, Castlehill, t 473 2067. The café in the Festival Centre, in a former church. Terrace.

Chez Jules, 1 Craigs Close, 29 Cockburn Street, t 225 7983; 61 Frederick Street, t 225 7983. Excellent value and very French.

The Elephant House, 21 George IV Bridge, t 220 5355. Good quality snacks and light meals among 600 elephants.

Engine Shed Café, 19 St Leonards Lane, t 662 0040. Popular students' lunch spot with a friendly atmosphere and home-cooked food.

Ferri's Restaurant, 1 Antigua Street, t 556 5592. Has a happy Italian atmosphere (genuine). Good for children and extremely reasonable.

Fruitmarket Gallery Café, 29 Market Street, t 225 2383. Stylish eaterie in the recently refurbished Fruitmarket Gallery.

Henderson's Salad Table, 94 Hanover Street, t 225 2131. Popular self-service vegetarian restaurant.

Howies, 4/6 Glanville Place, t 225 5553; 63 Dalry Road, t 313 3334; 208 Bruntsfield Place, t 221 1777. Good plain Scottish food in lively bistro-type restaurant.

La Bagatelle, 22 Brougham Place, t 229 0869. Small and intimate, with a French atmosphere.

Madogs, 38 George Street, t 225 3408. American-inspired cocktail bar specializing in exotic cocktails. It is known for its hamburgers, but there is a wide alternative choice.

Ndebele, 57 Home Street, t 221 1141. African café, gallery and deli, with an emphasis on South Africa.

Entertainment and Nightlife

The Tourist Information Centre at 3 Princes Street, just above the station, will advise on theatre and concert ticket availability, information about events in Edinburgh, and sell tickets. There are top-class concerts, opera, drama, ballet, variety shows, etc. in Edinburgh's theatres, and the latest films in the cinemas.

Theatres

The Festival Theatre, Nicolson Street, t 529 6000. Created from the old Empire, and large enough to stage any ambitious production.

Kings Theatre, Leven Street, t 229 1201. Restored to its original Georgian splendour.

National Centre for Dance in Scotland, Grassmarket, t 225 5525. A new centre for dance, with a programme of courses and performances.

Netherbow, High Street, t 556 9579. A multi-arts centre with a variety of shows and exhibitions.

Playhouse, at the top of Leith Walk, t 557 2590. Family entertainment, pop concerts.

Queen's Hall, Clerk Street, t 668 2019. Home of the Scottish Chamber Orchestra and Scottish Ensemble, and important jazz centre.

Royal Lyceum Theatre, Grindlay Street, near the Usher Hall, t 229 9697. One of Scotland's largest repertory companies.

Theatre Workshop, 34 Hamilton Place, t 226 5425.

Traverse Theatre, Cambridge Street, t 228 1404. An acclaimed experimental contemporary theatre renowned for its innovative productions.

Usher Hall, Lothian Road, t 228 1155. Concert venue.

Cinemas

Cameo, Home Street, t 228 4141. Arts cinema.

Dominion, Newbattle Terrace, t 447 2660/8450. Traditional old cinema.

Edinburgh Filmhouse, Lothian Road, t 228 2688. All the good films you missed, or long to see again, as well as new ones.

Odeon Film Centre, Clerk Street, t 667 7331/2. Same as above.

Odeon, Westside Plaza in Wester Hailes, t 453 1569. Multiplex.

UCI, Craig Park, t 0800 888 955. A 12-screen multiplex.

UCI, New Craighall, t 669 0777. Multi-screen.

UGC Cinema Megaplex Fountainpark, 130–32 Dundee Street, t 0870 902 0417.

The **Drum Complex** in Greenside Place, at the top of Leith Walk, is in the process of development into a **Warner Village**, which is expected to attract world premiere films. There will also be a casino, restaurants, a fitness centre and food shops.

Discovering Edinburgh

If your stay is limited, don't try to see the whole city. If you only have one day, your best bet is to confine your sightseeing to the Royal Mile. Start at the Castle, which takes a good two hours, and then wander down the hill towards Holyrood, lunching at one of the many places on the way and looking in at some of the dozens of tourist attractions you pass. Finish up at the Palace of Holyroodhouse and Holyrood Abbey. If you still have any energy left, climb Arthur's Seat (822ft) from the Holyrood car park, for a panorama of the city. (It doesn't take long, and you can drive most of the way.)

If you have two days, you should explore the New Town on the second day, including a couple of the art galleries or museums, with perhaps an hour or so browsing among the shops. If you have three days you should certainly visit the National Gallery, or the Scottish National Gallery of Modern Art: half a day at one of these is excellently counterbalanced by half a day in the Royal Botanic Garden.

For a while, then, Edinburgh retreated into the shadows, with brief leaps into the daylight, such as when the National Covenant was signed at Greyfriars in 1638, and when Cromwell occupied the city in 1650. The Act of Union in 1707 pushed it still further into oblivion, until Prince Charles Edward Stuart marched into the town in 1745 and captured Holyrood Palace and the hearts of the townspeople for five unreal weeks of feasting and triumph, before his march south.

From the death-throes of the Jacobite rebellion, peace finally emerged, and with it came the **Scottish Enlightenment**, that glorious explosion of culture and science that was born in Edinburgh and spread its tentacles worldwide (*see* **History**, pp.46–7). Walter Scott was largely responsible for the triumphal visit to Edinburgh of George IV, in 1822, who marched about resplendent in tartan and, some say, flesh-coloured tights, the first royal visit for more than 100 years (discounting that of Prince Charles).

In the middle of the 19th century Queen Victoria and Prince Albert discovered what the Queen called 'my dear, beloved Scotland', and the country suddenly became socially acceptable to southerners.

Old Town and New Town

One of the best legacies of the Enlightenment is Edinburgh's New Town, built in the 18th century. Before this, Edinburgh consisted of a warren of ancient buildings in the shadow of the Castle Rock: tall tenements, stacked together for want of space, teemed with people, vermin and disease. At the northern foot of the rock lay Nor' Loch, a stinking pond of effluent. Both Dr Johnson and Sydney Smith commented on the filth and smell of Edinburgh's streets. In 1767 the city fathers held a competition for a design to improve the town. The winner was 23-year-old James Craig, with his plan for a spacious town north of the Castle. Building began at once, and continued well into the 19th century when the Nor' Loch was drained and turned into gardens. The New Town is a masterpiece: elegant crescents, squares and gardens, lined with Georgian buildings, many cleaned to reveal their former pure stone (a highly controversial process because experts now suspect that the process damages the stone).

The Edinburgh Festival

The **Edinburgh International Festival of Music and Drama**, born in 1947, was conceived out of a desire to shake off the drabness of the post-war years. Its fathers were the Lord Provost, Sir John Falconer, Harry Harvey Wood of the British Council, and Rudolf Bing, the first artistic director. In that first year performers included the Glyndebourne Opera Company, the Hallé Orchestra, the Vienna State Orchestra, the Old Vic Theatre Company, the Sadler's Wells Ballet Company, and many more.

The Festival takes a theme each year and many of the performances and exhibitions relate to this. For three weeks in August and September, the city goes a little mad. Accommodation is booked months ahead and people dash about in a frenzy, trying to cram in as much as possible.

The **Fringe** started at the same time and has mushroomed to such an extent that it is now the world's largest arts festival, with more than 500 performances each day, by some 450 companies, sharing about 150 stages. Every spare inch is used: redundant kirks, halls, back rooms, basements, attics, schools, pavements. Students and drama companies come from all over to perform anything from monologues, poetry readings, street shows and acrobatics to full-scale drama and opera. Shows are staged all day and most of the night. It is impossible to see them all, and escalating prices are making the punters more selective. Tom Stoppard, Rowan Atkinson and Billy Connolly are among the many stars who were first launched through the Fringe.

The **Military Tattoo** usually starts a week before the Festival and runs for three weeks. It takes place on the Castle Esplanade (*1½ hours; every night except Sun; two performances on Sat*), and is one of the most popular attractions. Set against the backdrop of the floodlit Castle, it is a pageant of military display, with massed bands, pipes and drums, dancers, drills and tableaux. You can never be sure whether the climax is going to be a Bulgarian belly-dancer or a parade of Indian elephants. The Tattoo always ends with a lone piper, floodlit on the battlements, his haunting music reaching out across the dark to echo in your heart for ever.

The **Edinburgh International Film Festival** coincides with the first two weeks of the main Festival. There are screenings, discussions and conferences, and it is attended by some of the world's leading film-makers.

The **Edinburgh Book Festival** is a great literary bonanza spread through seven pavilions specially erected in Charlotte Square Gardens.

The **Edinburgh International Jazz and Blues Festival** presents top performers and bands from all over the world, with 80 hours of jazz daily throughout the city.

Only from the air is it possible to appreciate the symmetry of the New Town's formal design (described by some contemporary conservatives as 'windy parallelograms').

Edinburgh gained its affectionate sobriquet, 'Auld Reekie', in the days when reek (smoke) from the lums (chimneys) of the Old Town, lay over the city like a pall. The stones of the city are honed by a pervasive east wind: they say you can always spot a native of Edinburgh – when he rounds a corner anywhere in the world, his hand will fly instinctively to clutch at his hat.

The Old Town

Edinburgh Castle

Open April–Sept daily 9.30–6; Oct–Mar 9.30–5; adm.

The history of the Castle is the history of the city itself, and its position makes it the focus of attention. Allow at least two hours, more if possible, and try to go on a reasonably clear day to get full advantage of the views. The blue uniformed Castle guides, many of them ex-servicemen, are a fund of knowledge as they lead you upwards on the rough, cobbled pathways. You can also rent excellent audio tapes when you buy your ticket. The following itinerary covers the main attractions.

The **Esplanade**, below the Castle gate, slopes surprisingly steeply upwards: it is here that the Tattoo is staged (*see* opposite). Most Wednesday and Saturday evenings in May and June, the ancient, stirring ceremony of Beating the Retreat is also performed here, with pipes and drums; and it is now used to stage concerts and musicals. Beyond the entrance to the Esplanade, the **Witches' Well**, on the right, is near where over 300 witches were burned, between 1479 and 1722.

At the top of the Esplanade a drawbridge crosses a dry moat through a massive gateway, flanked by statues of Robert the Bruce and William Wallace. Ahead, the path slopes up to the right, towards the **Portcullis Gate**, which dates from 1574. Just before this, up on the left, is a memorial stone to Sir William Kirkcaldy of Grange, a colourful 16th-century character who helped murder the notorious Cardinal Beaton (*see* p.340) and was a leader of the Lords of the Congregation in the Reformation. Kirkcaldy was an accessory to the murder of Rizzio, Mary, Queen of Scots' secretary. Later, he received her surrender at Carberry Hill, and was mainly responsible for her final defeat at the Battle of Langside. After her imprisonment in England, he changed his loyalties and held Edinburgh Castle in her cause until he was forced to surrender, and was hanged.

Above the Portcullis Gate is **Constable's Tower**, later known as Argyll's Tower because the Marquess of Argyll was held in the dungeon here before his execution in 1661. The mixed construction of the steep path, a seam of cobbles between smooth stones, allowed grip for the horses and free-running tracks for the vehicles they pulled. The path snakes up past the Argyll Battery to the tourist administration area and shop. Beyond is the **Regimental Museum** of the Royal Scots, Britain's oldest infantry regiment, with trophies, uniforms, flags, weapons, and other memorabilia.

St Margaret's Chapel, on King's Bastion, is Norman and one of the oldest roofed buildings in Scotland. It is thought to have been built by Margaret after she moved to

Pontius Pilate's Bodyguard

The Royal Scots are known as Pontius Pilate's Bodyguard: there was a dispute with some French officers about which was the oldest regiment. 'We were on duty at the Crucifixion' declared the French. 'Had we been,' retorted the colonel of the Royal Scots (then called Le Regiment de Douglas), 'we should not have been asleep on duty.'

the Castle in 1076, though some believe it may have been built in her memory by her son, David I. Although often restored, this simple chapel must look much the same now as it did when it was built. Weddings and christenings are sometimes held here.

Beside the chapel, on King's Bastion, is **Mons Meg**, a mighty 15th-century cannon about whose history people disagree. Some say she was forged in Mons, in Belgium; others will tell you she was hastily cobbled together by a local blacksmith and his family to help James II when he took Threave Castle in 1455 and finally subdued the Black Douglases. This story has some credence, as the land given to the blacksmith as a reward was called Mollance, or Mons, and his wife's name was Meg. Whatever the true story, Mons Meg was taken to the Tower of London in 1754, but returned to its present home at the insistence of Sir Walter Scott.

Crown Square is signed to the right, off the path up to King's Bastion. The buildings around the square are the Scottish National War Memorial, the Crown Room, Queen Mary's Apartments, the Old Parliament or Banqueting Hall, and the Scottish United Services Museum.

The **Scottish National War Memorial**, on the right, is dignified and poignant. Designed by Sir Robert Lorimer and opened in 1927, it contains a Gallery of Honour divided into recesses, each containing a roll call of Scottish soldiers, sailors and airmen who gave their lives for their country. Stained-glass windows by Douglas Strachan depict war as part of human destiny, and carved reliefs illustrate all the services. There is a shrine opposite the entrance, built out of the rock.

The **Crown Room**, in the 15th-century Old Palace, has imaginative tableaux to pass the time while you queue to get in. The regalia in the glass case have their origins in medieval times and are thus older than the English crown jewels in London, which are almost all post-Restoration (Cromwell having destroyed the earlier ones). The crown, made of Scottish gold decorated with 94 pearls, 10 diamonds and many other precious stones, is said to have been used by Robert the Bruce in 1306. (It was set on his head by a brave woman, Isobel of Fife, Countess of Buchan, acting for her brother whose hereditary right it was to crown the king, but who was too frightened to do so. This lion-hearted woman was captured by the English and hung up in a cage from a wall in Berwick, as a punishment.) The crown was remodelled for James V in 1540 and was last used when Charles II was crowned at Scone in 1651. The glittering sword of state was given to James IV by Pope Julius II. During the Civil War, the Scottish regalia were hidden for safety (*see* 'Dunnottar Castle', p.399). After the Act of Union in 1707, they were packed away in a chest and forgotten for a hundred years, until that tireless patriot, Sir Walter Scott, came along. He organized a search and the regalia were discovered, in the same room in which they are now displayed.

Queen Mary's Apartments are also in the Old Palace, with the cupboard of a room in which Mary gave birth to James VI in 1566. An intriguing mystery hangs over that accouchement: in 1830 a tiny oak coffin was discovered, behind panelling in a recess in the room, containing the remains of an infant wrapped in silk, with a 'J' worked into the shroud. No one will ever know the story behind this relic: it was reinterred, carrying its secret with it, leaving our minds seething with speculation. It is worth remembering that it was crucial for Scotland's security that the queen gave birth to a live son. Mary had suffered some nasty shocks during her pregnancy, including witnessing the murder of her secretary, Rizzio. The room in which she laboured was so small that her loyal women could easily have blocked the view of the bed from the carousing nobles next door, gathered to witness the birth. It has been remarked that portraits of James VI show a definite similarity to portraits of John, second Earl of Mar, whose mother looked after the infant king after his birth.

The 15th-century **Banqueting Hall**, once the Old Parliament Hall and extensively rebuilt by James IV, is a vast chamber with a high open-timber roof and displays of weapons on the walls. It is still used for social gatherings on ceremonial occasions. In 1440 this was the setting for the infamous 'Black Dinner'. The Black Douglases were becoming too powerful for the liking of those who ruled Scotland on behalf of the 8-year-old James II. They summoned 14-year-old William, Earl of Douglas, and his younger brother, to attend a banquet in the presence of the king in this room. Legend has it that a black bull's head was brought in, signifying a death sentence. The two young Douglases were arrested, and executed on trumped-up charges of treason.

In one of the dungeons below the Banqueting Hall, the ninth Earl of Argyll was held before his execution in 1685. He was a staunch Protestant who supported Monmouth's rebellion against James VII/II, but he was defeated and executed. French prisoners were also imprisoned here during the Napoleonic wars. The **Scottish United Services Museum** covers the history, dress, weapons and equipment of all three services. On the way out, look over the northern and southern walls of the Esplanade: to the north lie Princes Street, the New Town, Leith and the Firth of Forth backed by the grey-blue hills of Fife; to the south, the Pentlands, Moorfoots and Lammermuirs and, on a clear day, the distant shape of Ben Lomond to the west.

The Royal Mile

A walk down the Royal Mile from the Castle to Holyrood could take days if you explore everything. (There are plenty of places for refreshment along the way.) It offers cameo glimpses into the past. From the 11th century onwards it was a warren of close-packed houses, shouldering each other for light and air, a maze of wynds, yards and stairways: a steaming, stinking, cauldron of humanity. During the 18th and 19th centuries, when the rich crossed the putrid Nor' Loch and began to build the New Town, the Old Town became the poor quarter, with many families to each tenement, huddled together in overcrowded squalor. These houses are now being restored and reinhabited. All the way along, closes with intriguing names open off either side.

Castle Hill

Castle Hill leads down the Royal Mile from the Esplanade. From here, Castle Wynd Steps on the right descend to the Grassmarket (*see* below). At the top is **Cannonball House**, so called from the ball embedded in its western gable, which is said to have been fired from the Castle towards Holyrood during its occupation by Prince Charles in 1745. **The Hub**, in the old Tolbooth Church on Castlehill (*open daily from 9.30;*

www.eif.co.uk/thehub), is the Festival Visitor Centre, with a booking office, exhibition area, shop and café-bar.

The **Scotch Whisky Heritage Centre** (*open daily 10–5.30; adm; www.whisky-heritage.co.uk*) is a series of tableaux with life-like models, sounds and smells, progressing from the illicit stills, smuggling and evasion of the Redcoats, through to the laird with his decanter. An audiovisual show explains (in seven languages) the process of whisky making and blending, and the tour ends with a free dram.

Over the road is the **Camera Obscura** (*open April–Oct daily 9.30–6, later in high summer; Nov–Mar 10–5; adm*). From here you can look at the city through a contraption of mirrors giving an intriguing, reflected aerial view. There are also view-finders and telescopes around the roof, and exhibitions.

The **Assembly Hall of the General Assembly of the Church of Scotland** (*public viewing of debates Wed 2.30–5.30, Thurs 9.30–12.30 and 2.30–5.30; tours Mon–Fri 10–12 and 2–4*) is usually the meeting place for the annual General Assembly, but until the new Parliament buildings near Holyrood are finished it is used for parliamentary sessions. It is on the site of a palace where Mary of Guise lived in the 16th century. Plays are staged in this magnificent hall during the Festival.

The **Tartan Weaving Mill and Exhibition** (*open Mon–Sat 9–5.30, Sun 10–5; adm*) is a working mill with demonstrations of the story of tartan 'from sheep to kilt'.

Lawnmarket

Castlehill runs into Lawnmarket. Not far down on the left is **Gladstone's Land** (*open April–Oct Mon–Sat 10–5, Sun 2–5; adm*). Dating from 1617, with its original arcaded front, this is a typical house of its period, expanding upwards to six storeys. Originally the home of a wealthy burgess, Thomas Gledstanes, it is furnished in the style of the time with painted ceilings.

17th-century **Lady Stair's House**, now the **Writers' Museum** (*open Mon–Sat 10–5*), is behind Gladstone's Land. It contains relics of those three literary giants: Burns, Scott

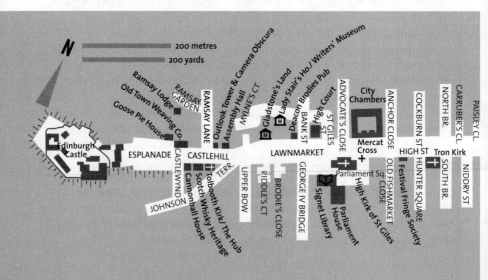

and Stevenson. Lady Stair was a leading hostess of Edinburgh society in the 18th century. You can see Burns' writing desk and Scott's chess board.

Brodie's Close, opposite Lady Stair's House, was the home of the model for Robert Louis Stevenson's character, Dr Jekyll. Deacon Brodie was a respectable citizen by day and a notorious thief by night. He also made furniture, including a linen press owned by Robert Louis Stevenson. He was hanged in 1788, on a drop he designed himself.

On the corner of Lawnmarket and George IV Bridge three brass studs in the road mark the site of the last public execution, in 1864. It is city tradition to spit on the heart-shaped stones in front of Parliament Square, a little further down. These, called the **Heart of Midlothian**, mark the site of the old city jail, demolished in 1817. It was here, in 1650, that the head of gallant Montrose was displayed on a pike.

St Giles Cathedral (*open Easter–Sept Mon–Fri 9–7, Sat 9–5, Sun 1–5; Oct–Easter Mon–Sat 9–5, Sun 1–5; www.stgiles.net; free guides*) lies just off Lawnmarket within Parliament Square, which covers the old churchyard. John Knox is buried somewhere around here, probably under the car park behind the cathedral where there is said to be a plaque on one of the parking slots. For some St Giles' unadorned Presbyterian gloom banishes all trace of the God whose house it claims to be. Correctly, it is the High Kirk of Edinburgh, and it is odd that a church that was once the centre of anti-Episcopal rioting, where clergy were physically assaulted for trying to retain Episcopalian ritual, is still referred to as a cathedral – a word that means the seat of the bishop. A church is thought to have stood here as early as the 9th century, but the present Gothic building dates from the 15th century. It has been much restored, not always to advantage, and contains many relics and monuments. Near the entrance to the side chapel, a tablet marks the spot where Jenny Geddes flung her stool at the dean, striking a blow for the Covenanters in the 17th century. The **Regimental Colours** of the Scottish regiments hang above the nave – historic banners embroidered with their battle honours. The Colours are treated with respect: people stand up and men salute when they are paraded. The **Chapel of the Thistle** (*adm*) was designed by

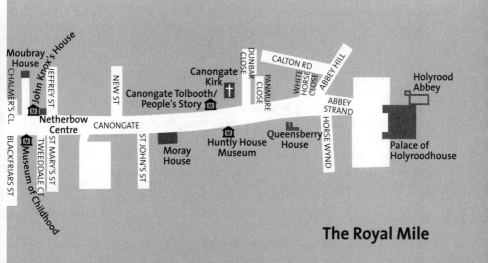

The Royal Mile

Robert Lorimer in 1911. Tiny and ornate, in honour of The Most Ancient and Most Noble Order of the Thistle, it is deliciously out of place among these dark, forbidding walls.

Parliament House (*open Tues–Fri*) is just behind St Giles. Now the Scottish Law Courts, it was the home of the Scottish Parliament until after the Union in 1707. The Great Hall has a hammerbeam roof and stained glass. A Greek façade, added in 1808, hides the original front, but you can see how it once looked from George IV Bridge, around the corner.

High Street

In the High Street leading on from Lawnmarket, the 17th-century **Tron Church**, a little way down past St Giles and no longer used as a church, is so called because of the tron, or weighing beam, that stood nearby. The tron checked the weights used by the merchants: those found using underweight measures were nailed to the tron by their ears. Many locals have hazy recollections of storming up the Mound at Hogmanay, just before midnight, and staggering down the High Street to gather at the Tron to salute the New Year. The church is now used as the Old Town Information Centre, with an exhibition area.

John Knox's House (*open Mon–Sat 10–5; July and Aug also Sun 12–5; adm*) dates from 1490 and still has an outside stair. Restoration revealed its original walls, fireplaces and painted ceilings. John Knox is believed to have lived here from 1561 to 1572, and it is thought he died in one of the upstairs rooms. Inside are relics of his life, with pictures of Edinburgh in the past. Somehow, his dynamic personality is stamped into the soul of the building. It is easy to dismiss him as a dark, melancholy fanatic, breathing fire and everlasting damnation, but there was much more to him than that. Knox served time as a galley slave before he made his name as a reformer. He had a sharp wit, a shrewd worldliness and more: at the age of 51 he took as his second wife a girl of 16 who bore him three daughters.

Next door is the **Netherbow Arts Centre**, with a studio, café, workshops, children's theatre, puppetry and storytelling.

The **Museum of Childhood** (*open Mon–Sat 10–5; July and Aug also Sun 12–5*) displays nursery memorabilia, including toys, games, books and medicines, and is as fascinating for grown-ups as for children. You can hear children chanting their tables in the 1930s, watch street games in the 1950s.

Canongate

After Netherbow Port, High Street becomes Canongate – the road up which the canons, or clerics, walked from Holyrood Abbey through Netherbow Gate into the walled town. Canongate was once the smart residential quarter of the aristocracy.

Canongate Tolbooth (*open Mon–Sat 10–5*), 1591, contains the **People's Story Museum**, depicting ordinary people's lives in Edinburgh from the late 18th century to the present. It is marvellously evocative of the sights, sounds and smells of the past: the debtors' prison, town crier, political tub thumpers, pub camaraderie, genteel tearoom talk, washhouse gossip, etc.

The **Brass Rubbing Centre** (*open April–Sept Mon–Sat 10–5; also Sun during Festival 12–5; charge for brass rubbing*) is in Chalmers Close. A collection of replicas moulded from Pictish stones, rare Scottish brasses and medieval church brasses is available for amateur brass rubbers, with experts on hand to instruct and supply materials.

Canongate Church, beside the Tolbooth, was built in 1688 for the congregation that James VII ousted from Holyrood Abbey, and is used by the Royal Family when they are in residence at Holyrood. Opposite, the **Museum of Edinburgh** (*open Mon–Sat 10–5; also Sun during Festival 2–5*) shows Edinburgh life through the centuries.

17th-century **Queensberry House** is being gobbled up by the new Scottish Parliament, and will become offices for the Presiding Officers. As you pass, spare a thought for the kitchen boy who used to turn the spit here. While the second Duke of Queensberry was busy accepting a bribe to help push through the Act of Union in 1707, his oldest son and heir, a homicidal lunatic, was equally busy roasting the kitchen boy on his spit. He was caught, but not before he had begun to eat his victim. The building site around Holyrood is to be the home of the **Scottish Parliament**. For the full horror story of its inception read *All the First Minister's Men* by David Black.

Dynamic Earth, on Holyrood Road (*open Easter–Oct daily 10–6; Nov–Mar Wed–Sun 10–5; adm; t (0131) 550 7800; www.dynamicearth.co.uk*), is the story of our planet. From a molten mass to a tropical rainforest you whirl through time with sight, sound and smell effects to help your imagination. The best bit is the birth of the universe, with an overpowering spectacle of crashing constellations and blinding flashes, and when you return to the present there are lots of clever exhibits to play with, like a population counter clicking up births and deaths as you watch. You can even create your own earthquake or check up on the weather back home.

The **Edinburgh Dungeon**, 31 Market Street (*open daily 10–6; longer in summer; adm; t (0131) 556 6700; www.thedungeons.com*), is a splendid new venture focusing on characters from Scottish history. The centrepiece is a witchfinder boat ride and a visit to Sawney Bean (the cannibal, *see* p.246). Actors play infamous characters depicting some of Edinburgh's most grisly history: Burke and Hare, Deacon Brodie, etc.

The Palace of Holyroodhouse

Open April–Oct daily 9.30–6; Nov–Mar daily 9.30–4.30;
closed during Royal and State visits; adm;
t (0131) 556 1096; www.the-royal-collection.org.uk.

Holyrood Palace is the Queen's official residence in Scotland. Built during the reign of James IV, around 1500, it took a severe bashing, with the abbey, during the 'Rough Wooing' in 1544. Mary, Queen of Scots came here, a high-spirited, sensual widow of 19, fresh from the French court, accustomed to French ways. Here she received Knox, and was berated by him for attending Mass in her chapel. Here, in 1565, she married dissolute Darnley, four years her junior, a vicious youth who suspected her of infidelity with her Italian secretary, Rizzio, and helped to murder him in front of her when she was six months pregnant. Finally, it was here that Mary married Bothwell, a squalid business that brought a swift end to her reign. Of happier memory were the five weeks in 1745 when Charles Edward Stuart, the Young Pretender, held court: riding out to review his troops, spreading his magnetic charm at the magnificent Court levees in the evening, the darling of Edinburgh society and focus of all female eyes.

In the 150ft-long picture gallery is one of Scotland's best practical jokes. The gallery holds 89 of the original 111 portraits of Scottish monarchs, commissioned by the government in 1684 and completed in two years by a Dutchman called James de Wet. Many of the portraits are of fictitious characters and many of them, as Walter Scott commented when he saw them, 'lived several centuries before the invention of oil paints'. De Wet was paid £120 per annum for this daunting commission of monarchs 'in large, royall postures'. One can only guess at the feelings of the official who received and hung these astonishing portrayals at a rate of more than one a week.

The turreted lodge on the edge of the palace grounds, on the left approaching from Canongate, is Queen Mary's bathhouse. Some say she bathed here in white wine. To mark the Golden Jubilee, the **Queen's Gallery** will open towards the end of 2002 in the former Holyrood Free Church, with changing exhibitions of paintings from the Print Room at Windsor Castle.

Holyrood Abbey

The history of Holyrood Abbey runs in tandem with that of the Castle. It was founded in 1128 by David I on the spot where, tradition has it, he was saved by a miracle from being gored to death by a wild stag. The name Holy Rood (or Cross) is said to come from a fragment of the True Cross, brought to Scotland by Queen Margaret in the 11th century and incorporated into the abbey by her son David. If this is true, the holy relic did not survive. Only a shell now, with a soaring Norman arch, the abbey is a beautiful silhouette against the sky. James II was born and crowned here in the 15th century, and he and his two successors were married in the church, as was Mary, Queen of Scots (to Darnley in 1565). Several monarchs were buried at Holyrood, and Charles I was crowned here as well as in London.

South of the Royal Mile

The **Grassmarket**, a long, wide rectangle, lies at the foot of Castle Wynd Steps, or down Victoria Street, off George IV Bridge just before the Central Library. It was the scene of several ignoble events. The cross in a railed enclosure at the foot of Victoria Street marks the site of the gallows where more than 100 Covenanters were hanged in the 17th century for refusing to give up their right to worship God in their own way. Another of the Grassmarket's victims was Captain Porteous. In 1736 a crowd became restless after an unpopular execution, just up the hill in the Lawnmarket. Porteous ordered the Guard to fire. Some people were killed and Porteous was tried for murder and acquitted. The angry mob dragged him from the Tolbooth Jail and administered their own justice, hanging him from a dyer's pole in the Grassmarket.

Part of the **Flodden Wall** can still be seen at the top of the steps in the Vennel (vennel meaning 'alley') from the southwest corner of the Grassmarket up to Heriot

Greyfriars Bobby

On down George IV Bridge, opposite the entrance to Chambers Street, is the statue of a Skye terrier, Greyfriars Bobby, who watched over his master's grave at Greyfriars for 14 years, from 1858. He was fed by local people and granted Edinburgh citizenship in order to save him from being destroyed as a stray dog.

Place. This wall was hastily built to protect the city after the defeat at Flodden in 1513, when the victorious English army seemed too close for comfort. The new huge **National Centre for Dance in Scotland** in the Grassmarket is now open (**t** (0131) 225 5525, for information). Both Burns and Wordsworth stayed in the 17th-century **White Hart Inn**, where you might like to finish your tour of the Old Town.

The **National Library of Scotland** (*open June–Oct Mon–Fri 10–5 (till 8 during the Festival), Sat 10–5, Sun 2–5; t (0131) 226 4531; www.nls.co.uk*), on George IV Bridge opposite the Central Library, was founded in 1682 and is one of the four largest libraries in Britain. As well as enjoying the right to claim a copy of every book published in the British Isles, the library owns a collection of illuminated manuscripts and documents relating to Scottish history, including the last letter Mary, Queen of Scots wrote to her cousin Elizabeth on the eve of her execution. There is also the written order that set in motion the Massacre of Glencoe in 1692.

The **Scottish Parliament Visitor Centre** on George IV Bridge has information about the interim accommodation and the proposed development of the Holyrood project.

Set back beyond Greyfriars Bobby, across Candlemaker Row, **Greyfriars Kirk** is another of the Old Town antiquities. The adoption and signing of the National Covenant took place here in 1638 – that 'great marriage day of this nation with God', as Lord Warriston called it. In fact it led to even greater bitterness, hatred and bloodshed than before. Ironically 1,400 Covenanters were imprisoned in the kirkyard in 1679. The graveyard contains some important gravestones.

The **Royal Museum of Scotland** (*open Mon–Sat 10–5 (Tues till 8), Sun 12–5; www.nms.ac.uk*), around the corner in Chambers Street, is a Victorian building with a soaring glass interior and a range of exhibits so diverse you could wander happily for days. Collections include art, archaeology, ethnology, natural history, technology and social history, covering the whole world. A new annexe, the **Museum of Scotland** (*same opening times*) opened on St Andrew's Day 1998, and covers the social history of Scotland from its earliest beginnings. Artefacts from the former Museum of Antiquities will be incorporated into what promises to be a fine display.

The **University Old College** (1789), in South Bridge beyond the museum, is of both aesthetic and morbid interest. It is Robert Adam's largest work in the city and contains examples of his distinctive interiors. The upper library was designed in 1830 by William Playfair. The building stands partly on ground that belonged to Kirk o' Field, where Darnley met his nasty end. **The Talbot Rice Art Centre** (*open Tues–Sat 10–5, daily during the Festival; www.trg.ed.ac.uk*), contains an old master gallery and an exhibition gallery. The Torrie Collection, with important paintings and bronzes, some of which date from the 16th century, came to the Talbot Rice from Sir James Erskine of Torrie. The exhibitions are mainly of contemporary art.

Princes Street

Princes Street is unique: which other city's main street has shops on one side of the road only and gardens backed by a cliff-top castle on the other? When the town planners built the New Town in the 19th century they drained the stinking Nor' Loch and agreed to leave the south side of Princes Street open, with no buildings – the effect is breathtaking. Coming down any of the side streets into Princes Street from the north, you see the silhouette of the roofs and spires of the Royal Mile on the ridge above, a frieze of architecture leading dramatically up to the Castle. Unbelievably, in the 1960s a scheme was nearly approved to develop the south side of the street with the same sort of buildings as you see on the north. It was only squashed because professionals who lived nearby in the New Town had influence to wield. Had the scheme been allowed, it would have ruined Edinburgh's most famous, unique feature. There was controversy when Waverley Station, a fine building, was built, because of its position.

The shops are uninspiring, mainly chain stores, and the wide pavement is usually jammed with shoppers, so cross the road and relax in **Princes Street Gardens** – in the summer, anyway. Terraced lawns and flowerbeds shaded by old trees make a haven from the exhausting jostle of the shops. Tame grey squirrels beg for scraps and fat pigeons strut fearlessly at your feet. From spring onwards you can join the Edinburgh office workers lying on the grass like holiday-makers on a beach at lunchtime; or sit in the open-air café in the piazza. The gardens' **Floral Clock**, a horticultural showpiece that was the first of its kind in the world, contains over 2,000 plants.

The **Scott Monument** (*open Mar–May and Oct Mon–Sat 9–6, Sun 10–6; June–Sept Mon–Sat 9–8, Sun 10–6; Nov–Feb Mon–Sat 9–4, Sun 10–4*), at the eastern end of the gardens, will be familiar from photographs. Its 287 steps lead to a panoramic view of the city. This very Victorian monument, erected in 1840, seems entirely suitable and just the sort Sir Walter might have designed for himself. He and his dog Maida look out from under a great canopy, set with niches containing 64 of his characters.

The New Town

Calton Hill rises beyond the east end of Princes Street, a well-known landmark on the Edinburgh skyline, with its 'ruined' Parthenon, built as a war memorial for the Napoleonic Wars and left unfinished when funds ran out. There are marvellous views from the 102ft **Nelson Monument** (*open April–Sept Mon 1–6, Tues–Sat 10–6; Oct–Mar Mon–Sat 10–3; adm*) at the top, erected in 1815 in memory of Admiral Lord Nelson's victory and death at the Battle of Trafalgar, 21 October 1805. It is an upturned telescope, designed by Robert Burn, with a time ball which is lowered each day as the one o'clock gun is fired from the Castle. The buildings of the old Royal Observatory are open as the **Old Edinburgh Experience** on application to the custodian. The present observatory is on Blackford Hill, due south, where there is a visitor centre (*open daily; adm*) where you can learn about the work of astronomers all over the world.

George Street runs parallel to Princes Street along the ridge to the north, with some of the city's best shops and vistas down the intersections towards the Firth of Forth and across to the hills of Fife. **St Andrew Square** lies at the east end of George Street, a mixture of old and new buildings, dignified but somehow lacking the character of other squares in the New Town. It is in the process of redevelopment, with a new bus station and a Harvey Nichols store (due to open Autumn 2002).

Charlotte Square, at the west end of George Street, is a distillation of all the elegant charm of the New Town. Robert Adam designed it, but died before it was finished: it is accepted as one of his masterpieces and renowned throughout Europe. The elegance of the buildings is outstanding, even when the square is full of cars.

The **Georgian House** (*open Mar–Oct Mon–Sat 10–5, Sun 2–5; Nov and Dec Mon–Sat 11–4, Sun 2–4; adm*) is on the north side of the square. Furnished in its original, late 18th-century style, it gives a picture of the domestic and social conditions of a wealthy family in those days. The **National Trust for Scotland**, next door at no. 28 (*gallery open Mon–Sat 10–5, Sun 12–5; shop open Mon–Sat 10–5.30*), has a display of 20th-century Scottish paintings and an 1820s drawing room.

The curious inverted cones on the houses in the square are link extinguishers – used by link boys who were employed to escort people home in the dark with flaming torches. They plunged the torch into the cone to extinguish it, saving the pitch for the next customer. These can be seen in other places, but it is unusual to find a whole square with them. A major conservation repair programme is underway, and the NTS hope to stimulate a major renaissance of the whole square.

North of Charlotte Square are a number of other fine crescents and squares. The Moray Estate was developed by James Gillespie Graham in 1823. The grand curves of Moray Place, Ainslie Place, Randolph Crescent and many more, surrounding attractive gardens and linked by well-proportioned streets, contrast with Craig's grid pattern in the first New Town development. Most of the buildings are still private houses and flats, and there has been little modern development. Many of the streets have retained their cobbles, making the New Town a noisy but very popular place to live.

Art Galleries

Edinburgh's art galleries would take weeks to explore thoroughly. If there is only time to explore one, it ought to be the National Gallery, described by the art historian Sir John Pope-Hennessy as 'the finest small gallery in the world'.

The National Galleries of Scotland (*www.natgalscot.ac.uk*) comprise the National Gallery, the National Portrait Gallery, the Gallery of Modern Art and the Dean Gallery, in Edinburgh, as well as the outposts of Paxton House, just outside Berwick-upon-Tweed, and Duff House, near Banff.

The **National Gallery of Scotland** (*open Mon–Sat 10–5, Sun 2–5; adm for special exhibitions; excellent free public lectures on individual paintings Fri 12.45*) stands at the foot of the Mound, across a piazza – a favourite haunt of buskers. The gallery, a neo-Grecian building designed by William Henry Playfair, was built in the middle of the

19th century. The first stone was laid by Prince Albert in 1850; a wing was added in 1978, and the end of the 1980s marked a complete refurbishment. The Director of the National Galleries of Scotland, Timothy Clifford, restored the gallery to Playfair's original conception, with the paintings crowded together (some say too much so) on walls whose colours are carefully chosen to fit the theme of each room. The result is stunning: burgundy walls in the main rooms are a striking foil for gilt frames and intensify the colours of the paintings. Clifford follows his contention that the gallery should provide a variety of vistas, as in an 18th-century landscape garden: sublime, contemplative, unexpected, diverting and even witty. Picture hanging is an art form in itself and Clifford has demonstrated this most effectively.

Among the gallery's Scottish paintings are works by William McTaggart; portraits by Allan Ramsay; and ebullient works by David Wilkie, whose 'social history' pictures sum up the life of ordinary people in the 18th and 19th centuries. There are several of Raeburn's portraits, including a self-portrait.

Downstairs, there is a library, a print room and a prints and drawings gallery. Every January 38 watercolours by Turner are displayed – the Vaughan Bequest – a collection whose colours are so delicate that they are only allowed into the light for one month each year.

In the main part of the gallery, on two floors, there is a large collection of European and British paintings. Poussin's *Seven Sacraments* are on their own for silent contemplation, in Room 5, off Room 4 where the rest of the Poussins hang, in a setting meant to be an evocation of the Poussin interiors. The marble floor is newly laid, the walls drab and dimly lit. The colours in the paintings are so rich and deep they are almost indigestible, and the faces glow with life. One of the most spectacular vistas in the gallery is that from Room 8, down the enfilade of wine-red galleries to the largest canvas in Scotland, *Alexander III King of Scots Saved from the Fury of a Stag by the Intrepid Intervention of Colin Fitzgerald* by Benjamin West.

A poignant story is attached to the portrait *The Hon Mrs Graham* by Gainsborough. In 1774, at the age of 17, Mary Cathcart married Thomas Graham. The couple adored each other, continuing to exchange passionate love letters until Mary died at the age of only 34. Thomas was so heartbroken he couldn't bear to look at this portrait, painted within the first year of marriage when she was still half a child. She glances uncertainly from beneath her plumed hat, dressed in a magnificent gown, giving the impression that she wishes the artist would hurry up so she can change into something more comfortable and curl up with a book. Thomas hid the painting away and it was forgotten until his heir inherited the property, found the portrait locked away in London, and gave it to Scotland on the proviso that it should never leave the country again.

The **Scottish National Portrait Gallery** (*open Mon–Sat 10–5, Sun 2–5; adm for special exhibitions; free lectures Wed 12.45*) is at the east end of Queen Street, and includes the Queen Street Café. From this building, opened in 1899, statues of illustrious Scots stare down at the street from Gothic niches in the façade, each carefully vetted for authenticity before erection between 1889 and 1906: John Knox, looking rather benign, Mary, Queen of Scots, William Wallace, Robert the Bruce, and many more.

Inside, an arcaded floor-to-roof hall with an upper gallery is decorated with murals and friezes depicting Scottish history, and these alone deserve hours of study. Painted by William Hole and commissioned in 1897, they display a remarkable talent. A processional frieze of Scottish characters over the centuries, all dated and named against a richly gilded background, is remarkable. No one has been left out: Caledonia, Scotland personified, sits as the alpha and omega, with Stone Age Man on one side and Thomas Carlyle on the other. The procession is endless.

As for the portraits themselves, it has to be said that the Scots are good subjects for portraits: they seem to have particularly strong faces. The scope in this gallery is vast and presents a history lesson, sewn together by many of Scotland's most famous people, painted by the leading artists of their times: Darnley, aged nine, by Hans Eworth, looking as if butter wouldn't melt in his mouth; his wife Mary, by an unknown artist, carrying all the sadness of her life in her enigmatic face; James VI/I, her son, by John de Critz, weak-faced and dour; the gruesome *Execution of Charles I*, artist unknown, with intricate detail and rich, gleaming colour. Paintings by Lely include one of John Maitland, Duke of Lauderdale, portraying the gross coarseness of an unprincipled Secretary of State who dominated Scotland after the Restoration.

The **Scottish National Gallery of Modern Art**, in Belford Road northwest of Princes Street (*open Mon–Sat 10–5, Sun 2–5; adm for some loan exhibitions; free lectures Mon 12.45*), was opened in 1984 in a neoclassical building designed by William Burn in the 1820s as a school for fatherless children at the bequest of John Watson. It stands back from a green sward dotted with trees and sculptures, some by Henry Moore. When the plan to form a separate gallery for modern art was finally executed, the trustees of the National Galleries of Scotland allocated a large proportion of their total purchase grant to the new gallery to allow it to catch up with the others. Thus significant examples of many of the great 20th-century movements were acquired before escalating prices made this prohibitive. It owns paintings and sculpture by key artists of all nationalities, and has also gained a number of important works through bequests and gifts. Altogether the gallery owns some 3,000 paintings, sculptures, drawings and prints, its greatest strengths being in works of German Expressionism, Surrealism and French art. There are two floors of galleries, with a licensed café in the basement and a shop.

The **Dean Gallery**, opposite the Gallery of Modern Art at 73 Belford Road (*open Mon–Sat 10–5, Sun 12–5; adm for special exhibitions*), is the newest part of the National Galleries, housing mostly contemporary art, particularly a fine Dada and Surrealist collection and archive, sculpture and graphic art.

The **Royal Scottish Academy** of painting, sculpture and architecture (*open Mon–Sat 10–5, Sun 2–5 during exhibitions; adm*) is beside the National Gallery, facing on to the Mound. It was founded in 1826 to promote fine arts in Scotland and holds two main exhibitions a year: the Annual Exhibition, in the summer, and the Festival Exhibition. These vary enormously and cover all aspects of fine art.

The **City Art Centre** (*open Mon–Sat 10–5, also Sun 2–5 during the Festival; adm for special exhibitions*) is tucked away behind Waverley Station. It houses the city's art collection, including many Scottish works, and holds a number of exhibitions from all over the world. There is a café next door.

The **Stills Gallery**, 23 Cockburn Street (*open Tues–Sat 10–5*), displays international photography, with a specialist bookshop and café.

Cathedrals

Among Edinburgh's many churches of all denominations, there are two other cathedrals apart from St Giles. **St Mary's Episcopal Cathedral** of 1879, in Palmerston Place west of Princes Street, has a central spire visible from all over the city. The cathedral's Music School is in the grounds of the late 17th-century Easter Coats House nearby. As well as services, the cathedral holds public concerts throughout the year.

St Mary's Catholic Cathedral is round the corner from York Place at the east end of Queen Street. Its all-male choir has been acclaimed as being among the best in the land, 'because they sing not as trained professionals, but with their hearts'. At the start of a High Mass the choir processes into the church, their voices swelling and deepening as they move forward filling the building with glorious sound.

Around Edinburgh

Holyrood Park and Surrounds

Holyrood Park stretches south and east of the palace. The steep hill rising abruptly to the south of the palace car park is **Arthur's Seat**, less of a slog than it looks. The easiest way up is from Dunsapie Loch to the east. The name has no connection with the legendary King Arthur; it might relate to Prince Arthur of Strathclyde, but it is more likely to be a corruption of *Ard Thor* – Gaelic for 'height of Thor'. Views from the top make the climb worthwhile. On the eve of May Day, crowds head up the slopes of Arthur's Seat, like colonies of ants. It is traditional to greet the dawn of May Day from the top, and most years there are well over 2,000 people there. **Salisbury Crags**, the rocky peaks west of Arthur's Seat, are part of the park. There are also three lochs, **Duddingston Loch** in the southeast being a bird sanctuary preserving a surprising variety of bird life so close to the city. The village of Duddingston, to the east of the loch, was the encampment for Prince Charles' army for six weeks in 1745 while he reigned in Holyrood Palace.

Meadowbank, northeast of Holyrood Park, is a huge leisure centre, which has twice been the venue for the Commonwealth Games.

Restalrig Church, just east of Meadowbank, was destroyed in 1560 by John Knox and his followers. They branded it 'a monument of idolatry' and pulled it apart. It was later restored. The small hexagonal chapel beside it, with a lovely groined roof resting on a central pillar, was the chapel of a college founded by James III in 1478. When it was restored in the 20th century the new floor was split open by a spring of water, believed to be one that used to cure eye diseases. The original chapel that stood over

Shopping

James Pringle Woollen Mill, Bangor Road, Leith. Tartans, tweeds and knitwear. You can usually find some tremendous bargains. They also have a 'trace your clan' computer.

Where to Stay

Malmaison, Tower Place, Leith, **t** (0131) 468 5000, *edinburgh@malmaison.com* (*moderate*). Award-winning classic contemporary hotel on the waterfront. Trendy.

Eating Out

If you want to combine a good meal with an out-of-town excursion, these restaurants within easy motoring distance have been classed among the top in Britain.

Champany Inn, Champany Corner, Linlithgow, **t** (01506) 834 532. Less than 15 miles from the city centre, and surely one of the best steak houses in Britain (*see* p.195).

Greywalls, Gullane (*see* p.183), **t** (01620) 842 144. Well worth the journey.

The Peat Inn, Cupar, **t** (01334) 840 206. In Fife, a little further away (*see* p.344).

La Potinière, 15 or so miles east along the coast at Gullane (*see* p.183), **t** (01620) 843 214. *Closed for 2002.*

Leith t (0131–)

On the waterfront at Leith there are several excellent seafood restaurants, with nautical atmospheres and tables outside.

Fishers, Tower Street/The Shore, **t** 554 5666 (*moderate*). Good seafood in convivial atmostphere.

(Fitz) Henry, 19 Shore Place, **t** 555 6625 (*moderate*). Delicious food in a warehouse brasserie.

Malmaison Brasserie, in the Malmaison hotel, **t** 555 6969 (*moderate*). Good food.

Martin Wishart, 54 The Shore, **t** 553 3557 (*moderate*). An excellent place with just the right ambience, and first-class food.

The Rock, Commercial Street, **t** 555 2225 (*moderate*). Warehouse on the waterfront. Good, simple food, well cooked.

The Shore, 3 The Shore, **t** 553 5080 (*moderate*). Converted pub with lots of character.

Skippers Bistro, 1a Dock Place, **t** 554 1018 (*moderate*). Bohemian atmosphere and friendly staff. The menu is changed twice a day: mouth-watering smoked salmon roulade and scallops.

The Vintners Room, The Vaults, 87 Giles Street, **t** 554 6767 (*moderate*). Candlelit meals in an old wine merchants' auction room in a warehouse. Cobbles, open fires and good food.

The Waterfront, 1 Dock Place, **t** 554 7127 (*moderate*). Attractive wine bar overlooking the water – it was once the waiting room for steamboat passengers.

Daniel's Bistro, 88 Commercial Quay, **t** 553 5933 (*cheap*). Splendid French food in a warehouse, with a conservatory and outside tables by the water.

Khublai Khan's Mongolian Restaurant, 43 Assembly Street, **t** 555 0005 (*cheap*). DIY barbeque and as much as you can eat.

the spring was called St Triduana. There was in fact no saint of that name, which comes instead from a three-day fast practised by the old Celtic Church.

The Royal Botanic Garden

Open April–Aug daily 9.30–7; Mar and Sept daily 9.30–6; Oct and Nov–Feb daily 9.30–5; www.rbge.org.uk.

The Botanic Garden, north of the city between Inverleith Row and Inverleith Terrace, deserves frequent visits to appreciate its ever-changing beauty. The herbaceous borders are spectacular, backed by a gigantic beech hedge. There are glasshouses and pavilions full of exotic vegetation, steamy-hot and lush as a tropical jungle. The rock garden is huge, full of rare alpine plants rising in miniature mountains from the water garden and sweeping lawns. There is none of that prim 'keep-off-the-grass' feeling in these gardens: they are beautifully kept but informal. In summer students lie on the lawns, studying and relaxing.

Warriston Cemetery

Not many people would think of seeking an hour or two of peace among the dead, but this can be done in Warriston Cemetery. Just to the east of the Botanic Garden follow the Water of Leith northwards, across Inverleith Row and along Warriston Road towards the crematorium. The cemetery was bought by a property speculator who then found that some of the graves were too recent to allow excavation. It is now a secret garden, tended just enough to clear the paths but not so much as to spoil its wild character, with forgotten graves overhung by trailing creepers, shaded by fine trees. You can wander in dappled sunlight, pausing to read inscriptions, brushing aside a swathe of old man's beard to examine a draped urn or a marble angel. There is no feeling of bereavement. Don't, however, go through the tunnel that leads under the road into an older part of the cemetery: there is an evil presence there, so tangible one almost receives a physical shock.

Leith

Ask at the Tourist Information Centre for Leith Walk leaflets, or go to 11 Madeira Place, *www.leithwalks.co.uk*. Also look at *www.edinburgh-waterfront.com*.

The **Water of Leith** rises in the Pentlands and flows over 24 miles to Leith, where it joins the Firth of Forth. It once powered about 80 water mills and was a safe anchorage for ships at Leith. A riverside walkway is being constructed for the 12-mile stretch to Balerno and will soon be finished. The **Visitor Centre**, 24 Lanark Road (*open April–Sept daily 10–4; Oct–Mar Wed–Sun 10–4; adm; t (0131) 455 7367; www.wateroffleith.edin.org*), tells the story of the river and its relation to the economy of the city.

Leith, to the northeast, is the historic port of Edinburgh. Formerly an area of high unemployment and destitution, it is now becoming fashionable as gentrification proceeds apace, and with the regeneration comes a rash of new housing and commercial centres, including the ambitious new **Ocean Terminal** shopping centre (*www.oceanterminal.com*), with the Royal Yacht Britannia anchored alongside. A number of wine bars, hotels, pubs and restaurants stand along the waterfront, some with outside tables from which you can watch maritime activity in the port. The English used to batter Leith during their many campaigns against Edinburgh. Mary, Queen of Scots landed here when she came back from France to take up her crown in 1561. One can't help wondering what a mixture of feelings – of hope, excitement and anxiety – raced through her mind as she received her first taste of Scottish hospitality. Two years before, her mother Mary de Guise-Lorraine had her headquarters here – probably in Water Street – during her struggles with the Lords of the Congregation.

Charles I played golf on **Leith Links** and it was while he was playing here in 1641 that he was stopped, mid-putt, and told the news of the Irish Rebellion. Cromwell built a fort in Leith, which the Jacobites captured in 1715. George IV landed in the port in 1822, on his celebrated visit to Edinburgh organized by Sir Walter Scott.

HMY *Britannia* (*open Jan–Mar and Oct–Dec Mon–Fri 10–3.30, Sat and Sun 9.30–4.30; April and May Mon–Fri 9.30–4, Sat and Sun 9.30–4.30; June–Sept daily 9.30–4.30; adm; www.royalyachtbritannia.co.uk*), built on the Clyde, has returned to the land of her birth after more than 40 years of ferrying Royals around the world. Early in 1998 she came to rest in the Port of Leith, to become part of the innovative **Ocean Terminal** complex. Visitors can explore four of her decks, unless one of the Royal Family happen to be exercising their prerogative to stay on board.

Andrew Lamb's House, in Burgess Street, is owned by the National Trust for Scotland. This four-storey building with a projecting staircase tower was built as a house and warehouse combined, and is now an old people's day centre. It was here that Mary was entertained on her arrival in 1561 by Andrew Lamb, one of the rich merchants of Leith. **Trinity House**, in Kirkgate, was founded as an almshouse in 1555, rebuilt in Victorian times and contains four portraits by Raeburn, which can be seen on request. The much-restored Church of St Mary, nearly opposite, was built in the 15th century.

At the **Clan Tartan Centre**, Leith Mills, 70/74 Bangor Road (*open Mon–Sat 9–5 (till 5.30 in summer), Sun 10–5; www.clantartan.com*), you can trace your tartan roots and pick up good woollens and bargains. The **Scotch Malt Whisky Society**, in The Vaults, 87 Giles Street (*open by arrangement only, t (0131) 554 3451; www.smws.com*), is for the serious connoisseur. It will arrange whisky tastings tailored to your requirements.

Dean Village and Stockbridge

Northwest of the city centre the main road north crosses the Dean Bridge, giving no hint of the **Dean Village** in the valley below. There was a grain-milling community here for 800 years, straggling along the Water of Leith. The old buildings have been restored and converted into flats and houses. You can walk for miles along this waterway, a peaceful haven close to the heart of a busy city. **Stockbridge**, adjacent, has become rather trendy, though it is still popular with students restocking their wardrobes from the secondhand shops.

Lauriston Castle

Open April–Oct Sat–Thurs 11–1 and 2–5;
Nov–Mar Sat and Sun 2–4; adm.

Lauriston Castle is further to the northwest, off Cramond Road South, overlooking the river in the suburb of Davidson's Mains. The original 16th-century tower was extended and is now a fine house which contains good paintings, furniture, tapestry and 'Blue John Ware'.

Edinburgh Zoo

Open April–Sept daily 9–6; Oct–Mar daily 9–4.30;
adm; www.edinburghzoo.org.uk.

Edinburgh Zoo, at Corstorphine, going west out of Edinburgh on the A8, is one of the biggest in Britain. The perimeter fence runs halfway up Corstorphine Hill and it is worth climbing the hill in the early morning to watch the sun flooding in over the Lothian Plain. Suddenly, close by, the harsh roar of an African beast bellows out to greet the dawn. There is a huge penguin pool and a restaurant.

Craigmillar Castle

Open April–Sept daily 9.30–6.30; Oct–Mar Mon–Wed
and Sat 9.30–4.30, Thurs 9.30–12, Sun 2–4; adm.

Craigmillar Castle is 3½ miles southwest of the city centre on the A68 – a route through open countryside in the days when Mary, Queen of Scots, used to ride out with her court. The ruins of the castle stand high above a straggle of modern buildings that threaten to overwhelm it from all sides, yet fail to diminish its splendour. These well-preserved walls, dating from the 14th century, have witnessed some of the darker moments of Scotland's history. In 1475 James III imprisoned his brother, John, Earl of Mar, in the keep, accusing him of 'conspiracy'. Later, Mar died from 'overzealous bloodletting'.

Craigmillar was Mary's favourite country retreat. The village nearby was known as Little France when the overflow from her court took lodgings there. She came here after the murder of her secretary, Rizzio, and it was here in 1566, at the Craigmillar Conference, that she was urged by her lords (including Bothwell) to divorce Darnley. She was torn by the conflict between her strict Catholic upbringing, her repugnance for her dissolute husband and her growing passion for Bothwell.

The banqueting hall on the first floor is served by four stairways, and it is easy to imagine it with hanging tapestries, straw on the flagged floor, blazing logs in the vast open hearth and a minstrel in the gallery below the barrel-vaulted ceiling. There are views from the roof across to Arthur's Seat, the Firth of Forth with the hills of Fife beyond, and the soft contours of the smoke-grey Pentlands on the southwestern horizon. The two ancient yew trees in the courtyard are relics from the days when they were believed to ward off evil spirits (a more prosaic explanation for their presence being that their wood was needed for making bows).

The Lothians

11

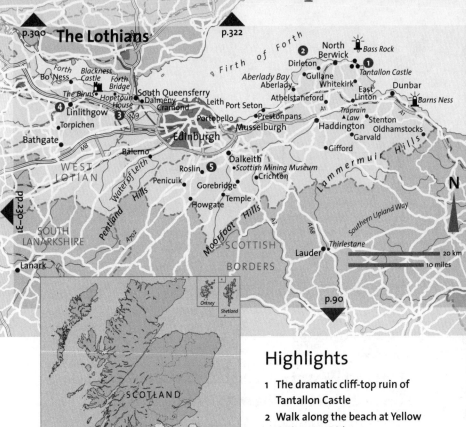

North Berwick ②
Bass Rock
Dirleton ①
Tantallon Castle
Firth of Forth
Aberlady Bay
Aberlady
Gullane
Whitekirk
Dunbar
East Linton
Barns Ness
Forth
Bo'Ness
Blackness Castle
Forth Bridge
South Queensferry
Hopetoun House
Dalmeny
Leith
Port Seton
Athelstaneford
A1
The Binns
Linlithgow ④ ③
M9
Cramond
Portobello
Prestonpans
Traprain Law
Stenton
Torpichen
Oldhamstocks
Musselburgh
Haddington
Garvald
Bathgate
M8
Balerno
Dalkeith
Gifford
WEST LOTIAN
Roslin ⑤
Scottish Mining Museum
Crichton
Lammermuir Hills
Water of Leith
Penicuik
Gorebridge
Pentland Hills
Howgate
Temple
Moorfoot Hills
A702
A7
A68
Southern Upland Way
N
SOUTH LANARKSHIRE
SCOTTISH BORDERS
Thirlestane
Lauder
Lanark
20 km
10 miles
p.90
Orkney
Shetland
SCOTLAND
NORTHERN IRELAND
ENGLAND

Highlights

1 The dramatic cliff-top ruin of Tantallon Castle
2 Walk along the beach at Yellow Craig, near Dirleton
3 Magnificent Hopetoun House
4 Linlithgow Palace, birthplace of Mary, Queen of Scots
5 Ornate carving at Rosslyn Chapel

Arriving in the Lothians from the Borders you come over the Lammermuir, Moorfoot or Pentland Hills and see the whole region laid out below you: an expanse of farmland punctuated with rust-red roofs and massive carbuncles of volcanic rock, with the glinting Firth beyond and the blue hills of Fife on the horizon. Your eye is drawn towards Edinburgh, dark and dense in the distance, dominated by Castle Rock and Arthur's Seat. There are 70-odd miles of coastline: sheer rock cliffs, wide golden sands, dunes tufted with marram grass, quaint little fishing harbours. Rivers and streams tumble from the hills and clatter across the plain to the sea. These once provided power for the mills and bring beauty and irrigation to the fertile land. While much of East Lothian is flat farmland stretching down to the coast with some good beaches, most of Midlothian and West Lothian is industrial with historic towns and buildings scattered throughout. The Lothians' roots go a long way down into prehistory. Stone-Age man left traces of hill forts. When the Romans arrived they were inhabited by the *Votadini*, with Traprain Law as the capital. The name may have been taken from their King Loth. After they faded into obscurity, the Lothians formed the northern part of Bernicia, inhabited by Britons. Lothian men were always independent; they kept aloof from the rest of Scotland until 1018 when Malcolm II defeated the Angles and drew Bernicia into his kingdom.

When Queen Margaret persuaded her husband to move the court to Edinburgh in the middle of the 11th century, the history of the Lothians became bound up with that of the capital. Invading armies swept through in both directions. When the monarchy was strong, so was the surrounding land; when anarchy prevailed, it was within range of the capital that the powerful lords were most aggressive. Much of Mary, Queen of Scots' brief reign was played out in the Lothians in the middle of the 16th century, and Prince Charles Edward Stuart's even briefer appearance dazzled the citizens of Lothian for six weeks when his army camped out at Duddingston near Edinburgh. When Scotland finally took on the mantle of peace, houses no longer needed to be fortresses. The cultural renaissance that erupted in Edinburgh, in the wake of the suppression of the Highlands, spread outwards in ripples of fine architecture and collections of art. Great mansions were built on vast estates, close to the capital, often financed by fortunes made from coal.

Coalmining is the Lothians' oldest industry, pioneered 800 years ago by medieval monks, whose primitive, shallow workings were the forerunners of today's deep mines. Coal was used to boil seawater to extract the salt, essential as a preservative before the days of refrigeration, and provided fuel for castle and cottage as well as for industry. Whole families toiled in the pits, and miners were bought and sold with their mines, like slaves. Only one open-cast mine is left now, where once there were hundreds. The Lady Victoria mine at Newtongrange has been cleverly exploited to create an interesting colliery museum.

With some of the most fertile land in Britain, agriculture plays an important part in the economy. In the mid-18th century landowners started to 'enclose' the land, turning the peasants' small uneconomic 'runrig' fields into larger fields. Farm steadings were built and new villages, such as Tyninghame, were created to house the displaced peasants who became farm labourers. Some worked in textile mills built along the rivers, or went down the mines. Today barley is the most important crop, used for malting and for feeding stock. Market gardening and vegetable growing are lucrative, with the markets of the ever-hungry capital on the doorstep. On the less fertile hill pastures to the south, cattle are bred and sold to farms on the plain to be fattened for market. Only sheep graze on the moors, often being moved down for the winter.

Tourism is important to the Lothians' economy. Although the region has Edinburgh for its centre, it is by no means just the city's dormitory.

The Coast East of Edinburgh: Barns Ness to Musselburgh

This stretch of coast is a paradise for naturalists, with nature reserves, sandy beaches, rugged rocks and a wealth of birds. The seaside towns are like English resorts, with rows of villas staring out to sea, genteel and trim.

A small detour off the A1, about 3 miles east of Dunbar, reaches **Barns Ness**: the road runs straight out to the lighthouse on a rock promontory beyond a campsite. There is a wildlife reserve, a geology trail with an old lime kiln, and bracing bathing from clean white sands.

Dunbar

Dunbar was an important fishing port 300 years ago, giving jobs to 20,000 workers. The harbour is quiet now, though it still has a small fishing fleet. Smuggling once flourished: in 1765 8,000lbs of contraband tobacco passed through the port. Today it is a rapidly developing holiday resort with reputedly the lowest rainfall and highest sunshine in Scotland. Edward I defeated the Scots here in 1295 and his son, Edward II, escaped from the harbour by sea, 19 years later, after his defeat at Bannockburn. In 1650 Cromwell fought and defeated the supporters of Charles II in Dunbar, killing 3,000 and taking 10,000 prisoners. While it was generally Cromwell's practice to order the execution of many of his prisoners, 1,000 of the Dunbar men were shipped down to help Vermuyden in his efforts to drain the Fenlands.

The town sprawls around a wide High Street, squared off at the north end by Lauderdale House, built by Robert Adam, once used as a barracks and now restored to flats. The 16th-century steepled **Town House** (*open April–Oct daily 12.30–4.30; www.dunbarmuseum.org*), in the middle of the High Street, is the oldest civic building in constant use in Scotland, with a local history and archaeology museum.

Dunbar Castle

The best view of the castle is from above, at the edge of Lauderdale House barrack square, and there is a board giving its history. One jagged, fang-like tower and a few scattered stones remain of what was once an extensive fortress guarding the gateway to the eastern plain, sprawled across sea-lashed rocks, overhanging the narrow entrance to the harbour. The original castle was built in the 11th century for Cospatrick, Earl of Northumbria, deposed by William the Conqueror and made Earl of

Black Agnes

The focus of many battles, Dunbar Castle's most stirring claim on the imagination was a siege in 1339 when Black Agnes, Countess of Dunbar, and her ladies held it for six weeks against the English. This brave woman mocked the great siege engine which was used against the castle. She and her ladies leant over the battlements and wiped the walls with their dainty handkerchiefs where the missiles had hit.

Tourist Information

Dunbar: 143 High Street, t (01368) 863 353, *www.dunbar.org.uk; open all year.*
North Berwick: Quality Street, t (01620) 892 197; *open all year.*

Where to Stay

North Berwick is packed with homely hotels and guesthouses, many overlooking the sea.
Greywalls Hotel, Muirfield, Gullane, t (01620) 842 144, *www.greywalls.co.uk (expensive).* Luxurious Lutyens-designed country house. One of the best hotels in Scotland, and the prices reflect this. A few years ago King Hussein and Queen Noor of Jordan ate here and were so impressed by the food that they pinched the chef; the replacement is just as good. *Open mid-April–Nov.*
The Marine Hotel, Cromwell Road, North Berwick, t 0870 400 129, *heritagehotels _north_berwick.marine@forte-hotels.com (expensive).* Dependable old-fashioned, comfortable hotel for golfers.
Open Arms Hotel, Dirleton, t (01620) 850 241, *openarms@clara.co.uk (expensive).* An unexpected treasure in a smallish village, family-run for the last 40 years. Up-market inn (1685) on the edge of the green overlooking the castle. Comfortable and peaceful, with open log fires, it has long been acclaimed for its food. People drive out from Edinburgh to eat here.
Craig En Gelt Hotel, Marine Road, Dunbar, t (01368) 862 287 *(moderate).* Overlooking the harbour and ruins of Dunbar Castle. Golf packages.
The Glebe House, Law Road, North Berwick, t (01620) 892 608, *j.a.scott@tesco.net (moderate).* Hospitable B&B in a very comfortable Georgian manse 2 minutes from the sea.
Kaimend, Hamilton Road, North Berwick, t (01620) 893 557, *shipping@tward.co.uk*

(moderate). Faces south and north over the golf course and the sea, with a beach only 300 yards away. Charlotte and Nigel Souter run the house as a cosy, lively home and they ply you with good food and comfort.
Inveresk House, Inveresk, Musselburgh, t (0131) 665 5855, *chute.inveresk@btinternet.com (moderate).* Splendid 16th-century rambling house dating, with lots of interesting stories. B&B in a great atmosphere.
Point Garry Hotel, West Bay Road, North Berwick, t (01620) 982 380 *(moderate).* Comfortable, family-run hotel; has good golf packages.
53 Eskside West, Musselburgh, t (0131) 665 2875 *(cheap).* Splendid, cosy B&B in an old terraced fisherman's cottage.
Blenheim House Hotel, Westgate, North Berwick, t (01620) 892 385 *(cheap).* Sea views, and golf next door.
The Castle Inn, Dirleton, t (01620) 850 221 *(cheap).* Old coaching inn overlooking the green. Friendly atmosphere.
Drum Mohr, Levenhall, nr Musselburgh, t (0131) 665 6867, *www.drummohr.org (cheap).* Award-winning campsite.
The Old Aberlady Inn, Main Street, Aberlady, t (01875) 870 503 *(cheap).* Cosy, homely inn.

Eating Out

Greywalls *(see above).* Will also give you a memorable meal if you can afford it. *Closed Oct and for a week in June.*
La Potinière, Gullane, t (01620) 843 214. Housed in what looks like a restored bus shelter on the main road. For 25 years proprietors David and Hilary Brown have served French country-style cooking of a quality that is outstanding as well as being remarkably cheap. *They've decided to take a break in 2002, but ring to see if they've reopened.*
Open Arms Hotel, Dirleton, *see above.*
Starfish, Dunbar, t (01368) 865 384. Bistro on the quay with delicious fresh seafood.

Dunbar by his cousin Malcolm Canmore. When Bothwell abducted Mary, Queen of Scots in 1567, he brought her to Dunbar Castle. It was to Dunbar that they fled, less than six weeks later. The castle was demolished by Mary's half-brother, Moray, after her final defeat. Later, Cromwell used its stones to improve the harbour.

Dunbar Harbour has cobbled quays around an outer and inner basin, restored warehouses, a coastguard station, working fishing boats, piles of netting and lobster creels, pleasure craft and the ever-vigilant lifeboat. Kittiwakes throng the rocks, their cries echoing above the ruined castle. In northerly and easterly gales, waves pour over the harbour walls. Picture it in the old days, the boats packed into the basins, men busy on deck, sorting and landing the catches, the quays alive with the chatter of women, gutting heaps of slithering silver herring.

The **John Muir Country Park**, on the western outskirts of town, is named after the 19th-century conservationist and explorer, born in Dunbar, who founded America's national parks. Acres of wild coastland surround the mouth of the Tyne, where you can walk along the cliffs, fish, sail, surf-ride, play golf, and enjoy the abundant wildlife.

The **Scottish Nuclear Come and See Programme** (*open Mar–Sep daily 9.30–4.30; Oct–Feb Mon–Fri 9.30–4.30, Sat and Sun 1–4.30; tours 10.30 (Mon–Fri only), 1.30, 3.30; freephone t 0800 250 255; www.snl.co.uk*), at Torness south of Dunbar, explains how nuclear energy affects us in the home. There are good walks and picnic areas nearby.

Whitekirk

Following the coast, take the A198 four miles west of Dunbar, and Whitekirk is a couple of miles further on. This was once the site of a holy well, now lost in the field opposite the church. Among the pilgrims who came here in the 15th century was a papal delegate, Aeneus Silvius de Piccolomini, who later became Pope Pius II. He walked barefooted in the snow from Dunbar to give thanks for his rescue from a shipwreck. This pilgrimage earned him rheumatism in his feet for the rest of his life. It is said he found the Scottish lassies 'forthcoming and eager to kiss everyone in sight'. The imposing 12th-century **church** dates was well restored after it was burnt by zealous suffragettes in 1914. The name Whitekirk for such a predominantly red building is explained by the former use of whitewash to cover the sandstone.

Tantallon Castle

Open April–Sept daily 9.30–6.30; Oct–Mar Mon–Wed and Sat 9.30–4.30, Thurs 9.30–12, Fri and Sun 2–4.30; adm.

14th-century Tantallon is a mile or so beyond Whitekirk. This dramatic ruin stands on the edge of a sheer cliff overhanging the sea between two bays. It was a stronghold of the powerful Douglas family who leased it (when it was a smaller fortalice in the 14th century) from the Earls of Fife – an unusual practice in those days. These were the Red Douglases, Earls of Angus, who 'rose upon the ruins of the Black' Douglases when they were subdued by James II. These Red Douglases became a menace to the Crown, ruling their domains with a total disregard for authority. They lived just as they pleased, especially when Margaret Tudor, the devious widow of James IV, married their leader, the Earl of Angus, in 1514, and they became arch manipulators in the power struggle over the boy-king, James V. They built on to and strengthened Tantallon, the perfect stronghold for this arrogantly audacious family.

The castle's massive curtain walls cut it off on its headland, making it impregnable against the impotent batterings of rivals, while supplies came in regularly by sea. It took Cromwell's artillery 12 days of devastating bombardment before Tantallon was eventually 'dinged doun'. The three landward ditches were dug to repel siege engines and invaders. The walls are 14ft thick, the well 100ft deep, bored through rock. Seen silhouetted against the sea, Tantallon is one of Scotland's most heart-stopping ruins.

North Berwick

North Berwick was created a Royal Burgh by Robert III around the end of the 14th century. It developed into a holiday and golfing resort during the 19th century. A compact, sunny town flanked by two bays with a rocky headland between, it is the main shopping centre for the area. Narrow, one-way streets, teeming with holiday-makers in summer, lead down to the sheltered harbour, full of boats, surrounded by warehouses converted into flats. Lobster creels, nets and fish-boxes mingle on the quay with the spars of pleasure boats and hulls of sail-boards and, just beyond, an open-air swimming pool built into the rock, high above the sea.

North Berwick Museum (*open April–Oct daily 11–5; www.northberwickmuseum.org*), on the upper floor of the old school, in School Road, displays local social history, archaeology and wildlife, with special exhibitions.

The **Scottish Seabird Centre**, on the harbour (*open summer daily 10–6; winter daily 10–4; adm; t (01620) 890 202, www.seabird.org*), recently opened by the Prince of Wales, is a splendid place for ornithologists of all ages. Spy cameras on the Bass Rock relay live pictures of puffins, gannets and so on, unselfconsciously living their daily lives.

The **Auld Kirk** stands on a rocky spit near the harbour. All you can see of this noto-rious 12th-century ruin today is the whitewashed nave, south aisle and foundations. When James VI/I was nearly drowned in a freak storm off the Bass Rock, he blamed a well-established coven of witches in North Berwick, alleging that some of them had had the temerity to row around his foundering ship in a sieve. The witches were arrested one dark night as they performed some nasty rituals in and around the Auld Kirk, presided over by their 'Devil', Francis, Earl of Bothwell, nephew of Mary's Bothwell, who lived at Hailes Castle nearby. The subsequent trial of 94 witches and six wizards was based on confessions extracted by gruesome torture and attended by the King who was inspired to write a book on the subject.

North Berwick Law is the volcanic rock that towers 613ft above the town. Climb its steep flank for a view out to sea, over to the hills of Fife and across the Lothian plain to the Lammermuirs, Moorfoots and Pentlands. This was one of a chain of warning beacons and in the Middle Ages was crowned by a fort. Now it is occupied by a watchtower, built to look for invaders during the Napoleonic Wars, and more modern buildings used in the First World War. There is also an arch made from the jawbone of a whale, a relic from the days of whale fishing in the North Sea.

The Bass Rock

The Bass Rock, one of Lothian's volcanic plugs, lies 1½ miles offshore from Tantallon. Standing 350ft high, a mile in circumference, its sheer-walled wedge is a landmark for sailors. Boat trips from North Berwick cruise around it, but permission is needed to land. St Baldred the hermit died on the rock in the 7th or 8th century and you can just make out where his cell was, halfway up, on a terrace on the south side. Near the lighthouse are the ruins of a castle owned by the Lauder family. In 1406 James I, the 12-year-old heir to the throne, sheltered on the Bass on his way to sanctuary in France. (His subsequent capture at sea and detention in London for 18 years proved to be greatly to Scotland's advantage, for he returned well educated and able to cope with the anarchy strangling his country.) Many Covenanters were imprisoned on the rock during the Killing Times in the 17th century. Later, four fugitive Jacobites held out there for four years, provisioned by the French. The Bass Rock is now a gannetry, as well as a haven for gulls, kittiwakes, puffins, fulmars and guillemots. You may even see seals. If you are sailing near its guano-whitened cliffs on a hot day, you won't miss it.

Dirleton

Three miles west of North Berwick, Dirleton is one of the prettiest villages in the area, with pantiled cottages, a 17th-century church, session house, old school and inns grouped around two wide, tree-lined greens.

Dirleton Castle and Garden (*open April–Sept daily 9.30–6.30; Oct–Mar Mon–Sat 9.30–4.30, Sun 2.30–4.30; adm*) is a 13th-century ruin overlooking the upper green from a rocky mound in the middle of the village. It was the last castle in the south of Scotland to resist Edward I, and was demolished by General Monk, for Cromwell, in 1650. Surrounded by lawns, a garden and a 17th-century bowling green, it has a 17th-century doo'cot containing 1,100 empty nests, a relic from when pigeon meat was a valuable supplement to the diet in the lean winter months. A coven of witches, possibly those of North Berwick, was imprisoned here before being half-strangled and publicly burnt at the stake on Dirleton Green. The gardens include a herbaceous border listed in the *Guinness Book of Records* as the longest in the world.

Yellow Craig, a sandy beach studded with dunes and backed by woodland, is reached by a lane leading a mile seawards from the eastern edge of Dirleton. It has a caravan park, picnic sites and a nature trail. The small hillock rising from the trees was the model for Spyglass Hill in Robert Louis Stevenson's *Treasure Island*. The sandy bay, fringed with buckthorn and marram grass, overlooks Fidra Island, a lump of black basalt rock, eroded by wind and sea. There was a Celtic monastery on Fidra. Romanized in 1165, it was a popular place for pilgrimages and its ruins can still be seen. (Boat trips are available from North Berwick.)

Gullane

Gullane is a seaside golfing mecca about a mile west of Dirleton. Pronunciations vary, from Gillan and Gullan, to Goolan: Gillan was once considered 'posh', but Gullan and Goolan date from further back. Church land until the Reformation, it developed into a holiday centre for the wealthy genteel, with **Muirfield** among its golf courses and a sandy beach to occupy non-golfing members of the family. The Open Golf Championship is regularly held at Muirfield. **St Andrew's Collegiate Church** is said to have fallen into ruin in the 16th century when James VI/I objected to the minister smoking tobacco and transferred the parish 2 miles east to Dirleton.

Gullane Hill was formed by wind-blown sand, a process that still continues. Sand has silted up Aberlady Bay on the west side of the hill and created a bird sanctuary and nature reserve, with over 200 recorded species of birds, including five species of tern. A footbridge leads from the roadside car park into the reserve. Many years ago, great sailing ships would have lain at anchor right up to the mouth of the river.

Luffness Castle (*not open to the public*) overlooks Aberlady Bay. It dates from the 16th century, with a 13th-century keep built on the site of a Norse camp. You can still see the moat, curtain walls and towers. It was built by the Scottish–Norman family de Lindsay, one of whom was Regent of Scotland when Alexander III was a boy. He died on a Crusade, bequeathing land to the monk who carried his embalmed body home. The ruins of the monastery, built on the promised gift of land, are near the castle, with the tomb and effigy of the crusading laird.

Aberlady

Aberlady, no more than a straggling village on the southwest shore of the bay, was a thriving trading port until the Peffer Burn silted up. Pantiled cottages border the main street, with the Quill Gallery, inns and a mercat cross that lost its top in the Reformation. In the church, with 15th-century tower and vaulted stone basement, is part of an 8th-century Celtic cross with interwoven bird carvings. The original 'louping-on stane' at the gate was the mounting block.

Myreton Motor Museum (*open April–Sept daily 10.30–4.30; adm; t (01875) 870 288*), signposted, a mile to the east, is a collection of vintage cars, old road signs, advertisements, petrol pumps, cycles, motorcycles, military vehicles and memorabilia from early motoring days (1896 onwards).

Long, rock-strewn **Gosford Sands**, less than a mile beyond Aberlady, overlook the Firth of Forth, cut by a network of tracks and picnic sites, backed by wind-sculpted trees. It can be scruffy, but it's not a bad place to stretch your legs or walk the dog.

Port Seton

Seton Collegiate Church (*open April–Sept daily 9.30–6.30; adm*) is just beyond Gosford Bay on the coast road. Built on the site of an earlier church, it was established as collegiate in 1492 and you can still see the ruins of the domestic buildings. In the church are effigies of the fifth Lord Seton and his wife: he was killed at Flodden in 1513; she built the transept and spire. Seton House, next door, has a collection of peacocks.

Seton Castle (*private*), an 18th-century building adjacent to the church, stands on the site of Seton Palace. It was frequently visited by Mary, Queen of Scots, of whom the Setons were loyal supporters. She came here with Darnley after Rizzio's murder and also the next year, with Bothwell, after Darnley's murder, when she took part in an archery contest, adding another nail to the coffin that was being built for her by her critics. The daughter of the house, Mary Seton, was one of the Queen's Four Marys. **Seton Sands**, nearby, is a holiday park with permanent caravans and facilities for those who prefer holidays crammed with entertainment.

Prestonpans

Prestonpans straggles along the coast to the east, forming an almost continuous waterside township with Port Seton, Cockenzie and Longniddry. It took its name from the open-air salt pans in which 12th-century monks from Newbattle Abbey used local coal to boil seawater from the Firth to extract the salt. It is an uninspiring sprawl, but its name will draw Jacobites like a magnet.

Go first to Meadowmill, between Prestonpans and Tranent. Looking from the viewpoint across grassland that now covers old colliery workings, it is hard to believe you are on the front line of the **Battle of Prestonpans**, when Prince Charles Edward Stuart defeated General Cope in a 15-minute dawn battle in September 1745. Cope established his army with Preston, Cockenzie and Port Seton behind them, a deep ditch and a boggy marsh in front and the 10ft wall of Preston House protecting their western flank. The Prince's army slipped in from the east as the sun rose, three men at a time down a narrow track, and overwhelmed the enemy by the ferocity and speed of their surprise attack, hacking their way through the Hanoverian lines with broadsword and dirk. The Hanoverians fled 'eskaped like rabets', as the Prince later reported to his father. The outcome so boosted the Prince's morale that he believed they were invincible. A cairn in a field beside the A1 commemorates the battle.

Off the coast road in Prestonpans, in the heart of the village, **Preston Tower** was built by the Hamiltons in the 15th century. Originally about 50ft high, it was burnt down by the English in 1544, quickly repaired, burnt down by Cromwell in 1650, and rebuilt again, this time with a two-storey addition on top, making it unique in Scotland. It is now the central feature of a new housing development, together with a boundary wall and a 17th-century lean-to doo'cot. The 17th-century **mercat cross** nearby is the only complete and unaltered cross of its kind in Scotland. It has a unicorn-crowned shaft rising from a circular base with pilasters and niches, and a turnpike stair to a platform from which public proclamations were read.

Prestongrange Industrial Heritage Museum (*open April–Oct daily 11–4; special 'steam days' on the first Sunday of each month; www.prestongrangemuseum.org*), on the western outskirts of Prestonpans, is on a former colliery site and covers 800 years of mining history. Outside, you can see an 1874 Cornish beam pumping engine with its five-storey engine house. The former power house is full of mining artefacts.

Musselburgh

Musselburgh, almost a suburb of Edinburgh, is at the mouth of the River Esk whose tidal flats were once carpeted with mussel beds. The Romans had a fort here to supply their camp at Inveresk; 5,000-year-old Bronze-Age relics have been excavated locally. On the direct route to Edinburgh, it was often sacked by invading English armies. In

1332 Robert the Bruce's nephew, Thomas Randolph, Earl of Moray and Regent of Scotland, fell ill and was given sanctuary from the English by the citizens of Musselburgh, until he died. The town was called the **Honest Toun** thereafter and Honest Toun celebrations are held every summer, with pageantry and entertainment.

From its beginnings, golf was played on **Musselburgh Links**, the oldest surviving course in the world although now a racecourse. James VI/I was an enthusiastic player and James IV is also believed to have played here. Cromwell stationed troops on the links in 1650 after his victory at Dunbar, while he 'sorted out' the district.

Fisherrow is Musselburgh's old harbour, with terraces of fishermen's cottages on the waterfront. On the quay, in a smart refurbished establishment, Mr Clark sells his own smoked salmon, among the most succulent in Scotland and well worth a visit.

The **Tolbooth**, at the east end of Musselburgh High Street near the mercat cross, was once the town prison. Its unusual 16th-century spire was built from material taken from the chapel of Our Lady of Loretto, nearby, when the Reformation decreed its demolition. The chapel, founded by a hermit, Thomas Douchtie, in 1533, became a healing centre for the sick. When its stones were recycled for secular use the Pope was so outraged he excommunicated the Honest Toun for 200 years.

The Battle of Pinkie was fought southeast of the town in 1547, one of Henry VIII's victories during his 'Rough Wooing'. **Pinkie House** (*open to the public Tues afternoons during the summer and Christmas terms*), opposite Loretto, is part of the school on the site of the chapel, an early 17th-century building with later additions. The gallery on the first floor has an arched timber ceiling painted in tempera by Italian artists.

Inveresk Lodge Gardens (*open April–Oct Mon–Fri 10–6, Sat and Sun 2–5; Nov–Mar Mon–Fri 10–4.30, Sun 2–5; adm*), a mile south of Musselburgh, are the gardens of a 17th-century house (*private*) run by the National Trust for Scotland and specializing in plants for small gardens. Just south of here is **Carberry Hill**, scene of the battle that resulted in Mary, Queen of Scots' surrender and capture. Mary, aged 25, proud to the last, prepared to watch the chivalric encounters that were to decide the issue. No one of suitable rank among the rebel nobles stepped forward to take up Bothwell's challenge. There was no fight and Mary decided her surrender and the promise of a safe conduct for Bothwell were the best solution. She embraced her new husband whose child she was carrying, and watched him ride off. She never saw him again.

The Coast West of Edinburgh: Cramond to Bo'ness

This stretch of coast is rich in large country houses linked by attractive walks along the shore, giving way to the industrial sprawl around Grangemouth to the west.

Cramond

Cramond, on the western fringe of Edinburgh, is an 18th-century village at the mouth of the River Almond as it flows into the Firth of Forth. Cramond means fort-on-the-river. The fort was Roman, built in about AD 142 to guard the harbour. Its

> ## The Goodman of Ballengeich
> To the south, beside an older Cramond Brig than the present 17th-century bridge, James V was violently attacked. The King was given to wandering about dressed as a humble farmer, calling himself the Goodman of Ballengeich. He was thus disguised when he was attacked by robbers, or, some say, by the family of a peasant girl to whom he was making love. He was rescued by a local man, Jock Howieson. The King rewarded him with a gift of land on condition that Howieson and his descendants should wash the hands and feet of all new sovereigns on their first visit to Scotland. The present Queen upheld the tradition in 1952.

foundations can still be seen by the church, with an illustrated plan. (In the summer, free conducted walks around the village start from the kirk at 3pm every Sunday.)

Dalmeny

Dalmeny, about 3 miles west of Cramond, is a group of cottages around a green, tucked away below the A90 some distance from Dalmeny House. The 12th-century **church**, dedicated to St Cuthbert, must be one of the finest gems of Norman architecture in Scotland. Its receding arches draw your eye towards a simple altar and east window. In the pulpit is a carved misericord, possibly unique, on which the weary preacher could surreptitiously sit between exhortations.

Dalmeny House (*open July and Aug Sun–Tues 2–5.30; adm; www.dalmeny.co.uk*) is a good mile northeast of the village, on the Forth. This fine example of Romantic–Gothic was built in 1815 for the Earl of Rosebery, whose family has lived here for more than 300 years. Although it isn't old in terms of history, it is a splendid mansion with a Gothic hammerbeamed hall, vaulted corridors and classical main rooms, as well as 18th-century French furniture, tapestries and porcelain, and a unique collection of Napoleonic memorabilia. Some of the paintings are very fine, especially the portraits. Queen Victoria stayed here with Prince Albert in 1842 and commented on the beauty of the setting – you can see why – and the 'excellent modern comforts' of the house, which might have had something to do with the plumbing. From the grounds you can walk along the shore to Cramond or South Queensferry.

South Queensferry

South Queensferry is 9 miles west of Edinburgh, where the Firth of Forth narrows to little more than a mile. In the 11th century Queen Margaret of Scotland established a free ferry here, to carry pilgrims to visit the holy shrines at Dunfermline and St Andrews. She built two hospices for the weary pilgrims, one on each bank. The ferry service continued (though latterly not free) until the opening of the road bridge in 1964, linking North Queensferry and South Queensferry. The four-span rail bridge, built between 1883 and 1890, was a tremendous engineering feat. Over a mile long, with the railway 157ft above the water, its painted surface would cover 135 acres.

Stretching away on either side are private estates with houses open to the public, farmland and woods with views across the water to the hills of Fife. The 16th-century **Hawes Inn** (*see* 'Where to Stay and Eat', opposite) stands on the site of the southern hospice, facing the old ferry ramp. Its view across the river is blinkered by the two bridges – a very different aspect from the days of Sir Walter Scott, who was often here and mentioned it in *The Antiquary*. In Robert Louis Stevenson's *Kidnapped*, David Balfour met Captain Hoseason at the Hawes Inn, in a bedroom 'heated like an oven by a great fire of coal', the captain having been 'carbonadoed in the tropic seas'.

The **Queensferry Museum** (*open Mon and Thurs–Sat 10–1 and 2.15–5, Sun 12–5; adm; www.cac.org.uk*), in Burgh Chambers, has local history exhibits, including a display on the building of the rail bridge.

Hopetoun House

Open April–Sept daily 10–5.30; adm;
www.hopetounhouse.com.

Hopetoun House is 2 miles west of Queensferry along the shore. It is one of Scotland's most magnificent mansions, built for and still lived in by the Hope family. Originally completed between 1699 and 1704 by the architect Sir William Bruce (who rebuilt Holyrood) for the first Earl of Hopetoun, it was rebuilt and enlarged by William Adam and his sons Robert and John between 1721 and 1754. To appreciate fully its classical beauty, go to the end of the avenue and look back at the house, a perfectly proportioned sweep of inspired architecture. Among its furnishings and treasures are paintings attributed to Van Dyck, Titian, Rubens and Rembrandt, some hung on walls lined with silk and damask. The gardens were modelled on those at Versailles and landscaped to give views across the Forth to the Lomond Hills. Now almost all reduced to lawns, the pattern can only be seen from aerial photographs. There is a deer park, rare St Kilda sheep and a nature trail, as well as walks along the river.

Festivals

September: Antique Dealers' Fair, Hopetoun House; a chance to pick up a bargain (for special arrangements for people with disabilities, call **t** (0131) 331 2451).

Sports and Activities

The **Maid of the Forth, t** (0131) 331 4857, *www.maidoftheforth.co.uk*, sails from Hawes Pier, under the bridge, to Inchcolm Island (*see* Fife, p.329), throughout the summer. Also cruises with BBQ, casino or private charter.

At Port Edgar, west of the Forth Road Bridge, there is a yacht marina in the former naval station, **HMS** *Lochinvar*, **t** (0131) 331 3330, with a launching ramp, races and regattas, water skiing, and sailing and wind-surfing lessons.

Scottish Railway Preservation Society, Bo'ness, **t** (01506) 822 298, *www.srps.org.uk*. Steam train rides on the Bo'ness and Kinneil Railway. *Open weekends, and on certain weekdays in summer.*

Where to Stay and Eat

Hawes Inn, South Queensferry, **t** (0131) 331 1990 (*moderate*). A traditional, historic inn, with pub food as well as *haute cuisine*. Also live jazz and blues on Mondays. If you stay, you can listen for the hushed voices of the pilgrims and the tramp of sailors' feet.

Priory Lodge, 8 The Loan, South Queensferry, **t** (0131) 331 4345, *calmyn@aol.com* (*moderate*). Good, no-nonsense guesthouse, 10 minutes from the airport. Comfortable and friendly.

Richmond Park Hotel, Bo'ness, **t** (01506) 823 213 (*moderate*). Comfortable, if somewhat lacking in character, with good views over the Firth to the Fife hills.

Dougal Philip's Walled Garden Centre (*open daily 10–5.30*), in the walled garden, is a real treat for gardeners. When exhausted, go to the licensed **restaurant** in the converted stables courtyard and indulge in smoked salmon, Aberdeen Angus beef, or the 'Hopetoun Delight' dessert – all home cooking.

House of the Binns

House open May–Sept daily 1.30–5.30 for guided tours only;
grounds open April–Oct daily 10–7; Nov–Mar daily 10–4; adm.

The House of the Binns is a couple of miles west along the river from Hopetoun. The curious name stems from *ben*, the Scottish word for 'hill'. The house, dating from 1630 with 19th-century Gothic embellishments, stands above parkland with views across the Forth. The moulded ceilings are very fine, and the rooms are beautifully furnished. The most intriguing aspect of a visit to the Binns is the memorabilia of the notorious Tam Dalyell (pronounced Dee-el), who raised the Royal Scots Greys here in 1681 and whose father built the house. Stories about General Tam, whose mortal remains were popularly believed to have been removed from the family vault at Abercorn, nearby, and carried to a far warmer resting place by the Devil himself, are as spine-chilling as they are apocryphal. Known to his troops as the 'Bluidy Muscovite', he was alleged to hold flagellation parties, to munch wine glasses and to have conversations with the Devil – stories richly embroidered by his Covenanting enemies. In the house is a heavy carved table that was recovered from a muddy pond where it had lain for 200 years, having been hurled there, it is said, by the Devil, a bad loser in a game of cards with Tam. Among the relics of this legendary man are his sword, his Bible and the comb with which he groomed his beard, having sworn after the execution of Charles I never to cut a hair of his head until the restoration of the monarchy. His descendant, also Tam Dalyell, is a Labour MP.

Blackness Castle

Open April–Sept daily 9.30–6.30; Oct–Mar Mon–Sat 9.30–4.30,
Sun 2–4.30, closed Thurs pm and Fri; adm.

Blackness Castle is a mile or so north of the House of the Binns. The castle juts into the Firth of Forth, its northern walls pointed like the prow of a massive battleship, lapped on three sides by the river. Its original date is unknown. The present tower was built in the 15th century when it was one of Scotland's most important fortresses. Besieged by Cromwell, it has in its time been a royal castle, a prison for Covenanters, a powder magazine and a youth hostel. When Scotland and England were joined by the Act of Union in 1707, Blackness was one of the four fortresses to be maintained at full military strength. If you look out across the water through the gun-slits in the curtain wall, you can almost hear the roar of cannon fire and smell the acrid tang of spent gunpowder.

The riverside village of **Blackness**, just along from the castle, was a medieval seaport, with wharves and warehouses, teeming with all the noise and smell and colour of a busy port which supplied the Royal Burgh of Linlithgow.

Bo'ness

Bo'ness or Borrowstownness, a couple of miles further west, is of historic rather than scenic interest. The Antonine Wall started a mile to the east, at Bridgeness. It was built by the Romans in AD 142 between Forth and Clyde in an abortive attempt to protect the south from the northern barbarians (*see* **History**, 'The Romans', p.35).

Kinneil Museum (*open Mon–Sat 12.30–4; adm*), next to Kinneil House a mile west of Bo'ness, is in converted 17th-century stables. They have Bo'ness pottery and cast-iron work, an exhibition of the estate's history going back 2,000 years, and an excavated fortlet from the Antonine Wall. Don't miss the bothy (hut) at the back where James Watt built his first steam engine while trying to solve the problem of flooding in a nearby mine in 1765.

The Hinterland: Linlithgow to Haddington

There is plenty of interest, both historical and aesthetic, on the way back eastwards, skirting the southern outskirts of Edinburgh. Don't be put off by built-up areas; they often conceal things worth seeing.

Linlithgow and Around

Linlithgow, 3 miles south of Bo'ness, lies in an oasis of rural tranquillity, surrounded by rounded hills and remote farming communities untouched by the ugly sprawl of industrial and mining development just out of sight beyond the horizon. There was a Pictish settlement here before the Romans came, and the first royal palace was recorded in the 12th century. Edward I had his headquarters in the town in 1301 and David II built a royal manor, destroyed by fire along with the town in 1424. The following year work began on the present palace. Since then the town has seen much of Scotland's history.

Linlithgow Palace

Open April–Sept daily 9.30–6.30; Oct–Mar Mon–Sat 9.30–4.30, Sun 2–4.30; adm.

The palace is one of the country's most poignant ruins. Only pigeons now inhabit the shell that stands on a slope of grass overlooking its own loch. Pinkish-ochre walls rise to five storeys, supported by flying buttresses: a roofless square with many of its rooms so well preserved that only a little imagination is needed to see how they must have been. Through its gateway in 1513 James IV rode out, against the advice of his lords, to lead his gallant army to tragic defeat at Flodden. The elaborate fountain in the quadrangle is said to have run with wine when James V gave it to Mary of Guise as a wedding present in 1538. Four years later their daughter was born in one of the upper chambers, ill-fated Mary who was proclaimed Queen of Scots within a week of her birth. Over-enthusiastic fuelling of domestic fires, possibly with bedding straw, by

General Hawley's troops who were garrisoned there on the night of 31 January 1746, reduced the palace to a smouldering shell. The swans on the loch add a royal touch: it is said they flew away when the Roundheads arrived and returned the day Charles II was crowned at Scone in 1649. Perhaps the best view of the palace is at night from the M9, from where it looks almost ethereal, floodlit against the dark sky.

St Michael's Church is so close to the palace that from a distance it seems to be part of it. As well as providing a place of worship for many of Scotland's monarchs, this large pre-Reformation church has had to endure much harsh treatment since its consecration in 1242. It was rebuilt after the fire of 1424; John Knox's followers despoiled it; Cromwell's soldiers stabled their horses in the aisle and left shot-holes in the walls. While praying for guidance and victory before Flodden, James IV saw a ghost which stood by the altar and warned him of his coming defeat. The original stone crown on the tower collapsed in 1820 and was replaced by the present astonishing laminated wood and aluminium 'crown of thorns' in 1964 – an unfortunate flight of fancy.

The **Linlithgow Story** (*open April–Oct Mon–Sat 10–5, Sun 1–4; adm; www. linlithgowstory.org.uk*), in Annet House in the High Street, tells the history of the area with displays and artefacts. The **Linlithgow Canal Centre** has a little museum (*open Easter–mid-Oct Sat and Sun 2–5, July and Aug daily; or by appointment,* **t** *(01506) 671 215; www.lucs.org.uk*) at the Manse Road basin, and runs boat trips on the canal to Avon Aqueduct (2½ hours), as well as shorter trips. There is a tearoom.

Cockleroy Hill is on the right, along a country lane due south of Linlithgow, signposted to Beecraigs Country Park. It is an easy 15-minute stroll through dense pines and up a gentle slope of turf and vivid green moss. Some say the name is derived from '*cuckold le roi*', and hints at an indiscretion by Mary of Guise, getting her own back for the philanderings of her husband, James V. Others, more prosaic, say the name stems from the Gaelic *cochull ruadh*, meaning red hood. The keenness of your eyes is the only limit to the horizon from here. A view indicator points out 36 landmarks, including Goat Fell, 66 miles away on Arran. You can see the ramparts of a Pictish hill fort beyond the indicator: their lookouts would have been able to give good warning of attack.

Torphichen Preceptory (*open April–Sept Sat 11–5, Sun 2–5; adm*), 2 miles further south, was founded in 1153 as the community of the Scottish Order of the Knights of St John of Jerusalem. The 15th-century tower and vaulted transepts are all that remain, together with the nave which was rebuilt in the 17th century and is now the parish kirk. It stands on the outskirts of the village, among lawns backed by bracken-covered hills, and is a good example of fortified church architecture. A folding green-baize table, in one of the box pews in the kirk, hinted at a less than spiritual attitude among past parishioners. One of the tombstones in the rather spooky churchyard is thought to be pre-Christian, and there are several with ancient primitive carvings.

Cairnpapple is less than a mile south again, in the Bathgate Hills. A bleak summit aptly known as 'windy ways', it has panoramic views, coast to coast, from the Bass Rock to Goat Fell. Follow the Historic Scotland signs to a parking bay from where a

Tourist Information

Linlithgow: Burgh Halls, The Cross, **t** (01506) 844 600; *open all year.*

Festivals

June: Riding of the Marches, Linlithgow; with a parade, bands and decorated floats.

Sports and Activities

Beecraigs Country Park, in the Bathgate Hills, between Linlithgow and Bathgate, **t** (01506) 844 516; *www.beecraigs.com.* 657 acres of woodland walks, a deer farm, a trout farm, water sports on the lake, fly fishing, archery, a keep-trim course, orienteering, rock climbing and exhibitions in the park centre. *Open daily 9–4.*

Where to Stay

Champany Inn, nr Linlithgow, **t** (01506) 834 532, *www.champany.com* (*expensive*). An exceptional inn, just off the M9, where you can stay, and eat like a king (*see below*).

Dalmahoy, Kirknewton, **t** (0131) 333 1845 (*expensive*). A comfortable Marriott hotel focused on golf, in the large annexe of the original Georgian house.

Houston House, Uphall (just off the A89), **t** (01506) 853 831, *info@houston.macdonald-hotels.co.uk* (*expensve*). 16th-century fortified tower house where Mary, Queen of Scots' advocate once lived. Pleasant garden, four-posters, and excellent food with a good wine list, served in a panelled dining room.

Norton House, Ingliston, **t** (0131) 333 1275 (*expensive*). One of Richard Branson's Virgin hotels – very swish and excellent food.

Ratho Hall, Baird Road, Ratho, **t** (0131) 335 3333, *www.countrymansions.com* (*moderate*). 18th-century with Adam embellishments. Very comfortable and hospitable, with dinner on request. Wolsey Lodge standards.

Craigs Holiday Lodges, Williamcraigs, Linlithgow, **t** (01506) 845 025, *www.craigslodges.freeserve.co.uk* (*cheap*). Fully equipped A-frame chalets, on a wooded hillside with panoramic views over the Forth Valley, with linen and a colour TV. Ideal for families

Highfield House, Kirknewton, **t** (01506) 881 489, *hhuntergordon@compuserve.com* (*cheap*). Good B&B in an old manse.

Mrs Inglis, Thornton, Edinburgh Road, Linlithgow, **t** (01506) 844 693, *inglisthornton@hotmail.com* (*cheap*). Comfortable Victorian B&B with big garden.

West Port Hotel, Linlithgow, **t** (01506) 847 456 (*cheap*). Friendly hotel.

Beecraigs Country Park, *see* above, **t** (01506) 844 510. Very good caravan site in splendid surroundings.

Craigbrae, Kirkliston, **t** (0131) 331 1205, *westmacott@compuserve.com.* Good B&B.

Eating Out

Champany's, Champany Corner, **t** (01506) 834 532 (*expensive*). Surely the best steak house in Britain. Don't expect instant service here: lobsters glare out from a bubbling tank; cuts of raw meat, hung to full maturity, are laid out for inspection; whole salmon, fresh from the river, gleam on a slab; mouthwatering vegetables tempt from a huge wicker basket. Soaked in a house marinade, the steaks are seared on charcoal: the combination of method, marinade and maturity make them food fit for the gods. No one could begrudge a penny of the cost. You can also stay here, *see* above.

Bridge Inn, Ratho, **t** (0131) 333 1320. An inn on the canal, with a canal-boat restaurant, cruises and dancing; good value for money.

The Four Marys, Main Street, Linlithgow. Popular pub which serves food.

Livingston's, Linlithgow, **t** (01506) 846 565. Bistro-style cottage with conservatory. Good food at reasonable prices.

short climb over turf leads to a lofty site that was used for ritual and burial, from possibly 2500 BC until the 1st century. An underground **cist** or tomb (*open April–Sept daily 9.30–6.30; adm*) has been reconstructed. It is an eerie feeling on that windswept plateau, trying to picture those ancient ceremonies and those 4,500-year-old tragedies and tears. (When the cist is shut you can get the key from the curator of the preceptory in Torphichen.)

The Pentland Hills, Moorfoots and Esk Valley

The Pentland Hills run southwest from Edinburgh, sprawling across a width of four to five miles; the high moorland is carpeted with heather, bracken and deer-hair grass and laced with reservoirs and streams. There are dozens of good walks, some along the old cattle-drove routes south. The highest peak is Scald Law (1,898ft). The Moorfoots run more or less parallel to the east, equally lovely with attractive villages at their feet. The North Esk rises in the Pentlands, the South Esk in the Moorfoots: they tumble out of their separate hills and rush into a turbulent marriage beyond Dalkeith and enter the sea as one.

Malleny House Garden (*open April–Oct daily 9.30–7; Nov–Mar daily 9.30–4; adm; t (0131) 449 2283; www.nts.org.uk*), in Balerno about 7 miles southwest of Edinburgh off the A70, is lapped by the Water of Leith. Although the 17th-century house is not open to the public, it is a perfect focal point for the formal garden, with its rare shrub roses, clipped yews, rhododendrons and many shrubs and plants. The saddle-backed dovecote behind the house has not been inhabited since 1961 when its residents perished from a surfeit of treated grain. The Georgian wing of the house is due to open soon.

Castlelaw

Castlelaw Iron-Age Fort (*open at all times*) is signed off the west side of the A702 and easily reached by a short climb through gorse scrub from the road. There is a souterrain, or earth-house, with a stone passage and chamber, surrounded by three ramparts, occupied in the 2nd century by Romans. Visit Castlelaw at dawn and walk to the top of Woodhouselee Hill, beyond. The sun, rising over the Moorfoot Hills, bathes the land in a pinkish light, with mist still clinging to the valley, well worth the early rise.

At the **Flotterstone Inn**, just south of Castlelaw on the A702 (*see* 'Eating Out', p.199), you can sit in the garden in summer beside the Glencorse Burn or walk up beside the burn for about a mile to the **Glencorse Reservoir**, a pine-fringed stretch of water reflecting the surrounding hills. Like most of the reservoirs in the Pentlands, it is stocked with brown and rainbow trout, and day permits are available for both bank and boat fishing. The exposed mud shore and receding water-line too often indicate a shortage of rainfall. The water covers the remains of the Chapel of St Katherine in the Hopes, drowned when the valley was flooded to make the reservoir. In the 13th century Sir William St Clair of Roslin had a bet with Robert the Bruce. He wagered his head against this Glencorse valley, that his hounds would kill a certain deer that had eluded all huntsmen before it reached the Glencorse Burn. The deer was brought down at the burn, St Clair won his land and built the chapel on the site in thanksgiving. (He was later killed, with James Douglas, on the way to the Holy Land with Bruce's heart in 1330 – *see* 'Dunfermline', p.326.)

Penicuik

The **Edinburgh Crystal Visitor Centre** (*open daily 10–5; adm; www.edinburgh-crystal.com*) in Penicuik (pronounced Pennycook), runs conducted tours showing the process of glassmaking: blowing, cutting, engraving, etc. A tourist information office is open here in summer.

The Penicuik to Bonnyrigg Walkway

The railway that used to link Penicuik with Bonnyrigg has been transformed into a 5-mile walk, following the course of the River North Esk, through Roslin Glen. Part of the wooded valley of the North Esk is preserved as a countryside park. You pass the remains of what was once Scotland's biggest gunpowder mill, supplying munitions for the Napoleonic Wars as well as for the First and Second World Wars.

Glencorse Kirk

Built in 1665, a mile northeast of Penicuik, Glencorse Kirk is roofless except for the tower, which was a 19th-century addition. In his youth Robert Louis Stevenson was a fairly regular attender, having walked over the Pentlands from Swanston. In a letter from the South Seas, he wrote to the local minister and novelist, S. R. Crockett, one of the Kailyard School of writers:

Go there and say a prayer for me. See that it is a sunny day; I would like it to be a Sunday. Stand on the right bank just where the road goes down in to the water, and shut your eyes; and if I don't appear to you...

Roslin

Roslin, or Rosslyn, is 3 miles east of Castlelaw in the lee of the Pentlands. A fairy-tale castle rises from trees near an historic chapel. To see it from the outside, park by the chapel and walk around the graveyard and over a narrow footbridge (once a draw-bridge) that dizzyingly spans the North Esk, far below. The castle stands high over Roslin Glen, with dripping dungeons, an ancient yew tree and legends of buried treasure. Dating from 1304, when the Lantern Tower was built, it was the home of the St Clair family who came to England with William the Conqueror and were lured north by offers of land from Malcolm Canmore. Sir William St Clair, third Earl of Orkney, lived here in sumptuous state in the 15th century, ate off gold plate, waited on by dozens of lords and ladies, and minted his own coins. When his wife, Elizabeth, went visiting, her mounted escort numbered two hundred. The castle was burnt and bombarded many times. In 1447 one of the women of the household scrambled under a bed to help a whelping bitch. Her candle set the bedding on fire and the old part of the castle was gutted. The castle suffered badly in the 16th century, when Hertford was obeying his king's order to 'put all to fire and sword' in Scotland. Part of the castle can be rented, *see* 'Where to Stay', p.198.

Tourist Information

Newtongrange: Scottish Mining Museum, t (0131) 663 4262; *open summer only.*
Penicuik: Edinburgh Crystal Visitor Centre, t (01968) 673 846; *open summer only.*

Sports and Activities

Hillend Dry Ski Slope, on the northern slope of the Pentland Hills, **t** (0131) 445 4433. The largest of its kind in Europe. You can hire equipment and instruction.

Where to Stay

Borthwick Castle, Gorebridge, **t** (01875) 820 514 (*expensive*), *see* below. Every stone drips with history: you can dine by candlelight in the great hall, lie in bed listening to the wind moaning, and picture Mary and Bothwell, so recently married, enjoying one of their few moments of happiness together.
Dalhousie Castle Hotel and Spa, Bonnyrigg, **t** (01875) 820 153, *www.dalhousiecastle.co.uk* (*expensive*). Slightly cheaper, a massive 800-year-old keep with turrets and battlements

and a great round tower. Sublime food is served in the barrel-vaulted dungeons. Just don't think about the ghastly tortures that went on down here: in the wine cellar, marks on the walls were made by prisoners who were hung upside down to die. There are ghosts, of course, including a walled-up Grey Lady, but the canny manageress won't say where in case honeymooners are frightened away. Four-poster beds in some of the rooms, a spring well (under the bridal suite), and a crypt, inside. Clay-pigeon shooting, croquet, riding and archery, outside.
Abbey Mains, 2 miles east of Haddington, **t** (01620) 823 286, *joyce.abbeymains@farmersweekly.net* (*moderate*). Large, stone farmhouse run by the Playfair family who have owned it for generations. David Playfair is a farmer and Joyce does the garden from which much of the excellent food is produced. No smoking.
Brown's Hotel, West Road, on the outskirts of Haddington, **t** (01620) 822 254, *www.browns-hotel.com* (*moderate*). Comfortable, elegant 19th-century town house with a nice garden and a good reputation for food.
Johnstounburn House, Humbie, **t** (01875) 833 696 (*moderate*). Very high-class, elegant

Rosslyn Chapel (*open Mar–Oct Mon–Sat 10–5, Sun 12–4.45; Nov–April till 4.30; adm; tickets from the gift shop and café next to the Roslin Inn; www.rosslyn-chapel.com*) was the creation of the flamboyant Sir William St Clair in the 15th century. Worried, perhaps, that he might have used his great wealth too self-indulgently, he decided towards the end of his life that he'd better atone for some of his extravagances before going on to meet his Maker. He therefore started building a church. The St Clairs are hereditary Grand Master Masons, and the church was to be the world's High Temple of Masonry. Dedicated to St Matthew and founded in 1446, it was designed to be an enormous cruciform collegiate church but was never finished. When William died in 1484, enthusiasm for the project dwindled and all that was completed was the present chapel, a chancel and part of the transept, with a vault below. A number of St Clairs are buried in the vault, some, it is said, still in armour. The interior is so richly carved that you get visual indigestion. Nearly every inch has been decorated with men and animals, birds and foliage, flowers and insects: there are the Seven Cardinal Virtues, the Seven Deadly Sins, the Dance of Death and a lot more besides, all created by the finest craftsmen of the day.

Your eye will be drawn inevitably to the famous **Apprentice Pillar** on the south side of the Lady Chapel. The pillar's carving is so delicate that it makes the rest seem

17th-century country house at the foot of the Lammermuirs, surrounded by 40 acres of park and gardens. It's comfortable and the food is excellent.

Markle House, East Linton, t (01620) 860 570, *mcguinness@marklehouse.fsnet.co.uk* (*moderate*). 18th-century family house for comfortable and hospitable B&B. Meals by arrangement.

The Mill House, Temple, t (01875) 830 253 (*moderate*). Very special cottage by the river, with memorable food, and peace and quiet.

The Original Hotel, Roslin, t (0131) 440 2384 (*moderate*). Small, friendly coaching inn with a candlelit restaurant and four-poster beds.

Prestonhall, Pathhead, t (01875) 320 949, *h.callander@ukgateway.net* (*moderate*). One of the finest Georgian houses in the south of Scotland, in 70 acres of parkland, where you get a warm welcome from Henry and Jackie Callander.

Royal Hotel, High Street, Penicuik, t (01968) 676 979, *faichney@compuserve.co.uk* (*moderate*). Comfortable 18th-century coaching inn.

Stair Arms Hotel, Pathhead, t (01875) 320 277 (*moderate*). Nice, but on the main A68. Comfortable, with reasonable food.

Laird and Dog Hotel, Lasswade, t (0131) 663 9219 (*cheap*). Small family hotel in the High Street, only 15 minutes from Edinburgh. It has a cosy atmosphere and is comfortable.

Roslin Castle, Roslin (*see* p.197), c/o The Landmark Trust, Shottesbrooke, Maidenhead, Berkshire, t (01628) 825 925. Self-catering accommodation in a restored part of the castle (sleeping 8).

Eating Out

Drovers Inn, East Linton, t (01620) 860 298. An old railway inn, full of character and antique furniture, in an attractive village. Try the char-grilled suckling pig, cooked Spanish style, with honey and ginger.

Flotterstone Inn, just south of Castlelaw on the A702, *see* p.196, t (01968) 673 717. Nice garden by the Glencorse Burn, and a good selection of dishes at reasonable prices.

The Pheasant, Haddington, (01620) 824 428. Traditional, lively pub.

Poldrate's, Haddington, t (01620) 826 882. Bistro in converted mill, *see* p.203.

The Waterside, Haddington, t (01620) 825 674. Nice bistro and restaurant beside the river.

almost crude. It was named by Sir Walter Scott, after a fictional account of the apprentice who carved it being killed by his master who was jealous of the quality of the apprentice's work.

Roslin Inn, now the curator's house beside the chapel, dates from 1662 and has had many illustrious visitors including Boswell, Johnson, Burns, Scott, the Wordsworths and Edward VII, who engraved a memorial to his visit on a window in 1859 when he was Prince of Wales. Not far to the west, in the Pentlands, the Battle of Rullion Green took place in 1666, when troops under General Tam Dalyell, Commander of the King's Army in Scotland, defeated an uprising of Covenanters. Dalyell permitted appalling reprisals and his name became synonomous with terror. He also appropriated several of the forfeited estates.

The **Howgate Inn** (*not open to the public*), a couple of miles south of Roslin, was another inn with literary associations: Walter Scott, Allan Ramsay, Dr John Brown, Henry Mackenzie and Robert Louis Stevenson were among its better-known customers. Dr John Brown wrote his memorable story *Rab and His Friends* about the dog who goes to Edinburgh every day with the Howgate carriers. (The carrier and his wife are buried in the churchyard of St Mungo's in Penicuik.)

Temple

Temple is a hamlet about 4 miles east of Howgate as the crow flies – an attractive 6-mile drive. In a tranquil churchyard, on a hillside beside a cascading burn, is the roofless ruin of a 14th-century church. It stands on the site of one built by the Knights Templar, the soldier-monks of the Crusades who had headquarters here until the Pope decided they were becoming too powerful and suppressed them in 1312.

Dalkeith

Dalkeith, 6 miles north of Temple and 6 miles southeast of Edinburgh on the A68, has a wide, cobbled main street, embraced by the North Esk and South Esk before they unite further north for their final sprint to the sea. In spite of being the junction of several main roads, it has a stately feeling about it, enhanced perhaps by its palace and the historic castles that surround it.

In **Dalkeith Country Park** (*open April–Oct daily 10–6; adm*) you can roam along the river among the trees. There is a 'tunnel walk', a woodland adventure play area, an 18th-century bridge and a ruined orangery. Although the palace is not open to the public it makes a splendid background to the park. Seat of the Scotts of Buccleuch since the 12th century, it is a large, reddish, neoclassical mansion. Designed in the 18th century by Sir John Vanburgh around an older castle, it has a recessed centre and two projecting wings, modelled on the Dutch Loo Palace. Here in 1572, when the palace was known as the Lion's Den, the notorious James Douglas, Earl of Morton, lay on his sick-bed and held the council which plotted to bring Mary, Queen of Scots to trial. George IV stayed here in 1822 during his state visit to Scotland, as did Queen Victoria, in 1842, when she remarked in her diary that she had 'tasted oatmeal porridge, which I think very good'.

The much-restored 12th-century **Collegiate Church of St Nicholas** is on the north side of Dalkeith High Street. In the roofless ruin of the 14th-century choir and apse, a double tomb is believed to contain the remains of the first Earl Morton and his wife, Johan, daughter of James I. It was here in 1445 that Aeneas Silvius, a papal diplomat, later Pope Pius II, was astonished to see 'black stones' being given to the poor as alms. Much travelled as he was, the Italian had never seen coal before.

The **Edinburgh Butterfly and Insect World** (*open summer daily 9.30–5.30; winter daily 10–5; adm; www.edinburgh-butterfly-world.co.uk*) is on the A7 two miles north of Dalkeith. In exotic rainforest, landscaped with tropical plants, waterfalls and lily ponds, butterflies from all over the world fly freely around. There are displays of insects, a tearoom, garden centre, tropical fish shop, playground and picnic area.

Newbattle Abbey (*conducted tours on written application to the warden*) lies a mile southeast of Dalkeith and can be clearly seen from the gate. It was founded for the Cistercians in the 12th century; after the Reformation it became the family seat of the Kerrs, later Marquesses of Lothian, who gave it to the nation as an adult education centre. In its heyday it was frequently visited by royalty: a murdered mistress of David II was buried here; James IV met his 14-year-old bride, Margaret Tudor, here; James V stayed here; and George IV came on his Scottish bonanza. The monks of Newbattle were among the first to work the local coalmines.

Lady Victoria Colliery, Newtongrange

Just south of Dalkeith, Lady Victoria Colliery was built by the Lothian Coal Company in 1890 and pioneered many techniques in the mechanization of coal cutting and haulage. Converted into the **Scottish Mining Museum** (*open daily 10–5; adm; www.scottishminingmuseum.com*), its award-winning displays take you on a trip through the highs and lows of an industry that was once the backbone of Scotland, and bring to life what it must have been like for the people who lived and worked here. The interiors of the pit village are interesting and evocative. Look out for the miner, pale and exhausted, slumped in front of the fire in his kitchen after his shift in the mine, a blanket round his shoulders, his long johns drying on a rail. There is a licensed Victorian tearoom, and a tourist information office in the summer.

A couple of miles east of Newtongrange, on Tyne Water, the **Vogrie Country Park** has wooded glens and gardens around a great mansion and a nine-hole golf course. Vogrie House, built in 1876, contains an interpretative centre showing the park's history. In the grounds are a variety of gardens, including the Garden of Peace and Friendship where foreign visitors can plant trees as a token of friendship. Lime in the soil encourages wild thyme and quaking grass. The Rhododendron Walk, leading to the house, is glorious in the spring when the rhododendrons and azaleas are in bloom on a sea of daffodils. There is a pond, waterfall and rockery at the end, in front of the house. There is a Tree Trail, as well as nature trails with roe deer and even badgers. Over 70 species of birds have been recorded: look for dippers, bobbing up and down on the stones on the river bank.

Arniston House (*open July–Sept Tues, Thurs and Sun 2–5, or by appointment, t (01875) 830 515; adm; www.arniston-house.co.uk*), at Gorebridge, is a mansion built in 1726 by William Adam for Robert Dundas, later Lord President of the Court of Session. Walter Scott was a frequent guest and recorded in his diary in 1828: 'I am always happy in finding myself in the old Oak Room at Arniston where I have drank many a merry bottle...' Home-baked teas and clay-pigeon shooting now replace the merry bottles.

Borthwick Castle

Borthwick Castle is 5 miles south of Dalkeith in a hamlet in the Moorfoot Hills, just off the A7. More than 500 years old, and the largest complete twin-towered keep in Scotland (sadly somewhat over-restored), it is now a private hotel (*see* 'Where to Stay', above) where guests dine in a stone-vaulted great hall with minstrels' gallery and hooded fireplace, and can sleep in the bedchambers once occupied by Mary, Queen of Scots and Bothwell. The ill-fated couple came here a month after their marriage. Insurgents surrounded them and Bothwell escaped through the postern gate, followed later by Mary, disguised as a man. It is said that prisoners were invited to jump the 13-foot gap between the two towers at a height of 80ft. If they succeeded, they were allowed to go free. There is an information centre beside the lodge at the gate. A right of way links Borthwick to Crichton Castle, an easy hour's walk.

Crichton Castle

Open April–Sept daily 9.30–6.30; adm.

14th-century Crichton Castle stands within sight and signalling distance of Borthwick, 2 miles to the northeast on a grassy plateau, high and isolated above a steep valley. Now a ruin, this was Bothwell's seat and it is said he kept his divorced wife here after his marriage to Mary. This, however, does not tie in with the belief that Mary came here for refuge after she escaped from Borthwick, on her way to meet up with Bothwell and run to Dunbar. In the courtyard you can see a delightful memento of Bothwell's nephew, Francis Stewart, Earl of Bothwell, the half-mad demonist, who travelled widely in Italy in the 16th century and brought back the idea for this Italianate piazza. Its walls are of a classical diamond design over pillars, making a remarkable contrast to the sturdy structure of the rest of the castle. Mary came here as a guest of Bothwell when she was newly arrived in Scotland, to dance at the wedding of his sister to her half-brother. The chapel-like ruin beyond is a fortified stable. **Crichton Collegiate Church**, half a mile to the north, has been in continuous use since it was built in 1449 and has marvellous barrel vaulting.

Soutra Aisle

Open all the time; t (01875) 833 248, for tours and lectures.

From Crichton, go east on the back road for a mile and a half to the A68 and then 3 miles or so southwest to Soutra. The B6368 climbs into the hills from here, taking you to Soutra Aisle, a small stone building with a mossy roof, so simple you might pass it off as a byre. In 1164 Malcolm IV founded a large hospice here, ideally sited far from the slums and sewers of the towns. Recent discoveries show that the medicine they practised was remarkably advanced, especially in the use of herbal remedies, which they even used as a form of anaesthetic. The hospice functioned for about 600 years. It incorporated the parish church in the 16th century, and a service is held there once a year. The public can attend periodic seminars and learn about some of the amazing discoveries that have been unearthed here.

Haddington

Haddington, peacefully spread along the banks of the River Tyne, was extensively restored by an enterprising town council a few years ago, with a lot of help from local inhabitants: the results are outstanding. The wedge-shaped market square is divided at one end by the fine William Adam **town house** whose church-like steeple was added by Gillespie Graham in 1831, and has a clock that still strikes the curfew at 10pm and 7am. Bright colour-washed houses front the main streets, with quaint wynds and courtyards leading off. Flood water from the river has been known to reach the steps of the mercat cross. Over 130 buildings in Haddington are listed as of special architectural or historic interest, and an illustrated booklet, *A Walk Round Haddington*, is sold locally. There is also an architectural trail map, on the wall of the town house.

The medieval **Church of St Mary** is one of Haddington's greatest treasures. Built by the river in the 14th century on the site of at least two previous churches, the chancel and transepts were roofless for 400 years after the Reformation until it was restored to its full glory in 1973. Concerts are often performed here, honoured by such musicians as Yehudi Menuhin and Louis Kentner. The size of the church gives an idea of the early prosperity of this area. John Knox, who was born nearby in 1505, worshipped in St Mary's. A plain slab on the floor has a moving inscription on it by Thomas Carlyle, to his wife Jane Welsh, daughter of a Haddington doctor. She is buried in the churchyard, having left instructions that she did not wish to be buried with her husband with whom she shared a tempestuous though loving relationship.

The **Jane Welsh Carlyle Museum** (*open April–Sept Wed–Sat 2–5; adm*), in Lodge Street, is in the restored dining room of her childhood home and tells of her life and times. The Regency gardens are charming.

Haddington House (1680), in Sidegate, is the headquarters and library of the Lamp of Lothian Trust, responsible for much of the restoration of the church and the cultural life of the town. Its restored 17th-century garden (with roses, herbs and a paved sunken garden) is reached from Pleached Alley.

The Poldrate Corn Mill is a three-storey 18th-century mill beside the Tyne at Victoria Bridge. Its undershot water wheel and cottages were also restored by the Lamp of Lothian Trust and it is now a community and arts centre. East of the river is the Nungate: malefactors were hanged from the hump-backed bridge, a gruesome thought as you look at the attractive river scene. The bridge led to the now vanished Abbey of Haddington, known until the Reformation as the *Lucerna Laudoniae*, the 'Lamp of Lothian', for its reputation as a lamp of spirituality and learning.

The **Museum of Flight**, in East Fortune Airfield (*open daily 10.30–5; adm; www.nms. ac.uk/flight*), has lots of planes, gliders and war memorabilia displayed in the old hangers of a Second World War airfield. There's a 100-year-old Hawk, the earliest surviving hang-glider in Scotland, Dick Emery's *Tiger Moth*, and masses more.

Traprain Law

Traprain Law dominates the plain east of Haddington, a massive whale-backed hump, part of a volcanic seam that includes North Berwick Law and the Bass Rock. Traprain, 734ft high, was the capital of the North British *Votadini* tribe, overlooking the 'Scottish Sea' whence invasion frequently threatened. The people lived on the fertile lands below, in times of danger retiring to the summit, where you can still see the remains of a fort. Traces of their occupation on the lower slopes include standing stones and souterrains. In 1919 a hoard of 4th-century Christian and pagan treasure, possibly buried by pirates, was excavated from the top of Traprain. The collection includes 160 silver-gilt bowls, goblets and clasps, which are on display in the Museum of Scotland in Edinburgh. Conservationists have managed to arrest stone-quarrying operations at the east end of the law and it is hoped the ugly gouged-out wedge will eventually be restored.

Hailes Castle, an open monument, is below Traprain on the northern side. The extensive ruin dates from the 13th century and was once a feudal stronghold. Built by

the Hepburns, later Earls of Bothwell, and demolished by Cromwell, it was strategically sited on what was then the main north–south highway and charged
extortionate tolls from passing travellers. The ruin stands beside a fast-flowing burn
on a grassy bank carpeted with snowdrops and daffodils in spring. You can still see
the water gate, bakehouse and vaulted pit prison into which prisoners were lowered
and left to perish. The 29-year-old lover of the wife of one of the lairds was incarcer-
ated here and his spirit is said to linger on, begging for a Christian burial.

Lennoxlove House

Open Easter–Oct Wed, Thurs, Sun and some Sats 2–4.30; adm;
good garden café/tearoom open all year daily 11–5;
t (01620) 823 720; www.lennoxlove.org.

Lennoxlove House is a mile south of Haddington on the B6369. Home of the Duke of
Hamilton, it stands in woodland, overlooking the Lammermuirs. The 15th-century
keep has parapet gargoyles, bartizans and a watchtower penthouse. In the keep and
17th- and 18th-century house are paintings by Raeburn, Van Dyck, Janssens, Lely,
Augustus John and de Lazlo, as well as porcelain and furniture. Look for the death
mask of Mary, Queen of Scots, and her silver casket in which were found the letters
(possibly forged) incriminating her in the murder of Darnley. The house got its name
from the 17th-century Duchess of Lennox, Frances Teresa Stuart, a favourite of Charles
II and possibly the model for the original Britannia on the pre-decimal coinage.

Preston Mill (*open April–Sept Mon–Sat 11–1 and 2–5; Oct Sat and Sun 1.30–4; adm*) lies
about 5 miles northeast of Haddington on the outskirts of East Linton. This delightful
mill, restored by the National Trust for Scotland, stands in a picture-postcard setting,
on a green beside the Tyne, where muscovy ducks and mallards bask in the shade of
apple trees. It is probably the only mill of its kind in working order. Built of warm red
sandstone and pantiles, it has a polygonal kiln with a ventilator, a working waterwheel and wooden machinery. Next door there is a small museum in an outbuilding.

Athelstaneford

Athelstaneford is a hamlet on a whinstone ridge a few miles north of Haddington.
Immediately noticeable is the St Andrew's Cross flying from a flagpole high above a
brass mural in the kirkyard. The mural is engraved with a scene from a Dark-Ages
battle between an invading Northumbrian army and the combined forces of the Picts
and Scots. Legend states that the temporarily allied kings, normally at loggerheads,
prayed for victory and were answered by seeing a saltire – the diagonal cross of
St Andrew (diagonal at St Andrew's request because he did not wish to emulate
Christ) – etched in cloud against a blue sky. When they then won their battle, the two
kings agreed to make the saltire the national flag of their united kingdoms, with St
Andrew as their patron saint, a resolution that was to be broken many times before it
became reality. The head of the defeated Athelstane was stuck on a spike on Inch
Garvie, an island near the Forth Bridge.

The **National Flag Heritage Centre** in the Main Street (*open April–Sept daily 10–5*) is a Saltire Memorial in the church, with an audiovisual dramatisation of the 9th-century battle.

Stenton

Stenton, 6 miles east of Haddington just off the A1, is a well-preserved village with a reputation for being one of the last places to have burnt witches, a practice for which it was notorious. A **tron** (tall timber weighing scales, used for measuring wool at the wool fairs) stands on one of the two tiny greens. Red sandstone cottages with pantiled roofs surround the greens, one with its original outside stairway. The old joiner's house lies below, with a picturesque courtyard, and beside it stands a farm with a wheelhouse. Near the school is the Smiddy and the **Oak Inn**, incorporating a picture gallery with frequently changing exhibitions by contemporary artists. Here, you can sit and enjoy an excellent light lunch surrounded by the paintings.

The 16th-century **Rood Well** was once a popular place for pilgrims. It's easy to miss, on the right as you enter the village from the A1, in a hollow carpeted with St John's Wort. Nearby, the ruins of the old kirk, with crow-stepped tower and dovecote, lie in the shadow of the tall pinnacles of the present church.

Pressmennan Glen, a long, wooded hanging valley, is a mile south of Stenton, reached by forking left at Stenton school. Bennet's Burn was dammed in 1819 to form this artificial loch, a deep, dark snake of water, haunt of wildfowl and trout. There is a forest trail that takes about 2 hours.

The Lammermuirs

South and east of Haddington, deep valleys cut into the rounded summits of the high moorland of the Lammermuir Hills. In summer sheep graze among wine-red heather, whins and cascading burns; skylarks sing and wild thyme scents the air. In winter the roads are often blocked with snow, and tractors go out from remote farm-steads to feed the sheep.

Garvald

Garvald, 3 miles south of Traprain Law, is a small redstone village nestling in a fold of the hills beside the fast flowing Papana Water. Behind a grille on the church wall and below a sundial dated 1633, you can see a metal neck-collar (the 'jougs') the height of a small man, where they tethered petty criminals for punishment.

Nunraw lies in trees above the village to the southeast, a 15th-century tower house with later additions. This massive red pile, founded as a nunnery in the 12th century and abandoned during the Reformation, was bought by Irish Cistercians in 1946. It was their monastery while they built their new abbey. Now the monks in black and white habits welcome all visitors who come here looking for God. The new abbey, **Sancta Maria**, is further up the hill on the right, a starkly simple, pale stone building, high on the hillside. In the long plain church, the many clear-glass windows look out

Where to Stay and Eat

Forbes Lodge, Gifford, **t** (01620) 810 212 (*moderate*). Owned and run by Lady Marioth Hay, whose family have lived in nearby Yester House (*see* below) since the 12th century. Stylish and traditional, and a splendid place to stay, enhanced by a charming hostess.

Tweeddale Arms Hotel, Gifford, **t** (01620) 810 240 (*moderate*). Listed Georgian building beside the Reformation church. It combines an 18th-century atmosphere with modern comforts, and the food is good.

Eaglescairnie Mains, Gifford, **t** (01620) 810 491, *williams.eagles@btinternet.com* (*cheap*). Delightful Georgian farmhouse B&B with pretty gardens and friendly hosts.

Elba Waterfall Cottage, in the Lammermuir Hills, **t** (01835) 870 779, **f** (01835) 870 417 (*cheap*). Self-catering in an old keeper's cottage near Abbey St Bathans (sleeping 5–6).

Goblin Ha' Hotel, Gifford, **t** (01620) 810 244 (*cheap*). An old-fashioned place known for its friendly staff. The cooking is country-style with bar suppers and special Sunday lunches. Beer garden and boules court.

over the moors. When the wind moans outside and the clouds race across the sky, it is perhaps easy to feel closer to the God people come here to seek.

Gifford

Gifford, 4½ miles south of Haddington, is a 17th-century village straggling around a wide main street. The entrance to Yester House (*private*), at the end of an avenue, is a graceful wrought-iron and gilded arch between redstone gatehouses with columned pillars topped by urns. On the estate there is the **Goblin Ha'**, a mighty underground hall with a high vaulted roof. According to tradition, this was built in the 13th century by Sir Hugo Gifford, who was known to be a wizard. Sir Walter Scott could not resist putting such a romantic place into 'Marmion' ('Of lofty roof and ample size, beneath the castle deep it lies').

In **Gifford Kirk** the 'laird's loft' was a withdrawing room, with a fireplace for the pampered laird and his family. There is an illustrated history of local buildings on a wall in the main street.

Whiteadder Reservoir lies in a bowl of the Lammermuirs just inside the Lothian border 8 miles to the southeast. There is a sheltered picnic site below the dam surrounded by clumps of trees, and a choice of good walks up into the hills.

Oldhamstocks

Oldhamstocks, 8 miles northeast of the reservoir on a plateau above a valley, has its cottages clustered around a wide green with a pump and cross. The name comes from the Saxon for 'old settlement'. As in Gifford, there is an illustrated board in the middle of the village giving the history of local buildings.

The **Watch Tower** (1824) in the kirkyard was used to watch over the graves in order to protect them from the lucrative practice of body-snatching. The 15th-century chancel of the kirk has a stone-slabbed roof. Don't miss the proclamation hanging in the porch, granting the village 'two frie fares yeirlie ...' and '...a werklie mercat for buying and selling of horse nolt, sheip meil, malt and all sort of grane, cloath, linnings, etc'. What an easy life our ancestors had, before spelling was standardized!

Glasgow

12

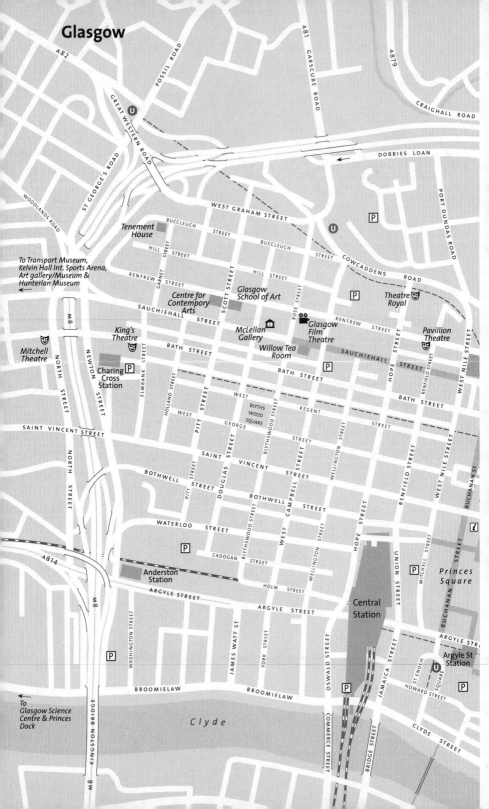

Glasgow

A82

A81

GARSCUBE ROAD

A879

CRAIGHALL ROAD

POSSIL ROAD

GREAT WESTERN ROAD

ST GEORGE'S ROAD

WOODLANDS ROAD

DOBBIES LOAN

PORT DUNDAS ROAD

WEST GRAHAM STREET

COWCADDENS ROAD

Tenement House

Buccleuch STREET

Buccleuch STREET

HILL STREET

HILL STREET

To Transport Museum,
Kelvin Hall Int. Sports Arena,
Art gallery/Museum &
Hunterian Museum

RENFREW STREET

GARNET STREET

SCOTT STREET

Centre for
Contempory
Arts

Glasgow
School of Art

ROSE STREET

Theatre
Royal

RENFREW STREET

SAUCHIEHALL

McLellan
Gallery

Glasgow Film
Theatre

HOPE STREET

Pavillion
Theatre

WEST NILE STREET

M8

King's
Theatre

NEWTON

ELMBANK STREET

BATH STREET

Willow Tea
Room

SAUCHIEHALL

STREET

Mitchell
Theatre

NORTH STREET

Charing
Cross
Station

BATH STREET

BATH STREET

HOLLAND STREET

PITT STREET

WEST

BLYTHS
WOOD
SQUARE

BUTHSWOOD STREET

REGENT

WELLINGTON STREET

STREET

SAINT VINCENT STREET

NORTH STREET

WEST

GEORGE

STREET

SAINT VINCENT STREET

DOUGLAS STREET

WEST CAMPBELL STREET

RENFIELD STREET

WEST NILE STREET

BUCHANAN STREET

BOTHWELL STREET

PITT STREET

BOTHWELL STREET

WELLINGTON STREET

HOPE STREET

WATERLOO STREET

CADOGAN STREET

BUTHSWOOD STREET

Princes
Square

A814

M8

Anderston
Station

ARGYLE STREET

HOLM STREET

ARGYLE STREET

Central
Station

UNION STREET

MITCHELL STREET

BUCHANAN STREET

ARGYLE STR

WASHINGTON STREET

JAMES WATT ST

YORK STREET

Argyle St
Station

ST ENOCH SQUARE

HOWARD STREET

To
Glasgow Science
Centre & Princes
Dock

KINGSTON BRIDGE

BROOMIELAW

BROOMIELAW

OSWALD STREET

COMMERCE STREET

BRIDGE STREET

JAMAICA STREET

CLYDE STREET

Clyde

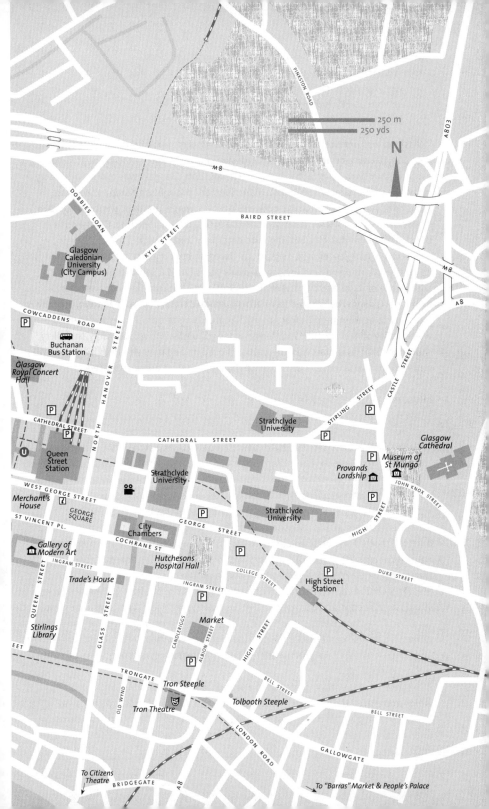

250 m
250 yds

N

PINKSTON ROAD

A803

M 8

M 8

A 8

BAIRD STREET

DOBBIES LOAN

KYLE STREET

CASTLE STREET

STIRLING STREET

Glasgow
Caledonian
University
(City Campus)

COWCADDENS ROAD

Buchanan
Bus Station

Glasgow
Royal Concert
Hall

NORTH HANOVER STREET

CATHEDRAL STREET

CATHEDRAL STREET

Strathclyde
University

Provands
Lordship

Museum of
St Mungo

Glasgow
Cathedral

JOHN KNOX STREET

Queen Street
Station

U

WEST GEORGE STREET

Merchant's
House

GEORGE
SQUARE

ST VINCENT PL.

Strathclyde
University

Strathclyde
University

HIGH STREET

GEORGE   STREET

City
Chambers

COCHRANE ST

Gallery of
Modern Art

INGRAM STREET

Trade's House

QUEEN STREET

GLASS STREET

Hutchesons
Hospital Hall

INGRAM STREET

COLLEGE STREET

High Street
Station

DUKE STREET

Stirlings
Library

EET

CANDLERIGGS

ALBION STREET

Market

HIGH STREET

TRONGATE

OLD WYND

Tron Steeple

Tron Theatre

Tolbooth Steeple

BELL STREET

BELL STREET

GALLOWGATE

To Citizens
Theatre

BRIDGEGATE

A 8

LONDON ROAD

To "Barras" Market & People's Palace

Beautiful city of Glasgow, with your streets so neat and clean,
Your stately mansions, and beautiful Green!
Likewise your beautiful bridges across the River Clyde,
And on your bonnie banks I would like to reside...

William McGonagall

Glasgow was once the ugly, boisterous, working-class hub of redundant industrial Scotland. Because of the flourishing Clydeside shipyards and all the associated heavy industry that grew up after the Industrial Revolution, Glasgow was particularly badly hit by the Depression of the 1930s. Unemployment brought hardship to seething warrens of slum tenements. But now, the 'Gorbals Image' (brilliantly encapsulated in *No Mean City*, by A. McArthur, written in the 1950s) has disappeared. Glasgow is a punchy, cosmopolitan city, buzzing with enterprise and vitality.

Edinburgh, with its Festival, its gracious Georgian buildings, its romantic past and its genteel Morningside ladies, was for many years lulled into a complacent acceptance of its role as cultural centre of Scotland. That complacency has been exploded: Glasgow celebrated its reign as Cultural Capital of Europe in 1990, only the sixth city to be nominated, after Athens, Florence, Amsterdam, Berlin and Paris, and was the City of Architecture and Design in 1999. Quietly, almost stealthily, that dirty, slum-infested tramp that was 'Glesca' has moved up and now vies with its grand rival for international attention. Only Glaswegians themselves are unsurprised.

History

When Edinburgh consisted of a cluster of huts around a wooden fort, St Mungo was busy in Glasgow establishing a church from which the present cathedral grew, on a site that had been consecrated by St Ninian two centuries before in the 4th century.

Assuming that legend is born from fragments of fact, a Pictish princess, possibly the daughter of King Loth, was banished from her father's court at Traprain Law in Lothian in the 6th century because of her liaison with an undesirable suitor. She was cast adrift in a coracle on the Firth of Forth, and landed at Culross in Fife. St Serf (or Servanus) took her in and cherished her during the birth of her son, Kentigern. St Serf baptized mother and babe and brought the child up, giving him the affectionate nickname of Mungo (or Munchu), the Latin–Welsh endearment for 'dearest friend'. Mungo became a missionary: in fulfilment of a prophecy, he took the bones of a holy man, Fergus, and carried them until God told him to stop. Glasgow Cathedral now stands on that spot, and the bones of Fergus are interred there. The town that grew up around the church was called Glas Cau (Gaelic for 'the dear green place'), and in the mild, dampish climate that prevails the land would certainly have been very green and fertile. Indeed, aerial photographs show a surprising amount of grass even now – over 70 parks in all.

Glasgow's coat of arms incorporates a salmon, a ring, a tree, a bird and a bell, all of which are related to the patron saint. Mungo saved the honour, and the life, of a queen by arranging for a ring that she had given her lover to be found in a salmon in the river, and returned to her to be shown to her suspicious husband. The tree is a branch that burned miraculously, enabling Mungo to rekindle the monastery fire that he had been entrusted to keep alight. The bird was a robin, a favourite of St Serf's, killed by accident and brought back to life by Mungo. The bell was one given to Mungo on his ordination and taken everywhere with him.

Glasgow's self-confident motto, 'Let Glasgow Flourish', stems from the more pious invocation that was inscribed on the 16th-century bell on the Tron Church: 'Let Glasgow Flourish Through the Preaching of the Word and Praising Thy Name'.

The city has played an important part in Scotland's history: in 1300 William Wallace defeated the English in a battle over what is now the upper end of the High Street. The university was founded in 1451 by Bishop Turnbull, only 40 years after St Andrews. Mary, Queen of Scots' final bid for power in 1568, after her escape from Leven Castle, took place at Langside, near Queen's Park. She watched the battle from her horse at Castle Knowe, riding forward into the mêlée to encourage her troops who were, even so, soon defeated. Cromwell came to Glasgow in 1650, and heard himself denounced as a 'sectary and blasphemer' by the Rector of the University, Zachary Boyd, in a two-hour sermon. (Cromwell took this public humiliation with rare humour, inviting Boyd to dinner and making him sit through three hours of prayer.) Prince Charles Edward Stuart lodged in the town on his way to Culloden in 1745.

Separated from America by the Atlantic Ocean, Glasgow merchants grew rich on the import of tobacco and sugar after the Union of Parliaments in 1707. The Clyde, once a shallow salmon river, was deepened by dredgers and the city flourished as a major port, developing into the world's leading shipbuilding centre. Glasgow reached its zenith in Victorian times, when it was the hub of mercantile and industrial Scotland, and it was then that so many of its fine buildings were built. Times of recession always hit hardest at areas of heavy industry, however, and Glasgow's docks are no longer the hives of activity that they were: Clydeside, badly bombed in the war, no longer reverberates to the ceaseless clang, clatter and fizzle of thriving shipyards, and the Clyde is no longer a busy waterway. To a certain extent, Glasgow has shaken itself free of dependence on heavy industry and has adapted its economy to embrace modern technology.

Modern Glasgow: Renaissance

No other Scottish city can rival Glasgow for its rich diversity of culture and entertainment. Home of the Scottish Opera, one of Scotland's most prestigious possessions, as well as the Royal Scottish National Orchestra and Scottish Ballet, Glasgow also has the Burrell Collection, attracting art lovers from all over the world. There are more than 20 top-class art galleries and museums, most of which are free. The Centre for Contemporary Arts is the best in Scotland, stimulating international interest. It mounts major art seasons with cross-cultural themes. Glasgow was recently said to rival Milan and Barcelona as one of the design capitals of the world.

Because the river flows through the heart of Glasgow, it is very much the main artery of the city, flanked by greens and quays, spanned by a network of bridges. A redevelopment programme has transformed the old docklands so that it is now possible to take a 'scenic' walk from Glasgow Green to Finnieston without danger of being hoisted up on a crane. Glasgow Green, the oldest public park in Britain, was the common grazing ground for the medieval city.

From any elevation on a clear day, the horizon is smudged by distant hills: to the north, beyond the modest Kilpatrick Hills and Campsie Fells, the great humps of Ben Lomond, Ben Venue and Ben Ledi, and the hills of Strathclyde in the west.

Architecturally, Glasgow is a curate's egg. Some of Britain's finest Victorian buildings stand adjacent to some of the 20th-century's worst examples of architectural sacrilege, mostly high-rise. The efficient motorway network, taking traffic through the heart of the city, has improved communications beyond belief, but heartrending acts of vandalism were committed to build it. The M8 effectively cuts the city centre in two, dividing the commercial side from what is now the West End and Glasgow University. Many of the older buildings have been cleaned recently: streets that used to be blackened by pollution have been restored to the warm glow of biscuit and red sandstone (a controversial measure as it has now been proved that the cleaning can damage the buildings).

Much of the suburbs are a jungle of ugly monsters, built in a misguided attempt to depopulate the slums. In time, as people move back into the rejuvenated inner city, these travesties of architecture may be replaced.

If comparisons must be made between Edinburgh and Glasgow, and perhaps this is inevitable with two major cities so close to each other, Glasgow is to Edinburgh what New York is to Washington. Glasgow today is a truly multicultural city, with large Italian and Asian communities. The native Glaswegian has strong Celtic blood, descended from the Irish who came over during the potato famine, and the deposed Highlanders driven from their crofts by sheep farmers.

The logo that announced the city's explosive rebirth in the early 1980s was a beaming yellow 'Mr Happy', with the words: 'Glasgow's miles better'. If this was a *double entendre*, it summed up the ebullient spirit of Scotland's most welcoming of cities. A new logo, 'Glasgow, the Friendly City', has been adopted recently in recognition of the warm-heartedness of the people of Glasgow, particularly towards visitors.

Central Glasgow

Glasgow Cathedral

Open April–Sept Mon–Sat 9.30–6, Sun 2–5; Oct–Mar closes at 4pm.

Glasgow Cathedral is on the site of the church built by St Mungo, and Glasgow grew up around it. It is the city's parish church, less than a mile east of the centre. There are still traces of the original stone building, dedicated in the presence of King David I in 1136 and rebuilt after a fire in 1197 in the lower church. The crypt, choir and tower were built in 1233, the rest being added at various stages in the succeeding years. During the destruction of church embellishment in the Reformation, the last Catholic Archbishop, James Beaton, stripped Glasgow Cathedral of its finery and carried the

Tourist Information

Glasgow t (0141–)

Glasgow: 11 George Square, t 204 4400, *enquiries@seeglasgow.com*, *www.seeglasgow.com*; *open all year*. As well as an information centre, this is a bureau de change, with booking facilities for accommodation – both local and national – theatres, concerts, etc., as well as coach and tour tickets. There are also tourist information services at Glasgow Airport, t 848 4440, and Hamilton Road Chef Services on the M74 northbound, t (01698) 285 590.

Getting There

By Air

Glasgow Airport, Scotland's international airport, t 887 1111, *www.baa.co.uk*, is 15 minutes from the city centre. It is served by flights from all major UK airports and offers many connections from Europe and North America. Prestwick Airport, t (01292) 511 000, *www.gpa.co.uk*, with transatlantic and international flights, is an hour away.

By Rail

There is a high-speed east-coast rail link with London, taking about 5 hours, as well as direct or connected links with all other major towns in the UK. For details ring National Rail Enquiries, t 08457 484 950. Also ask about Virgin Trains, who run the west-coast line.

By Road

There are direct motorway links with all major UK cities. A number of inter-city coaches operate between Glasgow, London and other main towns. This is usually the cheapest form of public transport and not uncomfortable.

Buchanan Bus Station, t 08705 505 050, for routes and prices; otherwise t 332 7133.

Getting Around

Scotrail, t 08457 484 950, *www.scotrail.co.uk*, offers some good travel pass tickets. The Roundabout Glasgow ticket (£3.50 adult, £1.75 child) gives unlimited rail travel for 10 miles from the city centre for a day. The Discovery ticket (£2.50) gives unlimited travel on the underground for a day. The Daytripper ticket (£7.50 1 adult and 2 children/£13 2 adults and 4 children) gives unlimited train travel for one day, including underground, most buses and some ferries in Strathclyde.

Buses run frequently in and around the city, and there are a large number of taxis. There is also an underground railway, 'The Subway', circling the city from Hillhead, north of Kelvingrove Park, round as far as Buchanan Street to the east, across the river to Shields and Kinning Park in the south and back round to Govan in the west, before recrossing the river to Partick. Because of the excellent motorway network, it is meant to be possible to get from the city centre to, for instance, the Burrell, way out in the suburbs, in a matter of minutes. A one-way system makes driving in the heart of the city remarkably unfraught.

The Travel Centre, St Enoch Square, t 332 7133, will help with most travel problems.
Buchanan Street Bus Station, t 332 7133.
Scottish Citylink Coaches, t 08705 505 050, *www.citylink.co.uk*.

Tours

City Sightseeing Glasgow Tour, 153 Queen Street, t 204 0444, *www.scotguide.com*. Hop-on-hop-off tours with local guide. Also architectural tours. *Mar–Nov*.
Clyde Marine Cruises, Princes Pier, Greenock, t (01475) 721 281, *www.clyde-marine.co.uk*. Day cruises in summer, on the Clyde and adjacent lochs.
Glasgow Ducks, 2nd floor George House, 36 North Hanover Street, t 572 8381. An unusual 90-minute tour in an amphibious bus.
Guide Friday – the Glasgow Tour, St Georges Building, 5 St Vincent Place, t 248 7644, *www.guide-friday.com*. Hop-on-hop-off open-top bus tour of the city with a guide. Departs every 30 minutes from George Square (*April–Oct*).
Mercat Tours, 4 Ochil Road, t 772 0022, *www.mercattours.com*. Themed walking tours: historic, gruesome, ghosts and ghouls. Depart from George Square.
Scottish Tourist Guides Association, t (01786) 447 784. Professionally trained guides can be

booked to lead informative Glasgow walks and tours. Also tours throughout Scotland. 18 languages available.

Scot Trek, 9 Lawrence Street, **t** 334 9232, *www.scot-trek.co.uk*. All sorts of guided walking tours, from 2-hour rambles to full-day or several-day tours in the area.

Walkabout Tours, 153 Queen Street, **t** 243 2437, *www.scotguide.com*. Audio-guided walking tours of the city centre and cathedral precinct.

Waverley Excursions, Anderson Quay, **t** 221 8152. The last sea-going paddle steamer in the world sails the Clyde estuary in summer.

Festivals

January/February: Celtic Connections; musicians from around the Celtic-speaking world descending upon Glasgow for an international celebration of traditional music at Glasgow Royal Concert Hall. Since 1993.

June: RSNO Proms; two weeks in the Royal Glasgow Concert Hall.

June/July: Glasgow International Jazz Festival; the city vibrates with folk music and jazz, indoors and out, played by groups from all over the world, especially Scandinavia and northern Europe, and musical gatherings go on far into the night.

August: World Pipe Band Championships.

Shopping

Glasgow's main shopping area radiates from **George Square** with branches of most leading chain stores. There are lots of leather shops at the eastern end of **Argyle Street**. Don't miss a visit to the '**Barras**' market, in Gallowgate, every weekend, *see* p.228.

Auld Alliance Bakery, opposite Mellis, just west of Kelvin Bridge on the Great Western Road. For the best bread. There are other gourmet grocers and wine shops on this street and many stay open late.

Buchanan Galleries, 220 Buchanan Street, **t** 333 9898, *www.buchanangalleries.co.uk*. A huge shopping complex, including a branch of John Lewis.

Cruise Clothes, Renfield Street. Trendy, cruisey clothes.

Designer Exchange, 3 Royal Exchange Court (off 17 Royal Exchange Square), **t** 221 6898. Good designer bargains 'as new'. Top names at affordable prices if you are lucky. *Open Tues–Sat 10–5.*

The Edinburgh Woollen Mill, 72 Nelson Mandela Place. For tweeds, tartans and woollen things.

Flip, Queen Street. Specialists in American-style clothes.

Hector Russell Kiltmaker, 110 Buchanan Street. For tweeds, tartans and woollen things.

Italian Centre, John Street. Designer shops such as Versace, Mondi and Emporio Armani, which was one of the first designer label stores to open in Glasgow and helped to put the Italian Centre on the map. There are restaurants, café-bars and a modern piazza adorned by contemporary artists and sculptors.

James Pringle Knitwear Company, 130 Buchanan Street. For tweeds, tartans and woollen things.

Mellis, just west of Kelvin Bridge on the Great Western Road. For the best cheese in Scotland.

Paddy's Market, Shipbank Lane. Glasgow's repository for second-hand clothes. The City Council tried to close it down because it didn't suit Glasgow's new image but there was such an outcry they couldn't. In the past, Irish immigrants sold their possessions here in order to subsist.

Princes Square, 48 Buchanan Street, **t** 221 0324, *www.princes-square.com*. A luxury specialist shopping area in a renovated 1841 square with cafés, restaurants, exhibitions and entertainment.

R. G. Lawrie Ltd, 10 Buchanan Street. For tweeds, tartans and woollen things.

St Enoch Centre, 55 St Enoch Square, **t** 204 3900, *www.stenoch.co.uk*. Over 85 stores under one huge glass roof.

Where to Stay

Glasgow t (0141–)

The following is just a selection, most within easy walk or reach of stations. The expensive hotels all have excellent restaurants. Also see *www.hotelsglasgow.com*.

Expensive

Arthouse Hotel, 129 Bath Street, t 221 6789, *www.arthousehotel.com*. New, modern, lively and stylish.

Carlton George Hotel, 44 West George Street, t 353 6373, *www.carltonhotels.co.uk*. City-centre de luxe, brand new with every possible comfort. 'Windows' is its very good rooftop restaurant.

Carrick, 377–83 Argyle Street, t 248 2355. 4-star modern building in the city centre, with all comforts and friendly staff.

Devonshire Hotel, 5 Devonshire Gardens, t 339 7878, *www.the-devonshire.co.uk*. Town house in the west end with majestic interior and de luxe accommodation.

Groucho St Judes, 190 Bath Street, t 352 8800, *www.grouchosaintjudes.com*. Excellent, small, rather exclusive hotel, in collaboration with London's Groucho Club, but not a club. Very good food.

Kelvin Park Lorne Hotel, 923 Sauchiehall Street, t 334 4891. The hotel has a friendly, relaxed atmosphere. Butlers Restaurant has been designed in manor-house style and the food is good and reasonable. Newbery's Bar is decorated in the style of Charles Rennie Mackintosh. Honeymoon couples get a special deal.

Malmaison Glasgow, 278 West George Street, t 221 6400, *www.malmaison.com*. Former flamboyant Greek Revival church, then a charmless office block, rescued by Ken McCulloch, failed rock star who also master-minded One Devonshire Gardens. There's a brasserie in the basement, *see* below.

Millennium Hotel, George Square, t 332 6711, *www.millennium-hotel.com*. Elegant, listed, 18th-century building, incorporating the house in which Sir William Burrell grew up. International cuisine is served in the conservatory or the Window on the Square Restaurant.

One Devonshire Gardens, Great Western Road, t 339 2001, *www.one-devonshire-gardens.co.uk*. Definitely the best hotel in Glasgow. Its restaurant, Amarylis, is also one of the best places to eat in town, *see* below.

Posthouse Glasgow City, Bothwell Street, t 0870 400 9032, *www.posthouse-hotels.com*. Large, ultra-modern, but friendly. Good food and very central.

Moderate

Albion Hotel, 405–7 North Woodside Road, t 339 8620, *www.glasgowhotelsandapartments.co.uk*. Warm hospitality 15 minutes from the airport, close to public transport.

Ambassador Hotel, 7 Kelvin Drive, t 946 1018, *www.glasgowhotelsandapartments.co.uk*. A mile from the city centre, overlooking the river and Botanic Gardens. Good value.

Babbity Bowster Hotel, Blackfriars Street, t 552 5055, *fraser@babbity.com*. Small and friendly with an old-style tavern atmosphere, peat burning on the fires and good food.

Central Hotel, Gordon Street, t 221 9680, *www.choicehotels.com*. Massive Victorian building in the city centre, with a warm welcome. The food is very reasonable; there is a carvery buffet and you can 'eat Scottish'.

Kirklee Hotel, 11 Kensington Gate, t 334 5555, *kirklee@clara.net*. In Glasgow West. Quiet and comfortable.

Manor Park Hotel, 28 Balshagray Drive, t 339 2143, *manorparkhotel@aol.com*. West End hotel with warm hospitality and the chance of chatting in (or listening to) Gaelic.

Merchant Lodge, 52 Virginia Street, t 552 2424. One of Glasgow's oldest buildings, originally home to tobacco lords, in a quiet backwater in Merchant City. Rejuvenated with attractive accommodation and some original features. Very good value. Lodge or B&B.

Victorian House, 212 Renfrew Street, t 332 0129. Four restored Victorian town houses near city centre, for good B&B. Very reasonable.

Cheap

Angus Hotel, 970 Sauchiehall Street, t 357 5155, *www.angushotelglasgow.co.uk*. Private terraced guesthouse/B&B overlooking Kelvingrove Park. Friendly atmosphere and comfortable rooms.

Charing Cross Tower, 10 Elmbank Gardens, t 221 1000, *www.charing-x.com*. Busy, convenient and unpretentious.

Old School House, 194 Renfrew Street, t 332 7600. Good lodge/B&B in a B-listed villa in its own gardens in a conservation area.

Queens Park, 10 Balvicar Drive, t 423 1123. Busy, convenient and unpretentious.

Townhouse Hotel, 21 Royal Crescent, t 332 9009. Overlooking private gardens in tree-lined crescent of elegant Victorian houses. Comfortable and friendly. B&B/Lodge.

Willow Hotel, 228 Renfrew Street, t 332 2332. Good value B&B in 3 terraced town houses.

Eating Out

Expensive

Amarylis, at One Devonshire Gardens, t 339 2001. Excellent meals in a luxurious setting (*see* above). Thoughtful service and mouth-watering menu. Ideal for a special occasion.

The Buttery, 652 Argyle Street, t 221 8188. Good food in the style and setting of a Victorian gentleman's club.

Puppet Theatre, 11 Ruthven Lane, t 339 8444. Probably your best bet if you want to splash out. Tempting food in a stylish setting.

Rococo, 202 West George Street, t 221 5004. Excellent upmarket restaurant with classic and contemporary menu, sumptuous setting, and an area for smokers outside.

Rogano, 11 Exchange Place, t 248 4055. Dates from 1876 but was remodelled in 1935 in classic Art Deco style. Renowned for its atmosphere and excellent seafood. Café Rogano, downstairs, is cheaper, and the food is just as good.

Moderate

78 St Vincent, the Phoenix building, 78 St Vincent Street, t 248 7878. Cosmopolitan, but predominantly French.

Air Organic, 36 Kelvingrove Street, t 564 5200. Not 100% organic, but as much as possible.

Alfredo's Bar, 146 West Nile Street, t 564 1270. Lively city-centre pub/restaurant with lots of special deals. *Open 8am–midnight.*

Arta, The Old Cheese Market, 13–19 Walls Street, t 552 2101. Splendid Mediterranean and tapas restaurant with inner courtyard and live entertainment.

Arthouse Grill, 129 Bath Street, t 221 6789. Good for seafood.

Auctioneers, North Court, St Vincent Place, t 229 5851. In what used to be McTears auction house, with very atmospheric decor.

Café Gandolfi, 64 Albion Street, t 552 6813. Bohemian and laid back, with stained glass and polished wood, and good Scottish food: try the cullen skink or smoked venison.

Café Source, 1 St Andrews Square, t 548 6020. Modern decor in 18th-century church. Proper meals or quick snacks.

Camerons, Glasgow Hilton, 1 William Street, t 204 5555. Very good food in a modern hotel.

Cantina del Rey, King's Court, Osborne Street/King Street, t 552 4044. Mexican food.

Cathedral House, 28–32 Cathedral Square, t 552 3519. Café-bar and restaurant with good views from the restaurant.

Le Chardon d'Or, 176 West Regent Street, t 248 3801. Stylish food in relaxed surroundings.

City Merchant, 97–99 Candleriggs, t 553 1577. Has a maritime mural in the dining room to complement the Scottish seafood theme, though the meat dishes should not be over-looked. A family-run restaurant, serving good food in a friendly atmosphere.

Di Maggio's Pizzeria, Royal Exchange Square, t 248 2111; 1038 Pollokshaws Road, t 632 8888; 163 West Nile Street, t 333 4999. Delicious and unusual pizzas and pasta. Set meals in the basement for under a fiver.

Gamba, 225a West George Street, t 572 0899. Very good, fairly new, seafood restaurant with several well-deserved awards, including Best Glasgow Restaurant. Mediterranean decor.

Gaucho Grill, 133 West George Street, t 204 5211. Very reasonable Argentinean steaks and wine. Book.

Glasgow Thistle, 36 Cambridge Street, t 332 3311. Garden café-restaurant in American style, or elegant Prince of Wales cocktail bar and restaurant.

Kama Sutra, 331 Sauchiehall Street, t 332 0055. A stylish Indian restaurant with love as its predominant theme – sensual appetizers, and framed scenes from the book adorning the walls.

Killermont Polo Club, in Maryhill Rd, t 964 5412. Referred to as an 'Indian restaurant from heaven', the food certainly is ambrosial – Goan-style mussels, orange tandoori duck or tandoori salmon. The interior is pure Raj: starched linen, pith helmets and pictures of polo ponies. The service is excellent.

Kooks, 1335 Argyle Street, t 334 9682. A smart continental-style bistro opposite Kelvingrove Art Gallery.

Malmaison Café Mal, in the Malmaison Hotel, 278 West George Street, t 572 1003, *see* above. Good Mediterranean ambience and food.

Malmaison Brasserie, in the basement of the Malmaison Hotel, as above. French food prepared from the freshest ingredients.

Mussel Inn, 157 Hope Street, **t** 572 1405. Very good seafood, fresh and simple, with nice informal atmosphere.

Nairns, 13 Woodside Crescent, **t** 353 0707. The brainchild of Nick Nairn (as seen on TV): delicious modern Scottish cuisine with an international twist (and a Michelin star) – in an elegant 18th-century town house. There are also four bedrooms.

Stravaigin, 28 Gibson Street, **t** 334 2665. Cosy, friendly, colourful and eclectic to the point of eccentricity, attracting plenty of locals. Try the rosemary-skewered Ullapool monkfish in black butter. **Stravaigin 2** is at 8 Ruthven Lane, **t** 334 7165.

Two Fat Ladies, 88 Dumbarton Road, **t** 339 1944. Named after the bingo-caller's jargon for 88 rather than the television cooks. Informal, with only 9 tables. Booking essential. The emphasis is on seafood, delicious enough to draw people in from afar.

Ubiquitous Chip, 12 Ashton Lane, **t** 334 5007. Plants, a waterfall, batiks and murals in a lively cobbled courtyard restaurant in a converted mews stable. Original and traditional recipes using the best Scottish ingredients.

Yes Restaurant and Brasserie, 22 West Nile Street, **t** 221 8044. Stylish café-bar and restaurant, with good choice of food in both.

Cheap

Good drinking places include the bar in the **Babbity Bowster**; the **Rat and Parrot**, John Street; **The Scotia**, Stockwell Street, which claims to be the oldest bar in Glasgow; **Victoria Bar**, Trongate; **Cottiers**, Hyndland Road; **Uisge Beatha**, Woodlands Road; and **Whistler's Mother**, Byres Road.

The Arches, 253 Argyle Street, **t** 565 1000. Vibrant café-bar with live music.

Babbity Bowster, Blackfriars Street, **t** 552 7774. Not only a friendly hotel but also serves first-class food in an upstairs restaurant (the mussels come highly recommended) and very good bar meals downstairs where you will rub shoulders with Glasgow's literati.

Baby Grand, 3 Elm Bank Gardens, Charing Cross, **t** 248 4942. Has been likened to a New York café, and specializes in fish dishes, accompanied by the baby grand, whose mood varies: jazz, soul, blues, requests.

Café Roberta, 84 Gordon Square, **t** 204 0860. Opposite Central Station, an authentic Italian coffee bar with home-made pasta, daily 'specials', sandwiches and good coffee.

Entresol Restaurant, at the Central Hotel (*see* above). The menu includes haggis, fillet of sole Bressay, whisky cream crowdie.

Ewington Hotel, 132 Queens Drive, **t** 423 1152. Serves west-coast fresh seafood, Aberdeen Angus beef and home-made soups such as delicious cullen skink.

Fazzi's, 67 Cambridge Street, **t** 332 0941. Unpretentious and friendly family-run Italian. Ideal for a pre- or post-theatre meal.

Fratelli Sarti, 121 Bath Street, **t** 204 0440. '100 per cent Italian'. You may have to queue at weekends but it's worth the wait. Try the spinach and ricotta gnocchi and baked pasta.

The Granary, 82 Howard Street, **t** 226 3770. Vegetarian café with healthy home-made food, very cheap. Try the aubergine and lentil moussaka or the homity pie.

Joe's Garage, Bank Street, **t** 339 5407. Good pizzas, pasta and unusual starters.

Nico's, Sauchiehall Street, **t** 332 5736. Good continental food.

Pizza Express, 151 Queen Street, **t** 221 3333. Modern, open-plan restaurant with above-average pizzas and pasta, and sometimes live jazz.

Entertainment

Top-class drama, music, ballet, variety shows, etc. can be found in Glasgow's theatres and cinemas. Also see *www.glasgow.gov.uk*.

Theatres and Music Venues

13th Note Club, 260 Clyde Street, **t** 221 0414, *www.13thnote.com*. Live dance music.

The Arches, 253 Argyle Street, **t** 565 1000, *www.thearches.co.uk*. In a series of Victorian railway arches, an exciting venue for theatre, music, nightclubs, exhibitions, fashion and cultural festivals.

BBC Scottish Symphony Orchestra, Queen Margaret Drive, **t** 338 2603, *www.bbc.co.uk/bbcsso*. Live broadcasts.

Centre for Contemporary Arts, 350 Sauchiehall Street, **t** 332 7521, *www.cca-glasgow.com*. New centre for international contemporary arts (*see* p.223).

Citizens Theatre, Gorbals Street, **t** 429 0022/8177, *www.citz.co.uk*. Glasgow's repertory theatre, opened in 1878 as a music hall, with main auditorium and two studio theatres, and an international reputation for British and European classics.

City Hall, Candleriggs, **t** 287 5024. A versatile stage where you can see anything from concerts by the Scottish Chamber Orchestra to traditional ceilidhs.

Glasgow Royal Concert Hall, **t** 353 8000. Specially designed by Sir Leslie Martin and opened by the Princess Royal in 1990, this modern complex has a 2,500-seat hall, two good restaurants, and conference facilities. Leading international orchestras perform classical music and jazz here, as well as the Glasgow-based Royal Scottish National Orchestra, BBC Scottish Symphony Orchestra and City of Glasgow Philharmonic.

Glasgow Theatre Club, Tron Theatre, 38 Parnie Street, **t** 552 4267, *www.tron.co.uk*. Built as a church at the end of the 18th century, on the original Tron steeple, it later became a theatre. The designers of the innovative redevelopment wanted to make 'an architectural statement on a pivotal corner of the Merchant City', a luminous focus for Glasgow Cross.

Henry Wood Hall, Claremont Street, **t** 225 3555, *www.rsno.org.uk*. Classical concert hall in what was Trinity Church. Now the administrative home of the Royal Scottish National Orchestra, and a venue for ceilidhs, weddings and meetings.

Kings Theatre, Bath Street, **t** 248 5153. Drama, family entertainment, musicals, amateur and touring shows.

Mitchell Theatre, Granville Street, **t** 287 4855. Meetings, lectures and amateur dramatics.

The Old FruitMarket, Albion Street, **t** 287 5024/5511. Popular venue for music festivals such as Celtic Connections, the Jazz Festival and Big Big Country. Also exhibitions and theatre.

Pavilion Theatre, 121 Renfield Street, **t** 332 1846. Family entertainment, variety, pop, rock, and pantomimes.

Royal Scottish Academy of Music and Drama, 100 Renfrew Street, **t** 332 4101, *www.rsamd.ac.uk*. Conservatoire for music and drama, also equipped as an arts centre.

St Andrews at the Square, 1 St Andrew Square, **t** 548 6020, *www.cafesource.co.uk*. 18th-century church with centre for Scottish music upstairs, and auditorium for concerts, ceilidhs, weddings, etc. downstairs.

Scottish Ballet, 261 West Princes Street, **t** 331 2931, *www.scottishballet.co.uk*. Headquarters of Scotland's national dance company, who also perform at the Theatre Royal.

Scottish Opera, 39 Elmbank Crescent, **t** 248 4567, *www.scottishopera.org.uk*. Headquarters of Scotland's national opera company, who also perform at the Theatre Royal.

The Stand Comedy Club, 333 Woodlands Road, **t** 0870 600 6055, *www.thestand.co.uk*. A purpose-built comedy club with live comedy Thurs, Fri, Sat and Sun. Booking advised.

Theatre Royal, Hope Street, **t** 332 3321, *www.theatreroyalglasgow.com*. Home of Scottish Opera and frequent host to the Scottish Ballet, Scottish Theatre Company, National Theatre, Ballet Rambert and other international companies.

Tramway Theatre, Albert Drive, **t** 422 2023, *www.tramway.org*. In a disused tram shed south of the river, with programmes of theatre and dance that are often quite avant-garde. It is many people's favourite Glasgow theatre.

Cinemas

Glasgow Film Theatre, Rose Street, **t** 332 6535, *www.gft.org.uk*. Two screens for cultural and classic films as well as new releases.

Odeon at the Quay, **t** 0870 505 0007. Off the Paisley Road south of the river (opposite Harry Ramsden's), a vast American 1950s-style cinema multiplex with 12 screens. Lit up at night, it is the focal point of a series of chain eateries and a Hot Shots Disco, built around an enormous car park.

Odeon Film Centre, 56 Renfield Street, **t** 332 3413, *www.odeon.co.uk*. Nine screens.

Discovering Glasgow

Don't try and cram all Glasgow into one day: if that is all the time you have, take a guided coach tour to orientate yourself in the morning, spend the afternoon at the Burrell Collection and Pollok House, or the Kelvingrove Art Gallery and Museum, and sample one of the many entertainments on offer in the evening. A must, if you want to know what's going on in and around Glasgow, is *The List*, a magazine published every two weeks (it also covers Edinburgh). Alternatively, go to the cathedral and the St Mungo Museum of Religious Life and Art in the morning, or to the Art Gallery and Museum, and the Hunterian Museum which is also at Kelvingrove Park.

Two days would allow you to do all of the above, and in three days you could take in a cruise on the Clyde and find time to wander through the older parts of the city.

treasures off to France, together with the archives, for safekeeping. Tragically, in the later turmoil of the French Revolution, these were lost and have never been found. In 1578, when the iconoclasts of the Reformation threatened to destroy the cathedral entirely, the city's trade guilds intervened and, miraculously, managed to prevent them: thus, today the cathedral is one of the finest examples of pre-Reformation Gothic architecture in Scotland. Although austere, like most Scottish churches, it is still very impressive.

St Mungo was buried here in 603. His tomb stands under a fan-vaulted ceiling among a forest of pillars in the lower church. In 1451 the Pope decreed that it was as meritorious to make a pilgrimage to Glasgow Cathedral as to Rome, and many thousands of pilgrims made their way here in medieval times. Look for the rood screen with fire-and-brimstone carvings of the Seven Deadly Sins on its corbels.

The cathedral stands on a grassy slope embedded with horizontal gravestones, backed by the Necropolis, on a hill behind. This gives a skyline of elaborate monuments, overshadowed by a Doric column from which John Knox keeps a stern eye on the city.

The **St Mungo Museum of Religious Life and Art** (*open Mon–Thurs and Sat 10–5, Fri and Sun 11–5*), next to the cathedral precinct, was the first museum of religion in the world and well worth a visit. The three galleries include an Art Gallery, Religious Life Gallery and Scottish Gallery, and there is a Buddhist Zen Garden. Salvador Dali's *Christ of St John of the Cross* is here.

Provand's Lordship

Open Mon–Thurs and Sat 10–5, Fri and Sun 11–5.

Provand's Lordship, in Castle Street opposite the cathedral, dates from 1471 and is Glasgow's only other pre-Reformation building of interest. Built as a priest's house and well preserved, it is a museum with 17th- and 18th-century furniture, tapestry and pictures, as well as the key of Leven Castle in Tayside, where Mary was imprisoned. She may have stayed in this house when she came to Glasgow in 1567 to visit her husband, Darnley, who was sick with some disfiguring disease diagnosed as anything from smallpox to syphilis. Whatever it was, she took him back to Edinburgh – and murder. Provand's Lordship is the oldest house in the city, visited by both James II and James IV during their reigns in the 15th and 16th centuries. Mysteriously, among its exhibits is an early 20th-century sweetie shop.

George Square

George Square is at the heart of the city, barely a quarter of an hour's stroll from the cathedral, along Castle Street and George Street. There is something continental about the square on a sunny day, like the main piazza of a Mediterranean town, where crowds gather to pass the time. Visitors in shirt sleeves, slung about with cameras, linger among the trees and statues. The square is a popular venue for demonstrations and the odd pop concert and other public events. At Christmas people bring their families to see the very special decorations, old fashioned and attractive with illuminated images of candles, swinging bells, angels, etc.

George Square is dominated by a **statue of Sir Walter Scott** on an 80ft-high column (first intended for a statue of George III). This mighty monument was the first to be set up in honour of Sir Walter, in 1837. He towers over Queen Victoria, Prince Albert, Robert Burns, James Watt, and many others, wearing his plaid across the wrong shoulder as was his custom.

The Italian Renaissance-style **City Chambers** (*open Mon–Fri 9–4.30*), topped by a wedding-cake concoction of cupolas and a soaring tower, forms the eastern side of the square. A free guided tour of its interior (*Mon–Fri 10.30 and 2.30 subject to availability and council business; t (0141) 287 2000; www.glasgow.gov.uk*) reveals the glories of its loggia, a great staircase, marble columns, soaring vaulted ceilings and a banqueting hall.

Just off George Square beyond the City Chambers lies the old **Merchant City**. Created in about 1750 as a planned development of gridded streets, it was here that the tobacco lords built their mansions and warehouses. These were the entrepreneurs of 18th-century Glasgow, who traded with the Americas, bringing to Scotland the three 'evils' of tobacco, rum and sugar, and they had money to spend. The area has recently become a focus for inner-city regeneration, with many of its fine buildings being restored. At its heart lies the Italian Centre. There is a Merchant City Trail leaflet obtainable from the National Trust for Scotland's centre in Hutcheson's Hall, 158 Ingram Street.

Museums and Galleries

The Gallery of Modern Art (*open Mon–Thurs and Sat 10–5, Fri and Sun 11–5*), in Royal Exchange Square just south of George Square via Queen Street, was opened in 1996 in one of the grandest of the tobacco merchants' houses, later the Royal Exchange and then the Central Library. The quality of the contents of the gallery is in the eye of the beholder. The elements – earth, air, fire and water – provide a loose theme, each allotted its own section, and the imagination is stretched, which may be the point. Of greater interest to conservation watchdogs is the intrusive mosaic on the pediment, which draws your eye as you approach. This garish ensemble, calling to mind kindergarten art, is thought by many to be inappropriate for such a fine, historic building. But the opening of the gallery has given a new focus to the square in an area where regeneration is vital: cafés with pavement tables are opening and charity shops are selling up to trendy bars and boutiques. There's a very good café upstairs.

The **Kelvingrove Art Gallery and Museum** (*open Mon–Thurs and Sat 10–5, Fri and Sun 11–5*) occupies a vast red-sandstone building on the western side of Kelvingrove Park about a mile or so west of the city centre. One of the best of its kind in Britain, this place needs several leisurely visits to be appreciated properly. Built as recently as 1901, it has a solid, Victorian feeling about it. An enormous central hall, sometimes used for organ recitals and special exhibitions, soars to the full height of the building.

The museum has archaeological collections, including a reconstruction of the Antonine Wall, and some Bronze-Age cists with their contents. There are also displays of armour, ethnological exhibits, natural history and social history. The engineering collection is so big that it is not possible to display everything: people with a special interest must ask at the enquiry desk.

The art gallery claims to have one of the finest collections of paintings owned by any city, beautifully displayed in upper galleries leading off the balcony that encircles the central hall. On the balcony there are sculptures (including works by Rodin and Epstein), ceramics, silver, jewellery and furniture displays (including work by Charles Rennie Mackintosh, the Glasgow-born architect who had a considerable influence on European design in the late 19th and early 20th centuries). The works of 'The Glasgow Boys' are well represented – that radical quintet, James Guthrie, John Lavery, George Henry, E. A. Hornel and Joseph Crawhall, who despised the mawkish paintings of their late 19th-century contemporaries, preferring to depict life more realistically and, some might feel, more crudely. Artists include Delacroix, Rubens, Rembrandt, Corot, Millet, Manet, Degas, Raeburn, Allan Ramsay, Reynolds, Hogarth, Whistler and Turner. There are lots of Impressionists and post-Impressionists, a Glasgow gallery, and a gallery for recent and contemporary paintings.

Kelvingrove Park is an ideal setting for the Art Gallery and Museum, with the River Kelvin flowing through its 85 acres. It was twice used for international exhibitions at the turn of the last century as well as for the Scottish National Exhibition in 1911. Concerts are performed several times a week in the summer, in the amphitheatre on the river bank. There are statues, fountains and a fine herbaceous border.

Glasgow University was founded in 1451, with just a few classes in the cathedral crypt. It then moved to the High Street, south of the Cathedral Square, and in 1870 was finally moved to Gilmorehill (above what is now Kelvingrove Park) where it now caters for more than 10,000 students. The **University of Glasgow Visitor Centre** (*University Avenue; open May–Sept Mon–Sat 9.30–5, Sun 2–5; t (0141) 330 5511*) is an award-winning, newly refurbished centre with touch-screen interactive displays and information systems, and a camera obscura.

The **Hunterian Museum** and **Hunterian Art Gallery** (*open Mon–Sat 9.30–5; www.hunterian.gla.ac.uk*) are in Hillhead Street, running north from the university and part of it. William Hunter was a student at Glasgow University in the 1730s. Having risen to fame and fortune as a physician, he left his collections of coins, paintings, prints, books, manuscripts, zoological, mineral and medical specimens to the university. The Hunterian Museum opened in 1807, Scotland's first public museum, and, since 1980, the Hunterian Art Gallery has been housed separately.

The museum has, as well as the world-famous Hunter Coin Cabinet, excellent geological, archaeological and ethnographical collections among its many exhibits. The art gallery's collection of work by **Whistler**, the contents of his studio at his death in 1903, is rivalled only by the collection in Washington's Freer Gallery. These paintings were inherited by Rosalind Birnie Philip, his sister-in-law, in whom he had instilled a determination that the English should not get their hands on work by a man whose genius they had failed to acknowledge. Rosalind gave a number of the paintings during her lifetime, on condition they should never leave the university. She bequeathed the remainder on her death in 1958. The present collection is made up of 80 paintings, over 100 pastels and several hundred watercolours, drawings and prints. Many of the works are unfinished.

The **Hunterian Art Gallery** houses the largest and most comprehensive print collection in Scotland, as well as paintings by Rembrandt, Chardin, Stubbs, Pissarro, Ramsay, Reynolds, Sisley and many more. Sculptures include work by Rodin, in the courtyard. It also boasts a comprehensive collection of work by Charles Rennie Mackintosh (1868–1928). One of Glasgow's talented sons, this architect and designer was a leading exponent of 'the Glasgow Style', which influenced the modern movement and had strong affinities with the Continental 'Art Nouveau' style, highly influential throughout Europe though less so in Britain. The **Mackintosh House** (*open 9.30–12.30 and 1.30–5*) is a reconstruction of No.6 Florentine Terrace nearby, now demolished, where he lived from 1906 to 1914. The rooms show all the decorations, alterations and improvements done to the original house by Mackintosh, together with some from his previous home at 120 Mains Street. For anyone who admires his austere approach to architecture and design, his clean, stark lines and manipulation of space and light, this is the finest existing example of his innovative flair and brilliance.

The **Glasgow School of Art** (*open Sept–June Mon–Fri 10–5, Sat 10–1, tours Mon–Fri 11 and 2, Sat 10.30 and 11.30; July and Aug Mon–Fri 11–5, Sat and Sun 10–3, tours Mon–Fri 11 and 2, Sat and Sun 10.30, 11.30 and 1; t (0141) 353 4526; www.gsa.ac.uk*), in Renfrew Street, was designed by Charles Rennie Mackintosh in 1896 and is believed by many to be his supreme architectural achievement. One of the best things about it is that it is still being used for the purpose for which it was built.

The **Willow Tea Room**, 217 Sauchiehall Street (*open Mon–Sat 9–5, Sun 12–5; www.willowtearooms.co.uk*), is another memorial to Mackintosh, its interior restored and furnished to his original design. It houses a jewellers and gift shop. Light meals are served in the 'Room de luxe and Gallery' (*Mon–Sat 9–4.30*).

The Headquarters of the Charles Rennie Mackintosh Society, in the former Queen's Cross Church at 870 Garscube Road, north of the Willow Tea Room (*open all year by arrangement, t (0141) 946 6600*), was built in 1897 in Mackintosh's Art

Nouveau–Gothic style, and is the only church he designed; it now has an information centre, reference library and book stall.

House for an Art Lover (*open April–Sept Sun–Thurs 10–4, Sat 10–3; Oct–Mar Sat and Sun 10–4; t (0141) 353 4770; adm; www.houseforanartlover.com*) in Bellahouston Park, Dumbreck Road, is based on Mackintosh's unrealized competition entry of 1901 for a German design magazine. Permanent exhibition rooms have been reproduced from his original portfolio designs and there is a postgraduate study centre for the Glasgow School of Art, a shop and a café.

The Lighthouse, Mitchell Street (*www.thelighthouse.co.uk*), is Scotland's Centre for Architecture, Design and the City, in the former offices of the *Glasgow Herald*, Mackintosh's first major public building. A legacy of 1999 when Glasgow was City of Architecture and Design, there are exhibits of the best local, national and international architecture and creative designs, as well as a Charles Rennie Mackintosh interpretation centre, cityscape views, a stylish café-bar and a shop.

The **Centre for Contemporary Arts** (*open Mon–Sat 11–6, Sun 12–5; t (0141) 332 7521; www.cca-glasgow.com*) at 350 Sauchiehall Street, formerly the Third Eye Centre, is partly housed in a Grecian building that caused a stir when it was designed by Alexander 'The Greek' Thomson in 1865. Thomson was Glasgow's, perhaps Scotland's, most important architect of the 19th century, only recently recognized by a growing public. Founded in 1975, this is Scotland's largest contemporary arts centre, containing galleries, a studio theatre, a bookshop, café-restaurant and bar. It holds an average of 30 exhibitions a year, and these exhibitions tour internationally as well as nationally. Programmes include drama, dance, music, readings, talks, films and festivals. The Centre has recently undergone major redevelopment, thanks to a £10.5million lottery grant, and it reopened in October 2001 with new and improved premises and an even more ambitious programme of events.

The **McLellan Galleries** (*opening varies with exhibitions; t (0141) 331 1854*), at 270 Sauchiehall Street, built in 1854, are specifically designed for touring and temporary art exhibitions.

The **Regimental Museum of the Royal Highland Fusiliers** (*open Mon–Fri 9–4.30, or by appointment; t (0141) 332 0961*) is at 518 Sauchiehall Street, with uniforms, pictures, medals, documents, photographs, trophies, and memorabilia, tracing the regiment's history back over 300 years.

The **Tenement House** (*open Mar–Oct daily 2–5; Nov–Feb by appointment; adm; t (0141) 333 0183*) at 145 Buccleuch Street a few blocks north of Sauchiehall Street, is a first-floor apartment in a red-sandstone tenement built in 1892, restored to give an insight into the living conditions of the lower middle-class family who lived here. Mrs Toward (Dressmaking, No Fitting Required), and her daughter Agnes, a shorthand typist, moved here in 1911 and Agnes remained until 1965 when she became too infirm to cope on her own. It is the epitome of genteel respectability, preserved as a time capsule of the first half of the 20th century. There are two rooms, as well as kitchen and bathroom, with the original kitchen range, period furniture and fittings. The National Trust for Scotland have set up an excellent social history project on the ground floor, displaying the development of tenement communities.

The **People's Palace** (*open Mon–Thurs and Sat 10–5, Fri and Sun 11–5*) is on the eastern side of Glasgow Green, half an hour's easy walk southeast of George Square, so called because it was built in 1898 as a cultural centre for the people in the East End of Glasgow. It is a museum devoted to the story of the city from 1175 to the present, including the growth of trades and industry, trade unions, labour movements, women's suffrage, entertainment and sport. Among its exhibits are a purse and a ring that belonged to Mary, Queen of Scots, a Bible that belonged to the notorious Archbishop Beaton, an organ built by James Watt, and portraits of many famous Glaswegians. There is a café, shop and an exotic winter garden, with tropical plants and birds.

The **Museum of Transport** (*open Mon–Thurs and Sat 10–5, Fri and Sun 11–5*) is in the Kelvin Hall in Argyle Street, across from Kelvingrove Park. It is one of the most renowned of its kind. Most forms of transport are represented, from bicycles and motor cycles and a painted, carved caravan, to six railway engines, some of which are 100 years old. There are trams, horse-drawn vehicles, commercial vehicles and cars. The Clyde room is a shipping gallery with models. Old photographs show many of the exhibits in use. Incorporated into the museum is a reconstruction of a 1930s street, with shops, a cinema, cars, delivery bikes and an underground station.

Scotland Street School (*open Mon–Thurs and Sat 10–5, Fri and Sun 11–5*), on the south side of the river, is a wonderful piece of architecture by Charles Rennie Mackintosh, particularly impressive when seen lit up at night from the M8. Each classroom is done as a reproduction of a different period of schooling – Victorian, wartime, etc. It's fascinating to see the facilities and equipment that were responsible for the education of some of Scotland's leading industrialists, economists, doctors, historians, artists, writers and academics. Well worth a visit.

The Burrell Collection

Open Mon–Thurs and Sat 10–5, Fri and Sun 11–5.

The Burrell Collection is 3 miles southwest of the city in Pollok Country Park, signposted off the main roads and motorways, and served by a good bus service. Buses 21, 23, 45, 48A and 57 run from the centre, and 34, 89 and 90 across the south of the city.

Opened in 1983, the Burrell is Glasgow's greatest treasure, attracting thousands of visitors from all over the world. The collection was given to the city by the wealthy industrialist Sir William Burrell (1861–1958) in 1944. Sir William joined his father's shipbuilding firm at the age of 15, and he had already begun to collect paintings, against the wishes of his father who would have preferred him to spend his money on more 'manly' pursuits. By the time he was 96, he had amassed some 8,000 objects, an average of two acquisitions a week. He was a careful collector, canny in his haggling, sometimes missing an important piece because he refused to pay inflated prices.

In 1971 a two-stage architectural competition was staged with an almost impossible brief: to design, not an institution, but a home in scale and in sympathy with the collection and the environment of the park. Had there not been a postal strike, causing the entry deadline to be extended, the winning design by Barry Gasson would not have been submitted in time. The building has won prestigious architectural awards. From the big car park it is all sharp angles, glass, red sandstone and wood, designed to give the best possible light and perspective to the treasures inside, making full use of the reflection of the trees and grounds of Pollok beyond the windows. Opulent courtyards and arcades create the illusion of being out of doors.

The breadth of Burrell's taste is astonishing. He was a traditionalist, with no time for the avant-garde, but within that scope his eye was caught by anything: prehistoric artefacts, oriental art, stained glass, porcelain, silver, paintings, sculpture, carpets, crystal and tapestries. The beauty and diversity of the collection dazzles the senses.

Reconstructions of the dining room, hall and drawing room of Hutton Castle, the Burrell's home on the Whiteadder near Berwick-on-Tweed, are incorporated into the building. Medieval stone and oak fireplaces and chimneypieces, antique furniture, tapestries, Eastern carpets, stained glass and the original soft furnishings, are all displayed with splendid effect.

There are objects from the ancient civilizations of Egypt, Iraq and Iran, Greece, the eastern Mediterranean and Italy. Among these can be seen: stone reliefs, bronzes, alabaster figures, an almost life-sized terracotta lion's head, amphoras, Greek earthenware vases, mosaics.

Almost a quarter of the collection is oriental. Chinese ceramics include polychrome figures from the Tang Dynasty (AD 618–907); porcelain from 14th-century Yuan and 15th-century Ming dynasties; every sort of domestic ware; and bright ceramic roof tiles with elaborate figures on them, to ward off evil spirits. Chinese bronzes include a 'champion vase': two cylinders joined by an eagle with outspread wings standing on a bear's head, probably awarded in archery contests. Chinese jades include jewellery, vessels, animals, fruit and figures. There are Japanese prints, ceramics from the Near East, and Near Eastern carpets.

From medieval Europe there is a 12th-century limestone portal from a church in Montron in France, looking entirely right in its ultra-modern setting, as does the magnificent 16th-century sandstone portal from Hornby Castle. Medieval church art and sculpture are also well represented.

Burrell looked on his medieval tapestries as being the most valuable part of his collection. Most were originally woven for churches and private houses and displayed as status symbols by ecclesiastics and nobles alike. The colours of some are still so rich it is hard to believe they were stitched over 500 years ago. Look for the 15th-century *Ferret Hunt* and *Hercules Initiating the Olympic Games*.

Another relic of the Middle Ages is stained glass, and not all of it comes from churches. There are vignettes of everyday life, including a jolly man warming his bare toes before a roaring fire and an industrious Dutchman making roof tiles.

Among decorative arts, the Burrell Collection includes exquisite porcelain, silver, gilt, glass, 'treen' (made of wood), needlework, furniture, armour and weapons.

Sir William Burrell started his collection with paintings and was still buying them two years before he died, 80 years later. As with the rest of his treasures, he seems to have had an astonishingly catholic taste, ranging from Degas and Cézanne to Bellini

and Hans Memling, whose *Annunciation* is rich in colour and yet simple in conception. There are a number of Impressionists and an assortment of prints and drawings.
Unfortunately some of the paintings are disappointingly hung and lit.

Among the sculpture in the collection is Rodin's *The Thinker*, a bronze from one of
the many casts of this best known of his works, in the original size. (*The Thinker* was
meant to be Dante, pondering the fate of mankind, crowning Rodin's magnum opus,
The Gates of Hell.)

Pollok House

Open Mon–Sat 10–5, Sun 11–5; **t** *(0141) 616 6410.*

Pollok House is in the same grounds as the Burrell Collection – a much older-estab-
lished showpiece, unfortunately now often neglected in favour of its magnificent
neighbour, although it is a lovely house in a fine setting. It was built in 1750 for the
Maxwell Macdonald family who gave it to Glasgow in 1966, along with 361 acres of
garden and parkland. It contains one of the finest collections of Spanish paintings to
be found anywhere in Britain, acquired by Sir William Stirling Maxwell when Spanish
art was neglected and underrated. The collection ranges from 16th-century Cosida,
across the whole field of Spanish painting, including El Greco, Murillo and Goya. There
are also many works by other European masters, 18th- and 19th-century furniture,
silver, ceramics and crystal. Look for the unusual astronomical clock, just like a standard grandfather clock until closer inspection reveals a face set with complicated
dials. Pollok Park has gardens designed by Sir John Stirling Maxwell, and there is a
Demonstration Garden, displaying all aspects of landscape gardening.

Other Attractions

Holmwood House (*open April–Oct daily 1.30–5.30, or by appointment,* **t** *(0141) 637
2129*), in Cathcart, south of the city, is in the process of restoration and well worth a
visit. Built in 1857 for James Couper, who made a fortune supplying the British
Government with paper during the Crimean War, Holmwood was designed by
Alexander 'The Greek' Thomson. In 1888 an admirer of Thomson wrote: 'The
Holmwood Villa has deprived us of either asking or answering the question: is an
architect an artist? If architecture be poetry in stone and lime – a great temple an epic
– this exquisite little gem, at once classic and picturesque, is as complete, self-
contained and polished as a sonnet.' Holmwood, last used as a convent school, was
rescued from redevelopment into flats and houses by the National Trust for Scotland
and it is hoped that eventually most of Thomson's original work will be restored.

The **Glasgow Science Centre**, 50 Pacific Quay (*mall open daily 10–6; tower open
Sun–Wed 10–6, Thurs–Sat 10–9;* **t** *(0141) 420 5000; www.gsc.org.uk*), is the perfect way
of entertaining bored techno kids of all ages, with interactive exhibits, a planetarium
and demo theatres. The 423-foot tower, weighing 440 tons, revolves 360°, with
galleries on past and future Glasgow, and amazing views.

The **Museum of Piping**, 30–34 McPhater Street (*open May–Sept daily 9–5; Oct–Mar Mon–Sat 9–5; t (0141) 353 0220; www.thepipingcentre.co.uk*), is probably the best museum for the history and music of the Highland bagpipe. The **College of Piping**, 16–24 Otago Street (*open Mon–Thurs 8.30–6, Fri 9–5; t (0141) 334 3587; www.college-of-piping.co.uk*), was established in 1944 and has a museum where you can hear and learn still more about Scotland's national instrument.

Hutcheson's Hall, 158 Ingram Street (*open Mon–Sat 10–5; t (0141) 5552 8391*), is an elegant city centre landmark – an A-listed building on the site of a 1641 hospice, which has been newly refurbished with a multimedia exhibition, Glasgow style, and work for sale by Glasgow designers.

Merchant Square, 71–3 Albion Street, Merchant City, is a vibrant city-centre meeting point, with bars, restaurants and shops, and regular events throughout the year.

The **Mitchell Library** (1874), North Street (*open Mon–Thurs 9–8, Fri and Sat 9–5; t (0141) 287 2999*), is the largest reference library in Europe, with over 1.5 million books.

The **Sharmanka Kinetic Gallery and Theatre**, 14 King Street (*performances Tues at 1, Thurs at 7, Sun at 3 and 6, or group bookings by appointment, t (0141) 552 7080; www.sharmanka.co.uk*), is an extraordinary theatre of mechanical sculptures: tiny carved figures and ingenious scrap perform Heath-Robinson/Hieronymous-Bosch ballet to music and lighting, telling the tragi–comic story of the struggle of the human spirit.

The **Tall Ship at Glasgow Harbour** (*100 Stobcross Road; open April–Sept daily 10–5; Oct–Mar daily 11–4; t (0141) 339 0631; www.thetallship.com*) is the *Glenlee*, one of the last surviving Clyde-built sailing ships (1896), which features exhibitions, events, a restaurant and a shop.

The **Scottish Football Museum**, Hampden Park (*open Mon–Sat 10–5, Sun 11–5; t (0141) 616 6100; www.scottishfootballmuseum.com*), is a celebration of the history of Scottish football in this £63 million refurbished stadium. The **Celtic Football Club Visitor Centre**, Celtic Park (*open Mon–Fri 10–2.45, Sat and Sun 11–2.45 (non-match days); t (0141) 551 4038; www.celticfc.co.uk*), is in the largest club in Britain, with tours of the museum and stadium. The **Rangers Football Club**, Ibrox Stadium, is open for tours only (*Sun 9.45–4.30; t 0870 600 1972; www.rangers.co.uk*).

The **Heatherbank Museum of Social Work**, Glasgow Caledonian University, Cowcaddens Road (*open Mon–Fri 9–4.30; t (0141) 331 8637*), is the only museum of its kind in the world, with over 2,500 slides of life in the 19th and early 20th centuries and a 5,000-volume reference library. The focus is on how the underprivileged were cared for in the past.

Outdoor Attractions

Glasgow Zoo Park (*open daily Nov–Feb 9.30–4, Mar–May and Sept–Oct 9.30–5, June–Aug 9.30–6; adm*) is in Calderpark, 6 miles southeast of the city on the A74, with all the animals you expect to see.

The **Fossil Grove** (*open April–Oct daily 12–5; park daily dawn–dusk*), in Victoria Park west of Kelvingrove, is unusual. In 1887 workmen, cutting a path across an old quarry, revealed a fragment of a 230-million-year-old forest. The weird stumps and roots were formed by the setting of mud within the bark of the trees, which, compressed for millions of years, became the coal that fired the Clydeside furnaces in the 20th century. The stresses and worries of yesterday and tomorrow seem trivial, seen in the perspective of this relic. The park has formal floral displays.

The **Botanic Gardens** (*open daily 7am–dusk; greenhouses daily 10–4.45*) lie beside the Great Western Road, north of Kelvingrove. They cover 42 acres with flowers, trees, shrubs and a famous collection of orchids. The **Kibble Palace**, a Victorian glass pavilion, houses a luscious collection of tree ferns, and plants from the temperate zones of the world.

'**The Barras**' (Barrows; *open Sat and Sun*), at Gallowgate north of Glasgow Green, is Glasgow's flea market. Over 800 traders sell anything you want from stalls, barrows and shops. This is a light-hearted place to idle away a sunny day. A good-humoured, jostling crowd fingers the bargains: beaten copper pots, leatherwork, straw mats, wicker baskets, silks and batiks, cottons and man-made fibres, cheap plastic junk, polished wood and plastic urns. One could be serenaded by a busker, touched for a fiver by a conscience-stabbing down-and-out, or have one's wallet slid dexterously from a pocket or bag as one haggles over the price of a strip of foam rubber.

The Clyde Valley and Ayrshire

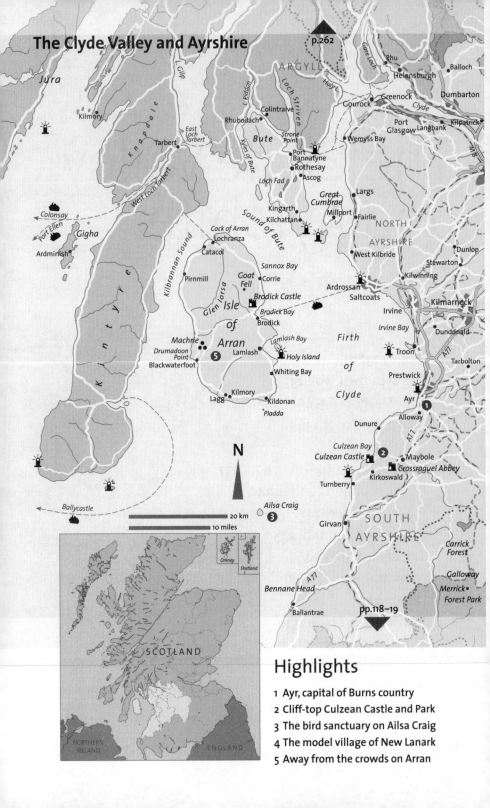

The Clyde Valley and Ayrshire

p.262

pp.118–19

Highlights

1 Ayr, capital of Burns country
2 Cliff-top Culzean Castle and Park
3 The bird sanctuary on Ailsa Craig
4 The model village of New Lanark
5 Away from the crowds on Arran

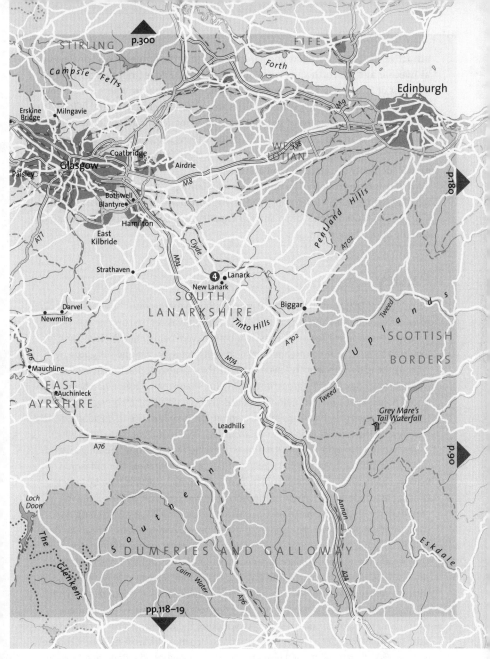

p.300

p.180

p.90

pp.118–19

Strathclyde embraced, until quite recently, much more than the broad valley of the Clyde. Now it has been appropriately renamed the Clyde Valley. Glasgow lies at its heart, surrounded by a straggle of vibrant, if not beautiful, satellite towns. To the south, a string of seaside resorts lines the sandy coast – Glasgow's playground – backed by farmland, rich in Covenanting history. (There's a Covenanting Trail.) North of the Clyde, uninspiring dormitory towns give way to the Campsie Fells with attractive villages, a few parks and gardens, a scrap of the Antonine Wall on Bar Hill at Twechar, and the Forth and Clyde Canal. The Erskine Bridge (toll) over the river to the west of Glasgow is a splendid sweep of modern engineering where once a tiny cable-ferry crossed the busy waterway. The area's economy has risen and fallen with Glasgow's. Since the decline of shipbuilding and its related industries, diversification into electronics and the silicon chip has brought a new prosperity to Clydeside towns. Most of them have a summer festival or civic week, with decorated streets and an excuse for plenty of entertainment and music.

Ayrshire is Burns country. The Burns National Heritage Park, Murdoch's Lone, Alloway, Ayr KA7 4PQ, **t** (01292) 443 700, *www.robertburns.org*, encompasses Burns Cottage and Museum, the Tam o'Shanter Experience, the Brig o'Doon, Alloway Kirk and the Burns Monument.

Paisley

Just west of Glasgow on the A737, Paisley's suburbs merge with those of the city. The town developed from a monastic community which was centred on the 12th-century abbey. At the time of the Union, muslin and linen were being manufactured and exported by boat. Sewing threads were also being spun by 1730 and silk gauze by 1760. By the early 18th century Paisley had the third largest population in Scotland, and it is now one of the 10 largest towns. In 1805 shawl manufacture had been introduced. Soldiers returning from India at the end of the 18th century brought with them the shawls they had acquired in Kashmir. The people of the town adapted these and created the distinctive Paisley design, based on segments of pine cones, which were Kashmiri in origin. But the Kashmir wool, which comes from Tibetan goats, proved too difficult to obtain in large quantities and shawls went out of fashion, leading to a decline in the industry. The first great thread mill was built by James Coats in 1826, but by 1841 a fifth of the workforce was unemployed, resulting in crippling poverty. Don't ever make the mistake of lumping Paisley with Glasgow. Paisley natives are known as 'buddies' and are linked by a fierce sense of camaraderie which has come down through many generations, deeply rooted in the cotton mills. They regard themselves as a homogeneous community as tightly woven as the shawls their ancestors created. The town has its annual festival in May.

Paisley Abbey (*open Mon–Sat 10–3.30, Sun for services only*) was founded in 1171 for Cluniac monks and was almost completely destroyed by Edward I. Rebuilt after Bannockburn, its tower collapsed in 1553, wrecking the nave, and it remained in this state for many years. The present restoration, which includes work by Robert Lorimer, is the parish church, a dignified building, austere but serene. The **Barochan Cross** in the abbey is a weathered 10th-century Celtic cross that once stood on a hillock overlooking Port Glasgow. The tombs of several of the Bruces are in the choir, under a stone-vaulted ceiling, and there is a chapel dedicated to St Mirin, a 6th-century saint who was adopted as Paisley's patron saint.

Paisley Museum and Art Gallery (*open Tues–Sat 10–5, Sun 2–5*) has a display of at least 500 Paisley shawls with their looms and design patterns. The **Sma' Shot**

Cottages (*open April–Sept Wed and Sat 12–4; www.smashot.com*), in George Place, are traditional 19th-century millworkers' two-storey houses with iron stairways, displaying social conditions in Victorian times. Each has its own theme and contemporary fittings. This delightful complex was initiated by a group of women, former employees from the cotton mills, who got together as a voluntary team and set it all up. On the first Saturday in July each year, they run an open day with parades and special events. **Coats Observatory** (*open Tues–Sat 10–5, Sun 2–5*), in Oakshaw Street, has had a continuous tradition of astronomical observation and meteorological recording since it was built in 1882. Built by the Coats (cotton) family in 1883, it is a working Victorian observatory with displays on astronomy, astronautics, seismology and meteorology. Weather permitting, there is a public telescopic viewing on Thursday evenings in winter.

South of the Clyde

All excursions south of the Clyde are an easy day trip from Glasgow. The M8/A8 runs west from the city and hugs the south bank of the Clyde, a vast mud flat at low tide and no longer the busy waterway it once was. It then becomes the A78 and runs down the coast, linking the seaside resort towns that are Glasgow's playgrounds.

Formakin (*open daily, 10–5; adm*), about a mile south along the B789 just after junction 31 on the motorway, was built by Robert Lorimer between 1903 and 1911. The buildings and landscaped grounds have been designed in the Arts and Crafts style, transformed from a meal mill and a few farm dwellings. You can walk in the restored gardens, visit the restaurant and gift shop in the old stable block and see rare animals on display in the old pigsty. Those with keen eyes should look out for stone monkeys clambering over ridges on the roof and a carved date stone above the entrance to the stable courtyard saying 1694, accompanied by DL – Damned Lie.

Finlaystone House and Gardens (*house open by appointment; grounds and garden open daily 10.30–5; adm; t (01475) 540 285; www.finlaystone.co.uk*) are about 20 minutes west of Glasgow just past Langbank. Dating from the 14th century and extended in 1760, the house belonged to the Cunninghams, Earls of Glencairn, for five centuries. The 14th Earl befriended Robert Burns who spent some time here and wrote a stirring poem, 'Lament for James, Earl of Glencairn'. John Knox was another of Finlaystone's better-known visitors. Owned and run by the Macmillan family, it is now a centre for the Clan Macmillan and home of its chief.

The house has exhibitions of Celtic art and Victoriana, and a collection of dolls from all around the world, and is sometimes the venue for concerts. The gardens are outstanding and as varied as the rooms in a house. A leaflet describes all the features, including a laurel hedge on a bank, cut once a year by a Flymo on water-skis. Landscaped in the 1830s and still being developed, its many 'rooms' open off sweeping lawns with magnificent views across the Firth of Clyde to the hills beyond. Look out for the ingenious Celtic Paving, near the bog garden and folly. This was laid in 1984 by the present chief's wife, instead of a maze. Its six circles and semi-circles

Tourist Information

Glasgow: Tourist Information Centre, 11 George Square, **t** (0141) 204 4400.

Festivals

May: Highland Games, Gourock.

Where to Stay and Eat

Gleddoch House Hotel, Langbank, **t** (01475) 540 711 (*expensive*). Converted family mansion in 250 acres overlooking the Clyde and Loch Lomond Hills; without doubt it is the pick of the bunch. It contains many of the original furnishings and pictures which give it the atmosphere of a private country house. Guests automatically become members of The Gleddoch Club, with free use of the 18-hole golf course, squash courts, snooker room and sauna. There is also riding. The food is renowned, the service excellent. Dogs are allowed in the rooms.

Manor Park Hotel, Skelmorlie, **t** (01475) 520 832 (*expensive*). On a hill overlooking magnificent views of gardens, hills and sea lochs on the Clyde coast. It is comfortable, the food and service are good and there are even peacocks in the grounds.

Inverkip Hotel, Inverkip, **t** (01475) 521 478 (*moderate*). Cosy, family-run coaching inn.

Victoria House, Main Street, Gourock, **t** (01475) 630 033. Well worth booking ahead to eat in this restaurant.

form a continuous line, adapted from a one-inch design in the *Book of Kells*. The **John Knox Tree** behind the house (moved 40 yards from around the corner in 1900 because the lady of the house complained it made the drawing room too dark for her to sew in) is a yew, said to have been where Knox held the first reformed Communion in the west of Scotland in 1556. There are also woodland walks, pick-your-own strawberries and raspberries, a tearoom (*open April–Sept*) and visitor centre and a play area.

Port Glasgow, Greenock and Gourock

Port Glasgow, Greenock and Gourock form a more or less continuous urban sprawl along the south bank of the Clyde. Once the hub of the mighty Clydeside shipbuilding industry, these towns were hit hardest by the Depression and for many years were a gloomy spectacle of dying shipyards and dole queues. But the tenacious spirit that is part of the Clydeside character is revitalizing the area: buildings are being cleaned up, enterprising new developments are replacing the skeletons of the shipyards, and a keen eye can pick out some fine architecture amongst the dreary tenements. Within a stone's throw inland, narrow lanes run through miles of unspoiled moor, dotted with gorse and heather and small villages.

Port Glasgow was built in the 17th century, the nearest deep-water port to the city. **Newark Castle** (*open April–Sept Mon–Sat 9.30–4.30, Sun 2–4.30; adm; www.historic-scotland.gov.uk*), east of the town, dates from the 16th century, with a 15th-century tower, and is said to be one of the best examples of a Scottish mansion house of this period. A solid, fortified pile on a green sward overlooking the river, it is still almost intact with courtyard, hall and a large number of chambers. In the days when it was a Maxwell stronghold, it was strategically placed with commanding views of the river. Also in Port Glasgow, there is a replica of the 25-tonne *Comet*, the first commercial steamship in Europe, an elegant craft built by John Wood in 1812. It had a 3-horse-power engine and dashed along at about 6 knots.

Merging with Port Glasgow's western suburbs, **Greenock** boasts some splendid Victorian architecture, including the Municipal Buildings, with a 245ft tower, and a classical-style custom house which is now a small **museum** (*open Mon–Fri 10–12.30 and 1.30–4*) with displays on customs and excise, including illicit distilling. The stained-glass windows in Old West Kirk on the Esplanade include work by pre-Raphaelites Burne-Jones, Rossetti and Morris. This was the first church to be built after the Reformation, in 1591, and the first Presbyterian church to be acknowledged by Parliament. It was moved here from its original site in 1920.

The **Maclean Museum and Art Gallery** (*open Mon–Sat 10–12 and 1–5*), in Union Street, has local and natural history exhibits, including model ships and information about James Watt who was born and educated in the town. The art gallery has work by Guthrie, another native of Greenock. Burns fans should go up Nelson Street to the cemetery, to see the **Tomb of Highland Mary** (*see* **Topics**, 'Two Enlightened Men', p.65), moved here when Old West Kirk was rebuilt. The original Burns Club was founded in Greenock in 1802. On Lyle Hill, above Greenock, the huge granite **Cross of Lorraine** – with its two transversals rising from a gigantic anchor – is the Free French Memorial. During the Second World War, Greenock was a Free French Naval Base and this is the memorial to the sailors who died in the Battle of the Atlantic.

Gourock, merging with Greenock, is on the shoulder where the Clyde swings round from the east to flow out to sea. Half resort, half port, it is the home of Caledonian MacBrayne (who run most of the west-coast ferries), and a yachting centre.

Granny Kempock's Stone, on Kempock Point beside the A78 overlooking the Firth, is a 6-foot-high block of grey stone dating from prehistoric times, thought to have been part of a Druid temple. Superstitious fishermen believed Granny Kempock commanded the sea. They laid offerings before her and walked around her seven times, begging for fair weather and good fishing. Newly married couples embraced her and asked for children. Today she is railed off, to prevent such familiarity.

Cloch Lighthouse, built in 1797, is an imposing white landmark on rocky Cloch Point, just west of the town, greeted with relief by homecoming sailors during wartime and by fishermen after a stormy night at sea.

Inverkip, a couple of miles south on the A78, has one of the biggest marinas in these parts, well supplied with chandlers and shore facilities. Skippers of bigger yachts should beware of the narrow, shallow entrance at low tide. A small back road east out of Inverkip leads up to **Cornalees Bridge** in the open moorland of **Clyde-Muirshiel Regional Park**. A nature trail here follows the aqueducts that used to supply the coastal towns with drinking water and power for the mills.

Captain Kidd

Captain William Kidd was born in Greenock in 1645 to a Covenanting minister. He went to sea as a boy privateer and earned a reputation for bravery, for which he received a reward of £150 from New York City. In 1696 he was given a ship with 30 guns and sent off to fight the French and capture pirates. A year later he got to Madagascar, the pirates' main headquarters, and, finding plunder more lucrative than government service, became a pirate himself. He was hanged in England in 1701.

Wemyss Bay is so called from the caves (weems) here, where Stone-Age nomads may have lived while making foraging expeditions from Ireland. There is a splendid Victorian station from which you can get ferries to Bute.

Down the Coast

The area from Skelmorlie to south of Irvine, including Arran and the Cumbraes, is known as Cunninghame.

Largs

Largs is easily the nicest of the Clyde resorts, with a history that adds stature to its bustling streets. Tucked in on a shelf below rolling moorland, with views across the Firth to Great Cumbrae and Bute, Largs was the theatre for a crucial, though rather ineffectual, battle in the 13th century. Old King Haakon of Norway, determined to dominate the Western Isles and worried that Alexander III had the same intention, launched his fleet from Kirkwall in Orkney in July 1263. The weather was appalling. The fleet battled round Cape Wrath and down the Minch as far as Skye, suffering much damage. In Skye they were joined by Magnus, King of Man, and a few others. Into the teeth of southwesterly gales they struggled on, past the Inner Hebrides and around the Mull of Kintyre. They were well into the Clyde by the end of September when they were caught by a gale which tore Haakon's ships from their moorings and drove them on to the Ayrshire coast at Largs. The sailors waded ashore to meet Alexander's army. There was a confusion of arrows and horses and then the Scots withdrew and allowed the Vikings to wade back to their ships and sail away. History doesn't relate *how* they managed to get those cumbersome long-boats off a lee-shore, nor *why* the Scots, with such a strategic advantage, allowed them to, but the outcome was conclusive. Haakon lost interest and died, and his successor, Erik, sold the Western Isles for less than £3,000 in 1266 and married Alexander's daughter Margaret. A phallic obelisk, known as the Pencil, on Bowen Craig south of the town, celebrates the battle, and every September hundreds of Scandinavians come to Largs to join in the Viking Festival. **Vikingar** (*open April–Sept Mon–Fri and Sun 10.30–5.30, Sat 12.30–5.30; Oct and Mar Mon–Fri and Sun 10.30–3.30, Sat 12.30–3.30; adm; t (01475) 689 777; www.vikingar.co.uk*), just north of the small pier, is a good exhibition of the history of the Vikings in Scotland, with suitable sound effects and videos.

Skelmorlie Aisle (*open June–Aug Mon–Fri 2–5*), just off Main Street by the old burial ground, is all that is left of a Renaissance church, converted into an elaborate mausoleum in 1636 for Sir Robert Montgomerie, a local dignitary. Of Italian design, it has intriguing carvings and is well worth a visit. If it is shut, the museum next door has the keys. The **Largs Historical Society Museum** (*open June–Sept daily 2–6; donation box*), in Kirkgate House, Manse Court, reconstructs the battle, and has exhibits of local history. The **Christian Heritage Museum** (*open April–Sept daily 10–5; adm*), in a Benedictine Monastery at 5 Mackerston Place, tells the history of Christian

monasticism in Britain and southwest Scotland, with some fine vestments an.
displays, as well as a café in the refectory, and a shop.

South of Largs to Kilmarnock

Kelburn Castle and Country Centre (*house open July and Aug daily 10–6, subject to
castle functions, or by appointment; adm; grounds Easter–Oct daily 10–6; adm; t (01475)
568 685; www.kelburncountrycentre.com*), on the A78 between Largs and Fairlie, offers
a good day out for the family. Kelburn has been the home of the Boyle family, Earls of
Glasgow since 1703, for 800 years, and Kelburn Castle, dating from the 13th century
with many later additions, is the home of the present Earl. The grounds feature wild
woodland, dramatic waterfalls and gorges, pools and grottos with wild flowers, ferns,
rare trees and shrubs, and a walled garden called The Plaisance, full of rare plants.
There is a licensed café, a lampoon-type Cartoon Exhibition depicting the history of
the Boyle family, and a museum with New Zealand exhibits. Other attractions include
a Commando Assault Course built by the Royal Marines, for adults; an Adventure
Course and Stockade, for younger Tarzans; guided walks and talks. There is also an
animals' and pets' corner, a riding centre, pony trekking and a new Secret Forest.

The **Scottish Nuclear Come and See Programme**, at Hunterston south of Largs (*open
Mar–Sept daily 9.30–4.30; Oct–Feb Mon–Fri 9.30–4.30, Sat and Sun 1–4.30; tours 10.30
(Mon–Fri only), 1.30 and 3.30; freephone t 0800 838 557; www.snl.co.uk*), describes how
nuclear energy affects us in the home. There are walks and picnics in the area.

The A78 runs through Fairlie and West Kilbride to Ardrossan and Saltcoats, a string
of unremarkable resort towns, some of which contain interesting museums and
visitor centres. The **West Kilbride Museum** (*open Tues–Sat 10–12 and 2–4*), for instance,
has costumes and a large collection of Ayrshire lace and embroidery. **Ardrossan** is the
port for the island of Arran (*see p.254*). **Saltcoats** was an important producer of salt in
the days of James V. **North Ayrshire Museum** (*open 10–1 and 2–5; closed Wed and Sun*)
at Kirkgate, Saltcoats, is in a late 18th-century church and shows aspects of local life.

At **Kilwinning**, east of Saltcoats, 17th-century **Dalgarven Mill** (*open Tues–Sun;
t (01294) 552 448; www.dalgarvenmill.org.uk*) is a working museum, with displays of
artefacts of the period and live models in authentic costume. At **Kilwinning Abbey**,
founded in the mid-12th century and now derelict, an annual archery competition for
the Papingo Trophy has been taking place for 600 years, the oldest such event in the
world. Kilwinning claims to be the first centre in Scotland of freemasonry. It was
introduced by the stonemasons working on the abbey.

Eglinton Country Park (*open Easter–Oct; t (01294) 551 776*), south of Kilwinning, is
landscaped with gardens, picnic sites, a visitor centre and walks, centred on the ruins
of **Eglinton Castle**. Here, in 1839, below the 100ft tower (now derelict), the Eglinton
Tournament took place: a whimsical Victorian longing for 'the good old days'.
Napoleon III took part as one of the knights, practising, no doubt, for his next abortive
attempt at the French throne the following year. In his novel *Endymion* Disraeli
borrows from this event.

mation

t (01475) 673 765.
294) 313 886.
reet, t (01563) 539 090.
Statue Square,

Arran Tourist Board,
15a Skye Road, t (01292) 678 100,
www.ayrshire-arran.com.

Festivals

Easter: Cycle Race, Girvan.
May: Carnival, Kilmarnock. **Folk Festival**, Girvan.
June: Burns Day, Kilmarnock. **Civic Week**, Girvan.
July: Harbour Festival, Irvine; over three days. **Horse show**, Kilmarnock.
August: Marymass, Irvine; week-long festival which culminates with a procession past the castle and the crowning of a queen; also a horse race alleged to be the longest in the world. **Festival of Leisure**, Kilmarnock.

Sports and Activities

Largs has a couple of golf courses, a National Sports Training Centre, a big swimming pool – and the sea. Three times a week the last sea-going paddle steamer, *Waverley*, sails from the pier to other resorts on the Clyde. Largs is also the port for **Great Cumbrae Island** (*see* p.253).
Largs Yacht Haven, south of town. Berths for over 500 yachts and all marina facilities: chandlers, a sea-school, diving equipment, provisions, sales, charter and repairs.
Clyde Muirshiel Country Park, *www. clydemuirshiel.co.uk*. 100 square miles of high roadless moorland near Largs. At Lochwinnoch there is a boating and fishing loch, with nature trails, picnic sites and information centres. *Organised events April–Sept.*

Irvine has splendid facilities including a seaside park and a Magnum Leisure Centre, with swimming pools, water-chutes, an ice rink, squash courts, theatre, cinema, restaurants, bars and cafés.
The Galleon Centre, Kilmarnock. Indoor leisure complex with swimming pools, ice rink, bowling hall, squash and badminton courts, a curling rink, sauna, fitness room, bar, etc.

Where to Stay and Eat

Blairquhan Castle, Straiton, Maybole, t (01655) 770 239, *www.blairquhan.co.uk* (*expensive*). Bookings for one party at a time (minimum 4 people). Very expensive and worth every penny. There's an art gallery and library.
Brig o'Doon, Alloway, t (01292) 442 466, *www.costley-hotels.co.uk* (*expensive*). By the River Doon and opposite the Burns Monument, its floodlit garden running down to the Brig o' Doon. Recently done up to a high standard. Good atmosphere.
Enterkine Country House, Annbank by Ayr, t (01292) 521 608, *www.enterkine.com* (*expensive*). Seriously expensive, retaining original Art Deco style. Only the best here, including the food.
The Ivy House Hotel, Alloway, t (01292) 442 336, *theivyhousealloway@hotmail.com* (*expensive*). Relaxed country house, recently refurbished. Very hospitable and good food.
Lochgreen House Hotel, Troon, t (01292) 313 343, *www.costley-hotels.co.uk* (*expensive*). Very comfortable hotel in 30 acres of garden and woodland.
Montgreenan Mansion House Hotel, Kilwinning, t (01294) 557 733 (*expensive*). A country house in 45 acres near a championship golf course.
Piersland Hotel, Troon, t (01292) 314 747, *www.piersland.co.uk* (*expensive*). Former home of Johnnie Walker family, overlooking Royal Troon's Open Championship golf course. Good atmosphere.

Irvine

Irvine, 3 miles south of Kilwinning, is Scotland's only coastal new town. Under its modern façade, its history goes back a long way. William Wallace was deserted by his followers here in 1297, when they signed a treaty with the English.

Scoretulloch House Hotel, Darvel, t (01560) 323 331, *www.scoretulloch.com* (*expensive*). A 'restaurant with rooms' on the edge of a grouse moor. Old, tranquil and splendid, with first-class comfort and food.

Thistle Hotel, Irvine, t (01294) 274 272, *www.thistlehotels.com* (*expensive*). Predictable hotel. Ultra-modern outside, the interior has arches and rattan, palms and bold carpets, and a stifling heating system. Some of the suites open on to a tropical lagoon with lush jungle, rocks, waterfalls, bridges and hot air.

Turnberry Hotel, Turnberry, t (01655) 331 000 (*expensive*). Vast golfing mecca on the coast, which has everything any golfer could possibly want.

Crosses Country House, Ballantrae, t (01465) 831 363 (*moderate*). Comfortable (Wolsey Lodge) country house in a secluded valley with 12 acres of garden and woodland and a Cordon Bleu cook.

Doonbrae, 40 Alloway Road, Ayr, t (01292) 442 511, *doonbrae@aol.com* (*moderate*). Cosy family house with meals by arrangement and relaxed hosts.

Elderslie Hotel, John Street, Largs, t (01475) 686 460 (*moderate*). Looks across to Cumbrae and Arran, and is nicely old-fashioned.

Finlayson Arms Hotel, Coylton, t (01292) 570 298 (*moderate*). Country pub/hotel.

Glenfoot, in Dundonald near Kilmarnock, t (01563) 850 311 (*moderate*). In attractive surroundings near 14th-century Dundonald Castle – a family home where you are well fed and cosseted in comfortable rooms.

Kings Arms Hotel, Dalrymple Street, in the middle of Girvan, t (01465) 713 322 (*moderate*). Where John Keats wrote 'A Tribute to Ailsa Craig' in the summer of 1818, three years before his death.

New Lanark Mill House and Self-catering Waterhouses, t (01555) 667 200, *www.newlanark.org* (*moderate*). A special place to stay, both in the hotel in the converted 18th-century cotton mill beside the river, and in the self-catering waterhouses (1–2 rooms).

Nether Underwood, near Symington, t (01563) 830 666, *www.netherunderwood.co.uk* (*moderate*). Modern country house in old walled garden. A Wolsey Lodge with excellent food and hospitality.

Skirling House, Skirling, near Biggar, t (01899) 860 274, *www.skirlinghouse.com* (*moderate*). A house by the village green, with pretty gardens and welcoming owners. Also two self-catering cottages.

Stair Inn, Stair, t (01292) 591 650, *www.stairinn.co.uk* (*moderate*). Small, cosy country inn, recently done up.

Loudoun Arms, Mauchline, t (01290) 51011 (*cheap*). Easy-going Irish host who serves generous breakfasts in a room lined with Burns murals.

Jolly Shepherd Hotel, Barr, near Girvan, t (01465) 861 233 (*cheap*). Friendly place with five bedrooms.

Kings Arms, Barr, t (01465) 861 230 (*cheap*). Small, unpretentious, whitewashed inn.

Poosie Nansies Inn, Mauchline, t (01290) 50316 (*cheap*). Burns fans should come here: echoing with memories, if not mod cons.

Braidlands, near Dalry, t (01294) 833 544. Cottage restaurant with first-class food.

Fins, Fairlie, near Largs, t (01475) 568 989. An excellent seafood bistro with a smokery. There is also a shop selling crafts.

Fouters, Academy Street, off Sandgate, Ayr, t (01292) 261 391. Very good restaurant.

Maccallums, Troon, t (01292) 319 339. A good seafood bistro at the ferry terminal.

Ristorante La Vigna, 40 Wellgate, Lanark, t (01555) 664 320. Excellent Italian food in jolly atmosphere.

Togs, Templehill, Troon. A really nice café.

Wheatsheaf Inn, Symington, t (01563) 830 307. A coaching inn with first-class pub food.

Wildings, 56 Montgomerie Street, Girvan, t (01465) 713 481. Restaurant serving a wide choice of good food.

The Big Idea (*open Mon–Fri 10–5 (last adm 3); Sat–Sun 10–6 (last adm 4); adm; t 08708 404 030, www.bigidea.org.uk*) is a splendid new attraction at the harbourside, opened for the millennium. Celebrating a thousand years of invention, this exhibition takes you through the world of inventions, creations and innovations. You can interact with the exhibits and use the workshop facilities to build your own inventions.

The **Scottish Maritime Museum** (*open daily 10–5; adm; www.scottishmaritime museum.org.uk*) is in Irvine harbour, once one of Glasgow's main ports, and includes working boats, a puffer, sailing boats and lifeboats. There is a collection of documents, artefacts and small craft, illustrating Scotland's sea-going heritage, as well as a tenement house, showing the 'room and kitchen' of a typical shipyard worker's dwelling at the turn of the last century, complete with range, utensils and drying laundry.

Glasgow Vennel (lane), the historic core of Irvine, was the main road to Glasgow until the end of the 17th century. Derelict and facing demolition in the 1970s, it was rescued and designated a conservation area in 1974. Its 18th- and 19th-century buildings are now restored and in use on an attractive cobbled street. **Glasgow Vennel Museum** (*open Mon, Tues and Thurs–Sat 10–1 and 2–5*), at nos.4 and 10, includes Burns' Lodgings, with a reconstruction of his attic room and the thatched Heckling Shop where he worked. Heckling was a well-paid but unpleasant job, involving separating the fibres of the flax plant from the stalk. It was backbreaking, dirty and smelly and the 22-year-old Burns loathed it, working from 10 to 12 hours a day. He suffered bad bouts of depression and it was during this time that he wrote 'Winter, A Dirge' and 'Prayer under the pressure of Violent Anguish':

...Sure Thou, Almighty, canst not act
From cruelty or wrath!
O, free my weary eyes from tears,
Or close them fast in death!

Fortunately the Almighty chose an alternative escape: on New Year's Eve 1781, during a drunken party in the Heckling Shop, Burns' aunt, Mrs Peacock, knocked over a candle which ignited the bundles of dry flax and demolished the shop. Burns remarked with glee: 'The shop burnt to ashes and left me like a true poet, not worth a sixpence.'

There is an **art gallery** in the the Vennel, with local and international exhibitions.

Kilmarnock and Around

Kilmarnock is the centre of industry in this area. The **Burns Monument**, in Kay Park, is a red-sandstone tower which is only viewable from the outside. Burns was closely associated with the town and his first collection of poems, *The Kilmarnock Poems*, was produced here by John Wilson in 1786, a 35-page volume containing 44 poems. Its success was immediate, rescuing the impoverished poet from emigration to Jamaica. **Kay Park** has a boating pond, children's play area, crazy golf and an assault course. The bowling club is the oldest in Britain – over 250 years old. Burns and his friends used to bowl here, pausing to quench their 'drouth' at the Kay Park Tavern, still there today.

The **Dick Institute** (*open Mon–Sat 10–5; t (01653) 554 343*), in Elmbank Avenue, has geological and archaeological exhibits, family archives and an art gallery. It is the finest library in Ayrshire and headquarters for the International Burns Federation.

Dean Castle and Country Park (*castle open summer daily 12–5; winter Sat and Sun 12–4; visitor centre summer daily 11–5; winter daily 11–4; country park always open; adm;*

www.deancastle.com) is in a wooded hollow in Dean Road, off Glasgow Road. The 14th-century fortified keep with a 15th-century palace contains collections of armour, weapons, old musical instruments and tapestries. There is a banqueting hall, old kitchens, a minstrel's gallery and a gloomy dungeon. A number of different events are held in the castle, including ancient warfare demonstrations, a jazz festival and fire-works in November. The 200-acre park has formal gardens, nature trails, a visitor centre, picnic sites, a Burns Garden, a riding centre and a ranger service. Tours of the park cover bird life, ecology, geology and industrial heritage. A garden is being culti-vated by groups of disabled people. There is a children's corner and a deer park.

East of Kilmarnock

Newmilns and **Darvel** are renowned for their lace and woollen industries, and tradi-tional Scottish bonnets are still made in **Stewarton**. Some of the mills have shops.

Dunlop is where Dunlop cheese was first made in the 17th century, from milk from Dunlop cows – now internationally famous as Ayrshires. When the Milk Marketing Board tried to export Dunlop cheese to England their customers, influenced by the name, complained it tasted rubbery: it is now called Scottish Cheddar and sells well.

On the way back to the coast from Kilmarnock on the A759, the rugged ruin of 13th-century **Dundonald Castle** (*open April–Sept daily 10–5; adm*), about 3 miles southwest of the outskirts, has recently been extensively renovated, with a visitor centre, and provides a good insight into medieval life. Dundonald was inhabited by the Fitzalans, Lord High Stewards, from whom the Stewart line descended. Robert II, the first Stewart king, died here in 1390, as did his son Robert III in 1406.

On the coast again, **Troon**, about 5 miles south of Irvine, is another seaside resort with sandy beaches and good golf courses. *Troone* means 'nose', referring to the craggy hook of land thrusting out into the sea with a lighthouse on the end. Lady Island, 3 miles off the point, is a bird sanctuary.

Prestwick

Prestwick was chosen as the site for an international airport because of its reputa-tion for being fog-free. **Bruce's Well** is in a railed enclosure surrounded by lawn and flowers in a residential area behind St Ninian's Church, south of the town and sign-posted from the Ayr road. Here, Robert the Bruce, probably in the early stages of the skin disease that killed him, is said to have struck at the ground with his lance in desperation because he was exhausted and parched with thirst. Water gushed from the ground and he was revived.

Ayr and Alloway

Ayr, merging with Prestwick, is the main holiday centre on this coast and seems almost to sparkle with friendliness. It is a spacious town bordering a long sweep of sandy beach, with wide roads and villas set far apart in pleasant gardens. In spring it is a riot of pink and red blossom, carpeted with bluebells and daffodils. There are two theatres, good shops, three golf courses, fishing, and a famous racecourse. There was a settlement here as far back as the 8th century. Early in his struggles for Scotland, Robert the Bruce burnt down 'The Barns of Ayr' (a temporary barracks) with 500 of Edward I's troops inside.

For many, Ayr is of supreme importance as the capital of Burns country. The **Auld Kirk**, down a wynd off the High Street on the banks of the river, is where Burns was baptized. Through Kirk Port, look for the morbid 'mort-safes' (1655), which were put over freshly filled graves to discourage body-snatchers. Cromwell supplied the funds to build this church, having used the old one as part of a fort, of which little remains.

The **Auld Brig** dates from the 13th century and was Ayr's only bridge until a new one was built in 1788 and replaced in 1877. Burns wrote a poem in which he watched the pretentious new bridge being built, through the contemptuous eyes of the old bridge, prophesying, with uncanny prescience, that the new bridge would not stand the test of time. 'I'll be a brig when ye're a shapeless cairn.' Sure enough, the new bridge had to be replaced after a flood in the 19th century.

Loudoun Hall is in Boat Vennel, one of the few places around here that has nothing to do with Burns. Among the oldest surviving examples of town-house architecture in the country, it was built for a rich merchant, in the late 15th century. It is being restored, having been condemned as a slum and threatened with a demolition order, and plans for its future are not yet certain.

Robert Burns was in fact born on 25 January 1759 in the village of **Alloway** now a suburb of Ayr to the south. Although he only lived there for seven years the atmosphere in Alloway is electric with his presence, and it would be difficult to go there and not catch mild Burns fever. Straggling round the River Doon, a cluster of buildings and monuments to the poet echo with his salty humour.

The **Tam o' Shanter Experience** (*open April–Sept daily 9–6; Oct–Mar daily 9–5; films adm*) is a good place from which to start a nostalgic Burns pilgrimage. As well as a visitor centre, shop and café, they have a Tam o'Shanter audiovisual show. Burns is frequently misunderstood: many of his admirers tend to deify him and miss the full flavour of his personality (*see* **Topics**, 'Two Enlightened Men', pp.61–66).

Burns Cottage and Museum (*open April–Sept daily 9–6; Oct–Mar Mon–Sat 10–4, Sun 12–4; adm*) is a simple white thatched cottage, the 'auld clay biggin' built by the poet's father, William, and the place where he was born. Family and animals shared the same roof in this long, low building – a practice that helped to warm the living quarters in winter, if also to make them rather smelly. The museum contains Burns memorabilia, including the family Bible and many original manuscripts. A recent addition is a Burns' Interpretation Gallery, with theme music.

...And, wow! Tam saw an unco sight!
Warlocks and witches in a dance:
Nae cotillion, brent new frae France,
But hornpipes, jigs, strathspeys, and reels,
Put life and mettle in their heels.

Alloway Kirk, across the road from the Tam o' Shanter Experience, is the scene of Tam's witches' orgy, when he was making his way home after a monumental bender with his 'trusty, drouthy crony – Souter Johnie'. Built in 1510, the kirk is a shell now, but you can peep in and see the very *winnock-bunker* 'window seat' where Old Nick sat, in the guise of a shaggy dog 'black and grim and large', and the tombs from which the dead held up lights to illuminate the witches' wild dance. Perhaps the poet was somewhat inebriated himself, when he came here one moonlit night and let the setting work on his imagination. The grave of William Burns, Robert's simple, devout father who died of overwork, lies in the shadow of the walls.

Burns Monument (*open same times as Burns Cottage above; adm*), overlooking the River Doon, is a fanciful Grecian-style temple on an Egyptian base, built in 1823. Fluted columns support a round, domed roof surmounted by an urn held up by three dolphins – symbols of Apollo, patron of the Muses. Inside, a simple chamber displays such treasures as Jean Armour's wedding ring and Highland Mary's Bible with a lock of her hair, books, papers, pictures and documents, including a photocopy of an original manuscript. A selection of Burns' work includes translations into Russian, made as early as 1800, and Esperanto. The gardens are full of unusual shrubs and trees: tulip trees, rare heathers, cultivated thistles and many more. In a pavilion – the Statue House – life-sized statues of such familiar characters as Tam o' Shanter and Souter Johnie sit in perpetual companionship, brought in from their original site in the garden where weather threatened erosion of their soft-stone bodies.

Brig o' Doon, beyond the monument on the right, is a 13th-century, single-arched bridge, soaring to a graceful peak, duplicated in reflection to form a frame for river scenery. This is the bridge over which Tam o' Shanter escaped on his Maggie, leaving the witches to their 'hornpipes, jigs, strathspeys and reels' in the kirk.

Around Ayr

Heading for Mauchline on the B743, turn off to **Tarbolton**. Burns lived here between the ages of 18 and 24. He joined the local dancing class 'to brush up my manners'. He also helped form the **Bachelors Club**, a debating society, in a 17th-century **thatched house** (*open Easter–Sept daily 1.30–5.30; Oct Sat and Sun 1.30–5.30; adm*). He was initiated into freemasonry here in 1781, in the upper room where the dancing classes were held, conveniently linked to the pub next door by an outside stair.

A somewhat incongruous pillar with a ball on top, in a field in Failford just outside Mauchline, is **Highland Mary's Monument**. Burns is said to have met Mary Campbell on this spot for the last time before she died.

Mauchline, northeast of Ayr on the B743, is an important step on the Burns Heritage Trail. A cul-de-sac in the centre of this unremarkable main road town leads to **Burns House Museum** (*open Easter–Sept Tues–Sat 10–5, or by appointment, t (01290) 550 045; www.robertburns.org*), where Burns installed his mistress, Jean Armour, and lived with her for a few months before and after their marriage in 1788. She gave birth to twins, for the second time, a week after they moved in. Furnished in the style of the period, it contains many relics of the poet. It was in the kirk above the **cottage** (*open June–Aug daily 2–4*) that Burns was forced to sit on the 'cutty stool' or stool of repentance, a humiliating punishment inflicted by the elders of the kirk because of his 'irregular marriage' with Jean. (It is said he refused to sit and stood defiantly beside the stool.) Four of his children are buried in the kirkyard, and a board shows the graves of many of his contemporaries who feature in his poems: Poosie Nansie, Tootie and the Bleth'rin Bitch. **Poosie Nansie's Tavern**, an ale shop and lodging house in Burns' day, is opposite the kirk. The tower on the northern edge of the town is another Burns Monument, erected in his memory in 1895, with a tourist information centre (*open Mon–Sat 9–5,* **t** *(01290) 551 916)*, an audiovisual display, 'Mauchline in the Time of Burns', and 'Local Industries Past and Present'. There are good views from the roof.

It is a short walk to **Ballochmyle Viaduct**, a unique structure over the River Ayr. In one curving arch of massive sandstone blocks, it spans 181ft across the river and is the largest and highest masonry arch railway bridge in Britain. A path along the north side of the river runs through a red sandstone gorge. Bronze-Age cup-and-ring markings can be seen on the sandstone a few yards from the path, discovered in 1987.

Dunure (*always accessible*) is a gaunt ruin on the edge of the cliff about 4 miles southwest of Alloway back on the coast road, the A719. Once one of the strongholds of the Kennedy family who ruled Ayrshire and considered themselves above the law, it has a conical dovecote, jagged walls, and a car park. Mary, Queen of Scots came here in 1563, when she toured her kingdom accompanied by a cavalcade of courtiers. It is said that in 1570 the Earl of Cassillis, Chief of the Kennedys, 'roasted' Allan Stewart, Commendator of nearby Crossraguel, in an attempt to persuade him to hand over the abbey lands. This gruesome event took place in the black vault, and so that 'rost suld not burne, but that it might rost in soppe, they spared not flambing with oyle'.

Going south from Dunure on the A719, watch out for **Electric Brae**, an optical illusion that makes your car appear to be going downhill when it is in fact going up.

Culzean Castle and Country Park (*castle open April–Oct daily 10.30–5.30, or by appointment; park open all year; adm;* **t** *(01655) 760 274)* overlooks Culzean Bay, and is the most visited of all National Trust for Scotland's properties. Pronounced 'Culain', the castle was built on top of the cliff in 1777 by Robert Adam, incorporating an ancient tower that was one of the Kennedy strongholds guarding the coast. Built with an eye to grandeur rather than defence, this sumptuous mansion is full of architectural marvels. There is the Round Drawing Room with a specially woven carpet, an Oval Staircase under a great glass dome, and a profusion of Adam mouldings. When Culzean was given over to the National Trust for Scotland in 1945, it was with the condition that an apartment be set aside for anyone whom Scotland might wish to honour. The first tenant for life was General Eisenhower.

The 565-acre country park was created in 1969, the first in Scotland, with a visitor centre in the Adam farm buildings, with exhibitions, a shop and a restaurant. The terraced gardens, with castellated walls enclosing a sunken fountain, are crammed with rare shrubs, palm trees, swathes of riotous colour and wafts of heady scent. There is a camellia house and orangery, a swan pond, aviary and deer park.

Maybole, a couple of miles east on the A77, has a tolbooth with a 17th-century tower and an important castle in the town centre, now used as offices, once stronghold of the Earls of Cassillis.

Crossraguel Abbey (*open April–Sept daily 9.30–6.30; adm*) is just to the south on the A77. Founded in 1244, it resisted the dissolution of the monasteries until, in 1592, the Reformation took its toll. It is a scattered ruin, giving a good idea of monastic life in those days. The 16th-century turreted gatehouse is particularly well preserved.

Kirkoswald is another step on the Burns Trail, 2 miles on towards the coast on the same road. Burns went to school here and bewailed that 'a charming Fillette who lived next door to the school overset my Trigonometry and set me off on a tangent from the sphere of my studies'. The poet learnt to drink here with John Davidson, the village cobbler, immortalized as 'Souter Johnie', in the poem 'Tam o' Shanter'. Tam was Douglas Graham of Shanter Farm, nearby. **Souter Johnie's Cottage** (*open April–Sept daily; adm*) was Davidson's home, a thatched cottage with a cobbler's workshop and Burns memorabilia. Life-sized statues of the Souter, Tam, the innkeeper and his wife are in the restored ale-house in the cottage garden. Both Davidson and Graham are buried in the churchyard, together with Kirkton Jean.

The castle at **Turnberry** is a scrap of a ruin on a cliff-top by the lighthouse, which stands on what was the castle's courtyard. Some people claim that Turnberry, rather than Lochmaben, was the birthplace of King Robert the Bruce. The castle was brought into the Bruce family by his mother, Margaret, and Robert's supporters used to meet here, to plot his accession to the throne.

Turnberry is internationally known as a golf centre, with two excellent courses and a huge hotel. It is incredible, looking at the velvet sward today, to think that these golf courses were surfaced with tarmac and used as an airfield during the war, while the hotel was requisitioned as a hospital.

Girvan to Ballantrae

About 6 miles south of Turnberry, **Girvan** is a typical Ayrshire resort, with good sandy beaches, golf courses, a harbour where pleasure-boats mingle with fishing trawlers, and easy access to the Galloway Forest Park to the east and south (*see* **Dumfries and Galloway, p.148**). **Knockcushan** is a public garden with an aviary, above the harbour. There used to be a hill fort here, and a stone commemorates the granting of a charter by Robert the Bruce, who administered justice from this hill.

Penkill Castle, 4 miles east of Girvan on the B734, an imposing 15th-century castle, was the home of the artist and poet William Bell Scott (1811–90), and a favourite haunt of his fellow Pre-Raphaelites, including William Morris and Dante Gabriel Rossetti, who wrote some of his poems here. It is now a private residence.

Boats (*for details t (01465) 713 219*) run from Girvan to **Ailsa Craig**, the 1,114ft-high volcanic lump rearing from the sea, 10 miles due west and known as Paddy's Milestone because it lies halfway between Glasgow and Belfast. At low tide you can walk its 2-mile circumference. From the top there are lovely, if rather windy, views over to Arran, Kintyre and the mainland. Ailsa Craig comes from the Gaelic for fairy rock, an incongruous name for the place where miscreant monks were sent to cool off, and where persecuted Catholics took refuge during the Reformation. It is now a bird sanctuary, including gannets and puffins: the guano smell is quite powerful on a warm day. A special granite used for making curling stones is quarried here.

Carleton Castle (*always accessible*), south of Girvan, was one of the watchtowers built by the Kennedys to defend the coast. A ballad tells of Sir John Cathcart of Carleton, who lived in the castle and pushed seven rich wives over the cliff. When it came to Mary Cullean, his eighth wife, he noticed she was wearing a sumptuous dress. He ordered her to remove it; coyly, she asked him to hide his eyes. When he obliged, she gave him a shove and over he went.

From **Bennane Head**, a few miles further south, there are views as far as Turnberry, Ailsa Craig, the Mull of Kintyre, and sometimes even Ireland. On the shore below lies ghastly **Sawney Bean's Cave**. Access is extremely difficult and only for the very sure-footed. In the 16th century it is said that a number of wealthy travellers, known to have passed through this area, vanished without trace. Local gossip led the authorities to this cave where they discovered Sawney Bean and his large, incestuously bred family, with an enormous quantity of human bones. Sawney and his ghoulish tribe had been living off the flesh, and the gold, of their unfortunate victims for years. Some accounts of the discovery of the cave describe a gruesome array of 'joints' pickled in brine or hanging from the roof like hams in a farmhouse kitchen. Sawney Bean and his family were taken to Edinburgh and executed.

Ballantrae, 3 miles south, was immortalized by Robert Louis Stevenson and twice tricked by literature. Burns wrote a song about the Stinchar valley, which carried the River Stinchar into the sea at Ballantrae, but fastidious editors changed it to: 'Beyond yon hill where Lugar flows', depriving Ballantrae of its rightful acclaim. Then Stevenson was attracted to the name of the place, and used it for his novel *The Master of Ballantrae*, but set the story further south in the Stewartry of Kirkcudbright.

Carrick Forest starts 8 miles due east of Girvan: wild, hilly country, studded with lochs and forests. **Loch Doon**, on the eastern edge of the forest, marks the border with Dumfries and Galloway. The castle on the southwest shore once stood on an island in the loch. When the Hydroelectric Board raised the level of the water, the ruined castle was dismantled and rebuilt on its present site. It used to be called Balliol Castle and was owned by King John Balliol.

The Clyde Valley

The A724/72 south from Glasgow follows the Clyde Valley, once renowned for orchards cultivated by the Romans. Although overshadowed by suburban development, there is plenty to see and do.

Summerlee Heritage Trust, in Coatbridge not far east of Glasgow (*open daily*), is 'Scotland's noisiest museum', a major industrial heritage museum, with working trams, steam and belt-driven engines, iron works, a coal mine and miners' cottages.

Drumpellier Country Park (*open April–Oct daily; adm*), Monklands, is 500 acres of heath, wood and moor around two lochs. There is a subtropical Butterfly House with brilliantly coloured butterflies living naturally among exotic hot-house plants.

About 3 miles east of Coatbridge, the **Weaver's Cottage Museum** (*open April–Sept daily 1.30–5.30; Oct Sat and Sun 1.30–5.30; weaving demonstrations most Fri, Sat and Sun; adm*), at Wellwynd, Airdrie, is good for social history. Airdrie used to be a prosperous handloom weaving town and the museum occupies two weavers' cottages (1780), illustrating the old 'but 'n' ben': the but for living and the ben for working. The museum's 'but 'n' ben's are rather sanitized versions of the originals which had no indoor plumbing: waste was chucked outside, and rats and bugs thrived.

Bothwell Castle, at Uddingston on the A74 (*open April–Sept daily 9.30–6.30; adm*), is an impressive red sandstone castle on the banks of the Clyde, said to have once been the largest and finest stone castle in Scotland. Dating from the 13th century and rebuilt in the 15th century, it was a stronghold of the powerful Black Douglases.

The **David Livingstone Centre**, at Blantyre (*open April–Oct Mon–Sat 10–5.30, Sun 12.30–5.30; Nov and Dec Mon–Sat 10.30–4.30; adm*), was the birthplace of the famous explorer and missionary in 1813. (He died in 1873, looking for the source of the Nile.) The 'single-end' tenement where he was born, and the cotton mill where he worked, give details of his life and the social conditions of the day. There is an Africa Pavilion, built in the shape of a cluster of rural African huts, illustrating African life today.

Carfin Grotto and Pilgrimage Centre, outside Motherwell (*open daily 10–5; t (01698) 268 941*), is an extraordinarily moving place despite the glitz, built in 1921 by despairing, striking miners. There is a replica Lourdes shrine among a range of holy shrines reflecting the history and tradition of pilgrimage across all religions.

Hamilton

Hamilton, the former county town of Lanarkshire, is a commercial and administrative centre. Originally called Cadzow, it was here that St Mungo converted King Rederech of Strathclyde to Christianity in 568. David I made the town a Royal Barony in the 12th century and this was superseded by a charter from James II, changing the name to Hamilton in recognition of the great landowning family in the area. In 1570 the town was sacked as reprisal for the Hamiltons' loyalty to Mary, Queen of Scots. Between 1770 and 1870 the population rose by 800 per cent, due to cotton and coal. By 1880 more than half Scotland's coal was produced in this area.

Hamilton Museum (*open Mon–Sat 10–5, Sun 12–5*), in Muir Street, dates from the 17th century and was once the Hamilton Arms Coaching Inn. It houses a transport museum, the 18th-century Assembly Room with original plasterwork, a musicians' gallery and a Victorian kitchen. Other displays are devoted to natural history, local industry and history. The **Cameronians Regimental Museum** is incorporated, with displays of uniforms, medals, banners and documents of this famous Covenanting regiment, now disbanded.

Alexander, 10th Duke of Hamilton, known as Il Magnifico, built the domed **Hamilton Mausoleum** in Strathclyde Park behind the museum, very prominent from the A74. In 1852 he had his ancestors removed from the graveyard of the old collegiate church and placed in the mausoleum. He installed an Egyptian sarcophagus on a marble

Festivals

June: Lanimer Day, Lanark; coincides with the Riding of the Marches.

Sports and Activities

Biggar Puppet Theatre, t (01899) 220 631. Miniature Victorian puppet theatre, tearoom, outdoor Victorian games and pets corner. Ring ahead. *Open Tues–Sat 10–4.30.*

M & D's Scotland's Theme Park, in Strathclyde Country Park at Motherwell, *www.scotlands themepark.com*. All the favourite attractions of a theme park and a huge rollercoaster 'tornado' too.

The Time Capsule, Monklands, in Coatbridge. Leisure centre designed around a swimming pool and ice rink. Themes span a million years, with prehistoric monsters, a swamp, volcano, frozen loch, River of Life, waterfall and much else.

pillar for himself but was worried that it would be too small to contain him. The story is told of his testy order, as he lay dying, to 'double me up; double me up', and it is even said that his feet had to be amputated to get him into the coffin. (The bodies were moved in 1921.) The chapel was never used as a place of worship, owing to a disconcerting echo lasting 15 seconds, said to be the longest echo in Britain (*open for tours April–Sept Sat, Sun and Wed 3pm; Oct–Mar Sat, Sun and Wed 2pm*). The park has a 200-acre loch, used for water sports, nature trails and a Roman bathhouse.

Calderglen Country Park, near East Kilbride, 5 miles west of Hamilton, has gardens and a children's zoo. About 7 miles southeast along the A726, **Strathaven Castle** dates from the 15th century and was once home of the Earls of Douglas and later the Dukes of Hamilton. The **John Hastie Museum** (*open Easter–Nov daily 9.30–5.30*), in Strathaven Park, has local history displays and relics from Covenanting times.

Chatelherault

Park open daily till sunset; hunting lodge Mon–Thurs and Sat 10.30–4.30, Sun 12.30–4.30; visitor centre Mon–Sat 10–5, Sun 12–5; adm.

Situated beyond the southern outskirts of Hamilton on the A74, this hunting lodge was built by William Adam in 1732 for the Duke of Hamilton, who also had the title Duke of Chatelherault. The buildings include gardeners' and keepers' bothies, stables, kennels, a banqueting hall, the Duke's apartments and kitchens. The mansion and part of the 18th-century park around Hamilton Palace, now demolished, were sold to the Scottish Office to help pay death duties. The gardens are being restored to their former grandeur. It is said the oaks in the park were planted by David I. The visitor centre illustrates the 18th-century characters who helped build Chatelherault.

Craignethan Castle

Open April–Sept daily 9.30–6.30; adm.

Craignethan Castle is southeast of Hamilton on the A72 at Crossford, reached across a green plateau where shaggy cattle roam among gnarled thorn trees. The castle materializes abruptly on a spur between the deeply eroded beds of the Water of Nethan and the Craignethan Burn. This 16th-century stronghold was destroyed after Mary, Queen of Scots was hounded from her throne – the Hamilton family who owned it had been loyal supporters of her cause. The well-preserved ruin has a keep, passages, basement and well, around an open courtyard. In 1962 excavations unearthed a rare 'caponier'. Buried for nearly 400 years, this dank, stone-roofed vault was built across the floor of a dry moat to protect 'handgunners' defending the castle. It contained bones of animals from the 16th-century gunners' hasty meals.

Although he denied it, Craignethan is believed to have been the inspiration for Tillietudlem Castle, in Walter Scott's novel, *Old Mortality*, home of the heroine Edith. A nearby halt on the long-disused branch railway was called Tillietudlem, in its honour.

Lanark

Lanark is southeast of Hamilton on a plateau above the upper reaches of the Clyde. Seen from afar it still looks like the compact, walled city it once was. The agricultural market centre for the area, it could be just another main-road town, with the A72 carrying heavy traffic through its centre. A closer look invites further exploration.

The main street is so broad that a long central flowerbed, studded with chain-linked pillars, divides it in two. It slopes between cheerfully painted houses and shop fronts to the 18th-century parish church standing like a bulwark at the bottom. The statue of William Wallace, in a canopied niche in the face of the colour-washed church tower, is an endearing sight: a huge, genial, Father Christmas-like figure who seems embarrassed by his bare, fat knees. He certainly doesn't look like the man who roused the Scots to rebellion in 1297. The statue was presented to the town in 1822 by its sculptor, Robert Forrest, who, it is said, was self-taught. This is easy to believe. William Wallace lived in Lanark, and when the English murdered his wife (or mistress) Marion Bradfute, it was here that he struck the first blow for Scottish independence.

New Lanark

It would be easy to dash through Lanark and miss New Lanark, a delightful back-water a mile to the south. Stop at the top, as the narrow road takes a final hairpin bend before descending, and admire the view down over the village to the distant Falls of Clyde. A mist of spray rises from the trees above a glint of foaming water; if the sun is shining it is a breath-catching view. New Lanark was built in 1784 as a model cotton manufacturing village by a rich industrialist, David Dale, and his partner, Richard Arkwright. Dale's son-in-law, Robert Owen, became manager of the estate in 1800 and instituted some radical innovations, including the founding of the first infant school in Britain. Owen's reforms for better working conditions and 'villages of unity' were the forerunners of today's cooperative societies. In an address to the inhabitants of New Lanark on New Year's Day 1816 Robert Owen said:

> ...*I know that society may be formed so as to exist without crime, without poverty, with health greatly improved, with little, if any, misery, and with intelligence and happiness increased a hundredfold; no obstacle whatsoever intervenes at this moment except ignorance to prevent such a state of society from becoming universal...*

Today **New Lanark World Heritage Village** is a monument to those days of reform, with no fewer than 29 awards in the past 40 years (*visitors centre open daily 11–5; adm; www.robert-owen.com; www.newlanark.org*). The old workers' houses have been brought back to life, austere but not ugly, uncluttered by architectural adornment, rising tall and plain from the street, some with outside stairways, overlooking the river. They are now much in demand not only as middle-class homes but also as affordable houses in a housing scheme. The bell that summoned the people to work or to pray still hangs high in its belfry. There are exhibitions illustrating the social history of this classic industrial village. The **New Millennium Experience** is a ride back through time to New Lanark in the 1820s, in the company of Harmony – a 'guide from the future'. **Annie McLeod's Story** is a 15-minute programme in the state-of-the-art theatre, with Annie's ghost telling her story of early 19th-century life in New Lanark. There are displays and exhibitions in various other buildings in the village including the Village Store, Robert Owen's house and the school. There is also the Edinburgh Woollen Mill's largest store in Scotland. New Lanark is hoping to be listed by UNESCO as a World Heritage Site.

The **Falls of Clyde Nature Reserve** can be reached on foot from the far end of New Lanark. A fenced path follows the Clyde a couple of miles upstream past the Falls of Corra Linn to those of Bonnington Linn. The river tumbles over black slabs of granite, overhung by pines, oaks and birches, spray rising like smoke. This stretch of the river, known as the Falls of Clyde and beloved of many artists, runs through Corehouse Nature Reserve. On the way is **Wallace's Tower**, or Corra Castle, too dangerous to enter but stirring to the imagination. It clings to a rock pinnacle high above Corra Linn, its walls rising directly from the edge of the sheer cliff. Although this reach of the Clyde is harnessed to serve the hydroelectric power stations and is thus robbed of much of its splendour, enough water remains to provide salmon with access to their spawning grounds up-river and to give dramatic effects as it pours over gigantic layered slabs of granite. Corra Linn drops 86 feet in a series of steps, to a dark still lagoon below, set in an amphitheatre of rock, and hung with damp vegetation and precariously rooted trees. **Bonnington Linn** is about a mile further on, with two branches of the river descending around a rock island.

Leadhills

Leadhills is 18 miles due south of Lanark as the crow flies. A pink road straggles over humpbacked bridges between drystone walls with views across farmland and smooth-turfed hills. Forest and pasture create a patchwork, green and brown and sepia, dotted with rural cottages, rising to desolate moor and peat bogs where the farms are linked by single telephone wires. High on this moorland, Leadhills is second only to nearby Wanlockhead (*see* p.145) as Scotland's highest village. In the small, windswept cemetery above the village lie the remains of John Taylor, who died at the age of 137, having worked for more than 100 years in the lead mills.

Allan Ramsay, the 17th-century poet, was born here, surrounded by hills alive with the ghosts of Covenanters who used their shelter for holding conventicles.

Biggar

Biggar, 10 miles southeast of Lanark on the A72, close to the Borders region, is a typical lowland market town, the main road running through its centre widening to form a market place. **Cadgers Brig** at the bottom of the town is the bridge where William Wallace is said to have crossed the burn dressed as a *cadger* (pedlar), on a spying mission. Actually the bridge is more likely to have been named after the cadgers who crossed it on market days. Biggar has several good museums.

Moat Park Heritage Centre (*open Mar–Oct Mon–Sat 10.30–5, Sun 2–5; adm*), at Kirkstyle in the town centre, is in a former church, adapted to show the history of the Upper Clyde and Tweed Valleys from the days of volcanoes and glaciers to the present. Among a collection of embroidery is the largest known patchwork quilt from the mid-19th century.

The **Gladstone Court Museum** (*open Mar–Oct Mon–Sat 10–12.30 and 2–5, Sun 2–5; adm*) is a reproduction of a Victorian street complete with grocer, photographer, dressmaker, bank, school, library, ironmonger, chemist, china merchant, etc.

Greenhill Covenanters House, at Burn Braes (*open May–Sept daily; when shut contact Moat Park, t (01899) 221 050; adm*), is a 17th-century farmhouse with strong Covenanting connections. It contains furniture and relics from those times, as well as a collection of dolls and rare breeds of animals and poultry.

Biggar also has the oldest surviving rural gasworks in Britain, built in 1839 and now the **Biggar Gasworks Museum** (*open June–Sept daily 2–5; adm*).

Tinto Hill, 2,320ft, 6 miles southwest of Biggar, west of the A73, dominates the land-scape for miles. It is a long but not arduous climb through scree and heather, and the views from the top are terrific. Keen eyes on a clear day will see 18 counties plus peaks in Cumberland, the tip of Ireland, the Bass Rock, Ailsa Craig, Arran and Jura. Tinto is wrapped in legend: William Wallace camped on the hill with his army in the 13th century, and there is a depression in a boulder at the top called, somewhat doubtfully, **Wallace's Thumbmark**. Tinto is derived from the Gaelic *teinteach* (place of fire), hinting that it may have been one of the sites for the Beltane fire rites, sometimes connected with human sacrifice.

North of the Clyde

Some say St Patrick was born at **Kilpatrick** a couple of miles west of the Erskine Bridge – a claim made by many other places on this coast down as far as Cumbria. Certainly he was captured near here in the 4th century and deported to Ireland as a slave. The Kilpatrick Hills are attractive moorland with rivers and reservoirs.

Dumbarton

Dumbarton is an industrial town about 3 miles west of the Erskine Bridge. Whisky has taken over in importance from the shipbuilding that once flourished on the waterfront. The famous clipper *Cutty Sark* was built in Dumbarton in 1869, named after the 'short shirts' seen by Tam o' Shanter when he watched the witches' orgy.

Dumbarton Castle (*open April–Sept daily 9.30–6.30; Oct–Mar Mon–Sat 9.30–4.30, Sun 2–4.30; adm*) stands high in a cleft in Dumbarton Rock overlooking the Clyde, a lump of volcanic basalt, site of a fortress since prehistoric times. The name is derived from *Dun Bretane* (Hill of the Britons). From about the 5th century this fortress rock was the centre of the kingdom of Strathclyde. It was a royal castle in the Middle Ages, later a barracks, and is now a museum. Mary, Queen of Scots sailed to France from here in 1548, aged five. A wall protects the front, shaped like the prow of a ship, with turret and guns. Up the steps, Wallace's Gatehouse is where William Wallace was imprisoned before being taken to his trial and barbaric execution in London in 1305. It was Sir John Monteith, Governor of Dumbarton Castle at the time, who finally betrayed Wallace.

The town of Dumbarton is modern, but there are a few old buildings, particularly 'Greit House', built in 1623, once the home of the Duke of Argyll, and the tower arch of the collegiate church of St Mary, founded by the Duchess of Albany in 1454.

The **Scottish Maritime Museum** (*open Mon–Sat 10–4; adm*), in Castle Street, has the oldest surviving experimental tank in the world, showing how wax and wooden scale models were used to test for such things as stability and resistance. It was the first tank of its kind, and was built in 1882 by William Denny and used for over 100 years.

Helensburgh

The A814 north from Dumbarton is narrow and twisting in some parts, clinging to the water most of the way and keeping company with the railway.

Helensburgh, at the mouth of the Gare Loch, 8 miles northwest of Dumbarton, is a resort built on a grid of wide streets, the town sloping up from the Clyde. Ferries cross the river to Gourock and pleasure cruises run from the pier. This is sailing territory, the water usually speckled with craft of all sizes. There are good shops, plenty of places to stay and lovely views across the Clyde. Helensburgh was the birthplace of John Logie Baird, one of the inventors of television.

The **Hill House** (*open April–Oct daily 1.30–5.30; adm*), overlooking the Clyde in Upper Colquhoun Street, was designed by Charles Rennie Mackintosh (*see* pp.221–2) for the publisher W. W. Blackie in 1902 and is his finest domestic work, demonstrating his flair for simplicity of line. Owned by the National Trust for Scotland, its gardens are being restored to Mackintosh's original design, and an audiovisual programme describes his life.

Glen Fruin, within easy walking distance of Helensburgh, is surrounded by beauty and solitude, serenaded by the clatter of streams flowing down from the hills. Climb **Ben Chaorach** and look down into the glen. You may hear the echo of war cries and pleadings for mercy. In 1603 there was a battle between the Colquhouns (pronounced Ka'hoon) and the MacGregors, arising from boundary disputes and accusations of cattle pilfering. The MacGregors slew not only the Colquhoun men, and their families who had been shut away in a barn for safety, but also a party of schoolboys who had been taken to watch the fun. The clan was proscribed in punishment.

Rhu, a mile west of Helensburgh, is another boating mecca, with woodland and lovely shrubs at **Glenarn Gardens** (*open Mar–June daily until sunset; adm*).

The Islands of the Clyde

Cumbrae

Great Cumbrae is so close to the Ayrshire mainland that it hardly counts as an island. Less than 4 miles in length and 2 miles in width, it has a 12-mile coastal road, ideal for bicycling. The highest point is 416ft.

Getting There

Just 7 minutes by roll-on, roll-off ferry from Largs (*every 15 minutes*).

Tourist Information

Largs: The Promenade, t (01475) 673 765.
Millport: Tourist Information Centre, t (01292) 678 100; *open Easter–Oct.*

Where to Stay and Eat

Cumbrae t (01475–)

There are a few hotels, guesthouses, B&Bs and self-catering places, and the latter might be your wisest choice. Book well ahead.
Amber Guest House, 1–3 Craig Street, Millport, t/f 530 532, *ambler@easynet.co.uk* (*cheap*). Family-run, on seafront.

College of the Holy Spirit, College Street, Millport, t 530 353, f 530 204, *tccumbrae@argyll.anglican.org* (*cheap*). Guesthouse and retreat attached to the cathedral.
Millerston House, West Bay Road, t 530 480 (*cheap*). Very reasonable and welcoming.
Royal George Hotel, Millport, t 530 301 (*cheap*). Overlooking the bay. Probably the best bet.
Mrs Elliott, t 530 040. Runs Sailaway Sea School, with a nice modernized cottage and water-sport activities on offer.
Mrs McLuckie, t (01324) 551 570. Runs a selection of flats in a house built by her family in 1794, on the seafront in Millport (sleeping 2–10).
Ritz Café, Millport. Wonderful, unpretentious 1950/'60s-style place run by Italian Scots since 1906. Food, served on formica tables, is of the 'mushy peas and vinegar' variety, and they have won awards for their ice cream.

Millport straggles around a wide bay looking south across the Tan to Little Cumbrae. A great many people go to Cumbrae in the summer, so don't expect to 'get away from it all'. The beaches are packed on a fine day. Water sports are popular and the National Water Sports Centre, based in Largs, caters for all kinds. Windsurfing is good off Millport beach.

Although Cumbrae is not ideal for the recluse, it has some interesting rock formations and good plant and animal life. The earliest village was at **Kirkton** about half a mile from the old pier in Millport, where the chapel was dedicated to St Columba in 1330 and replaced in 1612. The **'Cathedral of the Isles'** in Millport is the smallest cathedral in Britain, seating 100 people, designed by the important Victorian architect William Butterfield. This Victorian Gothic Episcopal collegiate church was consecrated in 1876. Its founder, George Frederick Boyle, later the Earl of Glasgow, had been involved in the Oxford Movement, and the cathedral was his attempt to revive the Episcopal Church in Scotland, complete with 'bells and smells'. The theological college that went with it was closed in 1885 and its buildings are now a retreat centre and basic holiday accommodation (*see above*).

The **Museum** (*temporarily closed due to fire; contact* **t** *(01292) 678 100*) shows the history of Millport and Cumbrae over the centuries. Boats run from Millport to Little Cumbrae. The ruined castle there was a residence of Robert II in the 14th century.

Arran

The miracle of Arran – Gaelic for *peaked island* – is that it has clung to its character despite the thousands of holiday-makers attracted every year by its beauty. It is slightly larger than the Isle of Wight: about 20 miles from north to south, 9 miles across and 56 miles in circumference. Often described as 'a microcosm of Scotland', it is divided in two by the Highland Boundary Fault that splits the mainland from northeast to southwest. The northern half is rough and hilly, its highest hill being Goat Fell; the southern half is gentler. Although hotels, guesthouses and chalet settlements ring the island, it is possible to roam inland for miles and feel surprisingly remote.

Arran was inhabited by Neolithic farmers before the dawn of recorded history, as its ancient stones and burial cairns prove. Since then its lovely landscape and mild climate have been put to many uses. The Irish Scots came over and settled in the early 6th century, making Arran part of the Kingdom of Dalriada. The Vikings held it for a time, until they were ousted by Somerled, Lord of the Isles, who was possibly of Norse descent himself. It became part of the Kingdom of Scotland in the Treaty of Perth in 1266. The Clearances took their toll in the 19th century when enclosed sheep farms drove out one-third of the population and killed Gaelic culture.

The main town and ferry terminal is Brodick – from the Norse *breidr vic*, broad bay – with a population of about 1,000. The other ferry terminal is at Lochranza in the north of the island, with crossings to Claonaig. There is so much to do on Arran it would be easier to list what is not available. Sea sports include: swimming, sailing, windsurfing, water skiing, sub-aqua diving and fishing. Land sports include: golf, riding, pony

Getting There

Ferries run between Ardrossan and Brodick, with train connections to Glasgow Central, about six times a day, four times on Sundays, taking 55 minutes. Ten sailings a day run between Claonaig and Lochranza, taking half an hour, with bus links to Brodick.

Caledonian MacBrayne, t (01475) 650 100/000.

Tourist Information

Brodick: The Pier, **t** (01770) 302 140; *www.arran-online.co.uk, www.arran.net.*

By far the best way to see the island is by bicycle (**t** (01770) 302 868/840 255/302 272).

Where to Stay

Arran t (01770–)

Auchrannie Country House Hotel, Brodick, **t** 302 234, **f** 302 812, *www.auchrannie.co.uk* (*expensive*). Modernized 19th-century mansion, 5 minutes from beach and golf course. Excellent food served in a conservatory-style restaurant. They have added a new Spa Resort complex which is more like a Travel Lodge.

Kilmichael Country House Hotel, Brodick, **t** 302 219, **f** 302 068, *www.kilmichael.com* (*expensive*). Down a lane out of the town, this is Arran's 'de luxe' country-house hotel where you will get excellent food and service in very elegant surroundings. Prices vary.

Apple Lodge, Lochranza, **t** 830 229, *applelodge@easicom.com* (*moderate*). Splendid, comfortable guesthouse in an old manse, with good views and good food. Take your own drink.

Butt Lodge Country House Hotel, Lochranza, **t** 830 240, *www.buttlodge.co.uk* (*moderate*). At the head of the sea loch, quiet and cosy, very comfortable, and the only 4-star hotel at the north end of the island.

Douglas Hotel, Brodick, **t** 302 155 (*moderate*). On the seafront, with live entertainment, dancing, sauna and a beauty salon.

Grange House, Whiting Bay, **t** 700 263 (*moderate*). On the Esplanade. Very friendly and comfortable.

Invercloy Hotel, Brodick, **t** 302 225, *invercloy-hotel@sol.co.uk* (*moderate*). Opposite a safe, sandy beach, with balconies in front and a friendly atmosphere. Dogs and children welcome.

Kinloch Hotel, overlooking the sea at Blackwaterfoot, **t** 860 444, **f** 860 447, *www.kinloch-arran.com* (*moderate*). Comfortable, modern eyesore with good food, indoor swimming pool, solarium, sauna, squash court and beauty salon.

Lagg Hotel, Kilmory, **t** 870 255, *thelagginn@connectfree.co.uk* (*moderate*). 18th-century coaching inn with 11 acres of garden running down to the Lagg Burn and good food.

Arran Hotel, on the seafront in Brodick, **t** 302 265 (*cheap*). Welcomes children.

Corrie Hotel, Corrie, **t** 810 273 (*cheap*). In the village, with the sea (and road) in front and Goatfell behind. A convivial atmosphere prevails, enhanced by the local bar.

Strathwhillan House, Brodick, **t** 302 331, *strathwhillan@talk21.com* (*cheap*). Very friendly guesthouse with views across Brodick Bay and good food.

Eating Out

Brodick Bar, Brodick. Large, informal and friendly, with accent on fresh local produce.

Creelers, by the Heritage Museum, Brodick, **t** 302 810. Try here for an evening out. The seafood is memorable, and you should book.

Kilmichael Hotel, *see* above. Probably the best place for a slap-up dinner.

trekking, tennis, squash, bowling and, of course, walking and climbing. Time spent bird-watching will reward you with sightings of rare species, and the flora and fauna of the island are diverse.

If it is raining in Brodick don't worry: Arran usually manages to show a smiling face for at least some of the day.

Brodick

Brodick is a large resort-village with plenty of hotels, guesthouses and B&Bs. It spreads around Brodick Bay overlooked by Brodick Castle, below which lies Old Brodick. New Brodick developed during the 19th century when larger vessels required more sophisticated facilities.

Brodick Castle (*castle open April–June and Sept–Oct daily 11–4.30 (last adm 4); July and Aug daily 11–5 (last adm 4.30); reception centre, shop and restaurant open daily 10–5; Nov and Dec also weekends 11–3 (restaurant open April–Oct till 5); walled garden open all year daily 9.30–5; park open all year daily 9.30–sunset; adm; t (01770) 302 202*) belongs to the National Trust for Scotland. The home of the Dukes of Hamilton, it was built in the 13th century on the site of a Viking fortress. Many of the treasures on display were brought to the castle by Susan Euphemia Beckford, who married the 10th Duke in 1810. She inherited them from her father, William Beckford, the reclusive, eccentric collector of fine art who built Fonthill Abbey in Wiltshire and wrote *Vathek*. The guidebook to the castle gives details of all the silver, porcelain, paintings and furnishings. The castle is a tall, stately building of red sandstone, facing the sea and surrounded by a range of hills dominated by Goat Fell. The gardens were rescued and replanted by the Duchess of Montrose, daughter of the 12th Duke who inherited the castle in 1895, with the help of her son-in-law, J. P. T. Boscawen of Tresco Abbey, which is why many of the plants and trees come from Tresco. The fabulous colours and pungent scents are exotic enough to have been part of the rich oriental settings in *Vathek* itself.

The **Isle of Arran Heritage Museum** (*open Easter–Oct Mon–Sat 10–5; adm*) occupies an 18th-century croft-farm on the edge of Brodick. The smithy, cottage and stable block illustrate changing conditions from the far past to the turn of the last century. Rooms in the cottage show nostalgic Victoriana, complete with black kettle on the hob and iron bedstead under the eaves.

The **Arran Chocolate Factory** (*t (01770) 302 595*) and **Arran Brewery Company** (*t (01770) 302 353*), both in Brodick, are worth noting for a rainy day.

Around the Island

The road around the island only loses the sea in a couple of places, while the String Road cuts through the middle from Brodick to Blackwaterfoot. Another road cuts through Glen Scorrodale from Lamlash to Lagg Inn.

Goat Fell (2,866ft), north of Brodick, dominates Arran. It is best attacked on a clear day; there are several ways up and the views from the top make the climb worthwhile. There won't be any goats – 'Goatfell' comes from *gaoith bheinn*, windy mountain – but you might see golden eagles gliding on air currents in a corrie below.

Corrie is about 6 miles north of Brodick. Its white cottages, trim colourful gardens, harbour, quay and beach have made it a favourite with artists.

Walk up into the glens that cut into the hinterland like spokes of a wheel. There are two at **Sannox** – delightful, secret places away from the road, with heather, lichens, mosses and alpine willow, and many rare wild flowers. The **Fallen Rocks**, beyond Sannox, are thought to be the relics of a landslip in the Palaeozoic Age which sent these massive boulders – some as big as houses – tumbling to the beach. This is a popular place for rock climbers. Sannox has a nine-hole golf course and a Pony Trekking Centre (**t** *(01770) 810 222*).

Lochranza, possibly from Loch of the *chaoruinn* (rowan), lies 2 miles southwest of the northern headland, Cock of Arran. The 13th/14th-century **Lochranza Castle** is a romantic ruin on the tidal flats, backed by hills. The castle is L-plan, three storeys high with a pit prison in the vaulted basement. It is said to have been a staging post for Robert the Bruce in 1307, when he returned from his famous encounter with the spider of Rathlin Island. Seen against a flaming sunset, this roofless shell is stunning. Lochranza has a nine-hole golf course.

The **Isle of Arran Distillery**, in Lochranza (*open April–Oct daily 10–5; restaurant and visitor centre; t (01770) 830 264; www.arranwhisky.com*), is open for tours.

Heading south from Lochranza down the west side of the island, the road clings to the sea with hills tumbling down almost to the beach. Steep-sided **Glen Catacol** runs inland up into the hills through beech, oak and larch, chestnut and fir, and vivid green ferns. **Thundergay**, 5 miles south of Lochranza, gets its strange name from *Tor-na-Gaoith* (hill-of-the-wind). Two miles further south, **Pirnmill** is derived from the bobbin mill that was here in the days when linen was an important industry in the island. The mill has now been converted into holiday flats. **Glen Iorsa** runs northeast through marshy bog land, hemmed in by barren hills. It is a great tract of lonely, waterlogged moor, lying below frowning crags cut by steep ravines and lochans.

The southwest quarter of Arran is rich in prehistoric remains. These include **Auchagallon Stone Circle**, 15 red sandstone blocks which once encircled a cairn; the **Farm Road Stone Circle** close by (within range of the nine-hole Machrie golf course); the **Machrie Standing Stones**, slim, primeval monoliths whose mysterious purpose is still unknown; and the **Kilmory Cairns**, at Lagg Inn.

King's Caves at Drumadoon, Blackwaterfoot, are where Robert the Bruce is said to have sheltered when returning to free Scotland from the stranglehold of English domination. Legend brings the 3rd-century warrior-poet Fingal (Fionn) MacCumhail here, father of Ossian and leader of the Feinn, who feature in the old sagas. There are rock carvings of typical Pictish hunting scenes and animals in the caves.

A lovely 10-mile walk takes you up **Glen Scorrodale** from **Sliddery** and along Sliddery Water to Lamlash Bay.

Kildonan, 6 miles east of Sliddery, is a sprawling farming village with a sandy beach. There are views from here of Pladda Island Lighthouse and Ailsa Craig, which rises like an iceberg 13 miles out to sea. Look for a large colony of Atlantic grey seals along the shore towards Bennan Head to the west. Unafraid and curious, they come quite close to the shore to inspect passers-by. The mysterious carcass of a large sea-creature, discovered here in 1981, baffled experts for some time until it was identified, with great disappointment, as a gigantic basking shark. Before the headland, a winding path used by smugglers in the 18th century hugs the cliffs and leads to the road above. **South Bank Farm Park** (*open Easter–Oct; adm*) has sheep dog demonstrations and rare breeds of farm animals and deer.

Whiting Bay, north of Kildonan, is a popular holiday village. Here, shops and hotels jostle with holiday cottages along the waterfront. There are also craft shops which specialize in leather, pottery and wood carving. A jewellery workshop, signposted at the north end of the village, sells locally made silver and gold jewellery. For evening entertainment, **Nags Bistro** has live music and a disco in the summer. There is an 18-hole golf course with fine views across the Firth of Clyde to the Ayrshire hills. **Glen Ashdale Falls** are signposted from the south end of the village, up a steep, wooded glen to where crystal water cascades down on to glistening rocks. The **Giant's Graves** (signposted) are a stone circle traditionally associated with Fionn MacCumhail.

Lamlash completes the circular tour of the island, 3 miles south of Brodick on Lamlash Bay, which is almost blocked at the mouth by Holy Island. This wonderfully safe anchorage, now a yachtsman's haven, has given shelter to many an important traveller. King Haakon and his fleet took refuge here after they had been defeated in the Battle of Largs in 1263, and in 1548 the ship carrying five-year-old Mary, Queen of Scots to France from Dumbarton sheltered here. Lamlash has annual sea angling competitions, renowned throughout Scotland.

Holy Island, a mile offshore, provides good shelter to the bay and was the site for an early Christian and medieval monastery, the ruins of which remain. St Molaise went into retreat in a cave on the western shore in the 6th century, now called St Molio's Cave. The Buddhist community from Samye Ling, in Eskdalemuir in the Borders, bought the island in 1992 to develop a meditation and retreat centre (**t** *(01387) 373 232; www.holyisland.org*).

Take home one of Arran's unique blends of mustard, locally made and sold at **Arran Provisions**, The Old Mill, Lamlash. The range is imaginative and they also do delicious jams, jellies, sauces, and chutneys. Another local speciality is Arran cheese – a Dunlop cheese made at The Creamery in Kilmory.

Bute

Bute is another holiday island, attracting many people in the summer, including Glaswegians who like to take a trip 'doon the watter'. Rothesay is a town of bright lights and tourist traps, a little run-down although great efforts are being made to revive it. Off season it has that feeling of being full of slightly peeling, empty boarding houses. There are plenty of hidden corners if you are prepared to walk to some of the less accessible beaches and coves, especially in the northwest. The **Kyles of Bute** are the narrow straits separating the island from the mainland in the northwest and northeast. Sailors exploring the coast will find a number of secret bays populated only by seals and sea birds. Mount Stuart, an incredible Gothic mansion, is the main home of the Bute family, who own the island as well as much else in Britain and have been revered patrons of the arts for generations.

There are angling competitions on the island, as well as a bowling tournament, three golf courses, tennis, riding, good fishing and every sort of water sport in wonderfully clear water. Nature lovers will appreciate the walking and bird-watching.

Getting There

A roll-on, roll-off car ferry runs frequently from Wemyss Bay to Rothesay, taking half an hour. The roll-on, roll-off car ferry from Colintraive in Argyll to Rhubodach, also has frequent sailings daily; the crossing takes 5 minutes.
Caledonian MacBrayne, t (01475) 650 100.

Tourist Information

Rothesay: Victoria Street, t (01700) 502 151, f 505 156, *www.rothesay-scotland.com; open all year.*

Festivals

May: Jazz Festival.
July: Folk Festival.
August: Bute Highland Games.

Where to Stay and Eat

Bute t (01700–)

P&J Hardy, Kames Castle, Port Bannatyne, t 504 500, *www.kames-castle.co.uk (expensive–moderate).* Six period cottages in a private estate on Kames Bay, around a 14th-century tower house.

Ardencraig Self Catering Holidays, t 504 550, *ardencraig@talk21.com (moderate–cheap).* Palladian mansion with 5 apartments and 7 chalets in 9 acres of gardens and woods overlooking the Firth of Clyde, 1½ miles from Rothesay.

Ardmory House Hotel and Restaurant, Ardbeg, t 502 346, *ardmory.house.hotel@ dial.pipex.com (moderate–cheap).* Small hotel overlooking the water. Comfortable and relaxed. **Cannon House Hotel**, Battery Place, Rothesay, t 502 819, f 505 725 *(moderate–cheap).* Georgian town house near the harbour, with views over the bay and the hills. Sailing available on their 40ft yacht.

Kingarth Hotel and Restaurant, t/f 831 662 *(moderate–cheap).* A country inn overlooking Kilchattan Bay.

St Blane's Hotel, Kilchattan Bay, t/f 831 224 *(moderate–cheap).* At the water's edge, with moorings for visiting yachtsmen. All the bedrooms are en suite and they run a courtesy bus, though you should take your car if you want to explore.

Ascog House, Ascog, on the coast southeast of Rothesay, t 503 372 *(cheap).* One of the best of the B&Bs, run by Mrs Watson in a farmhouse, nice and secluded and very friendly.

West End, 1 Gallowgate, Rothesay. Memorable fish and chips.

During the summer there is plenty of organized jollity to while away the evenings, and pleasure cruises for the day time.

Rothesay Castle (*open April–Sept daily 9.30–6.30; Oct–Mar Mon–Wed and Sat 9.30–4.30, Thurs 9.30–1, closed Fri; adm*) was built in 1098 in the days when Norsemen dominated the islands. It reverted to Scotland after the Battle of Largs in 1263. Added to over the centuries, and now one of the finest surviving medieval castles in Scotland, it is an impressive fortress with high curtain walls and drum towers enclosing a circular courtyard. King Robert the Bruce captured it in 1313 and it was his great-great-grandson who was first created Duke of Rothesay, a title held by the present Prince of Wales. The castle was used as a headquarters when both James IV and James V tried, with little success, to subdue the arrogant rule of the Lords of the Isles. Cromwell battered it badly during the Civil War and it was burned by Argyll in 1685 during the Monmouth Rebellion; it then lay in ruins until restoration began in the 19th century. The **Bute Museum** (*open April–Sept Mon–Sat 10.30–4.30, Sun 2.30–4.30; Oct–Mar Tues–Sat 2.30–4.30; adm*) is behind the castle. There are displays of Bute's geology, ancient history, maritime traditions, culture and natural history.

The **Winter Garden Visitors' Centre** in Victoria Street, in a restored 1920s seaside theatre, contains a heritage centre, cinema and bistro. **Rothesay Pavilion** is a multi-purpose entertainment centre with fun-filled family shows.

Mount Stuart (*open May–Sept Mon, Wed, Fri–Sun 11–5; grounds 10–6; April and Oct Sat and Sun; but times liable to alteration, **t** (01700) 503 877; www.mountstuart.com*) is 5 miles south of Rothesay. It only opened to the public in 1995 so has not yet become as familiar as other stately homes and is a remarkable monument to what money, determination and persistence can achieve. Home of the Butes, who are descended from Robert II, the present house has evolved from several predecessors and was conceived by the 3rd Marquess with the help of the architect Robert Rowand Anderson, who drew up the first plans in 1878. When the Marquess died in 1900, many of his grandiose plans were yet to be accomplished and interest waned. His heir advertised it for sale in 1920 'conditional to its complete demolition and removal by the Purchaser...' But no one was tempted and the house survived. In 1983 the 6th Marquess began full-scale renovation and restoration. He died 10 years later and his family agreed to honour his wish to open the house to the public. There are 300 acres of designed landscape and woodland. A major 'project' is underway in a large octagonal glass pavilion in the kitchen garden: a 'microcosm' of mountain and rainforest from Borneo and Papua New Guinea.

Ardencraig Gardens (*open May–Sept Mon–Fri 9.30–5, Sat and Sun 1–5*), south of Rothesay, supply plants for the whole island. As well as demonstration gardens and fish ponds, there are aviaries with exotic foreign birds. **Canada Hill**, above the town in the lower middle part of the island, is an easy walk and gives panoramic views of the Firth of Clyde, Argyll and Arran. **St Blane's Chapel**, on the southern toe of Bute, is a 12th-century ruin with a Norman arch, built on the site of a monastery founded by St Blane in the 6th century. **St Ninian's Chapel**, halfway up the west coast, on a point by a glorious sandy bay, is another early settlement. **Ettrick Bay**, further north, has a sandy beach.

Loch Lomond, Cowal, Kintyre, Argyll and Islands

14

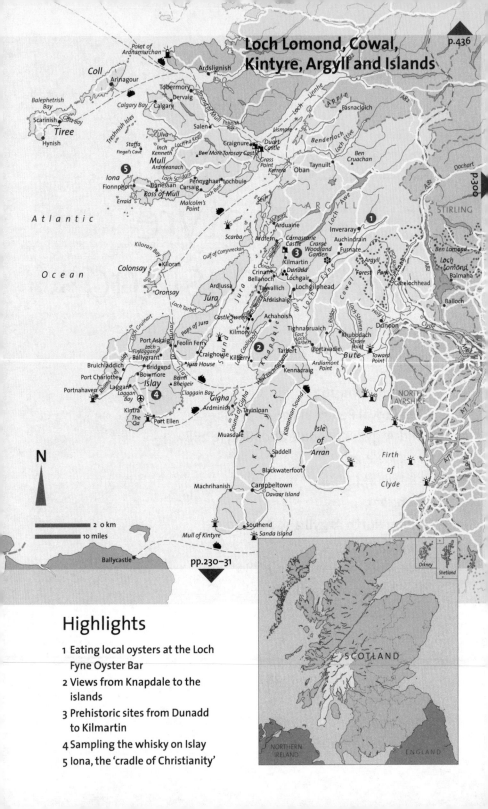

Loch Lomond, Cowal, Kintyre, Argyll and Islands

p.436

Highlights

1 Eating local oysters at the Loch Fyne Oyster Bar
2 Views from Knapdale to the islands
3 Prehistoric sites from Dunadd to Kilmartin
4 Sampling the whisky on Islay
5 Iona, the 'cradle of Christianity'

Because of their proximity to the densely populated city of Glasgow and its suburbs, and because of their natural beauty, Loch Lomond and the Cowal Peninsula are too popular for anyone wishing to get away from it all. The main routes become clogged with traffic in the tourist season and boats of every sort skim the water. Tourist traps abound, eating places fill up quickly, hotels need booking well in advance. But, in spite of this, it is possible to appreciate relative seclusion if you abandon your car, particularly in the Cowal Peninsula, and walk away from the roads.

Loch Lomond

The A82 along the west side gives views across the loch with its islands and anchorages, to the hills on the far side. This is particularly beautiful in the early morning when there is little traffic and mist clings to the glassy water as the sun rises over Ben Lomond. The loch is 24 miles from north to south, its southern end as much as 5 miles wide, narrowing to a long, thin neck in the north. The largest inland loch in Scotland, it is one of the most beautiful, though being so accessible it is also one of the most popular.

Balloch, at the south end of the loch, is a holiday resort with a marina. Balloch Castle Country Park is 200 acres of woodland, park and gardens on the shore of Loch Lomond. You can drive up the east side of the loch as far as Balmaha from where you can climb Ben Lomond.

Luss, on the west side, is a popular village with a kilt shop and bagpipe works. All this part of the country is owned by the Colquhoun family, whose former home, **Rossdhu House**, has been converted into an exclusive golf club with a 600-acre course and scenic ruins – a playground for celebrities.

'Loch Lomond'

Oh, I'll tak the high road,
An' you'll tak the low road,
An' I'll be in Scotland afore ye,
But me an' my true love will never meet again
On the bonnie, bonnie banks o' Loch Lomond.

The song 'Loch Lomond' was composed in Carlisle jail by Donald MacDonell of Keppoch, a Jacobite awaiting a trial that ended in his brutal death after Culloden. The English were capricious in their distribution of justice: some prisoners were arbitrarily sent to the gallows, others were set free and told to walk home. MacDonell, fairly sure of his fate, wrote that his spirit would get back to Scotland on the 'high road', swinging on the gallows, faster than his living companions on the low road. (Some people sing the first two lines differently: You'll take the high road – the normal route, and I'll take the low road – of death, but the first version is thought to be the original.)

Tourist Information

Balloch: Balloch Road, t (01389) 753 533, f 751 704, *www.visitsscottishheartlands.org*; *open all year.*

Where to Stay and Eat

Cameron House Hotel and Country Estate, t (01389) 755 565, *devere.cameron@ airtime.co.uk (expensive)*. On the shore of Loch Lomond, with a health club and golf course. All luxuries laid on.

Ardlui Hotel, t (01301) 704 243, *www.ardlui.co.uk (moderate)*. Small, delightful and friendly country hotel on the north tip of Loch Lomond, with moorings.

Cobbler Hotel, Arrochar, t (01301) 702 238, *www.cobblerhotel.co.uk (moderate)*. On the banks of Loch Lomond below Ben Arthur. Lively and gregarious, with live musical entertainment in the evenings.

Drovers' Inn, Inverarnan, t (01301) 704 234, *www.droversinn.com (moderate), see* below. Worth visiting for its ambience alone.

Duck Bay Hotel and Marina, on Loch Lomond, t (01389) 751 234, f 758 113 *(moderate)*. Lively spot for boating people.

Inverbeg Inn, near Luss, t (01436) 860 678, f 860 686, *inverbeg@onyx.net (moderate)*. Overlooks Loch Lomond, with a great atmosphere and good food.

The Lodge on Loch Lomond, Luss, t (01436) 860 201 *(moderate)*. Cosy rooms and good food.

Rowardennan Hotel, t (01360) 870 273, f 870 251 *(moderate)*. On the east side of Loch Lomond in the lee of Ben Lomond. Excellent value for its position.

Loch Lomond Youth Hostel, t (01389) 850 226, *www.syha.org.uk (cheap)*. Particularly grand youth hostel on Loch Lomond: an ex-baronial mansion with its own ghost.

The Old School House, Gartocharn, t/f (01389) 830 373, *bertiearmstrong@compuserve.com (cheap)*. Charming, comfortable, late 18th-century Wolsey Lodge, a mile from the loch. Good food and nice view. No smoking.

Tarbet Hotel, t (01301) 702 228, f 702 673 *(cheap)*. Scottish baronial-style mansion overlooking the loch. Comfortable modern interior, friendly staff and reasonable food.

Don't miss the **Drovers' Inn** at Inverarnan (*see* above), right up on the west side before the river widens into the loch: an atmospheric 20th-century interpretation of an 18th-century inn, established in 1705, it is very lively.

A number of cruise boats operate on the loch. The small islands scattered over the south end are steeped in history. **Inch Cailleach** (Island of the Old Women) was the burial place of the fierce MacGregor clan. It belongs to Scottish Natural Heritage and has trails and woodland paths. Ruined **Lennox Castle** on Inch Murrin (Isle of Spears) was where the Duchess of Albany retired, after James I slaughtered her husband, sons and father in 1425 (not without cause, *see* **History**, p.41).

There are plenty of places to launch small boats, and a number of boats for hire from the many marinas, holiday parks and water-sport centres lining the shore.

The Cowal Peninsula

The Cowal Peninsula attracts many climbers, sailors and holiday-makers in the summer. (Cowal derives from Comhal, who was a Dalriadic Scot.) The drive west from Tarbet through Glen Croe on the A83 is spectacular. The distinctive shape of **The Cobbler** (2,891ft) looms to the north of the road as it twists and climbs up the shoulder of **Beinn Ime** to **The Rest and Be Thankful** – which speaks for itself. The views from the car park here are worth stopping for. A stone commemorates the completion of this military road in 1750, part of a network constructed to try to keep order in

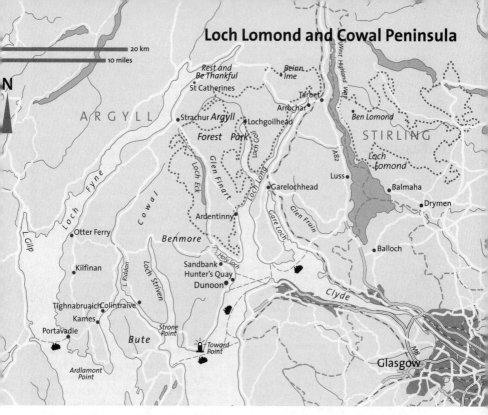

the Highlands after the Jacobite risings. Known as the **Arrochar Alps**, the hills around here offer excellent climbing for experts. Apart from The Cobbler and Beinn Ime, there are Beinn Narnain, Ben Vane and Ben Vorlich marching away to the northeast – all 'Munros' over 3,000ft.

The Cowal Peninsula stretches to the south, part of Argyll's misshapen lobster claw, washed on either side by Loch Long and Loch Fyne. **Carrick Castle** is a 14th-century ruin on a promontory in fjord-like Loch Goil. The Glen Mhoir approach down the B828 from The Rest and Be Thankful is dramatic, the road dropping from 1,000ft to sea level in 3 miles. This was where the Argylls kept their documents and their prisoners. A remote enough place in those days, the great shell of the keep is still impressive, even with its rash of water-sport enthusiasts nearby. The road ends here, but you can just see where the loch joins up with Loch Long, to the southeast. The area within the triangle formed by The Rest and Be Thankful, Loch Long and Loch Goil is known as **Argyll's Bowling Green**. A more unlikely name would be hard to find. Measuring 8 miles by 4, it includes 10 major summits and is only accessible on foot. Fantastic views can be had from the tops of the hills: a jigsaw of moor and hill, each irregular piece linked by a gleaming sliver of water.

The award-winning **European Sheep and Wool Centre**, at Lochgoilhead (*open Apr–Oct daily; adm*), is the first of its kind in Europe. There are 19 different breeds of sheep, demonstrations of shearing, and a shepherd and his dog working the sheep (*three shows daily at 11, 1 and 3; Sat by prior arrangement only*). There is a shop and a coffee shop.

Tourist Information

Dunoon: 7 Alexandra Parade, t (01369) 703 885, f 706 085, *www.cowal-dunoon.com*; *open all year.*

Festivals

Last Fri and Sat in August: Cowal Highland Gathering, t (01369) 703 206, *www. cowalgathering.com*; over a hundred years old and the largest in the world: over 150 pipe bands and the World Highland Dancing Championships.

Sports and Activities

Drimsynie Leisure Complex, Lochgoilhead. Heated swimming pool, jacuzzi, sauna, 9-hole golf course and restaurant.

Where to Stay

Creggans Inn, Strachur, on the shores of Loch Fyne, t (01369) 860 279, f 860 637, *www. creggansinn.co.uk* (*expensive*). 400-year-old inn known for its friendliness and food.
Ardentinny Hotel, on Loch Long, t (01369) 810 209, f 810 241, *janetadams1@hotmail.com* (*moderate*). Surrounded by rhododendrons. Boats can be hired from the hotel, and package holidays include visits to local attractions. The food is first class.
Ardfillayne Country House, West Bay, Dunoon, t (01369) 702 267, f 702 501 (*moderate*). A Victorian country house in 16 acres of woodland, with sea views. Very comfortable.
Ardtully Hotel, 297 Marine Parade, Dunoon, t (01369) 702 478 (*moderate*). Overlooking the Firth of Clyde, with a reputation for good service, comfort and food.
Castle Toward Outdoor Centre, by Dunoon, t (01369) 870 249, *www.actualreality scotland.com* (*moderate*). Multi-activity breaks, learning holidays and expeditions.

Colintraive Hotel, Colintraive, t/f (01700) 841 207, *kyleshotel@aol.com* (*moderate*). A small, family-run hotel with large bedrooms.
Dunans Castle, Glendaruel, t (01369) 820 380, f 820 213, *www.dunans-castle.co.uk* (*moderate*). Splendid castle guesthouse with friendly ghost, private chapel, salmon fishing, clays, archery and quad bikes all on the estate. Very good value and friendly.
Enmore Hotel, Marine Parade, Kirn, Dunoon. t (01369) 702 230, f 702 148, *www. enmorehotel.co.uk* (*moderate*). Small luxury hotel with squash courts, four-posters, jacuzzi, good food and sea views.
Kames Hotel, Kames, t (01700) 811 489, f 811 283, *www.kames-hotel.com* (*moderate*). Comfortable, friendly hotel overlooking the Kyles of Bute, on the seafront in Kames.
Royal Hotel, Tighnabruaich, t (01700) 811 239, f 811 300, *www.royalhotel.org.uk* (*moderate*). On the Kyles of Bute. Comfortable and hospitable, with fish and game a speciality.
Drimsynie House Hotel and Leisure Complex, Lochgoilhead, t (01301) 703 247, f 703 538, *www.drimsynie.co.uk* (*cheap*). Victorian mansion with mock battlements and turrets in wooded grounds overlooking Loch Goil, with a leisure complex, *see* above.
Esplanade Hotel, Dunoon, t (01369) 704 070, f 702 129, *www.ehd.co.uk* (*cheap*). Jovial hotel overlooking the traffic-free West Bay Promenade, a stone's throw from the pier.
Kyles Hotel, Tighnabruaich, t (01700) 811 674, f 811 721, *thekyleshotel@netscape.net* (*cheap*). Overlooks the Kyles and is very good value.
Rosscairn Hotel, Hunter Street, Dunoon, t/f (01369) 704 344, *www.rosscairn. freeserve.co.uk* (*cheap*). Victorian house in a quiet, residential area next to the 18-hole Cowal Golf Club. *Free golf Mar, April and Oct.*

Eating Out

The Oystercatcher, Otter Ferry, t (01700) 821 229. Excellent seafood, steaks and game cooked by French-born Alain. Free moorings for seafaring customers.

The B839 then runs northwest through **Hell's Glen**, a steep hanging valley overlooking Loch Fyne at its far end.

Loch Fyne is renowned for sea fishing and oysters. A string of villages line the loch: Cairndow, St Catherines and Strachur. Much of this area is covered by the Argyll Forest

Park. From Strachur the A815 runs south down forest-fringed Loch Eck. Branch left at the Whistlefield Hotel and take the long way round, down Glen Finart – more lovely views – to **Ardentinny**, a picturesque village with a sandy beach on Loch Long. The road hugs the shore to Strone Point and back northwest along Holy Loch. The loch is said to have been so named when a ship, carrying earth from the Holy Land intended as foundations for Glasgow Cathedral, foundered in a storm as it tried to get around the corner into the sheltered Clyde and finished up in this appendix of the river.

The **Benmore Botanic Garden** (*open Mar–Oct daily 9.30–6; adm*) is barely 2 miles north of the head of the loch. Planted in the last four decades of the 19th century and bought by the Younger family, famous for their ale, this garden was made over to the nation in 1928 and is now an offshoot of the Royal Botanic Garden in Edinburgh. In May and June the gardens blaze with yellow, orange, flame and crimson azaleas, and rhododendrons ranging from white to deep maroon. There is a splendid avenue of sequoias (giant Californian Wellingtonias).

Dunoon and Around

Dunoon is 5 miles south of the junction with the A815 and is the chief resort on the Cowal Peninsula. It was just a village until early in the 19th century, when rich merchants built villas and developed it into a resort. It is now a holiday base for the gregarious who intend to explore Cowal, and has been the destination for generations of Glaswegians taking their summer break '*doon the watter*'. In winter it goes into hibernation. The long, low sprawl of the town, washed by the Firth of Clyde, is backed by a crescent of blue-green tree-covered hills. Two ferry companies operate a service across the Clyde between Gourock and Dunoon – a 20-minute crossing. Dunoon is an ideal holiday centre on the threshold of good walking and climbing country. It is also at the heart of idyllic sailing water. For those who prefer to let someone else take the helm, there are cruises on the Firth of Clyde in summer.

Dunoon Castle, of which only a trace remains, dates from the 14th century. It was built on the site of an earlier fort, with a colourful history that kept it bouncing back and forth between English and Scottish hands like a ball in a game of catch. Edward I took it; Robert the Bruce snatched it back; Edward Balliol had a turn; only to be ousted by Robert II. In 1471 the Earls of Argyll were made Honorary Keepers by James III, on condition they paid the Crown a fee of a red rose, whenever demanded. When Queen Elizabeth II visited Dunoon in 1958, she was presented with a red rose without having to demand it. **Castle House Museum** (*open Easter–Oct Mon–Sat 10.30–4.30, Sun 2–4.30; adm; www.castle-housemuseum.org.com*), in Castle Gardens opposite the pier, was built in 1822 in the Gothic style with grandiose crenellations. There are exhibits of local history from Neolithic times to the present, with Highland Mary's Cottage, a Victorian schoolroom, parlour, kitchen, nursery, study, etc.

An attractive drive south from Dunoon takes you to Toward Point, with a lighthouse on the tip. To the west is the ruin of **Toward Castle**, a Lamont stronghold until 1646 when the Campbells of Argyll surrounded the castle, captured the inhabitants and murdered them. Understandably, the castle was then deserted and fell into ruin. The track beyond goes only halfway up the east side of Loch Striven.

The **Ardnadam Heritage Trail** starts at Sandbank a couple of miles northeast of Dunoon: a 2-mile route for those who enjoy organized exploring. It is dotted with information boards describing the local flora and fauna, as well as the site of an Iron-Age roundhouse.

Lazaretto Point, north of Dunoon on the A815, beyond Hunter's Quay, was the quarantine station for servicemen fighting in the Napoleonic Wars.

To explore the rest of the peninsula by car, take the B836 west from the head of Holy Loch to the head of Loch Striven and on to the A886. Here turn left and take the road down the east side of Loch Riddon to **Colintraive**, with views across to Tighnabruaich and the Kyles of Bute. Colintraive means 'Strait of Swimming', from when drovers swam their cattle across here. A car ferry runs from Colintraive to Bute (*see* p.258). The road then peters out, but it is possible to continue down to Strone Point and some way up the west shore of Loch Striven.

Return to the head of Loch Riddon on the A886, and take the A8003 down the west side, high above the Kyles of Bute with views in all directions. **Tighnabruaich** (house on the hill) and **Kames** are two popular resorts looking across the Kyles to Bute. A minor road runs on down to Ardlamont Point, the southernmost tip of the Cowal Peninsula, rising to 205ft. The waters of Loch Fyne, the Kyles of Bute, the Sound of Bute and Kilbrannan Sound meet beyond the foot of the headland.

From Ardlamont, go north about 4 miles to Millhouse and then west a couple of miles to **Portavadie**. With deep water offshore, this area was chosen as an oil-platform construction site and £14 million was spent on ground preparation. An enormous dry dock was built. But no one seemed to want any oil-platforms and the place stood unused. Eventually, the sea wall was breached, the dock flooded and the £14 million washed away.

From Millhouse, take the B8000 north, through Kilfinan, a hamlet where the hotel has 16th-century vaults and the church stands on a Celtic site. **Otter Ferry**, 3 miles to the north, takes its name from the Gaelic *oitir* (a sandbank): yachtsmen beware. The sandbank sticks out more than a mile into Loch Fyne, prominent at low tide but easy to trip up on when submerged by the flood tide. The Norsemen who fought in the Battle of Glendaruel in 1100 beached their longships side by side on the sand bar, clambered ashore and marched over the pass into Glendaruel 5 miles to the east. They were slaughtered by the Scots, who threw their bodies into the river: *ruel* is a corruption of the Gaelic for 'blood flowed'.

Mid-Argyll: Knapdale and Kintyre

This is walking country, where spectacular views unfold at every turn and many of the best places are inaccessible except on foot.

Loch Fyne, a long narrow arm of the sea, washes the western shore of the Cowal Peninsula. It seems to eat its way into the Highland landscape – a mixture of hill and forest, in some parts rising steeply from the water, in others rolling back in sweeps of farmland. At the head of the loch, near Cairndow, look for the long, whitewashed **Loch**

Fyne Oyster Bar (*see* p.271). It isn't cheap but it's well worth a visit, even if just for the seafood chowder. **Here We Are** (*t (01499) 600 350, www.hereweare-uk.com*), in a new building of local oak next to the Oyster Bar, is a visitor centre/community resource centre with exhibits about Cairndow. The adjacent **Tree Shop** specializes in specimen trees, indigenous Highland trees and shrubs. They also sell an extensive range of woodwork, basketwork, dried flowers and unusual presents.

At the head of Loch Shira, an appendix off the northwest corner of Loch Fyne, a track leads north up remote Glen Shira to a ruined cottage where Rob Roy hid for some time during one of his adventures.

Inveraray

Inveraray stands on the northwest shore of Loch Fyne, a gracious 18th-century town, curiously un-Scottish, built in a T-plan with the road north passing through an archway and the parish church on a mound, dividing the Main Street. Inveraray was once a small fishing village, always a domain of the Campbells of Argyll. Old Inveraray, clustered around the old castle, was sacked by Montrose in 1644. The present town was the creation of the third Duke of Argyll in 1743, employing Roger Morris and William Adam, both of whom died before the work was finished. John Adam, son of William, completed the job with the help of Robert Mylne. When he commissioned the building of the present castle, the Duke decided he wanted more privacy and moved his tenants out of sight and earshot.

Inveraray Bell Tower (*open May–Sept daily 10–1 and 2–5; adm*), adjacent to the Episcopalian church, was established in the 20th century by the 10th Duke of Argyll, its peal of 10 bells rung in memory of the Campbells who died in the First World War. The 126ft granite tower gives views over Loch Fyne and Inveraray, although it is rather an eyesore within the context of the rest of this elegant town.

Inveraray Jail (*open April–Oct daily 9.30–6; Nov–Mar daily 10–5; adm*), in Church Square, comprises the Old Prison, with ghastly cells where men, women, children and lunatics were crammed, complete with sound effects and smells; the New Prison (19th century), with improved conditions; the courtroom as it was in 1825 when men were deported to Australia for minor crimes; and many exhibitions, including one on crime and punishment, with details of medieval punishment – hanging, branding, tongue-boring and burning. You can also see the open-air cages called airing yards where prisoners took exercise. There is a souvenir shop.

Inveraray Castle (*open April–Oct Mon–Thurs, Sat and Sun; July and Aug also Fri 10–1 and 2–5.45, Sun 1–5.45; adm*) was built on the site of a 15th-century fortress, but the present castle dates from 1770, when the town was being built. The castle is a square pile, greenish and imposing, with round towers topped by conical witches' hats at the four corners, added in 1878 by the 8th Duke. Aiming at aggrandizement, he also added an additional floor with gabled dormers like the raised eyebrows of scandalized dowagers. Designed by Roger Morris, with help from William Morris who was Clerk of Works, and decorated by Robert Mylne, the castle may have been based on a sketch by Vanbrugh and is imposing rather than beautiful. A bad fire in 1975 destroyed the roof and top floor but these have been rebuilt. Magnificently decorated rooms provide

Tourist Information

Inveraray: Front Street, **t** (01499) 302 063, **f** 302 269; *open all year.*
Lochgilphead: Lochnell Street, **t** (01546) 602 344, **f** 606 254; *open April–Oct.*
Campbeltown: Mackinnon House, The Pier, **t** (01586) 552 056, **f** 553 291; *open all year.*

Where to Stay

Crinan Hotel, **t** (01546) 830 261 (*expensive*). Renowned for its lovely position overlooking the sea to the Sound of Jura, its comfort and its delicious food, *see below*. People come a long way to stay and eat here.
Stonefield Castle Hotel, Tarbert, **t** (01880) 820 836, **f** 820 929 (*expensive*). Overlooks Loch Fyne, with moorings, fine gardens, summer swimming pool, good food and good service.
Argyll Hotel, Inveraray, **t** (01499) 302 466, **f** 302 389, *www.the-argyll-hotel.co.uk* (*moderate*). Where Johnson and Boswell stayed, overlooking Loch Fyne, with just the right blend of history and comfort.
Columba Hotel, Tarbert, **t/f** (01880) 820 808, *www.columbahotel.com* (*moderate*). Listed Victorian house with sauna, gym and solarium on the shores of Loch Fyne overlooking the harbour; 'bargain breaks'.
Fernfield, Crinan, **t** (01546) 830 248, **f** 830 282 (*moderate*). B&B with dinner on request, overlooking Crinan Harbour. Very friendly and comfortable.
Fernpoint Hotel, by the pier in Inveraray, **t** (01499) 302 170, **f** 302 366, *fernpoint.hotel@virgin.net* (*moderate*). Georgian house with a spiral stair and wonderful 'executive suites' overlooking Loch Fyne. The public rooms aren't remarkable, but the food is good.
Galley of Lorne, Ardfern, **t/f** (01852) 500 284 (*moderate*). Traditional Highland inn on the shores of Loch Craignish, with a warm welcome and excellent seafood. There are barbecues on the terrace whenever possible, and a good range of malts.
Knock Cottage, Lochgair, **t/f** (01546) 886 331 (*moderate*). Wolsey Lodge in 10 acres of secluded wild gardens, loch and field, with lovely views over the sheltered anchorage of Lochgair. A cosy old croft house with nice modern additions and delicious food.
Loch Fyne Hotel, Inveraray, **t** (01499) 302 148, **f** 302 348 (*moderate*). Very pleasant hotel run by charming locals who maintain a relaxed, comfortable Highland atmosphere.
Lochgair Hotel, near Inveraray, **t/f** (01546) 886 333 (*moderate*). Family-run, easy-going and comfortable. There are boats for fishing.
Loch Melfort Hotel, Arduaine, **t** (01852) 200 233, **f** 200 214, *www.loch-melfort.co.uk* (*moderate*). Established a reputation for good service, comfort and excellent food. Yachtsmen swap Force Nine stories in the Chart Room Bar. The main house, built in 1900, gazes out across the sea. The six bedrooms are done up like guest rooms in a country house. An adjoining Cedar Wing, long and low, has 20 rooms, each with its own bathroom, balcony and picture window, facing south across the water. *Open Feb–Jan.*
Ormsary Estate Lodges, near Loch Caolisport, **t** (01880) 700 222 (*moderate*). 15 self-catering lodges (sleeping 2–6), well spaced out, comfortably furnished and well equipped. They have lovely views to the west in one of the most beautiful settings in Kintyre.
Royal Hotel, Main Street, Campbeltown, **t** (01586) 552 017 (*moderate*). Overlooks Campbeltown Loch from the harbour, with a 'traditional' atmosphere.
Skipness Castle, by Tarbert, **t** (01880) 760 207, **f** 760 208, *james@skipness-freeserve.co.uk* (*moderate*). A modern house built on to the

perfect settings for paintings, tapestries, Oriental and European porcelain, 18th-century furniture and many other treasures. Among the paintings are portraits by Kneller, Raeburn, Hoppner, Gainsborough, Batoni and Ramsay. The grounds, with old trees framing vistas over Loch Fyne, are reminiscent of an 18th-century painting. A folly overlooks Inveraray from a steep, wooded hilltop.

Auchindrain Museum (*open April–Sept daily 10–5; adm*), 6 miles south of Inveraray, is an old West Highland township with 18th- and 19th-century cottages and ruins of its Victorian predecessor, which burned down in 1969. Spectacular views down to Kilbrannan Sound. Friendly and comfortable, and the food in the Skipness Castle Seafood Cabin is excellent.

Tigh Na Truish, Clachan Bridge, see p.276, t (01852) 300 242 (*moderate*). Very special, atmospheric inn with B&B rooms and one self-catering cottage (sleeping 2).

Braleckan House, Inveraray, t (01499) 500 662 (*cheap*). 19th-century building restored to make two self-catering houses on a family farm. Both are peaceful and well equipped.

Cornaig, Kilmartin, t (01546) 510 224 (*cheap*). Very special B&B, with Mrs McAuslan.

Corranmore House, Ardfern, t/f (01852) 500 609 (*cheap*). B&B on a working farm in a lovely position on the water, with charming hosts and dinner by arrangement.

Cuilfail Hotel, Kilmelford, t (01852) 200 274, f 200 264, *info@cuilfail.co.uk* (*cheap*). A Victorian house built around an attractive old coaching inn. Excellent indoor BBQ.

Duachy Farm, Kilninver, t/f (01852) 316 244, *gillian.cadzow@tesco.net* (*cheap*). Delightful B&B on a trout loch, with a boat. Charming hosts and cosy rooms.

Escart, West Loch Tarbert, t (01880) 820801 (*cheap*). Traditional farmhouse B&B with far more character than most, and charming, hospitable owners. Beautifully sited overlooking West Loch Tarbert, it has dogs, cats and fowl, including peacocks.

George Hotel, Inveraray, t (01499) 302 111, f 302 098, *www.thegeorgehotel.co.uk* (*cheap*). Excellent value, and has been in the same family since 1720. Good pub food.

Killean Farmhouse, Inveraray, t (01499) 302 474 (*cheap*). Seven, well-equipped self-catering holiday cottages (sleeping 4–10). Also B&B.

Tarbert Hotel, Tarbert, t/f (01880) 820 264 (*cheap*). Right on the harbour, popular for *après*-sailing, friendliness and good value.

White Hart Hotel, Main Street, Campbeltown, t (01586) 552 440 (*cheap*). Family hotel on a busy corner.

Eating Out

The Anchorage, Tarbert, t (01880) 820 881. Said by some to be the best in the land, especially for seafood.

An Tairbeart, Tarbert, see p.274. Excellent meals with lots of fresh seafood.

The Cairn, Kilmartin, t (01546) 510 254. A nice bistro/restaurant. *Open Mar–Oct.*

Crinan Hotel, t (01546) 830 261, see above. Renowned for its delicious food, supplied daily by fishing boats that unload a short distance from the kitchen. For a cheaper and more relaxed meal, try the pub menu – the same chef and just as good.

George Hotel, Inveraray, t (01499) 302 111, see above. Good pub food.

Loch Fyne Oyster Bar, t (01499) 600 264, see pp.268–9. Excellent restaurant in an old farm building. The shop sells fresh and smoked seafood, including oysters from the local oyster beds, mussels, salmon and scampi; also venison, special cheeses, home-baked bread, sauces, and so on. Well worth making a detour for. *Open daily from 9am; mid-Mar–Oct last sitting 9pm; Nov–Mar 8pm.*

Skipness Castle Seafood Cabin, by Tarbert, t (01880) 760 207, see above.

The Smiddy, Smiddy Lane, Lochgilphead. The nicest place to eat in Lochgilphead: a vegetarian bistro-style establishment with excellent home cooking.

Tayvallich Inn, Loch Sween, t (01546) 870 282. Excellent bar and restaurant on the shores of Loch Sween; the seafood is particularly good – sea-to-plate fresh. Book in advance to be sure of a table.

outbuildings furnished in their original styles. On display are parlours, kitchens with box beds, byres, barns, a smiddy, and all the old utensils. There are demonstrations of the runrig – or strip-farming – methods prevalent in the Highlands until the end of the 18th century, when villages had communal tenancy of farmland and paid their rent jointly, in this case to the Argylls.

The name of **Furnace**, a couple of miles further on, is an unhappy reminder of the troubled times that reigned during the 18th century. It is so called from the charcoal-

burning smelting furnace, established here to utilize trees felled by order of the
Hanoverian government, so that rebel Highlanders still clinging to the Jacobite cause
would have less cover in which to hide.

Crarae Woodland Garden (*open Mar–Oct daily 9–6; winter daylight hours; adm*), 3
miles south, is one of Scotland's most beautiful 'wild' gardens. Captain (later Sir)
George Campbell took over the estate in 1926 and threw himself into developing this
luxuriant 'Himalayan Ravine'. He cut back the natural vegetation from the banks of
the Crarae Burn and planted the banks with 'exotics', paying careful attention to
create spectacular drifts of colour. Walks cross and recross a burn as it cascades over
falls and through a gorge among a spectacular variety of conifers, hardwoods and
shrubs. Early summer and autumn are most spectacular. A Neolithic chambered cairn,
dating back some 4,500 years and once of considerable size, was excavated in the
1950s and is a feature of the gardens.

Lochgilphead

Lochgilphead, 24 miles southwest of Inveraray, at the head of Loch Gilp, another
appendix off Loch Fyne, is a holiday resort as well as the shopping centre for the area,
with good shops around the wide main street that was once the market place. Loch
Gilp is mostly mud flats at low tide. This was a fishing village until the Crinan Canal
opened in 1801 and it became a convenient stopping-off place for boats. The population expanded to supply services for people passing through the canal; a lunatic
asylum and poor house were built. Now it is a busy town and the regional headquarters. The Mid Argyll Show takes place in Lochgilphead in August.

The **Crinan Canal** slices through the top of Knapdale from Ardrishaig on Loch Gilp to
Crinan on the west coast. It was built at the end of the 18th century and stretches for
9 miles, with 15 locks. It was designed to cut out the treacherous waters around the
Mull of Kintyre that inhibited trade between the west coast and Glasgow, and was
much used at first by commercial puffers, fishing boats and passenger craft. With the
decline of the herring industry and the introduction of rail and road networks, it lost
most of its commercial traffic and is now mainly used by pleasure boats, saving the
sailor 130 miles. Going down the canal in a small boat is a peaceful way of passing a
fine day, though you have to work the lock gates yourself, straining at the handles
that wind up the sluices in the massive wooden gates, and leaning on the great
timber arms that swing them open when the water either side is level. In 1847 Queen
Victoria sailed down the canal in a decorated barge drawn by horses ridden by postil-
ions dressed in scarlet, on her way to the Western Isles.

Crinan itself is a pretty hamlet on a rocky peninsula with a sheltered harbour,
popular with sailors, with the tidal gate between the canal and the open sea. The
Crinan Hotel is said to be one of the best in Scotland, overlooking the island-speckled
Sound of Jura; *see p.270.*

Knapdale

Knapdale is nearly an island. It runs south from Lochgilphead like a clenched fist, just managing to hang on to the long arm of Kintyre. This part of the west coast, on the Gulf Stream, is unbelievably lush in summer. Autumn is glorious: a wonderful range of colour paints the hills. So too is spring, when rhododendrons and azaleas are in bloom against the soft new green and the sparkle of water. Perhaps the best time of all, though, is November, when a light dusting of snow covers the last autumn leaves, and the water shows steel-grey against the hills etched in white. It is possible to drive right around the coast from Lochgilphead and across the middle from Inverneil to Achahoish. Along the coast each mile opens up a fresh view to the islands of Jura and Islay in the west, or down through layers of hills to distant lochs and the sea.

Kilberry, in the southwest corner of Knapdale on the B8024, has a collection of 9th- and 10th-century stones, and some from the Middle Ages, gathered up from the surrounding area and housed under cover in a steading, just north of the hamlet, signposted **Kilberry Stones** from the road. Marion Campbell, the archaeologist who collected the stones, lived in Kilberry Castle, a brooding pile, medieval in origin, remodelled in the 19th century by David Bryce, which has belonged to the Campbells of Kilberry for centuries. The food at the **Kilberry Inn** is good.

St Columba's Cave, 12 miles northwest of Kilberry on the western shore of Loch Caolisport (pronounced and sometimes spelt Killisport) near Ellary, is an enchanted spot, almost tangibly spiritual. There is an altar on the right with two crosses carved above, a smaller cave, reached by steps, traces of dwellings outside the cave and the ruin of a chapel. As its name indicates, tradition associates this cave with the saint's mission in Scotland. Excavations in the 19th century unearthed evidence that there was a settlement here as far back as 8000 BC, making St Columba comparatively modern.

Unfortunately, there is a private road with a locked gate so it is not possible to go on around the peninsula. You must backtrack via Lochgilphead to explore Loch Sween.

Castle Sween guards the entrance to Loch Sween from the eastern shore. Now alas surrounded by a caravan site, some say it is the oldest stone castle on the Scottish mainland. Dating from the 11th century, it is a great sprawl of a ruin, Norman in style, with buttresses. You can see the old ovens, the well and the original drain and rubbish-chute in the wall of the round tower, down which everything, including sewage, was indiscriminately cast. The castle was a stronghold of the MacSweens in the 12th and 13th centuries, but they lost their lands when they sided with the English in the 14th century. Robert the Bruce besieged it and installed the McNeills of Argyll to maintain it, one of whom married a MacMillan. Thus, Knapdale became MacMillan territory. The castle was destroyed in 1647 by Royalists fighting the cause of Charles I.

The 13th-century **Kilmory Knap Chapel** is on the southern tip of the peninsula north of Loch Caolisport. A glass roof protects the sculpted stones inside. The showpiece here is the **MacMillan's Cross**, elaborately carved in the 15th century, possibly by monks from the monastery at Kilberry.

Kintyre

An isthmus between East and West Loch Tarbert, straddled by the village of **Tarbert**, joins Kintyre to Knapdale. Here in the 11th century Malcolm Canmore struck a bargain with the Norwegian King Magnus Barelegs who was harassing him. He told Magnus he could claim any western island he could get to by boat with his rudder down. Magnus had his Vikings tow him across the isthmus – and claimed Kintyre as his. Tarbert comes from *an tairbeart* – isthmus; there are several in Scotland. This one is on an attractive bay with a backdrop of hills, popular with sailors, especially during regattas on Loch Fyne. Tarbert Castle, above the village, was renovated by Robert the Bruce in 1325 but is now no more than a pile of stones with a good view. There is a signed footpath.

An Tairbeart is a contemporary art centre with displays of local history and a Midge Factory. They also have excellent meals with lots of fresh seafood.

A road circles most of the coast of the peninsula, passing through villages and hamlets, most of which cater for summer visitors. The landscape is similar to that of Knapdale, cut by wooded valleys rising to hilly moorland. The east and west routes meet at **Campbeltown** at the head of Campbeltown Loch, a haven for boats in a westerly gale, and subject of that hopeful song: 'O Campbeltown Loch I wish you were whisky'. It is a holiday town and boating centre, and was once an important herring port, with 34 distilleries, of which two remain open. Although less than 40 miles from Glasgow as the crow flies, Campbeltown is about 135 miles by road. Although the town appears to be stolidly Victorian, it was founded in 1607. The 7th Earl of Argyll brought in Protestants from the Lowlands in an attempt (known as the Plantation Policy) to pacify what was then a rather troublesome area. James IV had problems here too and built Kilkerran Castle, now in ruins, in 1498 when he was desperately trying to bring the Lords of the Isles to heel. Flora Macdonald sailed to North Carolina from Campbeltown in 1774, emigrating with her family nearly 30 years after her brave actions helped save the life of Prince Charles Edward Stuart. William McTaggart, that great painter of Scottish life and scenery, was born in the town in 1835.

Campbeltown Museum (*open daily except Wed and Sun*), in Hall Street, has a demonstration of how vitrified forts were formed.

Davaar Island is a lump of rock at the mouth of the loch, accessible at low tide along a shingle spit – The Dhorlin – on the southern shore. It is marked by buoys and you must get the tides right unless you want to be cut off. (You have about 6 hours, which is more than enough.) Your destination is a cave on the eastern side of the island, the seventh cave along to your right. Here, in 1887, a man called Archibald Mackinnon secretly painted a picture of the Crucifixion on the rock, inspired by a dream. It is a moving picture after the style of El Greco, lit by a shaft of light that streams into the large cave through an aperture. In 1934, when the artist was 80, he returned to the cave and restored the painting.

Machrihanish, 6 miles west of Campbeltown and fully exposed to the fury of Atlantic gales, is a holiday village with a hotel, golf course, campsite and sandy beaches, as well as a token airport.

Mull of Kintyre

Southend, tucked around the corner to the east of the Mull of Kintyre, is another holiday village. There is a golf course and sandy beaches with dunes covered in marram grass, which offer shelter from the wind. Nothing remains today of Dunaverty Castle, which once stood above vicious rocks here, shrouded in uncomfortable memories. Three hundred of Montrose's men, fighting the cause of Charles I, were besieged there by the merciless Covenanter General, David Leslie. The Royalists, mostly Irish mercenaries, were forced by thirst to surrender and shamelessly massacred.

Keil, just west of Southend, has a flat rock traditionally regarded as the place where St Columba first landed in Scotland. Keen eyes will spot footprints burnt into the rock where he stood, turning his back on the land that had outlawed him.

From Southend you can hire a boat to **Sanda Island**, about 2 miles offshore. Robert the Bruce is said to have hidden here in 1306 on his way back from Rathlin Island, spurred on towards Bannockburn by the spider.

The **Mull of Kintyre**, the southern tip of the peninsula, is a rocky extremity with a lighthouse and sheer cliffs; dramatic in westerly gales. You must walk the final 1½ miles or so to the point, only 13 miles from Ireland. The Mull of Kintyre was the subject of a popular song by Paul McCartney, who bought a house close by.

About 19 miles on, take the B8001 to **Skipness Point**, where the ruins of a large 13th-century castle and chapel command the bay, built by the MacSweens to guard Kilbrannan Sound. In 1537 the then chatelaine, Janet Douglas, Lady Glamis, was burnt for witchcraft, accused of poisoning her husband and plotting to kill James V. The King was carrying out some 'cleansing', ridding his kingdom of the Douglases who had been a threat to his supremacy, and poor Janet had the misfortune to have been born a Douglas.

Lorne

The A816 runs up the west coast from Lochgilphead to Oban flirting with the sea, dipping and rising for 37 miles, with magnificent views as it kisses the coast. There are numerous side roads, tracks and footpaths, almost all of which are worth exploring. Walk up any of the glens to the east of the road and discover remote lochans hidden in the hills and wild moorland. To the west is the sea and miles of empty beaches with sand, rocks, cliffs and views of the islands.

Four miles northwest of Lochgilphead is all that is left of **Dunadd Fort**, capital of the kingdom of Dalriada from the 6th to the 9th centuries, a powerful political centre. It was the headquarters of early missionaries, including St Columba, until Kenneth MacAlpine moved the capital to Pictland. A rocky hillock above a meandering river is all that remains and, if you search carefully, a rock with carvings of a boar, some Ogham inscriptions (now protected)...and a footprint. Historians believe this was the place where kings were crowned and that St Columba crowned Aidan here in 574, using the disputed Stone of Destiny as the throne (*see* **Topics**, 'Stone of Destiny' p.66).

The footprint is indisputable, and only the most prosaic could resist the urge to stand in it and imagine those ancient ceremonies on this lofty site.

History has left a remarkable detritus of cairns, standing stones and prehistoric remains in this area. From Dunadd to **Kilmartin** is about 3 miles, packed with Stone-Age and Bronze-Age relics. Some of the cists have been reconstructed and you can go inside and see the carvings on the walls.

Kilmartin House (*open daily 10–5.30; adm; www.kilmartin.org*) is a museum of ancient culture by the church. The ticket lasts all day so an overview of the museum can be followed by a visit to the sites, and then a return to the museum to study particular sites in depth. This museum is worth making time for, as it provides an excellent preparation for exploring some of the 150-plus prehistoric sites in the area. It includes audiovisual presentations with authentic music; a 3-dimensional map; displays; hands-on exhibits; sound effects and much else. A converted barn serves delicious local products: nettle or comfrey soup, squat lobsters, crab claws – washed down with heather ale of bramble or silver birch wine.

Carnassarie Castle, 9 miles north of Lochgilphead, is the ruined home of John Carswell, first Protestant Bishop of the Isles, who in 1597 translated Knox's liturgy into Gaelic. It was the first Gaelic book ever to be published.

Lunga Wildlife Park, on the Ardfern Peninsula north of Loch Craignish, has indigenous animals and there is experimental white-fish farming in the loch.

Arduaine Gardens (*open daily 9.30–sunset*), run by the National Trust for Scotland just north on Loch Melfort, has subtropical plants as well as magnolias, rhododendrons and azaleas, a water garden and rock garden, and many rare trees and shrubs.

The island of **Seil** is a hook of land west of Loch Melfort – joined to the mainland by the much-photographed hump-backed Clachan Bridge, celebrated as 'the only bridge over the Atlantic', designed by Telford in 1792. Just over the bridge is *Tigh na Truish* – the house of the trousers – where Highlanders who had been off the island in the days of proscription would change back into the forbidden tartan kilts (*see* 'Where to Stay'). From this bridge a narrow road twists down to Easdale, scarred by old slate-quarry workings, flooded out in a terrible storm and no longer operating. Rows of traditional slate-workers cottages add atmosphere. There is a large souvenir shop/art gallery manned by a tartan-clad artist. Part of *Whisky Galore* was filmed here, many years ago, transforming the township into a stage set. The **Easdale Island Folk Museum and Slate Islands Heritage Trust Centre** (*open April–Oct daily 10.30–5.30; adm*) has exhibitions of the industrial and domestic history of these Slate Islands. **Seafari** runs daily trips from Easdale harbour (*1–3 hours; t (01852) 300 003*).

An Cala Garden (*open April–mid-Oct daily 10–6; adm*), on Seil, is a coastal garden designed in the 1930s to be seen as the foreground to a wonderful vista of sea and islands. It is laid out with meandering paths, streams, terraces, rockeries and formal beds, with ornamental trees and shrubs. An unexpected gem amidst the slate.

Oban, North Argyll and Appin

Oban

Oban – the little bay – is 37 miles north of Lochgilphead and is the gateway to the isles; unashamedly a holiday resort in summer, when the streets seethe with visitors and traffic; quiet and provincial in winter. Before the Victorians developed it into an important port and the principal town in Argyll, it was a mere hamlet with one inn. Now it is crammed with shops, hospitals and schools, serving a wide area. Hotels, guesthouses and neat villas offering bed and breakfast are numerous; cafés and restaurants are packed; and there is a fairly lively nightlife offering discos, public ceilidhs and family fun shows. In spite of all this Oban remains truly West Highland and unspoilt.

The first National Mod was held in Oban in 1892 and has often returned since. Because it is the main port for the Outer Isles, you will often hear Gaelic spoken on the pier and around the town.

The town rises steeply from a crescent-shaped bay, its main street fronting the harbour whence MacBrayne's steamers ply between Mull and the Inner and Outer Hebrides, and smaller ferries, fishing boats and pleasure craft come and go between the islands. The quays are thronged with people, cars and freight, loading and unloading. High above stands **McCaig's Folly**, a large replica of the Colosseum built in 1897 at a cost of £5,000 by a banker, McCaig, to give work to the unemployed and create a museum and observation tower as a memorial to his family. It was never finished but remains a prominent landmark.

The Catholic See of Argyll and the Western Isles has its well-attended cathedral, **St Columba's**, in Oban, overlooking the harbour. Although this area is predominantly Protestant, there are still communities which were left untouched by the Reformation.

Oban is a base for sub-aqua divers, with air supplies in the town and good under-water terrain. The Sound of Mull is littered with wrecks and the waters offer a wealth of marine life and cliff scenery. It is also ideal for sailing, with some fairly challenging, breathtakingly beautiful stretches, especially south through the Firth of Lorne to the Sound of Jura, past the infamous Corryvreckan whirlpool (*see p.287*).

Oban Distillery (*open Mon–Fri 9.30–5; Easter–Oct also Sat; adm*), in Stafford Street, gives 45-minute tours ending in a free dram. **World in Miniature** (*open Easter–Oct daily; adm*), on North Pier, is a display of miniature rooms, furniture, dioramas, and so on, all scaled at one inch: one foot.

Oban Rare Breeds Animal Park (*open end Mar–Oct daily 10–5.30; adm*) is a couple of miles on past the golf course, with unusual breeds of sheep, cattle, goats, pigs, poultry, ducks, deer, etc. It also has a pets' corner, nature trails, tearoom and shop.

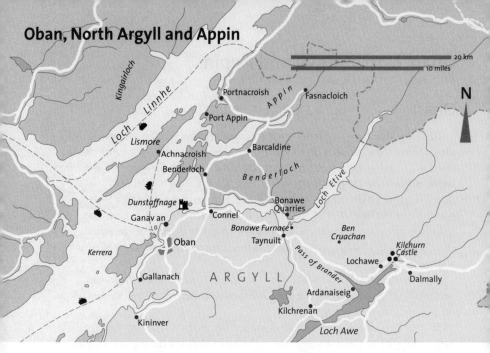

Oban, North Argyll and Appin

20 km
10 miles

N

Kingairloch

Loch Linnhe

Appin
Portnacroish
Fasnacloich
Port Appin

Lismore
Achnacroish
Benderloch
Barcaldine
Benderloch
Loch Etive

Dunstaffnage
Bonawe Quarries
Ganavan
Connel
Bonawe Furnace
Ben Cruachan
Kilchurn Castle
Oban
Taynuilt
Pass of Brander
Lochawe
Kerrera
Gallanach
ARGYLL
Dalmally
Ardanaiseig
Kilchrenan
Kininver
Loch Awe

Kerrera Island

From a point a couple of miles south of Oban on the Gallanach road, a 3-minute foot ferry runs on demand (*t (01631) 563 665*) across to Kerrera, the 4-mile-long island sheltering Oban from the worst of the southwesterlies that rip up the Firth of Lorne. Alexander II died in Horseshoe Bay in 1249 while trying to evict the Norsemen who held the island. Kerrera was a droving station between Mull and the mainland, cattle having to swim across from its northern tip.

Dunollie Castle, the ruin on a promontory guarding the north entrance to Oban Harbour, was the ancient stronghold of the MacDougall Lords of Lorne, one of the oldest clans in Scotland. **Ganavan Sands**, just to the north, is a good place to stretch your legs before a long ferry crossing, but not a place for a quiet day on the beach. It has a restaurant, bar, coffee shop, car park, play area, putting, donkey rides, water sports and a launching slip.

Lismore Island

From Oban, a car ferry runs 7 miles north to Lismore Island in Loch Linnhe (*taking 50 minutes; Mon–Sat up to 4 times a day*). There is also a 1-mile passenger-ferry crossing from Port Appin. You can hire bicycles at Port Appin and also on the island (*t (01631) 760 213*).

Lying at the entrance to Loch Linnhe between Morvern and the hammerhead of the Benderloch peninsula, Lismore is 10 miles long and 1½ miles wide, a limestone sliver overlaid with heather. *Lios mor* means great garden or enclosure. It was the seat of the diocese of Argyll from 1200 to 1507, in the days before Luther stirred up the Reformation. Traces of the miniature cathedral that was once here are incorporated into the parish church, built in 1749. The bishop's dwelling, the 13th-century **Achadun**

Tourist Information

Oban: Argyll Square, **t** (01631) 563 122, **f** 564 273; *open all year.*

Hebridean Princess, **t** (01756) 704 704, *www.hebridean.co.uk.* Luxurious and expensive cruises around the Western Isles.

Corryvreckan, **t** (01631) 770 246, *www.corryvreckan.co.uk.* 64ft yacht with experienced crew and good food. Runs 6–12-day trips for 10 passengers in summer.

Festivals

August: **Argyllshire Gathering**, Oban; one of the major Highland Games, with lots of piping and dancing and traditional games (much less formal than Royal Deeside).

September: **Oban Gala Day and Street Fair**; colourful carnival.

Where to Stay

Isle of Eriska, Ledaig, **t** (01631) 720 371, **f** 720 531, *www.eriska-hotel.co.uk* (*very expensive*). Scottish baronial pile, built in 1884, connected to the mainland by a bridge. Its proprietors, the Buchanan-Smiths, have created a magnificent private-house atmosphere, with everything you could wish for, including tremendous hospitality, roaring log fires and an excellent kitchen.

Invercreran Country House Hotel, Glen Creran, near Appin, **t** (01631) 730 414, **f** 730 532, *www.invercreran.com* (*expensive*). In a sheltered glen surrounded by hills. A well-run, comfortable hotel with an excellent dining room.

Ardanaiseig, Kilchrenan, **t** (01866) 833 333, **f** 833 222, *www.ardanaiseig-hotel.com* (*expensive–moderate*). Beneath Ben Cruachan on the shores of Loch Awe, in a garden of rhododendrons and azaleas. Scots Baronial mansion with a 'country house' atmosphere. The food is excellent, and the accommodation very comfortable.

Airds Hotel, Port Appin, **t** (01631) 730 236, **f** 730 535, *www.airds-hotel.com* (*moderate*). Overlooks Loch Linnhe, Lismore, Shuna and the Morvern hills; very comfortable, with

good food and friendly staff. *Open Mar–Jan, with special winter reductions.*

Alexandra Hotel, overlooking Oban Harbour, **t** (01631) 562 381, **f** 564 497 (*moderate*). Comfortable, old-fashioned, good-value seaside resort hotel, serving wholesome, if predictable, food. Some self-catering units.

Bridge of Awe Lodge, Taynuilt, **t** (01866) 822 642, **f** 822 510 (*moderate*). A comfortable lodge at the western end of the Pass of Brander, with antiques, and gardens running down to the River Awe. Excellent dinners by arrangement, and Wolsey Lodge standards of hospitality. Fishermen catered for.

Manor House, Gallanach Road, on Oban Bay, **t** (01631) 562 087, **f** 563 053 (*moderate*). Built by the Duke of Argyll in 1780 as his Oban retreat and later used as a dower house. It has marvellous views, is comfortable and serves good Scottish and French food, especially seafood.

The Pierhouse, Port Appin, **t** (01631) 730 302, **f** 730 400, *www.pierhousehotel.co.uk* (*moderate*). The old ferry house at the end of the pier, now an idyllic place to stay and also to eat delicious seafood in the bistro/restaurant, bar or patio.

Argyll Hotel, Oban, **t** (01631) 562 353 (*cheap*). Also in the town centre.

Barriemore Hotel, Oban, **t/f** (01631) 566 356 (*cheap*). Superior Victorian hotel overlooking the bay, with a friendly atmosphere.

Falls of Lora Hotel, Connel, **t** (01631) 710 483, **f** 710 694 (*cheap*). Overlooks Loch Etive, 5 miles north of Oban. Another of the old-fashioned-style hotels, it gives good service. Some of the rooms are expensive.

Eating Out

The Boxcar, 108 George Street, Oban. A good bistro. *Open evenings only.*

On the pier, Oban. A shed on the pier between the MacBrayne's ticket office and the town sells really fresh seafood snacks: baps generously filled with freshly cooked prawn or crab, still warm and outstandingly good.

The Pierhouse, Port Appin, **t** (01631) 730 302, *see above.*

The Studio, Craigard Road, Oban. Very reasonable, cheap meals.

Lady Rock

The boat from Oban to Mull passes Lady Rock, an islet off Lismore Lighthouse at the head of Loch Linnhe. In the 16th century, a Maclean of Lochbuie, disenchanted by his wife, tethered her to this rock. Passing fishermen took pity and released her and she fled to her father, Campbell of Inveraray. This irate chief invited Maclean to stay on the pretext of commiserating with him on the death of his wife. At the end of dinner, the 'deceased' wife confronted her husband, and her relatives set on him with broadswords.

Castle, is at the southwest end of the island, now a ruin. The overgrown, jagged ruin of **Coeffin Castle**, in the northwest, also dates from the 13th century. The remains of **Broch of Tirefour** stand on the northeast coast, overlooking the mainland. Lismore suffered badly from the 'Clearances' and the population dwindled from about 1,500 in 1775 to 600 by 1885. Today it stands at about 140.

Bachuil House contains the Bachuil Mor, or pastoral staff of St Moluag, the man who converted the island to Christianity in the 6th century. Moluag and Columba are said to have been rivals, the one being a Pict, the other a Celt.

There is a tearoom in the middle of the island.

North of Oban and Appin

Dunstaffnage Castle (*open April–Sept daily 9.30–6.30; Oct–Mar 9.30–4.30, but closed Thurs pm, Fri and Sun am; adm*) is 4 miles north of Oban on a rocky promontory guarding the entrance to Loch Etive, making it of vital strategic importance in the past. A splendid ruin, it seems to grow out of the rock. Parts of it stand over 60ft high, its massive walls more than 10ft thick, but its ancient glory is somewhat marred by a marine laboratory and housing developments. The first fort was founded around the 1st century BC, said to have been a recruiting centre for soldiers to fight the Romans. Flora Macdonald was held prisoner here for a few days after helping Prince Charles in 1746. Tradition holds that the Stone of Destiny came here from Dunadd, staying until Kenneth Macalpine moved it to Scone in an attempt to draw together his kingdom of Picts and Scots (*see* **Topics**, 'Stone of Destiny', p.66).

The A85 north from Oban and Dunstaffnage crosses the crooked finger of Loch Etive at Connel, where sea and loch are in constant turmoil trying to pour in and out through a bottleneck; Connel comes from *conghail* – tumultuous flood. The road loops round Loch Creran, clinging to the coast in places with more good views. This area is a rugged, mountainous hinterland laced with rivers and cascading burns, cut by Loch Etive.

About a mile north of the Connel Bridge, a minor road to the right runs 5 miles out to the northern shore of Loch Etive and **Ardchattan Priory Gardens** (*open April–Oct daily 9–6; adm*). The priory was founded in 1230 and was the meeting place of Robert the Bruce's Parliament in 1308, one of the last to be held in Gaelic. Among the ruins, burned by Cromwell's soldiers, some carved stones can still be seen. The gardens are at their best between July and September, with shrub roses, herbaceous borders and potentillas.

Bonawe (*open April–Sept Mon–Sat 9.30–6.30, Sun 2–6.30*), about 6 miles on around the north side of Loch Etive, is where an old iron ore smelter, of great importance during the Napoleonic Wars, has been preserved by Historic Scotland. This may sound boring but is well worth a visit if you are interested in the industrial and related social history of the country. This was an industrial community with cottages, a school, a laundry and everything else needed to serve the workforce and families.

Barcaldine Castle (*open July and Aug 11–5 and some school hols; adm; t (01631) 720 598*), built in 1609, is known as the black castle because of its dark stones. It played a tragic part in the massacre of Glencoe. Macdonald was stormbound here on his way to sign the oath of loyalty, and was thus too late (*see* p.460). There are underground passages and a ghost.

At Barcaldine, back on the A828, is the **Sea Life Centre** (*open summer daily 9–6; ring for winter times; adm; t (01631) 720 386*). Lots of sea creatures can be seen, some predictable, some nightmarish. They are returned to the sea at the end of the season – one wonders how long they survive having been spoon-fed for a year.

Port Appin, on the flat, marshy peninsula off the southwest tip of Appin, is an attractive little place with a pier and lovely views. There is a craft shop and an excellent bar/fish restaurant in what was the old ferry house – an excellent place to stop off for lunch (*see* above). The passenger ferry to Lismore runs from here.

Castle Stalker (*open by appointment; adm; t (01631) 730 234*), *Caisteal Stalcair* – castle of the hunter, off Portnacroish a few miles north, is a popular postcard/calendar picture on its small island at the mouth of Loch Laich. Former seat of the Stewarts of Appin, it dates back to about 1540. A small, grey tower house built over a pit prison, it has been well restored and you get a good view of it from the road. Keep an eye out for seals around here: they bask on the rocks in large numbers, flopping down into the water if disturbed, to pop up and stare balefully with great velvety eyes at intruders (*see* South Ballachulish, p.459, for the Appin Murder).

Kinlochlaich House Garden (*open April–Oct Mon–Sat 9.30–5.30, Sun 10.30–5.30; Nov–Mar closed Sun; adm*) includes a marvellous garden centre/nursery in lovely surroundings. They have cottages to let here (*t (01631) 730 342*).

The A85 east from Connel to Loch Awe is an attractive drive with views of Loch Etive, through the Pass of Brander below the looming bulk of **Ben Cruachan** (3,689ft). The **Cruachan Power Station** (*visitor centre open Easter–Nov daily 9.30–5; July and Aug daily 9.30–6; adm*), 6 miles beyond Taynuilt, is a great cavern hewn out of Ben Cruachan to accommodate an underground power house. Electric buses run through the tunnel of this glistening subterranean empire – not for the claustrophobic. Water is used from the Cruachan Reservoir to power turbines supplying electricity. (It is said that it takes so much of this electricity to pump the water back up to the reservoir that the turbines have to run very very fast in order to stand still.)

Anyone with the time and energy to climb Ben Cruachan will get some of the best views in Scotland from its summit. The **Pass of Brander**, through which the River Awe squeezes itself into Loch Etive, was carved out by the receding Ice Age 10,000 years ago. In 1309 the Black Douglas, fighting for Robert the Bruce, reversed an ambush by John MacDougall of Lorne, fighting for the English. In their frenzy to escape, many MacDougalls drowned. In spite of the MacDougall motto, *Buaidh no Bas* – conquer or die, John MacDougall escaped down the loch in his galley.

Loch Awe is a 23-mile-long serpent of water with thickly wooded shores, many islands, and more than its share of midges clinging to the dense vegetation. One of the largest freshwater lochs, it is renowned for its huge brown trout. The large Victorian building you see from the road is the **Loch Awe Hotel**, fairly hideous inside and out but with wonderful views from its terrace. **St Conan's Church**, in Lochawe village, is a synthesis of architectural styles from ancient Roman to Norman, designed at the turn of the last century by an eccentric Campbell.

Kilchurn Castle, best seen from a distance, on a commanding site at the north end of the loch, dates from 1440. It belonged to the Campbells of Breadalbane until it was taken over by Hanoverian troops in 1746, with the consent of the anti-Jacobite Campbells. The gale that destroyed the Tay Rail Bridge also demolished one of Kilchurn's turrets.

When the level of the loch is low, traces of several *crannogs* can be seen – man-made islands where early settlers built dwellings for protection against attack. Some of the islands were used as clan burial grounds, especially **Inchail**, where there is a ruined chapel dating from the 13th century and several graves of the Macarthur Clan. There are good walks either side of the loch. On the west side there is an information centre at **Inverliever**.

Ardanaiseig Gardens (*open April–Oct daily; adm*) are at the north end of the loch, east of the B845. They contain rhododendrons, azaleas, rare shrubs and trees and good views across the loch to Ben Cruachan.

White Corries Chairlift (*open May–Dec daily; Jan–April Sat and Sun only; adm*) is north of Tyndrum on the A82, almost on the border with the Highland Region. The lift climbs 2,100ft into the hills, with glorious views over Rannoch Moor and into Glencoe.

The Islands of Argyll

Gigha

Gigha (pronounced with a hard 'g' at the beginning and a silent 'g' in the middle – 'Ge'a') is said to be named after Gudey, Norse for God's Isle. Indeed this subtropical island is an earthly Garden of Eden, but some say it comes from the Norse *gja-ey*, cleft island. Although it is only 56 miles from Glasgow and 3 miles from the mainland, this low-lying, fertile lump, 7 miles long and never more than 1½ miles wide, has managed to retain a true island character. It is firmly on the tourist map, but even that has not spoiled its magic.

With at least 14 owners in 200 years the inhabitants have been dependent on the whims of landlords who often looked on the island as a business venture or a tycoon's

Getting There

There are twice-daily flights from Glasgow to Campbeltown (*weekdays only*), from where taxis go to the ferry terminus at Tayinloan (25 miles away). Or you can drive to Tayinloan, where you are encouraged to leave your car and hire a bicycle. The ferry runs approximately hourly and takes about 20 minutes.

For further information contact Caledonian MacBrayne, **t** (01475) 650 100.

Tourist Information

Campbeltown: Mackinnon House, The Pier, **t** (01586) 552 056, **f** 552 291; *open all year*. Or talk to the McSporran family in the shop.

Where to Stay and Eat

Gigha Hotel, t (01583) 505 254, **f** 505 244, *www.isle-of-gigha.co.uk* (*moderate*). Situated in the original 1789 inn, this is a perfect honeymoon retreat on this paradise island. Almost ranch-style, and not a bit grand, with a cosy lounge and cheerful bar/gossip-collecting centre. The food is good and the position lovely. They will arrange skippered fishing-boat hire, trips around the island, or golf. The hotel also operates six self-catering cottages, including Ardailly House.

Post Office House, t (01583) 505 251 (*moderate*). Seumas McSporran, needless to say, offers inexpensive accommodation here, where you can be sure you won't be disappointed.

toy. Changing hands again recently, Gigha has opted for community ownership, which means that, with a generous injection of public money, the inhabitants have bought the island for a song and will no doubt expect further subsidies to keep it going. As with other crofting community trusts, there are already problems: the big house is up for sale and some of the locals are beginning to talk about 'the good old days'. Time alone will tell. What the perpetrators of these communal buy-outs seem to forget when they talk about 'returning the land to the people' is that in the days before 'white settlers' the land never belonged to 'the people'. Some of the landowners may have been harsh, but a great many of them had considerable knowledge of land management and the means to implement it.

Perhaps the most influential of the incoming lairds in the 'good old days' was Colonel Sir James Horlick, whose malted beverages lulled the world to sleep and made him a fortune. He bought Gigha in 1944 and lived there till his death in 1972, indulging his passion for gardening. **Achamore House Gardens** (*open daily dawn–dusk; adm*) was the result. Thanks to the balmy Gulf Stream (not so balmy when you try swimming in it) giving an almost frost-free climate, the acidic soil, the already established trees and, of course, the Horlick fortune, these 50 acres are a riot of rhododendrons, camellias and azaleas in early summer, with many rarer exotic plants, shrubs and trees.

The village is **Ardminish**, where everything happens. Probably the most celebrated of Gigha's 120 residents is Seumas McSporran, a sturdy figure past his half-century with a genial smile almost as wide as his face. He has lived on the island for all but two years of his life and used to hold some 14 or 15 jobs. 'I had to consult a list to get up to date with them.' They included: sub-postmaster, postman, registrar, Pearl Assurance agent, special constable, fireman, ambulance driver, taxi driver and undertaker. He had a uniform or outfit to go with each job. His shop, a family concern, stocks most things you might need, and they will get things quickly from the mainland for you (**t** *(01583) 505 251*).

The ruined medieval church at **Kilchattan** dates from the 13th century. There are quite a few archaeological sites: cairns, standing stones, forts and duns. There is a nine-hole golf course, a visitor centre, a hotel and a Boathouse Bar. The Achamore creamery produces a very good cheese.

Islay

Islay (pronounced 'eye-la'), the most southerly of the Inner Hebrides, is some 15 miles off Kintyre, about 25 miles from north to south and 20 miles across at the widest point. Farmland rises to moors traversed by burns; rugged coastline gives way to open sweeps of beach. A favourite holiday island for bird-watchers, naturalists, photographers and artists, it also has much to interest archaeologists: the island has been inhabited since Neolithic times.

Excellent trout and salmon fishing can be found on the rivers Duich and Sorn, and on well-stocked lochs such as Gorm, Torrabus and Ballygrant. Boats can be hired locally for sea-angling, too. Warmed by the Gulf Stream, so they say, miles of sandy beaches offer swimming and sunbathing. The surf is sometimes good. Machrie's 18-hole golf course is well known.

Perhaps best known for its distinctive peaty malt whisky, Islay has a number of distilleries whose names are synonymous with this amber nectar: Laphroaig, Lagavulin, Ardbeg, Bowmore. The air is heavy with the pungent smell of smouldering peat. Now and then islanders tangle with conservationists who insist that the special Duich Moss peat, essential for the flavour of Islay whisky, should be preserved for rare Greenland white-fronted geese. At a stormy meeting not so long ago the islanders, furious at Green interference, argued that whisky was more vital to their survival than 'any bloody goose'. The distilleries welcome visitors.

Historically, Islay was the administrative capital of the Lords of the Isles and therefore of prime importance until the forfeiture of the Lordship in 1493. The civil headquarters were on two small islands on Loch Finlaggan. This was the centre of power for an administration which, at its zenith in the early 15th century, ruled all the islands off the west coast and almost the entire western seaboard from Cape Wrath to the Mull of Kintyre.

Port Ellen is the ferry arrival point at the south of the island. Port Ellen Distillery, built in 1815 and no longer in operation, dominates the skyline overlooking Leodamus Bay. A road runs around the coast northeastwards for about 10 miles and then gives way to a track. **Dunyvaig Castle** is the 14th-century ruin on a cliff, 3½ miles east of Port Ellen, stronghold of the Macdonalds of Islay in the days when the Lords of the Isles considered themselves above the authority of the Crown.

Kildalton Cross, beside ruined Kildalton Chapel 7 miles further north along this road, is an important survival of Celtic art. It is a 9th-century Celtic cross carved from a single block of blue stone and inscribed with early Christian symbols. Similar to one in Iona Abbey, it is one of the finest in the country. There was an early Christian chapel and a monastery here, too, before the present Kildalton Chapel was built by the Lords

Getting There

Ferries run to both Port Ellen and Port Askaig from Kennacraig in northwest Kintyre, taking about 2 hours (*3 times a day, Wed and Sun once a day*).
Caledonian MacBrayne, **t** (01475) 650 100.
Flights go daily from Campbeltown (*Mon–Fri*), and twice daily from Glasgow (*Mon–Sat*).
A local bus service links most of the island, with extra runs in the summer, and day tours of beauty spots and places of interest.

Tourist Information

Bowmore: The Square, **t** (01496) 810 254, **f** 810 363; *open all year.*
Campbeltown: Mackinnon House, The Pier, **t** (01586) 552 056, **f** 553 291; *open all year.*

Where to Stay and Eat

What you may miss in glamour, you will certainly gain in Highland hospitality, warmth and friendliness.

Port Charlotte Hotel, **t** (01496) 850 360, **f** 850 361, *carl@portcharlottehot.demon.co.uk* (*expensive–moderate*). Victorian house in the main street with a conservatory, and a garden going down to the sandy beach. It serves good food, especially seafood.
Bridgend Hotel, **t** (01496) 810 212, **f** 810 960 (*moderate*). Pretty garden and good food. *Open all year.*
Glenegedale House, by Port Ellen, **t** (01496) 302 147 (*moderate*). A 17th-century farmhouse near the airport and golf course, looking across Laggan Bay to the Atlantic.
Kilchoman House, by Bruichladdich, **t** (01496) 850 382, **f** 850 277, *ian@kilchoman.demon.co.uk* (*moderate*). Five self-catering cottages (sleeping 2–7) in 40 acres of farmland near a sandy beach, with a restaurant.
Kilmeny Farmhouse, Ballygrant, near Loch Finlaggan, **t/f** (01496) 840 668, *www.kilmeny.co.uk* (*moderate*). Cosy little 5-star guesthouse, with good views, de luxe awards and excellent food. No smoking.
Port Askaig Hotel, **t** (01496) 840 245, **f** 840 295 (*moderate*). Looks out over the harbour, and is attractive and cosy. *Open all year.*

of the Isles in the 14th century. It is roofless but substantial, and there are some late-medieval grave slabs inside.

Claggain Bay, beyond the chapel, is sandy with rocky pools, backed by Beinn Bheigeir (1,612ft), the highest hill in Islay.

The rugged **Oa Peninsula** (pronounced 'oh'), 5 miles southwest of Port Ellen, was a haunt of smugglers and illicit whisky distillers, who made cunning use of its sheer cliffs honeycombed with caves. One road crosses it, but most of the peninsula is only accessible on foot.

Machrie, northwest of the Oa, has an 18-hole golf course on the machair, and borders the sandy crescent of Laggan Bay.

Bowmore, about 9 miles north of Port Ellen, was the old capital and administrative centre of the island – seat of the Islay Parliament, a sort of feudal court. The village was built by Daniel Campbell the Younger in 1768 on the site of monastic lands, and was one of the earliest of Scotland's planned villages introduced by wealthy 'improvers' in the 18th century. The village is crowned by an intriguing, round church, Italian in design. Its shape deprives the devil of any corners in which to lurk.

Bowmore Distillery (*open all year for videos about distilling, guided tours and a dram*), established in 1779, claims to be the oldest legal distillery on Islay and is still privately owned.

Bridgend is a hamlet among woods at the head of Loch Indaal, with good beaches and a hotel. **Dun Nosebridge** is an Iron-Age fort 2½ miles to the southeast. **Islay**

Woollen Mill is an old working mill where you can watch tweed being woven and buy the products.

The Rhinns of Islay projects westwards like a great hammerhead, with wonderful walks and views. The award-winning **Museum of Islay Life** (*open Easter–Oct Mon–Sat 10–5, Sun 2–5; adm*) is in a converted church in **Port Charlotte**, on the southeast shore of the Rhinns. Exhibits cover the history of the island, with traditional craft work and tools, a maritime section and domestic artefacts. A lapidarium, below the museum, displays an important collection of carved stones dating from the 16th century.

There is a wildfowl sanctuary at **Ellister**, south of Port Charlotte, and an RSPB reserve at **Loch Gruinart** to the north. The **Islay Natural History Trust**, at the Field Centre, Port Charlotte (*open April–Oct, t (01496) 850 288*) has displays on local wildlife, as well as children's activities and a good reference library. **Portnahaven** is the southwest tip of Islay, with the green shores of Ireland only spitting distance away.

Ruined **Finlaggan Castle** stands on an islet in Loch Finlaggan, just off the road from Bowmore to Port Askaig. This was the main stronghold of the Macdonalds, Lords of the Isles. The 14 chiefs of the Lordship were summoned to council meetings here, to confer with their overlord. They came from all over the Kingdom of the Isles, many in coracles, accompanied by members of their clans. They were proud men, settling their disputes and problems independently of the Scottish Parliament, often with great wisdom and justice but often with bloodshed. There is a **visitor centre** (*open April–Oct; ask at Bowmore tourist information centre*), illustrating some of the intriguing history of those times and displaying archaeological remains unearthed by recent diggings.

Port Askaig is the other ferry terminal for the mainland and for Jura. The views across the narrow Sound of Islay to the Paps of Jura are glorious. There is a hotel and a roadless hinterland to the north.

Jura

Just off the northeast coast of Islay, Jura has very little tourist accommodation and is far less frequented, though more severely beautiful. Wild and rugged, it is famous for its deer, which are keenly stalked by the owners and guests of the sporting estates of which the island is comprised. Over 20 miles long and sparsely populated, it has a small village, Craighouse, a distillery and a hotel. Silver and white sandy beaches give way to rugged shingle which teems with wildfowl. Loch Tarbert almost cuts the island in two from the west. The three bosoms or Paps of Jura rear up at the south end of the island – the highest is 2,576ft. A single-track road runs south from the ferry, and then some way up the east coast. Most of the island is only accessible on foot. The west coast – private land – has some amazing caves, some of which have been adapted for temporary use by shepherds and, in recent years, a young woman artist.

In the 19th century Jura was the stepping stone for drovers taking cattle from Islay and Colonsay to the mainland markets, with two to three thousand cattle crossing every year. There were about 1,000 inhabitants 150 years ago; now there are less than

Getting There

There is no direct link with the mainland. A car ferry runs approximately every 45 minutes from Port Askaig on Islay to Feolin, taking 10 minutes (fewer ferries on Sundays).

Tourist Information

Campbeltown: Mackinnon House, The Pier, t (01586) 552 056, f 553 291.

Where to Stay and Eat

Exploration Jura, t 07899 912 116 (*moderate*). Mike and Joan Richardson offer rooms in their house (space for 4) and in a bunkhouse (for 6) (*April–Oct*). They also run guided hill walking or Land Rover tours of the island.

Jura Hotel, Craighouse, t (01496) 820 243, f 820 249, *jurahotel@aol.com* (*cheap*). All you could wish for: relaxed and friendly, with a lovely setting and good local food. Book.

200. Tourism is very low key, mainly geared for day visitors from Islay. Sportsmen who pay large sums for their pursuits aren't too keen on seeing hikers in their gun sights. Most of the locals work on crofts, for the Forestry Commission, as estate workers or in the distillery.

Craighouse, the only village, has the island's single hotel and the distillery.

Jura House Garden (*open all year; adm*) is an oasis on the southern shore. Its large walled garden was established in the middle of the 19th century to exploit the natural features and beauty of the area; thanks to the mild climate, exotic Australasian plants grow well here. Everything is organically produced and there is an attractive walk through woodland to the shore at Ardfin.

One of Jura's party tricks is the **Corryvreckan Whirlpool**, in the strait between its northern point and Scarba. Notorious to west-coast sailors it can be both lion and lamb. Flood tides meet around a steep pyramid rock 15ft below the surface, causing the whirlpool, whose noise has been heard, they say, 10 miles away. It roars like an express train and its mighty maw has been known to suck down whole boats, but at slack tide it can be approached by sea, its satin-smooth water ruffled by tiny eddies that pull gently at the boat without harm. In May 1946 George Orwell, renting **Barnhill**, 7 miles beyond Ardlussa, to write *1984*, misread the tide-table and capsized in the Corryvreckan with his 3-year-old adopted son and a couple of friends. Miraculously no one was drowned, but it can't have done much for his TB.

Colonsay and Oronsay

These two tiny islands, joined at low tide, lie 10 miles west of Jura, 25 miles from the mainland. To the west, the only thing between here and Canada is Du Hirteach Lighthouse. The landscape is made up of craggy hills, woods and a rocky coastline broken by silver sands. Their names are derived from the saints Columba and Oran who landed here on their way to Scotland from Ireland. Legend holds that when Columba discovered he could still see the shore of the land from which he had been exiled, he pressed on to Iona; whether from repugnance or sadness is not related. It is also said that he banished snakes from the two islands, as he did on Iona.

Getting There

There are 3 car ferries from Oban (*Mon, Wed and Fri*), taking 2½ hours. There is a boat from Kennacraig via Islay taking about the same time and allowing a 6-hour visit before it returns in the late afternoon (*only April–Sept Wed*). A tour bus meets this boat and takes visitors around the island.

Ring Caledonian MacBrayne, t (01475) 650 100, for seasonal details.

Tourist Information

Oban: Argyll Square, t (01631) 563 122, f 564 273.

Where to Stay and Eat

Colonsay Estate, t (01951) 200 312 (*moderate*). Self-catering in a number of estate houses.
Isle of Colonsay Hotel, Kiloran, t (01951) 200 316 (*moderate*). Small, family-run and the food is excellent, using local ingredients whenever possible. They run wild flower courses and provide free bikes. They also have self-catering chalets. Next door, Virago is an interesting bookshop with new and second-hand books on Scottish and West Highland themes.
Seaview, t (01951) 200 315 (*moderate*). The best guesthouse, which also has a self-catering flat for 2 people and 2 cottages.

The strand linking the two islands can submerge rapidly in the flood tide. Be aware of the tide-table if you want to spend time exploring the Priory on Oronsay: it dries out for about 3 hours either side of low tide.

Both islands have a high average of sunshine. Over 500 species of wild flowers can be found, including rare purple orchids, sea samphire and marsh helleborine. Bluebells and primroses bloom in the woods, wild irises flower in damp corners, harebells nod on the sand dunes and purple thrift clings to the rocks. Eucalyptus, palm trees and rare shrubs flourish in the mild climate. There are also over 150 different bird species.

Kiloran Bay, on the northwest of Colonsay, is probably the most unspoilt beach in all the islands. After a strong westerly wind there can be rollers good enough for surfing, though it can be dangerous.

Colonsay House Gardens (*open daily*) have subtropical shrubs and plants, rhododendrons, embothriums, meconopsis, magnolias and palm trees. The house was built in 1722 and is now holiday flats.

Wild goats roam the island, reputedly descended from survivors of a Spanish Armada wreck in 1588. Otters can be seen occasionally and there are lots of grey seals. **Balnahard** beach has hundreds of cowrie shells in the coves. **The Strand** is a beach a mile wide in the south of the island, festooned with mussels on the rocks and prawns in the pools.

For about 3 hours either side of low tide, the Strand becomes a causeway to Oronsay, an enchanted island populated by sheep and serenaded by skylarks. **St Oran's Chapel**, on Oronsay, is a ruined 14th-century priory, named after St Columba's faithful companion. Although the cloisters have collapsed, this is a splendid ruin with gravestones carved with boats and warriors and hunting scenes. A tall, carved Celtic cross stands at the entrance. Excavations revealed that Oronsay was inhabited in the Middle Stone Age. Certainly Norsemen lived here long before the present chapel was built by Columban monks.

Mull

Mull, 'isle-of-the-cool-high-bends', is the second largest of the Inner Hebrides after Skye, and merits a whole book to itself. It is shaped like a caricature of the British Isles, its southwestern peninsula kicking frivolously upwards. Encircled by 300 miles of rugged coastline, it is deeply cut by lochs with many wooded hillsides and secret corners, some easily reached by coastal roads, others only on foot. The western seaboard is sprinkled with islands: **Inch Kenneth**, **Ulva**, **Staffa** and, further west, the **Treshnish Isles** with **Coll** and **Tiree** beyond. There are plenty of boat trips to the islands, and some of the hotels charter their own boats. In addition, the locals will take you fishing or sightseeing. The whole coast is a sailor's paradise. Around the head of Loch Na Keal, about halfway down the west coast, there are steep cliffs fringed by sandy inlets. The hinterland is a mass of hills, dominated by **Ben More**, 3,169ft, in the west. There are some fine castles and an ancient pilgrim track across the Ross of Mull, taken by pilgrims to Iona.

Johnson and Boswell came to Mull during their tour of the Hebrides. Johnson lamented the lack of trees, attributing this to idleness, but applauded the French wine he was given.

There are more red deer on Mull than people: over 3,000 roam the island and the smaller fallow deer can be seen in the woods around Gruline and Salen. There are also polecats, weasels, stoats, mink, feral ferrets and otters. Wild white goats can be seen from Grass Point down to the Ross of Mull.

Unlike some other islands, the depopulation of 150 years has been reversed in Mull. With fishing, farming, tourism and building to employ them, fewer young people are seeking the bright lights of the mainland and there are a number of incomers who prefer insular peace and beauty to the materialistic scramble of the cities. However, there is not always perfect harmony between these 'white settlers' and the 'natives'.

Tobermory

Having stopped off at Craignure, the ferry sails up the Sound of Mull to Tobermory – the Well of St Mary – the 'capital' of Mull. Founded as a fishing village in 1789 on the site of an earlier Christian settlement, it has one of the most sheltered harbours in Scotland, tucked round behind a headland. The village clusters around the anchorage. Terraced houses, colour-washed in strong reds, pinks, yellows, blues and ochres, rise from the harbour up a steep, wooded bank. Yachstmen and fishermen jostle for mooring space.

Mull Museum (*open Easter–mid-Oct Mon–Sat; adm*), in an old baker's shop, is a concession to one of Mull's main industries – tourism. As well as giving an overview of the island's history, the museum tells the story of the wrecked galleon *Florencia*, relic of the Spanish Armada which lies in the bay beyond the harbour, still a focus of attention for treasure seekers today. The ship sought shelter here in a storm in 1588. Always hospitable, the islanders treated the Spaniards with courtesy, restocking their stores and entertaining them in grand style. But Scotsmen are thrifty as well as hospitable and, when rumour came that the *Florencia* was about to depart without

Getting There

There is an airfield on the island to which charter flights can be arranged from Glasgow.

Car ferries run frequently from Oban to Craignure (*40mins*); Oban–Tobermory (*c. 2hrs*) and Lochaline–Fishnish (*¼hr*). There is also a car ferry from Kilchoan to Tobermory in summer (*½hr*). You can get 'multi-stop' ferry tickets, which are much cheaper. Caledonian MacBrayne, t (01475) 650 100.

The Mull Experience, t (01680) 812 309/812 421 (*May–Sept only*). Coach trip which includes the Oban–Craignure ferry and a tour of the island, visiting Duart Castle, Torosay Castle and Gardens, and a ride on the Mull railway. Cars can be hired easily; most roads are single-track with passing places.

Tourist Information

Tobermory: t (01688) 302 182, f 302 145.
Craignure: t (01680) 812 377, f 812 497.
Oban: t (01631) 563 122, f 564 273.

Festivals

March: Drama Festival.
April: Music Festival.
July: Highland Games, Tobermory. **Children's Highland Games.**
August: West Highland Yachting Week; early in the month. **Salen Show**; including a dogshow.
October: Car Rally.

Sports and Activities

Wet- or dry-fly **trout fishing** is available in Mishnish Lochs, Loch Tor and Loch Frisa.

Licences, tackle and bait can be obtained from Brown's Ironmongers on Tobermory High Street, or the National Forestry Commission's office at the south end of Loch Frisa. You can also hire rods and boats.

Tobermory has a nine-hole **golf course**, with spectacular views, on the northern tip of the island, owned by the Western Isles Hotel.

Mull Little Theatre, Dervaig, 5 miles from Tobermory, t (01688) 302 828 (box office, t (01688) 400 377), *www.mulltheatre.org.uk*. Featured in the *Guinness Book of Records* as the smallest professional theatre in Britain, with 37 seats – until it lost that accolade by expanding to a massive 43. Professional productions in summer (six times a week); book well in advance. Amateur productions in winter. The theatre is close to **Druimard Country House Hotel**, *see* below, which serves pre- and post-show lunch or dinner.

Island Cruises

There are inter-island cruises to Staffa, Treshnish, Coll, Eigg, and Muck, in charter boats. Go well prepared: take a picnic and weatherproof clothing as conditions change quickly, and seasickness pills – the slow Atlantic swell can be disastrous for uneasy stomachs. You might see whales and dolphins. Book your cruise through:

Island Encounter Wildlife Safaris, at Aros, t (01680) 300 441.

Turus Mara, t 08000 858 7886.

Other Tours

Isle of Mull Land Rover Wildlife Expeditions, t (01688) 302 044, *www.scotlandwildlife.com*. Daily expeditions all year from Ulva House Hotel, Tobermory (lunch provided), on which you may see otters, eagles, porpoises, seals, and so on.

having paid its dues, a local man, Donald Maclean, went aboard to remonstrate. He was locked up in the ship's cell, but managed to escape. In retaliation he blew up the ship, together with the hoard of gold and treasure it was alleged to have been carrying. So far, only a few coins and cannon have been discovered, but the search continues. Divers should note, however, that the wreck is protected and it is forbidden to dive in its area.

The only **distillery** in Mull is in Tobermory (*open Easter–Oct Mon–Fri 10–5 for tours*). **An Tobar** (*open Mar–Dec daily 10–5.30*), in Argyll Terrace, is an arts centre and gallery,

Where to Stay

Druimard Country House, Dervaig, t/f (01688) 400 345, *www.druimard.co.uk (expensive)*. Luxurious Victorian country house hotel near the theatre *(see above)*. Excellent food.

Glengorm Castle, near Tobermory, t (01688) 302 321, *www.glengormcastle.co.uk (expensive)*. 4-star B&B in Victorian castle with spectacular views. Well worth the expense.

Western Isles Hotel, Tobermory, t (01688) 302 012, f 302 297 *(expensive–moderate)*. Massive Victorian pile, high above Tobermory with stunning views, old-world charm and traditional Highland hospitality. Good food.

Calgary Farmhouse and Dovecote Restaurant, Dervaig, t/f (01688) 400 256, *www.calgary.co.uk (moderate)*. Restaurant with rooms, *see below*.

Craignure Inn, Craignure, t (01680) 812 305, f 812 470, *www.craignure-inn.co.uk (moderate)*. Original 17th-century drovers' inn, now more genteel.

Druimnacroish Country House Hotel, Dervaig, t/f (01688) 400 274, *www.druimnacroish.co.uk (moderate)*. Lovely country house in a converted watermill, with excellent service.

Highland Cottage, Breadalbane Street, Tobermory, t (01688) 302 030, f 302 727, *www.highlandcottage.co.uk (moderate)*. Very stylish little hotel with excellent food.

Killiechronan House, t (01680) 300 403, f 300 463 *(moderate)*. A former estate house at the head of the loch. Very comfortable, with good food.

Tiroran House, on the north shore of Loch Scridain, t (01681) 705 232, f 705 240, *www.tiroran.com (moderate)*. Remote, with a lovely garden. Cosy and hospitable, with excellent food.

Tobermory Hotel, Tobermory, t (01688) 302 091, f 302 254, *www.thetobermoryhotel.com*

(moderate). Right on the waterfront, and full of character and boating camaraderie.

Ulva House Hotel, Strongarbh, Tobermory, t/f (01688) 302 044, *www.ulvahousehotel.co.uk (moderate)*. Cosy Victorian house with lovely sea views, good food and Land Rover expeditions, *see above*.

Pennygate Lodge, Craignure, t (01680 4) 812 333 *(cheap)*. Georgian manse in a lovely setting.

Redbay Cottage, Fionnphort, t (01681) 700 396 *(cheap)*. B&B in glorious position on the water. Lovely relaxed atmosphere. Dinner on request.

Staffa Cottage Guest House, overlooking Tobermory Bay, t/f (01688) 302 464 *(cheap)*. Charming 19th-century terraced cottage in a wooded garden. Supper cruises available.

Eating Out

Calgary Farmhouse and Dovecote Restaurant, Dervaig, t (01688) 400 256. Nice bistro/wine bar, with a gallery in summer, and rooms.

Druimard Country House, Dervaig, t (01688) 400 345. Pre- and post-theatre meals. Excellent food. Also a hotel, *see above*.

The Garden Barn, Tobermory, t 01688 302 235, *www.isleofmullcheese.co.uk*. Excellent farm enterprise, where the famous Mull cheese is made. *Open April–Sept Mon–Fri 10–4*.

The Mishnish, Tobermory, t (01688) 302 009, *www.mishnish.co.uk*. 'Good craic'.

Puffer Aground, in Salen, t (01680) 300 389. Good food; you should book.

Strongarbh House, Tobermory, t (01688) 32338. Serves good seafood and steak. Book at weekends. You can also stay here.

Ulva Heritage Centre, t (01688) 500 241, *see below*. Licensed tearoom with excellent oysters and Guinness. *Open Easter–Oct Mon–Fri 9–5; June–Aug also Sun*.

with exhibitions, music, workshops and talks. You can also enjoy coffee and cakes around the fire.

Going west on the B8073, look for three small, linked lochs where there is trout fishing. **Snake Pass**, beyond the last loch, is said to be the home of many adders. This is also the start of a good walk to Loch Frisa. On the hill down into **Dervaig** there is a cemetery at Kilmore, with some of the oldest gravestones on Mull. Filmgoers may recognize this as one of the sets for *Where Eight Bells Toll*.

The **Old Byre Heritage Centre** (*open Easter–mid-Oct daily; adm*), a mile beyond Dervaig, is a crofting museum with tableaux showing life at the time of the Highland Clearances, with the family and animals around the central fire, busy about their daily lives. A half-hour audiovisual programme illustrates further what life was like (*hourly from 10.30*).

The west-coast road gives views out to the scattering of islands that enhance the wonderful seascapes, especially when seen against a setting sun. There are good sandy beaches, particularly the one at **Calgary Bay**. Calgary was once a prosperous crofting community but its people were evicted and emigrated to Canada, establishing a town in the North West Territory in 1884. Nostalgic and homesick, they called their new town after their old home.

Boats run from Dervaig or Ulva to the **Treshnish Isles** and to **Staffa**, when the weather is fair. A new landing stage on Staffa makes access easier in rough weather and some cruises allow you an hour ashore. You can go into **Fingal's Cave** by boat, or walk around the side on a platform. This huge cathedral-like cavern is made up of columns of basalt, some hexagonal, truncated at different levels like organ pipes and of similar construction to Ireland's Giant's Causeway. The formation inspired Mendelssohn in 1829 to write the *Hebrides* overture.

Cruises which include **Lunga** in the Treshnish Isles are especially good during the nesting season. You are advised not to linger too long over the puffins at the start of your tour because they are so bewitching you may never see the rest of the island. They sit scratching, chatting and popping in and out of their burrows, an arm's length from you. There are also kittiwakes, razorbills, shags and guillemots, and lots of black rabbits.

The island of **Ulva** will be familiar to anyone who knows the poem 'Lord Ullin's Daughter', which tells the tale of 'The Chief of Ulva's Isle' and his lover, fleeing her father's wrath and drowning in the ferry, crossing to the island. Lord Ullin stood helpless on the shore, while:

The waters wild went o'er his child,
And he was left lamenting.

Ulva Heritage Centre (*open Easter–Oct Mon–Fri 9–5; June–Aug also Sun; adm*) is a restored thatched croft house and information centre, with a licensed tearoom.

Eas Forss is a waterfall that cascades over the cliff into a pool and then under a rock, arching into the sea, 10 miles from the Ulva ferry.

The walks and views all down the west coast are good. Much of the coastline is columned basalt with sandy bays and rock coves, with seals, guillemots, oyster-catchers and herons in the rock pools. Wild flowers are abundant: orchids, bright pink thrift and yellow irises.

Where the road turns south, before cutting back inland across the Ardmeanach peninsula, you can look out across the entrance to Loch na Keal to **Inch Kenneth**. This was the burial place of many Scottish kings and was visited by Johnson and Boswell in 1773, as guests of Sir Allan Maclean and his two daughters. Unity Mitford took refuge here with her family after her unfortunate association with Hitler and the

Nazis. To the right, **Tragedy Rock** is a huge boulder which crashed on to the cottage of a young local couple on the first night of their married life, 200 years ago, killing them both.

The **Ardmeanach Peninsula** is owned by the National Trust for Scotland. At Burgh on the southern tip, aptly named The Wilderness, MacCulloch's Tree is signed – a fossilized tree 50 million years old embedded in the shore. Sadly, much of it has been removed by fossil collectors.

The **Ross of Mull** is the southwest headland, with softer scenery. **Erraid**, the tidal islet off the southwest tip of the Ross, was once home to Robert Louis Stevenson, and it was here that David Balfour swam ashore from the wreck of the brig *Covenant* in *Kidnapped*. The island is now inhabited by members of the Findhorn Foundation, who contemplate the inner sanctity of their spiritual and holistic lives. **Uisken** on the south side, reached by a road from Bunessan, is a lovely beach with lonely crofts, mostly ruined – another village abandoned in the Clearances.

The **Isle of Mull Wine Company** at Bunessan welcomes visitors and will arrange tastings. They make the Isle of Mull Vermouth and The Mull Riveter, a blend of their own vermouth and bitters with vodka. Children will enjoy a visit to the **Angora Rabbit Farm** (*open Easter–Oct Sun–Fri 11–5; adm; there's a café*), at Ardtun near Bunessan, where they can see how their clipped coats are made into wool. Further east at Pennyghael, take the road south to Carsaig, a lovely spot where salmon fishermen still work. The amazing Carsaig Arches is a famous geological freak – a natural, jagged archway through the rock.

From the head of Loch Scridain the A849 goes inland back towards the east coast through Glen More. At Ardura a road turns south to Loch Buie, a lovely drive down past Loch Spelve and Loch Uisg. Moy Castle, at the end, now a ruin, was the ancestral home of the MacLaines of Lochbuie.

Duart Castle (*open May–mid-Oct daily 10.30–6; adm*) is about 5 miles northeast of the head of Loch Spelve, an impressive fortress on a headland guarding the approach to the Sound of Mull and clearly seen from the Oban ferry. It dates from the 12th century, and was the home of the Chiefs of Maclean until it was confiscated after the Jacobite rising in 1745. It was bought back and restored in 1912 by Sir Fitzroy Maclean, who was then the chief. He was a gallant Hussar colonel who had ridden with the Light Brigade in the Crimea and died at the age of 100, affectionately known as Old Man A Hundred. As well as the keep, visitors can see the cell where prisoners from the Spanish galleon *Florencia* were held after it had been sunk in Tobermory in 1588 by Donald Maclean. There are relics of the Maclean family in the main hall, with many of the gifts presented to the late Chief – who was among many other things, Chief Scout and Lord Chamberlain – during his world tours. There is also an exhibition of scouting throughout the Commonwealth, in the old staff rooms at the top of the castle.

Just south of Duart, the road to **Grass Point**, on Lochdon, was the old drovers' road for cattle and sheep from the outer isles, bound for mainland markets. It was also the landing point for pilgrims going to Iona. The seal on one of the rocks around the bay is of rather a different species to those living in the waters around Mull. It was the handiwork of the eminent sculptor, poet and writer, the late Lionel Leslie. First cousin of Winston Churchill, he and his wife Barbara came to live in the old Drover's Inn after the Second World War, building it up from a ruin with their own hands. Boatloads of visitors came over from Oban in the summer to have tea, buy local crafts and listen to the sculptor's stories. Even in his mid-eighties his wit was as sharp as the stone he could no longer see to carve. There are also bas reliefs of a deer, an eagle, fighting swans and horses on the walls of a roofless byre beside the house, in lasting memory of a great artist and a great man. The house has been done up for holiday lets.

Torosay Castle (*open mid-April–mid-Oct daily 10.30–5; gardens open all year; adm*) is a mile west as the crow flies, across Duart Bay. This 19th-century Scottish Baronial building, with all the embellishments so beloved by the Victorians, was designed by David Bryce. The 11 acres of terraced Italian-style gardens with a statue walk and water garden were laid out by Robert Lorimer. The house contains magnificent paintings of wildlife by Thorburn, Landseer and Peter Scott, and family portraits by Poynter, de Lazlo, Sargent and Carlos Sancha. There are also hunting trophies, a library and an archive room with photographs and scrapbooks going back over 100 years. In the high season boats run from Oban direct to Torosay. A **miniature railway** (260mm gauge) runs a mile and a half from Craignure Pier to the castle (*Easter–mid-Oct; adm*), the only passenger train service in the Hebrides.

The roofless, ruined church by the cemetery at **Salen** is unlikely to be restored. A wicked Maclean of Duart was buried here many years ago and the consequence was the roof blew off. Three times they put it back and three times it blew away, unable to settle over the remains of such a villain. Sadly, the 1st-century statue of the Virgin Mary that used to be in this church has been stolen.

Ruined **Aros Castle**, just across Salen Bay, dates from the 13th century and was one of the strongholds of the Lords of the Isles. It is thought to have been one of four castles whose surrender to Scotland was demanded by Alexander II in 1249. The Commissioner of James IV tried many of the rebellious island chiefs here in 1608.

Iona

No one can visit Mull without making a pilgrimage to the 'cradle of Christianity', though in fact St Ninian was spreading the word for nearly 150 years before St Columba founded his church on Iona in 563. 1997 was the 1,400th anniversary of Columba's death and was celebrated in many ways both on and off the island, with a fair amount of inter-denominational rivalry which must have amused that wise advocate of the One True Faith.

The island is beautiful – white cockle-shell sand and vivid green slopes, slashed with rust-red granite and painted with wild flowers. The powerful Irish saint, of royal descent, outlawed from his own land, came here with a few followers and set about converting the heathen Picts of Scotland to the Celtic Christianity of his homeland. Many Scots, Irish and Norse kings were buried on Iona, including Macbeth and Duncan.

When Johnson and Boswell came here in 1773, the abbey was a complete ruin. Johnson was deeply moved by the atmosphere: 'That man is little to be envied ... whose piety would not grow warmer among the ruins of Iona.' Today he may not have been so impressed.

In 1938 George Macleod, a controversial Presbyterian socialist who renounced an inherited title but accepted one bestowed by the State, settled a new community on the island and began the rebuilding of the monastery and domestic buildings. He believed that the church needed to get closer to the lives of ordinary people, and that practical and spiritual work in a community would be good training for people with vocations for public service of any sort. Thus the Iona Community was born. But George Macleod and most of his followers spoke no Gaelic; they were not Gaels and had no cultural ties with their adopted home. There could never be full integration, although the natural courtesy of the islanders forbade outward animosity towards the zealous incomers. Opinions differ about this historic abbey: for some, the sanctity of the restored abbey has been erased and they find it hard to kneel and say a prayer among the hugging and hand-holding and happy-clappery of the Community, surrounded by stalls selling postcards, souvenirs and booklets. Instead they find their peace in St Oran's Chapel and in the *Reilig Odrain* – the ancient burial ground – and in the remoter parts of the island. Mammon rules within the precincts, and even a ferryman has been known to ram a visiting boat innocently trespassing on his commercial berth.

But with only 2½ hours, day visitors haven't time to disrupt the real Iona. When the last boat leaves at about 5.30pm the native islanders emerge and get on with their lives. There is a well-stocked, licensed Spar shop selling delicious home-made bread, run by an astute local family who also run the only pub and an excellent restaurant. There is an up-market craft shop; a tourist-trap souvenir shop called Finlay Ross, with hairy socks, scented things and good books; and a marvellous little pottery with pieces that mirror the exceptional colours of the Iona land- and sea-scapes. And there is a tiny bookshop with a tiny doorway, across the road from the Columba Hotel,

Getting There

The passenger ferry from Fionnphort, on Mull, to Iona, takes 5 minutes. There is also a Sacred Isles Cruise, on certain days in summer, from Oban, via Staffa. They allow 2½ hours on Iona before the return journey.

Where to Stay and Eat

The Abbey, t (01681) 700 404 (*cheap*). Offers full board from March to December; very cheap and pretty spartan, which is good for the soul – monkish food and no licence. Visitors are expected to take part in the day-to-day activities of the community. There are also week-long courses: details from the wardens.

Argyll Hotel, t (01681) 700 334, **f** 700 510, *www.argyllhoteliona.co.uk* (*cheap*). Right on the water, built in 1868 as the inn, with 15 cosy bedrooms en suite, though some of the baths are so small you have to ablute in sections. The food is excellent.

Finlay Ross, t (01681) 700 357/365, **f** 700 562 (*cheap*). The souvenir shop does a good B&B.

St Columba Hotel, t (01681) 700 304, **f** 700 688, *columba@btinternet.com* (*cheap*). On rising ground north of the village, ½ mile from the jetty, with a rather crude seal lolling outside the front. It is popular with Americans so has plenty of mod cons.

selling, when it is open (which isn't that often), everything from rare books to tatty paperbacks.

The **Iona Heritage Centre** in Telford Manse (*open April–Oct Mon–Sat 10.30–4.30*) focuses on local history, and has a small shop and a café.

Iona is special, in spite of all the trappings and communal bonhomie. St Columba *was* here, all those years ago. Walk away from the designer Holy Place and climb the small hill, Dun I, to the north of the abbey. Look down on the restored buildings where so much attention has been paid to the Holy Fabric that they forgot to restore the Holy Spirit; on the trails of people with strap-hung cameras, chattering and munching. Stay very quiet and listen: you may catch a faint echo of ironic laughter, and feel a charismatic presence beside you. St Columba was known to have a well-developed sense of humour.

Coll and Tiree

Coll and Tiree, less than 11 miles off the northwest tip of Mull, are low islands which look barren from the sea but are charming, with green fields surrounded by an almost continuous string of deserted white beaches, where you may see many sea birds, seals and even otters. Sturdy cottages have rounded, thatched or tar-felted roofs to withstand the winter gales.

Coll

Coll is endearingly fish-shaped, about 13 miles long and 3 miles wide with a population of about 150. Sandy beaches, azure water, rocky coves, backed by machair strewn with wild flowers in spring, make this another away-from-it-all paradise. The record of sunshine is good (usually tempered by a persistent wind). Johnson and Boswell were forced to make an unscheduled stop on Coll due to bad weather. By the fifth day of their incarceration Johnson was pining for the mainland.

Two standing stones at Totronald, called *Na Sgeulachan* (the Tellers of Tales), are thought to be part of a pagan temple, and traces of prehistoric forts and duns scatter the island. Adamnan, St Columba's biographer, mentions it in his *Vita Sancti Columbae*. During the Norse occupation of the islands, Coll was the headquarters of Earl Gilli, brother-in-law of Sigurd, Ruler of the Orkneys and Hebrides in AD 1000. By the end of the 13th century it belonged to the MacDougalls of Lorne, from whom it was taken by Robert the Bruce because they opposed him. It passed to a second son of the Macleans of Duart in the early 1400s and remained in their keeping until 1856, when Hugh Maclean, last laird of Coll, was forced to sell his estates to pay for his extravagant lifestyle. John Stewart of Glenbuckie, factor to the Duke of Argyll, bought it, and his ruthlessly efficient farming methods resulted in mass emigration to Canada and Australia by the unfortunate crofters who could no longer afford his inflated rents (*see* **Topics**, 'Highland Clearances', p.52). Traces of their abandoned croft houses can be seen at the northern end of the island. The resident population is now about 130, with quite a few incomers and holiday-home owners. Coll, known for its

Getting There

Boats run from Oban (*daily exc Thurs and Sun*), taking 3 hours to Coll, 4½ to Tiree. Boats also run from Tobermory, taking 2 hours. For details, contact Caledonian MacBrayne, **t** (01475) 650 100. There are also flights to Tiree from Glasgow (*daily exc Sun*) and from Barra (*Tues–Thurs*).

Getting Around

You can hire cars very reasonably on Coll, which meet you at the ferry. Bicycles can also be hired and are the best way of getting about – except for the wind.

Tourist Information

Oban: Tourist Information Centre, **t** (01631) 563 122, **f** 564 273. Local knowledge is by far the best. Contact them for practical information before you go.

Where to Stay

Coll

Self-catering: one chalet and three flats in Arinagour, **t** (01879) 230 373 (*cheap*); a house, a bungalow and a bothy, c/o Estate Office, **t** (01879) 230 339 (*cheap*).

Achamore, **t** (01879) 230 430, *jim@achamore.freeserve.co.uk* (*cheap*). Very cheap and relaxed, in a splendid setting. Good for families.

Isle of Coll Hotel, at the head of Arinagour Bay, **t** (01879) 230 334, **f** 230 317 (*cheap*). Overlooking the Treshnish Islands, with six rooms and a jolly, Hebridean atmosphere.

Tigh-na-Mara Guest House, Arinagour, **t/f** (01879) 230 354 (*cheap*). Modern house with eight bedrooms overlooking the bay, with a restricted drinks licence.

Tigh Solas, Arinagour, **t/f** (01879) 230 333 (*cheap*). A modern bungalow. Very friendly.

Tiree

Don't expect the Ritz, but you will certainly find true island hospitality and kindness.

Balephetrish Guest House, overlooking Balephetrish Bay, **t** (01879) 220 549. Pebble-dash croft house (*cheap*).

Scarinish Hotel, Gott Bay, **t** (01879) 220 308, **f** 220 410 (*cheap*).

Tiree Lodge, Gott Bay, **t** (01879) 220 353, **f** 220 884 (*cheap*).

Self-catering is to be recommended and you can buy essential stores, though you should bring luxury food if it is important to you.

Kenovay Thatched Cottage, **t** (01505) 690 662. For the perfect honeymoon (it only sleeps two), a restored croft-bothy in the middle of the island, 10 minutes from the beach.

Lighthouse View, Scarinish, **t** (01828) 670 626/ **t** (0141) 778 1405. Sleeps six.

---

trout-filled lochs, has attracted a number of literati, and features now and then in glossy magazines. Sea fishing is also good, and local fishermen will take visitors out in their boats. Walking, bicycling, swimming, bird-watching, botany and relaxation are the chief occupations for visitors. There is a nine-hole golf course at **Arinagour**. This village has the main concentration of population, a trim place which lies around the western shore of Loch Eatharna, with trim cottages and gardens.

Breachacha Castle, at the southern end of the island, is now used as the headquarters for an adventure training school. The later (new) castle dates from 1750 and was described by Johnson as 'a tradesman's box' and by Boswell as 'a neat gentleman's house'. It was heightened and baronialized in the mid-19th century and is now almost beyond hope of restoration.

The economy depends mainly on farming, commercial fishing and tourism. A recent innovation is a small factory in Arinagour where a range of herbal skin-care products is made.

Tiree

Tiree, southwest of Coll, is about 12 miles long, and 7 miles at its widest, dwindling to less than 1 mile at its narrowest. Its name comes from *Tir Eth* (Land of Corn), dating from the days when it supplied corn to Iona. It is so low and flat that it has the Gaelic nickname *Tir fo Thuinn* (Land Below the Waves). It used to be famous for its snipe, before much of the ground was drained. The highest hill, **Ben Hynish**, is a 480ft pimple. It shares with Coll a reputation for glorious beaches, abundant wild flowers and birds, as well as a high average of sunshine. This, with its magnificent Atlantic rollers, has earned it the title 'Hawaii of the North'. Windsurfers come from all over Britain to compete in Tiree where conditions are first rate. During championship weeks, world-class windsurfing can be watched. Tiree also has a phenomenal population of hares.

Sandaig Museum (*open June–Sept Mon–Fri 2–4*) is in a restored thatched cottage, with exhibits of island life.

A standing stone near **Balinoe** is thought to have been part of a Druid temple. Many of the island names are Norse in origin, dating from the 400 years of Norse occupation from about 890 to 1266. Among the many ancient remains scattered over Tiree is **Dun Mor Broch** on **Vaul Bay** on the north coast. A well-preserved ruin, it is one of the tall, hollow towers probably built for refuge from Norse and other invaders. It is 30ft in diameter, its walls as much as 13ft thick.

Gott Bay is a 3½-mile crescent of sand, backed by rich machair carpeted with wild flowers. **Hynish** has a small dry dock, flooded by an elaborate system of fresh water from springs. **Skerryvore Museum** (*open daylight hours*), in the old signal tower at Hynish, tells the story of the construction of the Skerryvore Lighthouse, visible at the end of a telescope, built by the father of Robert Louis Stevenson. There is a young people's outdoor training centre based in the lighthouse cottages. On the north shore of **Balephetrish**, another good beach, *Clac Choire* (Stone of the Corrie) is a large granite boulder perched on a rocky base, a relic from the Ice Age. Decorated with intriguing prehistoric carvings, it is known locally as the Ringing Stone because of the metallic note it produces when struck. It is said that when *Clac Choire* shatters, Tiree will sink below the waves.

Views are marvellous all around the coast, especially those to the Treshnish Islands to the east, with the aircraft-carrier-shaped *Bac Mor* (The Dutchman's Cap). One of the best places to see the birdlife is under the sheer cliffs below Carnan Mor in the south. Look for the distinctive 'greenstone' on the beaches, found also in Iona. Tiree has a nine-hole golf course.

Central Scotland

15

Central Scotland

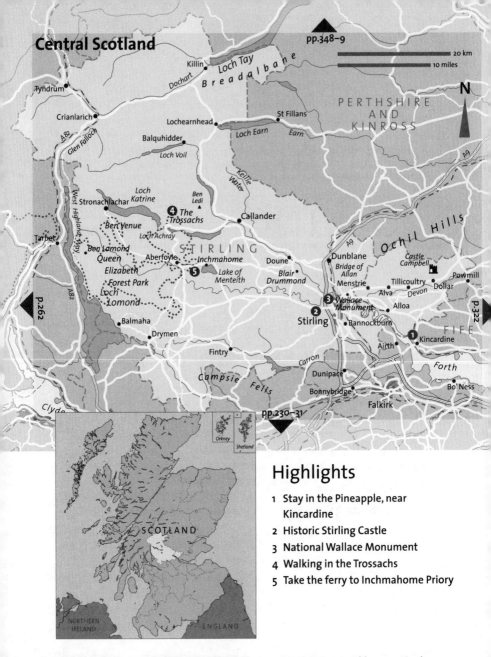

pp.348–9

20 km
10 miles

Tyndrum
Killin
Loch Tay
Dochart
Breadalbane

Crianlarich
Lochearnhead
St Fillans

PERTHSHIRE
AND
KINROSS

Balquhidder
Loch Earn
Earn

Clen Falloch
A82
Loch Voil

Kellie
Water

Loch
Katrine
Ben
Ledi

Stronachlachar
Loch Achray
4 The Trossachs
Callander

Ben Venue

Ben Lomond
Queen
Elizabeth
Forest Park
Loch
Lomond

West Highland Way

Tarbet

Aberfoyle
Inchmahome
5 Lake of Menteith
Doune

Blair
Drummond

STIRLING

Dunblane
Bridge of
Allan
Menstrie

Castle
Campbell

Ochil Hills

Tillicoultry
Alva
Devon
Powmill
Dollar

A9

3 Wallace Monument
Alloa

Balmaha

Drymen
2 Stirling
Bannockburn

Fintry

Airth
1 Kincardine

FIFE

Carron

Dunipace

Forth

Campsie Fells

Bonnybridge

Falkirk

Bo'Ness

Clyde

p.262

p.322

pp.230–31

N

Orkney
Shetland

SCOTLAND

NORTHERN
IRELAND
ENGLAND

Highlights

1 Stay in the Pineapple, near Kincardine
2 Historic Stirling Castle
3 National Wallace Monument
4 Walking in the Trossachs
5 Take the ferry to Inchmahome Priory

This is the heart of Scotland, with Stirling rearing up on a crag like a sentinel towards the east. Part of it is a densely populated industrial sprawl and part is flat and dreary, but there are many beauty spots and the long view is of hills all around and the promise of Highland scenery beyond. Small and compact, this area offers an astonishing variety of scenery, some of it lovely, but because it is so close to

Edinburgh and Glasgow it attracts many holiday-makers. The Trossachs, a subtle combination of loch, wooded slopes and crag backed by green and russet hills, are a magnet for tourists.

Within the protection of these hills, with no sea coast, the climate is gentle and often hot. Lush vegetation carpets the glens with vivid green ferns and mosses, and great slabs of forest – hardwood and conifer – climb the shoulders of the hills and give a glorious display in autumn. Further north is rugged moorland.

History

This was Pictland, home to those mysterious aboriginal settlers, indigenous long before the Irish Scots, the Angles and the Welsh began to push north, followed by the Romans, who built the Antonine Wall in AD 140. Hadrian's Wall, further south, had been built ten years previously but was not proving to be strong enough to deter the ferocious northerners. This new wall was built by Roman legionaries in a somewhat futile attempt to push the barbarians back and cut them off. It stretched 37 miles, from Old Kilpatrick on the Clyde to Bridgeness on the Forth, and you can see some of its best-preserved sections around Falkirk. If possible, go first to the Royal Museum of Scotland in Edinburgh or the Hunterian Museum in Glasgow, where there are excellent descriptions of how it was constructed as well as many relics. In spite of the enormous effort that went into the building of it, the wall was abandoned by the Romans after less than 25 years, and the Picts were left to their own devices.

Christianity crept in from the west, spread first by St Ninian's missionaries in the 4th century and then by those of St Columba in the 6th. The Picts were canny about change: you will find sacred stones carved with a combination of Christian and pagan symbols to appease any of their old gods who might be jealous. In the 9th century, when Kenneth Macalpine drew the Picts and Scots together, the Picts began to lose their identity as a dominant race and gradually faded from existence before their history could be recorded.

Stirling reflects the subsequent history of this central hub of Scotland: in 1297 William Wallace kindled the fire of rebellion against English suppression at Stirling Bridge, and Robert the Bruce refuelled the blaze in 1314 by defeating Edward II at Bannockburn. Stirling became a favourite royal residence, as well as an important fortress guarding one of the gateways to the Highlands. Prince Charles Edward Stuart wasted valuable time and resources laying siege to the castle in January 1746, but failed to capture it.

Today the region draws its wealth from the industrial belt in the southeast, from a thriving tourist trade, agriculture on the flat lands below the hills, and from sheep on the moors.

While you aren't likely to get the nose-to-tail traffic so familiar near popular resorts in England, you can expect frustration on twisting single-carriageway roads, when dozens of impatient drivers get trapped behind slow-moving, impassable caravans.

Falkirk, the Hillfoots and Stirling

The southern part of the Central Region around Falkirk is dominated by Stirling, on its cone of rock in the distance. Although not attractive, it is certainly dramatic, and contains unexpected treasures and a wealth of history. Beyond, where the Ochils guard the way north, fringed by the towns and villages of the Hillfoots, lie glens whose fast-flowing rivers once powered woollen mills supplied by sheep in the hills. In spite of its proximity to the industrial belt, this area has a peaceful, unspoilt charm.

Falkirk

Falkirk, deep in the heart of industrial Scotland, does not, on first acquaintance, tempt one to linger; but there is much history behind its modern face, and it should not be passed by too quickly. A pedestrian precinct within the High Street has made the town centre very much more attractive, and an enterprising council has plans for a number of other schemes that should revitalize the whole place. This is where the best-preserved sections of the Antonine Wall can be seen.

Falkirk was once one of the cattle drovers' main trysting places – it's hard to picture the scene now in the busy streets. Two battles were fought here: one in 1298, when William Wallace was defeated by Edward I, and one in 1746, when Prince Charles Edward Stuart, retreating north, turned to defeat the government forces who pursued him. His victory was partly due to the cowardice of the Hanoverian troops, many of whom, when confronted by the ferocity of the charging Highlanders, threw down their arms and fled.

Falkirk Museum (open Mon–Fri 10–5; April–Sept also Sun 2–5), in Orchard Street behind the main car park, is small but extremely interesting. Here you will find the history of the area, including a good section on the Antonine Wall, and details of the two battles. Prince Charles lodged in **Callendar House** (open Mon–Sat 10–5; April–Sept also Sun 2–5; adm), in Callendar Park, surrounded by woodland. This huge French château-style mansion has been restored to its former splendour. On display are a Georgian kitchen and an 1820s clockmaker, printer and general store. There is also a history of the house, a tearoom and gift shop. You can walk and play golf in the park.

The Antonine Wall

The Antonine Wall was an earth rampart consisting of a ditch with a military road running along its south side, and the displaced earth thrown up to create a wall on the north side. Forts were built at 2-mile intervals along its 37-mile length. A part of it can be seen in Callendar Park Housing Estate, to the east, and another at Watling Lodge, on the western outskirts of town by the canal. Here, just by the road, you can clearly see how the wall must have been, and there is a description board. To get the best idea of it, go to **Rough Castle**, well signposted 1½ miles from Bonnybridge, west of Falkirk (accessible at all times). Even the slag heaps that overshadow the plateau fail to detract from the queer feeling that you get, standing there thinking of those unfortunate legionaries, accustomed to gentler postings, condemned to this bleak place, menaced by a wild race of men who appeared from nowhere with blood-curdling war cries and primitive but lethal weapons. There are information boards to help the imagination, explaining where there was a fort, barracks, commander's house, granary, headquarters and a bathhouse.

North of Falkirk, and now closed, are the famous **Carron Ironworks**, a massive place founded in 1759, where Britain's cannons were once made. Robert Burns paid a visit to the works and was so horrified that he dashed off a quick verse:

We came na' here to view your works
In hopes to be mair wise,
But only lest we gang to hell
It may be no surprise!

West of Falkirk

The Carron Valley

The Carron Valley is surprisingly rural, even though it lies so close to the industrial belt. Five miles west of Falkirk, at Dunipace, the B818 takes you westwards along the River Carron for 6 miles to the reservoir. Just before this, a bridge reaches an island picnic spot, surrounded by the white tumult of the river. Less than a mile further on beyond the reservoir, just past Loch Walton, you can leave your car and walk across the bracken to the left to the Loup of Fintry. Here, the Endrick Water tumbles in long creaming falls to the valley below, filling the air with its noise and spray. **The Campsie Fells** guard the southwest of the Carron Valley, offering easy climbs with fine views.

Culcreuch Castle

Culcreuch, at Fintry 3 miles west of the falls, was built by the Galbraith clan in 1296. The Galbraiths lived here until their chief, Robert, had to flee to Ireland after a scandal in 1630. The castle has had various owners since then and is now a well-preserved mansion run as an hotel (*see p.304*), with the old keep incorporated. There is parkland, a walled garden, pinetum and loch.

North of Falkirk to the Hillfoots

The Pineapple

Instead of going straight up to Stirling on the motorway, take the A905 4 miles north of Falkirk, past the road to Kincardine Bridge. Past the Airth Castle Hotel turn off left on the B9124. Not far along the road, a clear sign directs you to The Pineapple (*grounds open 9.30–sunset*), an amazing garden folly, built as a retreat on the Dunmore estate in 1761. This is a relic from the times when the privileged classes could indulge their fancies with the help of a large labour force. A double wall

Central Scotland

304 Central Scotland

Tourist Information

Falkirk: The Steeple, High Street, **t** (01324) 620 244, **f** 638 440; *open all year.*
Stirling: 14 Dumbarton Road, **t** (01786) 475 019, **f** 450 039, *www.visitscottishheartlands.org*; *open all year.*
Open-top Heritage Bus Tour, **t** (01786) 475 019/479 901 (*summer only*).
Dunblane: Stirling Road, **t** (01786) 824 428; *open May–Sept.*

Festivals

July: Tartan Festival Fortnight, Stirling; celebration of all things Scottish, with dancing, ceilidhs, concerts, guided walks, medieval street stalls, period costumes and buskers. **Agricultural Show**, Doune and Dunblane.
August: Strathallan Highland Games, Bridge of Allan.

Shopping

Paton's Mill, Lower Mill Street, Tillicoultry. The place to buy Glen Gordon knitwear.
Sterling Mill, Tillicoultry. Built in 1846. Used as a barracks in the First World War, then a paper mill. Now a furniture warehouse, with gallery, shop, garden centre and restaurant.
Inverallan Hand Knitters, Shavelhaugh Loan, Alva. The largest hand-knitting company in Europe, employing about 2,000 knitters who work at home. Their patterns go back to AD 830 and are found in the *Book of Kells.*

Sports and Activities

Mariner Leisure Centre, Camelon, Falkirk. Pool with tropical décor and wave machine, chute, saunas, solarium, squash, multi-gym and restaurants. *Open daily 9am–11pm.*

Megazone, 104 Grahams Road, Falkirk, **t** (01324) 634 828. Laser game centre, with enemy players. *Open Mon 4pm–10pm, Tues–Fri 12–10pm, Sat and Sun 10am–10pm.*
Rainbow Slides Leisure Centre, Goosecroft Road, Stirling. Over 200 metres of translucent spiral water tubes filled with lighting and sound effects. Also a pool, solarium, sauna, steam room and café. *Open daily.*

Where to Stay and Eat

Gean House Hotel and Conference Centre, Alloa, **t** (01259) 219 275, **f** 226 411, *www.enterpriseaccommodation.co.uk* (*expensive*). Up-market hotel not just for conferences. Very luxurious and pampering.
Radisson SAS Airth Castle Hotel, near Kincardine, **t** (01324) 831 411, **f** 831 419, *www.radisson.com/stirlingshireuk* (*expensive*). The castle's history goes back to the early 14th century, but conversion to an hotel has somehow robbed it of any historical feeling, though it is extremely comfortable. Excellent food in the Dungeon Bar and restaurant. There's a health club and swimming pool and they'll organise 'Scottish pursuits' for you.
Black Bull Hotel, The Square, Killearn, **t** (01360) 550 215 (*moderate*). Very good food, great atmosphere and comfortable rooms.
Castle Campbell Hotel, Bridge Street, Dollar, **t/f** (01259) 742 519 (*moderate*). Very nice, small hotel right beside the Dollar Burn. Friendly and good value.
Culcreuch Castle, Fintry, **t** (01360) 860 555, **f** 860 556, *www.culcreuch.com* (*moderate*). 14th-century castle (*see p.303*), log-fire cosy and quirky, without pretentious frills, in 1,600 acres of parkland, with free fishing. There are four-posters, a dungeon, dining room/bar and sports centre, and eight Scandanavian-style lodges for self-catering.

surrounds a 14-acre garden, the space between the walls being for the circulation of hot air from furnaces. On top of the north wall is a vast stone pineapple, 45ft high, whose interior forms the domed roof of a circular chamber below. Pineapples were grown here in 1761, under hothouse conditions in the buildings flanking this centrepiece, with an army of stokers beavering away to feed the fires that provided the necessary heat. The buildings are now converted into a holiday home (*see above*).

Glenmiln House, Campsie Glen, t (01360) 311 322, f 310 501 (*moderate*). A Wolsey Lodge at the foot of the Campsie Fells in rural surroundings. Friendly and comfortable.

Harviestoun Country Hotel and Restaurant, Tillicoultry, t (01259) 752 522, f 752 523, *www.harviestouncountryhotel.com* (*moderate*). Small hotel in converted listed buildings below the Ochil Hills, with restaurant, coffee/gift shop and conference centre.

The Pineapple, near Kincardine, t (01628) 825 920, *see* p.303. A folly which you can rent for self-catering holidays through the Landmark Trust.

Strathallan Hotel, Chapel Place, Dollar t (01259) 742 205. Good pub food.

Unicorn Inn, Kincardine, t (01259) 730 704. Excise Street, near the bridge. A place to drive out of your way for: wonderful atmosphere and delicious food, especially the seafood. Spanish flavour.

Whinsmuir Country Inn, Powmill, t (01577) 840 595. Great meals in a relaxed, friendly atmosphere.

The Woolpack, Tillycoultry. Splendid old pub.

Stirling t (01786–)

Cromlix House, Dunblane, t 822 125, f 825 450, *www.cromlixhouse.com* (*expensive*). Typical large Victorian country house, imaginatively refurbished. It is luxuriously comfortable, the food, service and hospitality are excellent, and it has a magnificent chapel.

Hilton Dunblane Hydro Hotel, Dunblane, t 822 551, f 825 403, *www.dunblane.hilton.com* (*expensive*). Large, neo-Victorian hotel in 44 acres, comfortable and convenient in a grand setting with spectacular views. Indoor swimming pool, a whirlpool spa and sauna, all-weather tennis, crazy golf, an adventure playground and a gymnasium.

Stirling Highland Hotel, Spittal Street, Stirling, t 272 727, f 272 829 (*expensive*). The old High School, done up to the very highest standards of a luxury hotel, with leisure complex and a choice of restaurants.

Royal Hotel, Bridge of Allan, t 832 284, f 834 377, *www.royal-stirling.co.uk* (*expensive–moderate*). Newly done up, very luxurious and comfortable in the town centre.

Golden Lion Milton Hotel, King Street, Stirling, freephone t 0808 100 5556, f 469 400, *www.miltonhotels.com* (*moderate*). Dependable hotel. The décor is a bit glitzy for its 1786 origins, but it is comfortable and the food is good.

Kippenross, Dunblane, t 824 048, f 823 124 (*moderate*). Georgian house in a small family estate a mile outside Dunblane in delightful grounds. A Wolsey Lodge, it is comfortable and hospitable with good food. No smoking.

Mackeanston House, Doune, t 850 213, f 850 414 (*moderate*). A 17th-century farmhouse, with all the high standards of a Wolsey Lodge combined with a host who plays the pipes and a hostess who is an inspired cook.

Park Lodge Hotel, 32 Park Terrace, Stirling, t 474 862, f 449 748, *www.parklodge.net* (*moderate*). Partly Victorian, partly Georgian, charming mansion overlooking the park and Castle, in nice gardens. Some of the rooms are replicas of period rooms, with antique furniture and drapes, old paintings and ornaments, and there is a four-poster. *Haute cuisine* is on offer, and there's a good wine cellar.

Stirling Arms Hotel, Dunblane, t 822 156, f 825 300 (*moderate*). 17th-century coaching inn on the banks of the Allan Water. Good food in the Oak Room Restaurant.

West Plean, Denny Road, Stirling, t 812 208, f 480 550 (*cheap*). Charming farmhouse where you will be cosseted, kept cosy and well fed.

Cross Keys Hotel and Bar, Kippen, t 870 293. Splendid cheap pub food and grander meals.

Rumbling Bridge

It would be all too easy to cross the River Devon at Rumbling Bridge and miss the significance of its name, so narrow and steep is the gorge as you cross the bridge by car. A gate by the bridge gives access to steps, from where you can see this breathtaking chasm, 120ft deep and so narrow in places that you could shake hands with someone on the far side, if you were both acrobats.

The gorge was formed by the fast-moving water of melting ice sheets at the end of the last Ice Age, about 10,000 years ago. From an observation point, well fenced, you can see how the present bridge, built in 1816, spans the older one, built in 1713, with a queer, leap-frog effect. The lower bridge is an alarmingly narrow stone span lacking any sort of parapet, and this was once the main highway.

A securely fenced path, built by sappers, winds along the river from the bridge. Trees cling tenaciously to the steep limestone rock face of the gorge, as well as vivid green ferns, mosses and trailing vines, with the river rumbling over the rocks far below.

A short distance up from the bridge is **Maceachin's Cave**, a truly romantic spot where an escaping Jacobite, Hector Maceachin, hid after Culloden in 1746, having escaped from Castle Campbell (*see* below). He was hidden by the daughter of the local laird, Hannah Haig. How could they not have fallen in love in this wonderful setting? They did: and were married. You can walk a short distance up to Devil's Mill, where the thumping of the water on the boulders sounds like a mill grinding; it is so called because it didn't even stop for the Sabbath. Downstream from the bridge you get to **Cauldron Linn**, a double waterfall, impressive after rain.

Castle Campbell

Open April–Sept Mon–Sat 9.30–6.30, Sun 2–6.30; Oct–Mar Mon–Wed and Sat 9.30–4.30, Thurs 9.30–12.30, Sun 2–4.30; adm.

Castle Campbell is 3 miles west of Rumbling Bridge and a mile north of Dollar. Use a map and look out for the Historic Scotland signs, for the castle is not well signposted. Try to go on a fine day, preferably in autumn. The reasonably agile can park at the bottom, instead of driving up the rough track to the car park, and take the footpath up the burn, through steep, mossy, wooded banks; a secret place overhung with ferns where you must watch where you walk. The path crosses narrow foot bridges, offering sudden glimpses of cascading water through rocky ravines. Ahead, high up and apparently inaccessible, the castle soars in lofty isolation on a spur above the wooded ravines of the Burn of Care and the Burn of Sorrow, backed by a crescent of bracken-covered hills, which are copper-coloured in autumn. Enigmatically, the castle was once called *The Gloume* (Gloom), yet even with the dismal names of the two burns, it is the least gloomy of any place in the world. Seen in sunlight, with the trees at their autumnal best, it is a castle of enchantment.

The present castle dates from the 15th century, built on the site of an earlier fortress and acquired in marriage by the Campbells of Argyll, who changed its forbidding name by Act of Parliament in 1489. John Knox preached here in 1556, on the grassy slope now called Knox's Pulpit. Montrose's army tried (and failed) to take the castle in 1645. (Some of his troops, of the Maclean Clan, having a private feud with the Campbells, wanted an excuse to burn it.) General Monk was also here, nine years later, and his troops made a better job of destruction. A vaulted 'pend' leads into the court-yard, and a substantial amount of the ruin is intact. In the tower is the great hall with the entrance to the pit prison, on the right of the fireplace. From the roof there are views down across Dollar Glen and up into the hills.

The Hillfoots

The Hillfoot villages, strung out westwards from Rumbling Bridge under the Ochils, provide a scenic setting for the **Mill Trail Visitor Centre** (*open Jan–June and Oct–Dec daily 10–5; July–Sept daily 9–6*), where you can trace the history of the development of the woollen industry in Clackmannanshire. There is an audiovisual show, and gift, coffee and woollens shops. The villages of **Dollar**, **Tillicoultry**, **Alva** and **Menstrie** grew up at the foot of the Ochils, above the marshy bog of the plain, in the 16th century. The good grazing of the hills and the pure, soft water of the burns that ran down to feed the River Devon, were ideal for the foundation of what was to become a world-famous woollen industry, with easy access to the markets in Stirling, Edinburgh, Glasgow and Perth. As you follow the Mill Heritage Trail westwards from Dollar to Stirling, take time off to walk up any of the glens that run north into the Ochils, where the burns that used to drive the mills cascade downwards. The hills beyond are haunted by the ghosts of Covenanters who took refuge here.

Dollar is best known for its Academy, one of Scotland's leading schools, once called MacNabb's School. John MacNabb, who died at the beginning of the 19th century, was a local boy who made a fortune at sea and returned to his native land to share his wealth. The village straddles the tree-lined River Devon, with stone cottages whose gardens shout with colour in the summer, and Castle Campbell, high on its crag, floodlit at night – a most impressive sight. Dollar's milling tradition was the least developed in the Hillfoot villages, possibly because the local landowners were reluctant to encourage industry so close to the prestigious school. **Brunt Mill**, by the burn above the village, was built in 1820 and now belongs to the Academy.

Tillicoultry, less than 3 miles to the west, at the heart of the Mill Trail, has the **Clock Mill Heritage Centre** with all the information you could want: looms, workshops and an audiovisual show. There is also a tourist information centre. This village was producing cloth in Mary, Queen of Scots' day, and their coarse, hand-woven cloth became known nationally as Tillicoultry Serge.

Devon Way is a pleasant low-level, 3-mile walk, well signposted along the route of the old railway linking Dollar and Tillicoultry. **Mill Glen**, which you get to from the top of Upper Mill Street, takes you to Upper Glen and a string of waterfalls.

Alva, a couple of miles or so further west, is dominated by the massive six-storey Strude Mill, built in 1827 when the cottage-based woollen industry was being taken over by factories. If you walk up Alva Glen you see traces of a complex water system of pipes, weirs and overflow channels, once used to feed the waterwheel of the mill. There are several mill shops.

Menstrie, a couple of miles west of Alva, is another of the Hillfoot villages with a milling tradition. **Menstrie Castle** (*open Easter Sat and Sun 2–4; May–Sept Wed–Sun 2–4*) is a 16th-century tower house. It has been rather over-enthusiastically restored and rises from the middle of a housing development like a toy fort on the nursery floor amidst a clutter that should have been tidied away. It contains a Nova Scotia Exhibition Room, run by the National Trust for Scotland in honour of Sir William Alexander, who was born here. He was sent off to found a Scots colony in Canada in

1621, as a reward for his services to the Crown. He was an indifferent poet and an unpopular Secretary of State for Scotland, and one thing he would never have permitted is the building of a modern housing estate on his doorstep.

Still going west towards Stirling on the A91, just beyond Menstrie, look for a concealed entrance signed 'The Square'. This leads to the tiny village of **Blairlogie**, a delightful huddle of pretty old houses and a whitewashed church, built along narrow, winding streets on a ledge below the Ochils among orchards and colourful gardens. Blairlogie is one of the first of the Hillfoot communities. It grew up around its castle, a sturdy little fortress on a shelf above the village (*not open to the public*).

Alloa, 4½ miles southwest of Tillycoultry, has a fine medieval tower, **Alloa Tower**, in Alloa Park (*open April–Sept daily 1.30–5.30; Oct Sat and Sun 1.30–5.30; adm*). Recently restored and furnished with 18th-century interiors, this is one of Scotland's largest surviving 14th-century keeps, complete with its original dungeon and roof beams. This was once a stronghold of the Earls of Mar. Mary, Queen of Scots stayed here as a child, as did her son James and his son Henry. Mary returned here when she was married to Darnley.

Stirling

Stirling, backed by the Ochils, beckons to you from whichever way you approach. It rises abruptly from the flat plains: a fortress-crowned rock with a grey town clinging to its steep sides – a colourful, blood-stained history book. Because of its strategic position, guarding the route north, this was a fortress town since earliest times; bitterly fought over, bravely defended. Seven battlefields, including Bannockburn, lie within its shadow. Stuart monarchs held court here. In 1746 Prince Charles wasted precious time and equipment besieging it. The history of the town is encapsulated in the castle.

Stirling has flung itself into tourism with wholehearted gusto. (Some of this gusto, unfortunately, has allowed insensitive development to spoil parts of it, particularly around the station.) It is the ideal centre for a holiday, if you like plenty of organized fun. For the entire summer the town is ablaze with colour and excitement, humming with every sort of entertainment, exhibition and event, decorated with flowers and banners. There is an **Orientation Centre** opposite the Castle Esplanade, where you can find out exactly what is on offer. During the summer, an antique open-topped bus links the Old Town with the commercial centre.

Stirling Castle

Open April–Sept daily 9.30–6; Oct–Mar daily 9.30–5;
adm; ticket includes entry to the Argyll and Sutherland
Highlanders Museum in the Castle, and to Argyll's Lodging
in Castle Wynd.

Stirling Castle stands aloof above all the summer frivolity at its feet. Run by Historic Scotland, the Castle includes the **Royal Burgh of Stirling Visitor Centre** on the Castle

Esplanade (*open Jan–Mar and Nov–Dec daily 9.30–5; April–June and Sept–Oct daily 9.30–6; July and Aug daily 9–6.30*), which is a good place to mug up on the story of Stirling, with a multilingual audiovisual show, and sound and light exhibition, as well as viewpoints, a shop and tourist information.

Legend credits King Arthur with having taken the Castle from the Saxons, adding a touch of romance to a stronghold that seems otherwise too solid for the chivalric wisps of Arthurian tales. What is certain is that Alexander I died here; Henry II took it as part-payment for the release of William the Lion after the Battle of Alnwick; and that same William died here in 1214. In those days it would have been built of timber, superseded by masonry in the 13th century. Continual alteration and restoration have resulted in the Castle seen today, most of it 15th- and 16th-century, with Renaissance architecture added by James IV and James V.

One of the Castle's many memorials to its history is the **Douglas Room** where in 1452 James II summoned the eighth Earl of Douglas, whom he suspected of disloyalty, stabbed him to death and threw his body out of the window at the end of the passage. Tradition held that a skeleton, found in the garden in 1797, was that of Douglas. You can't help feeling sorry for the frantic king, trying to heave the gory remains through the window.

In the **Chapel Royal**, nine-month-old Mary was crowned Queen of Scots in 1543, surrounded by scheming nobles and a miasma of conflicting loyalties and ambitions. Mary lived in the Castle until she was taken to France at the age of five. The chapel was rebuilt by her son, James VI/I, who was baptised here, and is now the Memorial Hall for the Argyll and Sutherland Highlanders, whose headquarters are in the Castle. In the **Argyll and Sutherland Highlanders Museum** there is a good collection of regimental memorabilia, with some 15 Victoria Crosses won by members of the regiment.

In the **Lions' Den**, outside the palace, James III and James IV both kept lions. Catching and shipping them must have presented a terrible problem for whoever had the job of supplying them.

Floodlit at night, the Castle is transformed into a fairy-tale setting, visible from miles away. Various stirring events take place periodically on the Esplanade: Beating the Retreat, solo piping, massed pipe bands, all enhanced by the historic setting. **Ladies Rock**, in the Castle cemetery (access from the Esplanade or Castle Wynd), was the favourite vantage point for watching the Royal Tournaments in the valley below. the **Star Pyramid** is in memory of all who were martyred seeking religious freedom.

The **Beheading Stone**, on Gowan Hill (access from Upper Castlehill), is now covered in an iron cage. This gruesome block is believed to have caught the blood of many an important offender, including former Regent Murdoch, Duke of Albany, in 1425, two of his sons and his father-in-law, the Earl of Lennox (*see* **History**, p.41) – part of James I's Albany cleansing regime when he achieved his majority.

The Old Town

The old part of Stirling town is clustered up the hill to the Castle: Spittal Street leads up to St John's Street and Broad Street, which converge at the top to form Castle Wynd. A number of historic buildings line the steep, narrow streets, including the

Church of the Holy Rude, built uphill with the choir elevated, where Mary of Guise was made Regent for Mary, and where James VI/I was crowned. **Mar's Wark**, at the top of Broad Street, is the remains of a palace that was started in 1570 by the Earl of Mar but never finished; it was mostly destroyed during the Jacobite rising in 1746.

Argyll's Lodging, in Castle Wynd (*open same times as the Castle, and included in Castle ticket*), is a splendid example of a complete 17th-century town house. It was built by Sir William Alexander, founder of Nova Scotia (*see* Menstrie, p.307), and went to the Argylls on his death. Set back through an iron gate into a forecourt, it has been well restored by Historic Scotland, authentically recreated by craftsmen following detailed inventories from the 9th Earl of Argyll who lived here in 1680.

Stirling Old Town Jail (*open April–Sept daily 9.30–5; Oct daily 9.30–4.30; Nov–Mar daily 9.30–3.30; adm*), in St John Street, has 'living history performances', original cells, life-like models and a good view from the roof. It is a good reconstruction of life in the Victorian jail, built to replace the ghastly old Tolbooth jail. There is a new exhibition showing the daily life of a prisoner in a modern prison.

The **Tolbooth and Mercat Cross**, in Broad Street, was built in 1703 by Sir William Bruce. The court house and jail were added in 1809. Now it is a popular music venue, with a year-round arts programme. The unicorn on top of the Mercat Cross is known locally as 'the puggy'. Look out for the famous statue of **Rob Roy MacGregor** in Corn Exchange, showing his exceptionally long arms.

The **Kings Knot** – very prominent on the low ground as you come in from the west off the A9 – an octagonal stepped mound now grassed over, was once part of the magnificent formal gardens laid out below the Castle in about 1630. Opposite (where you can now see houses, a golf course and a public park) was Kings Park, the royal hunting grounds.

Smith Art Gallery and Museum (*open Tues–Sat 10.30–5, Sun 2–5*), Dumbarton Road, was founded in 1874. It provides an excellent introduction to the history of Stirling, and a constantly changing programme of exhibitions, demonstrations and lectures.

Around Stirling

Bannockburn Heritage Centre

Sir Robert the Bruce at Bannockburn
Beat the English in every wheel and turn,
And made them fly in great dismay
From off the field without delay...

from '*The Battle of Bannockburn*', by William McGonagall

A visit to Bannockburn is more of an historical pilgrimage than a search for scenic beauty. From Stirling follow the signs for **Bannockburn Heritage Centre** (*site open all year; heritage centre, shop and café open Mar and Nov–Dec daily 11–4.30; April–Oct daily 10–5.30; adm*), not for Bannockburn. The Battle of Bannockburn took place in 1314, over an area that is now mostly housing, less than 2 miles from Stirling.

The heritage centre is on higher ground, to the southwest, at Borestone Brae, where Bruce is said to have set up his standard the evening before the battle. You can see fragments of the 'bored-stone' with its socket hole in the visitor centre, where an audiovisual theatre gives a history of the battle.

If you walk through the hedge from the car park, you come to the imposing **Robert the Bruce Memorial Statue**. Bruce was that great general who won his battle mounted on a pony, a golden circlet on his helmet to identify himself, armed only with a battle-axe. He instructed his men to dig man-traps all over the plain, disguised with branches, and to scatter iron spikes, or calthrops, over the field. Before the battle, Bruce's army knelt to receive a blessing from a friar who walked among them with a crucifix in his hands. Edward mistook the situation and thought they were begging for mercy. 'They are,' he was told, 'but from God, my liege, not from us. Yonder men will win the day or die upon the field.' And, as every good Scot knows, Robert sent 'proud Edward's army...homeward tae think again'.

National Wallace Monument

Open Jan–Feb and Nov–Dec daily 10.30–4;
Mar–May and Oct daily 10–5; June and Sept daily 10–6;
July and Aug daily 9.30–6.30; adm.

A visit to Stirling is not complete without going to see the Wallace Monument. One and a half miles northeast of town on top of the 360-foot-tall Abbey Craig, it is almost as much of a landmark as the Castle: a Victorian monster of a tower, 220ft high with a mighty bronze statue of Wallace set in its wall above the door.

A steep, zigzagging climb from the car park is punctuated with seats where you can rest. The five floors contain a 'battle tent' with the talking head of Wallace, his sword and the story of the Battle of Stirling Bridge in 1297, which he is said to have directed from the top of Abbey Craig. (In the film *Braveheart*, fact was submerged in extravaganza and among the many liberties taken with history was the reason for his success in this battle. The English were in a hurry and trying to economize: they attacked over the bridge, which was too narrow, instead of fording the river not far away. The dead piled up, blocking the way, and those who did manage to get over foundered in the marsh beyond, giving Wallace the victory.) There is a Hall of Scotland's Heroes, with marble busts. Don't be daunted if you can't recognize them all: an audiovisual presentation fills you in on each of them. There is a 360° diorama of the surrounding landscape with the history described, and you can climb to a parapet below the crown of the monument for dizzying views across the Carse of Forth to the Castle on its rocky eminence above Stirling town. From here you can see seven battlefields, each of which played an important part in Scotland's history: Cambuskeneth, Stirling Bridge, Falkirk (two battles), Bannockburn, Sauchieburn and Sheriffmuir. There is a shop and café, woodland walks and a picnic area.

To complete your historic tour, you should visit **Stirling Old Bridge**, a mile north of the town off Drip Road; or you can look down on it from the Monument. This 15th-century stone bridge was the lowest crossing point over the River Forth for about 400 years, until Stirling New Bridge was built in 1831. Today's Old Bridge replaced several earlier ones nearby, including the wooden one which was the focal point of William Wallace's victory (*see* above).

Bridge of Allan

A couple of miles north of Stirling, Bridge of Allan was a spa town in Victorian times, visited by fashionable people from near and far. The **Museum Hall** is a fine piece of architecture lying derelict in the centre of town. Essential repairs have been carried out and it is to be restored, though unfortunately it is most likely that it will become private dwellings and remain closed to the public. There are some pleasant riverside walks, to remind you of Burns' 'Banks of Allan Water'. The University of Stirling is southeast of the town in the grounds of Airthrey Castle, designed by Robert Adam.

Dunblane

Requiescant In Pace

In March 1996 a madman called Thomas Hamilton, about whom many people had already expressed misgivings, walked into a primary school with two pistols and killed 13 small children and their teacher, and wounded several more. This unbelievable tragedy put Dunblane on the world map, and resulted in emotive and radical restrictions being imposed on firearms' licensing.

Dunblane, 4 miles north of Stirling and bypassed by the A9, is a small town built around its ancient cathedral in the valley of the Allan Water. A narrow main street leads up to the cathedral close, with some fine old buildings around it.

The **Queen Victoria School**, on the northern outskirts of town, is a state-endowed boarding school for the sons of servicemen, run on military lines, where the boys receive both a good education and a firm discipline not always found in fee-paying public schools.

Dunblane Cathedral (*open April–Sept Mon–Sat 9.30–12.30 and 9.30–6, Sun 2–6; Oct–Mar Mon–Sat 9.30–12.30 and 1.30–4, Sun 2–4*) was founded in 600 by St Blane of Bute, grandson of King Aidan of Dalriada, and still has parts of the old Celtic church in its red sandstone walls. Most of the present cathedral was commissioned by Bishop Clement in the mid-13th century. The roof was stripped after the Reformation, but it was restored in 1892 and is now the parish church. This Gothic building has an oval window that you can only see from the outside, decorated with carved leaves and flowers and called the Ruskin Window because John Ruskin praised it. After a visit to the cathedral, he said: 'I know not anything so perfect in its simplicity, and so beautiful, as far as it reaches, in all the Gothic with which I am acquainted.'

Three poignant stone slabs in the cathedral are memorials to Margaret Drummond and her two sisters, all poisoned in 1502 by scheming nobles. James IV was in love with Margaret. (Some go further and say he was secretly married to her.) Politicians desired a union with England, and Margaret Drummond was a threat to this plan. Why her luckless sisters had to be eliminated as well remains a mystery – perhaps they all ate from the same dish. Within a year of this awful crime, James married 14-year-old Margaret Tudor and found himself the brother-in-law of bellicose Henry VIII.

The **Cathedral Museum and Library** (*open June–Sept Mon–Sat 10.30–12.30 and 1.30–4.30; donation box*) is in the cathedral close. The museum was the Dean's House, built in 1624, and displays local history.

Blair Drummond Safari and Adventure Park

Open April–Oct daily 10–4.30; adm.

Blair Drummond Safari Park is on the River Teith, 7 miles to the southwest. In one of Scotland's more enthusiastic attempts to cater for whole families on holiday, you can see lions, giraffes, tigers, hippopotami and other exotic animals, or take a boat trip on the lake and see a chimp island, or take a 'Flying Fox' cable slide across the lake. This children's bonanza includes aquatic mammal shows, a pets' corner, an adventure playground, a 3D 'Cinema 180', an 'Astraglide', picnic areas, shops, amusement arcades, restaurants and a bar for exhausted parents. The house, which is a school for disabled children, is not open to the public.

Doune

Doune, 3 miles west of Dunblane, is a small, winding village with wooded hills rising in folds to the north. Ironically (in the light of the terrible Dunblane shooting incident) in the 17th and 18th centuries this was an important pistol-making town, with three factories to support the industry, and the drove road linking Highlands and Lowlands for carrying the pistols to market. The coat of arms has crossed pistols on it.

Stand in the attractive, triangular market square and try to picture the scene when it was a 17th-century sheep and cattle market, to which people flocked from miles around. There would have been ramshackle stalls selling broth and ale; a press of wild-looking men from the hills, herding their beasts; smoke from fires; and the smell of animals and the unwashed. It was a living, seething scene, full of bawdy jokes and raucous laughter, with underlying tension and sharp eyes on the watch for trouble between Covenanters and soldiers.

The **Bridge** was apparently built by Robert Spittal in 1535. Spittal was tailor to the wife of James IV. (He also founded Spittal's Hospital in Stirling, so the Queen must have paid him well.) Spittal is said to have been refused passage on the ferry that preceded the bridge because he had no money on him. He built the bridge to spite the unfortunate ferryman.

The **Doune Motor Museum** (*open April–Nov daily 10–5; adm*) contains Lord Moray's collection of vintage cars, mostly in working order. The collection includes Hispano-Suiza, Bentley, Jaguar, Aston Martin, Lagonda and the second oldest Rolls-Royce in the world. There is a tarmac track, about a mile long, for racing hill climbs: during hill-climb weekends the Motor Museum and café are open only to people attending the climb. A number of other events take place here throughout the summer, including car rallies and radio-controlled aeroplane rallies.

Doune Castle

*Open April–Sept daily 9.30–6.30; Oct–Mar Mon–Wed and
Sat 9.30–4.30, Thurs 9.30–12.30, Sun 2–4.30; adm.*

Doune Castle is one of Scotland's best-preserved medieval castle ruins. Built in the 14th century by Robert, Duke of Albany, and his son, Murdoch, it was annexed by the Crown after the wholesale execution of the Albany family by James I. James IV gave it to his Queen, Margaret Tudor, who in turn passed it to her second husband, Henry Stuart, Lord Methven. Later it passed to the Earls of Moray who still own it; the Bonnie Earl of Moray who, in the ballad, came 'soondin' through the toon', lived here.

The gatehouse is a self-contained complex, complete with its own water supply in case of siege. Built around a large courtyard, it is protected by two rivers and a deep moat. A long, vaulted passage leads into the courtyard with a vaulted chamber on the right where Prince Charles put the prisoners he took at the Battle of Falkirk, having captured the castle. More recently it was used for the filming of the BBC production of *Ivanhoe*.

The **Lord's Hall**, on the first floor of the main tower, has two magnificent fireplaces side by side, and a window from the steward's room beyond the thick wall. Picture it when it was filled with smoke from the two blazing fires, with rushes on the floor, dogs squabbling over bones, and a throng of people jostling for attention from the nobles at the high table.

The gardens were created in the early 19th century by the tenth Earl of Moray. They include a walled garden, a pinetum, shrubs, and woodland walks through the glen.

The Trossachs

Callander

Once beyond Doune, you begin to feel the lure of the Highlands. Callander, 8 miles from Doune and a good holiday centre for this area, is a sturdy town to the east of the Trossachs, overshadowed by Ben Ledi. The town was rebuilt to its present wide design by military architects in the wake of Prince Charles, perhaps because it is easier for rebels to hold a town if the streets are narrow and houses close together. Older television addicts might experience a sense of *déjà vu*, for this was Dr Finlay's *Tannochbrae*. It also features in *The Country Diary of an Edwardian Lady*.

From here you are within easy reach of the Trossachs and invigorating walks up through wooded glens on to the moors, with streams and rivers rushing down to fill Loch Lubnaig and the River Teith. Walk up to the Bracklinn Falls and remind yourself that Sir Walter Scott once rode his horse across here for a bet: or to the Falls of Leny and watch out for the water sprites, dancing in the spray-mist.

In the summer Callander is the stage for a variety of entertainments such as organized ceilidhs, open-air pipe-band concerts and Highland dancing, as well as wild-life slide shows.

The **Rob Roy & Trossachs Visitor Centre** (*open Mar–May and Oct–Dec daily 10–5; June daily 9.30–6; July and Aug daily 9–7; Sept daily 10–6; Jan and Feb daily 11–4.30; adm to audiovisual & exhibition*), in Ancaster Square, tells the life of the Highland folk hero. There's traditional entertainment on summer evenings.

It has to be said that if it hadn't been for Sir Walter Scott, and to a lesser extent Wordsworth and his sister Dorothy, the Trossachs would never have appeared so indelibly on the tourist map. When *Lady of the Lake* was first read by an avid public, the Trossachs became the 'in' place for travellers to the north, and its overrated beauty became a legend. This 'beauty spot' image stuck, heartily endorsed by local inn keepers and hoteliers, assisted by its situation so conveniently close to the increasingly densely populated towns to the south.

There is no one particular thing to see in and around the Trossachs. The scenery is attractive if you have not already been spoiled by the Highlands. Preferably explored outside the tourist season, this area is best appreciated on foot. Even in the high season, most sightseers prefer to stay within sight of their cars and few are on the prowl before ten o'clock in the morning. Avoid weekends. You have only to make an early start and get away from the roads to shake off the feeling of claustrophobia that can attack when there are too many people. Autumn and early spring are the best time in this land of forested ravines and gullies.

Although people tend to refer to the whole of the area between Callander and Lochearnhead to the east, and Loch Lomond to the west, as the Trossachs, in fact the Trossachs proper is only the gorge that runs from Loch Achray to Loch Katrine, a rugged pass barely a mile long. Locals will give you two meanings for this strange name: 'bristly country' or 'the crossing place'; no one is sure which is correct. Thick woods often obscure the view, but now and then you get a hint of the magic that enchanted Sir Walter Scott. The road twists and climbs through gorse and bracken and very green moor, past rhododendrons, with plenty of footpaths leading off.

Loch Katrine

Loch Katrine, 9 miles west of Callander, is the setting for Walter Scott's *Lady of the Lake*. Ellen's Isle is named after the heroine of the poem. You can take a trip in the Victorian steamer *Sir Walter Scott* from Trossachs Pier to Stronachlachar (*see p.316*). As you watch the passing shore, picture fair Ellen being wooed by the mysterious James FitzJames, who bore a remarkable resemblance to James V, the monarch who enjoyed roaming the countryside disguised as the Goodman of Ballengiech. A prosaic guide will tell you that this loch is also Glasgow's water supply. Because of this, there is a large notice at the pier forbidding you to swim, paddle, picnic, fish, camp, light fires or throw coins in the loch (though why anyone should feel the urge to throw their money into a loch is a mystery). There is a café and souvenir shops at the pier.

To get the best view of the loch, forget the boat trip and put on your walking boots. There is an easy climb up **Ben Venue** (2,393ft) from Achray on the western shore of Loch Achray, about 8 miles west of Callander on the A827: it's about 5½ miles and takes under 5 hours. Take the track from behind the Loch Achray Hotel and head west

Tourist Information

Callander: Rob Roy & Trossachs Visitor Centre, Ancaster Square, t (01877) 330 342, f 330 784; *open Mar–Dec daily; Jan and Feb Sat and Sun*. **Aberfoyle**: t (01877) 382 352, f 382 153; *open April–Oct.*

Festivals

August: International Highland Games, Callander.

Sports and Activities

The Victorian steamer *Sir Walter Scott*, t (01877) 376 316, *www.lochkatrine.org.uk*. 45-minute cruises along Loch Katrine from Trossachs Pier to Stronachlachar. *Easter–Oct sailings from Trossachs Pier daily at 11 (exc Sat), 1.45 and 3.15.*

Where to Stay and Eat

Roman Camp Country House Hotel, Callander, t (01877) 300 003, f 331 533, *www.roman-camp-hotel.co.uk (expensive)*. In 20 acres of garden beside the River Teith, on which you can fish. Comfortable 17th-century hotel with Victorian and modern additions, once a hunting lodge of the Dukes of Perth. Good food. James Barrie once stayed.

Bridgend House Hotel, Bridge Street, Callander, t (01877) 330 130 *(moderate)*. Faces the road with a mock-Tudor face hiding an 18th-century heart. Views to Ben Ledi, four-poster beds and a pretty garden.

Creagan House, Strathyre, t (01877) 384 638, f 384 319, *mail@creaganhouse.fsnet.co.uk (moderate)*. A really cosy, friendly 'restaurant with rooms'. Delicious food.

Forest Hills Hotel, Kinlochard, near Aberfoyle, t (01877) 387277 *(moderate)*. Big country house hotel with plush leisure centre, including a swimming pool, set in 20 acres of informal gardens overlooking Loch Ard. Also luxury self-catering apartments.

Invertrossachs Country House, near Callander, t (01877) 331 126, f 331 229, *www.invertrossachs.co.uk (moderate)*. Large Edwardian house with lots of character on Loch Venachar, in 33 acres of woods and garden. Self-catering apartments also available to let.

through the Pass of Achray. There are various ways up, and it can be quite boggy in places, but the views from the two peaks make the climb worth while.

Aberfoyle

Aberfoyle guards the southern approach to the Trossachs and is a lively holiday centre. The road north, 'Duke's Pass', is too densely wooded to give more than a glimpse of the lochs below. Walter Scott made his first notes for *Rob Roy* in the dining room of the village manse.

The **Scottish Wool Centre** *(open daily; adm)* displays the history of sheep and wool in Scotland over 2,000 years, with films, sheepdog demonstrations, spinning and weaving, a children's farm, shop and restaurant.

The **Queen Elizabeth Forest Park Visitor Centre** *(Forest Drive open April and May–Sept; visitor centre Mar–Oct daily 10–6; Nov–Feb daily 11–4)* is a modern stone building just before you come down into Aberfoyle, with an ornamental lake and walks. In the lodge, displays illustrate the wildlife and vegetation of the 75,000-acre park to the west, and there is a shop and café. The park is very much 'Designer Highlands', groomed for the thousands of pairs of boots and bicycle wheels that traverse it each year, but there are still parts of it off the beaten trails, and some good hills to climb: Ben Lomond (3,192ft) and Ben Vrackie (1,922ft) are two of the best.

Lake Hotel, Port of Menteith, t (01877) 385 258, f 385 671, *www.lake-of-menteith-hotel.com* (*moderate*). Right on Scotland's only lake, looking across to Inchmahome. They've retained much of the Art Deco furniture and decor, and the food is good.

Lochearnhead Hotel, t (01567) 830 229, f 830 364, *gus@lochhot.freeserve.co.uk* (*moderate*). A family-run hotel right on the loch.

Stronvar House, Balquhidder, t (01877) 384 688, f 384 230, *www.stronvar.co.uk* (*moderate*). Splendid self-catering house in a laird's mansion with crow-stepped gables overlooking Loch Voil, 5 bedrooms, four-posters and a Bygones Museum (for guests only). The house has an intriguing history.

Brook Linn Country House, Callander, t/f (01877) 330 103, *derek@blinn. freeserve.co.uk* (*cheap*). Victorian house with spectacular views from a 2-acre garden, and the food isn't bad (the dining room is no smoking). *Only open May–Nov.*

Clachan Cottage Hotel, Lochearnhead, t (01567) 830 247, f 830 300, *www. clachancottagehotel.com* (*cheap*). Charming old white cottage overlooking Loch Earn, with lovely views. What it may lack in sophistication is made up for in atmosphere.

Leny House, near Callander, t/f (01877) 331 078, *www.lenyestate.com* (*cheap*). Country mansion in parkland with good views. Very comfortable and welcoming. Also a first-class range of self-catering establishments – of all sorts from capacious houses to tiny log cabins.

Monachyle Mhor, near Balquhidder, t (01877) 384 622, f 384 305, *www.monachylemhor.com* (*cheap*). Pink-harled farmhouse gem with nice views and the right atmosphere. Go for a room in the courtyard annexe if you can. Its public bar is a lively centre for the local community of an evening.

Norrieston, Thornhill, t (01786) 850 234, *sue.duke@btinternet.com* (*cheap*). Mrs Duke provides a warm, friendly welcome and exceptional self-catering in a wing of a charming house.

Ben Ledi Café, Callander. For an unpretentious, satisfying café meal.

The Byre, Brig o'Turk, t (01877) 376 292. Bar with blackboard menu, and restaurant.

The Café, Brig o'Turk, t (01877) 376 267. Good plain food.

Myrtle Inn, just south of Callander on A84, t (01877) 330 919. A good place for a meal.

Inchmahome Priory

Always accessible, but the weather dictates the running of the ferry, for which you pay. Ferry runs April–Sept daily 9.30–6.30; last trip home 7pm; t (01877) 385 294.

Before going on north from Callander, follow the A81 6 miles southwest to Lake of Menteith and take the ferry to Inchmahome Priory, a semi-roofed ruin on the largest island of the three on the lake. Founded for Augustinians in 1238, the priory was a refuge for Mary, Queen of Scots for a short while before she was sent off to France to grow up out of range of Henry VIII's 'Rough Wooing'. It is nice to think of the little girl in the garden now called Queen Mary's Bower, playing hide-and-seek, perhaps, with the indulgent monks.

A surprising number of pilgrims come here to see the grave of Robert Cunninghame Graham, the 'rebel laird' of the estate, who died in Buenos Aires in 1936 aged 84. This flamboyant character travelled extensively in South America, Spain and Morocco; married a Chilean poetess; was imprisoned for 'illegal assembly' in 1887 (a Socialist demo in Trafalgar Square); was elected first president of the Scottish Labour Party in 1888; and wrote many travel books, essays and short stories. He was a close friend of both Joseph Conrad and W. H. Hudson.

The **Farmlife Centre** (*open May–Oct daily; adm*) at Dunaverig Farm, 2 miles west of Thornhill, has traditional farm buildings with old farm implements, machinery and memorabilia, farm animals, adventure playground, nature trails, shop and tearoom.

Balquhidder

A famous man is Robin Hood,
The English ballad-singer's joy!
And Scotland has a thief as good,
An outlaw of as daring mood;
She has her brave Rob Roy...

from 'Rob Roy's Grave', by William Wordsworth

Another popular literary association in this area is at Balquhidder on Loch Voil, north of the Trossachs, 10 miles or so north of Callander, and just west of the A84. This is where **Rob Roy** lived, died and is buried. This colourful, Robin Hood-like character, much romanticized by both Sir Walter Scott and Liam Neeson, lived between 1671 and 1734, son of Macgregor of Glengyle. Rob Roy started life peacefully enough as a herdsman, but the Macgregors had been outlawed for their bloodthirsty habits and life was hard. He took to cattle rustling and smuggling, robbing the rich to pay the poor, and legends of his daring escapades and narrow escapes around Loch Katrine make good reading and stirring films, even if, in reality, he was no doubt a rogue and a menace to his neighbours. He died uncharacteristically in his bed and was buried in Balquhidder churchyard. You can't miss the grave: Clan Gregor have been unable to resist the temptation to 'do it up'. The 'MacGregor Despite Them' refers to the proscription of the clan.

Lochearnhead

Fourteen miles north of Callander on the A84, you come to Lochearnhead, on the western corner of Loch Earn. There are several good hotels here, and a boating and water-skiing centre. The loch runs 7 miles east to St Fillans, a ribbon of water sheltered by hills, and an ideal place for a holiday.

Breadalbane

Called after the Earls of Breadalbane (pronounced Bred-awl-bn, with the emphasis on the middle syllable) who used to own most of it, the land north of the Trossachs is your overture to the Highlands. In the days before the clan system was abolished, many bitter battles were fought for supremacy over these hills and moors. Campbells, MacNabs, MacGregors and MacLarens contested every inch, committing ghastly atrocities to wreak revenge on each other. You are likely to find a different sort of tourist here: more energetic, striding out with knapsack and climbing boots. It is rugged territory, where you may see roe deer and golden eagles, tumbling rivers, spectacular falls and dark lochs. For botanists there are masses of wild flowers and unusual plants. Cut by the glens of the rivers Dochart and Lochay, and veined by the network of burns that pour out of the hills to feed them, this is walking and climbing country, backed by the massive hills of Strathclyde to the northwest.

Killin

Killin is about 7 miles north of Lochearnhead, a couple of miles off the A85 on the A827. White-harled cottages with pretty gardens, jolly hotels and eating places, and tartan-hung tourist traps add to the picture-postcard scene. When snow lies on the hills there is an almost alpine feel. It sits astride an old bridge, under which the Falls of Dochart carry the River Dochart in a tumble of falls and rapids, swirling down through the village into Loch Tay, long and deep between two ranges of hills.

On **Inchbuie** (or Innes Bhuidhe, the Yellow Island), the lower of two islets below the old bridge in Killin, is the burial ground of the MacNabs, an aggressive clan who ruled the district until they emigrated to Canada in the 19th century, forever at loggerheads with the neighbouring clans of Neish and Gregor. The Breadalbane Centre has the key to the burial ground. St Fillan, who died around AD 777, is thought to have lived nearby, and the centre displays eight 'healing stones' that bear his name. Each stone represents the part of the body it will heal.

The **Breadalbane Folklore Centre** (*open Mar–May and Oct daily 10–5; June and Sept daily 10–6; July and Aug daily 9.30–6.30; Feb Sat and Sun 10–4; closed Nov–Jan; adm*) gives a good insight into the life and legends of Breadalbane, covering the history of the leading clans of the area, stories of the saints, and details of flora and fauna.

Finlarig Castle, hidden among trees on a primrose-carpeted mound, half a mile north of Killin past the cemetery, is a dangerous ruin now. It was the seat of the sinister-sounding Black Duncan of the Cowl, a fierce Campbell chief. All that remains is a stark keep and a separate building with a coat of arms on it, possibly a chapel. Close to the tower, you can still see a gruesome 'beheading-pit'. It is said that it was the privilege of the gentry to be beheaded, while the common people were hanged from a tree. Beyond the ruin are two 20th-century graves with simple Celtic crosses: Sir Gavin Campbell, Marquess of Breadalbane, and his wife of 50 years, Lady Alma.

Crianlarich

From Killin the A85 goes about 11 miles southwest to Crianlarich, tucked in among the moors. Isolated but by no means deserted, it has the somewhat incongruously urban-sounding title of 'railway junction'. This is where the railway lines from Oban and Fort William join up on their progress south. The West Highland Line, from Glasgow to Mallaig, takes you through such glorious scenery that it is worth travelling on it for the journey itself. The station is unmanned and rather ramshackle now, but in its midst, like an oasis in the desert, is a cosy café where travellers waiting for a connection sit contentedly munching bacon butties and drinking hot coffee.

There are usually a number of knapsack-burdened people striding around Crianlarich in climbing boots and anoraks: the 90-mile West Highland Way passes by on its way from Milngavie (pronounced Mull-guy) to Fort William, and this is a

Tourist Information

Killin: Breadalbane Folklore Centre, Falls of Dochart, **t** (01567) 820 254, **f** 820 764; *open Mar–Nov daily; Dec–Feb Sat and Sun only*.

Tyndrum: Main Street, **t** (01838) 400 246, **f** 400 530; *open April–Oct*.

Where to Stay and Eat

Ardeonaig Hotel, near Killin, **t** (01567) 820 400, **f** 820 282, *www.ardeonaighotel.co.uk* (*moderate*). A former drovers' inn (1680), on the south side of Loch Tay.

Morenish Lodge Hotel, near Killin, **t/f** (01567) 820 258, *www.morenishlodgehotel.co.uk* (*moderate*). Built in 1750 as a shooting lodge for the Earl of Breadalbane, looking south over Loch Tay with Ben Lawers to the north. A comfortable, attractive haven with pretty rooms, good food and charming owners.

Falls of Dochart Hotel, Killin, **t** (01567) 820 270, **f** 820 439 (*cheap*). Good value hotel overlooking the bridge. The rooms are all en suite, and there's a cosy bar/restaurant, the Salmon Lie (*cheap*), in a converted smithy, with stone walls, a log stove and very reasonable food.

Invervey Hotel, Tyndrum, **t** (01838) 400 219, **f** 400 280 (*cheap*). A friendly, family-run hotel, convivial and lively.

Lodge House, Crianlarich, **t** (01838) 300 276, *www.lodgehouse.co.uk* (*cheap*). A good place for walkers, situated on a knoll beside the road.

Morenish House, near Killin, **t** (01567) 820 220 (*cheap*). The nicest self-catering place in the area, on the north side of Loch Tay in an old farmhouse beautifully converted and equipped.

Portnellan Lodges, Crianlarich, **t** (01838) 300 284, **f** 300 332, *www.portnellan.co.uk*. Very well-equipped self-catering lodges and cottages with splendid views (sleeping 2–8). Bar/club room available, as well as fishing, boating, bikes, canoes and golf.

favourite staging post. Three road-routes also meet in Crianlarich: south to Loch Lomond, northwest to Oban and Fort William, and northeast to Pitlochry.

Tyndrum

Tyndrum is 5 miles north on the A82, nestling in a glacial valley and another junction of three roads, south, north and west, where the cattle drovers used to meet up on their way to markets at Falkirk and Crieff. Some years ago this tiny settlement acquired 'gold rush' status. Extensive gold mining in the area led to the speculation that this was about to become an important gold centre in Britain, and some rather 'utility' accommodation was built. The gold fever seems to have died down now, though you may occasionally find a loner, hopefully panning. The emphasis has shifted to tourism, and some outsized hotels have been built to the detriment of the scenery. This is now a place to stop off en route to the western Highlands and for walkers and climbers. There are walks in all directions, and well over a dozen Monros within conquering distance: take a good map, stick to the accepted codes of practice, and you can spend happy weeks in these hills.

Fife

Fife

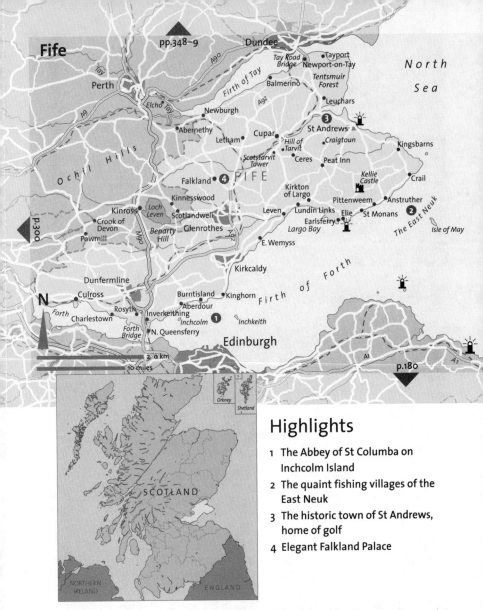

pp.348-9

North Sea

Dundee
Tay Road Bridge
Tayport
Newport-on-Tay
Tentsmuir Forest
Balmerino
Leuchars
Perth
Elcho
Newburgh
3 St Andrews
Craigtoun
Kingsbarns
Abernethy
Cupar
Hill of Tarvit
Letham
Scotstarvit Tower
Ceres
Peat Inn
Crail
Ochil Hills
Falkland **4** FIFE
Kellie Castle
Kinnesswood
Kirkton of Largo
Pittenweem
Anstruther
Kinross
Loch Leven
Scotlandwell
Leven
Lundin Links
Elie
St Monans **2**
Crook of Devon
Beparty Hill
Glenrothes
Earlsferry
Largo Bay
The East Neuk
Powmill
E. Wemyss
Isle of May
Kirkcaldy
Firth of Forth
Dunfermline
Culross
Burntisland
Kinghorn
Aberdour
N
Forth
Charlestown
Rosyth
Inverkeithing
Inchcolm **1**
Inchkeith
Forth Bridge
N. Queensferry
Edinburgh

2 0 km
10 miles

p.180

Orkney
Shetland

SCOTLAND

NORTHERN IRELAND
ENGLAND

Highlights

1 The Abbey of St Columba on Inchcolm Island
2 The quaint fishing villages of the East Neuk
3 The historic town of St Andrews, home of golf
4 Elegant Falkland Palace

Fife sticks out between the Firth of Forth and the Firth of Tay, thrusting its nose into the North Sea like the head of an aggressive Scottie dog, with the M90 as its collar, Dunfermline as its name-tag and St Andrews as its beady eyes. Bordered thus on three sides by water, it has a disproportionate coastline for its size. Industrial towns in the south give way to fishing villages around the East Neuk, strung out along miles of sandy beaches. Filmgoers may recognize the sands around St Andrews as those used for the running scenes in *Chariots of Fire*. A flattish landscape of open spaces and vast skies with sweeping views over farmland and clumps of trees is broken by humps like Largo Law, and the Lomond Hills on the western boundary. A network of rivers, lochs and reservoirs provides agricultural irrigation and some fishing. You won't find dramatic scenery, but Fife has an elusive charm. The Tay supports the remnants of the salmon netting industry and has abundant wildlife. Fife takes its share of battering when the wind is in the east, but it has a higher average of sunshine and less rainfall than most of the rest of Britain.

Abernethy, just over the border in Perthshire, was once a Pictish capital, whose overspill left many prehistoric sites to be excavated in the whole area. Two of Fife's towns have an ancient history: Dunfermline was the capital in the 11th century, and some say St Andrews received the shipwrecked remains of that saint in the 4th century. Geographically isolated, this used to be a region people went to, but not through, until the Tay Road Bridge was opened in 1966. When new boundaries were planned in 1975, Fife was to be split horizontally, one half to become part of Tayside and the other part of Lothian. But the planners reckoned without the people of Fife, who protested so violently that they remained intact. There were once seven Celtic kingdoms, now there is only one. With the recent revision of regions, proud little Fife has retained her identity and reverted to her ancient title: The Kingdom of Fife.

Coal mining and heavy and light industry in the southwest corner give way to agriculture in the fertile hinterland. Fishing is still a way of life for some. Tourism, especially around the coast, plays an important part in the economy, including, as everyone knows, golf.

The South Coast

The south coast of Fife is the northern shore of the Firth of Forth, a string of industrial towns and villages whose people have toiled in coal mines and dockyards, factories and fishing boats. (The holiday resorts that serve these towns are popular in the summer; on a hot day their beaches can be as overcrowded as those of the Costa Brava.) Among the sprawl of utility buildings, there lurk hidden gems.

Culross

Going anticlockwise around the coast, the first stop will be at Culross (pronounced Coo-rus). This miniature town on the shore of the Firth of Forth has been restored by the National Trust for Scotland over the past 50 years. A showpiece Royal Burgh of the 16th and 17th centuries, it looks almost exactly as it must have done in those days, though, like most museums, it can never replicate the smell and teeming, boisterous splurge of life as it was.

Culross was once one of the largest ports in Scotland, comparable in importance to Liverpool. It traded in coal, iron, fish, hand-loom weaving and salt, extracted from sea water in salt pans heated by local coal. The combination of the Industrial Revolution and a bad storm that silted up the port severely damaged the economy, and the town became a backwater until 1932 when the National Trust moved in.

Tourist Information

Dunfermline: 1 High Street, **t** (01383) 720 999, www.dunfermlineonline.net.
Kirkcaldy: 19 Whytecauseway, **t** (01592) 267 775.
Forth Bridges: c/o Queensferry Lodge Hotel, St Margaret's Head, North Queensferry, **t** (01383) 417 759.

Festivals

June: Civic Week, Dunfermline; an excuse for festivities, parades and entertainment.
April: the **Links Market,** Kirkcaldy; the largest and oldest fair in Britain – the Esplanade is closed for five days and a great gala of events is presented with plenty of music, colour, pomp and ceremony.

Where to Stay and Eat

Balbirnie House Hotel, Markinch, **t** (01592) 610 066, www.balbirnie.co.uk (expensive). 18th-century, grade A listed, de luxe country house in its own 400-acre park with 18-hole golf course and excellent food.

Belvedere Hotel, West Wemyss, **t** (01592) 654 167, www.thebelvederehotel.com (expensive–cheap). A cluster of white cottages in a good position overlooking the Forth. Comfortable rooms and excellent food.

Dundonald Arms Hotel, Mid Causeway, Culross, **t** (01383) 882 443 (moderate). Small, 17th-century inn: cosy and friendly, with nice food and atmosphere.

Dunnikier House Hotel, Dunnikier Park, Kirkcaldy, **t** (01592) 268 393, www.dunnikier-house-hotel.co.uk (moderate). Comfortable hotel with friendly service.

Garvock House Hotel, St Johns Drive, Transy, Dunfermline, **t** (01383) 621 067, www.garvock.co.uk (moderate). Country house in woodland setting near the centre.

Keavil House Hotel, Crossford, nr Dunfermline, **t** (01383) 736 258, www.keavilhouse.co.uk (moderate). Comfortable hotel with good food, and a leisure club in the gardens.

King Malcolm Hotel, Queensferry Road, Dunfermline, **t** (01383) 722 611, kingmalcolmhotel@hotmail.com (moderate). All the modern trimmings and excellent food; convenient and comfortable, if somewhat characterless.

Queensferry Lodge Hotel, North Queensferry, **t** (01383) 410 000 (moderate). All modern

Historically, Culross was the site of a 5th- or 6th-century religious foundation presided over by St Serf (or Servanus), and St Kentigern was born here. Leave your car on the outskirts of the old part and explore the steep, narrow, cobbled streets on foot.

The **Palace** (open 1 April or Easter, whichever is earlier–Sept daily 1.30–5; Oct also Sat and Sun; adm; **t** (01383) 880 359) was built in 1597 by a prosperous merchant, Sir George Bruce, overlooking the river which in those days came much closer to the town. Standing within a walled court, with crow-stepped gables, decorated dormer windows and pantiled roofs, its garden rising steeply behind with terraced walks, the whole complex is most attractive. Bruce, trading local salt for valuable glass, cheated James VI of window tax by incorporating half-shutters of wood into the windows. You won't find a better example of a Scottish laird's house anywhere else. Bruce's private counting house, through an iron door, is stone-vaulted, fireproof and has safes sunk into the walls. The painted ceiling, with allegorical figures, Latin texts and 'improving' admonishments, is on the second floor and is one of the best in Scotland.

The **Town House** or **Tolbooth** (open same times as Palace; adm), built in 1626, is on the right of the palace. It has a double outside stair and was restored, and the tower added, in 1783. The National Trust for Scotland has its headquarters here, and you can see an audiovisual show in the visitor centre telling the history of the town and showing how it was rescued from decay. You can see the iron house, or prison, on the comforts and conveniences, with panoramic views of the River Forth, tourist information, craft and interpretation centre.

Rescobie House, Leslie, north of Glenrothes, t (01592) 749 555, *www.rescobie-hotel.co.uk* (*moderate*). Probably the most elegant hotel in the area. Peaceful place to stay, secluded and creeper-clad, in 2 acres of lovely garden and grounds. Homely, with sporting prints on the walls, antique furniture and log fires. A good base for golfing.

Woodside Hotel, Aberdour, t (01383) 860 328, *www.woodside-hotel.co.uk* (*moderate*). Right in the middle of Aberdour, with good hospitality, and good seafood.

Clarke Cottage Guest House, 139 Halbeath Road, Dunfermline, t (01383) 735 935, *clarke-cottage@ukonline.co.uk* (*cheap*). Victorian house with first-class facilities for people with disabilities.

Forth View Hotel, Hawkcraig Point, Aberdour, t (01380) 860 402 (*cheap*). Small, secluded place, on the water at Hawkcraig Point, with gorgeous views, near Silver Sands Beach and the golf course. The food isn't at all bad. *Open April–Oct.*

Halfway House Hotel, Kingseat, Dunfermline, t (01383) 731 661 (*cheap*). Well-placed for the motorway, and very adequate.

Hawkcraig House, Aberdour, t (01383) 860 335 (*cheap*). A gem, and perhaps the nicest place to stay in these parts – the old ferryman's house at Hawkcraig Point, on the water's edge overlooking the harbour and Inchcolm Island. Only two rooms, so book well in advance. You can lean out of the window and watch the seals and birds. The home-cooked food is excellent. Bring your own wine. No credit cards. *Open mid-Mar–Oct.*

Inchview Hotel, 69 Kinghorn Road, Burntisland, t (01592) 872 239 (*cheap*). Listed Georgian building overlooking Pettycur Bay – not wildly exciting, but comfortable with good food. Golf packages.

St Mungo's Cottage, Low Causeway, Culross, t (01383) 882 102, *martinpjackson@hotmail.com* (*cheap*). Cheap and friendly B&B.

Town House Hotel, Markinch High Street, Markinch, t (01592) 756 459, *townhouse@ecosse.net* (*cheap*). A bargain. The owner/proprietor does the cooking and makes you feel thoroughly at home.

The Channel Restaurant, North Queensferry, t (01383) 412 567. Excellent bistro serving good, simple food.

Old Rectory, Dysart, Kirkcaldy, t (01592) 651 211. First-class meals in nice atmosphere.

ground floor, the council room with a painted ceiling, and the debtors' room. The 'high tolbooth' or turret was apparently used for witch-spotting. The tron, or public weighing scales, stood outside the tolbooth, where traders' measures could be checked against the standard weights to curb cheating.

The **Study** (*open Easter–Sept daily 1.30–5; adm*) is an L-plan, late 16th-century house with a turnpike stair and a small room at the top of its tower, which gave it its name. It is reached by climbing steep, narrow streets, cobbled and paved, behind the Town House until you get to a tiny asymmetrical market place with a reconstructed mercat cross. Inside the house is a small museum with furniture, pottery, pewter of the period and maps illustrating the early town.

The **Little Houses of Culross**, which are privately occupied, can be enjoyed from the outside. They are good examples of the domestic architecture of the relatively humble working-class people of those days, in apparently random positions against each other, straggling up the narrow streets.

Culross Abbey (*open daily*) was founded in 1215 for Cistercian monks on the site of St Serf's church. The present parish church (1300), was rebuilt in 1633 from the original choir and central tower. Inside is a spectacular alabaster monument in memory of Sir George Bruce, who built the palace.

East from Culross, just along the shore, is the ruin of **St Mungo's Chapel** (*always accessible*). Built in 1513, it commemorated the spot where a Pictish princess, after escaping the wrath of her family, landed and gave birth to St Kentigern, affectionately known as Mungo. Across the Forth the flaming stacks of the refinery at Grangemouth are strangely ethereal when seen through the haze they create, or in the half-light, against a darkening sky, reflected in the water.

Charlestown to Dunfermline

Undulating farmland reaches inland, with narrow lanes and sudden splendid views. Along the shore you pass through picturesque harbours and villages such as **Charlestown**, an 18th-century village surrounding a green on a wooded plateau above the Forth. Charlestown Harbour, a small haven that dries out at low tide, was built by the 18th-century laird, the 5th Earl of Elgin, for sailing ships bringing iron ore and carrying away locally quarried lime. This is Bruce country, for the Earls of Elgin trace their descent from King Robert. It was the 7th Earl who 'acquired' the ancient Greek marble sculptures (now called the Elgin Marbles), and sold them to the British Museum in 1816 for £35,000. (The Parthenon was being used by the Turks, who were then occupying Athens, for target practice.) These marbles continue to be a bone of contention between Britain and Greece. Just before the Second World War they were cleaned, emerging so pristine that the public were outraged and the Assistant Keeper in the Department of Greek and Roman Antiquities was unfairly forced to resign.

Limekilns, a mile east of Charlestown, is an old-world village whose pretty cottages were lived in by the seamen who worked the ships out of Charlestown. Although those days are gone, there is still a great feeling of community here in the riverside settlement. The Ship Inn is a nice fisherman's pub.

Oakley, a few miles inland, is a strongly Catholic mining village built to house workers in the Comrie Colliery, many of whom came from declining areas in the west. The church, endowed in 1958 by the Catholic laird, the late Captain Smith-Sligo, has some beautiful stained glass, and woodwork carved by a local craftsman.

Dunfermline

Dunfermline was once the capital of Scotland. Hub of the southwest corner of Fife, it is dominated by the abbey and palace that stand above the town like sentinels. The town falls away from this crowning glory, an endearing mixture of Scottish Baronial, modern industrial and ancient ruins. Dunfermline means 'fort-by-the-crooked-pool', after a fort that stood in what is now Pittencrief Park.

King Malcolm Canmore lived in Dunfermline in the middle of the 11th century. He was an unremarkable, blood-thirsty, perhaps rather boorish, man, until along came saintly Margaret, an English princess. Margaret and her brother Edgar Atheling, heir to Edward the Confessor, had been usurped by William the Conqueror and forced to flee. She married Malcolm in 1067 and set about anglicizing Scotland, both culturally and ecclesiastically. Edward I held court here during his campaigns against the Scots at the end of the 13th century; Charles II agreed to accept the Covenant while staying in Dunfermline in 1651.

The town is probably best known today as the birthplace of **Andrew Carnegie** (1835–1919), the son of a linen weaver, who went to America and made a fortune in steel. One of the best-known philanthropists of the modern world, he used his millions for the benefit of mankind in numerous ways. To his home town he gave Pittencrief Park, the public baths, a library and an annual Festival of Music and Art.

The **Abbey** (*open April–Sept Mon–Sat 9.30–6.30, Sun 2–6.30; Oct–Mar Mon–Sat 9.30–4.30, Sun 2–4.30, but closed Thurs pm and Fri pm; adm*) is reached by steps from a terraced car park. The church, much restored, stands adjacent to the ruined monastery buildings and palace, which are linked to each other by a pend. It is hard to believe, when you look at these remains, that in the 13th century they were said to be 'big enough to hold two sovereigns with their retinues, at the same time, without inconvenience to one another'. There was a Culdee Chapel on the site where Malcolm Canmore, a widower, married Margaret. Two years later the queen, horrified by the lax ways of the Celtic Church, began to build a new church to be administered in the English manner to which she was accustomed. When she endowed the Benedictine priory, she set up a shrine with a relic of the True Cross and encouraged pilgrims to come from miles away to venerate it.

The present church stands on the foundations of Margaret's church, some of which you can see through iron grilles in the floor. Frequently sacked and burned over the centuries, today's building is a jigsaw of different styles, the nave dating from 1128 and the massive buttresses from the 16th century. In 1818 workmen unearthed a vault with a stone coffin in it, containing a skeleton wrapped in thin sheets of lead. Shreds of cloth of gold clung to the bones and the breastbone had been sawn through, almost conclusively proving that this was the coffin of Robert the Bruce. Bruce died in 1329 having begged Sir James Douglas to carry his heart to Palestine and bury it in Jerusalem. (He had always intended to make a pilgrimage to the Holy Land in atonement for murdering his rival for the throne, Red Comyn.) Douglas set off with the heart but was killed in Spain in battle with the Moors. The heart was retrieved from the battlefield, returned to Scotland and buried in Melrose Abbey, where it is today. Bruce's remains were reinterred; a brass plate under the pulpit, set in Italian porphyry, marks the spot.

Malcolm Canmore and Queen Margaret died within a few days of each other in 1093, and their shrine is against the outside wall of the present abbey, where the Lady Chapel once stood. The abbey succeeded Iona as the burial place for Scottish kings.

The ruined **Palace** (*open same times as Abbey*), still magnificent, especially against an evening sky, was built when Margaret and Malcolm married. You can imagine the queen, walking up each day from Malcolm's Tower, now a ruin in Pittencrief Park below, to inspect the progress of her new home. Although she would have preferred to have been a nun rather than a queen, Margaret loved fine clothes and exotic furnishings, and no doubt her palace was very splendid. It provided an admirable setting for her task of 'refining' the rough, Celtic ways of her husband's court.

Pittencrieff Glen is reached through a gate opposite the west door of the abbey. When Andrew Carnegie was a boy, before he emigrated to Pennsylvania to make his fortune, he was forbidden entrance to the privately owned park. He never forgot this, and when he returned with his millions he bought it and gave it to the people of Dunfermline so that 'no wee child should ever feel locked oot of it, as I was'. So anyone can now roam among shrubs and flowers and trees, along the steep-sided, wooded glen where birds sing and a burn tumbles down over its rocky bed, and no child is ever 'locked oot'. It is a beautiful place. **Pittencrieff House** (*open daily*) was built in 1610. It, too, was bought by Carnegie, and makes a good focal point in the park. Inside there are displays of local history, costumes and an art gallery.

The **Andrew Carnegie Museum** (*open April–Oct Mon–Sat 11–5, Sun 2–5; handloom demonstrations May–Oct first Fri of the month; adm*), in Moodie Street, is the small cottage where Carnegie was born. The rooms are furnished as they were in his lifetime, and the millionaire himself, remarkably lifelike in waxen effigy, sits at his desk in his study, looking rather stern, perhaps planning where to bestow his next gift.

Abbot House Heritage Centre, Maygate (*open daily 10–5; adm*), reveals 1,000 years of local history in a marvellous old building whose gardens lead into the Abbey grounds.

Dunfermline Museum (*open Mon–Fri by appointment, t (01383) 313 838*) is at Viewfield. This Victorian villa has displays on local history, including the weaving and linen industries, both of which enriched the town in the past.

East Towards Kirkcaldy

Rosyth

Rosyth is 3 miles south of Dunfermline, on the shore of the Forth. Its dockyard, now privatized, has played an important part in British naval history over the years. At one time it was the only naval dockyard where the entire fleet could anchor at any state of the tide. Naval ships still come as far up as the dockyard, and great oil tankers lie at anchor, waiting to take on oil from the artificial island just east of the rail bridge. This is the terminal of the pipeline from the North Sea oil fields. A ferry link from Rosyth to Zeebrugge is started in May 2002 (visit *www.superfast.com* for more details).

St Margaret's Hope is east of the dockyard, near the foot of the Forth Road Bridge. Tradition has it that it was at this rocky promontory that Queen Margaret landed in Scotland for the first time.

North Queensferry

North Queensferry was originally the northern terminal of the ferry established by Queen Margaret to carry pilgrims to Dunfermline. It remained a ferry terminal until the road bridge was opened in 1964, and is now a backwater with a big yacht marina.

In **Deep Sea World** (*open April–June and Sept–Oct daily 10–6; July and Aug daily 10–6.30; Nov–Mar daily 11–5; adm; www.deepseaworld.com*), you go through an aquarium in an underwater, transparent viewing tunnel and come literally face to face with the fish. It is an extraordinary experience as you encounter sharks and piranha so close you can almost – but reassuringly, not quite – touch them. There is also a pirate exhibition, an audiovisual theatre, shop and café.

Inverkeithing

It is worth stopping off in Inverkeithing, an older place than you might think at first glance – granted a Royal Charter in 1165. Behind the busy central square in the High Street, the 14th-century **Greyfriars Hospice** (*in the process of refurbishment; call t (01383) 313 838*), restored as a community centre, has a small museum, crammed with items of local historical interest – religious, military, industrial and domestic.

Dalgety Bay

Keeping to the shore road, east of Inverkeithing you come to Dalgety Bay, now fringed by a sprawling residential development, but haunted by ghosts. **Donibristle House** stands on the site of the house where, in 1592, 'the Bonnie Earl of Moray' was murdered by an avenging Huntly on the order of the king. There are many versions of the murder story, one being that there was a tunnel from the house down which the unfortunate earl tried to flee, but because his hair had been set alight by his enemies he acted as a living torch for his pursuers. The house has suffered several catastrophes in the more recent past. A fire in 1858 caused the central block of its H plan to be removed leaving two large wings connected by subterranean passages. Another fire in 1985 destroyed the west wing. The house has been restored and is part of an up-market housing development – its history and character sadly sacrificed to Mammon.

St Bridget's Church, further along the shore of Dalgety Bay, is an unexpected little ruin right beside the water, its mossy banks dotted with tumbled headstones. It was dedicated in 1244; the eastern part of the church is the oldest. It was a two-storey kirk with a burial vault and laird's loft.

Aberdour

Aberdour, just east of the Forth Road Bridge, is a popular resort, known for its silver sands. There is a lovely sandy beach just east of the old town, and plenty here for a family holiday: golf, water sports, a sailing centre and a little harbour. The picturesque town has a cluster of medieval buildings above it, overlooking the sea. **St Fillan's Church** is part Norman, part 16th-century, like an enchanting miniature cathedral, with a leper-squint in the west wall and an atmosphere of peace and timelessness.

Aberdour Castle (*open April–Sept Mon–Sat 9.30–6.30, Sun 2–6; Oct–Mar Mon–Wed and Sat 9.30–4, Thurs 9.30–12.30, Sun 2–4; adm*) stands close by on 14th-century foundations, and still has its original tower. It was added to in succeeding centuries and is an imposing, rather gloomy place, but it adds majesty to the overall scene. The circular **Dovecote** is part of the castle complex.

Inchcolm

A boat runs from Hawkcraig Point in Aberdour (*t (01383) 830 665*), to the small island of Inchcolm, across Mortimer's Deep, the watery grave of poor Sir Patrick Spens. Inchcolm is a perfect place to visit on a fine day, the boat trip making it more special.

There are usually a few private boats at anchor in the harbour, with much good-natured 'giving way' to the official cruise boats. On calm days the water is often ruffled by the wakes of powerboats and waterskiers.

The **Abbey of St Columba** (*open April–Sept; adm; cruises run from North Queensferry July and Aug, and from South Queensferry April–Oct, weather permitting; for times t (0131) 331 4857 or (01383) 823 332*) is just next door to the landing jetty, overlooking a small rocky bay. It was founded in 1123 for Augustinian monks by Alexander I. A Columban monk-hermit who lived on the island saved the King when his boat foundered on the rocky shore; building the abbey was the King's act of gratitude. There is a rough cell at the northwest corner which could have been the hermit's. Although it was often sacked by the English and desecrated during the Reformation, the abbey has been restored and looks a little too new, but the monastic buildings are the best you will find in Scotland. You can see the 13th-century octagonal chapter house with stone roof, and a 14th-century cloister with chambers above.

Burntisland

Burntisland, 3 miles east of Aberdour, once famous for shipbuilding, is now more popular as a holiday resort, its boatyards closed down. The town climbs from the water and on a fine day in summer the beach resembles that of any Mediterranean resort, with scant room to lay a lilo.

The octagonal **Church of St Columba** was the first to be built in Scotland after the Reformation. It was copied from a church in Amsterdam and has a central pulpit and galleries reached by outside stairs. The tower, added in 1749, is joined to the corners of the church by great flying arches. The General Assembly of the Church of Scotland was held here in 1601, when, in the presence of James VI, it was proposed that there should be a new translation of the Bible, the Authorized Version, published in 1611.

Agricola is said to have used the natural harbour for his fleet in about AD 83 – it's strange to think of those Roman galleys at anchor where fibre-glass pleasure boats are now moored.

Rossend Castle is a 15th-century tower house that was saved from demolition and restored. Now it is one of Burntisland's treasures. It is used as offices but can be seen from the outside. It was here that an ardent French poet, Pierre de Chastelard, hid himself in Mary, Queen of Scots' bedroom in 1563, a crazy escapade that cost him his life. He was executed in St Andrews and died reciting poetry and crying 'adieu, thou most beautiful and most cruel Princess in the world'. He had already been caught hiding in her rooms at Holyrood.

Kinghorn

At Kinghorn, a couple of miles further along the coast, you will see a Victorian monument beside the road in the shape of a Celtic cross. This is where Alexander III was thrown from his horse and killed, an event which altered the course of Scottish history. The King had been sitting in council with his lords in Edinburgh. They had eaten well and washed down their meal with plenty of wine. He set off to return to his wife of six months, Jolande, whom he had married in a desperate attempt to get himself an heir. There was a violent storm, but he insisted on being taken across the Forth at Queensferry. On the far side he refused to shelter till daybreak but set off, galloping eastwards towards Pettycur where his queen awaited him. His horse stumbled on the edge of the cliff at Kinghorn and that was the end of the King, thus fulfilling a prophecy made at his wedding feast in Jedburgh. The country was plunged into many years of bitter conflict and power struggles. Kinghorn is now a holiday resort, with a sandy beach, good hotels, a golf course and campsites.

Inchkeith Island

You need to hire a boat to go out to the island of Inchkeith, southeast of Burntisland. Its strategic position in the Firth of Forth has made it an important defensive stronghold over many centuries, ever since Mary de Guise-Lorraine (mother of Mary, Queen of Scots) invited her French compatriots to fortify and occupy the island to defend Scotland's shores from English invasion. The island was used in the last two World Wars to defend Rosyth dockyard and the rail bridge. It is now occupied only by the lighthouse keepers and by thousands of seagulls.

The story is told of an experiment that was tried by that innovative monarch, James IV. He wanted to see what language a child would speak if it had no example to follow. He sent two infants to the island with a totally dumb woman as their nurse. Some say that the children grew up speaking excellent Hebrew, others that they emerged from the experiment speaking fluent Gaelic.

Kirkcaldy

Once known as 'the Lang Toun', Kirkcaldy (pronounced Kirkoddy) stretches along the coast 3 miles north of Kinghorn. It is a busy seaport, industrial centre, holiday resort, and Fife's main shopping town, with 4 miles of seafront and an esplanade whose retaining wall was built in the early 1920s in an effort to relieve unemployment as much as to hold back the pounding sea.

Linen, weaving and textiles were the town's first occupations, until a weaver of sailcloth, Michael Nairn, turned his talents to the invention of linoleum, which erupted into a major industry. It is said that at the height of the linoleum boom you could smell Kirkcaldy from many miles away. With the development of synthetic fibres and more sophisticated floor coverings, the town's industry has diversified tremendously. Among Kirkcaldy's famous sons are the architects Robert and James Adam, and Adam Smith, a brilliant scholar and philosopher who wrote, among other learned works, *Inquiry into the Nature and Causes of the Wealth of Nations* in 1776.

If you explore the heart of Kirkcaldy you will find more than just a modern town full of good shops and busy streets. In the older parts you can come upon delightful little wynds and courtyards, and old houses with pantiled roofs and crow-stepped gables, as for example in the eastern suburb of **Dysart**.

Dysart is full of character, with a picturesque harbour below the ancient battlement tower of St Serf's Church. In the old days Dutch traders in tall-masted sailing ships came here to barter, exchanging cart-wheels, kegs and pipes for local coal, salt, beer and cured fish.

Kirkcaldy Museum and Art Gallery (*open Mon–Sat 10.30–5, Sun 2–5*) is in the War Memorial Gardens, next to the station. It has a good archaeological collection, with 300-million-year-old fossils, as well as displays on local social history, natural history and industry, including the process of linoleum making. The art gallery has work by many Scottish artists including William McTaggart, that great master who captured simple everyday life and familiar scenes so well. Among other artists are Peploe, Lowry, Sickert and Raeburn. There are also displays of the local Wemyss Ware pottery. (Incorporated is the Café Wemyss, which closes at 4.30pm.)

The **McDouall Stuart Museum** (*open June–Aug Mon–Sat 2–5*) is an award-winning museum in Fitzroy Street, Dysart, in a building restored by the National Trust for Scotland. The house, which has a lintel dated 1575, was the birthplace of John McDouall Stuart, who in 1866 was the first man to cross Australia from south to north through the central desert. The museum tells you all about Stuart and his fascinating, and often hair-raising, expeditions, including his encounters with Aborigines and Australian wildlife.

Kirkcaldy has several parks: **Beveridge Park**, with flower gardens and a boating lake; **Dunnikier Park**, to the northwest, with a nature trail and golf course, shaded by cedar trees; and **Ravenscraig Park**, along the shore beyond Dysart.

Ravenscraig Castle

Open May–Sept daily 10–7; Oct–April daily 10–3; adm.

Ravenscraig towers dramatically above Ravenscraig Park, on a rocky promontory overlooking the river. This substantial ruin dates from 1460 when James II intended it as a dower house for his wife. He lost interest in it when she died. James III gave it to the Earl of Orkney in exchange for Kirkwall Castle, which he had long coveted, and it was finally demolished for Cromwell in 1651 by General Monk. It was the first castle in Britain to be designed for defence by and against cannon shot, and you can still see the wide gun loops in the massively thick walls. The views over the Forth made it a splendid vantage point against invasion. Sir Walter Scott called it Ravenshough, in his poem 'Rosabelle'. Near the castle, the steps that lead from the high-rise flats in Nether Road down to the beach should number 39, and are said to have inspired John Buchan, though he moved his 39 steps several hundred miles south.

Kirkcaldy to Glenrothes

West and East Wemyss

West Wemyss is 1½ miles, and East Wemyss 3 miles, east of Dysart. They are so called from the many 'weems', or caves, in this bit of the coast. People have sheltered in these caves for thousands of years, and the graffiti they left behind is fascinating, possibly dating back to the Bronze Age (2500 BC). Owing to erosion they are not at the moment safe to explore, but a campaign to Save Wemyss' Caves is under way. The villages are characterized by their colliers' cottages, some of which are in dire need of rescue. The ruin just east of East Wemyss is called **Macduff's Castle**, and was once the stronghold of the Thanes of Fife.

Leven

Leven,along the coast from the castle on Largo Bay, is another holiday centre with a good beach and plenty of holiday facilities, including golf and fishing. It is hard to believe that the harbour was once a busy port, used to ship in provisions to the Royal Palace of Falkland. It silted up and is now a car park and swimming pool complex.

In **Silverburn Estate and Animal Farm** (*open all year*), east of Leven near the beach, you can walk in the woods and gardens and observe the wildlife, including, if you are lucky, red squirrels. There are paddocks where the Silverburn Shetland ponies graze if they are not pulling carts in the park, and in spring there are usually foals to see, as well as pygmy goats from Africa and pot-bellied pigs from Vietnam.

Lethem Glen, on the northern outskirts of Leven, is another nature centre, with displays and information about wildlife, a 45-minute nature trail, and a pets' corner for young children.

Lundin Links, also on Largo Bay, is yet another family holiday resort. It has a sandy beach, sea fishing and golf. The standing stones just to the west are thought to have been part of a Druid temple.

Glenrothes

Five miles inland from either Kirkcaldy or Leven, Glenrothes was built in 1949 as the second (after East Kilbride) of Scotland's post-war new towns. Its original purpose was to house the workers in a new coal mine which never materialized. Light industries found homes here instead, and only the gregarious who enjoy masses of organized, modern entertainment would be tempted to spend a holiday here. The town is new and unbeautiful: the entertainments cover all tastes from indoor swimming, bowling, snooker, skating and curling, to outdoor gliding, parachuting, hang-gliding and golf.

East Neuk

Neuk is a Scots word meaning 'corner', and that is exactly what this small wedge of land is, jutting off the eastern edge of Fife from Largo Bay to St Andrews, coming to a point at Fife Ness. This is a genteel holiday centre, where you are more likely to stumble on quaint pantiled cottages with neat, bright gardens than on fun-parks. On a nice day, tour the fishing villages that ring the East Neuk, each with its own character. In medieval Scotland there was much sea-trade with Europe and Scandinavia. Scottish wool, coal, leather and cured fish were exchanged for timber and manufactured goods. As well as goods, however, fashions were exchanged: crow-stepped gables, for instance, are of Flemish origin. When trade declined, fishing took over, particularly for herring, and was at its height in the 19th century. Now these little ports are less busy. Built around picturesque harbours, crow-stepped houses rise in steep terraces, joined by twisting cobbled streets and wynds. The very names of these villages suggest stoic Scots dependability with no frills and flounces: Pittenweem, Anstruther, Crail – names to be reckoned with. The beaches are gorgeous and less populated than those further south, and the hinterland is pleasant farmland, with St Andrews providing plenty in the way of history and culture.

Around the South Coast of East Neuk

Largo

Largo, at the head of Largo Bay, 3 miles northeast of Leven, was once an important fishing centre. It is now mainly residential, and popular in summer with its golden crescent of sand. While you are here, climb the volcanic cone of Largo Law, where an ancient chief is said to have been buried, dressed in silver armour. There are good views of Fife from the top.

Elie and Earlsferry

Elie and Earlsferry, at the eastern end of Largo Bay, 6 miles from Largo, are more or less one place. Both are popular resorts with lovely sandy beaches where, if you look carefully, you may find garnets in the sand. Earlsferry is the place where Macduff, Earl of Fife, is believed to have hidden from Macbeth in the 11th century in a cave at Kincraig Point, before being ferried to Dunbar.

St Monans

St Monans, 3 miles northeast, has a cluster of charming old houses reaching down to the sea. When the wind is in the southeast the spray rises over the churchyard wall to wash the gravestones in the cemetery of a small fishermen's church that stands on the edge of the water. The foundations of this church date from 1362 when David II dedicated it to St Monans, or Mirren, an Irish missionary, in gratitude for a miraculous recovery from an arrow wound. The unusual T shape of the church is because the nave was never built.

The town rises steeply from a double harbour, an attractive network of narrow, twisting streets and restored old houses. **Miller's Yard** was established in 1747. Although it ceased boatbuilding in 1993, a number of employees still do boat repairs.

Pittenweem

Pittenweem ('place-of-the-cave'), a mile up the coast, is the home port of the East Neuk fishing fleets, with a thriving fish market. It is an attractive town, its old harbour often crammed with fishing boats, its quays stacked with fish boxes and gear. It is well worth getting up early in the morning to see the fish market in full fling.

The National Trust for Scotland has done tremendous work on several of the buildings in the town. These include **Kellie Lodging**, a tower that juts into the High Street,

The Real Robinson Crusoe

Look out for the statue of Alexander Selkirk, who was born in Lower Largo in 1676. Selkirk was a wild young man who ran away to sea, quarrelled with his captain and was dumped, at his own request, on the uninhabited island of Juan Fernandez, where he existed for five years until he was rescued. He and his story were immortalized by Daniel Defoe in his novel *Robinson Crusoe*.

and **The Gyles**, a group of 16th- and 17th-century houses by the harbour. You can see the remains of a priory in the grounds of the Episcopal church (1114), whose Augustinian monks established a shrine in St Fillans Cave, where services are still occasionally held.

Kellie Castle

Open April–Sept daily 1.30–5.30; Oct Sat and Sun
1.30–5.30; grounds open all year daily 9.30–sunset; adm.

Kellie Castle is 3 miles inland on the B9171. Some of it dates from the 14th century, but it is mostly an impressive pile of mainly 16th- and 17th-century domestic architecture, in landscaped gardens. It was rescued from decay in 1875 by Professor James Lorimer, whose son, the famous architect Robert Lorimer, designed the walled garden, the garden house, walled doo'cot and some internal decoration, and whose grandson, the sculptor Hew Lorimer, is the resident custodian. It has some splendid plaster work and painted panelling.

Anstruther

Anstruther, a mile up the coast from Pittenweem and contracted to 'Anst'er' by locals, was once an important fishing centre but is now better known as a holiday resort. It has, however, hung on to its link with its fishing past, and there are guided historical walks around the town (*end June–end Sept*).

The **Scottish Fisheries Museum and Aquarium** (*open April–Oct Mon–Sat 10–5.30, Sun 11–5; Nov–Mar Mon–Sat 10–4.30, Sun 2–4.30; adm; www.scottish-fisheries-museum.org*), at the head of the harbour, gives a unique insight into the life and work of a fishing community, with interiors of a typical fisherman's home – complete with wife, baby and cradle. There is a Fife fishing boat on display, known as Fifie.

The Isle of May

Boats run from Anstruther and Crail to the Isle of May,
weather permitting; t (01333) 310 103; 4–5 hours for the trip.

The Isle of May is the largest of the four islands that command the entrance to the Firth of Forth, once of vital strategic importance. The island, 1 mile long and about a quarter of a mile in width, has an intriguing history stretching back into the dark ages and embroidered with legend, all told in *The Story of the May Island*, published by Largo Field Studies Society in Upper Largo. 'The May' became a National Nature Reserve in 1956, since when the seabird population has increased dramatically. Look

Tourist Information

St Andrews: 70 Market Street, **t** (01334) 472 021; *open all year.*

Anstruther: Scottish Fisheries Museum, Harbourhead, **t** (01333) 311 073; *open April–Sept.*

Crail: Crail Museum and Heritage Centre, 62–4 Market Gate, **t** (01333) 450 869; *open April–Sept.*

Festivals

Spring: the **Kate Kennedy Pageant**, St Andrews; *c.* 60 students parade the streets in costume. Kate, the niece of one of the founders of the university, was so beautiful that all the students were in love with her. The pageant is all-male: Kate is played by a first-year student, and all the others are members of the Kate Kennedy Club, dressed as famous Scottish figures, past and present.

March: Festival of Food and Wine, St Andrews.

April: Annual Golf Week, St Andrews.

May: Country Fair, Craigtoun Country Park near St Andrews.

July: Elie Fair. Holiday Fair Week, Anstruther. **Festival Week**, Crail. **Highland Games**, St Andrews.

August: Arts Festival, Pittenweem. **Lammas Fair**, St Andrews; Scotland's oldest surviving medieval market, with stalls and booths in the streets – a bright, colourful carnival that lasts for two days.

October: Dunhill Nations Cup Golf, St Andrews.

30 November: St Andrews Day.

Sports and Activities

Byre Theatre, St Andrews, **t** (01334) 475 000. Productions throughout the year. Began its life in a cowshed of the Old Abbey Street Dairy Farm, hence its name.

Crawford Arts Centre, St Andrews, *www. crawfordarts.free-online.co.uk.* Changing programme of art exhibitions, professional theatre and music performances. *Open Mon–Sat 10–5, Sun 2–5.*

East Neuk Outdoors, Anstruther, **t** (01333) 311 929. Activity holidays with abseiling, archery, boardsailing, canoeing, climbing, coastal walks, cycling, bird-watching, historic tours and special activities for children. They have a playgroup for 2–5 year olds.

St Andrews Aquarium, *www. standrewsaquarium.co.uk.* A good place to occupy children (though not so good as the one in North Queensferry). There is a 'Catch' beach restaurant and bar. *Open daily 10–6; July and Aug daily 10–9.*

Where to Stay and Eat

Rufflets Country House Hotel, Strathkinness Low Road, St Andrews, **t** (01334) 472 594, *www.rufflets.co.uk (expensive).* A real treat, in 10 acres of award-winning gardens, with superb food, and quiet, friendly service. Run by the same family for more than 35 years. Special winter rates.

St Andrews Old Course Hotel, St Andrews **t** (01334) 474 371, *www.oldcoursehotel.co.uk (expensive).* Very swish and very expensive, with free use of spa facilities. It overlooks the Old Course, and has its own championship course. Mouth-watering food.

Cambo Estate, Kingsbarns, **t** (01333) 450 313, *www.camboestate.com (moderate).* B&B in a marvellous country house with lovely views and ancestral rooms. Also self-catering apartments and cottages, some with four-posters.

The Craw's Nest, Anstruther, **t** (01333) 310 691, *crawsnest@compuserve.com (moderate).* Built as a manse in 1703, and extended considerably. A bit impersonal, but comfortable. Dinner-dances and special off-season, extended-stay reductions.

The Golf Hotel, Elie, **t** (01333) 330 209, *www.golfhotel.co.uk (moderate).* Friendly and comfortable.

for the puffins with their unreal-looking striped beaks, living in burrows in the turf (puffins are only ashore for a few weeks, so check first if you want to see them), and the incredible camouflage of nesting eider ducks, which manage to stay totally

Lundin Links Hotel, Lundin Links, t (01333) 320 207, *www.lundin-links-hotel.co.uk* (*moderate*). Mock-Tudor house with an air of solemn respectability. Surrounded by golf courses, close to the beach. Golfing breaks.

Old Manor Hotel, Lundin Links, t (01333) 320 368, *www.oldmanorhotel.co.uk* (*moderate*). Overlooks the golf course and the sea, with excellent food. Special rates for long stays.

Rusacks, Pilmour Links, St Andrews, t (01334) 474 321, *www.heritage-hotels.com* (*moderate*). Built in 1887, overlooks the Old Course. Very comfortable and prestigious with excellent food.

The Smuggler's Inn, Anstruther, t (01333) 310 506, *smuggs106@aol.com* (*moderate*). Three hundred years of atmosphere overlooking the harbour. You eat well here, in great comfort with cosy log fires. Special deals available.

Ashbank, Lucklawhill, Balmullo, t (01334) 870 807, *alison.outlaw@talk21.com* (*cheap*). Very comfortable, cosy B&B. Dinner on request.

Falside Smiddy, Boarhills, St Andrews, t (01334) 880 479, *birk@falside.freeserve.co.uk* (*cheap*). Converted 18th-century smiddy. Very cosy, with delicious dinner by arrangement.

Kinkell, 2 miles out of St Andrews on the Crail road, t (01334) 472 003, *www.kinkell.com* (*cheap*). Family home on a farm which runs down to the sea, within easy walking distance of the Rock & Spindle beach. A Wolsey Lodge with tennis and croquet on the lawns.

Little Carron Cottage, Little Carron Gardens, St Andrews, t (01334) 474 039, *www.carron10.freeserve.co.uk* (*cheap*). B&B in an attractive converted farmhouse with riverside walk to town centre.

St Michaels Inn, Leuchars, t (01334) 839 220 (*cheap*). Cosy, traditional inn only 10 minutes from St Andrews and very good value.

Selcraig House, Nethergate, Crail, t (01333) 450 697, *margaretselcraig@compuserve.com* (*cheap*). Friendly 18th-century guesthouse.

Bouquet Garni, Elie, t (01333) 330 374. Excellent food.

The Cabin Seafood Restaurant, St Monans, t (01333) 730 327. Just what it says – and very good.

The Cellar, Anstruther, behind the Fisheries Museum, t (01333) 310 378. Really good local seafood – very jolly.

The Fish Bar, on the front in Anstruther. Excellent fish and chips.

Grange Inn, Grange Road, St Andrews, t (01334) 472 670. A good pub/restaurant.

Ship Inn, Elie, t (01333) 330 246. Popular place for good pub meals and summer barbecues in the garden by the beach. Excellent steaks and seafood. You can also stay here.

West Port, 170–2 South Street, St Andrews, t (01334) 473 186. Very good restaurant with a varied menu.

Self-catering

The Hermitage, Anstruther, t (01333) 310 909. Very attractive, homely restored old house with a couple of suites (each sleeping 4).

Kingask Country Cottages, St Andrews, t (01334) 472 011, *kcc@easynet.co.uk* (*moderate*). 12 exclusive holiday cottages and a luxury country house, for well-equipped self-catering.

Montaquhanie Holiday Homes, near St Andrews, t (01382) 330 252. A variety of elegant town houses in St Andrews, cottages, farmhouses and country house apartments (sleeping 2–12). Very well equipped, with a range of prices.

Morton of Pitmilly, Kingsbarns, t (01334) 880 466. Luxury holiday houses in a converted farm courtyard, with indoor heated pool and sauna, fitness room, games room, floodlit tennis court, putting green, and lots more.

St Andrews University, t (01334) 462 000. 74 self-catering houses provided by the university during university holidays: a bit different, but very good value.

Woodland Holidays, Kincaple, t (01334) 850 217, *www.woodlandholidays.co.uk*. Pinewood Scandinavian chalets among trees, 3 miles west of St Andrews. They provide linen, blankets, televisions and lots more. No pets.

motionless within only a few feet of the path. Other birds include guillemots, razorbills and kittiwakes. You are more than likely to see seals here, too.

The remains of a beacon in the middle of the island are from the first Scottish lighthouse, built in 1636. The tower was at least twice the height of today's, and it had a huge brazier on top that burned coal at the rate of between one to four tonnes a night, depending on the wind. It needed stoking every 20 minutes, was invisible upwind, and was easily confused with the lights of the saltpans along the mainland shores. In a storm in 1792, sulphurous fumes from the cinders of the beacon killed the lighthouse keeper and his family, seven in all, as they slept. The present lighthouse was built by Robert Stevenson, grandfather of the writer, in 1816.

Before you go on up the coast, take a trip inland to the **Secret Bunker** (*open April–Oct daily 10–5; adm; www.secretbunker.co.uk*) at Trywood. This is an authentic relic from the Cold War, an underground labyrinth in a hillside, one of several in which central government and military commanders would have set up shop, and lived, in order to run the country in a nuclear war. It is a fascinating place, equipped exactly as it was – a 1950s time-warp.

Crail

Crail is another well-restored fishing town with one of the prettiest harbours in Fife, created a Royal Burgh in 1310 and granted the right to trade on the Sabbath. Picturesque colour-washed houses and cobbled streets lead down to the harbour and its crow-stepped customs house. The **Church of St Mary** is 12th century. The large blue stone at its gate is said to have been hurled there by the Devil from the Isle of May, out to sea. You can see an 8th-century Pictish cross slab in the church, and in Victoria Gardens the early Christian **Sauchope Stone**. The restored **Tolbooth** is early 16th-century. The **Crail Museum and Heritage Centre** (*open Easter week and June–Sept Mon–Sat 10–1 and 2–5; mid-April Sun 2–5; May daily 2–5; adm; t (01333) 450 869*) tells much of the history of this ancient town, and has a tourist information centre.

Kingsbarns

From Crail, the coast road turns northwest towards St Andrews and you lose the sea for a while. You come first to Kingsbarns, 3 miles from Crail, whose name will tell you that this is good farmland. There is a nice story attached to the original owners of **Pitmillie**, just north of the village. In the 11th century, before Malcolm Canmore was king, he asked a stranger for the loan of 'a few pennies'. 'Not a few: mony pennies', came the munificent reply. King Malcolm did not forget. When he came into power he granted his benefactor land here and the family became known as 'Moneypenny'.

St Andrews

St Andrews, 10 miles beyond Crail, unfolds below you: its ghosts beckon irresistibly. Many of the stones used to build the older houses came from the ruined cathedral on the eastern edge of town, towards which the three main streets lead. Scotland's oldest university, founded in 1411, is now the living heart of the town whose medieval spirit is kept young in many ways. For instance, you might see the Sunday parade of students processing from the chapel in the scarlet medieval gowns that were introduced so that they could be spotted easily when entering brothels. (Divinity students wear black gowns: presumably they were above suspicion.) There are organised tours of the university's historic buildings, usually twice a day from June to August (**t** *(01334) 476 161*). Or you might even spot Prince William, the eldest son of Prince Charles and Princess Diana, second in line to the throne, who chose to read for a Fine Art Degree at St Andrews University, ensuring that there will be a waiting list for aspiring students for the next few years, as well as a lucrative tourist boom.

Andrew, brother of Simon Peter and the first disciple to be called by Jesus, was 'the most gentle of the Apostles'. Among his many converts was the wife of the Roman Governor of Patrae. The governor was so furious and jealous of his wife's conversion that he had Andrew crucified. (Andrew asked to be tied to an X-shaped cross so that he should not appear to be emulating Christ.) According to legend, St Rule, who was custodian of the saint's remains in Patrae some time between the 4th and 8th centuries, had a vision of an angel who ordered him to take five of Andrew's bones, sail to the western edge of the world and build a city in his honour. Rule set off and was shipwrecked on the rocks just to the west of today's harbour. He hurried ashore and enshrined the sacred relics on the headland where the ruins of the 12th-century cathedral now stand. The shrine became a place of worship for Christian pilgrims from far and wide and a special ferry was kept on the River Forth to transport them. St Andrew became Scotland's patron saint; his white cross on a blue ground became the national flag (the 'silver saltire'); and the city where his sacred relics lay enshrined became the ecclesiastical capital of Scotland.

St Andrews Cathedral (*open April–Sept Mon–Sat 9.30–6.30, Sun 2–6; Oct–Mar Mon–Sat 9.30–4.30, Sun 2–4; adm; www.saint-andrews.co.uk*), founded in 1160, was once the largest cathedral in Scotland. Medieval pilgrims came in their thousands to pray at one of its 31 altars. It is strange to stand in front of the remains of the high altar and recall that Robert the Bruce stood here at the consecration of the cathedral in 1318, 160 years after the building began. Here too stood James V and Mary of Guise-Lorraine at the ceremony of their marriage. In 1559 that zealous reformer John Knox preached some stirring sermons on the 'cleansing of the temple' and roused his congregations to such hysteria that they stripped the cathedral of its glorious embellishments and riches, leaving it to decay into ruin. Even as a ruin it is magnificent. A great twin-towered façade soars towards the sky, surrounded by neat green turf, graves, the foundations of the priory, a few massive walls and a Norman arch. The **Cathedral Museum** is full of interesting relics, including a unique sarcophagus. **St Rule's Tower** is also within the precinct, a gaunt chaperone. Here the holy relics were kept until the cathedral was completed. If you feel energetic you can climb the 158 steps inside the tower and see wonderful views of the town and out to sea. **The Pends**, now roofless, was the vaulted gatehouse entrance to the cathedral precinct. Dating from the 14th century, it is said that it will collapse when the wisest man in Christendom walks through the arch. The prophecy doesn't include women so the Pends still stands.

St Andrews Castle (*open same times as the cathedral; adm*) is northwest of the cathedral on a rocky headland overhanging the sea beyond a deep moat. Now a ruin, it was built as the Bishop's Palace at the end of the 12th century and it witnessed some extremely nasty incidents in the bloodstained history of the Scottish Church. George Wishart, the ardent Protestant reformer, was burned at the stake in front of the castle in 1545, and tradition tells of the notorious Catholic Cardinal Beaton, lying on velvet cushions inside the castle, watching his death throes. Whether this is true or not, Beaton paid for Wishart's life with his own. A worldly, immoral man, the Cardinal did not hesitate to plead for mercy on account of his priestly status two months later, when he was stabbed to death by a party of avenging Reformers. His body was hung over the battlements and then slung into the 'bottle dungeon', a fearsome rock pit, where it was preserved in salt until its discovery more than a year later. After the murder the Reformers held the castle against a siege, having been joined by John Knox and others, before they were all captured and sent off to serve time as galley slaves. Knox was a close friend of Wishart; it was to be 14 years before he returned to stir the reforming pot again.

The castle fell into ruin in the 17th century but you can still see the bottle dungeon. A large number of the Reformers were imprisoned in this hell-hole: it is hard to believe that many can have survived. Beaton's apartments are thought to have been in the tower to the southwest.

One of the features of the castle is the mine and counter mine, tunnelled through the rock during the siege that followed Beaton's murder in 1546–7. The besiegers started their tunnel but were frustrated by the defenders who tried to intercept them. Uncertainty about who was where led to abandonment. The galleries were later useful as secret tunnels in those days of intrigue.

The **Church of St Salvator** is among St Andrews' many fine university buildings. In North Street, it was founded as the University Chapel by Bishop Kennedy in 1450, uncle of the beautiful Kate who is fêted in the April pageant. The Bishop's tomb is in the church, along with a magnificent mace from his time which is still carried on ceremonial occasions. The pulpit was the one John Knox preached from, carried here from the parish church; he thumped out his message on that very wood.

Patrick Hamilton, the proto-martyr of the Reformation, was burned for his Lutheran heresy in front of St Salvator's College in 1528. Archbishop James Beaton, uncle of the notorious Cardinal, was mainly responsible for his persecution. Above the site of his death you can see an impression of his face engraved in the stone wall, said to have been left there when his soul flew out of the flames as he died.

The **Royal and Ancient Golf Club** makes history pale into insignificance for golfers. Known to the cognoscenti as the R and A, this world-famous establishment determines the rules of the game, although it is by no means Scotland's oldest club. The club house is open to members only. The autumn Golf Meeting at the end of September is the main event of the year, and when you see the preparations beforehand (the tents and booths and marquees) you would imagine an army was preparing for a major battle. It is at this meeting that the Captain for the Year plays himself into office, watched by thousands of anxious eyes, in case he should miss that important ball. Of the four courses, 'The Old' is the most famous.

The **British Golf Museum** (*open Easter–mid-Oct daily 9.30–5; Nov–Easter Mon and Thurs–Sun 11–3; adm; www.britishgolfmuseum.co.uk*), opposite the R and A, is a must for golfers – everything you didn't know about the history of golf and a lot more besides, going back to its conception 500 years ago, with ball-by-ball reminiscences.

St Leonard's College, founded in 1512 and no longer extant, was on the present site of St Leonard's Girls' School, beyond Abbey Street (known to its inmates as The Prison). Many ardent reformers, including John Knox it is thought, studied at the college, and the term 'to have drunk at St Leonard's Well' was coined from those times, meaning to have listened to the Protestant doctrine. The library of St Leonard's School is in Queen Mary's House in South Street, where Mary is believed to have stayed in 1563, taking a holiday with her ladies from the burdens of State affairs. While she was there she planted a thorn tree that still flourishes in the quadrangle of St Mary's College.

West Port at the end of South Street, built in 1589, was the main entrance to the old city. It gives a good idea of what it must have been like in the days when a town could literally shut its gates and defend itself from within.

In North Street, there is the **St Andrews Preservation Trust** in a 17th-century building, where you can learn more about all the treasures in this ancient city.

Don't miss the picturesque **harbour**. The main pier was rebuilt in the 17th century with stones from the ruined cathedral and castle.

Craigtoun Country Park (*open April–Sept daily 10.30–6; adm*), 2 miles south of St Andrews, is 50 acres of parkland surrounding Mount Melville House, now a hospital. The park has an Italian garden, a Dutch village surrounded by an ornamental lake built in 1918, a Rio Grande Miniature Railway, putting, bowling, trampolines, shops, a licensed restaurant and a picnic area. There are nature walks and a ranger service, too.

Leuchars

The railway line to St Andrews was closed some years ago and Leuchars, 5½ miles northwest, is now the station that serves the town. In the village of Leuchars you could easily miss one of the best relics of Norman architecture in Scotland. Only an apse and chancel remain, incorporated into the parish church, with an arcaded exterior to the apse. If you look carefully you can see the axe marks of the ancient masons on the blind arches and pilasters. It is a pity that the modern church is so plain, but perhaps its dullness offsets the triumph of the Norman part.

The peace of this part of Fife is often interrupted by low-flying planes working from the RAF base nearby.

South of the Tay

The north coast of Fife is less developed than that of the East Neuk and has more of an estuary feeling, with views of the river over the mud flats and a rich bird life. Inland it is all farms and towns and villages with sturdy names like Auchtermuchty and Strathmiglo – pronounced Strathmigla. Falkland, with its splendid palace, lies at the heart of this area which has several other interesting ruins as well.

Tentsmuir Forest

Going north towards the Tay you come to the Tentsmuir Forest, a couple of miles northeast of Leuchars. Pines grow right down to the broad, sandy beach, providing shade for summer picnics. Keep your eyes skinned for deer, and families of seals sunning themselves on the sands, as well as lots of different birds.

Tayport and Newport-on-Tay

Tayport and Newport-on-Tay, 5½ miles north of Leuchars, are holiday resorts on the southern shores of the Firth of Tay. Both claim to have had the oldest ferry in Scotland, and it seems likely that boats might have run from both places since earliest times when they were crude settlements. Neolithic remains have been excavated on this northeastern corner of Fife.

The Tay Rail Bridge

So the train mov'd slowly along the Bridge of Tay,
Until it was about midway,
Then the central girders with a crash gave way,
And down went the train and passengers into the Tay!
The Storm Fiend did loudly bray,
Because ninety lives had been taken away,
On the last Sabbath day of 1879,
Which will be remember'd for a very long time.
William McGonagall

The southern approach to the Tay rail bridge is a short distance west of the one that collapsed in a gale on 28 December 1879, sending a train and about 100 passengers into the water, a disaster that shocked the world and still brings a shiver of horror to hearts today. Stumps of the piers of the original bridge can still be seen on the north side. Anyone who has not read the account of the disaster as told by that astonishing poet William McGonagall should do so at the first possible opportunity.

The new rail bridge, built only a few years later, is a graceful construction curving across the river like a 2-mile memorial to the disaster. The road bridge, 2 miles downstream, is a toll bridge.

Balmerino Abbey

Balmerino Abbey (*always accessible*) is a ruin 3 miles west of the rail bridge on a hill overlooking the river. It was founded for Cistercians in the 13th century by Alexander II, whose mother is buried here. It was mostly destroyed by the English in 1547, during the 'Rough Wooing', and a later attempt to restore it was foiled by the Reformation. The last Lord Balmerino was a brave old man, beheaded as a Jacobite in 1746. Seen against a stormy sky, it is a poignant shell, with just the entrance to the chapter house and the roofless sacristy standing among farm buildings.

Lindores Abbey

The scattered remains of Lindores Abbey (*always accessible*) are 8 miles southwest, just before Newburgh, and also overlooking the Firth of Tay. This abbey was an important religious community until it was secularized in 1600. The main entrance arch and part of the west tower still stand in jagged isolation, all that remain of a place that witnessed the savage burning of exquisitely illuminated Mass books, and manuscripts by John Knox. Lindores was founded in the 12th century for Benedictines, and numbered among its many pilgrims several Scottish monarchs.

Newburgh

Newburgh, 13 miles southwest of Newport, almost on the border with Tayside, is a Royal Burgh with a pretty little harbour. On the hill to the south of town you can see the remains of Macduff's Cross, the legendary place of sanctuary for any Macduff who had committed a murder in hot blood. To achieve pardon, the murderer had to touch the cross, wash himself nine times at Ninewells nearby, and forfeit nine cows, each to be tied to the cross.

Laing Museum (*open April–Sept Mon–Fri 11–6, Sat and Sun 2–5; Oct–Mar Wed and Fri 12–4, Sun 2–5*) has exhibitions of fossil fish discovered in Dura Den, a feature on Scottish emigration, and Victorian displays including a reconstructed Victorian study.

Falkland

Falkland, 9 miles south of Newburgh, is an ancient town, clinging to the lower slopes of the Lomond Hills, looking across the Howe of Fife. The rich farmland that you see now was once a forest full of deer and wild boar. Many of the 17th- to 19th-century buildings have been restored, making it a delightful place to wander about in, especially on a fine day when the sun plays tricks with the old stones, dappled with light and shade.

Wander along the High Street, beyond the palace gates, through the Market Square, and up the Maspie Burn on to East Lomond Law. From here, the landscape is all rolling hills, rounded hillocks, and attractive villages with stone cottages and pantiled roofs. This is the Howe of Fife, 'howe' meaning sheltered place.

Falkland Palace

Open April–May and Sept–Oct Mon–Sat 11–5.30, Sun 1.30–5.30;
June–Aug Mon–Sat 10–5.30, Sun 1.30–5.30; adm.

Falkland Palace was built in the 15th and 16th centuries as a hunting lodge for the Stuarts. Much of it has been restored, giving an example of early Renaissance architecture – compact and ornate, its massive walls and barred windows a reminder that even hunting lodges had to be fortified. The south wing is the best preserved, with an elaborate façade, mullioned windows and a gate house flanked by round towers.

Festivals

June: Gala Week, Cupar.

Where to Stay

Craigsanquhar House, by Cupar, **t** (01334) 653 426, www.craigsanquhar.com (*expensive*). Quiet and comfortable hotel in 36 acres. Good food.

Fernie Castle Hotel, near Letham, **t** (01337) 810 381, www.ferniecastle.demon.co.uk (*expensive*). A must for castle addicts. Built in 1510 in 30 acres of park and woods, this is a prince among castles, with a round tower and a prize-winning French chef. Well placed for golfers, and well worth the price.

The Weaver's House, Auchtermuchty, **t** (01337) 828 496 (*expensive*). A very well set-up cottage for self-catering (sleeping 6).

Cunnoquhie, Letham, **t** (01337) 810 237 (*moderate*). 18th-century shooting lodge, with later additions, on a hill top with gorgeous views. Now a Wolsey Lodge, and a minor stately home: comfortable, easy-going grandeur and good food.

Eden House Hotel, 2 Pitscottie Road, Cupar, **t** (01334) 652 510, www.eden-group.com (*moderate*). Victorian house overlooking Haugh Park. Good food.

Gorno Grove House, Strathmiglo, **t** (01337) 860 483, sandymatthew@compuserve.com (*moderate*). Above the village with lovely views and a garden-in-the-making. A Wolsey Lodge, informal, relaxed and comfortable.

The Peat Inn, Peat Inn, **t** (01334) 840 206 (*moderate*). Former coaching inn, a first-class hotel with 8 mini-suites decorated in whimsical French style. For restaurant, *see* below.

Sandford Country House Hotel, near Wormit on the Firth of Tay, **t** (01382) 541 802,

www.sandfordhotelfife.com (*moderate*). Listed country house built around a courtyard garden, with comfortable rooms and good food. Special golf packages.

Covenanter Hotel, The Square, Falkland, **t** (01337) 857 224, www.covenanterhotel.com (*cheap*). Family-run 17th-century coaching inn with an excellent bistro and restaurant, attractive and cosy.

Redlands Country Lodge, near Ladybank, **t** (01337) 31091 (*cheap*). A little different, in lovely gardens surrounded by open country, with self-contained and comfortable pine log-cabin bedrooms. Excellent food, golf, fishing, shooting and pony-trekking.

Westfield House, Westfield Road, Cupar, **t** (01334) 655 699, westfieldhouse@standrews4.freeserve.co.uk (*cheap*). B&B in B-listed Georgian house in nice garden.

Eating Out

The Covenanter Restaurant, in the Covenanter Hotel, Falkland, *see* above.

Eden House Hotel, Pitscottie Road, Cupar, *see* above. If you want something cheaper, this will serve you a very reasonable meal.

Ostler's Close, Cupar, **t** (01334) 655 574. Splendid restaurant/bistro off Main Street.

The Peat Inn, at the junction of the B940/941, Peat Inn, **t** (01334) 840 206. People travel a long way to eat in this 18th-century inn. It's a true French auberge, complete with Michelin star, modelled on the proprietors' favourite establishment in Vonnas, France, with decor and ambience to match. The food is accurately aimed at discerning taste buds, the wine list is excellent and the service unbeatable. You can also stay, *see* above.

St Michael's Inn, St Michaels, **t** (01334) 839 220. Good roadside pub and restaurant.

It was in an earlier castle on this site, in 1402, that the heir to the throne, the Duke of Rothesay, was starved to death by the ambitious and greedy Duke of Albany. Falkland was annexed by the Crown when James I eliminated the powerful Albany family by the simple, if somewhat drastic, method of murdering all their menfolk. The elegance of the architecture was enhanced by French masons employed by James IV and then by his son James V. James V came to Falkland in 1542 after his defeat at Solway Moss. He died here, a broken man, having just heard of the birth of his daughter, Mary. He prophesied on his death bed that his infant daughter would be the last of the Stuarts to rule Scotland.

The palace was restored from complete ruin in 1887 by the Hereditary Keeper, the third Marquess of Bute, who also rescued the gardens and many of the houses in the town. The original Royal Tennis Court (1539) is still in use as one of Britain's few 'royal' or 'real' tennis courts. Perhaps Queen Mary had a game here. She certainly played golf, and is known to have come often to Falkland on hunting expeditions.

Cupar

Cupar, 10 miles northeast of Falkland, heading back to St Andrews, was once the administrative centre of Fife, and is still the headquarters for North East Fife District Council. It has elegant 18th-century houses built of mellow, honey-coloured stone. In 1276 Alexander III held an Assembly of the Three Estates in Cupar, made up of the Church, the burghers and the aristocracy. It was this that inspired Sir David Lindsay, who lived nearby, to write *Ane Pleasant Satyre of the Thrie Estaitis*, holding them up to ridicule. The play has been revived in a greatly shortened form, and is aired now and then during the Edinburgh Festival.

The **Scottish Deer Centre** (*open April–Oct daily 10–6; Nov–Mar daily 10–5; adm*) is 3 miles west of Cupar on the A91. Children will enjoy seeing deer at close quarters and even touching them, and there is lots to see and do in the visitor centre in the Georgian courtyard, which has a restaurant. Outside there is a farm walk, nature trail and falconry centre.

Hill of Tarvit

Open Easter, May, June and Sept daily 1.30–5.30;
July and Aug 11–5.30; Oct Sat and Sun only;
grounds all year daily 9.30–sunset; adm.

Hill of Tarvit is a mansion 2 miles south of Cupar. Dating from 1696 and splendidly remodelled by Robert Lorimer in 1906, the house has a nice lived-in feeling. The collection of treasures inside includes tapestries, porcelain, paintings and 18th-century English and French furniture. There is also an Edwardian laundry where you can almost see steam from the boiling sheets in the copper and feel the ache of the women's tired muscles at the end of the day. The gardens are laid out in French style with box hedges and yews; there is a woodland walk and a hilltop 'toposcope'. The view of the house from the garden, with a double flight of steps leading up to the terrace, is lovely.

Scotstarvit Tower, opposite Hill of Tarvit (*open same times as Hill of Tarvit*), is a five-storey, 16th-century tower house with battlements and turrets. It was the home of John Scott, a 16th- and 17th-century scholar and mapmaker in the days when new routes were opening up all around the globe.

Pitlessie

Pitlessie, 4 miles southwest of Cupar, will be familiar to fans of David Wilkie, from his famous painting *Pitlessie Fair*. The artist was born at Cults Manse nearby in 1785, and many of his paintings of everyday life were set locally, so you find yourself looking around for one of his jovial, bucolic peasants. Sadly the manse was destroyed by fire in 1926, together with a wealth of wall paintings done by Wilkie in his youth.

Ceres, Peat Inn, Magus Muir and Old Dairsie

In Ceres, 4 miles east of Pitlessie, pantiled cottages surround a green on which there are annual games, dating from victory celebrations after Bannockburn in 1314.

The **Fife Folk Museum** (*open Easter weekend and mid-May–Oct Mon–Thurs, Sat and Sun 2–5; adm*) is spread between a restored 17th-century tolbooth weigh house, two cottages and out of doors. This award-winning museum has collections of the domestic and agricultural tools and equipment in daily use before the invention of electricity and the petrol engine. Don't miss the dungeons in the tolbooth. There are also two nature trails from the village, planned by the Scottish Wildlife Trust, of botanical and geological interest.

Peat Inn, 3 miles to the southeast, is a hamlet that takes its name from its inn. It is well worth a detour to this inn, where you can eat as good a meal as you could hope for anywhere in the country, and stay the night (*see above*).

Magus Muir is 3 miles north of Peat Inn and just south of Strathkinness. This grisly spot is where a party of Covenanters butchered Archbishop Sharp in 1679, in the presence of his daughter. Sharp's attempts to restore Episcopacy to Scotland had not been entirely straightforward and he had won for himself universal detestation. This was hardly surprising when you remember that he went, as a Presbyterian, to plead the Covenanters' cause with Charles II and returned as the consecrated Bishop of St Andrews.

Old Dairsie, about 3 miles west of Magus Muir, has a bridge over the River Eden that was built by Archbishop Beaton in 1522. **Dairsie Castle** (*in the process of restoration*), where David II spent part of his youth, lies above the river. The Kirk of Dairsie, St Mary's, was built in 1621 by Archbishop Spottiswood in an attempt to bring the English Church to Scotland. It is a mixture of Gothic and classical, with an octagonal belfry, in a peaceful graveyard. Dura Den is a wooded gorge south of the bridge, where a large number of fossils have been found. These fossils gave vital clues to the formation of land and life here, over many millions of years. Beside the Ceres Burn that cuts the gorge are the ruins of several linen and jute mills, once an important part of the Fife economy.

Kinross-shire, Perthshire, Angus and Dundee

p.436

Cairnwell
Devil's Elbow

Spittal of Glenshee

④ *Glen Shee*

Bruar Falls

Blair Castle
Blair Atholl

Tayforest ⑤ *Queen's View*
Park

Kinloch Rannoch

⑤ *Foss* *Loch Tummel*

Loch Rannoch

Schiehallion ▲

Ben Vrackie

Killiecrankie
Pass of Killiecrankie
Pitlochry

Loch Faskally

Garry

Tummel

Ballinluig

Strathardle

A93

Bridge of Cally

Castle Menzies ● Aberfeldy

Glen Lyon

Fortingall

● Bridge of Balgie

Fearnan ● Kenmore

Ben Lawers ▲

PERTHSHIRE

AND

KINROSS

Amulree

Loch of Lowes
Dunkeld ● Birnam

Tay

Bankfoot ●

Loch Tay

B r e a d a l b a n e

Loch Lednock

Glen Lednock

Lednock

St Fillans ●

Glen Almond

Sma' Glen

Huntingtower Castle

Scone Palace

①

p.262

Loch Earn *Earn*

Comrie ● Crieff

● Innerpeffray

Perth

A9

Drummond Castle

Muthill ●

Tullibardine ●

Loch Katrine

S T I R L I N G

Callander ●

Braco ●

Auchterarder ●

O c h i l   H i l l s

A9

p.300

Kinross ●

Crook of Devon ●

M90

Orkney Shetland

SCOTLAND

NORTHERN IRELAND

ENGLAND

Highlights

1 Scone Palace, near Perth

2 Arbroath Abbey, home of the Declaration of Independence

3 Glamis Castle, the most haunted castle in Scotland

4 Skiing at Glenshee

5 Lochs Tummel and Rannoch

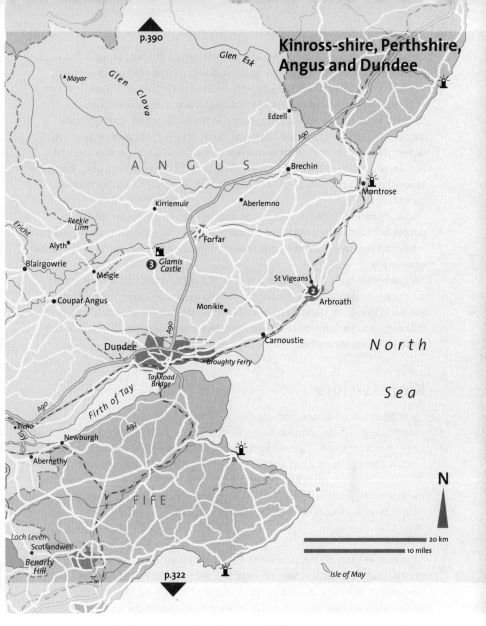

p.390

Kinross-shire, Perthshire, Angus and Dundee

Glen Esk

Mayar

Glen Clova

ᴬ N G U S

Edzell

A90

Brechin

Montrose

Kirriemuir

Aberlemno

Reekie Linn

Forfar

Ericht

Alyth

3 Glamis Castle

Blairgowrie

Meigle

St Vigeans

Coupar Angus

Monikie

2 Arbroath

A90

Dundee

Carnoustie

Broughty Ferry

North

Tay Road Bridge

Sea

A90

Firth of Tay

A92

Eicho

Tay

Newburgh

Abernethy

N

F I F E

Loch Leven

Scotlandwell

20 km

Benarty Hill

p.322

10 miles

Isle of May

The sun shines kindly on this eastern part of the Scottish mainland, and a keen wind hones its coast. In winter the peaks glisten with snow; in summer the hills and moors are bruised with purple heather. Birch, conifer and hardwood trees shade the glens, giving a blaze of metallic colours in autumn: bronze, gold, copper, rust.

Once the centre of the Pictish kingdom, hill forts and stone circles in this region are haunted by the ghosts of the Picts. The Romans came and went in the 1st and 2nd centuries. They built sophisticated fortifications but failed to subdue the Picts, who reigned supreme, with their own kings and culture. They gradually absorbed

Christianity as it crept in from the west and left carved stones to prove it. The Vikings swooped in from the sea, but were beaten off. In the middle of the 9th century Kenneth Macalpine united Dalriada in the west with Pictland, and Scone, just north of Perth, became the capital until the middle of the 15th century, with nearby Dunkeld an important ecclesiastical centre. In the turbulent 17th century many battles – political, religious and territorial – were fought in the narrow passes that linked north and south. The Battle of Killiecrankie, in 1689, was perhaps the best known, when the Highlanders almost annihilated the Government's army. Control of several strategic castles was hotly disputed half a century later, during the final Jacobite rebellion.

Agriculture and fishing have been the main sources of income for these rural people, with little industrialization except around Dundee. Whisky distilling plays an important part in the economy, and tourism is growing fast, backed up by the revival of old crafts.

Many people hurry through this part of Scotland, blind to its attractions in their rush to get to the Highlands proper. They miss a great deal. Approaching through Kinross in the south, the main routes into Perthshire and Angus radiate from Perth, following the river valleys like the wavering legs of a giant spider. That is how this guide will cover the region.

Kinross-shire

Scotland's second-smallest county, Kinross-shire, is dominated by Loch Leven within a semicircle of hills. You come in from the south on the M90, with the loch stretching away to your right and a tantalizing thickening of the skyline ahead, beckoning you towards the Highlands. If you aren't concentrating, the motorway will whisk you through it and away past Perth before you can blink. Don't be put off by the fact that the Tourist Information Centre is in a motorway service station: it is friendly and incredibly well stocked with literature and information.

Kinross

The market town of Kinross lies at the heart of farming country. The tolbooth dates from the early 17th century, later repaired and decorated by Robert Adam whose descendants still live at Blairadam House, nearby. The thriving woollen industry goes back many years to when wool and linen were hand-spun in the cottages. Kinross was once the only place where cashmere was spun in Britain. The goat hair is imported, but there are plans among Scottish farmers to establish Scottish goat farms which, it is thought, could be an important addition to the economy. In the 17th century Kinross was famous for making cutlery, until Sheffield stole the market in the 19th century.

The garden of **Kinross House** (*open April–Sept daily 10–6; adm*) is well worth a visit and, although the house itself isn't open to the public, you get a good view of it. Sir William Bruce, political mover-and-shaker around the time of the Restoration and

Kinross-shire **351**

Tourist Information

Kinross: Service Area, Junction 6, A90, **t** (01577) 863 680; *open all year.*

Festivals

Autumn: International Fly Fishing Championships, Loch Leven.

Where to Stay

Nivingston House Country Hotel and Restaurant, Cleish, **t** (01577) 850 216, **f** 850 238, *www.nivingstonhousehotel.co.uk* (*expensive*). Victorian mansion at the foot of the hills, in 12 acres of landscaped gardens with terrific views. Log fires and delicious, candle-lit dinners cooked by a gold-medallist chef. A memorable place to stay

Windlestrae Hotel, Kinross, **t** (01577) 863 217, **f** 864 733, *windlestrae@corushotels.com* (*expensive*). Upmarket country town hotel with 4 swish suites as well as rooms with jacuzzi/whirlpools. Good, varied food.

Gartwhinzean Hotel, by Kinross, **t** (01577) 840 595, **f** 840 779 (*moderate*). Comfortable, friendly hotel with good food.

Hamish and Frances Lindsay, Caplawhead, by Yetts o'Muckhart, **t** (01259) 781 556, *hamish-frances@caplawhead.freeserve.co.uk* (*moderate*). Charming comfortable B&B.

Lomond Country Inn, Kinnesswood, **t** (01592) 840 253 (*moderate*). Just as good, with a lovely view across Loch Leven from the dining room. Fishing permits available.

Muirs Inn, Kinross, **t/f** (01577) 862 270 (*moderate*). Traditional inn atmosphere and excellent home-cooked food.

Bein Inn, Glenfarg, **t** (01577) 830 216 (*cheap*). Old country inn, with public rooms full of character and a reasonable restaurant.

Kirklands Hotel, Kinross, **t** (01577) 863 313, **f** 863 313, *www.kirklandshotel.com* (*cheap*). Old coaching inn.

The Old Manse, Arngask, Glenfarg, **t/f** (01577) 830 394 (*cheap*). Lovely Georgian manse, run as a Wolsey Lodge with style and friendly hospitality.

Eating Out

Croftbank House Hotel and Restaurant, Station Road, Kinross, **t** (01577) 863 819. Gourmets should try this 'restaurant with rooms'. People come a long way to eat the food prepared by the chef-patron, who has won the Scottish 'Chef of the Year' award. B&B is cheap (there are only 4 rooms), so you can afford to splash out on dinner.

Grouse and Claret, Heatheryford (junction 6, M90), **t** (01577) 864 212, **f** 864 920, *grouseandclaret@lineone.net*. Good game and fish dishes in the dining room, which overlooks the loch. Also an enterprising list of events, and fishermen can try their skills in the Fishery. You can stay here.

a capable architect, believed in the importance of harmony between house, garden and landscape. He acquired the Kinross estate some time in the 1670s and is said to have intended a house for the Duke of York – James VII/II – in 1685 at the time of his accession. But James' short reign was over within three years and Bruce decided to keep the magnificent Palladian mansion for himself and concentrate on creating a suitable setting for it. He died in 1710, leaving this glorious garden running down to Loch Leven with Loch Leven Castle on its island as a theatrical backdrop.

Loch Leven

Loch Leven is by no means Scotland's most beautiful stretch of water, but it has an irresistible fascination. It is renowned in the fishing world for its unique pink trout, and international fishing competitions are held here frequently. As a nature reserve, it gives refuge to a large variety of migratory wildfowl: pink-footed and greylag geese and many different breeds of duck. They come from their northern nesting grounds in the autumn, between 10,000 and 20,000 of them, and graze the surrounding farmland during the winter. The haunting sound of them, coming in on the evening flight in arrowhead formation, is one of the most poignant in the world. In the early morning or at dusk you can hear a marvellous low symphony of chattering birds: little runs and trills of sound; murmurs and mutterings and an occasional squawk as a fussy mother calls her family to order. On the southern shore of the loch, **Vane Farm** (*open daily till dusk; adm*) is an RSPB visitor centre, with panoramic views from **Benarty Hill**, behind.

The largest island on the loch is **St Serf's Inch**, where Culdee (Servants of God) monks lived, in the now-ruined priory, in the 8th century.

Loch Leven Castle (*open April–Sept daily from 9.30; last ferry 5.15, weather and ferryman permitting; adm, including ferry from Kinross Pier*) is on **Castle Island**. Anyone with a drop of romance in their veins will be compelled to make this pilgrimage, crossing the olive green water in the wake of Mary, Queen of Scots.

The solid-looking ruin, with forbidding tower and curtain wall against a backdrop of trees, dates from the 14th century. As you step ashore, think back to when Mary arrived here as a prisoner, over 400 years ago. It was a June day in 1567. Mary was in ragged clothes, her hair shorn from her days as a fugitive. She was wretched from her defeat at Carberry Hill; already pregnant from her all-too-short marriage with Bothwell; exhausted, sick and utterly despairing. How must she have felt, as she landed at the little jetty into the custody of unsympathetic Lady Douglas? Not long after her arrival she suffered a devastating haemorrhage and miscarriage of – it is said – twins. She stayed in the castle for 11 months, during which time she so charmed an 18-year-old youth, William Douglas, that he helped her to escape. He rowed her ashore, throwing the keys of the locked castle into the loch (whence they were recovered, 300 years later). Mary's elusive spirit haunts this castle more than almost any other of the places she visited.

Kinnesswood is a tiny hamlet tucked into the foot of West Lomond, 4 miles from Kinross on the eastern side of Loch Leven. In the old days the villagers used to make vellum from calf skin and parchment from sheep skin – an art they learnt from monks in the 8th century. Walk up Puddin Wynd to the humble cottage where **Michael Bruce**, the 'Gentle Poet of Loch Leven', was born in 1746. This little memorial museum (*keys from Buchans garage in the village*) contains letters and books of the poet who could read the Bible at the age of four, wrote many paraphrases familiar to Scottish churchgoers, including 'O God of Bethel', and died at the age of 21. The views are good from Bishop Hill beyond the kirk car park.

The well at **Scotlandwell**, about a mile to the southeast, is fed by a spring of very clear, pure water that bubbles up through the sand and is reputed to cure leprosy. It was first recorded by the Romans.

Burleigh Castle (*key held at farm, opposite*), in the care of Historic Scotland, is a mile north of the loch and dates from 1500. It was the seat of the Balfours of Burleigh who were visited here several times by James VI.

At **Crook of Devon** (where some wag added 'Twinned with the Thief of Baghdad' to the road sign), 6 miles west of Kinross on the A977, there is a fish farm where you can feed the fish with pelleted food or try to fish them out of the tanks. They sell delicious fresh and smoked trout. The pub has excellent food.

Abernethy

Strictly speaking, Abernethy is in Perthshire, not Kinross, but it is en route to Perth from the south. You should take exit 9 from the motorway, 11 miles north of Kinross, and go 4 miles east on the A913.

It would be easy to dismiss Abernethy as 'just another village', but that would be a mistake. The Romans certainly sailed this far up the Tay and left the remains of a fort just to the south. More important, however, Abernethy was once a mighty Pictish kingdom. The 74-foot, tapering **tower** (*open April–Sept daily*), whose lower part dates from the 9th century, is one of only two such on the mainland of Scotland, the other in Brechin. When Abernethy was the centre of the Celtic Church, this tower provided the clergy with an almost impregnable refuge, as well as an excellent lookout in times of threatened invasion. The upper part dates from the 11th century, with a 7th-century stone carved with Pictish symbols set into the base. Also set into the wall is the 'jougs', an iron neck collar by which malefactors were chained for punishment. The design of these towers came over from Ireland with the missionary priests.

It was here in Abernethy, below the Ochil Hills, that Malcolm Canmore was forced to kneel and pay token homage to William the Conqueror in 1071. William had come north, conducting such a brilliant campaign against Scotland that Malcolm's humiliating capitulation seemed the only way to prevent the country being devastated. Perhaps he had his fingers crossed; perhaps he intended to acknowledge William as his overlord only in connection with his English estates. Whatever his motive, he allowed his son by his first marriage, Duncan, to be taken as a hostage to England, and his submission was to create centuries of unrest in both countries.

Perth

Some call Perth 'the gateway to the Highlands'. It may not be the only gateway, but it is an ideal centre from which to explore the more popular areas in the southern Highlands. Anyone arriving for the first time should have Walter Scott's *The Fair Maid of Perth* as a companion. As you come down into the city from the motorway you get a fine view of the town, spread out below, around the Tay. This view, 'new' since the building of the motorway, is in fact the old one, extolled by Scott in the first few pages of introduction to *The Fair Maid*. Two wide green parks, North and South Inch, unfold on either side, with a collage of spires reaching for the sky.

History

Perth was the first place where it was easy to bridge the river. Agricola established a Roman camp here and called it Bertha (from *Aber-tha*, mouth of the Tay), and his soldiers felt at home because the Tay reminded them of the Tiber. They must have been feeling *very* homesick. Traces of their old city wall can still be seen in Albert Close off George Street. It was a thriving port in the old days and is now an important live-stock market at the centre of a productive agricultural area. Its fine setting earned Perth the title 'The Fair City' in the past, and a recent transformation has done much to restore it to that status. In the days before conservation became fashionable, many of its old buildings were replaced by utilitarian monsters that are little short of archi-tectural vandalism, but now, with traffic-free shopping streets and award-winning floral displays, Perth is once again an attractive town, especially when the sun is shining. If you poke around you will find traces of the past, and there are some very fine late-Georgian terraces, especially around the Inches, and nice vistas of the river. When a new Marks and Spencer store was being built in the High Street some time ago, the remains of a medieval market were unearthed, resulting in a valuable stay of execution. A new bypass has considerably eased traffic congestion in the town centre.

Perth doesn't appear in the records until the 12th century. A devastating flood destroyed Old Perth in 1210, and William the Lion granted a Royal Charter to the town that was built in its place the same year. It was the capital of Scotland for a while, until the middle of the 15th century.

The mysterious drama of the Gowrie Conspiracy took place in 1600, in the now demolished Gowrie House. James I/VI was lured to an upstairs room by the Earl of Gowrie and his brother, Alexander Ruthven (to rhyme with driven), and his life was in some way threatened. He shouted for his lords through an open window and was rescued, Gowrie and Ruthven both killed in the confusion. The whole affair was shrouded in much speculation, with hints of homosexual motives mingled with suggestions that the King set the thing up in order to get rid of the brothers, whose ruthless political ambition was notorious.

City Sights

Perth Art Gallery and Museum (*open Mon–Sat 10–5*), in George Street, has local history displays and an exhibition showing the growth of the whisky industry which plays an important part in the economy of the area. It is one of the oldest museums in Britain.

The Battle of the Clans

Among the city's more colourful events was the Battle of the Clans, so graphi-cally woven by Scott into the convoluted plot of *The Fair Maid*. This was a contest between the Clans Chattan and Quhele (pronounced Kay), to establish who should take precedence in battle – a hotly disputed honour in those swash-buckling days.

Thirty men from each side were to fight in a tournament on the North Inch, watched by King Robert III (1390–1406), his wife and court. One of the Clan Chattan lost his nerve at the last moment and fled. The rule was that the two sides must be matched man-for-man, so a blacksmith, small and bandylegged, offered to stand in for the price of half a French crown. All but one of the Quhele Clan were slaughtered. Among the survivors of the Chattans was the blacksmith, who had done more than anyone else to secure victory (he is Scott's Henry, who wins the hand of virginal Catharine).

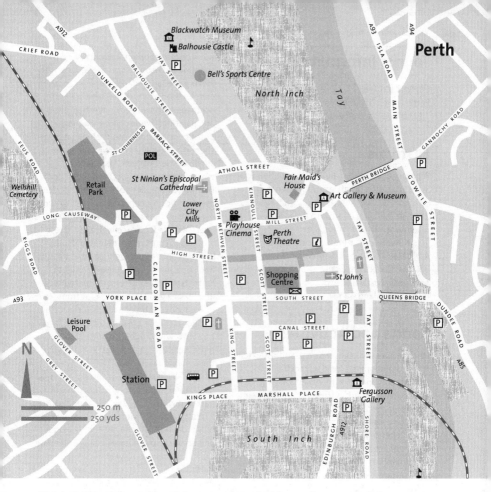

St John's Church (*open Mon–Fri 10–12 and 2–4; Sunday services 9.30 and 11*) was founded in 1126 by David I, recorded as The Kirk of the Holy Cross of St John the Baptist. Most of the present building dates from the 15th century and it is the oldest surviving building in the city, to which it gave its alternative name, St John's Toun (the football team is St Johnstone). Edward III is said to have killed his brother the Earl of Cornwall here in 1335; James I and the heart of Alexander III are thought to have been buried here; Montrose used it as a prison; Cromwell as a court of justice. Kings Charles I and II and Prince Charles Edward Stuart all worshipped here. It is hard to believe that this now almost starkly plain interior was the setting for John Knox's iconoclastic sermon in 1559, inciting his followers to purge all churches of idolatry – the sermon that led to the destruction of so many beautiful churches and monasteries, together with their priceless contents. St John's had at least 40 richly decorated altars dedicated to saints – a heartbreaking thought. Of the few treasures that were rescued are the 16th-century German Cellini Cup given to Mary of Guise by the Pope, 17th-century chalices and a 16th-century baptismal basin. The War Memorial Chapel was designed by Robert Lorimer when the church was restored in 1923. The church is used for concerts and is an excellent setting for *Murder in the Cathedral*.

Tourist Information

Perth t (01738–)
Perth: Lower City Mills, West Mill Street,
t 450 600; *open all year.*

Festivals

February and October: Bull Sales; whether you
are interested in cattle farming or not, this
wonderful assembly of bucolics has faces as
rich in character as any in a David Wilkie
painting. Farmers from far and wide pay
astronomic prices for the finest bulls.
**April/May and August/September: Perth
Races**; steeplechase only.
May: Perth Festival of Arts.
August: Highland Games.

Sports and Activities

Perth Leisure Pool, Glover Street. Sophisticated
pool with flumes, a 'wild water channel',
whirlpools and an outdoor section which is
open in winter. It has the reputation of being
the best in Scotland, with more than
700,000 visitors a year. *Open daily; adm.*
Perth Repertory Theatre, t 621 031. High
standard of performances and varied
programmes. Also a bar, coffee house and
restaurant.

Where to Stay

Unless you have set your heart on staying in
the city, don't. The best places, in all price
ranges, lie on its perimeter, and some are well
worth going the extra distance.

Expensive
Ballathie House Hotel, Kinclaven, not far north
of Perth, t (01250) 883 268, f 883 396,
www.ballathiehousehotel.com. Overgrown
shooting lodge on a 1,500-acre estate overlooking the Tay. Elegantly done up and well
endowed with mod cons. There are four-
poster or canopied beds, ancestral furniture
and paintings, *haute cuisine*, croquet, tennis,
putting, trout and salmon fishing and
shooting. It even has its own helipad.
Dupplin Castle, t 623 224, **f** 444 140,
www.dupplin.co.uk. Only 10 minutes from
Perth, an impressive 20th-century replacement of the original castle in lovely grounds
overlooking the Earn Valley. The ambience is
'gracious', the food excellent, and there are
all kinds of country-gentleman pursuits.
Isle of Skye Toby Hotel, Dundee Road, t 624 471,
f 493 902, *www.isleofskyeperth.co.uk.* In
Perth itself. Large, impersonal and comfortable, with a good view of the Tay from some
of the rooms. Rather business-focused.
Kinfauns Castle, on the outskirts, t 620 777,
f 620 778, *www.kinfaunscastle.co.uk.* Even
more expensive. A huge castle, with everything you could ever want.
Murrayshall House Hotel, Scone, t 551 171, f 552
595. Country house hotel in 300 acres of
parkland with an 18-hole, par 73 golf course,
a multiple-award-winning chef (emphasis
on good wholesome fayre), tennis, croquet
and bowls. Also shooting, fishing and riding.

Moderate
Campsie Hill, Guildtown, t (01821) 640 325,
f 640 785, *campsie@globalnet.co.uk.* A
Wolsey Lodge run by its owners, as a relaxed
hospitable family home. The house is attractive with nice gardens overlooking the Tay
and views 30 miles to the west.
Huntingtower Hotel, Crieff Road, t 583 771,
www.huntingtowerhotel.co.uk. Discreetly
modernized house in a secluded garden,
with nice rooms in the main house and
'lodge suites' dotted around the grounds.
Excellent food and friendly and helpful staff.

The **Fair Maid's House**, behind Charlotte Street (*closed at the moment but can be
seen from the outside*), is believed to have been the home chosen by Walter Scott for
virtuous Catharine Glover, The Fair Maid of Perth. It stands on the site of a medieval,
timbered castle, Scott's Glover's Hall. One of the oldest buildings in town, it is now a
mere cottage with medieval traces, of little interest beyond its literary association. It
has been so enthusiastically restored that it resembles a stage set.

Jarvis Hotel, West Mill Street, t 628 281, f 643 423. Converted 15th-century water mill (with the water still running) in a quiet, central area, with comfortable rooms and two restaurants.

Lovat Hotel, Glasgow Road, t 636 555, f 643 123, email@lovat.co.uk. Comfortable. Good food in the conservatory, restaurant and bistro.

The Quality Hotel at the Station, Leonard Street, t 624 141, f 639 912. One of Perth's dowagers – splendidly Victorian but with gracious concessions to modern comfort, in nice gardens only 5 minutes from the centre.

Queen's Hotel, Leonard Street, t 442 222, f 638 496, email@queensperth.co.uk. A big hotel by the train and bus stations, with lots of leisure facilities including a swimming pool and gym. Good food in two restaurants.

Royal George, Tay Street, t 624 455, f 630 345, www.theroyalgeorgehotel.co.uk. This place got its Royal appendage from a visit paid by Queen Victoria in 1848. It is a good old-fashioned Trust House, right on the river.

Salutation Hotel, 34 South Street, t 630 066, f 633 598, salutation@perth.fsnet.co.uk. One of the oldest hotels in Scotland, established in 1699, with strong Jacobite connections. Prince Charles had his headquarters here for a while. (He stayed in room 20; his Ops Room is now a meeting room.) Considerably more comfortable today, it has the largest Adam-style window in Scotland in its dining room.

Sunbank House Hotel, 50 Dundee Road, t 624 882, f 442 515, www.sunbankhouse.com. Early Victorian house only a short walk from the town centre, with a proper garden and views of the Tay. The food is excellent.

Cheap

Over Kinfauns, t 860 538, f 860 803, maclehose@overkinfauns.sol.co.uk. Hospitable guesthouse in a newly done up farmhouse overlooking the Tay. Historic site on Coronation Walk used for royal progress between Falkland and Scone in days gone by. Delicious dinners by arrangement.

Eating Out

1774, North Port, t 451 774. Cheerful bistro with old-world atmosphere.

Almondbank Inn, at Almondbank just west on the A9 to Crieff, t 583 242. Traditional old pub on the river, with first-class, very reasonable food. Booking advisable at popular times.

Betty's, opposite the art gallery in George Street. Splendid tearoom serving memorable home-made cakes and good savoury snacks. Closes at 5.30pm.

The Bridges, Tay Street, t 625 484. Good cooking – play spot the difference between the ostrich and Scottish beef steaks!

Exceed, 65 South Methven Street, t 621 189. Imaginative tapas bar in a converted seed store.

Greyfriars, South Street. One of the best pubs, intimate and convivial.

Holdgate's, 146 South Street, t 636 922. Good old-fashioned fish and chips. Founded in 1901 and still going strong.

Keracher's, South Street, t 449 777. Excellent fish restaurant/oyster bar with game dishes, too.

The Lemon Tree, 29 Skinnergate, t 442 689. Wholefood café with mouthwatering home-baking and coffee. Above a gift shop near the back entrance to M&S.

Let's Eat, Kinnoull Street, t 643 377. Award-winning food in a bistro-type atmosphere.

Let's Eat Again, George Street, t 633 771. Reasonably priced, especially the bar meals. The fish/seafood is the thing to go for. If in doubt try the bouillabaisse.

Marcello's, South Street. First-class takeaway pizzas. Open till 11pm, and midnight on Fri and Sat.

Blackfriars Street, nearby, was the site of the long-vanished Blackfriars Monastery, where James I was murdered in 1437. The story of Catherine Douglas, Catherine 'Bar-Lass', who supposedly tried to bar the door to the murderers by using her arm as a bolt, is a 16th-century legend.

The **Fergusson Gallery** (open Mon–Sat 10–5), in the Round House in Marshall Place, is devoted to the work of the Scottish painter and leader of the Scottish 'Colourist' movement, J. D. Fergusson, and his contemporaries. Fergusson's statuesque round-bosomed women are not to everyone's taste, but his landscapes are a joy and some of his sculptures are very fine. Though he was a Perthshire man he worked mainly in France. The **Round House** used to be the city waterworks, and from a distance resembles a mosque with its minaret.

Lower City Mills, in West Mill Street (*open April–Nov Mon–Sat 10–5; adm; shop open all year*), is a restored Georgian oatmeal mill which once produced porridge for prisons all over Britain.

Balhousie Castle, a heavily restored 15th-century Scottish baronial castle beyond Rose Terrace on the west side of North Inch, was the home of the Earls of Kinnoull. Now the Regimental Headquarters of the Black Watch, it houses its **Regimental Museum** (*open May–Sept Mon–Sat 10–4.30; Oct–April Mon–Fri 10–3.30*). The Black Watch – so called because of their dark tartan – was raised in 1739 to help the government pacify the rebellious Highlanders who were gathering momentum for their final bid for independence in 1745. There is a comprehensive display of the history of this famous regiment, with uniforms, weapons, pictures, documents, photographs and trophies, all recording its many honours and triumphs.

At **Bridgend**, at the east end of Perth Bridge, there is an old toll house which still has the notice of charges for sheep, horses, etc., which put modern prices to shame.

Branklyn Gardens (*open Mar–Oct daily 9.30–dusk; adm*), off Dundee Road, were designed in 1910 by John Renton, a local estate agent, and his wife. Although only covering about 2 acres, skilful planning and unexpected vistas make them seem much larger – an excellent outing for garden planners.

Around Perth

Kinnoull Hill rises 729ft above the town, barely a mile to the east. An easy stroll from the car park in Corsie Hill Road to the surprisingly extensive summit gives a bird's-eye view of the geological 'Highland Line' that divides the Highlands from the Lowlands.

Caithness Glass Factory (*open April–Oct Mon–Sat 9–5, Sun 10–5; Nov–Mar Mon–Sat 9–5, Sun 12–5*), off the bypass at the turn-off to Inverness, demonstrates glass blowing and manufacture, and there is a good shop and restaurant.

Elcho Castle (*open April–Sept daily 9.30–6.30; adm*) is a ruin 4 miles southeast of Perth. This is one of the more interesting of the later Scottish castles, having been both defensive and yet incorporating palace-like comforts. The square tower with a crow-stepped gable dates from the 15th century. The huge kitchen has a fireplace as big as a small room, and there are traces of fine plasterwork in the hall on the first floor. The bedrooms above had en-suite garderobes. James III granted the lands of Elcho to John de Wemyss in 1468. A subsequent Sir John de Wemyss became the first Earl of Wemyss under Charles I but sided with the Parliamentarians in the Civil War.

The **Perth Mart Visitor Centre**, just off the A85 Crieff road (*open Mon–Sat 9–5.30, Sun 10–5*) is next to the Cattle Auction Market, with shops and Farm Life exhibitions. A visit to the Bull Sales is memorable for the atmosphere (*see* above).

Scone Palace

Open April–Oct daily 9.30–5.15; adm;
www.scone-palace.co.uk.

Scone Palace is 2 miles north of Perth on the A93. Pronounced 'Scoon', the palace is a 19th-century restoration of 16th-century and earlier buildings, with battlements, a toy fort façade and the original gateway. In 1297 Edward I stole the Stone of Scone and took it to London (*see* **History**, 'Stone of Destiny', p.66).

The abbey and palace that stood here in the 16th century were destroyed by John Knox's followers, after he had denounced 'idolatry' in his sermon from St John's in 1559. Now a popular tourist attraction, this neo-Gothic pile is of historical rather than aesthetic interest, though it contains some fine porcelain, 17th- and 18th-century ivories, 18th-century clocks, French furniture and memorabilia, including Marie Antoinette's writing desk and bed hangings embroidered by Mary, Queen of Scots. The walls are lined with Lyons silk. Prince Albert is said to have used the ancient bog-oak floor of the long gallery as a curling rink, which might not have amused his wife. There is a coffee shop serving home-baked food, a gift shop and gardens with a playground and pinetum.

The **Perth Hunt Racecourse**, the most northerly in Britain, is in the palace grounds in a marvellous setting.

Huntingtower Castle

Open April–Sept daily 9.30–6; Oct–Mar Mon–Wed,
Thurs and Sat 9.30–4.30, Sun 2–4.30; adm.

Huntingtower Castle is 3 miles northwest of Perth on the Crieff Road. Built by the Ruthven family in the 15th century and formerly called House of Ruthven, or Ruthven Castle, this was the scene of the Ruthven Raid in 1582 when the Earl of Gowrie and several Protestant nobles captured and held 15-year-old James VI for 10 months as a hostage, against a demand that some of the royal favourites be dismissed. The plot failed and the earl was executed two years later for his part in the kidnap, and the succeeding earl and his brother were subsequently killed as a result of the Gowrie Conspiracy in 1600 (*see* above). James then proscribed the name Ruthven and the castle became Huntingtower. In 1670 it passed to the Earl of Atholl whose grandson, Lord George Murray, Prince Charles' commander, was born here in 1694. The castle fell into ruin and was rescued by the state in 1900. There isn't a lot to see apart from some 16th-century painted walls and ceilings; it is more a place of historic interest.

Angus and Perthshire: East of the A9

Angus lies to the east of Perthshire and the A9, north of the Firth of Tay, south of Aberdeenshire. The coastal plain consists of gently rolling farmland in the Carse of Gowrie, running back up into the Sidlaw Hills where winter can linger into spring, and from whose southern slopes you can get magnificent views across the Firth of Tay to

Fife. The coast is rugged red sandstone with sandy bays. The rest of the land east of
the A9 is Perthshire, and here you are in the Highlands with all the wonderful range
of scenery they contain. Perth is the hub from which all the following routes lead.

Antiques lovers should visit **Rait Village** (*open daily 10–5*; **t** *(01821) 670 379/205*), just
off the A9 on the way to Dundee. Individual showrooms in Georgian farm steadings
have masses for browser and collector alike.

Dundee

'Twas in the month of December, and in the year 1883,
That a monster whale came to Dundee,
Resolved for a few days to sport and play,
And devour the small fishes in the silvery Tay.

                  from 'The Famous Tay Whale', by William McGonagall

Dundee, fourth-largest town in Scotland and administrative headquarters for the
area, is 22 miles northeast of Perth on the Firth of Tay.

Although the history of the town goes way back, there is little to show for it architecturally: what was not destroyed by the English and by the Reformation, the
Dundonians replaced, in the name of modernization and progress. The architectural
vandalism of the 1950s and 1960s, however, is now being replaced by more dignified
modern developments.

Traces of Bronze-Age settlements have been found locally, and a number of Pictish
stones underline the importance of this area in the Dark Ages. 'Dundee Law', with the
remains of a Roman hill fort on top, is the highest point of the city, a volcanic lump
(571ft/174m) just north of the centre – an excellent place from which to get a bird's-
eye view of the whole area.

History

Kenneth Macalpine used Dundee as his headquarters in 834, when he was
campaigning for the union of Picts and Scots. William the Lion granted it a Royal
Charter in 1190. William Wallace went to school in Dundee (which claims, in competition with Lanark, that it was here he tangled with authority and was outlawed). It was
the first town in Scotland to adopt the reformed religion and it took George Wishart
as its paragon, suffering badly as a result, when he was burned at the stake in 1546.
Hereford pounded the town for Henry VIII during the 'Rough Wooing'; Montrose
stormed it in 1645 during the Civil War; and General Monk occupied it in 1651. In 1689
James VII raised his standard on The Law, after William and Mary had been declared
King and Queen of Scotland. Fickle in their loyalties, the Dundonians swung between
the Jacobite and the Hanoverian causes, conferring the Freedom of the Burgh on
Butcher Cumberland after his victory at Culloden.

In 1889 Queen Victoria granted Dundee a charter confirming all previous charters
given since the 12th century, one of which, from Charles I, allowed rights over

revenues earned from the river – including salmon fishing. She also made it a city and a county in its own right so that, strictly speaking, it is not part of Angus.

When the great surge of energy swept through Scotland during the Scottish Enlightenment, Dundee earned its popular alliterative description as the town of **Jam, Jute and Journalism**. Towards the end of the 18th century Mr Keiller, a local grocer, bought a bargain crate of oranges, down at the docks. They proved too bitter to sell, so frugal Mrs Keiller boiled them up with sugar and water and made delicious orange jam. This caught on, and in 1797 the Keillers opened their famous jam business. There are various explanations for the name marmalade. One is that it comes from *marmelo* (quince); another, accepting that Mrs Keiller was not the first to make orange jam, that when it was made for Mary, Queen of Scots she announced that it was good for *ma malade*. The original white stone jars in which Keiller's marmalade was sold are collectors' pieces.

The jute industry, helped by whale oil from a flourishing whaling fleet, blossomed in the early 19th century, introduced by people from Angus who settled in Calcutta. Dundee became a 'boom-town', with factories and tenements shooting up like mushrooms. This prosperity lasted for 100 years until India learned to develop her raw jute and materials became scarce. Until as late as the 1950s up to 7,000 people were employed at the jute mills, and there are many who remember the flood of people pouring out of the mill gates at five o'clock. Some of the old mills have been restored: one, opposite the police station, a handsome, mid 19th-century building, has been converted into a number of small workshops. The industry has diversified in recent years and includes oil-related enterprises. Whaling remained an important industry for many years, with large numbers of boats going from Dundee as far as the Arctic.

One of the by-products of the jute boom was the arrival in Dundee of many hundreds of Catholic Highlanders and Irish, dispossessed by the potato famine and land clearance, flocking to find work in the jute mills. As a result, the city today is about one-third Catholic, an unusually high proportion for the east of Scotland.

Journalism, the third of Dundee's Js, is the great Thomson and Leng empire. This autocratic publishing firm, which has no truck with unions or Catholics, is renowned for its wholesome, unsalacious publications, which include the *Sunday Post*, *People's Friend*, the *Dandy*, the *Beano* and dozens more. Until 1992 the *Dundee Courier* was the last reputable daily newspaper to have no news on the front page.

Dundee cake, a rich, dark, fruit cake with sliced almonds on top, finds its way on to tea tables all over the world.

Dundee University was founded in 1883 and incorporated with that of St Andrews in 1889, but became independent again in 1967.

The present rail bridge, carrying the main line from London to Aberdeen, was finished in 1887, and is the longest rail bridge in Britain – 2 miles 73 yards. The road bridge, one of the longest in Europe at 1½ miles, was opened in 1966 by the Queen Mother. There is a central walkway. (*See* p.342 for the Tay Bridge Disaster.)

Despite its ancient history, Dundee is a modern city catering for modern tastes, bursting with young enterprise rather than inherited culture. Among the city's imaginative innovations is its public art. In 1982 artists sponsored by the Manpower

Tourist Information

Dundee t (01382–)
Dundee: 21 Castle Street, **t** 527 527,
www.dundeecity.gov.uk; *open all year.*

Festivals

Summer entertainments include a number
of events both on and off the water, and jazz
and folk festivals in theatres, pubs and clubs.
July: Highland Games.

Shopping

Dens Road Market, on the hill to the north of
the town centre. Lively place for collectors of
cheap junk and bric-a-brac; the stalls are in
sheds or undercover. Same boisterous atmosphere as Glasgow's 'Barras' market.

Sports and Activities

**Dundee Contemporary Arts Centre and Jute
Café Bar**, 152 Nethergate, *www.dca.org.uk*. A
weekly programme of arts activities, films,
exhibitions, classes and tours, and a shop.
Open daily from 10.30; shop closed Mon.
Dundee Rep Theatre, Tay Square, **t** 223 530,
www.dundeereptheatre.co.uk. Scotland's
only resident company producing large-
scale dramas throughout the year.

Olympia Leisure Centre, Earl Grey Place, **t** 434
888. Will occupy the children on a rainy day.

Where to Stay

Expensive
Hilton Dundee Hotel, on the waterfront in Earl
Grey Place, **t** 229 271. Splendid views over the
Tay, and every possible convenience (leisure
club with pool, sauna and whirlpool), but no
character. Packages available.
Invercarse Hotel, 371 Perth Road, **t** 669 231. A
silk merchant's mansion in Victorian times,
now converted with modern comforts.
Swallow Hotel, Kingsway West, Invergowrie,
t 631 200. Victorian mansion in nice grounds,
with modern extensions, conservatory
garden restaurant, leisure club with pool,
spa and gym. Packages offered.

Moderate
Fort Hotel, 58 Fort Street, Broughty Ferry, **t** 737
999. Recently done up, and friendly.
Grosvenor Hotel, 312 Perth Road, **t** 642 991.
Comfortable Victorian listed building overlooking the Tay, near the centre. Friendly.
Hotel Broughty Ferry, 16 West Queen Street,
Broughty Ferry, **t** 280 027. Friendly hotel with
a swimming pool.
Queen's Hotel, 160 Nethergate, **t** 322 515,
www.queenshotel-dundee.com. Near the
waterfront and comfortably Victorian and
gracious, central and well run.

Services Commission and the Scottish Development Agency went on to the streets
with their paints and tools and got to work. The result is a stimulating trail of open-
air sculpture, ceramics, murals, mosaics and every sort of graphic and plastic art. Start
at the corner of Nethergate and Marketgait, and wander. You'll trip over examples
wherever you go. It is a remarkable achievement.

City Sights

Dundee has three city churches under one roof, just west of City Square, forming a
large, cruciform building surrounded on three sides by a pedestrian shopping
precinct. The **Old Steeple**, or St Mary's Tower (*open April–Sept Mon–Sat 10–5, Sun 12–4;
Oct–Mar Mon–Sat 11–4, Sun 12–4; adm; www.oldsteeple.co.uk*), Dundee's oldest
surviving building, is 15th century, the only part that remains of the pre-Reformation
church that stood here since the 12th century. Forty-five-minute tours take you
through the building, including the fully operational belfry and the parapet with
stunning views.

Shaftesbury Hotel, 1 Hyndford Street, t 669
216, *www.shaftesbury-hotel.co.uk*. Former
Jute baron's mansion, in a quiet acre in the
west end. Friendly and comfortable.

West Park Villas, 319 Perth Road, t 647 181.
Good B&B and longer stays. *Open June–Sept.*

Woodlands, 13 Panmure Terrace, Broughty
Ferry, t 840 033. Comfortable country house
in nice grounds, with pool and gym.

Cheap

Downfield Inn, 530 Strathmartine Road, t 826
633. Small and friendly, on a bus route to the
city centre and conveniently near Downfield
golf course.

Fisherman's Tavern Hotel, 10–14 Fort Street,
Broughty Ferry, t 775 941, *www.fishermans-
tavern-hotel.co.uk*. Converted traditional
cottage on Broughty beach with a secluded
garden. Very cosy, with good pub food.

Invermark House, 23 Monifieth Road,
Broughty Ferry, t 739 430, *sharon@inver-
markhouse.fsnet.co.uk*. Large, modernised
Victorian guesthouse in a nice garden near
the town centre. Friendly atmosphere.

Eating Out

The Agacan, 113 Perth Road, t 644 227. Delicious
Turkish food, spit-roast meat and arty décor.
Open Tues–Sun from 5pm; closed Mon.

Café Buongiorno, 11 Bank Street, t 221 179.
Jolly Italian atmosphere.

Café Montmartre, Gray Street, Broughty Ferry,
t 739 313. Delightful French bistro. *Open
Mon–Sat dinner only.*

Deep Sea, 81 Nethergate. First-class fish and
chips.

Fisherman's Tavern, Broughty Ferry (*see
above*). Good pub food.

Frasers, 594 Brook Street, Broughty Ferry, t 730
890. Good French food, reasonably priced, in
a relaxed atmosphere.

Jute, the Art Centre, Perth Road, t 432 000.
Splendid, fun place for lively snacks and
meals. *Open daily 10.30am–midnight.*

Pizza Express, 31 Albert Square, t 226 677.
Excellent pizzas. *Open daily lunch only.*

Raffles, 18 Perth Road, t 226 344. Popular
restaurant near the university with reasonable, unfussy food at reasonable prices.
Closed Mon.

Ship Inn, 121 Fisher Street, on the waterfront
at Broughty Ferry, t 779176. Very good
food in the upstairs restaurant with the
accent on Scottish ingredients, and pub
food in the lounge bar downstairs.
Advisable to book.

Visocchi's, 40 Gray Street, Broughty Ferry,
t 779 297. Italian snacks and ices.

Entertainment

Mardi Gras, South Ward Street, t 205 551.
Lively nightclub for those who like
loud music.

The **Howf** (burial ground or meeting-place) is northwest of the square. It was once
the orchard of the Greyfriars Monastery, founded in the 13th century. Mary, Queen of
Scots gave the land to the city and it became a cemetery. You can still see a number of
old gravestones with curious inscriptions.

McManus Art Galleries and Museum (*open Mon–Sat 10–5.30, Thurs till 7, Sun
12.30–4*), a Victorian Gothic building in Albert Square north of City Square, is the
Central Museum and Art Gallery. Exhibitions cover local history, archaeology and
wildlife, including the Tay whale, and a guide to the development of the town from
the Iron Age: the Picts, the Jute, social history and even the Tay Bridge disaster.

The art gallery contains work by Flemish, Dutch, French and British artists, with
some lovely Scottish paintings and frequent modern exhibitions. Among the
paintings in the permanent collection are seascapes by McTaggart, landscapes by
James McIntoch Patrick, works by Landseer and Millais, and the Pre-Raphaelite
Dante's Dream by Rossetti.

Look out for the Wishart Arch, an old gateway at Cowgate. It is so called because it was from here that the reformer George Wishart preached during the plague of 1544, two years before he was burned for heresy by Cardinal Beaton (*see* p.340).

Discovery (*open April–Oct Mon–Sat 10–5, Sun 11–5; Nov–Mar Mon–Sat 10–4, Sun 11–4; adm; www.rrsdiscovery.com*), on Discovery Quay, is the research ship used by Captain Scott for the first of his two expeditions to the Antarctic in 1901. Built in Dundee, this tall-masted, thick-hulled beauty now rides out her berthed retirement equipped with smells and sounds and life-sized models that transform her into a fantasyland surrounded by tourist traps. The cosy living quarters, the gleaming brass and wood-work, even the penguin in the oven, all make Captain Scott's expeditions look rather a lark. The reality was one long struggle for survival in deep-freeze temperatures and sullen or mountainous seas, with *Titanic*-type icebergs knocking on the hull and death an ever-present threat. There is a visitor centre adjacent where you can watch an introductory film and, perhaps, get a little nearer to what life was really like for those brave men.

Much more 'authentic', though less spectacular as a result, HM Frigate *Unicorn* is in Victoria Dock (*open same times as* Discovery, *except Jan–Mar closed weekends; adm; www.frigateunicorn.org*), a 46-gun wooden warship, launched at Chatham in 1824. She is the oldest British-built ship still afloat, the most completely preserved wooden sailing ship in the world, and the fourth-oldest ship afloat in the world, a unique survivor from the transitional period between wooden sailing ships and iron steamships. She was never fully rigged and never engaged in enemy action; for some years she was a prison hulk.

Verdant Works, in West Henderson's Wynd (*open April–Oct Mon–Sat 10–5, Sun 11–5; Nov–Mar Mon–Sat 10–4, Sun 11–4; adm; www.verdantworks.com*), is a working jute mill, and fascinating. The story of Dundee's relationship to the jute industry is most imaginatively demonstrated, from India to the end product. There are computer displays and hands-on activities, the authentic atmosphere of the machine room, and the social history of the workers.

Sensation, at Green Market (*open summer daily from 10am; call **t** (01382) 228 800, for winter times; adm; www.sensation-dundee.com*), is a live science centre, not for the over-squeamish, with over 60 interactive exhibits including keyhole surgery!

Shaws Sweet Factory, Visitor Centre and Shop, in the Keillers Building (*34 Mains Loan; open Mar–May and Sept–Dec Wed 1.30–4; June–Aug Mon–Fri 11–4, exc closed last week July and 1st week Aug; www.shawsdundee.co.uk*), is a 1950s-style workshop, with machinery dating from 1936. The sweets are handmade from recipes dating from 1879.

On top of Balgay Hill, northwest of City Square, **Mills Observatory** (*open April–Sept Tues–Fri 11–5, Sat and Sun 12.30–4; Oct–Mar Mon–Fri 4–10, Sat and Sun 12.30–4: special opening times for celestial events such as eclipses; www.mills-observatory.co.uk*) has telescopes, displays on astronomy and space exploration, a lecture room and a small planetarium. There is an audiovisual programme, an astronomer in residence, and a shop. Even without the telescopes, the view from up here is good, and when the skies are clear on winter evenings it is easy to get hooked on star-gazing.

Camperdown Park, further northwest, one of Dundee's 28 parks and gardens, was opened by the present Queen in 1946, when she was still Princess Elizabeth. It consists of about 400 acres of wooded parkland and garden with rare trees, a golf course, tennis courts, and a wildlife centre with bears, lynx, arctic foxes, pine marten, etc. There is a wildlife trail for children, and special events. Camperdown House, the mansion in the middle, was designed by William Burn in 1828 and contains a restaurant. **Clatto Country Park**, in Dalmahoy Drive off the A972, is a reservoir area with 24 acres of water sheltered by woods, popular for windsurfing and sailing. (You can hire equipment.) **Dundee University Botanic Gardens** (*open Mar–Oct Mon–Sat 10–4.30, Sun 11–4; Nov–Feb Mon–Sat 10–3.30, Sun 11–3; adm*), on Riverside Drive, has an award-winning visitor centre and landscaped gardens with native and exotic plants, both outside and in tropical and temperate pavilions.

Outside the Centre

Claypotts Castle (*not open to the public*) jumps out at you from a nightmare housing development just off the busy junction of the A92 and B978. One of the few castles in Scotland to remain unaltered since it was built in the 16th century, Claypotts is a four-storied Z-plan tower house with two round towers, crow-stepped gables, tiny windows, massive stonework and parapet walks. Incongruous as the setting now is, the castle somehow manages to retain a certain dignity, shrugging off the clutter of modern suburbia that sprawls at its feet. It belonged to the Grahams of Claverhouse, but was forfeited and given to the Douglas family after the famous 'Bonnie Dundee', Earl of Claverhouse, was killed at the Battle of Killiecrankie. Keep an eye out for the ghost that haunts its chambers, the vengeful spirit of a favoured maid servant who was unfairly deposed by a jealous rival. You can only see the castle from the outside.

Broughty Ferry, dominated by its castle, is on the coast road, 4 miles to the east. Although the fishing fleet has long vanished, a number of fisher cottages remain in the narrow wynds and courtyards off Fisher Street, steeped in the seafaring history of the community. It is easy to imagine the old fishermen mending their nets on the shore by their boats, drawn up above the tide. The village still mourns the tragic loss of its lifeboat *Mona* in 1959, with her crew of eight brave men, stranded and capsized on nearby Budden Sands in one of the ferocious gales that sweep this coast. The beach stretches away to the east in a long, sandy crescent.

Ancient Castle of Broughty Ferry
With walls as strong as Londonderry;
Near by the sea-shore,
Where oft is heard and has been heard the cannon's roar
In the present day and days of yore,
Loudly echoing from shore to shore.
from 'Broughty Ferry', by William McGonagall

Broughty Castle and Museum (*open April–Sept Mon–Sat 10–4, Sun 12.30–4; Oct–Mar closed Mon*) stands on a rocky promontory, towering over a tiny harbour that dries out at low tide. Built in the 15th century on the site of a Pictish fort, it had a commanding position guarding the entrance to the firth, from which to levy tolls from ships wanting to come up the river. The Gray family who owned the castle also controlled the ferry linking Broughty with Fife. The fourth Lord Gray sided with the English during the 'Rough Wooing' and allowed English troops to occupy this strategic strong-hold for three years until the French managed to recapture it for the Scots in 1550. Extensively restored in 1860, it is now a museum devoted mainly to the whaling industry that once flourished along this coast, and to the ecology of the Tay – much needed, as the pollution is bad here.

Two miles inland from Broughty Ferry, Historic Scotland signs point to **Ardestie**, on the A92, and **Carlungie**, a mile to the north, two well-preserved souterrains. These underground earthhouses, once covered by stone roofs, have chambers and passages which were the byres and silos of Pictish farmers in the 1st and 2nd centuries. It is thought they did not live in these souterrains, but nothing is certain about the Picts and they may have used them as places of refuge.

At **Monikie**, 5 miles north of Broughty Ferry on the archaeological detour, there is a country park around the reservoir, with walks, boating and picnic sites. You get splendid views from up here, down over fertile farmland to the distant coast where the constantly shifting sandbanks have claimed many ships over the centuries. The trees on the ridge above are sculpted into curious wedge shapes by the strong prevailing wind.

East from Dundee, Along the Coast

Carnoustie

Back on the coast road, Carnoustie, 10 miles east of Dundee, is a holiday resort and golf centre, with a championship course. Right on the sea, the town is a popular place in summer, with its own musical society, plenty of holiday activities and a conference centre which seats 500 people.

Barry Mill, two miles west of Carnoustie (*open April–Sept daily 11–5; Oct Sat and Sun 11–5*) is an early 19th-century working corn mill, with exhibitions on the history and role the mill played in the community, and some attractive walks.

Arbroath

Arbroath is 17 miles northeast of Dundee. The massive ruin of the red sandstone abbey rises from the heart of the town, surrounded by lawns and flowerbeds, the hub of a holiday resort and fishing centre. The Declaration of Independence was signed in the abbey in 1320 after Robert the Bruce's victory at Bannockburn, establishing Scotland's independence from England.

The most famous quote from this document has been an inspiration for many generations of aspiring nationalists, and indeed was used as the basis for the American Declaration of Independence:

...for as long as but a hundred of us remain alive, never will we on any conditions be brought under English rule. It is in truth not for glory, nor riches, nor honours that we fight, but for freedom – for that alone, which no honest man gives up but with life itself.

Perhaps Arbroath is best known now as the home of the 'smokie' – haddock smoked over wood-chip fires in the backyards of the fishertown between the harbour and the abbey. Many of the cottages display signs indicating that they sell the freshly smoked fish, and anyone who has not tried an Arbroath smokie should do so. One of the nicest ways to eat them is cold, with brown bread and butter, plenty of lemon juice and copious grindings of black pepper.

Arbroath Abbey (*open April–Sept Mon–Sat 9.30–6.30, Sun 2–6.30; Oct–Mar Mon–Sat 9.30–4.30, Sun 2–4.30; adm*) was founded by William the Lion in 1178 and dedicated to Thomas à Becket who had recently been murdered in Canterbury Cathedral. You can see William's tomb in the sacristy. The abbey holds a very special place in Scottish history: the original Declaration of Independence, written here in stirring Latin by its Abbot, Bernard of Linton, Chancellor of Scotland, is in Charter House, in Edinburgh, but you can buy a copy of it here, with translation. The abbey managed to survive the Reformation until 1606, when it was made a temporal lordship. Its final decay was due to neglect rather than vandalism or deliberate destruction. Parts of the ruin date from the 13th century, including the gable of the south transept and the west façade with its tower and entrance. They used to put lamps in the round window high above the south transept, as a landmark for ships at sea. The abbot's house is now the **museum**, with displays illustrating the domestic life of the religious community and a collection of Scottish medieval art.

Signal Tower Museum (*open July and Aug Mon–Sat 10–5, Sun 2–5; Sept–June Mon–Sat 10–5*) is a museum with exhibitions of local interest. It was originally built in 1813 as the signalling station for the Bell Rock Lighthouse, and its displays include fishing, the flax industry, archaeology and natural history. There is an **art gallery** in the library, which has works by Brueghel as well as a good variety of Scottish paintings.

From **Whiting Ness**, north of the wide promenade, you can walk for miles along the cliff top, with the sea pounding restlessly at the redstone rocks below, honeycombed with caves and deep inlets. Wild flowers cling to the steep slopes: thrift, vetch and sea grasses. The lonely cry of curlews with long, curved beaks and the shrill 'kubik-kubik' of black and white oystercatchers with vivid orange beaks can be heard over the booming waves. From the narrow path you get views over a sea dotted with trawlers, tankers, coasters and small boats. If the visibility is good, you should be able to see the **Bell Rock Lighthouse**, 12 miles out to the east and familiar to anyone who knows Southey's 'Ballad of the Inchcape Rock'. The Abbot of Arbroath fixed a warning bell on the hazardous rock to warn off mariners. Sir Ralph the Rover, a notorious pirate with a grudge against the abbot, cut the bell adrift. Later, sailing home in a fog, the pirate was wrecked on the rock. *Nemo me impune lacessit.*

Tourist Information

Carnoustie: t (01241) 852 258; *open April–Sept.*
Arbroath: Market Place, **t** (01241) 872 609; *open all year.*
Montrose: t (01674) 672 000; *open April–Sept.*

Festivals

July: Highland Games, Arbroath. **Donkey Derby**, Arbroath.
August: Flower Show, Arbroath.
September: Festival of Highland Dancing, Arbroath.

Where to Stay and Eat

Letham Grange Resort Hotel, Colliston, by Arbroath, **t** (01241) 890 373, *www. lethamgrange.co.uk* (*expensive*). Restored Victorian mansion in a sporting estate, with two golf courses and an indoor ice rink. Stylish, comfortable and well run. Good food.

Montrose Park Hotel, Mid Links, Montrose, **t** (01674) 663 400, *www.montrosepark.co.uk* (*expensive–moderate*). Quiet but central. Comfortable rooms and a dining room serving 'Scottish fayre'.

George Hotel, 22 George Street, Montrose, **t** (01674) 675 050, *www.thegeorge-montrose.co.uk* (*moderate*). Large, central and friendly.

Idvies House, Letham, **t** (01307) 818 787, *www.idvies.racetek.co.uk* (*moderate*). Attractive Victorian house run by its owners, with nice bedrooms including a four-poster room, a squash court and a billiard room.

Links Hotel, Mid Links, Montrose, **t** (01674) 671 000, *www.linkshotel.com* (*moderate*). Similar to the Montrose Park, with a bistro-style terrace restaurant and a nightclub.

The Old Manor, Panbridge, Carnoustie, contact Mrs Pape **t** (01241) 854 804, *www.carnoustiecottage.com* (*moderate–cheap*). Sea views from well-equipped self-catering cottage (sleeping 4 plus 2).

Auchmithie Hotel, Auchmithie, just north of Arbroath, **t** (01241) 873 010 (*cheap*). Splendid friendly place overlooking the harbour and the sandstone cliffs. Children welcome, and there is courtesy transport (within reason).

Glencoul House, Justinhaugh, contact Mrs Kirby **t** (01307) 860 248 (*cheap*). An old stone farmhouse.

The Wee Anchor, The Old Brewhouse, 3–5 High Street, Arbroath, **t** (01241) 879 945 (*cheap*). Traditional fisherman's cottage for self-catering at Seagate, the original harbour and now a conservation area. Central heating and cosy fire (sleeping 4).

The But 'n' Ben, Auchmithie, north of Arbroath, **t** (01241) 877 223. Cosy cottages converted into lively restaurant. Good seafood.

Gordons, Inverkeilor, **t** (01241) 830 364. Convenient restaurant on the A92, with modern and traditional dishes.

The cliff path takes you to **Auchmithie**, 3 miles to the north. Referred to as Musselcraig, in Walter Scott's *The Antiquary*, it is an ancient, picturesque village believed to have been the fishing centre in the old days. In the 18th century fishermen carried on a flourishing lobster trade with London, and it was here that the smokie industry was born. It is built on a rocky ridge above a tiny harbour with a flat chequerboard of farmland stretching away inland. The caves along this coast were much used by smugglers in the 18th century.

St Vigeans

As you come out of Arbroath going north on the A92, take the road signposted to St Vigeans, on the left. After less than a mile, park at the railway bridge and cross the Brothock Burn by footbridge to discover this gem of a hamlet, nestling out of sight below modern housing developments. A small red sandstone church is perched on top of a steep pre-Christian mound, 40ft high, like an upturned basin, neatly kept and studded with gravestones. This was once the parish church of Arbroath, predating the abbey by about 80 years. Extensive restoration over the years has more or less obliterated its early 12th-century origins, but there are still a few traces inside, and the tower dates from the 15th century. During one of its restorations, 32 carved stones were collected, some of which had been in the kirk and some used as part of its fabric. They were moved across to one of the red sandstone cottages with stone-slabbed roofs that form a semicircle at the foot of the mound. This is now the **St Vigeans Museum** (*open April–Sept daily 9.30–6; key at No. 7 at other times*). These Pictish and Celtic stones are well displayed and comprehensively explained. The **Drosten Stone** has one of the few inscriptions in Roman letters to be found on such stones, suggesting that the Picts were more literate than is often supposed. The first word is Drosten, the rest too worn to be more than guessed at. Even if archaeology bores you stiff, you will be intrigued by the intricate carvings on these ancient stones.

Redcastle (*always accessible*) is 7 miles up the coast. A 15th-century ruin jutting out on a cliff high above the sea, it dominates the sandy crescent of Lunan Bay below. To reach it you have to climb up a short, steepish path through trees and whins. The castle was built on the site of an old fort to protect the coast from Danish pirates, and William the Lion lived here while he was building Arbroath Abbey. It witnessed several battles and was partly demolished during one that sprang from a feud between its occupant and her divorced husband.

Look out for the **Elephant Rock** on Lunan Bay, between Usan and Boddin – you can't mistake this fossilized pachyderm as it lumbers out to sea.

Montrose

Beautiful town of Montrose, I will now commence my lay,
And I will write in praise of thee without dismay,
And in spite of all your foes,
I will venture to call thee Bonnie Montrose.
from 'Montrose', by William McGonagall

Montrose is almost on an island, with sea to the east, the River South Esk to the south, and a wide tidal basin to the west. There is a spacious feeling about the town: the middle section of the High Street is as wide as a market square. You can still see a few of the houses that were built gable-end on to the street, leading through to narrow closes and secret courtyards. Records tell of a Danish invasion in 980. The castle that once guarded the town was taken over by Edward I in 1296 and destroyed by William Wallace a year later. It was from here that Sir James Douglas embarked, carrying the heart of Robert the Bruce, on its abortive pilgrimage to the Holy Land (*see p.327*). James Graham, the Marquis of Montrose, was born in Old Montrose on the south side of the tidal basin in 1612. In 1715 the first of the Jacobite Rebellions ended ignominiously in Montrose when the Old Pretender set sail back to France from here.

A tenth of the world's population of pink-footed geese migrate to Montrose's tidal basin every November from their Arctic breeding grounds. This great wildfowl sanctuary is a marvellous place in winter, when you can hear the ceaseless grumble and chatter of the birds as they feed on the mud flats and the haunting sound they make as they circle in from the sky. It is remarkable to find such a wild haven so close to the town with its docks and shipping, its sturdy buildings and oil-related prosperity. **Montrose Basin Wildlife Centre** (*open April–Oct daily 10.30–5; Nov–Mar daily 10.30–4; t (01674) 676 336*), run by the Scottish Wildlife Trust at Rossie Braes, has a splendid observation room from which to view the birds and roosts.

A profitable slave trade flourished briefly in Montrose, and smuggling was a thriving activity in the 18th century. Because of its out-of-the-way situation, and a shortage of customs officers, the strongly Jacobite population had no conscience about defrauding a Hanoverian government of its income from excise duty. The words 'Mare Ditat' (the sea enriches) are aptly inscribed on the Montrose coat of arms. The undulating countryside has several good golf courses. In July the town holds its Rose Queen Ceremony and in August a Flower Show and Highland Games.

The **House of Dun** (*open Easter weekend, May–June and Sept daily 1.30–5.30; July and Aug daily 11–5.30; Oct Sat and Sun 1.30–5.30; adm; gardens and grounds open all year daily 9.30–sunset*), 3 miles west of Montrose, is a modest-sized Palladian house overlooking Montrose Basin. It was designed by William Adam in 1730 for David Erskine, Lord Dun. One of his descendants married Augusta, the natural daughter of William IV and Mrs Jordan, who created the lovely garden. It has flamboyant plasterwork in the saloon and much of the original furniture, found hidden away when the house was resurrected. Outside, there are woodland walks and exhibitions, including weaving displays and bothies containing a keeper's room and a potting shed.

Inland Angus

Brechin

Returning to Perth on the inland route, Brechin is 9 miles west of Montrose, sprawled up a steep bank above the South Esk in fertile Strathmore.

You can get a rather cluttered overview of the local history in a small **museum** in St Ninian Square (*open Tues and Thurs 9.30–6, Wed 9.30–8, Fri and Sat 9.30–5*).

The **Cathedral** and **Tower** are the focal points of this ancient town. These red sandstone buildings are perched above the twisting wynds, little courtyards and houses built gable-end on to the road. The tapering tower, restored in 1960, is one of only two such towers in mainland Scotland (the other is in Abernethy). Dating from 990, the tower's door is 6ft above the ground, giving the inhabitants greater security. The feet of the crucified Christ, carved on the lintel, are uncrossed, indicating an Irish influence in the design. (There are 76 of these towers in Ireland today.)

Now a parish church, the cathedral dates from the 13th century and was restored in 1900. The Pictish stones inside have interesting carvings on them, and you can also see a 16th-century font and some 17th-century pewter and silver.

Maison Dieu, off Market Street, is a single wall with a pointed, arched door, three narrow windows and a piscina – all that remains of an almshouse, hospice and chapel founded in 1256.

Brechin Castle Centre, at Haughmuir (*open summer Mon–Sat 9–6, Sun 10–6; winter Mon–Sat 9–5, Sun 10–5; adm; www.brechincastlecentre.co.uk*), is part of the Dalhousie Estates, with a country park, adventure playground, miniature railway, farm trail, etc. The highlight is **Pictavia** (*www.pictavia.org.uk*), with imaginative Pictish displays about our enigmatic ancestors.

Around Brechin

Six miles north of Brechin on the B966, **Edzell**, in the valley of the North Esk, is one of the places visited by Queen Victoria. The 19th-century Dalhousie Arch was erected in 1887 in memory of the 13th Earl of Dalhousie and his countess, who died within hours of each other.

Edzell Castle (*open April–Sept Mon–Sat 9.30–6.30, Sun 2–6.30; Oct–Mar Mon–Wed and Sat 9.30–4.30, Thurs 9.30–1, Sun 2–4.30; adm*) is a 16th-century ruin forming a red backdrop to the Pleasance, a walled garden designed by David Lindsay, Lord Edzell, in 1604. Even if your taste runs to gardens that overflow with soft lines and merging shapes, you cannot but be impressed by this horribly immaculate formal garden. It is modelled on the gardens at Nuremberg, and the flower-filled recesses in the walls are intricate heraldic emblems, concealing gun loops. A beautifully kept box hedge, bordering rose beds, has been clipped to spell out the somewhat phlegmatic Lindsay family motto: *Dum spiro spero* (While I breathe I hope). The foundations of a bath house were excavated in the corner of the garden in 1855, revealing a bath and a dressing and reclining room with a fireplace.

Mary, Queen of Scots held a council in the castle in 1562, and it was garrisoned by Cromwell's troops in 1651. A grisly story is told of a curse put on the Earl's family at Edzell by a gypsy, after they had ordered her two dumb sons to be hanged for poaching. Lady Crawford died the same day and her husband was torn apart by wolves a year later.

The **Caterthuns** are 6 miles southwest of Edzell, at Menmuir. These are two Iron-Age hill forts on a ridge, the higher one having spilled its masonry down the hill to mix with the lower. The original enclosing wall must have been as much as 40ft thick. If you follow the wooded valley of West Water from here up into the hills towards Loch Lee, you are following in the footsteps of Macbeth, as he fled from Dunsinane.

Before you go on towards Forfar, you should explore **Glen Esk** running north into the Grampians, carved by the North Esk and its tributaries. **Glenesk Folk Museum** (*open Easter weekend–May Sat–Mon 12–6; June–mid-Oct daily 12–6; adm*) is 10 miles north-west of Edzell at Tarfside. Once a shooting lodge, it contains exhibits showing what life was like in this area from about 1800 onwards, and there is a tearoom and craft/gift shop. All the Angus glens, such as Glen Isla and Glen Clova, are lovely.

Finavon Castle (*always accessible*) is 6 miles southwest of Brechin on the A94, a jagged ruin overgrown by nettles and scrub. It doesn't look much of a place now, until you look up at the 86ft tower and think of the day when the notorious Earl Beardie Crawford hanged his minstrel from a hook somewhere at the top. This he did because the wretched minstrel had foretold Earl Beardie's defeat at the Battle of Brechin in

Tourist Information

Brechin: t (01356) 623 050; *open April–Sept.*
Forfar: t (01307) 467 876; *open April–Sept.*
Kirriemuir: t (01575) 574 097; *open April–Sept.*
Blairgowrie: 26 Wellmeadow, **t** (01250) 872
960; ski information line, **t** (01250) 875 800;
open all year.

Festivals

August: Highland Games, Birnam.

Where to Stay and Eat

Castleton House Hotel, Glamis, **t** (01307)
840 340 (*expensive*). Select country house
hotel (6 de luxe rooms) in 11 acres of garden
and woods, 3 miles from the castle. First-
class food, fishing, shooting, stalking
and golf.

Drumnacree House, St Ninians Road, Alyth,
t (01828) 632 194 (*moderate*). Very friendly
hosts. The Oven Bistro serves good food,
made from local produce, with a varied
menu. It's very popular, so essential to book
in advance.

Finavon Hotel, by Forfar, **t** (01307) 850 234,
www.finavonhotel.demon.co.uk (*moderate*).
Attractive coaching inn on the banks of the
River South Esk. Cosy and informal, with
children's play area.

Glenesk Hotel, High Street, Edzell, **t** (01356)
648 319 (*moderate*). Family-run hotel next to
a golf course, with its own leisure complex
(pod, spa, sauna) and comfortable rooms.

Panmure Arms, 52 High Street, Edzell, **t** (01356)
648 950, *www.panmurearmshotel.co.uk*
(*moderate*). Newly done up and comfortable,
with friendly service.

Royal Hotel, Castle Street, Forfar, **t** (01307) 462
691 (*moderate*). Lively, former coaching inn
in the centre, with bustle and atmosphere.

Blibberhill, Brechin, run by Mrs Wendy
Stewart, **t** (01307) 830 323 (*cheap*). Old farmhouse run by a young family who will make
you so welcome you won't want to leave.

Cosy Neuk, 41 Westfield Loan, Forfar, contact
Mrs Graham **t** (01307) 464 553.

Peel Farm Coffee and Craft Shop, near Alyth,
just north of Reekie Linn. Farmhouse baking.

Picturesque, High Street, Edzell, **t** (01356) 648
699. Tiny tearoom serving delicious home-
made goodies. Also an eccentric, gallery/
shop with original paintings and pottery.

1452. The history of the Lindsay family is full of bloodcurdling stories, and it is for these
that the ruin is memorable, rather than for its appearance.

Take the little back road that climbs and twists 2 miles southeast from Finavon, up
over the hills through rugged scenery of dry stone walls and moorland, where black-
faced sheep graze the turf between patches of bracken and gorse. As you come down
the far side of the ridge, **Finavon Hill** is on your left. It is a short climb to one of the
finest vitrified Iron-Age hill forts in the land, in a shallow depression at the top. Its
shape and turf-covered ramparts are easily seen, and there is a central spring, or well.
Excavations in the 1930s revealed evidence of metal working, pot making and
weaving on this lofty summit with its glorious views up Strathmore to the Mearns
and west to Blairgowrie. It is strange to think of those tough Picts busy up here,
striving to exist on the hill top, keen-eyed and ever alert for danger.

If you are interested in the early settlers, go on down the back road from Finavon to
the B9134 and turn left a few hundred yards to **Aberlemno**. This tiny hamlet has four
remarkable Pictish stones. Three stand beside the road. The finest, however, is in the
churchyard. The carvings on this stone, 7ft high, are amazingly clear: a Celtic cross on
one side, flanked by intertwined creatures, and a stirring battle scene on the other, all
with intricate detail. This stone is believed to mark the grave of a Pictish king,
Feradach. The little kirk is simple and charming. Inside, an 18th-century Bible has dates
printed at the top of each page: the date of Genesis is set at 4004 BC.

Hatton, Ogilvy, Glamis, contact Mrs Jarron t (01307) 840 229 (*cheap*). On a family-run farm.

Kinloch House Hotel, near Blairgowrie, t (01250) 884 237, f 884 333, *www.kinlochhouse.com* (*expensive*). Gracious living in a typical early Victorian Scottish country house with oak-panelled hall, gallery, antique furniture and paintings, in 20 acres of wooded grounds. High-class food, shooting, fishing and golf.

Pitlochry Hydro, Blairgowrie, t (01796) 472 666, f 472 788, *www.shearingsholidays.co.uk* (*expensive*). An imposing stone building above the town overlooking the Tummel Valley. It has an indoor swimming pool, jacuzzi, sauna, solarium and gymnasium.

Ashintully Castle, Kirkmichael, Blairgowrie, t (01250) 881 237, f 881 490, *carol.steel@virgin.net* (*moderate*). Dating from 1583, was modernized in 1969 without spoiling its character. Well secluded in 3,000 acres, run as a sheep farm and sporting estate. A Wolsey Lodge with *cordon bleu* cooking and lots of outdoor activities on offer to guests.

Angus Hotel, Blairgowrie, t (01250) 872 455, f 875 615, *www.theangus.freeserve.co.uk*

(*moderate*). Large and rambling with an indoor swimming pool, sauna, solarium and spa. Golf and fishing on the doorstep and, though its size makes it a bit impersonal, it is comfortable, well run and convenient.

Altamount House, Coupar Angus Road, Blairgowrie, t (01250) 873 512, *altamounthouse@aol.com* (*moderate*). Georgian manor house in 6 acres. Nice rooms and good food.

Lochside Lodge, Bridgend of Lintrathen, t (01575) 560 340. Excellent food in converted farm steading (and you can stay here).

Clova Hotel, at the head of Glen Clova, t (01575) 550 222 (*cheap*). Outdoor activities.

Glenisla Hotel, Kirkton of Glenisla, t (01575) 582 223, f 582 203, *www.glenisla-hotel.co.uk* (*cheap*). Homely 17th-century coaching inn, with oak beams and atmosphere.

Dalmunzie House Hotel, Glenshee, t (01250) 885 224, f 885 225, *dalmunzie@aol.com* (*moderate*). Known as 'the Hotel in the Hills' – a vast Highland mansion in 6,000 acres with a nine-hole golf course, tennis courts, fishing, shooting and stalking. Comfortable, with log fires and good Scottish cooking, and only 5 miles from the ski slopes.

Bridge of Cally Hotel, t (01250) 886 231 (*cheap*). Cosy and friendly and very reasonable.

Pitmuies Garden (*open Easter–Oct daily 10–5; adm*), off the A932 to Forfar, is an outstanding garden, around an 18th-century house, with masses of spring bulbs, roses, herbaceous borders and many shrubs. There is a waterside walk and fine old trees. Look out for Guthrie Castle (*private*), close by on the main road. The entrance was built about 150 years ago to disguise a bridge on the old railway.

Restenneth Priory (*always accessible*) is 5 miles southwest of Aberlemno, just before you get to Forfar on the B9134. Surrounded by gently sloping meadows and scattered trees, it rises from a bowl of marshy ground that was once a peninsula jutting into a loch which was drained in the 18th century. In AD 710 Nechan, High King of the Picts, was baptized here by St Boniface. Nechan used Northumbrian masons to build a church in Romanesque style, possibly to celebrate his victory over the King of Northumbria at the Battle of Nechtansmere. In the 13th century Augustinian monks built a priory on the same site, incorporating the original tower. It is a tranquil place, the old stones rising from green sward. You can almost hear the voices of those far-off monks, chanting plainsong, as you stand in the ruined choir. An infant son of Robert the Bruce is believed to have been buried here.

Forfar

Just southwest of Restenneth, the busy town of Forfar has little left to see of its history. Once a thriving jute and linen milling centre, it now produces synthetic textiles, as well as tartans and tweeds. The **town and county hall** is early 19th century, designed by William Playfair, with a splendid council chamber in which you can see paintings by Raeburn, Romney, Hoppner and Opie. The town centre is attractive, with cobbled streets and warm sandstone buildings swirling around an island on which the town hall stands. Just around the corner in West High Street is the **Meffan Institute Museum and Art Gallery** (*open Mon–Sat 10–5*) which houses, as well as the library, a small museum of local interest in which you can see the dreadful **Forfar Bridle**. This is a metal collar, hinged to clip around the neck, with a prong in front to gag the unfortunate women who wore it while being burned at the stake as witches in the 17th century. There are some good displays with stirring sound effects. Forfar Loch, west of the town, is a so-called pleasure park, with picnic areas around an uninspiring small stretch of water.

Forfar to Perth via Glamis

Glamis

The southern route on the A94 takes you first to Glamis (pronounced *Glahms*), a hamlet in a wooded hollow just off the main road. History-steeped **Glamis Castle** (*open April–Oct daily 10.30–5.30 (last adm 4.45); July and Aug opens at 10; 50min guided tours; adm*) is approached down a wide tree-lined avenue from the top of which the pink-grey castle stands out against the distant hills, all angles, towers, wings, turrets and heraldic embellishments. It is grand rather than beautiful. Queen Elizabeth, the late Queen Mother, who died in March 2002 aged nearly 102, spent much of her childhood at Glamis, and her daughter, Princess Margaret, was born here. It's well worth getting the excellent guide book.

The land was granted to the Lyon family, Earls of Strathmore, by King Robert II in 1372, and it was their descendants who became Earls of Glamis, Kinghorne and Strathmore. Glamis has the reputation for being the most haunted castle in Scotland, and many are the spine-chilling tales that have been born from its stones. No one dares to enter the sealed crypt where huge red-bearded Beardie Crawford played cards with the Devil on the Sabbath; no one can account for the window that looks out from a chamber that does not exist on an upper floor.

The present castle dates mostly from the 17th century, with bits of the older building incorporated, including King Malcolm's room where Malcolm II is said to have died. The oldest part is Duncan's Hall, traditionally the setting for Shakespeare's *Macbeth*.

There are formal 19th-century Italian gardens and extensive parkland. A licensed restaurant sells light lunches and teas and there's a playground and quality shops selling gifts, books, small antiques, garden products and paintings by Scottish artists.

The **Angus Folk Museum** (*open April–June and Sept daily 11–5; July and Aug daily 10–5; Oct Sat and Sun 11–5 (last adm 4.30); adm*) is in Kirkwynd in the village beyond the castle, past the Strathmore Arms and a thatched cottage that is a rare sight among the pantiles and slates in this area. In the care of the National Trust for Scotland, the museum is in a terrace of picturesque early 19th-century cottages, meticulously restored in 1957, with stone-slabbed roofs and flagged floors. There are over 1,000 things to see, including a kitchen from 1807 with all the original fittings and furnishings, and a collection of agricultural tools and equipment. The museum gives a picture of how country people lived up to 200 years ago. There is even a Victorian manse parlour.

The **Glamis Stone** is in the garden of today's manse, opposite the museum, visible from the road. This 9-foot-high stone has intricate Pictish carvings. It is also called King Malcolm's Stone, from the belief that Malcolm II was buried here in 1034, having died in the castle. In fact, the stone is of an earlier date, possibly 9th century.

If ancient stones are what you enjoy, you will find plenty more nearby including **St Orland's**, or the **Crossans Stone**, standing 7ft tall in a field by the railway 2 miles to the north. This slender, repaired stone has carvings showing men in a boat.

Meigle

Meigle, nearly 7 miles southwest of Glamis, is the legendary burial place for King Arthur's poor faithless Guinevere. It also has a remarkable collection of early Christian Pictish stones. **Meigle Museum** (*open April–Nov Mon–Sat 9.30–12.30 and 1.30–6, Sun 2–6; adm*), in the old school, contains about 30 stones from the 6th to the 10th centuries, almost all found in or near the old churchyard. The carvings disprove any idea that the Picts were half-naked savages: they show elaborate clothing, weapons and equipment, and an unquestionably civilized culture. The large stone in the centre is thought to be Queen Guinevere's gravestone and portrays Daniel in the Lion's Den, possibly symbolizing Guinevere being torn apart by wild beasts. Beautifully displayed, with a descriptive leaflet, these stones stir the imagination, and are said to be one of the finest collections of Dark-Age sculpture in Western Europe.

Coupar Angus

Coupar Angus, about 5 miles southwest of Meigle, is in the Tay Valley and is a good centre from which to tour this area. It is a market town, very typical of the area, and so called to distinguish it from Cupar Fife.

Only the gatehouse remains of a once flourishing Cistercian abbey, beside the Dundee road. It was built about 1164 by Malcolm IV and destroyed in 1559. The parish church stands on the site of the old monks' chapel and you can still see the remains of the original piers from the nave. From Coupar Angus it is about 12 miles back to Perth, passing Perth Aerodrome.

Forfar to Perth via Blairgowrie

Kirriemuir

If you take the northern route back to Perth from Forfar on the A926, Kirriemuir is 6 miles to the west, on a hillside with a straggle of narrow streets lined by picturesque houses. This jute-manufacturing town is where J. M. Barrie was born. He renamed it 'Thrums' in the series of novels he wrote based on small-town life in Scotland. The house where Barrie was born, 9 Brechin Road, is maintained by the National Trust for Scotland as a museum, **Barrie's Birthplace** (*open April–Sept Mon–Sat 11–5.30, Sun 1.30–5.30; Oct Sat 11–5.30, Sun 1.30–5.30; adm*). It contains a nostalgic collection of manuscripts, letters, personal possessions and mementoes of the writer who belonged to that group known as 'The Kailyard School' at the end of the 19th century. These Kailyard writers exploited a sentimental, romantic image of life in Scotland that brought them a certain amount of contempt from their critics. Their naivety was blown by George Douglas in *The House with Green Shutters* which, according to J. B. Priestley, 'let the east wind into this cosy chamber of fiction'. However much people may despise whimsicality, no one can deny the talent of the man who created Peter Pan, Mary Rose, Dear Brutus and the Admirable Crichton. James Barrie was made a Freeman of Kirriemuir, and was buried in the churchyard in 1937.

Kirriemuir Gateway to the Glens Museum (*open Mon–Sat 10–5, Thurs 1–5*) is in the 17th-century Town House in the High Street, which was once the jail and courthouse. There is a model of the town in 1604, and interesting displays following the history and social history of the area.

A **Camera Obscura** (*open April–Sept daily 1–4*), in the Barrie Pavilion above the town, gives a panoramic view of Strathmore by an ingenious method of reflection.

You should make time to go north from Kirriemuir to explore some of the glens that stretch back into the Grampians – Glen Clova, Glen Prosen, Glen Isla: each with a mass of tributary glens like the veins of a feather, with tumbling rivers and tranquil lochs, hidden away among the hills.

It is worth making a detour from Kirriemuir to see **Reekie Linn**. It is about 9 miles due west and, if you've got a good map, the back roads are very attractive. Park at the Bridge of Craigisla and take the footpath through the wood. Reekie Linn is a dramatic waterfall haunted by water sprites and kelpies. The River Isla, constricted by narrow rock cliffs, pours into a deep gorge in a single cascade, the spray rising like smoke, stirring the dark waters of the river into tumult. The path takes you to a spur jutting out level with the top of the falls. If you suffer from vertigo you should go along to the right and see them from further off.

Barry Hill is beside the road about 3 miles south of the falls, just short of Alyth. It is a short, steep climb through whins and bracken, over turf honeycombed by rabbits. On top are the ruins of a large Pictish fort in a shallow depression. The oblong shape is very clear with round turrets and ramparts. Romance clings to these stones. If you believe the Scottish versions of the Arthurian legends, Queen Guinevere was imprisoned in this fort by King Arthur because of her love affair with a Pictish prince. If this was true, the captive queen had glorious views to comfort her.

Alyth, below the hill, is a pleasant little milling town bisected by the Alyth Burn.

Blairgowrie

Blairgowrie, 5 miles southwest of Alyth, beside fast-flowing Ericht Water, is a popular tourist centre all the year round, much favoured by golfers. Old mills still stand along the river, some derelict, some converted into dwellings and at least one open to the public. In summer there are the Highlands to explore, and in winter you can ski at the resort of Glenshee. The fertile soil produces abundant raspberry crops. This is magic walking country: fast-flowing rivers slice through steep mountain glens, with sudden glimpses of snow-capped peaks massing on the horizon.

Glen Shee

Glen Shee runs north from Blairgowrie into the Grampian region and is one of Scotland's main skiing centres. Its challenging pistes are often icy and demanding, especially the Tiger run, best left to experienced skiers, but in the right conditions there is scope for everyone. Weather conditions can be extreme, roads sometimes becoming impassable in snow. For skiing information, ring the Ski Hotline, **t** 09001 654 656. **Strathardle** forks off west of Glen Shee from the **Bridge of Cally** where the River Ardle and Black Water converge: another good launching pad for climbers and walkers in lovely surroundings.

Birnam

Be lion-mettled, proud, and take no care
Who chafes, who frets, or where conspirers are:
Macbeth shall never vanquish'd be until
Great Birnam wood to high Dunsinane Hill
Shall come against him.
William Shakespeare, *Macbeth*, Act 4, scene 1; witches' prophecy

Birnam, about 14 miles north of Perth, bypassed by the A9, is a village familiar to all lovers of Shakespeare. From Birnam Hill you can see Dunsinnan, or Dunsinane, 12 miles to the southeast – opinions and tastes dictate the spelling. Macbeth, in his castle on 'Dunsinane Hill', confidently believed the witches' prophecy that he was immortal until 'Birnam Forest come to Dunsinane'. Meanwhile, Malcolm was busy instructing his soldiers to camouflage themselves with branches from the trees in Birnam Wood and march on Dunsinane. There are remains of a fort on Dunsinane Hill, thought to be Macbeth's. Some of the trees in Birnam Wood are thought to date from the original forest.

South of Birnam on the A9 you pass signs to **Bankfoot**, where there is a visitor centre with restaurant, shops (outdoor clothes, gifts and so on), a play area and **The Macbeth Experience**, a multimedia exhibition that aims to bring history to life.

Along the A9: Dunkeld and Pitlochry

Dunkeld

Fifteen miles north of Perth, just off the A9, Dunkeld – the fort of the Celts – is an old cathedral town on the banks of the Tay, sheltered by wooded hills and much favoured by fishermen. Its history goes back to when it was a refuge for Pictish kings.

Being close to the ancient capital of Scone, Dunkeld became a stronghold of Columban monks who founded an abbey here in 729, having been driven from Iona by Norsemen. They enshrined holy relics of St Columba in their abbey. The saint himself is believed to have come to Dunkeld in the 6th century and to have founded some sort of religious establishment with the help of St Mungo. There is a St Colm's Well nearby.

Dunkeld suffered badly during the Covenanting Wars, and it was here that the Cameronians, extreme Covenanters, held the town against a troop of Highlanders in 1689. Triumphant after Killiecrankie, the Highlanders stormed the town, whereupon the Cameronians set fire to most of its buildings, driving the Highlanders out and securing eventual supremacy for William and Mary.

Dunkeld Cathedral (*always accessible*) is a substantial ruin beside the River Tay. The choir has been restored and is the parish church. The nave and great northwest tower date from the 15th century. The original medieval cathedral, which took two centuries to build, was only entire for about 60 years before the Reformers reduced it to a roofless ruin. Ironically, it contains the rather splendid tomb and effigy of the Wolf of Badenoch, who was a keen destroyer of churches, including Elgin Cathedral.

The **Little Houses**, lining Cathedral Street, were built after the destruction of the town in 1689 and were saved from demolition by the National Trust for Scotland in 1950. Well restored and privately occupied, they form a delightful approach to the cathedral and give the old part of town a unique character.

The Hermitage, signed from the A9 just beyond Dunkeld, is an 18th-century folly with dramatic views from Ossian's Hall to the Falls of Braan.

The **Beatrix Potter Exhibition**, in Birnam (*open daily 10–5; adm; www.birnaminstitute.com*), is a splendid tribute to her genius. Born in 1866, Potter spent many childhood holidays in Scotland, at Dalguise, and the freedom of her days here was a great influence on her love of nature, sketching and storytelling.

Loch of the Lowes

A couple of miles northeast of Dunkeld, Loch of the Lowes is a nature reserve where you can watch ospreys from a hide. These large brown and white sea eagles, cousins to the falcon, are common in America, where they nest on every navigation mark in the estuaries. Here, they are a rare, protected species, though their numbers are increasing slightly now that their nesting sites are so fiercely protected. There is a **wildlife centre** (*open April–Sept; adm; t (01350) 727 337*), with observation hide, displays and a shop.

Pitlochry

Pitlochry, 13 miles north of Dunkeld on the A9, is in the middle of Scotland, cradled by hills, with Ben Vrackie (2,759ft) looming to the north. With above-average hours of sunshine and below-average rainfall, this has been a popular holiday town since Queen Victoria, staying at Blair Atholl, declared it to be one of the finest resorts in

Tourist Information

Dunkeld: t (01350) 727 688; *open all year*.
Pitlochry: 22 Atholl Road, **t** (01796) 472 215/751; *open all year*.

Festivals

May: Highland Games, Blair Atholl.
May–October: Annual Summer Festival, Pitlochry; plays, concerts and Fringe events.
September: Highland Games, Pitlochry.

Shopping

Dunkeld Smokehouse, at Springfields, Dunkeld. Sells excellent smoked products, and will also smoke any fish you may have been lucky enough to catch.

House of Bruar, to the right of the A9, 10 miles north of Pitlochry, *www.houseofbruar.com*. Fairly recent venture, now considered 'the 'Harrods of the North', selling classy stuff at classy prices. A magnet for serious shoppers, with country clothes, a food hall, china, glass, gifts, library, restaurants and a heather and alpine nursery. Worth a visit, if only to look. *Open daily 9–5.30.*

Where to Stay and Eat

Hilton Dunkeld House, **t** (01350) 727 771, **f** 728 924, *reservations_dunkeld@hilton.com* (*expensive*). Lovely house, once the home of the Duke of Atholl, in 280 acres on the Tay. Has just about everything you could ask for except simplicity: swimming pool, sauna, spa bath, steam room, solarium and multi-gym; tennis courts, croquet, salmon and trout fishing, mixed game shooting and 4x4 off-road driving. Hermits and stoics, beware.

Kinnaird, Dalguise, near Dunkeld, **t** (01796) 482 440, **f** 482 289, *www.kinnairdestate.com* (*expensive*). Very expensive former shooting

lodge run as a private country house, with all the trimmings.

Auchnahyle, Pitlochry, **t** (01796) 472 318, **f** 473 657 (*moderate*). Wolsey Lodge in an 18th-century farmhouse with a nice garden surrounded by fields and lovely views. Wonderful hospitality and delicious food.

Dunfallandy House, Logierait Road, Pitlochry, **t** (01796) 472 648, **f** 472 017, *dunfalhse@aol.com* (*moderate*). Lovely old house, with delightful rooms. Accent on organic food. Extremely good value.

Knockendarroch House Hotel, Higher Oakfield, Pitlochry, **t** (01796) 473 473, **f** 474 068, *www.knockendarroch.co.uk* (*moderate*). Country house in mature gardens with good views, only 3 minutes' walk from the town centre. Relaxed and comfortable. Theatre dinners and transport service.

Atholl Palace, Pitlochry, **t** (01796) 472 400, **f** 473 036, *www.corushotel.com* (*moderate*). Large, comfortable pile overlooking the town and the Tummel Valley from 48 acres of nice garden and parkland. Outdoor pool, tennis, etc, and good verandah restaurant.

Pine Trees Hotel and Garden Restaurant, Strathview Terrace, Pitlochry, **t** (01796) 472 121 **f** 472 460, *www.pinetreeshotel.co.uk* (*moderate*). Victorian house in 10 acres, 5 minutes from the centre. Very comfortable and good food.

Fisher's Hotel, Atholl Road, Pitlochry, **t** (01796) 472 000, **f** 473 949 (*cheap*). Large, old-fashioned and comfortable, but rather busy.

Atholl Arms Hotel, Blair Atholl, **t** (01796) 481 205, **f** 481 550, *www.athollarmshotel.co.uk* (*moderate*). 19th-century coaching inn on the main street, with a splendid dining room in what once was the castle's ballroom.

Killiecrankie Hotel and Restaurant, **t** (01796) 473 220, **f** 472 451, *www.killiecrankiehotel. co.uk* (*expensive*). Once a dower house, then a Victorian manse, in pleasant grounds close to the Soldier's Leap. The staff tend to wear kilts and the food is excellent.

Europe. This royal stamp of approval resulted in many fine houses and mansions being built in the area, with spas that are now hotels. Today it is hard to believe it was once a remote hamlet. There were no roads north of Dunkeld until General Wade built his network of military roads after the Jacobite uprisings, linking the trouble-spots in the Highlands. In spite of its popularity – it gets very crowded in the summer and caters well for its tourists – it manages to retain a leisurely, strolling atmosphere, a perfect centre from which to explore the Highlands. The rivers Tummel and Garry converge from their valleys into Loch Faskally, 2 miles to the north, and hurry through the town to join the Tay at Ballinluig to the south. The main street is cheerful, with its bright façades, hotels and shops, distilleries and, not far off the road, hydroelectric development.

The **Hydroelectric Dam and Fish Ladder** (*open daily 10–5.30*) has an observation chamber from which to see the ingenious method of ensuring the salmon cycle is not broken. Thousands of salmon are 'lifted' annually and you can watch them through glass walls. Sometimes you can see sealice clinging to the fish, showing that they have come fresh from the sea. There is also a **Visitor Centre and Exhibition**, with a description of all the activities throughout the country and in the Loch Tummel group in particular. Few can deny that the hydroelectric schemes often enhance rather than spoil the Highland scenery.

Blair Atholl Distillery (*open Easter–Sept Mon–Sat 9–5, Sun 12–4; Oct, Nov and Mar Mon–Fri 9–5; Dec and Feb restricted hours; adm*), on the southern edge of Pitlochry, has a visitor centre. There are conducted tours with a free dram, a coffee shop, a bar with snacks and a shop selling whisky.

Edradour Distillery (*open Mar–Oct Mon–Sat 9.30–5, Sun 12–5; Nov–mid-Dec Mon–Sat 10–3.30; Jan and Feb shop only 10–4; tours in winter are weather-dependent: ring first, t (01796) 472 095; www.edradour.co.uk*) is the smallest in Scotland, hidden in the hills, less than 3 miles east of Pitlochry. It was founded in 1825 by a group of local farmers, a small complex of whitewashed buildings under neat grey slate roofs, tucked into a hollow beside the Edradour Burn. Here, after a conducted tour of the distillery – virtually unchanged since Victorian times – you get your free dram in a cosy barn before a peat and log fire.

Walking in this area is endlessly rewarding; every path you choose reveals fresh beauty and unexpected views. There are waterfalls and gorges festooned with lush ferns; woods and hills; rivers running fast over shallow rocky beds.

Pass of Killiecrankie

Six thousand Veterans practised in War's game,
Tried Men, at Killicranky were arrayed
Against an equal Host that wore the Plaid,
Shepherds and Herdsmen. – Like a whirlwind came
The Highlanders, the slaughter spread like flame;
from a sonnet by William Wordsworth

The road north from Pitlochry climbs along the upper slope of the Pass of Killiecrankie, a recently opened section of road that cost a great deal of money and took considerable skill to engineer. It clings precariously to the densely wooded gorge where, far below, the River Garry cuts its way through to join up with the Tummel. At the far end of the pass, about 3 miles from Pitlochry, there is a National Trust for Scotland **visitor centre** (*open April–Oct daily 10–5.30; adm*), with a pictorial description of the history of the Battle of Killiecrankie. Graham of Claverhouse, 'Bonnie Dundee', and his brave Jacobite Highlanders charged the British Army under General Mackay in 1689, in an attempt to depose William of Orange and restore James VII/II to the throne. The British were almost annihilated by the wild Highlanders, but Claverhouse was mortally wounded and his death, leaving his army leaderless, ensured the subsequent victory of the government troops three weeks later at Dunkeld.

You can walk down to the river from the visitor centre, past the terrifying **Soldier's Leap**, an 18-foot jump across the gorge, said to have been made by one of Mackay's soldiers, escaping from the Highlanders. Queen Victoria walked along this path and noted its great beauty in her diary in 1844.

Blair Atholl

Three miles north of Killiecrankie, the new road bypasses the village of Blair Atholl, giving a good view of **Blair Castle** (*open April–Oct daily 10–6; tours in winter by arrangement; adm; t (01796) 481 207, www.blair-castle.co.uk*), from across the river. This white, turreted baronial castle is the home of the Duke of Atholl, dating from 1269 though much Victorianized. It has seen many famous visitors: Mary, Queen of Scots stayed here; Claverhouse stayed here before the Battle of Killiecrankie and it was here that his body lay after the battle; Prince Charles accepted hospitality here on his march south in 1745; Cumberland garrisoned his troops here the following year, during which time the Duke of Atholl's brother, Lord George Murray, inflicted severe damage on the castle in his attempts to win it back; Queen Victoria visited the castle in 1844 and explored the whole area with tireless enthusiasm and energy. She granted the Duke of Atholl the privilege of being the only British subject allowed to retain a private army, the Atholl Highlanders.

The rooms are numbered and there is an excellent, readable guide book. Look for the Tapestry Room, hung with rich tapestries and containing a sumptuous four-poster bed topped by two vases of ostrich feathers. The Old Scots Room is furnished in the style of a simple cottage living room, complete with box bed, cradle and spinning wheel. There is much to see, from arms and armour, to Jacobite relics, china, toys, furniture, lace, paintings (including portraits by Lely, Ramsay and Raeburn) and even a natural history museum. There is a licensed self-service restaurant and, if you want to impress your friends, there is a separate dining room for private parties of up to 50 people. If you really want to splash out, you can also use the ballroom for up to 200 people, a truly noble setting for a knees-up, its panelled walls hung with a forest of antlers and acres of ancestral portraits under a timber-ribbed roof.

Beyond Blair Atholl is good walking and climbing country, over moor and scree, with lovely views. A nice walk is that to the **Bruar Falls**, well signed about 3 miles to the west; you can park by the road. A short walk takes you up to the falls, where the River Bruar cascades down through rocky chasms and over great gleaming slabs of granite. Robert Burns came up here when he was a guest of the Duke of Atholl. He was so disgusted by the treeless moorland that then surrounded the falls that he dashed off a poem, 'The Humble Petition of Bruar Water', and dispatched it to the Duke:

Would then my noble master please,
To grant my highest wishes,
He'll shade the bank wi' towering trees,
And bonie spreading bushes.

This plea, as you can see, found its mark and inspired the fourth Duke of Atholl to plant the trees now growing there. Walk on beyond the falls up the path for another mile or so, through birches and rhododendrons. A bridge then takes you over the stream and down the other side, making a round trip of about 2½ miles.

Perthshire: West of the A9

Lochs Tummel and Rannoch

If you take the B8019 west from Pitlochry, you should start humming Harry Lauder's famous song 'The Road to the Isles': 'by Tummel and Loch Rannoch and Lochaber I will go...' The drive out to Rannoch Station, on the northern side of lochs Tummel and Rannoch to where the road ends and back along the south side, is a round trip of about 65 miles. The scenery is beautiful, dominated by the great cone of **Schiehallion** in the south, with a kaleidoscope of vistas through the trees and the wasteland of Rannoch Moor stretching away to the west. Loch Tummel is less dramatic than Loch Rannoch, its gentler scenery reshaped by the hydroelectric development.

Queen's View, on Loch Tummel 2 miles up from the dam, was so called before Queen Victoria visited it in 1866. Perhaps Mary, Queen of Scots also stood on the promontory and looked down to the water, glinting in the sunlight, far below.

The **Tay Forest Centre** (*open April–Oct daily 9.30–5; donation box*) is at the southeast corner of the loch. Here you can learn about the geography and ecology of the area and how to find the Black Wood, south of Loch Rannoch, with part of the remains of the old Caledonian Forest.

Harry Lauder must have taken to the moors when he was 'walking with his crummock to the isles', because the road ends at Rannoch Station.

Five miles south of Pitlochry, the A827 takes you 10 miles west to Aberfeldy, and then out through Strath Tay to Loch Tay, a memorable drive especially in late summer, winding through small villages, with the river shaded by overhanging trees, backed by the hills beyond.

Aberfeldy

Let Fortune's gifts at random flee,
They ne'er shall draw a wish frae me,
Supremely blest wi' love and thee
In the birks of Aberfeldy.
                                    'The Birks of Aberfeldie', by Robert Burns

Aberfeldy is a pleasant little town on the Urlar Burn at its confluence with the River Tay. Robert Burns' poem refers to the silver birches beside the burn. The bridge over the Tay was built by General Wade in 1733 and is said to be the best of the many he was responsible for during his arduous task of trying to link up all the remote trouble-spots in the Highlands during the Jacobite uprisings. (Some argue that it is spoilt by its four incongruous obelisks.) The dramatic **Falls of Moness** are just a short stroll south of the town.

The **Black Watch Monument**, a kilted soldier, is at the south end of the bridge, erected in 1887 to commemorate the raising of the Black Watch in 1739.

The **Oatmeal Mill** (*open Easter–Oct Mon–Sat 10–4.30, Sun 11–4.30; adm*), in Mill Street, shows the process of milling raw grain into oatmeal, and you can buy the finished products.

Castle Menzies (*open April–mid-Oct Mon–Sat 10.30–5, Sun 2–5; adm*), a mile west of Aberfeldy, is a 16th-century, Z-plan fortified tower house, with carved gables over its dormers. Well restored after centuries of neglect, it belongs to the Clan Menzies (pronounced Mingies) Society and houses their Clan Museum. It was built by the Menzies, who lived in it for 400 years. It was rescued by the Clan Society in 1972 and the results of their long, arduous and extremely expensive labours are praiseworthy, particularly because they have avoided over-restoring this splendid fortress and have resisted the temptation to fill it with irrelevant clutter. There are a few desultory showcases of memorabilia, but on the whole the rooms are empty. There is a Prince Charlie's Room, where the prince stayed for two nights on his way to Culloden. All donations go to the continued restoration and upkeep of the castle, and there is a nice café and small shop.

Loch Tay, 5 miles west of Aberfeldy, is a long, dark snake of water under the brooding hulk of Ben Lawers, Perthshire's highest hill (3,984ft). All types of water sports take place on the loch, though keen fishermen might wish otherwise.

Ben Lawers is well worth climbing on a clear day, if you are fit – allow about 3 hours. At the top you can see from the Atlantic to the North Sea. There are masses of mountain flowers and birds, including kestrel, buzzard, red grouse, golden plover and curlew. Needless to say, there is a **visitor centre** (*open April–Sept daily 10–5*), for those who like their wildlife in consumer packages, off the A827 6 miles northeast of Killin. Run by the National Trust for Scotland, who care for the southern slopes of the hill, there are the inevitable booklets, information sheets and audiovisual programmes together with bossy instructions about what to wear and take if you climb the hill. (For which they can be forgiven: the Mountain Rescue people are frequently called out to risk their lives rescuing idiots who would do better to confine their outdoor activities to their gardens.)

Kenmore, at the head of the loch, was built for estate workers at **Taymouth Castle** in 1760 by the fourth Earl of Breadalbane and is now a conservation village. The gigantic castle was one of the most magnificent of Scotland's neo-Gothic palaces and has had a long and complex architectural history. It started life as a 16th-century keep – Balloch Castle – until the first Earl of Breadalbane decided to smarten it up in 1733 with the help of William Adam and subsequently many others, who tinkered around with the original plan, demolishing and building, until a whole new wing was added in honour of a visit by Queen Victoria in 1842. She was the first to dine in the new

Tourist Information

Aberfeldy: The Square, **t** (01887) 820 276; *open all year.*
Crieff: High Street, **t** (01764) 652 578; *open all year.*
Auchterarder: 90 High Street, **t** (01764) 663 450; *open all year.*

Festivals

Hogmanay: **Flambeaux Procession**, Comrie; at midnight the villagers parade around in a torchlit procession, followed by much revelry (from the ancient pagan fire-festivals to drive off evil spirits for the coming year).

Where to Stay and Eat

Loch Rannoch Hotel, **t** (01882) 632 201 (*moderate*). A former Victorian shooting lodge in 250 acres beside the loch. Convivial rather than cosy, with indoor pool, jacuzzi, sauna, solarium, steam bath, squash, tennis, sailing, windsurfing, canoeing, dry-ski slope, snooker, bicycles, fishing, plus live musical entertainment and Highland dancing evenings.

Bunrannoch House, Kinloch Rannoch, **t** (01882) 632 407 (*cheap*). Stay here if you possibly can, for hospitality at its best. A tall, thin Victorian ex-shooting lodge, run by its owner who is an outstanding cook, and knows how to make you feel at home.
Guinach House, Aberfeldy, **t** (01887) 820 251/237, **f** 829 607 (*moderate*). Family-run country house hotel in 3-acre garden. Comfortable and good food.
Invervar Lodge, Glenlyon, Aberfeldy, **t** (01887) 877 206, **f** 877 223 (*moderate*). High-class B&B with gourmet dinner by arrangement. Bring your own wine.
Farleyer House Hotel, Weem, by Aberfeldy, **t** (01887) 820 332, **f** 829 430, *www.farleyer.com* (*expensive*). 15th-century country house in 30 acres in the Tay Valley, with good fishing and a 6-hole golf course. Guests have access to the Kenmore Club's leisure facilites: swimming, all-weather tennis, etc. Also five 18-hole courses nearby.
Ailean Chraggan Hotel, Weem, by Aberfeldy, **t** (01887) 820 346, **f** 829 009, *aileanchraggan @btconnect.com* (*moderate*). Small, friendly, family-run hotel with comfortable rooms, fishing and excellent food, especially when there's fresh fish in straight from the west coast.

dining room and sleep in the new apartments, and was delighted by everything – the castle, the fantastic welcome she received, and the grounds. Now empty and for sale, already a victim of thieves stealing some of its fittings, it forms a dismal centrepiece to a golf course, in a bowl-shaped landscape in which many rustic lodges and other ancillary buildings are all part of the integral design. You can drive right past it, and there are boats for hire for fishing on the loch.

Before leaving Kenmore, turn left out of the castle gate and follow the loch round on the minor road a few hundred yards to the **Crannog** (*open April–Oct daily 10–4.30; in winter by appointment; adm; **t** (01887) 830 583; www.crannog.co.uk*). It would be easy to miss this and a shame to do so. It looks like a makeshift boat house or shelter, but when you cross the flimsy approach over the water you find a splendid reconstruction of a crannog, based on careful underwater research. The interior is almost cosy, with its high thatched roof, thatched walls, central fire and hay-scattered floor, surprisingly large with semi-partitions for semi-privacy.

If you can't climb Ben Lawers, you can drive around it – about 25 miles in all. Leave the A827 at Fearnan on Loch Tay and take the back road along Glen Lyon, Scotland's longest glen, to **Bridge of Balgie**, and then drive south through the hills, back to the loch past the NTS visitor centre. You can complete the circle on the main road along

Kenmore Hotel, Kenmore, t (01887) 830 205, f 830 262, *www.kenmorehotel.com* (*moderate*). Scotland's oldest inn (they say, in company with several others), since 1572, with its own salmon fishing and rights over Loch Tay. It has a 'traditional' atmosphere – nice old codgers in the bar, an original Burns' poem over the mantelpiece and a golf course on the estate.

Fortingall Hotel, Fortingall, t/f (01887) 830 367, *www.hotel@fortingall.com* (*moderate*). Splendidly informal, old-fashioned hotel, cosy, unspoilt and friendly, and next door to the famous yew tree.

Crieff Hydro Hotel, Crieff, t (01764) 655 555, f 653 087, *www.crieffhydro.com* (*moderate*). Still run by descendants of its founders, this hotel beams down on the town like a respectable dowager, with its splendid glass pavilion in front, indoor swimming pool, riding, tennis, free golf, sailing, windsurfing and waterskiing. Evening activities include dancing, films, discos and competitions.

Drummond Arms Hotel, St Fillans, t (01764) 685 212 (*moderate*). Quiet and unspoiled in an increasingly popular area, with friendly staff and a nicely relaxed atmosphere.

Four Seasons Hotel, St Fillans, t (01764) 685 333, f 685 444 (*moderate*). Recently refurbished, with an excellent reputation for food. Comfortable A-frame chalets behind the hotel give privacy.

Gleneagles Hotel, Auchterarder, freephone (UK) t 0800 328 4010, t (01764) 662 231, f 662 134, *www.gleneagles.com* (*expensive*). Scotland's only 5-star hotel. If you get fed up with the sauna, the solarium, the jacuzzi, the gymnasium, the shooting, the fishing, the snooker, the swimming, the squash, the bowling, the croquet and the tennis, you can always fall back on a round of golf. The 5-star rating embraces the chef as well as everything else. Prices and details on application (comfort doesn't come cheap).

Auchterarder House Hotel, t (01764) 663 646, f 662 939, *www.wrensgroup.com* (*expensive*). Victorian mansion in the hills, in 17 acres. Very luxurious and gracious.

Collearn House Hotel, Auchterarder, t (01764) 663 553, f 662 376, *www.collearnhotel.co.uk* (*moderate*). Restored Victorian country house, secluded but not remote, in 9 acres of nice gardens. Comfortable and elegant.

Duchally Country Estate, Glen Eagles, t (01764) 663 071, f 662 464, *www.duchally.com* (*moderate*). Excellent, rather rambling country house built in 1883 in 27 acres. Good food and comfortable rooms.

the loch back to Fearnan, but the nicest way to see Loch Tay by car is on the minor road that hugs the southern shore.

At **Fortingall**, 2 miles to the northwest as the crow flies, the pathetic vestige of a yew tree in the churchyard is said to be over 3,000 years old – Europe's oldest living object. This delightful little village has a single street of cottages, some thatched and rather English in character, and an intriguing legend. Some say that Pontius Pilate was born here, son of a Roman officer who had been sent on a peace mission to the Picts in **Dun Geal**, a fort on the steep, rocky hill behind the village. True or not, it adds romance to an already enchanted spot. You should try to abandon your car in this area: it is marvellous walking and climbing territory.

From Kenmore, take the narrow back road through Glen Quaich to **Amulree**, 9 miles south of Aberfeldy. This was an important junction of the old drove roads, where drovers broke their lonely journeys to exchange news and banter.

The Sma' Glen

The Sma' Glen is the moorland valley through which the A822 descends from Amulree to Crieff. It follows the River Almond as it thunders down over rapids and falls, with hills rising steeply to about 2,000ft on either side. You might see salmon leaping in September and October; the best place for this is the **Buchanty Spout**, in Glenalmond on the B8063, just off the A822.

After Newton, look out on the left of the road for **Ossian's Stone**, which is said to mark the grave of Ossian, the legendary Gaelic hero and bard who spent many years in fairyland until he was baptized by St Patrick. The stone was in fact moved to its present position by General Wade's road-builders when it blocked the path of one of their roads. Traces of a prehistoric burial, found when they lifted the stone, were given a reburial in a secret place by local Highlanders who were convinced that they were indeed the remains of the poet. Wordsworth thought so too:

> In this still place, remote from men,
> Sleeps Ossian, in the narrow glen.

Crieff

Crieff, about 12 miles south of Amulree, was once the centre for the biggest cattle tryst in Scotland and is now a Highland holiday town. Built on a steep hill facing south over the valley of the River Earn, it is dominated from the north by the Knock of Crieff, 911ft high, a woodland area with footpaths and good views from the top.

Nothing much is old in the town today. It was sacked and destroyed by Highlanders during the Jacobite rebellion. Later, a bleaching and tanning industry brought prosperity to its people. It became a spa town in the 19th century and there are faint echoes of Victorian splendour from the Crieff Hydro Hotel, above the town, with its glass domes and pavilions.

House of Grouse Distillery (*open Feb–Dec Mon–Sat 9.30–6, Sun 12–6, last tour 4.30; Jan–Feb Mon–Fri 11.30–4, last tour 2.30*) is the oldest in Scotland. Conducted tours show all stages of whisky distilling. The tour includes a taste, and a visit to the award-winning **Visitors' Heritage Centre**, with an audiovisual show, exhibitions, a whisky museum and retail shop.

Crieff Visitor Centre (*open April–Oct daily 9–5.30; Nov–Mar daily 10–4*) demonstrates the making of Perthshire's Paperweights, Buchan Pottery stoneware and wildlife sculptures. There is a video presentation, showroom, restaurant and plant centre.

Bookworms should slip off to **Innerpeffray Library** (*open Feb–Nov Mon–Wed, Fri and Sat 10–12.45 and 2–4.45, Sun 2–4; adm*), 4 miles southeast of town. An unlikely track through farm buildings takes you to the oldest public library in Scotland, entirely isolated in its little complex of house, chapel and school house. In Roman times this was on the main route between England and Scotland. The library, founded by the third Lord Madderty (or Maddertie) in the attic of the adjacent chapel in the mid-1600s, and moved here in 1762, was established 'for the education of the people, especially young students in the area...' It flourished until after the First World War when the public's reading habits changed and were better served by municipal lending libraries. Among the collection of old and antiquarian books, mostly religious or classical, is the Bible printed in 1508 and carried by Montrose when he was finally defeated at the Battle of Carbisdale in 1650. If you are good on scripture, look out for the *Treacle Bible*, one of many so called because the early translation of: 'Is there no balm in Gilead?' – Jeremiah 8, v. 22 – was: 'Is there no treacle..?'. There are wonderful treasures here: try to talk with Ted Powell, the present curator and a real enthusiast.

Two miles south of Crieff, **Drummond Castle Gardens** (*open Easter weekend and May–Oct daily 2–6; adm; castle not open to the public*) are approached down a mile-long tree-lined avenue. The sundial is dated 1630 and there are flowers and shrubs in a formal Italian setting against the backdrop of the castle. Founded in 1491, this was the setting for a terrible murder in 1502. Margaret Drummond and her sisters were poisoned, to prevent James IV from making Margaret his queen. Cromwell did his best to destroy the castle, and it was deliberately damaged in 1745 by its owner, the Duchess of Perth, to prevent Hanoverian troops from capturing it. More recently the gardens were used at the end of the film *Rob Roy*, when Rob himself meets the Duke of Montrose and they wander through the topiary.

Comrie

Comrie, 6 miles west of Crieff along the River Earn, is an attractive conservation village. Because it lies on the Highland Line – the geological fault that divides Highland and Lowland Scotland – more seismological tremors have been recorded here than anywhere else in Britain. Shocks were especially common during the 19th century: in recent years tremors have never done more than rattle the village teacups.

Earthquake House was built in 1874 to house one of the earliest seismographs in the world. They have a model of the original instrument as well as a modern one, in use, and a chart recorder. It isn't open to the public but there are exhibits on view from outside.

Just north of Comrie, and a pleasant walk, **Deil's Cauldron** is an impressive waterfall carrying the River Lednock down to meet the River Earn.

Fowlis Wester is a hamlet 5 miles east of Crieff. Here, 13th-century St Beans Church has a leper squint, an 8th-century Pictish stone and a fine lychgate – the roofed gateway to the churchyard where coffins could await the arrival of the priest, sheltered from the elements.

St Fillans, on Loch Earn 6 miles further west, is a popular holiday resort for anyone who enjoys sailing, water-skiing and windsurfing. It is also a good centre for walking and climbing.

Muthill is a conservation village 3 miles south of Crieff, with late 18th- and early 19th-century houses delightfully unspoiled. Muthill (pronounced Mew-thill) is derived from Moot Hill (hill of meeting). The older village was razed by retreating Highlanders after the Battle of Sheriffmuir in 1715, and rebuilt by the Drummond Earls of Perth. **Muthill Folk Museum** (*for opening times, t (01764) 652 578; donations*) has exhibits illustrating past domestic life in the village. Also in Muthill are the ruins of a once-important pre-Reformation church with its 12th-century Norman tower.

A couple of miles to the east of Muthill, **Tullibardine Chapel** is one of the very few of its kind that has been preserved intact since before the Reformation. Cruciform, built of red sandstone, it was founded as a collegiate church in 1445 by Sir David Murray, whose arms and those of his wife can be seen on the inside west wall. Since the Reformation it has been used as a burial vault for the Drummond Earls of Perth.

Gleneagles Hotel

About 6 miles south of Muthill, and a mile or so west of the village and station, Gleneagles Hotel is Scotland's premier golfing mecca, whose internationally famous courses lie along the edge of the Muir of Ochill, looking towards the Ochil Hills and Glen Devon – *see* above.

Braco and Auchterarder

Ardoch Roman Camp is at **Braco**, about 4 miles west of Gleneagles Hotel. Grass-covered earthworks are all that remain of a Roman fort dating from the 2nd century. It was once big enough to house as many as 40,000 men. You can still see the shape of it – a great rectangle with ditches and ramparts. Here, in wooden dwellings, the Romans tried to subdue the barbaric tribes who swooped down on them from the hills and glens and forests. The old Roman road runs north of Muthill and then east towards Perth, and an overgrown arch beside the bridge over the River Knaik is all that remains of the Roman bridge.

Auchterarder is 8 to 10 miles southeast of Crieff, depending on which road you take, tucked in under the northern slopes of the Ochil Hills. This is another holiday centre, with a golf course, good fishing and walks.

Aberdeen and the Grampians

18

Aberdeen and the Grampians

Moray Firth
Findhorn Bay
Burghead
Lossiemouth
Spey Bay
Portknockie
Findochty
Cullen
Whitehills
Gardenstown
Troup Head
Aberdour Bay
Pennan
Rosehearty
Kinnairds Head
Fraserburgh
Inverallochy
Findhorn
Elgin
Spynie Palace
Buckie
Sandend
Portsoy
Banff
Macduff
Duff House
New Aberdour
Kinloss
Brodie Castle
Forres
A96
Fochabers
Deveron
Mormond Hill
Crimond
Loch of Strathbeg
Rattray Head

5 Pluscarden Abbey
Keith
Turriff
Ugie
Peterhead
Bullers of Buchan
Boddam

M O R A Y
Craigellachie
strath Isla
A96
Dufftown
Huntly
Fyvie Castle
Fyvie
Haddo House
Mintlaw
Cruden Bay

Ballindalloch
Clashindarroch Forest
Insch
Tolquhon Castle
Tarves
Pitmedden
Colliston
Newburgh

4 Glenlivet
Glen Livet
Pitcapie
Inverurie
A90

Tomintoul
Lecht Road
Kildrummy
Glenbuchat Castle
Kildrummy Castle
Bridge of Buchat
Glenkindie
Bennachie
A B E R D E E N S H I R E
Alford
Kintore
A96
Torsterram
Lerwick
Stromness

Corgarff Castle
Castle Fraser
Bridge of Don
Aberdeen **1**

Tarland
Lumphanan
Hill of Fare
Drum Castle
Peterculter
Maryculter
Dee

Aboyne
Dinnet
Crathes Castle
A93
Banchory

3 Balmoral Castle
Crathie
Ballater
Glen Tanar

Linn of Dee
Inverey
Braemar
G r a m p i a n   M o u n t a i n s
Lochnager
Loch Muick

Stonehaven **2**
Dunnottar Castle

N

Fasque
Kinneff
Fettercairn
Arbuthnott
Inverbervie
Laurencekirk
pp.348-9

2 0 km
10 miles

SCOTLAND

Orkney
Shetland

NORTHERN IRELAND
ENGLAND

Highlights

1 Aberdeen, the granite city
2 Spectacular Dunnottar Castle
3 Balmoral, the royal holiday home
4 The Malt Whisky Trail
5 Timeless Pluscarden Abbey

The shires of Kincardine, Aberdeen, Banff and Moray comprise the shoulder of Scotland that juts out into the North Sea below the neck of Caithness and Sutherland. The name Grampian, by which this area has been known until recently, has a forbidding and stark ring to it, totally unjustified. It is a fertile land veined with rivers, half-girt by sea and backed by mountains. Routes, along the coast and inland following the straths and glens of famous rivers, radiate from Aberdeen like the ribs of an outspread fan. From the Cairngorms and Grampians in the west, a series of ravines and waterfalls, wooded glens and heathery straths carries the River Dee through forest and moorland to the east coast. Further north the River Don makes more gentle progress to the sea and, north again, the Spey completes its journey through very attractive country to join the sea at Tugnet.

Moors give way to undulating farmland that forms a wide coastal plain, patchworked with neat fields. The coast road links a chain of fishing towns and villages with sheltered harbours offering refuge from the wild North Sea. The coastline is both rugged and gentle – gaunt rock cliffs interspersed with long sweeps of clean sand.

History

Many prehistoric remains tell of early settlement on the fertile plains, but the region didn't feature much in history books until Kenneth Macalpine united its Picts with the Dalriada Scots in the 9th century. One of the Comyns, who came over with William the Conqueror, made his way north, married the daughter of a local chief and rapidly gained supremacy in the area. The Comyns, Earls of Buchan, were as much of a threat to Robert the Bruce's ambition to rule Scotland as the English. In 1307 he came north and crushed them in a couple of decisive battles.

With the Comyns effectively subdued, the Gordon family clambered to power. They ruled the land like despots for about 250 years, becoming Earls of Huntly, too big for their boots. Being so far from the seat of government their dominance didn't seem threatening until Mary, Queen of Scots came to the throne in 1561. Sir John Gordon, third son of the 4th Earl of Huntly, was then rash enough to boast of his aspirations to be consort to the widowed queen. Mary raged north with an army to curb such impertinence. Having hanged the Huntly Governor of Inverness Castle for refusing to admit her, she stormed into Aberdeen and disposed of the 4th Earl and Sir John. From then on, except for an occasional rumble of rebellion, the city of Aberdeen was loyal to the Crown and disinclined to rally to the Jacobite standard.

In the middle of the 19th century Prince Albert and Queen Victoria discovered Scotland and built Balmoral. From then on a stampede of tartan-clad southerners overran Deeside and its environs, enthusing over the scenic splendours. They tiptoed after deer, slaughtered game and hooked fish, integrating with the landed families. They built or refurbished a series of baronial mansions and castles to enhance their status. Balmoral is still the holiday home of the British Royal Family and even today the struggle for royal recognition goes on among some residents.

The oil boom of the 1970s brought great prosperity to Aberdeenshire, whose wealth had relied previously on farming, fishing, granite, textiles and paper. Land prices soared; property speculators thrived. But now that oil in established offshore oilfields is past its peak, many of the jobs that went with its exploitation will suffer. A number of upwardly mobile incomers have taken advantage of plummeting land prices and this area is gradually changing hands, though a number of the old landed families remain. To wring a living from vast estates, some are forced to supplement farming revenues by opening their castles and stately homes to the public and squeezing fortunes out of trigger-happy sportsmen and fishermen.

This was the home of the Gordon Highlanders, raised in 1794 by the Duke of Gordon to fight the Napoleonic Wars. They wore the Gordon tartan and it is said that the Duchess of Gordon helped in a recruiting drive by giving a kiss and a silver shilling to each volunteer. (She was well over 40 and described as 'well run'.) The Gordons have recently been amalgamated with the Queen's Own Highlanders, a regiment just as proud, formed from the amalgamated regiments of the Seaforth Highlanders whose roots went back to 1778, and the Queen's Own Cameron Highlanders, raised in 1793. They are now called simply The Highlanders.

From June to September the tartan-tinged air vibrates with the skirl of pipes and the thud of the caber, as towns stage exuberant Highland Games. These unique Scottish gatherings, dating from the 11th century when Malcolm Canmore held contests to find the best soldiers for his struggles against the Normans, are usually well supplied with beer tents and sideshows. The most popular is probably the Braemar Highland Gathering in September, due to the presence of the Royal Family.

One of Grampian's attractions is the 70-mile **Malt Whisky Trail** that takes in conducted tours of eight distilleries where some of the best-known malts are produced. There is also a Castle Trail, a Victorian Heritage Trail and a Coastal Trail.

Aberdeen

Aberdeen is the obvious place from which to begin to explore this area. It is an ever-changing city, the third largest in Scotland, hiding its true nature under a brittle, cosmopolitan exterior. Always a great port as well as a fish and cattle market, exporting granite, textiles and paper, Aberdeen suddenly found itself in the centre of an oil boom in the 1970s. Country and Western music emanated from dignified old buildings; bars and restaurants changed their characters overnight; American accents were two-a-penny and the opening ceremony of the American Club was like a visit to Texas. Property prices soared; entrepreneurs flourished.

Somehow, through all this, Aberdeen managed to retain its character. The Granite City, they call it, and it softens this austere title by decking its streets and parks with what must be some of the most spectacular displays of roses in the British Isles.

No oil boom could change the silvery-granite splendour of the Georgian part of the city, with gracious terraces, squares and crescents; nor the solid Victorian buildings that accompanied the 19th-century prosperity brought to the city by astute merchants; nor the long, wide sweep of Union Street; nor even, for all the smart new buildings, the waterfront. Expensive oil-rig supply vessels can never spoil the character of the harbour – a salty old reprobate smelling of fish.

Anyone wishing to trace their ancestors and their roots should go to the **Aberdeen and North East Family History Society**, 164 King Street (*t (01224) 646 323; open Mon–Fri 10–4, Tues and Fri also 7pm–10pm, Sat 10–1*), which has a wide range of reference books, microfiche, microfilm and so on for genealogical research. Basic advice is given free, and there are research guides, maps and local history material for sale.

History

Aberdeen was granted a Royal Charter by William the Lion in 1179, now preserved in the Town House in Union Street, endorsing an earlier one granted by David I. William Wallace is said to have burned 100 ships in the harbour in the 13th century. Robert Bruce held a council here in 1308. As a reward for the loyal support of the citizens, who forced the English to surrender their hold on the castle, he gave the city its coat of arms and the motto *Bon Accord*. Edward III burned down Aberdeen in 1336.

The Gordon clan, incomers from Berwickshire and Lothian who had dominated this northeastern corner for 250 years, overreached themselves in their ambition for power and began to eye the throne. Mary, Queen of Scots was forced by her Protestant half-brother, Moray, to come north in an attempt to quell them. The Countess of Huntly, however, had been promised by a local witch that, after his death, the Earl's body would lie in the Tolbooth in Aberdeen, entirely unwounded from any battle he cared to fight. She begged her husband to stand up to Mary so he summoned his army and fought. He was defeated and he and his son were captured. The shock brought on a massive heart attack which killed him. His unwounded body was taken to the Tolbooth. Mary executed Sir John Gordon and ordered the posthumous trial of the embalmed body of his father for treason.

Montrose sacked the city in 1644, fighting for the cause of Charles I. General Monk occupied it during the mid-17th century when he was Governor of Scotland for Cromwell. Although nominally Jacobite, the citizens of Aberdeen were not enthusiastic supporters of the cause.

City Sights

The area known as **Old Aberdeen**, northwest of the city centre, is best explored on foot; parking is almost impossible. Start at the little **Brig o' Balgownie**, a Gothic bridge spanning the River Don near its mouth, and the oldest medieval bridge in Scotland, built by Richard the Mason (affectionately known as Dick the Cement), on the orders of Robert the Bruce. Not so very long ago the unrestricted discharge of effluent from mills and factories up the river so polluted the water that you had to hold your nose here. Stricter control and conservation have had their effect and the Don flows cleaner now, the salmon once again making their way upstream to spawn. On the north side of the bridge you can see a terrace of old stone cottages with colourful gardens; the one nearest the bridge was once an ale-house on the drove road. Walk away from the bridge and look back at the simple pointed arch, reflected in the water.

Stroll through **Seaton Park** to twin-spired, fortified **St Machar's Cathedral** (*open daily 9–5*) in the Chanonry, the oldest granite building in Aberdeen and the only granite cathedral in the world. Founded in 1157, St Machar's stands on a promontory overlooking the Don, taking its name from the saint who founded a Celtic church here in the 6th century. A 14th-century red sandstone arch is all that remains of an older building, in contrast to the simple dignity of the later granite. Look for the oak heraldic ceiling, added in 1520, with 48 heraldic shields.

Old Aberdeen grew up around the cathedral, an independent burgh with its own council and charter. Today cobbled streets and charming old houses, some of which

Tourist Information

Aberdeen t (01224–)

Aberdeen: Provost Ross' House, Shiprow, t 288 828, *www.aberdeencity.gov.uk*; *open all year.*

Festivals

March/April: Scottish Connection; celebrating all things Scottish. Scottish Fiddle Orchestra Concert. Granite City Car Rally.
May: Marathon Road Race.
June: Aberdeen Highland Games. Bon Accord Carnival Parade. Aberdeen Festival.
July: International Football Festival.
August: Clydesdale Horse Show. Summer Flower Show. International Youth Festival.
November/December: Christmas Shopping Festival. St Nicholas Festival.

Sports and Activities

Beach Leisure Centre, t 647 647. Wave machines, water cannons and jet streams; aerobics, keep-fit training and ball games; and the Linx Ice Arena for skating, curling, dance, hockey and disco. Plus a crêche, café and bar. *Open daily 8.30am–10.30pm.*
His Majesty's Theatre, Rosemount Viaduct, t 641 122. The town's main theatre, built in 1906, seating 1,500 people. Its programmes include ballet, opera and concerts.

Where to Stay

Expensive

Altens Thistle Hotel, Souter Head Road, t 877 000. Comfortable, with an outdoor heated pool and good, expensive food.
Ardoe House, South Deeside Road, Blairs, t 867 355, *www.macdonaldhotels.co.uk*. Baronial-style mansion overlooking the Dee Valley on the outskirts. Elegant and comfortable, and the food is excellent.

Copthorne Hotel, Huntly Street, t 630 404, *reservations.aberdeen@mill-cop.com*. City-centre hotel off Union Street and near the Catholic Cathedral. The decor is fanciful, with fluted columns and fountains, and it has a good restaurant, Poachers, and Mac's Bar for more relaxed entertainment.
Marcliffe at Pitfodels, North Deeside Road, Cults, t 861 000, *www.marcliffe.com*. A 'Small Luxury Hotel of the World' – and with good reason. Worth every penny.
Patio Hotel, Beach Boulevard, t 633 339, *patioab@globalnet.co.uk*. Busy hotel, with leisure facilities near beach and city centre.
Simpson's Hotel Bar/Brasserie, 59 Queens Road, t 327 777, *address@simpsonshotel.co.uk*. Nor far from the city centre. Quite de luxe.
Skene House Rosemount, 96 Rosemount Viaduct, t 645 971; **Skene House Holburn**, 6 Union Grove, t 580 000; **Skene House Whitehall**, 2 Whitehall Place, t 646 600; *www.skene-house.co.uk*. Excellent serviced apartments, with suites from 1 to 3 bedrooms, with sitting room, kitchen and 1 to2 bathrooms (£60–200 per suite).
Thistle Aberdeen Airport, Aberdeen Airport, Argyll Road, Dyce, t 725 252. Convenient and comfortable, if somewhat tasteless.
Thistle Aberdeen Caledonian, overlooking Union Terrace Gardens in the city centre, t 640 233, *aberdeen.caledonian@thistle.co.uk*. Modern fittings, good food, sun-beds and a sauna, but not much character.

Moderate

Atholl Hotel, Kings Gate, t 323 505, *www.atholl-aberdeen.com*. Typical Aberdeen granite town house in the West End; no frills, but respectable and very comfortable. Golf, fishing, shooting and distillery tours can be arranged.

date back to 1500, give an air of tranquillity undisturbed by the roar of the modern city beyond. Near the cathedral, **Cruickshank Botanic Gardens** (*open Mon–Fri 9–4.30; May–Sept also Sat and Sun 2–5*) belong to the university, with extensive collections of shrubs, herbaceous and Alpine plants, and a rock and water garden.

King's College Chapel (*open Mon–Sat 9–5, Sun 11am service (term time) then 12–4*), in the High Street, stands on a green sward with a distinctive 'crowned' tower and

Cults Hotel, Cults, **t** 867 632, *thecults@ vagabond-hotels.com*. Nice, family-run hotel, fairly recently done up, with good food and comfortable rooms.

Hilton Aberdeen Tree Tops Hotel, Springfield Road, **t** 313 377. In wooded landscaped grounds, 10 minutes from the city centre. There's a pool and leisure complex for guests, and excellent food in a split-level Regency-style restaurant. (Some rooms are *expensive*.)

Imperial Hotel, Stirling Street, **t** 589 101. Central, with an imposing frontage that makes you think of top hats and carriages. Good service, and the food's not bad.

Inn at the Park, 3–4 Deemount Terrace, **t** 583 699, *info@innattheparkhotel.co.uk*. A nice, small hotel. Comfortable and hospitable.

Jarvis Aberdeen City Hotel, Market Street, **t** 582 255, *www.jarvis.co.uk*. Central and comfortable.

Jarvis Aberdeen Hotel, Great Western Road, **t** 318 724, *www.jarvis.co.uk*. Marginally cheaper than its sister hotel, above.

Maryculter House Hotel, South Deeside Road, **t** 732 124, *www.maryculterhousehotel.co.uk*. Country house in wooded grounds on the banks of the Dee, 8 miles from city centre.

Old Mill Inn, South Deeside Road, **t** 733 212, *www.oldmillinn.co.uk*. Delightful country inn, 5 miles from the city centre, next to Storybook Glen.

Palm Court Hotel, 81 Seafield Road, in the West End, **t** 310 351. Has been restored to splendid Palm Court ambience – lively, friendly and comfortable.

Cheap

Beeches Private Hotel, **t** 586 413. Homely.

Dunavon House Hotel, 60 Victoria Street, Dyce, **t** 722 483. Close to the airport, with a good restaurant.

Ewood House, 12 Kings Gate, **t** 648 408. Very nice, cheap hotel.

Eating Out

Most of the hotels serve good food, especially the **Marcliffe at Pitfodels**.

The Ashvale, 46 Great Western Road, **t** 596 981. Top-of-the-market fish and chips, as well as other things.

Atlantis, at the Mariner Hotel, 439 Great Western Road, **t** 591 403. Some of the best, fresh seafood you will get around here.

La Bonne Baguette, Correction Wynd, off Union Street, **t** 644 445. Excellent French snacks. *Open daytime only*.

The Courtyard Restaurant, 1 Alford Lane, west end of Union Street, **t** 213 795. Good food.

Four Mile House, Kingswells, **t** 740 318. Good restaurant.

Howies Restaurant, 50 Chapel Street, **t** 639 500. Specializes in Scottish dishes with a dash of French, using fresh local produce. Relaxed atmosphere.

The Lair Hillock Inn and Crynoch Restaurant, **t** (01569) 730 001, **t** 0800 074 1095. About 10 miles southwest of the city, on a road junction near Netherley, and worth the effort. The food and atmosphere are first class, and it has won several well-deserved awards.

Les Amis, 58–60 Justice Mill Lane, **t** 584 599. French restaurant specializing in seafood.

The Lemon Tree, 5 West North Street, **t** 642 230. Lively restaurant/bar with theatre upstairs for music and entertainment.

Owlies, Littlejohn Street, **t** 649 267. Owned by the same people as Silver Darling, but cheaper. Good French food in a bohemian setting.

Poldinos, 7 Little Belmont Street, **t** 647 777. Excellent pizzas.

The Prince of Wales, 7 St Nicholas Lane. Splendid pub with cheap food and a great atmosphere.

Silver Darling, Pocra Quay, **t** 576 229. Good seafood and lively dockside atmosphere – though quite pricey.

buttressed walls. This was Aberdeen's first university, founded in 1495, in the reign of James IV. Its chapel, first Catholic then Protestant, is now interdenominational. The tomb of its founder, Bishop William Elphinstone, is a magnificent sarcophagus outside the chapel, supported by figures of the Seven Virtues. **King's College Visitor Centre** (*open Mon–Sat 10–5, Sun 12–5; adm*), in the former University Library, tells the story of 500 years of the university and its students, and there is a coffee shop.

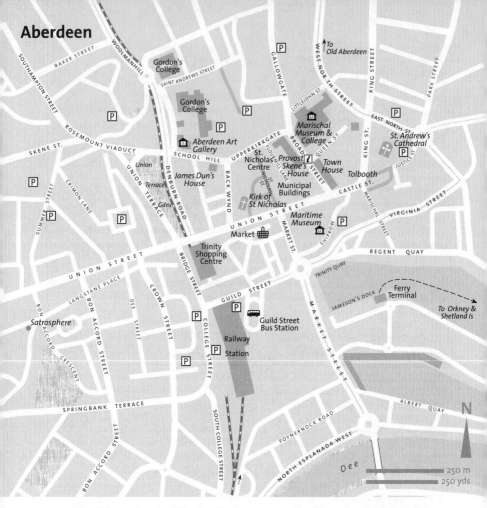

Aberdeen

At the **Planetarium** (*2nd floor Gallowgate Centre*, **t** *(01224) 612 130; ring for times*), you can take a guided tour of the universe, to the furthest galaxies.

Marischal College (pronounced Marshal), Broad Street, in the city centre, was founded in 1593 as a Protestant rival to King's, the two colleges being united to form Aberdeen University in 1860. The present building is an edifice of soaring pinnacles, a neo-Gothic granite fantasy glittering with mica, its roots in the 19th century with some of the older parts incorporated. The granite façade was added in 1906. The **Marischal Museum** (*open Mon–Fri 10–5, Sun 2–5*) has local, classical, Egyptian and Chinese antiquities, and illustrates evolving cultures of the world.

Provost Skene's House (*open Mon–Sat 10–5, Sun 1–4*) is opposite the college. Now a museum, this well-restored building dates from 1545. It was named after one of its owners, Sir George Skene, who was Provost of Aberdeen in 1676 and responsible for extensive renovation of the house. Butcher Cumberland lodged here from February until April 1746, on his way to defeat Prince Charles at Culloden. In those days the house formed two dwellings, both of which suffered considerable losses from the misbehaviour of the Duke and his officers. They made free with the stocks of provisions: coals, candles, ales and other liquors in the cellars. They milked the cow, spoiled the bed and table linen, and robbed their landlady of her hoard of precious sugar. It is a fascinating museum with some of the original decoration. The Painted Gallery, known as the Chapel, on the second floor of the west wing, revealed traces of religious paintings in 17th-century style, showing that medieval ideas and imagery persisted in this northeastern corner of Scotland far into the Reformation period. On the top floor, exhibits illustrate the history and domestic life of Aberdeen over the ages. There is a coffee shop in the original kitchen.

The **Tolbooth**, on the corner of Broad and Castle streets, was built in 1627. Its ancient town jail with original cells was the stage for the death of the 4th Earl of Huntly after his wife's witch had misleadingly promised him immunity from battle scars.

From the Tolbooth, go up Union Street to the **Kirk of St Nicholas** (*open May–Sept Mon–Fri 12–4, Sat 1–3; Oct–April (by appointment with Church office) Mon–Fri 10–1; Sunday service 11am; June–Sept also 9.30am; **t** (01224) 643 494*). The old parish church stands among trees in a peaceful churchyard bordered by Upperkirkgate and Back Wynd. Its 48-bell carillon rings out across the roar of the city. Founded in the 12th century and split in two at the Reformation, the present building dates from 1752. In the east part, the little stone-vaulted crypt-chapel, St Mary's, is 14th century. Witches were imprisoned down here in the 17th century; you can see the rings to which they were chained. More prosaically, the chapel has also been used as a plumber's workshop and an early Victorian soup-kitchen. The **Oil Industry Chapel** is in the church.

There are markets all year round at **Castlegate**, Union Street, which has been the centre of civic life since the 12th century.

Aberdeen Art Gallery (*open Mon–Sat 10–5, Sun 2–5*) is in Schoolhill. Among the many things to see here are 20th-century British paintings and sculptures, Raeburn portraits, works by Zoffany, Romney, Reynolds, Augustus John and Ben Nicholson, and an important collection of Scottish domestic silver and glass. There are also regular exhibitions, music, dance, poetry readings and films, a reference library, gallery shop, print room and café.

The **Village** (*open Mon–Sat 10–12, Sun 2.30–4.30; closed Thurs; adm*), 120 Rosemount Place, is an excellent place to take the children. With hands-on activities, they are transported to the ancient and third worlds on imaginative and instructive journeys.

The **Maritime Museum** (*open Mon–Sat 10–5, Sun 12–5*) is in Provost Ross' House, Shiprow, north of Trinity Quay and the Upper Dock. Overlooking the harbour, it is one of the oldest houses in the town and a fine example of early Scottish domestic architecture. Displays include Aberdeen's maritime heritage of fishing, shipbuilding and trade, and models of offshore oil installations.

Aberdeen Harbour is a conglomeration of seafaring life: fine old buildings line the waterfront where fishing boats are packed into the inner basins, some old and rusty, some so sophisticated that they need an electronic genius to operate them. If you want to see another face of Aberdeen, get up early one weekday morning and visit the **fish market** before the sales start at 7.30am. The action starts at around 4.30am and the earlier you go, the more impressive it is. As one of Britain's major fishing ports, Aberdeen exports hundreds of tonnes of fish daily. The boats dock in the cold pre-dawn, and box after box of fish is unloaded and stacked in open-sided warehouses. Fishermen with resilient faces toil at the final stages of their demanding job, their rich, salty humour warming the often bitterly cold air. Then the auction begins, in an unintelligible language of grunts, yells, mutterings and gestures.

Satrosphere (*179 Constitution Street; open April–Oct Mon–Sat 10–5, Sun 1.30–5; Nov–Mar Mon, Wed–Fri 10–4, Sat 10–5, Sun 1.30–5; adm; www.satrosphere.net*), near the beach opposite the Patio Hotel, is a marvellous science and technology centre where you can find out about such subjects as prisms, light, lasers, etc., and you are encouraged to take part in do-it-yourself experiments. This is a discovery place for all ages, whether science is your thing or not. You could easily spend a whole day here.

Glover House (*79 Balgownie Road, t (01224) 709 303; open by appointment Tues–Sat 10.30–4.30, Sun 1.30–4.30; adm*) tells the story of the rise of Thomas Blake Glover, a remarkable man who was born in Fraserburgh in 1838, went to Japan in 1859, and there played an extraordinarily vital part in the modernization and industrialization of a country that had been closed to foreigners for about 300 years. His relationship with a Japanese woman may have inspired Puccini's opera, *Madame Butterfly*.

The **Gordon Highlanders Regimental Museum** (*open April–Oct Tues–Sat 10.30–4.30, Sun 1.30–4.30; or by appointment, t (01224) 311 200; adm*), in Viewfield Road, has exhibitions displaying the uniforms, pictures, medals, letters and documents, weapons and memorabilia of this famous, locally recruited regiment. The Gordon Highlanders fought with distinction all over the world, and are now amalgamated with the Queens Own Highlanders (Camerons and Seaforths) to form part of the Highlanders. There is an audiovisual theatre, shop and tearoom.

Duthie Park Winter Gardens (*open Dec–Mar daily 9.30–4; April and Nov daily 9.30–5; May–Sept daily 9.30–9pm; Oct daily 9.30–10.30pm*), south of the city on the banks of the Dee, were recently hailed as Scotland's top tourist attraction. The glasshouse extension makes them the largest glassed gardens in Europe. They include a Japanese Garden, the biggest collection of cacti in Britain, birds, fish and turtles. Sit under a palm tree in mid-winter and picture yourself in some tropical paradise. Outside, in **Duthie Park**, there is a licensed restaurant, a play area, boating pond, Victorian bandstand and a Rose Mound, which brings on a severe attack of gardener's elbow as you contemplate the pruning season.

Hazelhead Park, not much more than a mile from the city centre along Queens Road, is a splendid, spacious place with a maze, gardens, a mini-zoo and a tearoom.

Footdee, known locally in the inimitable Aberdonian accent as 'Fittie', is a fishing village at the mouth of the Dee. The early 19th-century houses were designed by the fisherfolk themselves. Come here in an easterly gale and watch the sea breaking high over the harbour walls.

Another place from which to watch the changing moods of the sea is **Girdleness Lighthouse** in Walker Park, the grassy headland that juts eastwards from the other side of the harbour. You get a bird's-eye view of the harbour and the city from here.

A sandy beach stretches 2 miles northwards from the harbour, backed by dunes matted with marram grass and fringed by golf courses and an amusement park. The whole strip is called **Aberdeen Fun Beach**, and there are restaurants and bars to revive you. Bathing in the North Sea is only for the hardy: watch out for undercurrents.

The Grampians

The Coast South of Aberdeen

The A92 south from Aberdeen takes you along the coast, with the North Sea stretching away to the horizon, always busy with shipping. When the wind is in the east, big seas pound the beaches and cliffs, sending up great plumes of spray.

Stonehaven

Stonehaven is a holiday resort town 14 miles south of Aberdeen, as sturdy as its name implies, crouched around a bay below red sandstone cliffs. The sheltered harbour is now mainly used by pleasure boats. Stonehaven has a heated open-air swimming pool, a golf course, boating and windsurfing, fishing and sea-angling, and an indoor leisure centre with swimming pool.

The **Tolbooth Museum** (*open May–Oct Wed–Mon 2–4.30*) is a 16th-century building on the quay by the north pier, displaying local history and archaeology, with a special emphasis on fishing. The building was a storehouse of the Earls Marischal, later used as a prison. In 1748 and 1749 three Episcopal priests were imprisoned here for their insistence in following the old religion. During their incarceration women came from all over the county, smuggling babies in creels on their backs, to hold them up to the barred windows so that the priests could baptize them.

Dunnottar Castle (*open Easter–Oct Mon–Sat 9–6, Sun 2–5; Nov–Easter Mon–Fri 9–sunset; adm*) is about 2 miles south of Stonehaven, just off the A92. This spectacular ruined fortress stands high on a rocky promontory towering 160ft above the boiling sea, protected to landward by a deep natural cleft. It has been written: 'Dunnottar speaks with an audible voice; every cave has a record, every turret a tongue.' A Pictish fort stood here in the Dark Ages, and one of the earliest Christian chapels. The fort was replaced by a primitive castle in the 13th century. William Wallace stormed the English garrison in 1297, burning down the church where they had taken refuge, but failing to take the castle. Dunnottar was a stronghold of the Earls Marischal of Scotland from the 14th century. The extensive ruins include a great square tower and the chapel, built by Sir William Keith in 1392, and a gatehouse, built in 1575, said to be the strongest in Scotland. In 1645 the 7th Earl Marischal, a stubborn Covenanter, withstood a siege by Montrose, who took his revenge by laying waste to Stonehaven and the surrounding lands. His actions are recorded by a chronicler as having left the country 'utterlie spoilzeit plunderit and undone'.

During the Civil War the Scottish Regalia were brought to Dunnottar for safety. The castle was besieged in 1652, but the governor refused to surrender until the Regalia had been smuggled out in the apron of the local minister's wife, Mrs Grainger, and in

Tourist Information

Stonehaven t (01569–)
Stonehaven: 66 Allardice Street, **t** 762 806;
open April–Oct.

Festivals

July: Highland Games, Stonehaven.
New Year's Eve: Swinging the Fireballs;
ceremony going back to pagan times when
fireballs were swung through the streets to
ward off evil spirits.

Where to Stay and Eat

Alexander Guest House, 36 Arduthie Road,
Stonehaven, **t** 762 265, *www.alexanderguest
house.com* (*moderate–cheap*). Family-run,
licensed guesthouse, with warm welcome.
Arduthie House, Ann Street, Stonehaven, **t** 762
381, *arduthie@talk21.com* (*moderate–cheap*).

Excellent guesthouse in a big villa overlooking the sea. Every need is catered for and
the breakfasts are above average.
Dunnottar Mains Farm, Dunnottar, **t** 762 621,
dunnottar@ecosse.net (*moderate–cheap*).
Good B&B.
Heugh Hotel, Westfield Road, Stonehaven,
t 762 379 (*moderate–cheap*). Comfortable,
turreted granite baronial mansion, with oak
panelling, nice grounds and good food.
Marine Hotel, Shorehead, Stonehaven, **t** 762
155 (*moderate–cheap*). Right on the waterfront in the harbour. The staff are friendly
and they cater for children.
Mrs Bowman, 11 Urie Crescent, Stonehaven,
t 763 111, *sirdhana.stonehaven@virgin.net*
(*moderate–cheap*). Good B&B.
Mrs Craib, Car-Lyn-Vale, Rickarton, Stonehaven,
t 762 406 (*moderate–cheap*). Good B&B.
Tewel Farmhouse, Tewel, **t** 762 306
(*moderate–cheap*). Good B&B.
The Tolbooth, Stonehaven, **t** 762 287. Excellent
seafood in an old tolbooth on the harbour.

a bundle of flax carried by her servant. They were hidden in the kirk at Kinneff and kept safe until the Restoration of the Monarchy.

In 1685 167 Covenanters were imprisoned at Dunnottar in such awful conditions that you can almost sense the horror now, looking at the 'Whigs Vault' where many of them were confined: 'ankle deep in mire, with one window to the sea, they had not the least accommodation for sitting, leaning or lying and were perfectly stifled for want of air and no access to ease nature'. Some tried to escape through the window that overlooks the sea, but were recaptured and cruelly tortured. Many died. It was a chapter in the history of the castle that seems to overshadow it, even now adding a gloomy touch to the very well-preserved ruins. The castle was used as the setting for Zeffirelli's film *Hamlet*.

Dunnottar's history is further commemorated in the 18th-century kirk at **Kinneff**, 7 miles to the south just off the A92. Parts of the old kirk are incorporated into the current building and include those parts in which the Scottish Regalia were hidden for nine years by the Rev. James Grainger. The hiding place was under the flagstone below the pulpit. You can see memorials to Grainger, his wife, and to Sir George Ogilvy, Governor of Dunnottar Castle at the time.

Fowlsheugh is an RSPB reserve, signed off the A92 3 miles south of Stonehaven. Always open, but best in spring and summer, this is home to one of the largest sea-bird colonies in Scotland. From May to July boat trips run twice weekly from Stonehaven harbour (*for details **t** (01224) 624 824*).

Catterline, about 5 miles south of Stonehaven, is a picturesque old fishing village where it is often possible to see seals in the bay.

Inverbervie

Inverbervie is a milling town just to the south on the banks of Bervie Water. Here in 1341, at Craig David on the north shore, David II and his wife, Joan, were driven ashore by a storm while returning from nine years' exile in France. King's Step is the rock where David is said to have stepped ashore. He granted the town a Royal Charter the following year. There is also a memorial to Hercules Linton, the man who designed the famous clipper *Cutty Sark*. Today, this wild, rugged coastline offers little refuge from the ferocious storms that often rage in from the North Sea. The villagers take what shelter they can from harbours built into the cliffs. The sheltered area to the west is called Howe of the Mearns, with forest trails and picnic sites.

Glenbervie, just off the A94, is 6 miles southwest of Stonehaven. It was the home of the ancestors of Robert Burns and you can see the family tombstone and a cairn in memory of the poet, whose father emigrated west to Ayr.

The **Grassic Gibbon Centre** (*open April–Oct daily 10–4.30; adm*), at Arbuthnott, is a memorial to Lewis Grassic Gibbon (James Leslie Mitchell), the writer whose powerful Scottish prose in his trilogy *A Scots Quair* brings to life the Mearns at the beginning of the 20th century. He spent his childhood here and used recognizable local settings in his books. There is a coffee shop, gift/book shop and visitors' centre.

From here you can make a quick detour inland through Laurencekirk to **Fettercairn**, where you can tour the **Fettercairn Distillery** (*open May–Sept Mon–Sat 10–4.30*), and on to Fasque, often missed by tourists hurrying north on the main road. While you are here, go a few miles north on the B974 – a glorious drive over bald, rolling hills – and climb Cairn o' Mount for fantastic views.

Fasque

Open May–Sept daily 11–5.30; or by arrangement,
t (01561) 340 569; adm.

Just to the north of Fettercairn, with its turreted arch into the village commemorating a visit by Queen Victoria and Prince Albert in 1861, Fasque is down a side road to the left. This delightful, rambling mansion is for Victoriana addicts. The house, built in 1809, was the home of the Gladstones, including one of Britain's best-known prime ministers, W. E. Gladstone – he who chewed each mouthful a hundred times to aid digestion. He spent his honeymoon here before moving to Wales. Fasque, still owned by the family, has managed to preserve all the marvellous relics of Victorian times without becoming like a museum. Nothing seems to have changed for a hundred years. The kitchens are a joy and you can see portraits of all the family servants. A slightly ramshackle air hangs over the whole fascinating place and you expect to be summoned to tea by a butler at any moment.

Royal Deeside

The River Dee is born high in the Cairngorms, to the west. It boils down through steep-sided ravines, thunders over precipices gathering myriad tributaries from corries in the surrounding hills, foams through the deer forests of Mar, ripples at a suitably majestic pace past Balmoral Castle, and meets the North Sea in Aberdeen.

Deeside is perhaps best of all in autumn, when the rich blaze of colour is unforgettable. In winter the landscape becomes a dramatic sweep of snow-covered hills and torrents of ice: a skier's delight, with the Glenshee and the Lecht ski centres. In summer, with a good map and sensible equipment, you could spend a whole holiday exploring the hills and valleys of the Cairngorms and Grampians.

Peterculter and Maryculter

Leaving Aberdeen on the A93 west, you pass Peterculter and Maryculter (both pronounced kooter), once a Roman camp. William the Lion granted the lands to the Knights Templar, who built a chapel to St Mary in the late 12th century. Its ruins can still be seen in Templars' Park on the south bank of the river. The coloured statue of Rob Roy standing above the Leuchar's Burn has no historic significance. It was originally a ship's figurehead and has been replaced twice since it was erected.

Children and adults alike will enjoy **Storybook Glen** (*open Mar–Oct daily 10–6; Nov–Feb Sat and Sun 11–4; adm*), off South Deeside Road in Maryculter. A host of familiar characters are ingeniously arranged among flowers, streams and waterfalls.

The **Blairs Museum** (*South Deeside Road, Blairs; open May–Oct Tues–Sun 12–4; Nov–April by appointment; t (01224) 863 767, www.blairs.net*) tells 500 years of history in the former Blairs College, a Catholic seminary in a peaceful estate. There are a wealth of exhibits on ecclesiastical matters, Mary, Queen of Scots, and so on.

Drum Castle (*castle open Easter–May daily 1.30–5.30; June–Aug daily 11–5.30; Sept daily and Oct Sat and Sun 1.30–5.30; gardens open same dates 10–6; grounds open daily 9.30–sunset adm*), about 3 miles to the west, is one of the three oldest tower houses in Scotland. A massive granite tower, built towards the end of the 13th century, adjoins a mansion built in 1619. Robert the Bruce gave Drum to his standard bearer, William de Irwin, in 1324, and it remained in the possession of the family until the late Mr H. Q. Forbes Irvine left it to the National Trust for Scotland in 1975. It contains antique furniture, silver, portraits, family treasures and relics. The grounds are lovely, with an oak wood, rare trees and shrubs, sweeping lawns, nature trails, and a café.

Crathes Castle and Gardens

Castle open April–Sept daily 10.30–5.30; Oct daily 10.30–4.30; visitor centre, shop, restaurant, plant sales, gardens and grounds open all year daily 9.30–sunset; adm.

Crathes is 5 miles beyond Drum. Although familiar to many, it is still a pleasant surprise when seen in reality. The Burnett family had been granted lands north of the Dee by Robert the Bruce early in the 14th century, and it was Alexander Burnett who,

The Green Lady

Crathes has its ghosts, notably the Green Lady, who, dressed in green and carrying a baby in her arms, haunts certain rooms. A baby's skeleton was unearthed under the hearthstone in the Green Lady's room during the 19th century, and the story is told of a young girl, under the laird's protection, giving birth to a baby, fathered by one of the servants. Mother and infant died, under mysterious circumstances.

in 1552, decided to move from his stronghold on an island in the Loch of Leys nearby, and build a modern house, in keeping with his status as laird. The castle took many years to complete and is one of the best examples of Scottish domestic architecture as it developed from the previously necessary fortified dwellings – a style that was to die out within 60 years. When a Victorian extension, overlooking the upper garden, was burnt down in 1966, it was agreed to restore the castle to its present, original proportions. The interior is just as it was, with painted decorations on the beams and woodwork, allegorical designs, proverbs and biblical texts. You can also see some of the original furnishings, as well as many other treasures. The little ivory hunting horn in the main hall symbolizes the Burnetts' right of tenure over part of the Royal Forest, given them by Robert the Bruce. The gardens are a delight in every season. They consist of a series of small, interlinked gardens, like rooms in a house, each with its own motif and character – a profusion of colours, scents and blended textures. There are also nature trails in the grounds.

Banchory

Banchory, about 3 miles beyond Crathes, is a pleasant, sheltered town on the Dee. It rises in layers of terraced streets, backed by the **Hill o' Fare** (1,545ft) to the north, and rolling hills to the south. You catch an air of genteel respectability as you stroll among its antique shops and high-class boutiques.

Banchory Museum (*open Easter weekend 11–1 and 2–4.30; May, June and Sept Mon–Sat 11–1 and 2–4.30; July and Aug Mon–Sat 11–1 and 2–4.30, Sun 2–4.30; Oct Sat 11–1 and 2–4.30*), in Bridge Street, tells the history of the area.

In the 5th century St Ternan, a local man and follower of St Ninian, established a monastery where the churchyard now is, and you can still see traces of its medieval successor. Incorporated into the walls of the manse, carved wheel-crosses date from this early Christian period. Palaeolithic flints, excavated nearby, suggest a very early settlement. There is a golf course by the river, and the salmon fishing is renowned. Walk to the south of the town, where the Dee is joined by the Feugh, at **Bridge of Feugh**. The footbridge above the rapids is a good place from which to watch the salmon leaping up the ledges to get to their spawning grounds. There are forest and riverside walks as well as energetic hill climbs.

Aboyne

Aboyne, 13 miles to the west, is famous for its annual Highland Games (*see* p.404). It is a good base from which to explore this part of Deeside, and there are some excellent walks in the area. Follow the Water of Tanar, southwest of town, through Glen

Tourist Information

Banchory: Bridge Street, t (01330) 822 000; *open April–Oct.*

Ballater: Station Square, t (01339) 755 306; *open April–Oct.*

Crathie: The Car Park, t (01339) 742 414; *open April–Oct.*

Braemar: The Mews, t (01339) 741 600; *open all year.*

Festivals

August: **Highland Games**, Aboyne; all the traditional activities – tossing the caber, putting the weight, piping and dancing. **Highland Games**, Ballater; in Monaltrie Park, with a Hill Race to Craig Cailleach, south of the bridge. **Victoria Week**, Ballater.

September: **Highland Gathering**, Braemar, *see* below.

Where to Stay and Eat

Balgonie Country House Hotel, Ballater, t (01339) 755 482, *balgoniech@aol.com* (*expensive–moderate*). Comfortable, with old-fashioned hospitality and excellent food.

Banchory Lodge Hotel, Banchory, t (01330) 822 625, *www.banchorylodge.co.uk* (*expensive–moderate*). Georgian house beside where the Water of Feugh flows into the Dee. Old-world hospitality and decent food. Popular with the fishing fraternity.

Burnett Arms Hotel, High Street, Banchory, t (01330) 824 944, *theburnett@ email.msn.com* (*expensive–moderate*). Well-modernised 19th-century coaching inn in the middle of town. Friendly service.

Darroch Learg Hotel, Ballater, t (01339) 755 443, *www.darrochlearg.co.uk* (*expensive–moderate*). Worth a visit for the views alone. Traditional granite country house in 5 acres of garden, with views across the golf course to Lochnagar. Comfortable and friendly with an excellent restaurant. *Closed Jan.*

Dinnet House, Aboyne, t (01339) 885 332, *dinnet@dinnet.force9.co.uk* (*expensive–moderate*). Castle-style Victorian shooting lodge overlooking the Dee with extensive grounds and moorland. It is an attractive, comfortable Wolsey Lodge, and your hostess is an excellent cook. No smoking.

The Green Inn Restaurant with Rooms, Victoria Road, Ballater, t (01339) 755 701 (*expensive–moderate*). First-class food with top-quality ingredients. Worth staying. Book.

Hazelhurst Lodge Gallery Hotel Restaurant, Aboyne, t (01339) 886 921 (*expensive–moderate*). Really friendly little place, with only four bedrooms and excellent candlelit dinners. Arty interior and friendly people.

Hilton Craigendarroch, Braemar Road, Ballater, t (01339) 755 858 (*expensive–moderate*). Posh country-club-type establishment with lots of leisure facilities including pool, sauna, steam room, gym, squash, snooker, beauty salon, dry skiing, golf, fishing and shooting. It overlooks the Dee, and the food served in its restaurant is good.

Tanar, in whose woods you can see remnants of the old Caledonian Forest. Tanar oak was much used in the 19th century for the building of ships in Aberdeen. The **Braeloine Visitor Centre** (*open April–Sept Wed–Mon 10–5; Oct–Mar Thurs–Mon 10–5; adm for cars*) is 5 miles up the glen, with educational information on local wildlife, farming and forestry, as well as advice on where to walk. There are several tracks leading south over the hills, one of which, Fir Mount, is thought to be the route taken by Macbeth as he fled from Dunsinane to his death at Lumphanan.

    Lumphanan is 5 miles northeast of Aboyne. The **Peel Ring** is a medieval motte with wall, earthworks and ditches, and is believed to be where Macbeth fought his final battle against Malcolm Canmore in 1057. Macbeth's Cairn, in a circle of trees on the hillside, marks the spot where he is said to have died, crying: 'Lay on Macduff; and damn'd be him that first cries "Hold enough!"' (Actually, Shakespeare sets the death scene at Dunsinane.)

Raemoir House Hotel, Raemoir, near Banchory, t (01330) 824 884, *www.raemoir.com* (*expensive–moderate*). 18th-century mansion, converted from a private house in 1943, with tapestries, antiques, all mod cons, first-class food, tennis, a mini 9-hole golf course, and shooting, game fishing and stalking in season. There are also four self-catering apartments in the coach house available to let.

Tor-Na-Coille Hotel, Inchmarlo Road, Banchory, t (01330) 822 242, *tornacoille@btinternet.com* (*expensive–moderate*). Privately owned hotel with a variety of deserved awards, including for food. Very friendly. (Lift to all floors.)

Tullich Lodge, Ballater, t (01339) 755 406 (*expensive–moderate*). Victorian baronial mansion with individual atmosphere, nice rooms and a set menu, usually delicious.

Braemar Lodge Hotel, Glenshee Road, Braemar, t (01339) 741 627 (*moderate*). Splendid easy-going family hotel, where you feel quite at home. Also 4 log cabins for self-catering (sleeping 6).

Cambus O'May Hotel, near Ballater, t (01339) 755 428, *www.cambusomayhotel.co.uk* (*moderate*). An attractive, family-run country house overlooking the Dee. Good food and good service.

Invercauld Arms Hotel, Braemar, t (01339) 741 605, *info@invercauldarms-hotel-braemar.com* (*moderate*). On the spot where the Earl of Mar raised the Jacobite standard in 1715: there's a plaque to commemorate the occasion. Some of the rooms overlook the river, and the staff are very friendly.

Lys-Na-Greyne House, Aboyne, t (01339) 887 397 (*moderate*). Very special, welcoming guesthouse on the banks of the Dee. Dinner and packed lunches by arrangement.

Mar Lodge Apartments, Braemar, bookings via the NTS, t (0131) 243 9331, *www.nts.org.uk* (*moderate*). Five luxury apartments in a former royal hunting lodge in 77,500 acres (sleeping 5–15).

Monaltrie Hotel, Bridge Square, Ballater, t (01339) 755 417, *www.monaltriehotel.com* (*moderate*). Comfortable hotel by the Dee.

Deeside Hotel, Braemar Road, Ballater, t (01339) 755 420 (*cheap*). Comfortable, friendly family hotel with two downstairs bedrooms and a large garden.

Gairnshiel Lodge, Glengairn, Ballater, t (01339) 755 582, *www.gairnshiellodge.co.uk* (*cheap*). Delightful mountain lodge, very secluded, informal and cosy – and good value. King George VI dined here with his brother, the abdicated Edward VIII, Duke of Windsor, who was not allowed to darken the doors of royal establishments.

Glen Lui Hotel, Ballater, t (01339) 755 402, *www.glen-lui-hotel.co.uk* (*cheap*). Excellent value, comfortable rooms and good food. Special breaks include wine tastings.

Loch Kinord Hotel, Dinnet, t (01339) 885 229, *www.loch-kinord-hotel.com* (*cheap*). Good value and friendly hotel.

Milton Restaurant, just east of Banchory, t (01330) 844 566. Good food and crafts/gifts in an old farm steading.

White Cottage, Aboyne, t (01339) 886 265. Reasonable food in a cottagey atmosphere.

Tarland

Tarland, less than 5 miles northwest of Aboyne, is an old-world village set around a square, and is the centre of the MacRobert Trust – a huge complex of farming and charitable foundations.

Walk a short way to the east, beyond the golf course, to the well-preserved souter-rain, **Culsh Earth House**, by Culsh Farmhouse. Its roofing slabs are intact over a large chamber – you will need a torch to see inside.

Another prehistoric feature is **Tomnaverie Stone Circle**, on a rocky hillock a mile to the southeast, unexcavated and recumbent, probably dating from 1800 BC.

From Tarland, drive around Scar Hill on the B9119 and back to the A93 at **Dinnet**. The **National Nature Reserve** here covers heathland, scrub and birchwood, with old oaks and fenland.

Ballater

Ballater, 11 miles west of Aboyne, used to be the end of the line for the Royal Train, before the railway was closed. It's a popular holiday centre in the summer, in wooded moorland where you can roam for miles, discovering fresh enchantment at every turn.

The town developed in the late 18th century after an old woman discovered the healing powers of the spring water at the foot of Pannanich Hill. Her discovery was exploited by an ex-Jacobite, Francis Farquharson of Monaltrie, 20 years after his exile and near-execution, following Culloden. This enterprising entrepreneur built an inn at the hamlet of Cobbletown of Dalmuchie and developed it into a spa, which quickly became fashionable. After Queen Victoria fell in love with Scotland and came to Balmoral, the whole area developed into the prosperous place it is today.

The **Old Royal Station**, in Station Square (*open April, May and Oct Mon–Sat 10–1 and 2–5, Sun 1–5; June and Sept Mon–Sat 10–6, Sun 1–6; July and Aug Mon–Sat 9.30–7, Sun 1–7; Nov–Mar Sat and Sun 10–5*), has been lovingly restored to its Victorian splendour and celebrates 100 years of royal use. The Deeside line was extended to Ballater in 1866 and the station built so that Queen Victoria and her entourage could alight near Balmoral. The line was used until 1965, just before the station closed. You can see Queen Victoria's waiting room, plus audiovisual and interpretative displays.

The **McEwan Gallery** (*t (01339) 755 429; ring if it's closed*) is a treasure-trove of 18th-century paintings, pottery and books in a lovely house. The views from **Ballater Golf Course**, sweeping away to the hills, must be distracting enough to kill concentration on the game. There are some sizeable hills to climb, with panoramic views and always the sound of rushing water and the song of skylarks and linnets.

Balmoral

Gardens, grounds, ballroom and coach house
open mid-April–31 July daily 10–5; also June
and July Sun 10–5; adm; www.balmoralcastle.com.

Balmoral is another of those places so familiar from photographs that its reality is almost an anticlimax. Queen Victoria lost her heart to 'this dear Paradise', and she and Prince Albert bought the estate and the old castle in 1852, for £31,000. The old building, however, was too small for the royal household, and Prince Albert commissioned the building of the present granite mansion in 1853, a Scottish baronial edifice designed by William Smith of Aberdeen. It is still the Royal Family's holiday home.

The parts of the castle open to the public include exhibits of paintings, works of art and a tartan collection in the ballroom; an exhibition of royal heraldry, commemorative china, photographs and wildlife in the carriage hall; carriages and work by the Upper Deeside Arts Society in the stables; country walks, gift shops, a cafeteria, pony trekking and pony cart rides (when ponies are available) in the gardens. Walk up the hill behind the house to Victoria's monument to her beloved Albert. She spent a lot of time mourning him up here.

Crathie Church (*open April–Oct Mon–Sat 9.30–5, Sun 2–5; Sunday service 11.30*), just north of the castle, was built in 1895 to replace a series of previous churches whose origins went back to the 9th century. It is attended by members of the Royal Family when they are on holiday.

Lochnagar towers over the Balmoral area, among 11 peaks over 3,000ft high: massive sentinels, reflected in the waters of Loch Muick to the south. This scenery inspired Byron to write:

England! thy beauties are tame and domestic
To one who has roved o'er the mountains afar:
Oh, for the crags that are wild and majestic!
The steep frowning glories of dark Lochnagar.

More recently, Lochnagar inspired another writer, the present Prince of Wales, to write a delightful story, *The Old Man of Lochnagar*, to amuse his brothers during a cruise in the royal yacht.

Royal Lochnagar Distillery (*open Easter–Sept Mon–Sat 10–5, Sun 12–4; Oct–Easter Mon–Fri 10–4; last tour one hour before closing; adm*) was founded in 1845.

A good 8-mile walk starts at **Spittal of Glenmuick**, northeast of Loch Muick, and goes round the loch anticlockwise to the southwest corner and then across to the Dubh (black) Loch, deep in a corrie among brooding cliffs. You are about 2,000ft up here, and ice lingers on the water well into summer. Watch out for golden eagles soaring overhead on long, splay-tipped wings. Less rare than they used to be, they are still a protected species, hated by sheep farmers. Another bird of prey you might see up here, also protected, is the peregrine falcon, plummeting to earth at speeds of 112 miles per hour. In autumn you might hear the roaring of rutting stags.

Braemar

Braemar is a very popular holiday centre surrounded by beautiful scenery.

Braemar Castle (*open April–Oct Mon–Thurs, Sat and Sun 10–6; July and Aug daily 10–6; adm*) is a massive turreted fortress, built by the Earl of Mar in 1628. It was burnt by the Farquharsons in 1689 and garrisoned by the English after the Jacobite risings in 1715 and 1745 to protect the military road from Perth. The castle has barrel-vaulted ceilings, a sinister pit prison, spiral stairways and gun loops. Look for the carved graffiti on the internal woodwork, left by off-duty soldiers in the 18th century.

Braemar Royal Highland Gathering is held every year on the first Saturday in September, drawing upwards of 20,000 people. It includes all the traditional events, both athletic and musical, together with plenty of stalls and sideshows. The Royal Family attend the games, which might be why it is one of the biggest events of its kind in Scotland. The origins of these Highland Games are said to date from the 11th century, when Malcolm Canmore held contests to find the best soldiers for his struggles against the Normans.

Braemar Highland Heritage Centre (*open May–Sept daily 9–6; Oct–April Mon–Fri 9–5, Sat and Sun 10–5*) has audiovisual presentations and exhibitions on the history and landscape of the area, the Highland Gathering and royal bits and pieces.

Linn of Dee

A tour of about 12 miles takes you west from Braemar through the wooded Dee Valley to the Linn of Dee. It is an attractive and popular drive. The traffic can be tedious as the narrow road winds up through birches, with splendid views to the Cairngorms. Park at **Inverey** and walk the couple of miles on to the Linn of Dee. The narrow, rocky gorge is about 150 yards long, and the river boils through this bottle-neck in a tumultuous frenzy, filling the air with noise and a haze of spray. This lovely place is best appreciated early or late in the day.

Experienced walkers should try the famous **Lairig Ghru**, a testing walk from Linn of Dee over the Cairngorms to Aviemore.

Another walk from Inverey is south up the Ey Burn to the **Colonel's Bed**. The Colonel was John Farquharson of Inverey, a legendary character known as the Black Colonel, who used to ride his horse up sheer rock slopes and summon his servants by firing at a shield on the wall which rang like a bell when hit by a bullet. The Colonel's Bed is a ledge of rock in a gorge through which the Ey runs, where the Black Colonel hid after his castle had been burnt down by government troops following the Battle of Killiecrankie in 1689.

Aberdeen to Tomintoul

The A944 takes you west from Aberdeen through farm and moorland towards the hills. Less spectacular than Deeside, it is nevertheless attractive country with several prosperous private estates.

Castle Fraser

Open Easter weekend, May and Sept daily 1.30–5.30;
June–Aug daily 11–5.30; Oct Sat and Sun 1.30–5.30; adm;
gardens and grounds open daily 9.30–sunset; adm.

Castle Fraser is about 15 miles from Aberdeen, to the north of the road. It is one of the most spectacular of the Castles of Mar, Z-plan, dating from the 16th century and incorporating an earlier castle. The Great Hall conjures dreams of feudal lairds. Look for the eavesdropping device known as the 'Laird's Lug'. If you look closely at the great heraldic panel on the north side you can see the inscription 'I Bel', left by one of the Bel family, who were important master masons, very active in Aberdeenshire. They may also have helped to build both Crathes Castle and Craigievar Castle, near Kintocher. An exhibition off the courtyard tells the story of the Castles of Mar. There are also plants, a shop, tearoom, playground and walks; also events most Sundays.

Alford

Montrose fought one of his victorious battles against the Covenanters in 1645 near Alford (pronounced Arford), 10 miles further west, on the ground between the village and the bridge over the Don. A sad story hangs over **Terpersie Castle** (1561), rebuilt and lived in by its restorer, 4 miles northwest of Alford. The last owner, George Gordon, fought for Prince Charles at Culloden. He fled to the castle after the battle, to lie low until the worst of the reprisals were over. His young children, unaware of the threat, revealed that 'papa was at home' to his pursuers. He was captured in the castle and later executed.

Alford is on the Castle Trail, and in the old cattle mart there's a **Rural Life Heritage Centre** (*open April–Oct Mon–Sat 10–5, Sun 1–5*) with a working water mill, and a museum of rural life and social history. Also in the village is the **Grampian Transport Museum** (*open April–Oct daily 10–5*), with 'hands on' and 'climb aboard' exhibits, and the **Alford Valley Railway** (*ring for times and steam engine trips, **t** (01975) 562 811; adm*), a narrow-gauge passenger railway which runs half-hour trips.

Landacraig Garden Gallery and Nursery, between Alford and Kildrummy (*open May–Sept Mon–Sat 10–5, Sun 2–6*), is a delightful walled garden with exhibitions of paintings and sculpture.

Kildrummy Castle

Open April–Sept daily 9.30–6–30; adm.

Kildrummy is a ruined courtyard castle 10 miles west of Alford on the A97. Founded in the early 13th century, it is one of the most impressive and historic of the castles in this area. Edward I captured it and altered its design. Robert the Bruce sent his wife and children here when he went into exile on Rathlin Island in 1306. The story is told of a treacherous blacksmith who betrayed the fugitives to the English in return for their promise of 'as much gold as he could carry'. He set fire to the castle, whose inhabitants surrendered, receiving as his reward the molten gold, poured down his throat. The English executed Nigel Bruce, Robert's brother; the garrison was 'hangyt and drawyn' but Robert's intrepid wife, Elizabeth, escaped with her children and fled north to Tain. In 1404 Alexander Stewart, son of the Wolf of Badenoch, kidnapped the Countess of Mar, having killed her husband in order to widow her, and forcibly married her, to gain the title of Mar. The castle was destroyed because of the part it played in the 1715 rebellion. It is an extensive ruin, with a broad ditch and curtain wall, round towers, a keep and gatehouse.

Kildrummy Castle Gardens (*open April–Oct daily; adm*) were created when a Colonel Ogston bought the old castle in 1898 and built himself a modern pile in its lee. They include a Japanese rock and water garden, built in the quarry from which stone was taken for the castle, and a replica of Old Aberdeen's Brig o' Balgownie, spanning the stream among shrubs and alpines.

Two miles to the south, at **Glenkindie**, you can see a well-preserved earth house in a clump of trees, its short entrance passage leading to two chambers under massive roof slabs. You need a torch for the inner chamber.

From Glenkindie, follow the course of the Don through the valley of Strathdon and up into the hills to the west for less than 3 miles. 16th-century **Glenbuchat Castle** stands by the road at Bridge of Buchat. It was the seat of 'Old Glenbucket' (sic), a staunch Jacobite, who died in exile in France after Culloden.

Corgarff Castle

Open April–Sept daily 9.30–6.30;
Oct–Mar Sat 9.30–4.30, Sun 2–4.30; adm.

This is a stark, 16th-century tower house, within a star-shaped wall with gun loops. One terrible day in 1571, the family of the laird, Alexander Forbes, was besieged here by supporters of the deposed Mary, Queen of Scots. In her husband's absence, Forbes' wife refused to surrender. Edom o'Gordon ordered that the castle be burned, and she died in the flames, with her entire family and household. Corgarff was used by Jacobites in both 1715 and 1745. In 1748, in the aftermath of Culloden, the Hanoverians converted it into a garrison post and barracks to guard the military road from Perth to Fort George. In the 19th century the castle was used by the Redcoats in their unpopular campaign against whisky smuggling. Recently reconstructed rooms are excellent.

This is skiing country, for hardy skiers who don't need too many sophisticated lifts and resorts. The **Lecht Road**, from Corgarff to Tomintoul, is part of the military road built by the Hanoverians after Culloden. It rises steeply from 1,330 to 2,100ft within a distance of about 3 miles. The wild moorland is frequently cut off by snow in winter when fierce winds cause high drifts: remote farms and communities can be isolated for days. **Lecht Mine**, in the hills north of the Lecht Road near Well of Lecht, is where lead was mined between 1730 and 1737. The ore was taken on pack horses over the hills to Nethy Bridge where there was timber for smelting. Later it became a manganese ore mine, but fell into disrepair when the price of ore fell.

Tomintoul

Tomintoul, 8 miles northwest of Corgarff, is second only to Dalwhinnie as the highest village in the Highlands, at 1,150ft. Pronounced 'Tommin-towl', the name comes from the Gaelic *Tom-an-t-sabhal*, meaning 'hill of the barn'. The village lies along a gentle ridge flanked on one side by the River Avon (pronounced 'Arn'), famous for the clarity of its water, and on the other by Conglass Water. It is easy to drive through in a hurry and miss the attractions of this lofty, wild territory. Walkers will discover glens hidden in folds of the hills, with tumbling burns and tiny lochans, rich in bird, animal and plant life.

Tomintoul Museum and Visitor Centre (*open May and Oct Mon–Fri 10–4; June–Sept Mon–Sat 10–4*) is in an old baker's shop in the square. Displays include a reconstructed farm kitchen with all the old implements, a blacksmith's shop, a peat-cutting exhibition, and information on wildlife, climate, landscape and geology.

Glenlivet

Glenlivet, running north to the Spey, is not only at the heart of malt whisky country but also a settled farming area. In 1594 1,500 local men routed 10,000 Highlanders at the Battle of Glenlivet, and after the 1745 rising army units were garrisoned in Glenlivet to maintain order and to try to stamp out the illicit distilling of whisky. Catholicism has remained strong here, especially in the secluded Braes of Glenlivet where, in the 18th century, the Seminary of Scalen was the only place in Scotland for

Tourist Information

Alford: Station Yard, **t** (01975) 562 052;
  open April–Oct.
Tomintoul: The Square, **t** (01807) 580 285;
  open April–Oct.

Festivals

3rd Saturday in July: Highland Games,
  Tomintoul and Strathavon.

Sports and Activities

The **Lecht Ski Centre** is at the summit of the
Lecht Road (*see* below), with several ski tows,
a dry ski slope, ski school, ski hire, and a café
and crêche. A little further on is the
Glenmulliach Nordic Ski Centre for cross-
country skiers, with ski hire and tuition and
miles of trails.

Where to Stay and Eat

Kildrummy Castle Hotel, by Alford, **t** (01975)
571 288, *www.kildrummycastlehotel.co.uk*
(*expensive*). Slightly overawed by its own
grandeur, with all the style of a country
mansion and the comforts of a modern first-
class hotel; in gardens and woods

overlooking the castle from which it takes
its name. It has a good restaurant and offers
skiing, fishing and shooting packages.
Gordon Hotel, The Square, Tomintoul, **t** (01807)
580 206 (*moderate*). Good food and a
relaxed, informal atmosphere. Up to 50%
discount on last-minute bookings.
Lynturk Home Farm, Alford, **t** (01975) 562 504,
f 563 517 (*moderate*). Listed Georgian farmhouse (1762), recently extended by a
descendant of the founder of Aberdeen
Angus cattle. Run as a hospitable Wolsey
Lodge with cordon bleu cooking.
Minmore House Hotel, Glenlivet, **t** (01807) 590
378, *minmorehouse@ukonline.co.uk*
(*moderate*). Very comfortable and friendly.
Allargue, Corgarff, **t** (01975) 651 452 (*cheap*).
Mr and Mrs Tuck have a charming, well-
equipped, modernized cottage at the head
of the Don, with marvellous views.
Allargue Arms Hotel, Corgarff, by Strathdon,
t (01975) 651 410, *www.allargue.demon.co.uk*
(*cheap*). Close to the Lecht slopes in
gorgeous scenery. Very friendly and relaxed.
Colquhonnie Hotel, Strathdon, **t** (01975) 651
210, *www.colquhonnie-hotel.co.uk* (*cheap*).
Small family-run hotel with good home
cooking. Child friendly.
Glenavon Hotel, Tomintoul, **t** (01807) 580 218
(*cheap*). Small, family-run and very friendly,
with a big welcome for children and dogs.
A good base for skiing.

young men to train for the priesthood. The college survived several attacks by
Hanoverian soldiers and was finally moved to become Blairs College, near Aberdeen.
The building at Scalen is being restored as a museum – a beautiful remote spot. The
estate is open all year for walking, bicycling, skiing and riding.

Tomnavoulin Distillery (*open mid-Mar–Oct Mon–Sat 9–5*) is about 5 miles north of
Tomintoul on the B9008, and is one of the eight on the Malt Whisky Trail. It gives the
usual tour, audiovisual show and free dram, and claims to be the most attractive and
friendly of them all. Opinions may differ on this, depending on how many free drams
have already been tucked away, if you are doing the whole trail.

The **Glenlivet Distillery Visitor Centre** (*open April–Oct Mon–Sat 10–4, Sun 12.30–4;
adm; no children under 8*), also on the trail, was founded as an illicit still in 1746 by a
fugitive Jacobite after Culloden. (He changed his name from Gow to Smith because
Gow, being the anglicized spelling of the Gaelic equivalent to Smith, was liable to
arouse suspicion.) The distillery was subsequently made legal by his grandson. It
offers the usual tours and a 10-minute audiovisual show, 'The Ballad of The Glenlivet'.
There is a coffee shop and salad bar and a gift shop.

Aberdeen to Elgin

The A96 is the main road from Aberdeen to Inverness via Elgin, flanked by rich farm-land and studded with ancient castles. Along the minor roads lie farming communities in pleasant, undulating scenery.

About 10 miles from Aberdeen is the village of **Kintore**, a Royal Burgh since 1506. Its town hall, with outside stairs, was built in 1737. The church has a 16th-century taber-nacle decorated with painted angels on a panel. A Pictish stone in the graveyard has both Christian and Pictish carvings – perhaps a good example of how careful those early Christians were not to offend any pagan gods that just might exist in spite of what the missionaries said. (The more prosaic explanation is that the converted Picts recycled the old stones after their conversion.)

Little Treasures, at Petersfield, Kemnay (*open June–Aug and Dec Mon–Sat 10–5, Sun 1–5; Sept–Nov and Jan–May Fri, Sat and Mon 10–5, Sun 1–5; adm*) is a dolls' house, toy museum and shop, with some intriguing exhibits. **Monymusk Arts Trust**, just west of Kemnay (*open May–Sept daily*), is a collection of art, crafts, musical events and a museum of agricultural reforms, with interesting 18th- and 19th-century maps.

Inverurie, 16 miles from Aberdeen, is surrounded by Pictish remains. The **Carnegie Museum** (*open Mon and Wed–Fri 2–4.30, Sat 10–1 and 2–4*) has an interesting perma-nent archaeological exhibition. It also stages three 'thematic' exhibitions each year. The **Bass** is a 60ft-high motte, just outside the town, the site of a 12th-century castle. Mary, Queen of Scots visited a castle on this site in 1562. Pictish stones in the cemetery have clear carvings on them.

Brandsbutt Stone, north of Inverurie, has clear Pictish symbols and Ogham inscrip-tions, dating from the 8th century. The **Harlaw Monument** is a red granite obelisk marking the site of a particularly bloody clan battle in 1411. The cause of this carnage was the Countess of Ross. She renounced her inheritance to become a nun, leaving two uncles to fight for it: Donald, Lord of the Isles, and Buchan, son of Regent Albany. Donald was beaten, lost his claim to the title, and was forced to swear allegiance to the Crown at a time when the Lords of the Isles considered themselves to be kings. Not much further along the road, the **Loanhead Stone Circle** is a burial cairn marked by a ring of standing stones surrounding a mass of smaller ones.

Pitcaple Castle (*private*) is on the A96 south of Loanhead, a 15th- to 16th-century Z-plan tower house with 19th-century additions including two round towers. It is still a family home. Mary, Queen of Scots came here in 1562 and danced on the lawn, as did her great-grandson, Charles II, in 1650. The tree under which these two monarchs danced was replaced with a red maple by Queen Mary in 1923. Also in 1650, Montrose was brought here, a prisoner, renounced by the king for whom he had fought, on his way to execution in Edinburgh. A mile south of Pitcaple, the 9th-century **Maiden Stone** is thought to be one of the finest early Christian monuments. It is 10ft high and has a Celtic cross and Pictish symbols.

Bennachie is the long, wooded ridge rising to 1,733ft to the south, with an Iron-Age hill fort on **Mither Tap**, one of the peaks. Bennachie dominates the skyline all around with its distinctively shaped top. Many claim it to be the site of the Battle of Mons

Graupius, where Agricola penetrated the northeast and defeated the tribes in AD 83. Forestry Enterprise has developed some signposted walks, and the **Bennachie Centre** (*open April–Oct Tues–Sun 10–5; Nov–Mar Wed–Sun 10–5*), in Esson's car park by Chapel of Garioch, has 'an interpretation of the social and natural history' of the area.

The **Picardy Stone**, dating from the 7th or 8th century, is about 13 miles northwest of Inverurie on the B9002. Its Pictish symbols include a serpent, mirror and the mysterious 'spectacles' that are featured so often in those ancient carvings.

Leith Hall

Open Easter weekend and May–Sept daily 1.30–5.30;
Oct Sat and Sun 1.30–5.30; adm; garden and grounds
open all year 9.30–sunset; donation.

Leith Hall is 4 miles west of the Picardy Stone, down an avenue. The earliest part of the house dates from 1650, a tower house with turrets and gables, with further wings added during the 18th and 19th centuries, around a central courtyard. In the exhibition room, you can see a writing case presented to Andrew Hay, the laird, by Prince Charles on the eve of Culloden, and the official pardon given to him after he had fought for the prince. Andrew Hay, known as 'The Gentle Jacobite', was a philanthropic man, 7ft 2in tall. The grounds include a zigzag herbaceous border, a rock garden, a pond walk with observation hide, a picnic area and a flock of Soay sheep. There are 18th-century stables and an ice house.

Eight miles north of Leith Hall, you pass through **Strath Bogie**, with **Clashindarroch Forest** to the west, cut by picturesque valleys.

Archaeolink, Oyne Village, Insch (*open April–Oct daily 11–5; adm*), is a journey 6,000 years back in time, with reconstructions, an audiovisual show, restaurant and shop.

Huntly, 38 miles northwest of Aberdeen, is an 18th-century town on the plain, surrounded by hills, lapped by the rivers Deveron and Bogie. **Brander Museum** (*open Tues–Sat 2–4.30*), in the library in Main Square, gives a good grounding in local history, with 'thematic' exhibitions and displays on local celebrities. **Glendronach Distillery** is open on weekdays for tours. **North East Falconry Centre** (*ring to check times, t (01466) 760 328; adm*), at nearby Cairnie, flies eagles, owls and falcons daily.

Huntly Castle

Open April–Sept Mon–Sat 9.30–6.30, Sun 2–6.30;
Oct–Mar Mon–Wed Sat 9.30–4.30, Thurs 9.30–1,
Fri and Sun 2–4.30; adm.

Huntly (once Strathbogie) Castle is the ruin of a stately 17th-century palace in a wooded park above Deveron Water. It was the seat of the Marquesses of Huntly (the Gay Gordons), the most powerful family in this part of Scotland until the middle of the 16th century. The 12th-century fortress on the motte was owned by the Earl of Fife, a Gaelic Norman. Robert the Bruce convalesced here in 1307 after an illness. Just before the Battle of Bannockburn, the laird turned against Bruce. After the battle, his lands were forfeited and given to Sir Adam Gordon of Huntly, a supporter of Bruce.

Tourist Information

Inverurie: 18 High Street, t (01467) 625 800;
 open all year.
Huntly: 9a The Square, t (01466) 792 255;
 open April–Oct.
Dufftown: The Square, t (01340) 820 501;
 open April–Oct.
Elgin: 17 High Street, t (01343) 542 666;
 open all year.

Festivals

**Second weekend in June: Festival of
 Traditional Music and Song,** Keith.
July: Highland Games, Elgin. **Highland Games,**
 Dufftown.
August: Agricultural Show, Keith.
September: Fiddlers' Rally, Elgin.

Sports and Activities

Keith and Dufftown Railway, Dufftown
 Station, t (01340) 821 181. For train buffs.
 Class 108 diesel rail car, the *Spirit of Speyside*,
 which puffs along between Dufftown and

Keith through picturesque scenery.
*Open Easter–mid-Oct Sat and Sun; ring
for details.*

Where to Stay and Eat

Craigellachie Hotel, Craigellachie, t (01340) 881
 204, *www.craigellachie.com* (*expensive*).
 Large, comfortable hotel, with plenty of
 atmosphere and style, and good food.
**Macdonald Thainstone House Hotel and
 Country Club,** Inverurie, t (01467) 621 643,
 info@thainstone.macdonald-hotels.co.uk
 (*expensive*). Palladian country house
 surrounded by meadows and woods, with a
 comfortable, easy-going atmosphere, lots of
 leisure facilities and excellent food.
Mansefield House Hotel, Mayne Road, Elgin,
 t (01343) 540 883, *www.mansefieldhouse
 hotel.com* (*expensive*). Elegant, comfortable,
 former manse near town centre, with
 restaurant specializing in seafood.
Mansion House Hotel, The Haugh, Elgin,
 t (01343) 548 811, *reception@mhelgin.co.uk*
 (*expensive*). Elegant, comfortable mock-
 castle town house by the river.

In those days the fortress was made of wood, which was gradually replaced by stone. It was finally destroyed during the Civil War of 1452, in the reign of James II. James IV was a frequent visitor, during an era when the Gordon Earls of Huntly were at the zenith of their power, and it was here that he witnessed the marriage between Catherine Gordon and Perkin Warbeck in 1496. Warbeck was a Flemish impostor, Pretender to the English throne, claiming to be Richard, Duke of York, the younger of the two 'princes in the tower'. It suited the Scottish king to encourage his claims, but Warbeck met his comeuppance in the Tower of London and was executed in 1499.

The rise and fall of the Gordons was reflected in the rise and fall of Huntly Castle, until the second Marquis of Huntly lost his head for supporting Charles I, having first been imprisoned in the castle. Don't miss the awful dungeons and the basement passage walls marked by the graffiti of the dungeon guards. The carved fireplaces and heraldic doorway are splendid.

Dufftown

Dufftown, 10 miles west of Huntly, was founded in 1817 by James Duff, 4th Earl of Fife, to give employment after the Napoleonic Wars. Dufftown is known as the capital of Scotland's malt whisky distilling, giving rise to an old couplet:

*Rome was built on seven hills
Dufftown stands on seven stills.*

Pittodrie House Hotel, Pitcaple, t (01467) 681 444, *info@pittodrie.macdonald-hotels.co.uk* (*expensive*). 15th-century pile overlooking farmland with Bennachie towering above. Antiques, tapestries and fine paintings, cordon bleu food, squash, tennis, billiards, croquet and clay-pigeon shooting.

Blackhills Estate, by Elgin, t (01343) 842 223, *www.blackhills.co.uk* (*expensive–cheap*). Five very luxurious cottages in the lovely grounds of Blackhills House (sleeping 4–10).

Carden Self Catering, Alves, near Elgin, t (01343) 850 222, *www.carden.co.uk* (*moderate*). Luxury farm/courtyard cottages with lovely views, tennis and games room.

Delnashaugh Inn, Ballindalloch, t (01807) 500 255 (*moderate*). Nicely done-up drovers inn.

Glenlivet House, Ballindalloch, t (01807) 590 376, *www.glenlivethouse.co.uk* (*moderate*). Large Victorian country house to let to one party only. Either full board or self-catering (sleeping 22). Good position and views.

Gordon Arms Hotel, The Square, Huntly, t (01466) 792 288, *www.gordonarms. demon.co.uk* (*moderate*). Hospitable and comfortable.

Grange House, nr Keith, t (01542) 870 206 (*moderate*). Delightful, homely guesthouse.

Highlander Inn, Craigellachie, t (01340) 881 446, *highinn@aol.com* (*moderate*). Comfortable, cosy inn on the banks of the River Spey.

Huntly Hotel, The Square, Huntly, t (01466) 792 703 (*moderate*). An alternative to the above.

Kintore Arms Hotel, High Street, Inverurie, t (01467) 621 367, *www.kintorearmshotel. co.uk* (*moderate*). Family-run and hospitable.

Strathburn Hotel, Burghmuir Drive, Inverurie, t (01467) 624 422, *www.strathburn-hotel.co.uk* (*moderate*). Very modern, with all mod cons. Light and bright, with good food.

Westfield House, near Elgin, t (01343) 547 308 (*moderate*). Splendid 16th-century house. Comfortable and hospitable.

Castle Hotel, Huntly, t (01466) 792 696, *castlehot@enterprise.net* (*moderate–cheap*). Former home to the Dukes of Gordon, an 18th-century country house behind the ruins of Huntly Castle. Unpretentious, with a friendly atmosphere and lots of character.

Gordon Arms Hotel, in Fochabers High Street, t (01343) 820 508 (*moderate–cheap*). Old coaching inn with excellent food.

Good barley, peat and the right sort of water are the three essential ingredients for whisky making, and this area has them all. The **Glenfiddich Distillery** (*open April–mid-Oct Mon–Sat 9.30–4.30, Sun 12–4.30; mid-Oct–Mar Mon–Fri 9.30–4.30*) is part of the Malt Whisky Trail. It was founded by William Grant who produced the first bottling on Christmas Day 1887. This is one of only two distilleries to have its own bottling plant. The audiovisual show is in six languages and you get your free dram at the end.

Dufftown Museum (*open April–Oct daily 10–5*), in the Clock Tower, has a collection of local photographs and information about Lord Mount Stephen who founded the Canadian Pacific Railway.

Auchindoun Castle (*plainly visible on a steep hill above the River Fiddich but unsafe and not open to the public*), 2 miles southeast of Dufftown, is a massive three-storey

The Clock that Hanged MacPherson

The clock on the battlemented tower at the junction of the four main streets is known as 'the clock that hanged MacPherson'. MacPherson was an infamous free-booter who was condemned to death in Banff, to the north, in 1700 for robbing the rich and giving to the poor. A local petition for his reprieve was successful, but Lord Braco, the Sheriff of Banff, who loathed MacPherson, advanced the clock by an hour and hanged him before the reprieve arrived. The clock was subsequently removed from Banff and installed in this tower.

keep, enclosed by prehistoric earthworks. It was built by Robert Cochran, who was one of the favourites of James III and was hanged by enraged barons in 1482. In 1689 a party of Jacobites gathered within these walls to hold a council of war after the death of their gallant leader, Graham of Claverhouse (Bonnie Dundee) at Killiecrankie.

Some of the stones from Auchindoun were removed and used in the building of **Balvenie Castle** (*open April–Sept Mon–Sat 9.30–6.30, Sun 2–6.30; adm*), a mile north of Dufftown, next to the Glenfiddich Distillery. Now a ruin, this was a 14th-century stronghold owned by the Comyns. Edward I was a visitor in 1304; Mary, Queen of Scots spent two nights here in 1562 while campaigning against the powerful Gordons; Montrose took refuge here in 1644; victorious Jacobites occupied the castle in 1689 after Killiecrankie; and Cumberland's troops occupied it in 1746.

Mortlach Parish Church, on the southern edge of town, is one of the oldest places of Christian worship in Scotland, believed to have been founded in 566 by St Moluag, a contemporary of Columba. There are monsters, beasts and a horseman carved on the weathered Pictish cross in the graveyard, and an earlier Pictish stone in the porch. Substantially reconstructed in 1876 and again in 1931, it still has traces of an earlier building. There is a leper squint in the north wall and the lancet windows date from the 13th century. The watchtower in the graveyard, now used as a power house, was originally used to keep watch for body-snatchers.

Speyside Cooperage Visitor Centre (*open Mon–Thurs 9.30–4.30, Fri 9.30–4; adm*) at Craigellachie, 4 miles north of Dufftown, displays the cooper's craft over thousands of years, and you can watch coopers at work. There are tastings from March.

A slight detour takes in three more distilleries on the Malt Whisky Trail: **Cardhu** (*open Nov–Feb Mon–Fri 11–3; Mar–June and Oct Mon–Fri 10–4.30; July–Sept Mon–Fri 10–6, Sat 9.30–4.30, Sun 11–4; adm*), at Knockando, about 6 miles west of Craigellachie; **Tamdhu** (*open April–Oct Mon–Fri; June–Sept Mon–Sat*), also at Knockando; and **Glenfarclas** (*open April–Sept Mon–Fri 10–5; June–Sept also Sat 10–5; Oct–Mar Mon–Fri 10–4; adm*) at Ballindalloch, on the A95.

Ballindalloch Castle (*open Easter–Sept daily 10–5; adm*), close to the distillery, is one of the few castles to be lived in continuously by its original family, the Macpherson-Grants, since 1546. The fortified 16th-century tower house is flanked by later additions down to Victorian times, and some of the interior is impressive. There are nice grounds, too, and a tearoom and shop.

The eighth distillery on the Malt Whisky Trail is **Glen Grant** (*open April–Oct Mon–Sat 10–4, Sun 12.30–4; adm*), at Rothes, about 3 miles north of Craigellachie.

Keith

Keith is 11 miles northwest of Huntly on the Isla, the hub of an area of rich farmland. The present town was developed in the late 18th and early 19th centuries but its history goes back to at least 700 when St Maelrubha of Applecross converted the inhabitants to Christianity. Scotland's post-Reformation saint, St John Ogilvie, was born in 1580 at Drumnakeith. He studied in Europe and returned to preach to his own people. He was hanged in 1615 for refusing to take the anti-Catholic oath of loyalty to the Crown. Beatified in 1929, he was canonized in 1976. There is a statue of him in the

Roman Doric-style Catholic church. This building, partly copied from Santa Maria degli Angeli in Rome, comes as a surprise in an area that is not given to church ornamentation. It was built in 1830, helped by a donation from Charles X of France, who took refuge in Scotland after he was exiled, and gave the picture over the altar, *The Incredulity of St Thomas* by François Dubois. The stained-glass windows are by Father Ninian Sloane of Pluscarden Abbey. The imposing copper dome was added in 1915.

The **Scottish Tartans Museum**, on Mid Street (*t (01542) 888 419*), tells the history and development of tartan and kilts, with 700 examples on display.

Strathisla Distillery (*open April–Oct Mon–Sat 10–4, Sun 12.30–4; adm*), nearby, is another stop on the Malt Whisky Trail.

Fochabers

Fochabers, northwest of Keith on the Spey, is a good base from which to explore this area, with riverside walks, excellent fishing and proximity to the Malt Whisky Trail. The village grew in the shadow of the walls of Gordon Castle, which provided employment for most of the people in the old days. It was moved to its present site in the 18th century to make room for an extension of the castle. Part of the High Street is conserved and the buildings are much as they were when first built.

The Spey, with only 4 miles left in its race to the sea, runs slower now through shingle banks that threaten to close the mouth which had to be dredged four times in the 20th century, most recently in 1989. Salmon netting has been carried out for centuries from the spit at Tugnet, just down the river at Spey Bay, and this estuary region is rich in birds: kittiwakes, fulmars, cormorants, sandpipers, curlews, teal, ringed plovers, gannets, terns, shelduck, heron and osprey, to name but a few.

The northern section of the **Speyside Way** goes south from Spey Bay for 30 miles to Ballindalloch (*ring t (01340) 881 266, for details of maps, etc.*); from there, if you are still feeling energetic, it's only another 15 miles to Tomintoul. The walk begins at **Tugnet Ice House** (*open May–Sept daily 11–4*), built in 1830 to store ice for packing the netted salmon and now a visitor centre with an exhibition on the salmon-fishing industry, as well as information about local wildlife.

Fochabers Folk Museum (*open April–Oct daily 9.30–1 and 2–6; Nov–Mar daily 9.30–1 and 2–5; adm*), in the High Street, has the largest collection of horse-drawn vehicles in the north of Scotland, and a mass of memorabilia from the days of service to the castle. There is a reconstructed village shop from the turn of the last century, before the days of plastic wrappings and prepacked food.

Baxters Highland Village (*open daily 9–5.30; no factory tours at weekends or during factory holidays: t (01343) 820 393; www.baxters.com*) is a mile west of Fochabers. George Baxter was a gardener at Gordon Castle 120 years ago. He opened a grocery shop in Fochabers and sold jam made by his wife, Margaret. From this simple beginning evolved a business that has been handed down through the family to the present, producing a wide range of food that can be bought all over the world. The Duke of Richmond and Gordon, Baxter's old boss, took a keen interest and personally measured out the site for the factory one Sunday on his way home from church. You can see a Victorian kitchen similar to the one where the first Mrs Baxter tried out new recipes, and the modern kitchen where they are still experimenting to create new products. There are guided tours, an audiovisual show, shops, and a restaurant.

Elgin

Elgin, on the banks of the River Lossie, is the administrative and commercial capital of Moray, a busy market for the prosperous farms of the region, and a popular holiday centre. The ruined cathedral is one of Scotland's jewels. The town, at first sight sturdy and austerely granite, invites closer inspection. Wander through it and you will discover a number of fine old buildings, excellently proportioned with delightful embellishments, and intriguing glimpses into wynds and closes. Elgin is drenched in history, and is an excellent centre for exploring the northwest corner of Grampian.

First mentioned in history books in 1190, Elgin was the northern limit of Edward I's progress through the country. The town was partly burned by the Wolf of Badenoch in 1390, and again in a struggle for power between the Douglases and Huntlys in 1452. James II of Scotland used Elgin as a royal residence in the 15th century, and Prince Charles lodged at Thunderton House for 11 days before the Battle of Culloden.

Elgin Cathedral (open April–Sept daily 9.30–6.30; Oct–Mar Mon–Wed and Sat 9.30–4.30, Thurs 9.30–12.30, Sun 2–4.30; adm) stands on grass beside the river, a soaring symphony of arches, towers and windows, fretted against the sky. It was founded in 1224 and damaged by fire in 1270. In 1390 the Wolf of Badenoch, the wild and vicious natural son of Robert II, having been excommunicated by the bishop, burned down both town and cathedral, which contained treasures and valuable documents and manuscripts, with his 'wyld, wykked Helandmen'. After many ups and downs, the cathedral was stripped of its lead in 1567, by order of the Privy Council, in order to raise funds for defence. This act of authorized sacrilege was rewarded by the sinking of the ship that carried the lead. In 1650 Cromwell's troops did their worst to what remained, tearing down a beautiful rood screen and smashing the tracery of the west window. In spite of all this, peace and sanctity cling to this mellow ruin.

In the **Bishop's House**, just northwest of the cathedral, you can see a wing of the Precentor's Manse, with a 16th-century coat of arms on the wall.

Elgin Museum (open April–Oct Mon–Fri 10–5, Sat 11–4, Sun 2–5; adm) is in an Italian-style building in the High Street, with a collection of old red sandstone, Permian and Triassic fossils, as well as Bronze-Age relics and natural history displays. **Little Cross**, also in the High Street (1733), replaced an earlier one erected in 1402. In the old days this was the place of public punishment, with stocks and jougs. **Lady Hill**, opposite the post office in the High Street, bears only scant remains of the castle which once stood here, occupied by Edward I in 1296. The column (1839) and statue (1855) were put up in memory of the 5th and last Duke of Gordon.

Moray Motor Museum (open Easter–Oct daily 11–5; adm) is in an old converted mill in Bridge Street. The small collection of vintage cars and motorbikes includes a stately 1929 Rolls-Royce Phantom I, a 1913 Douglas motorbike, and a macho 1939 SS100, gleaming red.

Old Mills (*open April–Sept Tues–Sun 10–5; adm*), west of town on the Lossie, is a working meal mill dating from 1793. You can watch the milling in progress and learn what it's all about in the Old Mills Visitor Centre.

Johnstons Cashmere Visitors Centre (*open Mon–Sat 9–5.30; June–Oct also Sun 11–5*) at Newmill, east of town, is the only Scottish mill creating cashmere from the fibre to the garment. It tells the story of cashmere, and has a coffee shop and a mill shop. .

Spynie Palace

Open April–Sept daily 9.30–6.30;
Oct–Mar Sat 9.30–4.30, Sun 2–4.30; adm.

The ruins of Spynie Palace are a couple of miles north of Elgin – there is access to a small car park from the Elgin–Lossiemouth road. This was the castle of the Bishops of Moray in the 13th to 17th centuries. At one time the sea reached as far as the hillock on which the palace stands, with a good harbour and town. The sea then threw up a bar of sand and shingle across the mouth of the estuary, cutting off Spynie and turning the area into a loch surrounded by marshland. In 1808 a canal was built by Thomas Telford to drain the loch into the sea 5 miles north at Lossiemouth. Great floods in 1829 destroyed all the works and the loch grew again until the 1860s. The old palace saw much history. Mary, Queen of Scots stayed there in 1562 during her tour of the north, and it became a refuge for Covenanters in 1654, during Montrose's campaigns. James Ramsay MacDonald, Britain's first Labour Prime Minister, was buried in Spynie churchyard in 1937.

Pluscarden Abbey

Open all the time; www.pluscardenabbey.org.

Pluscarden Abbey, about 5 miles southwest of Elgin, is one of Grampian's jewels. Lying in a sheltered valley below a ridge of wooded hills, Pluscarden represents an act of faith that must be an inspiration to believer and non-believer alike, and is spiritually uplifting. The original abbey was founded by Alexander II in 1230 for an order of white-habited monks, the Valliscaulians, whose mother house was in France. It suffered damage at the hands of Edward I of England in 1303, and far worse damage from the Wolf of Badenoch, during his revenge on the Bishop of Elgin in 1390. In 1454 it took in Benedictines from Urquhart Priory (founded in 1124), for economic as well as political reasons. Just before the Reformation took off, a greedy, scheming prior, Alexander Dunbar, anticipating what was to come, managed to 'redistribute' priory funds and lands in favour of his family. He died in 1560, and by the end of that century the priory had passed into the authority of a lay commendator. The estate passed through various hands, gradually falling into disrepair and ruin; there are no remains.

In 1943 the Pluscarden lands were given to the Benedictine community of Prinknash Abbey, near Gloucester, a breakaway community from an Anglican order, whose proposals for doctrinal reform had caused some of its monks to rebel and become Roman Catholic. This order of converted Benedictines started rebuilding Pluscarden in 1948 and today you can see what they have achieved: a truly remarkable feat.

The choir and transepts are entire, as are the domestic buildings. The interior is a haven of timeless tranquillity, lit by a rich glow of colour from the modern stained-glass windows and overlaid by a lingering smell of incense. If you are lucky, you may hear, filtering through the walls from the Lady Chapel, the sound of the monks singing their daily office in Gregorian chant. You can go into the transept aisles, now a public chapel, and kneel at the south end to look through a wide squint into the Lady Chapel. Monks, dressed in coarse white habits, busy about their work on the land, add a medieval touch to Pluscarden. (*For enquiries about retreats, ring* **t** *(01343) 890 257.*)

Aberdeen to Turriff

The northeast shoulder of Grampian, well clear of the dramatic hills and spectacular glens further west, is mainly flattish farmland, studded with clumps of trees and a maze of burns and small rivers.

Pitmedden Garden and Museum of Farming Life

Open May–Sept daily 10–5.30; adm.

Pitmedden is best reached along the rural lanes to the east of the A947, north of Aberdeen. The garden was created by Sir Alexander Seton who inherited Pitmedden in 1667; and restored by the National Trust for Scotland in 1952. July and August are the best months to see this splendid recreation of a formal 17th-century garden, split-level with an upper garden and terraces overlooking the Great Garden. Sir Alexander modelled three out of the four symmetrical parterres on floral designs first used in Holyrood in 1647, in honour of Charles I. The fourth depicts the Seton coat of arms. Pillared gates lead into the Great Garden, down a graceful twin stairway, with two ogee-roofed pavilions. There is a fountain in each garden and no fewer than 27 sundials. You can see Sir Alexander's bathhouse in one of the two-storied pavilions, and a key to all the flowers in the garden. (The two 'thunder houses' are rare in Scotland.) In the other pavilion is an exhibition on the evolution of formal gardens. The **Museum of Farming Life** has a collection of agricultural and domestic implements. You can walk around the 100-acre estate, through attractive woods and farmland, and there is the usual adventure playground, picnic area and visitor centre.

Tolquhon Castle

Open April–Sept daily 9.30–6.30; Oct–Mar Sat 9.30–4.30,
Sun 2–4.30; adm.

Tolquhon Castle is a roofless ruin, a mile northwest of Pitmedden. Once the seat of the Forbes family, a 16th-century quadrangular mansion was built on to an early 15th-century rectangular tower. The forbidding fortress exterior hides a domestic residential inner court. You can still see the kitchen, cellars and stairways, with the hall and laird's room (which has a private stair to the kitchen) on the first floor. An inscription on the gatehouse is an endearing trumpet blast from the laird who did so much to enlarge the original castle: 'Al this wark, excep the auld tour, was begun be William Forbes 15 Aprile 1584, and endit be him 20 October 1589.'

William Forbes' master mason was Thomas Leiper, of a renowned family of masons, and it was he who designed the elaborate Gothic tomb of William and his wife, Elizabeth Gordon, in the church at **Tarves** a couple of miles north. It is rich in Renaissance detail, with statuettes of the couple standing on either side.

Haddo House and Garden

Open Easter–Sept daily 1.30–5.30; Oct Sat and Sun 1.30–5.30; adm; t (01651) 851 440.

Haddo is a fine Georgian mansion built in 1732 by William Adam on the site of House of Kellie, home of the Gordons of Haddo, Lords of Aberdeen, for over 500 years and burned down by Covenanters. The house stands in a park surrounded by lovely gardens, showing all William Adam's mastery of symmetrical design. It contains antique furniture, pictures and treasures in its elegant rooms. The stained-glass window in the chapel is by Burne-Jones. Haddo has developed its own choral society, with a theatre, beside the house. This is one of Scotland's leading musical bodies with productions of opera and concerts starring international artists. (If you are interested, write to the Choral Secretary, Haddo House, Grampian. Seating is limited.)

Fyvie Castle

Castle open April, May and Sept daily 1.30–5.30; June–Aug daily 11–5.30; Oct Sat and Sun 1.30–5.30; grounds open April–Oct daily 9.30–sunset; adm.

Fyvie dates from the 13th century, and has been described as the 'crowning glory of Scottish baronial architecture'. It stands on a mound above a bend in the River Ythan, approached up a long drive that skirts the lake among trees and rhododendrons. In the days when kings moved from house to house, William the Lion used to visit Fyvie. It passed through many hands over the centuries and its five towers represent its five dynasties of lairds: Prestons, Meldrums, Setons, Gordons and Leiths. The National Trust for Scotland acquired it from the late Sir Andrew Forbes-Leith in 1984. The splendid structure incorporates substantial remains of the medieval Fyvie. The square

Festivals

August: Turriff Show; two-day event – one of the largest agricultural events in Europe, attracting over 50,000 people each year.

Where to Stay and Eat

Meldrum House Hotel, Oldmeldrum, t (01651) 872 294, *www.meldrumhouse.com* (*expensive*). Comfortable, old-fashioned hospitality.

Fife Arms Hotel, The Square, Turriff, t (01888) 563 468 (*moderate*). Very reasonable.

The Redgarth, Kirkbrae, Oldmeldrum, t (01651) 872 353 (*moderate*). Friendly, family-run inn with comfortable rooms and a good menu.

Meikle Camaloun, Fyvie, t (01651) 891 319 (*cheap*). Attractive, very reasonable farmhouse guesthouse run by Mrs Wyness.

Delgatie Castle, see p.422, t (01888) 563 479, *www.delgatiecastle.co.uk*. Self-catering flats. Prices vary.

and round towers soar to a mass of corner turrets, conical roofs and corbels, and inside there is an impressive wheel stair.

Alexander Forbes-Leith bought the estate in 1889. He used the fortune that he had made in the American steel industry to restore the castle, sweeping away many of the ugly additions that had been added over the years, and filling it with treasures that can still be seen today, including the finest portraits by Gainsborough, Romney, Opie and Raeburn. The *pièce de résistance*, perhaps, is the 18th-century portrait of Colonel William Gordon, by Pompeo Batoni – a romantic study of a patrician colonel, standing in rich silken tartan, gazing somewhat disdainfully at a statue of Roma.

Gight Castle is a scant ivy-clad ruin east of Fyvie, by the River Ythan, reached by a footpath off the B9005. There isn't a signpost, but look for a turning by the scrapyard near Cottown. It dates from about 1560 and is associated with a particularly wild branch of the Gordon family, infamous for murders and suspiciously sudden deaths. Watch out for the Hagberry Pot, close to the castle – a bottomless pit reputed to be a direct route to Hell. The 13th Laird of Gight was Catherine Gordon who married 'Mad' Jack Byron. Their son was George Gordon, Lord Byron. Mad Jack, alas, was a compulsive gambler and gambled the castle away long before the birth of his talented son.

Turriff

Turriff, at the confluence of the River Deveron and the Water of Idoch, is a red sandstone town, first mentioned in the 6th century when the Gaelic poet Ossian described it as the capital of a Pictish prince, Lathmon. It is believed that St Congan founded a monastery near the village in the 8th century. The old church at the end of Castle Street, now a ruin, existed in the 11th century, and in 1179 Knights Templar – soldier monks of the crusades – were given land in Turriff to found their second Scottish base. The 20ft mercat cross in Castle Street is 16th century. The town is still remembered for 'The Trot of Turriff' in 1639, when a party of Royalists defeated the Covenanters in the first skirmish of the Civil War. More recently, Turriff hit the national news in 1913, when a local farmer, Robert Paterson, refused to join Lloyd George's National Health Insurance Scheme. One of his cows was impounded and the sheriff officers tried to sell it in the town, to cover the National Insurance payments Paterson owed. There was a riot, and the officers were chased out of town. Attempts to sell the cow in Aberdeen were also unsuccessful, and finally Paterson's neighbours bought it and gave it back to him. The 'Turra Coo' was front-page news.

Delgatie Castle (*open April–Oct daily 11–5; adm*), 2 miles east of Turriff, a 12th-century L-plan tower house with later additions, is home of the Clan Hay. Inside there are pictures, weapons, the widest turnpike stair in Scotland, and 16th-century painted ceilings which are believed to caricature people who lived in the castle at the time. Mary, Queen of Scots stayed here for three days in 1562, and there is a portrait of her in the room she used. Part of the castle is now self-catering holiday flats (*see* above).

17th-century **Eden Castle**, north of Turriff (*not open to the public*), is a ruin with a grisly legend. The wife of a tenant on the estate asked the laird to control her wild son. He did so by drowning the boy in the river, and the mother's subsequent curse caused the castle to fall down. All that remains now is the tower.

The Coast: Aberdeen to Forres

Heading north from Aberdeen on the coast road, you see another face of Grampian: miles of sandy beaches interspersed with rock cliffs, bordering an endless stretch of ocean to the east and north. Fishing towns and villages are strung out along the way, each with its legends of seafaring adventures and smuggling. Inland lie prosperous farms and good fishing rivers, and there are a number of golf courses, both coastal and inland.

The A92 takes you through **Bridge of Don**, past the sadly neglected barracks that were once the home of the Gordon Highlanders. Long, dune-backed beaches fringed by brambly golf courses, and an army firing range, stretch north for 6 miles to **Balmedie Country Park**. Further up, the **Ythan Estuary** cuts into the dunes at **Newburgh**, and from here to **Collieston** a vast nature reserve comprises heath, dunes, pasture and cliff: a haven for both ornithologist and botanist. Collieston is a picturesque village with a harbour, very similar to the villages in the East Neuk of Fife. T. E. Lawrence wrote much of *The Seven Pillars of Wisdom* here.

The sandy sweep of **Cruden Bay**, about 5 miles north of Collieston, is where the pipeline comes in from the Forties Oil Field, over 100 miles out in the North Sea. The name Cruden comes from *croju-dane*, meaning slaughter of the Danes. This refers to a bloody battle between Malcolm II and the Danes in 1012, led by Canute, later King of England. The Scots won and the Danes withdrew, undertaking to leave Scotland alone. Canute then turned his attention to England, which he conquered four years later. Once a tiny fishing hamlet, Cruden Bay was to be a luxurious holiday resort at the end of the 19th century. The Great North of Scotland Railway Company built a huge 55-bedroom hotel with tennis courts, croquet lawns, bowling greens and a championship golf course. However, it was too isolated. The project failed, and the hotel was demolished after the war.

Whinnyfold, the cliff-top village at the south of Cruden Bay, once had 24 fishing boats, despite not having a harbour. The boats were drawn up on the shingle beach and the fish laid out on the stones to dry. The jagged rocks off here – the Scours of Cruden – have claimed many wrecks. It is said that at a certain time of year the bodies of those who have perished during the previous 12 months come out of the sea to join their spirits in heaven or hell. (This legend inspired Bram Stoker to write *Mystery of the Sea*. It is said that Stoker was inspired by Slains when he wrote *Dracula*, and used Cruden Bay for the setting when the vampire comes ashore to vampirize the unfortunate Lucy. He used to holiday in the area and finally retired to Whinnyfold.)

New Slains Castle

Walk north from Cruden Bay a couple of miles along the cliffs till you get to New Slains Castle (*always accessible*). This extensive ruin stands high above the sea, which rages at its feet in rough weather. It was built by the 9th Earl of Erroll in 1598 to replace Old Slains Castle, further south, of which only a fragment remains. Old Slains was destroyed by James VI to punish Erroll for taking part in a revolt of Catholic nobles. 'New' Slains is a splendid, awe-inspiring ruin, and its extremely dangerous situation makes it unsuitable for children to visit unaccompanied. It is amusing to walk among its massive, rather gloomy walls and recall Johnson and Boswell's visit in 1773. Johnson was most impressed by its position, writing:

> when the winds beat with violence it must enjoy all the terrifick grandeur of the tempestuous ocean ... the walls of one of the towers seem only a continuation of the perpendicular rock, the foot of which is beaten by the waves.

Boswell, always fastidious about his comforts, wrote:

> I had a most elegant room: but there was a fire in it which blazed; and the sea, to which my windows looked, roared; and the pillows were made of the feathers of some sea-fowl which had to me a disagreeable smell: so that by all these causes I was kept awake a good while.

Slains reached its zenith at the turn of the last century when the 19th Earl, a philanthropic man, created what has been described as a mini welfare state in the district and played host to many writers, actors, musicians and singers. As a result of crippling death duties, taxation and the 19th Earl's generosity, his heir was forced to sell the castle to an absentee landlord who allowed it to fall into disrepair.

Johnson and Boswell also visited the **Bullers of Buchan**, just north of Slains Castle. Here the sea has eroded a sheer 200-foot rock chasm, into which the water pounds through a natural archway. Bullers means 'boilers'. Johnson wrote of this: 'which no man can see with indifference, who has either sense of danger or delight in rarity'. Much to the horror of Boswell, Johnson insisted on exploring the cavern by boat, writing later: 'If I had any malice against a walking spirit, instead of laying him in the Red Sea, I would condemn him to reside in the Buller of Buchan.'

Buchan means 'the land at the bend in the ocean', and was the name of Scotland's most northeasterly corner where the North Sea meets the Moray Firth. **Boddam**, about 3 miles north of Slains, is an old fishing village on Buchan Ness, the most easterly point on the mainland. There is a pleasant 19th-century character in the older parts of Boddam, though it is hard to believe they once boasted 85 herring drifters and 13 curing yards. All the fishing boats now operate out of Peterhead.

Peterhead

Peterhead, originally called Peterugie, is a couple of miles north near the mouth of the River Ugie, and is known locally as the 'Blue Toon'. It is the most easterly town on the Scottish mainland. The first harbour was built in 1593 and the town has always been linked with fishing, from early times when the first fishermen used lines to catch cod and ling. Whaling began in 1788 and Peterhead quickly became the leading whaling port in Britain, until herring fishing took over in 1818. By 1836 260 boats fished out of Peterhead, rising to over 400 by the middle of the century. During this time extensive, deep-water harbours were built, so that when fishing boats grew larger and could no longer use the smaller ports, Peterhead flourished. Although herring fishing is dying fast, the town continues to prosper, with white fish as its main catch. It is now the largest white-fish port in Europe with over 400 highly sophisticated boats. It was also ideally placed to cope with the influx of sea traffic during the oil-boom of the 1970s.

Peterhead was a popular spa town in the 17th, 18th and 19th centuries, and the remains of a mineral well and some baths can still be seen by the lifeboat shed. Burns was one of the many people who took the waters here. Surrounded by sandy beaches, golf courses and dunes, it is the largest town in the northeast after Aberdeen. Many of the houses are built of local pink granite.

The **Harbour**, with its three main basins, is an energetic place, with boats coming and going; vessels being refitted, repaired, repainted; chandlers and all the clutter of a seafaring port. The **Fishmarket**, as in Aberdeen, is a place to visit early in the morning when the boats are landing their catches in up to 14,000 boxes. Business starts at 8.30am (*exc Sun*), but you are best to go well before this to get the full flavour of this salty industry. Catches include whiting, haddock, sole, cod, mackerel and herring.

Peterhead Maritime Heritage, at the Lido (*open April–Oct Mon–Sat 11–4, Sun 12–4; call **t** (01779) 473 000, for winter times*), tells the maritime history of the area. Also a café, shop and playground.

The **Town House**, built in 1788, has a spire 125ft high. The statue in front is of Field Marshal Keith, born in Peterhead, who became Frederick the Great of Prussia's most trusted general, killed in battle in 1758.

The **Arbuthnot Museum and Art Gallery** (*open Mon, Tues, Thurs–Sat 11–1 and 2–4.30, Wed 11–1*) is in Arbuthnot House. Displays include fishing, whaling, local history and a coin collection.

Deer Abbey (*officially open Thurs–Sun, but the caretaker is usually here and will let people in at any reasonable time*) is 9 miles west of Peterhead. This insubstantial ruin was a Cistercian monastery founded in 1219 by Comyn, Earl of Buchan. It thrived until the late 16th century, and you can see the ground plan quite clearly, though most of the masonry was taken away for other uses.

Aden Country Park and Aberdeenshire Farming Museum (*park open Mar–Oct daily 7am–10pm; Nov–Feb daily 7am–7pm; Heritage Centre May–Sept daily 11–4.30; April–Oct Sat and Sun 12–4.30; adm*) is a mile west of Mintlaw, near Deer Abbey. The semicircular farm steading, restored from almost total dereliction, was inspired by the French wife of a former laird. Reconstructions show past and present farming life in this agricultural area – you can almost smell the oatcakes cooking on the griddle. Audiovisual shows and exhibitions give further information on the life of estate staff at the turn of the last century. There is a shop, a café, a picnic area and separate campsite. Aden (pronounced 'Adden') stands in a country park around the consolidated ruin of the old mansion, with nature trails and all the trimmings.

Along the Coast to Fraserburgh

Back to the coast, the villages along this northeast corner are unspoiled and soaked in seafaring history, their deserted sands a hermit's dream. Many of the original fisher cottages remain, sturdy and low, their gable-ends to the sea, to take the full force of winter storms. In some of the villages the old tradition of painting the houses with oil paint to protect them from the weather has become a competitive attempt to produce the most striking colour. The result is splendidly cheerful.

Rattray is a wild, unfrequented area south of Loch of Strathbeg, about 6 miles north of Peterhead. Once a thriving fishing port and Royal Burgh, its records go back to the 12th century, to the days when the loch was open to the sea. In 1720 a great storm caused the dunes to shift, cutting off the loch and silting up the harbour. Today all that remains is a ruined chapel, said to have been built in the 13th century in memory of the son of the Earl of Buchan who drowned in a well there, and the remains of a Comyn fortress in the process of excavation by Aberdeen University.

You will find no trace today of **Cox Haven**, or Cockshafen, a hamlet that existed in the 18th century around the Strathbeg Burn, somewhere north of Rattray. Thought to have been refugees from religious persecution in Holland, the people are believed to have held curious ritualistic ceremonies connected with 'fresh water' dolphins that were stranded in Loch of Strathbeg during the storm that cut it off from the sea. The community was completely wiped out during a cholera epidemic in the 19th century.

Loch of Strathbeg Nature Reserve (*entry by written permission only; write to The Warden, Loch of Strathbeg Nature Reserve, Crimonmogate, Fraserburgh*) covers 2,300 acres including the loch, with over 180 different birds recorded, including such rarities as the Caspian tern with its black crown and heavy orange-red bill, the pied-billed grebe from North America – such a rare visitor to Scotland that only five have been seen since 1963 – and the red-footed falcon with bright red patches round its eyes as well as red feet. There are two hides.

Crimond, just west of the loch on the main road, has two claims to fame. Its clock shows 61 minutes to the hour – a slip of the clockmaker's hand – and the Crimond version of the 23rd Psalm was composed by Jessie Seymour Irvine, daughter of the local manse.

On the southern slopes of **Mormond**, the hill to the west of the main road and the highest point in this area (768ft), the glittering white quartzite horse and stag were cut out of the hill in the 18th century by a Captain Fraser, possibly as memorials. Fraser built the now ruined hunting lodge above the horse.

Cairnbulg and **Inverallochy**, one either side of the B9107 about 3 miles north of Loch of Strathbeg, are among the oldest coastal settlements in the area with their original fisher cottages. One of these, known as '**Maggie's Hoosie**', has been restored and fitted out to show life in a 19th-century fishing community (*open April–Sept daily 2–4.30; adm*).

Fraserburgh

Across Fraserburgh Bay from Cairnbulg Point, Fraserburgh stands on the shoulder of Grampian at Kinnairds Head, a great slate rock thrusting into the North Sea and the Moray Firth. It is not a beautiful town, but an unmistakable tang of the sea lurks in its bones, giving it great character, and its 3 miles of dune-backed beach have won international awards for cleanliness. Known locally as the Broch – Scots word for burgh – the town began as a village called Faithlie. The Frasers bought the lands of Faithlie in

Tourist Information

Fraserburgh: 3 Saltoun Square, **t** (01346) 518 325; *open April–Oct.*
Banff: Collie Lodge, **t** (01261) 812 419; *open April–Oct.*
Forres: 116 High Street, **t** (01309) 672 938; *open April–Oct.*
Central Buchan Tourism Group publish a leaflet, 'Walks Roon Aboot Buchan', with 33 walks that take in places of interest.

Festivals

June: Highland Games, Burghead.
July: Highland Games, Forres. **Yacht Race,** Banff; to or from (alternate years) Stavanger in Norway.
September: Banff Golf Week.

Where to Stay and Eat

Knockomie Hotel, Forres, **t** (01309) 673 146, *www.knockomie.co.uk (expensive–moderate).* Comfortable, homely country-house hotel with all mod cons.
Ramnee Hotel, Forres, **t** (01309) 672 410, *ramneehotel@btconnect.com (expensive–moderate).* Elegant, comfortable Edwardian country house. Good food.
Banff Links Hotel, Banff, **t** (01261) 812 414 *(moderate).* Good-value Georgian house overlooking the Moray Firth. Special breaks.
Brough House, Milton Brodie, near Forres, **t** (01343) 850 617 *(moderate).* A Wolsey Lodge, beautifully furnished, comfortable, secluded and peaceful. Excellent food.
Fife Lodge Hotel, Banff, **t** (01261) 812 436 *(moderate).* A comfortable historic building

overlooking the River Deveron and Duff House Gardens. Good traditional cooking.
Saplinbrae House Hotel, Old Deer, **t** (01771) 623 515 *(moderate).* Nice old country house in 400 acres, with shooting, fishing and pony trekking. The food is good.
Tufted Duck, St Combs, Fraserburgh, **t** (01346) 582 481 *(moderate).* Cheery and comfortable, overlooking the sea. Excellent food.
Udny Arms Hotel, Main Street, Newburgh, **t** (01358) 789 444, *www.udny.co.uk (moderate).* Family-run hotel overlooking the Ythan estuary and golf course. Good food.
Waterside Inn, Fraserburgh Road, Peterhead, **t** (01779) 471 121, *www.waterside-inn.co.uk (moderate).* Large, modern hotel with leisure club, pool, and award-winning chefs.
Blervie, Forres, **t** (01309) 672 358, *meiklejohn@btinternet.com (cheap).* Grade A listed house, built in 1776 from the stones of Blervie castle. A friendly Wolsey Lodge with elegant rooms, attractive furnishings and antiques. The food is excellent.
Crown and Anchor Inn, Findhorn, **t** (01309) 690 243 *(cheap).* 18th-century coaching inn on the bay – friendly, with free boats.
The Findhorn Foundation, t (01309) 690 311 *(cheap).* Perfect if you want to meditate on spiritual awareness and personal growth. Details and prices on application.
Neptune Guest House and Verdant Restaurant, Forres, **t** (01309) 674 387 *(cheap).* 18th-century town house with vegetarian food, organic wines and monastic beer.
Skerrybrae Hotel, Lossiemouth, **t** (01343) 812 040 *(cheap).* Typical seaside hotel, on the edge of the golf course. Near the sea, with splendid views and friendly atmosphere.
Fagins, Whitehills, near Banff, **t** (01261) 861 321. Good plain cooking and seafood.

1504 and began developing the town. The first harbour was built in 1546, and in the 1570s Sir Alexander Fraser built a castle on Kinnairds Head. At the peak of the herring boom, during the last 30 years of the 19th century, more than 1,000 drifters would land their fish during the season which ran from July to September. Today the town is a major white-fish port, and the harbour is an increasingly busy commercial port.

Kinnairds Head Lighthouse is the oldest in Scotland and the original was built on to the castle in 1787. Next door is the **Museum of Scottish Lighthouses** (*open April–Oct Mon–Sat 10–6, Sun 12–6; Nov–Mar Mon–Sat 10–4, Sun 12–4; adm; www.lighthouse museum.co.uk*). As well as a major exhibition of artefacts from Scottish lighthouses, the visit includes a tour to the top of the lighthouse.

The **Wine Tower** (*access by arrangement with the tourist board*), overlooking the cove beside the lighthouse, is thought to have originally been a chapel dating from the 16th century and then perhaps a watch tower. It is a strange building, with three floors which have no connecting stairs. Six carved pendants attached to the arched room have been acclaimed as the finest examples of late 16th-century three-dimensional heraldry in Scotland.

The **Mercat Cross**, in Saltoun Square, is dated 1736 but thought to have been carved around 1603, as it is the only one in Scotland to show the royal arms of both the old Kingdom of Scotland and the new United Kingdom. The carved **Moses Stone** inside the South Church, dated 1613, is all that remains of the University of Fraserburgh, a short-lived establishment that attracted many students for a brief time when there was a cholera epidemic in Aberdeen.

Fraserburgh to Macduff

Rosehearty, about 4 miles west of Fraserburgh, is one of the oldest ports in Scotland. A party of Danes is said to have been shipwrecked here early in the 14th century. They were absorbed by the crofting community whom they taught to fish, an industry that was to swell to vast proportions along this coast. In the mid-19th century Rosehearty rivalled Fraserburgh as a fishing port, but when the herring fishing declined Fraserburgh's railway link and larger harbour drew the new steam drifters and Rosehearty's industry dwindled.

Pitsligo Castle (*always accessible*), half a mile to the south, was built by the Frasers in 1424 and is now a large and impressive ruin with 9-foot-thick walls. Originally the square keep had three rooms, one on top of the other: a vaulted kitchen, a vaulted banqueting hall, and at the top a sleeping apartment with 24 beds. It was extended into a courtyard castle in the 1570s and has been partly renovated.

The last laird was Alexander Forbes, 4th and last Lord Pitsligo, a fervent Jacobite who was forced into hiding when his lands were forfeited after Culloden in 1746. He dressed in rags and hid in caves or in the houses of his tenants for 46 years until he died at the age of 84. He is remembered for his generosity to the poor. The castle was bought by one of his descendants, an American multimillionaire, Malcolm Forbes, who is said to have plans for turning it into a heritage centre.

New Aberdour, a mile inland from Aberdour Bay, west of Rosehearty, was built in 1798 to succeed an earlier village on the bay. Saints Columba and Drostan are said to have landed here around AD 597 and founded a Celtic monastery at **Old Deer**, some 10 miles southeast as the crow flies. *The Book of Deer* came from here – one of the most precious literary relics of the Celtic church – a 9th-century Latin manuscript of parts of the New Testament, with Gaelic notes in the margin. It is now in the Fitzwilliam Library in Cambridge. Ruined **Old Aberdour Church** stands above the Dour Burn on the road down to the bay. It was founded by the two saints, and part of it is Norman. The old font is said to have held the miracle-working bones of St Drostan, and the oldest readable gravestone is dated 1440.

The broad sweep of Aberdour Bay is popular with holiday-makers, with rock pools and caves. At low tide you can get away from the crowds by walking around the headlands to more deserted stretches of clean sand. Not many have heard of Jane Whyte, whose memorial can be seen on the ruin of a woollen mill where she lived on the bay. In 1884 this brave lass saved the lives of 15 men, shipwrecked when their steamer ran aground during a storm. She struggled through raging seas to carry a line out to the ship along which the seamen could escape.

Dundarag Castle (*privately owned; can be visited with permission from the owner, who lives in the gatehouse*) is a ruin on the cliffs above Aberdour Bay to the northeast. Dun Dearg – Red Fort – was probably Pictish before it was turned into a monastery by St Drostan. It later became a Comyn stronghold and was destroyed by Robert the Bruce in 1308. Quickly refortified, it was as quickly re-demolished, this time in the 16th century by the English.

Rocky **Ceard's Cove**, west of Aberdour Bay, has a hermit's cave, where an antisocial retired sailor lived in the 1920s and 1930s.

Pennan, on the western side of Aberdour Bay, is a picturesque village on a ledge below high red sandstone cliffs, with a pebbly beach running down to the sea. You have to be practically on top of the village before you see it. If it seems familiar to filmgoers, it was one of the settings for *Local Hero*, including the public telephone box from which the central character made his reports to his American boss. (Other settings were at Arisaig and Morar.) The smuggling of liquor and silk ran a close second to fishing as the main industry here, with lots of secret coves and caves in which to evade the exciseman.

Bronze-Age **Fort Fiddes**, on a promontory above sandy **Cullykhan Bay**, west of Pennan, is said to be the earliest industrial site in Europe. Beads from the Rhine region are among the artefacts excavated from the ruins by archaeologists, suggesting that the inhabitants traded with the Continent as far back as 700 BC. It's an impressive site, overlooking the sheer face of Lion Head and the deep gash in the cliff called Hell's Lum (chimney).

Troup Head is a massive red sandstone headland beyond the bay, separating Pennan from **Crovie** (pronounced Crivvie), which is reached either by a narrow footpath along the bottom of the cliff or by a steep, zigzag road with a 1 in 5 gradient. It clings to the foot of the cliffs, its cottages with one gable-end practically in the sea and the other tucked into the rock. This tiny village once had nearly 100 fishermen and over 60 boats. A tremendous gale in 1953 drove many of the villagers to seek a more sheltered home, and Crovie was temporarily deserted.

Gardenstown, a mile to the west, is larger, built on the cliff that rises from Gamrie Bay in a series of narrow terraces. The road through the village descends steeply in a series of hair-raising bends, dropping from roof level behind a house to run level with the door in front. The original Seatown is at the bottom, with narrow footpaths and huddled, whitewashed cottages. This lower bit, severely threatened by the gale that depopulated Crovie, was saved by the newly built seawall.

There were no inland villages in Buchan before the 18th century. Between 1750 and 1850 local landowners built a succession of 'planned' villages, to house and employ displaced tenants during a period of 'enclosures' for estate improvement. These little inland villages have down-to-earth names: Auchnagatt, Longside, Maud, Mintlaw,

Stuartfield, Cuminestown, Fetterangus, New Blyth, New Leeds, New Pitsligo, Strichen. Dotted over the hinterland, each of them retains a strong community spirit and many of the traditional trades continue to flourish.

Macduff

Macduff is a fishing town west of Gardenstown, at the foot of the Hill of Doune beside the Deveron estuary. It developed as a spa when the **Well of Tarlair**, a mineral spring just east of town, was found in 1770 to have healing properties. Health fanatics used to flock to drink the waters until the well dried up. (It was blown up by a mine in the last war and is now a derelict swimming pool.) Macduff stands around a four-basin harbour, with a thriving fish market and a customs house. Next to the Doune Church there is an anchor, 13ft long and weighing more than 3 tonnes. It is believed to be from an 18th-century sailing ship, and was dragged up in a fishing net. It was placed here by the Town Cross to symbolize the town's long association with the sea. The Harbour Master organizes tours of the harbour on Wednesday afternoons and Friday mornings in July and August. If you climb the hill to the 70-foot-high octagonal War Memorial Tower, you get splendid views of the rugged coastline.

Macduff Marine Aquarium, in the High Street (*open daily 10–5; adm*), has displays of Moray Firth marine life, a kelp reef, ray tank, touch pools, and feed and dive shows.

Banff

Banff, less than 2 miles west of Macduff, is an old county town looking across the Deveron Estuary and Banff Bay. From the 16th to the 18th century the landed gentry built themselves elegant town houses in Banff, to retreat to during the winter months when their castles became too cold and draughty. The town's history goes back to 1120 when it was one of the Hanseatic trading towns sending ships as far afield as the Mediterranean and the Baltic, carrying hides, wool, sheepskin and salted salmon. Smuggling was rife. Banff was an important herring fishing port, with 90 boats and an annual export of 30,000 barrels of herring, until the harbour silted up after a storm and caused the Deveron to change course. The fleet then moved across the bay to Macduff.

Duff House (*open April–Oct daily 11–5; Nov–Mar Thurs–Sun 11–4; adm; www.duff-house.com*), beside the golf course, has been extensively restored. The Duff family, later Earls of Fife, made a considerable fortune buying up land from impoverished lairds just before the Union in 1707. The house is among the finest works of Georgian Baroque architecture in Britain, and could accurately be described as unique. Its original design, by William Adam, included flanking pavilions which were never built, hence its rather tall stark appearance. In its time, it has been a hotel, a hospital and a prisoner-of-war-camp. It is now an out-station of the National Galleries of Scotland, as well as a splendid country house, and there is a café and shop.

Banff Castle, now a municipal building, was also designed by William Adam, built on the site of a medieval fortress of which the moat remains.

Banff Museum (*open June–Sept Mon–Sat 2–4.30*) has a collection of armour, costumes, burial urns, silver and local natural history.

Plaques have been put up on many of Banff's finest old buildings, and you can get a *Royal and Ancient Banff* booklet from the tourist information centre, giving details of a town walk. They also do a 'Walkman Tour of Banff', on tape.

A 2-mile walk south along the river from Duff House takes you to **Bridge of Alvah**, a single-arched, vertigo-inducing bridge built high across a gorge of the Deveron.

Banff to Buckie

Whitehills, just west of Banff, is the smallest village to retain its own fishing fleet and daily fishmarket. It is another place where the 19th-century cottages, built gable-end to the sea for protection from storms, are unchanged. In the *New Statistical Account of 1845* the Rev. A. Anderson wrote of a prosperous fishing village whose villagers were 'cleanly in their habits', so that 'fish cured by them has a superior reputation'. He also noted that the women of Whitehills were dominant over the men, claimed the proceeds of the white-fish market, and were of a 'superior comeliness'.

Whitehills is built around **Knock Head**, said to be where grey rats first came ashore in Scotland from a wreck. There is a sandy beach to the east, at Boyndie Bay. The **Red Well**, near the shore past the caravan park, is a beehive-shaped house built by the Romans to protect a spring with a high iron content. At the spring and autumn equinox the first rays of the sun, rising over Troup Head 10 miles away, illuminate the interior of the well while the surrounding area is still in complete darkness. It is thought the well must have been some sort of calendar.

Boyne Castle is a ruin in a wooded valley above the Burn of Boyne, not far to the west. It was built by the Ogilvy family in 1580, and in those days was a great complex with four corner towers, four storeys high. The Ogilvys lost their estate after Culloden, and the castle eventually fell into ruin.

Portsoy is a fishing town, less than 5 miles west of Whitehills, built around a 17th-century harbour. Many of the 17th- and 18th-century buildings were restored in the 1960s, and a large part of the town is preserved as a conservation area. Among the buildings to look out for are the **Old Star Inn** (1727) and **Soy House**, possibly built in 1690 and the oldest house in town. Green and pink Portsoy marble was cut from a seam of serpentine which runs across the hills west of the harbour, and provided two chimney pieces for Louis XIV's palace at Versailles. The **Portsoy Marble Workshop and Pottery** at Shorehead (*open April–Sept Mon–Sat 9–5; Oct–Mar Mon–Sat 10–5*) continues to make things out of the local marble and sell small samples in the form of paperweights and knick-knacks.

Fordyce, 3 miles southwest of Portsoy, nestles under Durn Hill. This cluster of cottages among narrow streets, with a small late 16th-century tower and quaint church, has won many conservation awards.

Sandend, a couple of miles north on the coast, is a 19th-century fishing village much painted by artists and said to have the smallest harbour in Scotland. It stands on the western arm of Sandend Bay, one of the most popular beaches in the area.

Findlater Castle is a spectacular three-storey ruin built into a rock face beyond Sandend, its windows overlooking a sheer drop of 50ft to the sea. Built as a fortress by the Ogilvys in 1455, it was unsuccessfully besieged in 1562 by Mary, Queen of Scots when she was trying to subdue the powerful Gordons. Although easy to get to, the castle is highly dangerous and children should be tethered.

Cullen, about 3 miles further west, is tucked in under a steep hill overlooking Cullen Bay – a sweep of white sand on which are curious red sandstone rocks called the 'Three Kings of Cullen'. The small harbour, once busy with herring boats, is now mainly used for pleasure craft. One of the things you notice here is the series of railway viaducts which divide the sea town from the upper town. They were built in 1886 because the Countess of Seafield refused to allow the railway line to cross the grounds of Cullen House. The village specialized in smoked haddock and the local delicacy, 'cullen skink', is a fish stew based on smoked haddock. George Macdonald, a 19th-century Congregationalist minister who was rejected by his congregation and had to support his family of 11 by writing, set two of his novels in Cullen, *Malcolm* and *The Marquis of Lossie*. He is better known, however, for being the author of *The Princess and the Goblin*.

Portknockie, 3 miles west of Cullen, had to be built on the clifftop because there was no room between the water and the foot of the cliff, and has wonderful views across the firth to the hills of Sutherland and Caithness. Its harbour is the only one in the area that is accessible at lowest tides. An archaeological dig revealed the remains of an Iron-Age fort on the promontory.

Findochty, a couple of miles further west, is a striking example of villages whose houses are painted in brightly coloured oil paints, vying with each other for effect. The old smugglers' route to Buckie ran along the edge of the Strathlene Golf Course and beach. In the old days the pack ponies of the nightriders, with their hoofs muffled, would not have had the footbridges and steps.

Buckie

Buckie is another 2 miles on, taking the A942 around the coast, overlooking **Spey Bay**. This long town is an important fishing base, with all the attendant maritime establishments: chandlers, boat builders, ice works, a fish market and the largest scampi-processing factory in Scotland. It's a solid, unpretentious town with the fisher houses typical of the area. Some are restored, with external stone steps going up to what used to be the net loft on the upper floor.

Buckie Drifter (*open April–Oct Mon–Sat 10–5, Sun 12–5; adm*) tells the story of the herring industry and of those who depend upon it. The mouth of the River Spey is about 3 miles to the west. A footbridge crosses the river on the old railway viaduct and you can walk an invigorating 8 miles along the beach to Lossiemouth. Spey Bay is also the beginning – or end – of the Speyside Way, which goes south to Ballindalloch and Tomintoul, via Tugnet.

Lossiemouth

Lossiemouth is a popular resort with a pretty harbour and two good beaches. It is also a busy fishing port. It developed as the port for Elgin, 5 miles to the south, after sand and shingle silted up the previous port at Spynie (*see* p.419). Ramsay MacDonald, Britain's first Labour Prime Minister, was born here in 1866 and his house is marked with a plaque. There is a reconstruction of his study in the **Lossiemouth Fisheries and Community Museum** (*open May–Sept Mon–Sat 10–5*), as well as exhibits relating to the fishing industry of the area.

This stretch of windswept coast has great sweeps of sand, rich in wildfowl. The peace is frequently shattered by low-flying planes from RAF Lossiemouth.

Burghead

At Burghead, 7 miles west of Lossiemouth, there are traces of both Iron-Age and Norse forts. In the Iron-Age fort you can go down steps to what is called the 'Roman Well', probably an early Christian baptistry, fed by a natural spring. In common with many communities, Burghead re-enacts ancient ceremonies that were performed to scare away evil spirits. In a ceremony called 'Burning the Clavie', a lighted tar barrel is carried through the streets every 11 January – the old-style New Year's Eve – unless it falls on a Sunday, when the ceremony takes place a day earlier.

Findhorn Bay

Findhorn is a village, 7 miles on along the coast, on the eastern arm of Findhorn Bay, a large expanse of tidal flats which dry out at low tide. If the name is familiar it may be because of the local sailing club's challenge for the America's Cup in 1991.

Findhorn in Time and Tide (*open May and Sept Sat and Sun 2–5; June–Aug Wed–Mon 2–5; adm*) is in two salmon fishery huts by the Culbin Sands Hotel. One hut is a recon-structed salmon fisher's bothy and the other traces Findhorn's history.

In the huge caravan park, there is the **Findhorn Foundation** (*guided tours summer Mon, Wed, Fri, Sat and Sun at 2pm, t (01309) 690 880*), an international community of some 200 members, founded in 1962 as a centre for 'spiritual and holistic education'. The inhabitants stroll about, smiling politely and somewhat vacantly, and you will need determination to get through their apparent unwillingness to communicate with strangers. Their *modus vivendi* is meant to demonstrate cooperation with nature and with the sacred in all aspects of life. There are nature gardens, ecological build-ings, sewage treatment and 'innovative architecture'.

In the village of **Kinloss**, on the southern edge of Findhorn Bay, the small overgrown ruin of Kinloss Abbey was once an important Cistercian centre. It was founded by David I who was led there by a dove after he had lost his way in the forest.

Much of this coastline has changed dramatically over the years as a result of the storms that batter it. The **Culbin Sands**, stretching away to the west of Findhorn Bay, were built up over the years by wind-blown sand until 1694, when a mighty storm finished the job, engulfing all the farmland and buildings in its path. The sands now cover 3,600 acres of dunes and marram grass.

Forres

Forres, a scant 3 miles southwest of Kinloss, has a long history going back to before the mythical day when Shakespeare's Macbeth and Banquo met the witches on the blasted heath, on their way to the town to attend the court of King Duncan. The loca-tion of the heath is fairly flexible, including Macbeth's Hillock, 5 miles west, and Knock of Alves, 8 miles east. The town preserves its medieval layout, with the main street widening to form the market place, linked to parallel streets by a series of narrow lanes. Forres has well-kept parks, especially Grant Park at the foot of Cluny Hill, which is a riot of colour in summer, with amazing floral sculptures. The town won a certificate of commendation in the European 'Entente Florale' in 1990. **Nelson Tower** (*open May–Sept Tues–Sun 2–4*), on top of the hill, is a landmark for miles and has good views of the Moray Firth.

The **Crimean Memorial Obelisk**, at the west end of the High Street, stands on the site of Forres Castle, where King Duncan held his court. The **Falconer Museum** (*open May–Oct Mon–Sat 10–5; Nov–April Mon–Fri 10–5*), also in the High Street, gives you an idea of the town's history. It has displays of natural and social history, fossils and archaeology, and temporary exhibitions. The **Witch's Stone**, in Victoria Road, is thought to date from Pictish times and to have been used as an altar to the Sun God. It marks the site where one of three barrels, containing three condemned witches, came to rest, having been rolled down Cluny Hill.

Sueno's Stone, on the northeastern outskirts of the town, is an outstanding example of a Pictish sculpted stone. It stands over 20ft high, a slender sandstone shaft dating from the 9th or 10th century. It is clearly carved with a battle scene on one side, full of bodies and heads and weapons, around a broch, with a cross on the reverse side (probably a cenotaph commemorating a victory). Its once splendid setting, overlooking the Moray Firth, has been necessarily diminished by encasing the stone in a protective building, without which it was doomed to erosion.

Darnaway Castle, seat of the Earls of Moray, has a magnificent 15th-century oak hammerbeam roof. Among the Stuart portraits is one of the murdered 'Bonnie Earl'.

Randolph's Leap at Logie, 7½ miles south of Forres on the B9007, should be called Cumming's Leap. Robert the Bruce gave land belonging to the Cummings to Thomas Randolph, Earl of Moray. The Cummings raided Darnaway Castle in retaliation but were forced to flee. Alistair Cumming leapt across the narrow gap above this impressive gorge to evade pursuit.

Brodie Castle

*Open Easter or 1 April if earlier–Sept Mon–Sat 11–5.30,
Sun 1.30–5.30; Oct Sat 11–5.30, Sun 1.30–5.30;
grounds April–Oct daily 9.30–sunset; adm.*

Brodie is about 5 miles west of Forres. It was built on land given to the Brodies by Malcolm IV in 1160 and owned by them until the present day. Part of the existing building dates from the 17th century, rebuilt after the castle was destroyed in 1645. There are also 18th- and 19th-century additions. It is a pale cream-coloured building, with conical turrets and coats of arms on the outer walls, approached down a beech avenue. The castle contains French furniture and English, Continental and Chinese porcelain and paintings. There are woodland walks by a 4-acre loch, a picnic area, adventure playground, car park and shop.

The Highlands

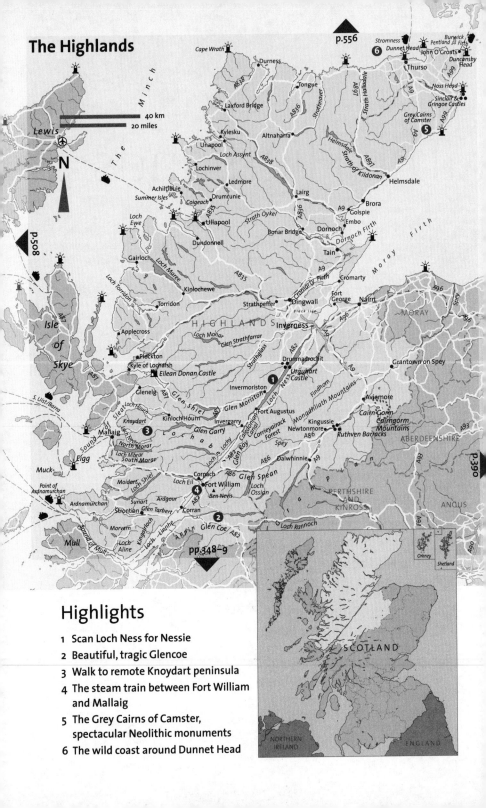

The Highlands

p.556

Cape Wrath
Durness
Tongue
Laxford Bridge

Lewis

The Minch

40 km
20 miles

N

Kylesku
Unapool
Loch Assynt
Altnaharra
Lochinver
Ledmore
Achiltibuie
Drumrunie
Summer Isles
Coigeach
Ullapool
Loch Ewe
Dundonnell

Strath Halladale
Strathnaver
Strath of Kildonan
Helmsdale

Stromness
Dunnet Head
John O'Groats
Thurso
Burwick
Pentland Firth
Duncansby Head
Noss Head
Sinclair & Gringoe Castles
Grey Cairns of Camster

p.508

Gairloch
Loch Maree
Loch Torridon
Kinlochewe
Torridon
Applecross

Isle of Skye

S Uist/Barra

Plockton
Kyle of Lochalsh
Eilean Donan Castle
Glenelg
Glen Shiel
Invermoriston

Knoydart
Kinloch Hourn
Invergarry
Glen Garry
Mallaig
North Morar
Loch Morar
South Morar

Eigg
Muck
Point of Ardnamurchan
Ardnamurchan
Moidart
Loch Shiel
Sunart
Ardgour
Strontian
Glen Tarbert
Corran
Corpach
Loch Eil
Fort William
Ben Nevis

Lairg
Bonar Bridge
Strath Oykel
Strathpeffer
Dingwall

HIGHLANDS
Inverness

Loch Monar
Glen Strathfarrar
Strathglass
Drumnadrochit
Urquhart Castle
Loch Ness
Fort Augustus
Caledonian Canal
Corrieyairack Forest
Kingussie
Newtonmore
Ruthven Barracks
Dalwhinnie

Golspie
Embo
Dornoch
Dornoch Firth
Tain

Helmsdale
Brora

Cromarty Firth
Fort George
Nairn
Cromarty
Black Isle

Moray Firth
MORAY

Grantown on Spey

Findhorn
Monadhliath Mountains
Aviemore
Cairn Gorm
Cairngorm Mountains
ABERDEENSHIRE

Glen Roy
Glen Spean
Loch Ossian
Loch Rannoch

p.390

ANGUS

PERTHSHIRE AND KINROSS

Mull
Morvern
Loch Aline
Sound of Mull
Kingairloch
Loch Linnhe
Glen Coe
Appin

pp.348-9

Orkney
Shetland

SCOTLAND

NORTHERN IRELAND
ENGLAND

Highlights

1 Scan Loch Ness for Nessie

2 Beautiful, tragic Glencoe

3 Walk to remote Knoydart peninsula

4 The steam train between Fort William and Mallaig

5 The Grey Cairns of Camster, spectacular Neolithic monuments

6 The wild coast around Dunnet Head

Behold her, single in the field,
Yon solitary Highland Lass!
Reaping and singing by herself;
Stop here, or gently pass!
Alone she cuts, and binds the grain,
And sings a melancholy strain;
O listen! for the Vale profound
Is overflowing with the sound.

from 'The Solitary Reaper', by William Wordsworth

Until relatively recently, when Jacobites made a bid for the English throne, the Highlands were so isolated geographically that few outsiders ventured into them. Communication between remote communities, cut off by mountain ranges and huge tracts of water, was arduous and almost entirely by boat. The people turned westwards and across to the islands for their culture: to the east lay remoteness and barbarism. It was only after 1715 and the first Jacobite rising that General Wade's planned road system evolved and people like Dr Johnson were able to travel about and 'discover' this untapped source of purple prose.

The Battle of Culloden sparked off the death of the clan system and contributed to the mass exodus that took place over the succeeding century or so. All that remains are tumbled stones, where villages of crofters once squeezed a living from the poor soil, subsisting under the protection of their chief.

Agriculture, fishing and tourism are the main occupation of Highlanders. Major roads are excellent, but it is often necessary to drive long distances to get around mountains and sea lochs. Many of the minor roads are single track, with passing bays (infuriating in the caravan season).

In the remoter parts, not much has changed in the last hundred years or so. There may be kit houses and new hotels with picture windows, pile carpets and bathrooms en suite, but the people who staff them are not very impressed by these modern trappings. In the vicinity there are probably a dozen derelict vehicles, discarded over the last 20 years. The surrounding countryside is littered with rusting beer cans and empty whisky bottles, and it would not be surprising to find a live sheep among the inhabitants of a cottage kitchen. It was in the Highlands, particularly in the west, that you used to find the old bards and tellers of folk tales handed down orally over the centuries. These days you must go to the islands to find them. In those parts of the Highlands that were untouched by the Reformation, and by the banning of fun and gaiety by the stern Calvinists, you will find the best fiddlers and pipers.

Highland Games are a popular summer diversion throughout the region, usually less showy than the smart dress parades of the more fashionable area dominated by the Grampians. A piper practises a pibroch behind a shed, pacing with precise steps, while his rival faces a row of intent judges in the ring. Little girls in full Highland costume perform the intricate steps of a sword dance on a wooden platform. A huge man with bulging biceps totters under the weight of a gigantic caber; another heaves a cannonball-weight across the grass; another a javelin. Young men hurl themselves up and over a high jump. There are side shows and stalls, hot-dog stands, fish and chips, and always a well-attended beer tent. Sometimes these games were fairs, organized by clan chiefs, but they usually had a serious purpose: the chief would be talent-spotting for fit men for his army.

Look out for **sheepdog trials**, where these intelligent animals are put through their paces. There can be few things more stirring than to see a first-class pair of dogs working a flock of sheep, controlled by a minimum of monosyllabic or whistled commands. The Great Glen Sheepdog Trials, in Fort William in July, is one of the best of these, and there are often smaller trials at agricultural shows.

Inverness

As the capital of the Highlands, with its newly acquired 'city' status, and the junction of many routes, Inverness – from *Inbhir*, mouth of the River Ness – is a good place from which to explore the Highland area. The River Ness flows through the heart of the city, converging with the northern end of the Caledonian Canal. The first settlement grew up 5,000 years ago at the first place where people could ford it at low tide, the sea and hills forcing travellers from all directions to pass through a bottleneck. Being also the navigable limit of the Moray Firth, with a good sheltered harbour at the river mouth, Inverness became a focal point for trade routes. Although not outstandingly beautiful, parts of Inverness have a certain sturdy charm, and the riverside is attractive. Perhaps the best view is from the bridge below Bridge Street. Fishermen stand thigh-deep in the fast-flowing River Ness, flanked by well-proportioned houses and churches. When the sun shines, it is a curiously continental picture.

Its sheltered position beside the sea made Inverness a natural place for trade to develop, and it has been an important centre from earliest times. In the Middle Ages it developed as a port and ship-building centre, with trade links with Europe. It was often the focal point of clashes between Highland and Island chiefs, who ruled their lands like kings, and the Scottish Crown, ever trying to subdue them. It is now the communications and administrative centre for the north of Scotland.

St Columba is recorded by his biographer, St Adamnan, as having visited the Pictish King Brude in a castle somewhere near the River Ness in AD 565 and converted him and his people to Christianity. This could have been on Craig Phadrig, the small hill just west of the city which still has the remains of a 4th-century vitrified fort. It is more likely, however, that Brude's stronghold stood on Castle Hill where the castle stands today.

Historical fact and poetic fiction have become so inextricably interwoven around the story of Macbeth and his bloodstained journey to the throne that there are several different claims for the true setting for King Duncan's murder. The most reliable sources say the deed was done in a house near Elgin in 1039, not in Macbeth's castle in Inverness, which was almost certainly at the eastern end of The Crown, still referred to as Auldcastle; and it is believed that Malcolm Canmore destroyed **Inverness Castle** in revenge for Duncan's death. A new castle was built in the 12th

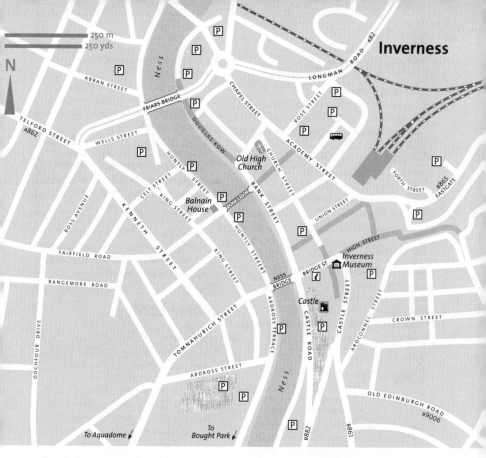

century on the site of the present one, and was much abused in subsequent years. The English occupied it in the War of Independence and Robert the Bruce destroyed it. Its successor became the hub of conflict between Highlanders and those trying to subdue their wild ways. Mary, Queen of Scots hanged its rebellious governor from the ramparts when he refused her entry in 1562. Jacobites occupied it in 1715 and 1745, and blew it up in February 1746 to keep it from government hands. The present castle was built in the 19th century and looks brand new, its pinkish walls rising from the small hill exactly like a toy fort. It houses the law courts and local government offices.

The city centre is compact, with the Station Square in the middle, dominated by a splendid war memorial statue of a Cameron Highlander, erected in 1893 to mark the centenary of the Camerons – the local regiment. (They were first amalgamated in the early 1960s with the Seaforth Highlanders to become the Queen's Own Highlanders, and then with the Gordon Highlanders to become The Highlanders.)

Inverness Museum and Art Gallery (*open Mon–Sat 9–5*) in Castle Wynd, between the castle and the town hall, has interpretations of the social and natural history of the Highlands, and exhibitions of silver, weapons, Jacobite memorabilia and paintings. There are often interesting talks and slide shows, and there's a shop and coffee shop. The **Castle Gallery**, in Castle Street, displays work by important contemporary artists, and sells up-market gifts and craft work.

Tourist Information

Inverness t (01463–)
Inverness: Castle Wynd, **t** 234 353; *open all year.*
Guide Friday, at the Railway Station, **t** 224 000.
Tours in an open-top double-decker bus
(*May–early Oct daily*).
Ken White Tours, **t** 223 168. Personally
conducted minibus tours, including Loch
Ness. Maximum 16 people.
Tartan Taxis, **t** 233 033. Tours over a wide area,
including to Skye.

Festivals

March: Folk Festival.
July: Highland Games.
August: Festival Week; Cadet Tattoo.
September: Northern Meeting Piping
Competition; the finest pipers compete for
prestigious awards.

Shopping

The Mill Shop, Holm Woollen Mills (James
Pringle), off Dores Road in the western
suburbs. A good place to stock up on woollens, tweeds, kilts, rugs, etc. There are factory
tours, a Clan Tartan Centre and a restaurant,
as well as the interior of a crofter's living
room on the way in. You can usually find
some good bargains. *Open daily.*

Sports and Activities

Eden Court Theatre, **t** 234 234/239 841.
Warner Bros Multiplex Cinema, Eastfieldway,
t 711 175.
Ten Pin Bowling, 167 Culduthel Road, **t** 235 100.
Bucht Park Ice Rink, **t** 235 711; **Aquadome**, **t** 667
500; **Sports Centre**, **t** 667 505.

Moray Firth Dolphin Cruises, Shore Street
Quay, **t** 717 900.
Caley Cruisers, Canal Road, **t** 236 328,
www.caleycruisers.co.uk. Run by Jim and
Elizabeth Hogan, with a fleet of 50 cruise
boats with all mod cons. Sleeps 2–8.
Jacobite Cruise, from Tomnahurich Bridge,
t 233 999, *www.jacobitecruises.co.uk.*
Includes a stop off at Urquhart Castle.
Castle Cruises Loch Ness, **t** (01456) 450 695,
www.lochnesscruises.com. From opposite
the car park in Drumnadrochit.
Loch Ness and Great Glen Cruise Co., **t**/**f** 711
913, *www.lochnessboat.com.* Splendid old
converted barge runs 3–6-night cruises from
Top Lock, Canal Road (*April–Oct and winter
charter; £600 for 3 nights*).

Where to Stay

Expensive
Culloden House Hotel, 3 miles east of the
city, **t** 790 461, **f** 792 181, *www.culloden-
house.co.uk.* The best option within easy
reach of the city: Georgian mansion built
around a Jacobean castle near the battlefield, bought by an American millionaire
who traces his roots back to the time of
Robert the Bruce. This was the Jacobite
headquarters for the battle and was where
Prince Charles spent the night before his
defeat. Some 30 Highlanders took refuge
here after the battle and were slaughtered
by Cumberland's men. A mound marks their
burial ground. The house was destroyed by
fire soon after the battle and replaced in
1772 by the present mansion. It has elegant,
Adam-style décor, four-posters, amazing
bathrooms and food worth staying in for.
Bunchrew House Hotel, on the Beauly Firth
about 5 miles west of Inverness, **t** 234 917,
f 710 260, *www.bunchrew-inverness.co.uk.*

St Andrew's Episcopal Cathedral is to the south. An imposing, pinkish building on
the banks of the river, it was built between 1866 and 1874, with an octagonal chapter
house and an elaborate interior. Eden Court, beyond the cathedral, is a glass edifice
built in 1976, incorporating the 19th-century house of Bishop Eden. It is an 800-seat
multipurpose theatre, conference centre and art gallery, with an excellent restaurant.
Ambitious programmes are laid on throughout the year: concerts, ballet, drama, the
latest films and many art exhibitions.

A homely, peaceful Victorian mansion with a late-Georgian core in 15 acres of attractive garden and grounds, with turrets and towers, and excellent food.
Dunain Park Hotel, t 230 512, **f** 224 532, *www.dunainparkhotel.co.uk.* Quiet mansion house hotel, with friendly staff, small covered pool and food that people travel for.
Jarvis Caledonian Hotel, Church Street, **t** 235 181, **f** 711 206. Large and impersonal, but convenient, backing on to the river.
Glenmoriston Town House Hotel, 20 Ness Bank, **t** 223 777, **f** 712 378, *glenmoriston@cali.co.uk.* Very spoiling, small hotel on the river, with elegant rooms and a good restaurant, La Riviera, *see below.*

Moderate
Royal Highland Hotel, Academy Street, **t** 321 926, *www.royalhighlandhotelco.uk.* The old Station Hotel, in the town centre. Traditional and comfortable, with an air of genteel respectability and an Agatha Christie foyer.
Columba Hotel, Ness Walk, **t** 231 391, **f** 715 526. Large, impersonal and rather busy, but convenient and central, overlooking the river, with all the essentials. Friendly staff.
Culduthel Lodge, Culduthel Road, **t/f** 240 089. Comfortable hotel in quiet area, with friendly service.
Maple Court Hotel, 12 Ness Walk, **t** 230 330, **f** 237 700, *www.macleodhotels.co.uk/maple-court.* Smallish hotel in nice grounds beside the river. Good seafood in its Chandlery Seafood Restaurant.
Drumossie Hotel, on the A9 to Perth 3 miles out of town, **t** 236 451, **f** 712 858 (*moderate*). Modern, with views over the Moray Firth.

Cheap
Clisham House, 43 Fairfield Road, **t** 239 965, **f** 239 854, *www.clisham.dircon.co.uk.* Small,

friendly and quiet, within easy walking distance of the city centre. Very good value.
Felstead House, 18 Ness Bank, **t/f** 231 634. On the river opposite Eden Court. Family-run and unpretentious with warm Highland hospitality.
Glendruidh House, Old Edinburgh Road, **t** 226 499, **f** 710 745. Delightful, family-run hotel overlooking the Moray Firth and the city.
Heathmount Inn, Heathmont, **t** 235 877, **f** 715 749, *www.heathmountinn.co.uk.* Nice pub atmosphere and comfortable bedrooms.
Farr Mains, by Inverness, **t** (01808) 251 205, **f** 251 466, *c&jmurray@farrmains.freeserve.co.uk* (*cheap*). Very comfortable family home with true Highland hospitality, great atmosphere, dinner on request, and you might be allowed to feed the llamas.

Eating Out
See Culloden House, Dunain Park and Maple Court hotels, above.
Number One, Greig Street, **t** 226 200. At the end of the pedestrian bridge over the river, part of Café One. Small, very high-quality, expensive and worth it.
La Riviera, Ness Walk, **t** 223 777. Italian-style adjunct to the Glen Moriston Hotel, overlooking the water, where the food is delicious, particularly the seafood.
Chili Palmers, Queensgate. Continental-style bar with a warm welcome.
Eden Court Theatre. Good self-serve food, for drop-in refreshment.
Riva, Ness Walk, **t** 237 377. Delicious Italian food, pastries and coffee.
The Mustard Seed, 16 Fraser Street, **t** 220 220. Overlooking the River Ness. Excellent reputation both for food and service.
The Herbivore, 38 Eastgate Street, **t** 231 075. Popular and very good value.

Ness Islands, up-river away from Eden Court, form a public park spread over a series of small islands in the River Ness. They are linked by footbridges, with views down the river towards the city.

Tomnahurich – Hill of the Yews, sometimes called Hill of the Fairies – is the small, boat-shaped hillock to the southwest. Two wandering fiddlers, Thomas and Farquhar, were lured to Tomnahurich by the Fairy Queen, to play for a night's dancing. In the morning they found the town and its people strangely altered and everyone laughing at them. The 'night' had lasted a hundred years. They crept into a church for refuge – and crumbled into dust. Tomnahurich is now the city's cemetery, with many elaborate monuments clinging to the steep, wooded sides and a splendid viewing point from the top. Below lie the environs of Inverness, with neat villas, well-kept gardens and an air of respectability.

The northern entrance to the **Caledonian Canal** is in the western suburbs. It was constructed in the 19th century by Thomas Telford, and much used in the old days by boats wishing to avoid the long and often hazardous slog around the north coast. Still used by fishing boats, it now offers a perfect way for sailors to explore the Great Glen. Cabin cruisers can be hired from the marinas just down from the entrance, and passenger cruises operate in the summer.

The 19th-century **Cameron Barracks** stands on Knockentinnel – the Rallying Hill – a high ridge above Millburn Road on the eastern edge of Inverness: a wise old sentinel guarding the city. From here, many a brave young Cameron Highlander walked out, newly trained, to give his life so that his Highland home should remain free.

Around Inverness, to Nairn

The south side of the Moray Firth is flattish open farmland, with views across to the Black Isle and the hills of Easter Ross.

Culloden

Taking the back roads east of the A96 Culloden is about 5 miles east of Inverness. Start at the first-class **visitor centre** on the edge of the battlefield (*open April–Oct daily 9–6; Nov–Mar daily 10–4; adm for audiovisual show and cottage; battleground always accessible, with guided tours in summer*). The audiovisual show gives details of the battle, on 16 April 1746, when Prince Charles Edward Stuart and his 5,000 exhausted, starving and ill-equipped Highlanders were defeated by the Duke of Cumberland, son of George II, and his 9,000 well-trained and well-equipped men. During that battle 1,200 Highlanders fell; many more were butchered by order of the Duke as they lay wounded. Accounts of the Prince's reaction to the failure of his dreams vary: some say he tried to rally his Highlanders; some that he had to be held back from galloping forward to a hero's death; others are less starry-eyed.

Whatever is true, one thing is sure: he was led away and hidden by loyal High-landers for five months, with a price of £30,000 on his head, until he returned to the Continent in a French frigate, to live out the rest of his life there in wretched, debauched exile.

As well as exhibitions and displays, the visitor centre has a study room for school parties, with a library and Jacobite relics. In addition there is a coffee shop and restau-rant, and a very good bookshop with a comprehensive range of Scottish publications.

The old **cottage**, outside, is the only building to survive the battle. It was still inhab-ited at the beginning of the 20th century and is now a folk museum with its old furnishings and domestic equipment; as well as taped music and Gaelic.

On the **battlefield** wooden plaques tell which clan fought where and how the battle progressed. There are clan graves, communal burial sites with headstones bearing clan names, and a memorial cairn, erected in 1881. On the edge of the bleak battle site is the Well of the Dead where wounded Highlanders were slain as they drank water to revive themselves. A single stone bears the inscription: 'The English were buried here.' The flat stone beyond the visitor centre is called the Cumberland Stone, thought to have been the vantage point from which the Duke viewed the battle.

The **Clava Cairns** are signed a mile east of Culloden. These form a remarkable Stone- and Bronze-Age burial site, possibly dating from 2000 BC. Three large burial cairns in a glade of beech trees take you back to the prehistoric rituals that would have accompanied the internment of those farmers and herdsmen so many years ago. Two of the cairns have passages leading into them; the third has curious stone strips radiating from it like the spokes of a wheel. Each is surrounded by a circle of standing stones, some inscribed with cup-and-ring symbols. Excavations revealed traces of cremated human bones, pottery and other remains: memorials of people who were alive nearly 4,000 years ago.

Kilravock Castle (*open Wed for guided tours, but ring first: t (01667) 493 258; grounds open Mon–Sat; adm*) is 5 miles northeast of Culloden, still keeping to the back roads. Dating from the 15th century, this castle has been preserved almost intact because the owners never had enough money to mess about with its original design. In 1190 a Norman called Rose came north, married into a local family and settled on these lands. Kilravock (pronounced Kilrawk) has been the home of the Rose chiefs ever since. Among its relics are two reminders of Culloden – a punch bowl and a pair of leather thigh boots. Rose of Kilravock entertained Prince Charles before the battle and offered punch from this bowl. He was not a Jacobite, but the Prince had ridden over to call on him and no true Highlander refuses hospitality. Shortly afterwards, Cumberland came blustering up, flushed with celebration of his 25th birthday: 'I hear, sir, you've been entertaining my cousin!' Rose explained and was excused. Cumberland, for some inexplicable reason, left his boots behind. These two relics are an ironic reflection of the two people associated with them: Prince Charles, merry and charismatic, who later drowned his failure in alcohol; Butcher Cumberland, brash, gross and cruel – very much a jackboot image. The gardens and grounds are lovely, especially in spring. Prince Charles walked here with his host and watched young trees being planted. He remarked on the contrast between this peaceful scene and the commotion that was going on all around, preparing for the battle. Some of the beautiful old trees today must be the ones that were being planted. (Kilravock is now a 'Christian Guest House': *see* 'Where to Stay', below.)

Cawdor

The name Cawdor (pronounced Cawder), 8 miles northeast of Culloden, is familiar to anyone who has read Shakespeare's *Macbeth*. Within moments of having been told by the witches he is to become Thane of Cawdor, Macbeth is told that the king has indeed bestowed the title on him. The fulfilment of this prophecy encourages him to bring about the final one, that he would be king, by murdering King Duncan in 1040. His Cawdor, however, was of an earlier date.

Cawdor Castle (*open May–mid-Oct daily 10–5.30; adm; www.cawdorcastle.com*) dates from 1372, when the central tower was built, more than 300 years after Macbeth's perfidy. Domestic buildings were added in the 16th century and later remodelled. Protected by a gully on one side and a dry moat on the other, the castle, floodlit at night, has a walled garden, ablaze with colour in the summer. Entry is over a drawbridge, and it feels like a living home, rather than a museum, probably because it is still lived in. It is easy to imagine it in medieval times, with its winding stairways and massive walls. Among the things to see are Flemish tapestries, paintings, weapons, household equipment and family heirlooms. Carbon dating has confirmed that the scrap of an ancient tree, railed off in the basement, is older than the castle, thus authenticating an old story. The original founder, Thane William, was granted a licence to build himself a fortress. He was told in a dream to load a donkey with panniers of gold and build a castle wherever it stopped. He obeyed and the donkey stopped for a rest in the shade of a thorn tree around which Thane William built his castle. Outside there are nature trails, a nine-hole mini-golf course, putting green and picnic spots, as well as a licensed restaurant and souvenir shop. You could easily spend a day here.

In a conservation area, Cawdor village, straggling around the castle grounds, is not at all typical of Scotland: its peaceful cosiness matches that of the castle. The church is 17th century, built in thanksgiving by the twelfth Lord Cawdor after he was saved from a shipwreck.

Fort George

*Open April–Sept daily 9–6.30; Oct–Mar Mon–Sat 9.30–4.30, Sun 2–4.30; adm; entry includes Regimental Museum of the Queen's Own Highlanders, but ring to confirm winter opening times, **t** (01667) 462 777.*

Fort George is about 8 miles northwest of Cawdor on the B9006, on a windswept promontory jutting out into the Moray Firth. It is the most unspoilt example of an artillery fort in Europe. Built between 1748 and 1769, to replace 'Old' Fort George in Inverness (destroyed by Prince Charles in 1746), it is a classic 18th-century fortress. The defences include the traditional outer works: ravelin, ditch, bastion and rampart, designed by William Skinnor who was in his day the leading expert on artillery fortification. The government contractor who built it was John Adam, oldest son of architect William Adam, and brother of Robert.

Passing through the forbidding fortifications, one is brought to a delighted standstill by the mellow pink sandstone garrison buildings, their impeccable 18th-century proportions mercifully unscarred by Victorian or later 'improvement'.

The fort was built to house a garrison large enough to overawe Jacobite support in the Highlands, but by the time it was completed the Jacobite threat was finally dead, so it has never had a history of conflict. It became a base where a long series of regiments was mustered and equipped and whence they embarked for service in

Festivals

July: Holiday Week, Nairn. **Vintage Car Rally**, Nairn.

August: Highland Games, Nairn. **Fairground Fortnight**, Nairn. **Farmers Show**, Nairn.

Sports and Activities

The Little Theatre, in Fishertown, Nairn. Small theatre with a repertory company who perform every Wednesday in the summer.

Where to Stay and Eat

Nairn t (01667–)

Kilravock Castle, Croy, t 493 258, f 493 213, *info@kilravockcastle.com* (*moderate–cheap*). Historic old castle (where Prince Charles dined before Culloden, *see* below) in peaceful grounds near the river. The emphasis now is very much on God: grace before meals, Bible readings and comment at breakfast and dinner; no drink – though naughty guests have been known to smuggle bottles into their cells and smoke up the chimney.

Birkwood, near Croy, t 493 376, *newilkinson@hotmail.com*. Splendid separate apartment for B&B in nice house with good views. Comfortable, friendly and delicious breakfasts.

Cawdor Tavern, Cawdor. Dark wood and velvet interior, decorated with ornamental plates and hunting scenes. A bust of Shakespeare gazes benignly over the saloon where they serve good food.

Newton Hotel, Nairn, t 453 144, f 454 026 (*moderate*). Recommended as one of Nairn's best: friendly, quiet and with excellent food.

Clifton Hotel, Nairn, t 453 119, f 452 836, *www.clifton-hotel.co.uk* (*moderate*). A uniquely special place in every way: style, gracious living, convivial atmosphere and charm. Excellent food.

Carnach House Hotel, Inverness Road, Nairn, t 452 094, f 452 994 (*moderate*). Comfortable, peaceful hotel in 8 acres overlooking the Moray Firth.

Golf View Hotel, Nairn, t 452 301, f 455 267 (*moderate*). Overlooking the Firth, close to the golf course, with a leisure club, tennis courts, swimming pool, sauna, games room and regular entertainment.

Alton Burn Hotel, Nairn, t 452 051, f 456 697, *enquiries@altonburn.co.uk* (*moderate*). Spacious family hotel with the emphasis on golf. Peaceful setting overlooking Nairn golf course and the Moray Firth.

Claymore House Hotel, Stabank Road, Nairn, t 453 731, f 455 290, *www.claymorehouse-hotel.com* (*moderate*). Comfortable, friendly, smallish hotel.

Invernairne Hotel, Thurlow Road, Nairn, t 452 039, f 456 760 (*moderate*). Family-run hotel overlooking the Moray Firth, with private path to beach. Good 3-night offers.

Sunnybrae Hotel, Marine Road, Nairn, t 452 309, f 454 860 (*moderate*). Small cosy, family hotel in wonderful position, with good food.

The Longhouse, Nairn. Expensive restaurant with seriously good food.

Boath House, Auldearn, near Nairn, t 454 896, f 455 469, *www.boath-house.com* (*moderate*). Gracious living in lovely house with beautiful grounds and delicious food.

America, the West Indies, the Middle East, India and South Africa. In 1881, when each British infantry regiment was allocated its own territorial recruiting area and home base, Fort George became the depot of the Seaforth Highlanders. Generations of Highland soldiers trained there for colonial service, for two World Wars and for modern Cold War campaigns.

You can see splendid reconstructions of life for the soldiers here in the 18th century, and magnificent views over the Moray Firth where dolphins are often spotted.

The regiments of the garrison change over every two years, and they have the privilege of living in barracks that are the oldest in the world still occupied by a battalion of British infantry.

The **Regimental Museum of the Queen's Own Highlanders** is in the fort. Formed in 1961 by the amalgamation of the Seaforth Highlanders and the Queen's Own Cameron Highlanders, they are the present-day descendants of the two historic regiments of the northern Highlands – now amalgamated with the Gordon Highlanders to become The Highlanders. In the building formerly used by the Lieutenant Governor, the Queen's Own Highlanders preserve a superb collection of uniforms, pictures, medals, weapons, colours, artefacts and treasures, representing nearly every major campaign fought by the British Army over the past 200 years. The splendour of red coat and tartan, the glitter of gilt plate and dirk, the glint of steel broadsword and bayonet, cannot fail to stir the imagination. With its history, its atmosphere and its garrison, Fort George is unique in being a 20th-century military base where the 18th century lives on.

Nairn

Nairn, not quite 9 miles east of Fort George, is a seaside holiday town, sometimes called the Brighton of the North. On the mouth of the River Nairn, it has sandy beaches along the Moray Firth, two golf courses and a reputation for a high average of sunshine. (In Victorian times a Dr Grigor put Nairn on the map by recommending it to his patients as 'one of the healthiest spots in Britain'.) Imposing houses built by retired Victorian Empire-builders and trim villas with neat gardens give it an aura of old-fashioned gentility.

Originally called Invernairn, the old fishertown is a collection of restored cottages. In the **Nairn Fishertown Museum** (*open June–Sept Mon–Sat 10.30–12.30; adm*), in Laing Hall, King Street, you can see photographs and articles relating to the Moray Firth and the herring fisheries during the steam drifter era. There are also displays of domestic life in a fishing community. (Nairn now has a yacht marina, but no longer any local fishing boats.)

Nairn Museum, in Viewfield Drive (*open May–Sept Mon–Sat 10–4.30*), has displays of local and natural history, archaeology, geology, ethnology, and temporary exhibitions.

South of Inverness

Inverness to Kingussie

The Spey, Scotland's second-longest river, is born high in the hills above Loch Laggan, 40 miles south of Inverness, and cuts across the southeast corner of the Highlands. Beginning as a mere stream, it gathers momentum as it flows east and then north to the sea near Buckie, fed by many burns that drain from the hills on either side, turning it into a rushing tumult of water. Running between the great Cairngorms in the east and the Monadhliath Mountains to the west, the Spey is famous for its astonishing natural beauty. In spring fresh green shows through winter brown and snow still caps the mountains; in summer it is a patchwork of mulberry heather, emerald bracken, sparkling water and grey granite; in autumn snow already dusts the hills, a backdrop to the splendour of the turning leaves; in winter a white Alpine world dazzles and enchants. Leave the main roads and explore the minor roads and tracks.

Grantown-on-Spey

About 26 miles down the A9 from Inverness, branch left at Carrbridge on the A938. Grantown-on-Spey, 10 miles east, is one of Speyside's tourist centres, a Georgian town at the junction of several routes. On the banks of the River Spey and surrounded by trees, the town was founded in 1776 by Sir James Grant, one of the Highland's 'improving lairds'. With the development of skiing in the hills, this area is popular all year round. The **Grantown Museum and Heritage Trust** (*open all year*) displays the history of the town.

Revack (Gaelic for smooth hollow) **Highland Estate** (*open daily 10–6*), on the B970 between Grantown and Nethy Bridge, is 15,000 acres surrounding a shooting lodge built in 1860 when Queen Victoria made the Highlands fashionable. There is a good gift shop, with gourmet food, a licensed restaurant, a plant centre which specializes in orchids, and lovely walks.

The **Loch Garten Osprey Centre** (*open April–Aug daily 10–6; adm*), 8 miles south of Grantown-on-Spey, is known for its breeding ospreys. Americans, accustomed to seeing these 'fish-hawks' in countless numbers nesting in their rivers and estuaries, are amused by the security surrounding Scotland's few pairs, but it must be remembered that before the mid-1950s (when one pair set up their nest in a tree at Loch Garten) they had not been seen in Britain for almost 50 years. When an over-enthusiastic egg thief robbed this precious nest in 1958, precautions had to be taken. Now, it is not so unusual to see the slow, flapping flight of one of these brown and white birds, or hear its shrill, cheeping cry. The nature reserve has a lot more than ospreys for anyone who will stand still and observe. Its bird life includes blackcock, capercaillie and crossbills, and among the animals are red squirrels and deer. In winter the haunting cry of geese and the eerie honk of whooper swans float across the waters of Loch Garten.

Boat of Garten, west of the loch, is so called after the ferry that operated here until a bridge was built in 1898. It is the home of the **Strathspey Steam Railway Company**, *see above*. While you are in the area, visit the **Tomatin Distillery** (*open Mon–Fri 9–5, May–Sept also Sat 10–12.30*), Scotland's largest malt whisky distillery and the first to be acquired by the Japanese, in 1985, with guided tours and a free dram. Tomatin is derived from a Gaelic word meaning 'the hill of the juniper bushes' – curious for a whisky distillery.

Award-winning **Speyside Heather** (*open daily 9–6; www.heathercentre.com*), 6 miles from Grantown, grows over 300 different heathers; its visitors' centre will give advice on growing them at home. There is a restaurant, shop and antiques.

Aviemore

Aviemore, about 14 miles southwest of Grantown-on-Spey, is a thriving tourist centre and dormitory for the Cairngorm ski resort, teeming with energetic holiday-makers. Dominated by the Cairngorms, with several peaks over 3,000ft, this area has

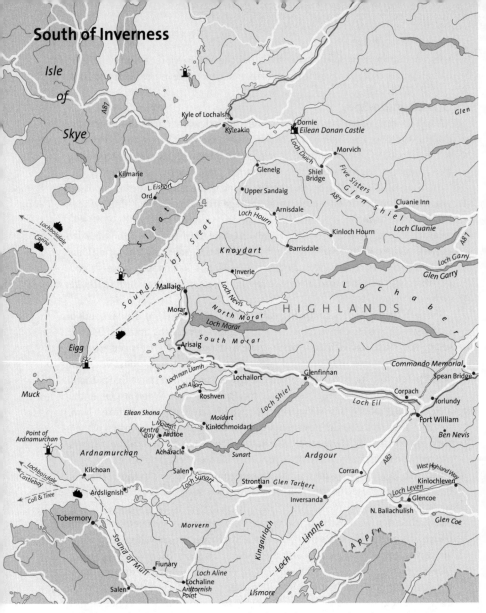

South of Inverness

Isle
of
Skye

A87

Kyle of Lochalsh
Kyleakin

Dornie
Eilean Donan Castle
Morvich

Loch Duich

Kilmarie

L. Eishort
Ord
Glenelg
Shiel
Bridge

Five Sisters

Glen Shiel

A87

Upper Sandaig
Arnisdale

Cluanie Inn

Loch Hourn
Kinloch Hourn
Loch Cluanie

Lochboisdale
Canna

Sleat

Sound of Sleat

Knoydart
Barrisdale
Inverie

Loch Garry
Glen Garry

A87

Loch aber

HIGHLANDS

Mallaig
Loch Nevis
North Morar
Loch Morar

Morar

South Morar

Eigg

Arisaig

Commando Memorial
Spean Bridge

Muck

Loch nan Uamh
Loch Ailort
Lochailort
Glenfinnan

Loch Shiel
Loch Eil
Corpach

Torlundy

Roshven

Eilean Shona
L. Moidart
Kentra Bay
Ardtoe

Moidart
Kinlochmoidart

Fort William

Ben Nevis

Point of
Ardnamurchan

Ardnamurchan
Acharacle
Sunart
Ardgour

A82

West Highland Way

Lochboisdale
Castlebay
Kilchoan
Salen

Loch Sunart
Strontian Glen Tarbert

Corran

Kinlochleven

Coll & Tiree
Ardslignish

Inversanda
Loch Leven
Glencoe

N. Ballachulish

Tobermory

Morvern

Kingairloch

Loch Linnhe

A R D G O U R

Glen Coe

Sound of Mull
Fiunary
Loch Aline
Lochaline
Ardtornish
Point

Lismore

Salen

some of Scotland's grandest scenery. It is hard to believe, now, that this was once no more than a railway station on the main line to Inverness, without even a pub. In the 1960s it was put on the tourist map as one of the first 'designer resorts' – hence many of the rather unfortunate buildings today. The skiing is centred on **Cairngorm**, to the southeast, with about 30 runs spread over two valleys. It is short on black runs but challenging enough for most people who don't mind capricious weather – it can be Arctic on the higher pistes. A new funicular railway has opened, taking visitors up to the **Ptarmigan Centre** at 3,600ft. (*Ski Hotline, t 09001 654 655; Cairngorm Centre, t (01479) 861 261. There is a café/bar and shop.*)

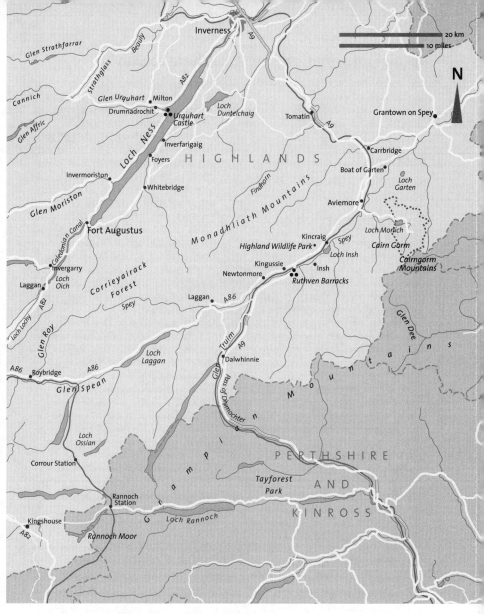

Throughout the year the surrounding countryside is a kaleidoscope of anoraks and knapsacks, psychedelic skiing clothes, or shorts and T-shirts. Within spitting distance of this hub of sporting activity lie heather-clad moors, mountains, valleys, tumbling burns and beautiful lochs. **Rothiemurchus Visitor Centre** (*open daily 9–5.30, t (01479) 812 345; adm; www.rothiemurchus.net*) gives an insight into everyday life on a working Highland estate. There is lots to see and do: walking, fishing, clay pigeon shooting, 4x4 driving, wildlife and shops. The **Cairngorm Reindeer Centre** (*open April–Oct for visits at 11am and 2.30pm; winter 11am only; t (01479) 861 228; adm*), at Glenmore, has Britain's only herd of reindeer, living free on the slopes of the Cairngorms.

Tourist Information

Grantown-on-Spey: 54 High Street, t/f (01497) 872 773; *open all year.*
Aviemore: Grampian Road, t (01479) 810 363, f 811 063; *open all year.*

Festivals

June: Highland Games, Grantown-on-Spey.

Sports and Activities

Strathspey Steam Railway Company, Boat of Garten, t (01479) 810 725. Has its own station, some remnants of the old Highland railway (closed in 1965) and a museum of railway memorabilia. You can travel the very scenic route between Boat of Garten and Aviemore in a steam train. *Regular trips June–Sept; enthusiasts' trips at other times.*
Aviemore Mountain Resort. A bewildering choice of activity: an ice rink and curling rink, a theatre/cinema, a ballroom, an artificial ski slope, a games room, squash courts, go-kart track, and children's outdoor amusements. There are also cafés and restaurants, bistros and bars, gift shops, craft shops, souvenir stalls, amusement arcades and discos.
Loch Morlich Watersports Centre, 5 miles east of Aviemore, t (01479) 861 221. Sailing courses, equipment hire, café, camping and caravanning. *Open May–Oct.*
Loch Insh Watersports and Skiing Centre, t (01540) 651 272, www.lochinsh.com. Courses in canoeing, windsurfing, sailing, swimming and skiing. Also accommodation and restaurant, *see below. Open April–Oct.*

Where to Stay

Grant Arms, Grantown-on-Spey, t (01479) 872 526, f 873 589 (*moderate*). Rather austere-looking, old-fashioned grey pile in the town centre, but managed by nice people.
Garth Hotel, Castle Road, Grantown-on-Spey, t (01479) 872 836, f 872 116 (*moderate*). Just off the square, a 17th-century black and white building in 4 acres of gardens. Atmospheric, comfortable and good food.
Tyree House Hotel, in The Square, Grantown-on-Spey, t (01479) 872 615 (*moderate*). Good value without too many frills.
Muckrach Lodge Hotel and Restaurant, Dulnain Bridge, t (01479) 851 257, f 851 325, www.muckrachlodge.co.uk (*moderate*). Comfortable, old family home set in attractive grounds, with good food. Very good value.
Auchendean Lodge Hotel, Dulnain Bridge, t/f (01479) 851 347, www.auchendean.com (*moderate*). Very special, small, elegant hotel with excellent food, including local chanterelles, wild venison and wild strawberries – and advice on wine and the best malt.
The Boat Hotel, Boat of Garten, t (01479) 831 258, f 831 414 (*moderate*). Near the loch, with 6 miles of fishing on the Spey, and a good reputation for food.
The Old Ferryman's House, Boat of Garten, t/f (01479) 831 370 (*cheap*). Very cosy, relaxed B&B with dinner on request. Delicious food and great hospitality.
Dalrachney Lodge Hotel, Carrbridge, t (01479) 841 252, f 841 383, www.dalrachney.co.uk (*expensive–moderate*). Comfortable hotel in 16 acres, and the food is excellent.

Kincraig Highland Wildlife Park (*open daily 10–6; adm; www.kincraig.com/wildlife*) is 6 miles southwest of Aviemore. Animals which once roamed free over the Highlands live here in a natural setting: boar, wolves, bears, bison and many more. You drive through the park and must leave pets in the kennels provided. There are also aviaries with indigenous birds such as capercaillie, eagles and hawks, and an exhibition on man and fauna in the Highlands.

Leault Farm, at Kincraig (*t (01540) 651 310*), has demonstrations by working sheepdogs: 10-team border collies, shearing, and lots of other sheep farm activities.

Loch Insh, a mile southeast of Kincraig, is formed by a widening of the river and is surrounded by blue hills and trees. You can take part in all kinds of water sports here, and there's accommodation and a restaurant (*see above*).

Carrbridge Hotel, Carrbridge, t (01479) 841 202 (*moderate*). Old-established, rambling, easy-going, full of character and very friendly.

Feith Mhor Country House, Carrbridge, t (01479) 841 621, *feithmhor@btinternet.com* (*moderate*). Charming Victorian house with good home cooking and friendly staff.

Cairn Hotel, Carrbridge, t (01479) 841 212, f 841 362, *cairn.carrbridge@talk21.com* (*moderate*). Old-fashioned and cosy.

Fairwinds Hotel, Carrbridge, t (01479) 841 240, *fairwindsinfo@tesco.net* (*moderate*). Small and cosy with a huge conservatory.

Hilton Coylumbridge, Aviemore, t (01479) 811 811, f 811 309 (*moderate*). Predictable, with all mod cons but not a lot of character.

Hilton Aviemore, Aviemore, t (01479) 810 681, f 810 534 (*moderate*). As above.

Smiffy's, Grampian Road, Aviemore, t (01479) 810 190. The best fish and chips in the area.

Loch Morlich Watersports Centre, 5 miles east of Aviemore, *see above*, t (01479) 861 221. Camping and caravanning. *Open May–Oct.*

Loch Insh Watersports and Skiing Centre, t (01540) 651 272, *www.lochinsh.com*. Cosy self-catering log chalets or B&B. Also Boathouse Restaurant, *see below*.

Duke of Gordon Hotel, Kingussie, t (01540) 661 302, f 661 989, *dukegor@dial.pipex.com* (*moderate*). Recently done up at vast expense, this hotel was mentioned by Queen Victoria in her diary. All the trimmings, including a piper.

The Cross, Tweed Mill Brae, Kingussie, t (01540) 661 166, f 661 080, *www.thecross.co.uk* (*moderate*). On the outskirts of town, a restaurant with charming rooms, *see below*.

Columba House Hotel and Restaurant, Manse Road, Kingussie, t (01540) 661 402, f 611 652, *www.columba-hotel.co.uk* (*moderate*). Delightfully homely former manse with a large walled garden, croquet and traditional Scottish food.

Osprey Hotel, Ruthven Road, Kingussie, t/f (01540) 661 510, *www.ospreyhotel.co.uk* (*moderate*). Nice old house with no pretensions and lots of character. Very good value.

Eagle View Guest House, Newtonmore, t (01540) 673 675, f 633 675, *eagleview@aol.com* (*moderate*). Splendid, attractive house with wonderfully friendly owners. The rooms are comfortable and the food good, with three-course evening meals.

Drumlaggan, Balgowan, just beyond Laggan, t/f (01528) 544 242 (*moderate*). Idyllic retreat with a difference, conveniently placed between the ski slopes of Aviemore and Fort William. Perfect for walking or skiing holidays, with a civilized family atmosphere, excellent food and wonderful hosts.

Eating Out

Tomatin Inn, Tomatin, t (01808) 511 291. Local colour and good value.

Craggan Mill Restaurant, on the Grantown–Dulnain Bridge road, t (01479) 872 288. In a picturesque water mill, with good food, a craft shop and gallery.

Boathouse Restaurant, Loch Insh Watersports and Skiing Centre, t (01540) 651 272. Good restaurant attached to first-class watersports centre, *see above*.

The Cross, Kingussie, *see above*. A 'restaurant with rooms' in a converted tweed mill. The food (*expensive*) is the best you will get in the area and has won many awards.

The white 18th-century church on a rocky point at the northern end of the loch was built on a site said to have been used by Druids, and used continually for Christian worship since the 6th century. Inside is an 8th-century hand-bell, shaken to call the faithful to worship, before the days of bells in steeples. The **Rock Wood Ponds**, south-east of the loch, teem with wildlife.

The gaunt shell of **Ruthven Barracks** (pronounced by some to rhyme with driven) stands on a hillock east of the A9, 5 miles southwest of Kincraig, dramatically floodlit at night. On the site of a stronghold of the Wolf of Badenoch, notorious son of Robert II, it was built after the 1715 Jacobite uprising to discourage further rebellion, and extended by General Wade in 1734.

Prince Charles captured it from government troops during his ascendancy, and it was here, after Culloden, that some 1,500 surviving Jacobites assembled, awaiting their Prince. They waited in vain, until they received the message that the cause was dead and they must now fend for themselves. On the day after the battle, Lord George Murray sat down in the barracks and wrote a long, bitter letter to the Prince, resentfully listing all the blunders that had contributed to their defeat. Prince Charles never forgave him. Before disbanding to return to the homes they had so eagerly left, the loyal Highlanders, abandoned by their leader, kindly blew Ruthven up to save it from the enemy.

Kingussie and Newtonmore

Kingussie, a mile to the west and bypassed by the A9, is another popular holiday resort. Derived from the Gaelic *cinn giuthasich*, meaning 'at the head of the first', and pronounced 'Kin-yewsie', it has one main street, backed by lovely Highland scenery. The Badenoch and Strathspey Music Festival is held here in March.

The **Highland Folk Museum** (*t (01540) 661 307, www.highlandfolk.com; Kingussie site open mid-April–Sept Mon–Sat 9.30–5.30; winter for guided tours only; adm; Newtonmore site open mid-April–Aug daily 10.30–5.30; Sept and Oct Mon–Fri 11–4.30, Sat and Sun ring to check; adm*) is a must for anyone interested in Highland life and folklore. It is on two sites, Kingussie and Newtonmore, 2½ miles apart and well worth the detour from the A9 – follow the signs. (Allow 1½ hours for Kingussie and 3 hours for Newtonmore.) It was founded in Iona in the 1930s and later moved here under the control of the universities of Glasgow, Edinburgh, St Andrews and Aberdeen. Beautifully arranged, both indoors and out, the two sites include an authentic blackhouse from Lewis, built by someone who was raised in one, a clack mill (named from its 'clacking' noise), and many exhibits of farming and domestic life, including a salmon smokehouse. At Newtonmore there is a reconstructed early 18th-century Highland township with animals.

Waltzing Waters, in Newtonmore (*open Feb–early Dec daily; shows lasting 45mins, from 11 to 5 every hour on the hour, evening show 8.30; adm*), is an indoor 'water, light and music spectacular' that defies description: go and see it.

From Kingussie south to the Tayside Border, the A9 runs through Glen Truim to **Dalwhinnie**, backed by hills, forest and moor, crossing the border through the Pass of Drumochter. Very isolated and unpopulated, this is not an area for running out of petrol on a winter's night.

The A86, west from Kingussie to Glen Roy and Spean Bridge, runs through glens flanked by steep hills, the road dipping and climbing beside **Loch Laggan**. Cars should be abandoned to walk up valleys into the hills, past secret lochans and hidden glens.

Inverness to Glencoe via the Great Glen

Some 400 million years ago, the landmass of Scotland split apart along what is now the Great Glen, the fissure being eroded by glaciers in the Ice Age until the final retreat of the ice as recently as 10,000 years ago. The Caledonian Canal, a waterway through the glen, was surveyed by James Watt in 1773. Thomas Telford started work on construction in 1803, and completed it in 1821. Of its 60-mile length, 22 miles is true canal; the rest takes advantage of the natural lochs and rivers in the rift. The Great Glen, starting with Loch Ness, is spectacular, and the best way to enjoy it is by boat. (*See* Inverness for boat hire.)

Loch Ness

Loch Ness is world famous, thanks to Nessie. It is also extremely beautiful. About 23 miles long and an average of a mile wide, its steep wooded banks form a wind-funnel, causing surprisingly rough seas at times. Depths of 900ft have been recorded, deeper than much of the North Sea. Before the road system was established, Loch Ness was the main artery of communication between the east and west.

Feelings run high over Nessie – the Loch Ness Monster – known to the cognoscenti as *Nessiteras rhombopteryx*. Sceptics may scoff, but St Adamnan, not given to telling fibs, records a sighting of her in his biography of St Columba, when they were sailing up the loch to convert Inverness. Columba, it seems, had a calming effect on her when she threatened one of his monks, and she has never been troublesome again. Setting aside whisky-induced hallucinations and wishful-thinking sightings, many eye-witness accounts of Nessie come from people whose honesty and integrity are beyond doubt. A 16th-century chronicle describes 'a terrible beast issuing out of the water early one morning about midsummer, knocking down trees and killing three men with its tail'. A monk who was organist in Westminster Cathedral saw her in 1973, and several of the monks at Fort Augustus Abbey have seen her. Thirty hotel guests saw two humps appear in an explosion of surf, and cruise half a mile before sinking, in 1961. Bertram Mills was sufficiently convinced to offer £20,000 to have Nessie delivered alive to his circus. It is impossible to drive down Loch Ness without scanning the dark waters hopefully. Anyone who spends a night at anchor in a boat on the loch will find themselves starting up in the darkness every time a ripple slaps the hull. In the film *Loch Ness*, it is depicted incorrectly as tidal.

There are two roads down Loch Ness from Inverness: the A82 is the main road down the west side, with views of the loch and quite a lot of traffic in summer. The B862/852 is much less frequented, very attractive, but with not so many views of the loch, some sections of it being inland.

You have a choice of two **Loch Ness Monster Visitor Centres**, in keen competition at Drumnadrochit, 15 miles down from Inverness on the A82, with all the information known or dreamed up about Nessie: films, documents, photographs, possible explanations, models, sonar rooms, etc. – a study for sceptic and credulous alike. You won't actually learn anything from these places except that, despite all our modern technology, microchips, satellites and robots on Mars, Nessie remains a delightful enigma.

Urquhart Castle (*open April–Sept daily 9.30–6.30; Oct–Mar Mon–Sat 9.30–4.30; adm*) is just beyond Drumnadrochit on the southern tip of Urquhart Bay, overlooking Loch Ness, with free off-road parking from where there is an overview of the whole layout. A jagged keep rises from crumbling walls against a backdrop of loch and hills beyond. This was once one of the largest castles in Scotland, dating from the 14th century.

Tourist Information

Fort William: Cameron Centre, Cameron Square, t (01397) 703 781, f 705 184; *open all year*.

Festivals

End of June/beginning of July: Great Glen Sheepdog Trials, Fort William.
July: Great Glen Gala, Fort Augustus. **Highland Games**, Fort William.
August: Lochaber Agricultural Show, Fort William.

Shopping

Spean Bridge Woollen Mill. Good for traditional Scottish tweeds and woollens; also weaving demonstrations and a restaurant. *Open daily*.
Ben Nevis Woollen Mill, Belford Road, Fort William. Quality clothes, bargains, gifts, snacks and clan/tartan research. You can also collect your official certificate for completing the 95-mile West Highland Way.

Sports and Activities

Sea Island Cruises, Town Pier, Fort William, t (01374) 207 135. Cruises along Loch Linnhe to look for seals and wildlife. *April–Oct daily, weather permitting;* 1¼ *hours*.
Jacobite Steam Train, c/o West Coast Railway Company, t (01524) 732 100; bookings, t (01463) 239 026. Fort William station to Mallaig following the 'road to the isles' through glorious scenery. It stops at Glenfinnan and allows about 2 hours in Mallaig. Booking essential. *Late June–Sept*.

Where to Stay and Eat

Loch Ness Lodge Hotel, Drumnadrochit, t (01456) 450 342, f 450 429, *info@lochness-centre.com* (*moderate*). Comfortable, friendly hotel perched above Loch Ness, with a visitor centre, and a 200-seat cinema.
Old Pier House, Fort Augustus, t (01320) 366 418, f 366 770 (*moderate*). Unquestionably the nicest place to stay on Loch Ness, a Highland farmhouse on the shore, also run as a riding centre. The MacKenzie family are multilingual, and daughter Sasha is a well-known Celtic harpist with a wonderful voice. There's also an idyllic log cabin.
Lovat Arms Hotel, Fort Augustus, t (01320) 366 206/4, f 666 677, *lovatarmshotel@hotmail.com* (*moderate*). Comfortable, overlooking Loch Ness and the abbey. Good food.
Knockie Lodge Hotel, Whitebridge, t (01456) 486 276, f 486 389, *www.knockielodge.co.uk* (*expensive*). Rambling pile overlooking Loch Ness, now a select country house hotel.
Glengarry Castle Hotel, Invergarry, t (01809) 501 254, f 501 207, *www.glengarry.net* (*moderate*). Rather grim-looking pile with the ruins of Invergarry Castle in the grounds, where the seven severed heads were presented to the chief of the MacDonells of Glengarry (*see* p.456). Extremely comfortable hotel in a lovely position overlooking Loch Oich, with friendly hosts, four-posters and a relaxed family atmosphere. *Open Mar–Nov*.
Invergarry Hotel, t (01809) 501 206, f 501 400, *www.invergarry.net* (*cheap*). Nice, and cheap.
Corriegour Lodge Hotel, Loch Lochy, t (01397) 712 685, f 712 696, *www.corriegour-lodge-hotel.com* (*moderate*). Victorian hunting lodge above the loch, with loch-view conservatory dining room, good food and comfort.
Old Pines, Spean Bridge, t (01397) 712 324, f 712 433, *www.oldpines.co.uk* (*moderate*). A restaurant with rooms. Delightfully informal, family-orientated home with excellent food and comfortable rooms, catering for children. Babysitting available.
Spean Bridge Hotel, t (01397) 712 250, f 712 001 (*moderate*). Old-fashioned, comfortable and jolly.
Invergloy House, Spean Bridge, t/f (01397) 712 681, *www.invergloy-house.co.uk* (*cheap*). Very

---

Built on the site of a vitrified fort, it was given to John Grant of Freuchie in 1509 by James IV. In 1692 it was blown up to save it from Jacobite hands. Romantics say that Nessie lives in a subterranean cave below the castle. A new visitor centre tells you all you want to know.

peaceful B&B in a converted stables, with views of Loch Lochy.

The Old Station Restaurant, Spean Bridge, t (01397) 712 535. First-class snacks, soup, sandwiches, meals and home baking (*Tues–Sun 11–5.30*). Also excellent dinner (*Fri and Sat until 9*). The train still stops here.

Glenspean Lodge Hotel, Roybridge, t (01397) 712 223, f 712 660 (*moderate*). Turreted Highland lodge in 5 acres. Good position, friendly family hosts and good food.

Roybridge Hotel, t (01397) 712 201 (*cheap*). Pleasant, well-run hotel at the entrance to Glen Roy, with passable food.

Inverlochy Castle Hotel, at Torlundy, 3 miles north of Fort William, t (01397) 702 177, f 702 953, www.inverlochy.co.uk (*expensive*). Grand Victorian mansion, *see* p.458 – so exclusive it doesn't publish its prices. (Not to be confused with Old Inverlochy Castle.)

The Grange, Grange Road, Fort William, t (01397) 705 516, f 701 595 (*moderate*). Peaceful, comfortable B&B overlooking Loch Linnhe.

Alexandra Milton Hotel, The Parade, Fort William, t (01397) 702 241, f 705 554, www.miltonhotels.com (*cheap*). Dependable hotel which has been revamped.

The Crannog Seafood Restaurant, Town Pier, Fort William, t (01397) 705 589. A converted bait store overlooking Loch Linnhe, with a distinctive red roof and verandah for eating outside in good weather. The memorable seafood comes virtually from sea to plate, and is reasonably priced.

No.4, Cameron Square, Fort William, t (01397) 704 222. Highly acclaimed restaurant.

Lochaber Siding, Fort William Station, t (01397) 701 843. Newly opened coffee shop/travel centre/craft shop.

Ardgour House, by Fort William, t (01413) 376 669 (*cheap*). Self-catering mansion (sleeping 22), former home of the MacLeans of Ardgour, in 6 acres of private garden with fishing. There is a heated swimming pool, sauna, spa pool, billiard room and lots more.

Tangasdale, Corpach, t (01397) 772 591 (*cheap*). Stay in this bungalow for Miss MacPhee's hospitality and the feeling of being in a genuine Gaelic-speaking home.

Ballachulish House, t (01855) 811 266, f 811 498 (*moderate*). 18th-century laird's house overlooking Loch Linnhe and the Morven Hills, once home of the Stewarts of Ballachulish, with strong Jacobite connections. It was burnt down by Hanoverian troops in 1746, and rebuilt. Its owners understand Highland hospitality. Charming, welcoming and full of atmosphere, with excellent food.

Ballachulish Hotel, t (01855) 811 606, f 821 463, www.freedomglen.co.uk (*moderate*). In a marvellous position overlooking the water, and the food is good.

Ardsheal House, Kentallen of Appin, t (01631) 740 227, f 740 342, www.ardsheal.co.uk (*moderate*). Real-home atmosphere, lovely views and roaring fires. The original 16th-century house has been obscured by solid Victorian additions. First-class food, wines, malts and hospitality. *Open Mar–Oct or by arrangement.*

Druimgrianach, Cuil Bay, Duror, t (01631) 740 286 (*cheap*). A friendly family house on Loch Linnhe for B&B.

Clachaig Inn, 2 miles east of Glencoe village, t (01855) 811 252, f 811 679, www.glencoe-scotland.co.uk (*cheap, see below*). Good-value hotel/hostel, with some self-catering chalets. A convivial centre for climbers, and walkers – always seems to be full of dejected people 'waiting for the weather'.

Kings House Hotel, Glencoe, t (01855) 851 259, f 259 216, www.kingy.com (*moderate–cheap*). Claims to be Scotland's oldest inn (*see* p.460). An excellent base for walkers and climbers, with a jolly 'outward bound' atmosphere, in dramatic surroundings.

Calasona, Onich, t (01855) 821 291 (*cheap*). Very cosy, clean, modern B&B run by a friendly young couple, the Macalpins. The scenery is stunning, and you have the run of the sitting room, with TV, delicious home-made biscuits and a tea/coffee tray.

At **Balbeg**, about 4 miles on, is the memorial cairn to John Cobb who was killed in 1952, trying to break the world water speed record on Loch Ness' measured mile. The memorial is inscribed in Gaelic: 'Honour to the brave and to the humble.'

Fort Augustus

Fort Augustus, on the southern end of Loch Ness, is the halfway halt down the Great Glen, a popular tourist centre with an ancient history. It was a base for St Columba and the early missionaries when travelling from Iona to convert the east. There is a pre-Christian crannog, Cherry Island, just to the north in Loch Ness.

The town's original name was Kilcumein (burial place of Cumein who was one of St Columba's followers). After the Jacobite rising in 1715, barracks were built in the town to quell further rebellion, and there are still traces of the old buildings behind the Lovat Arms Hotel. General Wade made his headquarters here in 1724, and in 1729 began the building of the fort beside the loch. It was named Augustus after William Augustus, Duke of Cumberland, at that time the fat, eight-year-old schoolboy son of George II, who was to go down in history as Butcher Cumberland. Jacobites took the fort in 1745 and held it until after Culloden. Lord Lovat bought the ruins and presented them to a Benedictine community in 1876, for the founding of an abbey which became a public school until it closed in 1993. The monks kept it alive until recently, but were forced to put it up for sale. It is now privately owned, alas, but the cloisters and gardens are open to the public.

The **Clansman Centre** (*open April–Oct daily; adm*), beside the bridge over the canal, shows how the clans survived in the Highlands, with live presentations and a talk in a Highland turf house. You can be photographed in authentic Highland costume.

The **Caledonian Canal Heritage Centre** (*open April–Oct; adm*) is in a converted lock-keeper's cottage beside the ladder of locks. It gives a comprehensive history of the canal, and has a good gift shop.

Around Loch Ness

To complete a circular tour of Loch Ness, rather than go on down the Great Glen, take the B862 from Fort Augustus back up the east side, which is prettier and quieter. Part of the way is one of General Wade's military roads, built in anticipation of further Jacobite uprisings.

Just after Whitebridge, 10 miles from Fort Augustus, the road forks. The left fork goes to **Foyers**, where there are woodland walks and a spectacular waterfall (except in very dry weather). From Inverfarigaig, about 3 miles northeast of Foyers, back to Inverness, there are a number of excavated remains of burial chambers, forts and cairns, some in good condition, including a vitrified Iron-Age fort, at **Ashie Moor**, west of Loch Duntelchaig.

Down the Glen

Going on down the Great Glen from Fort Augustus, **Tobar nan Ceann** is the 'Well of the Heads' monument beside the road on the western shore of Loch Oich. An obelisk supports the bronze heads of seven men, held together by a dirk through their hair. Beyond, steps lead through a damp tunnel to a sinister well underneath. This is where Iain Lom MacDonell, poet of his clan, washed the severed heads of the murderers of his chief, Alasdair MacDonell, 12th Chief of Keppoch, and his brother Ranald, in 1663. He presented the washed heads to MacDonell of Glengarry, who had refused to help

Lowlanders Defeated at Highbridge

At Highbridge, a couple of miles west of Spean Bridge, one of General Wade's most remarkable bridges was built across the 100-foot gorge of the River Spean. It is ruined now, but still spectacular.

Three days before the raising of the standard at Glenfinnan, two companies of government troops surrendered to a handful of Jacobite Macdonalds here in the first 'engagement' of the '45. The two companies of the Royal Scots were on their way to Fort William as reinforcements at a time when it was known that the local Highlanders were restless. They had heard a great din of pipes and noise and believed themselves to be in the midst of a mighty army. They were ambushed at the bridge by about 10 cunningly sited Highlanders and routed. The engagement, which may have been the catalyst that decided those of the chiefs who had not yet committed themselves to joining the Rising, was commemorated by the pibroch 'The Rout of the Lowland Captain'.

him avenge the murder. It was the 15th Chief MacDonell of Glengarry who erected the monument in the 19th century. Inscribed in English, Gaelic, French and Latin are the words: 'this ample and summary vengeance'.

A little further down, at **Laggan** between Loch Lochy and Loch Oich, there was a ferocious clan battle in 1544 between the Frasers and the Macdonalds. It was called *Blàr-na-léine* – the Battle of the Shirts: because it was so hot they all threw off their cumbersome plaids and fought in their shirts. Of the 1,000 men engaged, only 12 survived. The casualties included the entire Fraser hierarchy, leaving Clan Fraser leaderless: fortunately 80 of the gentlemen's wives had been left pregnant and each one produced a male heir. The recent TV series *Monarch of the Glen* was filmed near here.

Several routes meet at **Spean Bridge**, about 12 miles south down Loch Lochy. Just short of the village is the much-photographed **Commando Memorial** by Scott Sutherland, erected in 1952. A bronze group of commandos stands on a high promontory looking out over the view towards Ben Nevis and Lochaber, surrounded by the harsh terrain where they trained during the Second World War. The simplicity of the statue is dramatic.

Glen Roy is a slight detour from Roybridge, 3 miles east of Spean Bridge on the A86. At first it seems just another glen, with the River Roy tumbling down through wooded gorges to flatten out and meander at a more stately pace across the valley floor, bare hills rising on either side. Stop at the large observation car park some way along and look down the valley. A number of horizontal lines run across the hillside, quite high up, each line exactly matched by one on the opposite side of the valley. These '**Parallel Roads**' are terraces left by the receding glacier that once filled the valley. They are geologically famous because of their clarity, and date from a late Ice-Age build-up about 11,000 years ago. Glen Roy used to be well populated, but like so many others in this area it is now virtually empty. Walk on up the Roy and then follow the track east to Loch Spey where the Spey rises in the hills south of the Corrieyairack Pass, very close to the source of the Roy.

The **Corrieyairack Pass** was an important military route and it was once possible to take a carriage through to Fort Augustus on Wade's road, now just a track. Prince Charles set up an ambush here in 1745, hoping to catch General Cope's men on their way to Fort Augustus. Cope got wind of the plan and wisely decided against his march, thus thwarting and thoroughly annoying the Prince.

Northwest of Spean Bridge, at Achnacarry, the **Clan Cameron Museum** (*open mid-April–mid-Oct daily 2–5*) covers Clan Cameron, Lochaber, the Jacobite risings and the use of the estate for commando training in the Second World War. It also has a section on the Cameron Highlanders.

On the western route down the Great Glen (B8004), **Strome** is the site of Bonnie Dundee's headquarters, where he mustered the clans loyal to James VII before Killecrankie. At **Erracht** close by, tucked away up a track, a cairn was unveiled in 1993 by Colonel Sir Donald Cameron of Lochiel to commemorate Alan Cameron of Erracht, the founder of the 79th Highlanders, raised in 1793. Cameron was born in the little house above the cairn.

Continuing on down the Great Glen from Spean Bridge on the A82, you pass some rather unexpected ranch-style buildings, weathered now from their original sickly yellow, with 'Great Glen Cattle Ranch' emblazoned on their walls. During the post-war years of hardship and shortage, Mr Joseph William Hobbs, an Englishman who had spent many years on ranches in Canada, decided to open a ranch in Scotland and produce 'beef in quantity'. It was a great success and these old buildings were part of the enterprise. Mr Hobbs lived in Inverlochy Castle, a baronial mansion built for the 3rd Lord Abinger in 1863, and now the very expensive Inverlochy Castle Hotel (*see* p.455). Queen Victoria stayed here, and the plot for John Buchan's *John Macnab* was based on a true story which had its roots in the castle in 1887.

Old Inverlochy Castle, now a crumbling ruin at the mouth of the Lochy, has been stabilized by Historic Scotland as a consolidated ruin. Dating from the 13th century, it has a walled courtyard and round corner towers, one of which was the keep, and a water gate. The castle was once a stronghold of the Comyns and scene of several battles, including one in 1645 in which Montrose defeated a Covenanter army under Argyll with a loss of 1,500 men. This was one of the greatest feats of arms in Scottish history. The first Argyll knew of Montrose's presence was the sound of the pibroch: 'Sons of the dogs, come out and get flesh.' Legend tells of a Pictish settlement on this site, where King Archaius signed a treaty with Charlemagne in 790.

Fort William

Fort William is 10 miles southwest of Spean Bridge and is the southern gateway to the Caledonian Canal. It is a tourist resort, shopping centre for the whole of this area and hub of several routes. It lies in the lee of Ben Nevis, Britain's highest mountain (4,406ft) – a massive lump, with the choice of several routes to the top depending on expertise and physical fitness.

The fort for which the town was named was demolished in the 19th century to make way for the railway. It was first built by General Monk in 1655, an earth construction that proved to be of insufficient strength when put to the test by rebellious Highlanders later in the century. It was then rebuilt in stone, withstanding Jacobite attacks in 1715 and 1746. The town was named Maryburgh after the wife of King William III, before being named in honour of the king himself. It grew up around the railway and is Victorian and sturdy, with a cheerful holiday atmosphere. For Gaelic speakers its official name is still *An Gearasdan* – the Garrison.

The **West Highland Museum** (*open Mon–Sat 10–4/5; July and Aug also Sun 2–5; adm*), in Cameron Square, is crammed with interesting history, natural history and folk exhibits. It has been upgraded without spoiling its traditional features: display cases are modelled on those of the 1890s but have modern lighting. It is almost a 'museum of a museum', enhanced by modern technology, with a series of well-laid-out rooms. Montrose's helmet and many Jacobite relics are displayed. The most popular exhibit is the 'secret' portrait of the prince, used in the days when loyal Jacobites toasted 'the king across the water': a meaningless blur of paint on a tray, until you view it from the right angle on the a curved metal cylinder or glass when it is transformed into a recognizable portrait. The museum has two more of these 'anamorphic' paintings, both 'naughty pictures' for voyeurist gentlemen.

You can pass a contented hour or so leaning over the rails beside the long ladder of locks that brings the Caledonian Canal down to the level of the sea. The locks are used by fishing boats and pleasure craft, and the gates are hydraulically operated, the water boiling through sluices until the level is equal either side. Eight of the 11 locks that link Loch Linnhe with the canal are called **Neptune's Staircase**, a rise of 72ft in 500 yards, which presented Telford with an enormous problem when he built the canal (opened in 1882). Loch Linnhe is always busy with pleasure boats in the summer.

Treasures of the Earth, on the A830 out of Fort William to Corpach (*open daily; adm*), is a crystal and gem stone exhibition – rather sparkling in ultra-violet light.

Aonach Mhor ski area (**t** (01397) 705 825), developed in 1989, is accessible off the A82, 7 miles northeast of town. It has the only cablecar in Scotland – the Nevis Range Gondola – and is a popular and fast-expanding skiing resort. Although the weather is unpredictable, there are some excellent runs for all standards of skier, and the Corrie Dubh, with a new chairlift, holds snow late in the season. The Gondola runs daily throughout the year and gives access to lofty walks in summer. There is some challenging rock climbing here, too. From the top of Ben Nevis on a clear day you can see Ben Lomond near Glasgow, the Cairngorms, the Cuillins in Skye and the Outer Hebrides. The tourist route to the top starts at Achintee Farm about a mile southeast of the town on the way into Glen Nevis; it is well signed, well trodden and seldom empty. You are advised to allow about 7 hours to get to the top and back.

A fast road runs along the east side of Loch Linnhe to the **Ballachulish** (pronounced Balla-hoolish) **Bridge**, 13 miles to the south. The bridge spans a narrow constriction between lochs Linnhe and Leven, where not so long ago a small car ferry used to slither and slide on the fast current. In **South Ballachulish** look out for the stark, stone memorial to James Stewart, on a hillock just above the bridge, with a bitter inscription. Stewart was falsely hanged for the 'Appin Murder' in 1752, on which Robert Louis Stevenson based *Kidnapped* and its sequel, *Catriona*. The staunchly Jacobite Stewarts of Appin had to forfeit their lands after Culloden. The Crown factor, Colin Campbell of Glenure, known as the Red Fox, took delight in evicting Stewarts in favour of Campbells. He was assassinated during one of his forays and James Stewart was unjustly used as a scapegoat, tried before the Duke of Argyll at Inveraray by a jury of 11 Campbells, found guilty and hanged. The rough stone on top of the monument came from his farm. A memorial cairn marks the site of the Red Fox's murder in the Wood of Lettermore, about a mile west of Ballachulish, near the road.

Ballachulish was the centre for Scotland's biggest slate quarry, still full of slate but no longer used because imported slate is now much cheaper. Some of the slate workers' cottages have been converted into a teashop, craft shops, etc.

Glencoe

Glencoe is 4 miles to the east. This dramatic pass, with raw peaks reaching up on either side, is slashed by white scars of cascading water. In good weather, away from the road, Glencoe is staggeringly beautiful, with creaming burns and falls, glistening rocks and hidden lochs and glens. But when the weather closes in, there is an unmistakable aura of doom, enhanced by its well-known history. *Glen Coe* means 'Glen of Weeping', and many tears were shed on 13 February 1692. MacDonald of Glencoe, late with his oath of allegiance to King William III, provided the government with an excuse to get rid of his troublesome clan. It was an affair of the greatest possible dishonour. Campbell of Glenlyon billeted himself and 128 soldiers with the MacDonalds for several days, living as guests and accepting the generous hospitality that was such an integral part of Highland life. Glenlyon's company, acting on higher authority, rose one dawn and massacred their hosts as they slept. About 40 of the clan were slaughtered including the chief and his family. Tradition has it that the Glenlyon's piper, who was called MacKenzie, played to warn the MacDonalds. No one can drive through the glen 300 years later and not glance up into the hills and remember that bitter morning. You can almost hear the cries of the women and children, and see the bloodstains in the snow. The **Massacre Memorial**, in the village of Glencoe, is a tall, slender cross – a poignant reminder of senseless slaughter.

Glencoe Folk Museum (*open Easter–Sept Mon–Sat; adm*) is in Glencoe village. It contains many Jacobite and historic exhibits, domestic implements, weapons, costumes, photographs, dolls and dolls' houses, tools, and much else, all housed in a group of thatched houses. The **National Trust for Scotland Visitor Centre** (*open Mar–Oct daily; site open all year*) is 2 miles east of the village, full of information about the massacre, with advice on mountaineering and walking, and Ranger-led walks.

The resident warden in the Clachaig Inn (*see above*) will advise about good walks and climbing in the glen, where there is some of the most challenging mountaineering in the country, much of which is not suitable for amateurs. There is a chairlift and T-bars for skiers at the head of the glen, and good skiing on Meall a Bhuiridh, when conditions are right.

The 17th-century **Kings House**, on the left beyond the Pass, is said to be one of Scotland's oldest licensed inns. It was used as a barracks for the troops of George III after Culloden, hence its name, and has a colourful history. Its tap room was notorious in the days of cattle droving. It is now a hotel, with the original inn still at its heart.

White Corries Ski Centre, a little further on, has the longest vertical descent in Scotland – 2,600ft – and plenty of challenging skiing on Meall a Bhuiridh for those who don't mind capricious weather. Snow lingers long in Glencoe, and the skiing season continues well into the spring. (Ski Hotline, **t** 09001 654 658.)

The **Devil's Staircase** is a zigzag track, part of the West Highland Way and former military route constructed by Caulfeild in the 1740s, climbing from Altnafeadth at the head of Glencoe, across a ridge and down to Kinlochleven. It is a steepish walk with views across the glen to Buachaille Etive Mor.

Beyond Glencoe, **Rannoch Moor** stretches away to the east, a vast swampy waste-land, unpopulated except by birds, bleak even in summer. Plans to extend the West Highland Line across this most desolate of moors in the 19th century, so it could link up with Perthshire, were abandoned after a group of railway executives set out over the moor to survey it, got lost, spent the night in a bog and nearly died of exposure.

Loch Ossian is about 17 miles northeast of Glencoe as the crow flies, tucked into a valley surrounded by hills and inaccessible by road. There is a youth hostel (**t** (01397) 732 207), and the train stops at Corrour Station, where there is a new café for travellers. The energetic should get out the map and attack it on foot. It is a lovely 10-mile tramp from Black Corries Lodge, over the shoulder of Stob na Cruaiche, around the eastern end of Blackwater Reservoir and along the course of the railway.

Kinlochleven, at the head of Loch Leven, was a big iron ore smelter, founded to bring employment at the beginning of the 20th century and now closed. Most of the houses were built for the workers.

West of the Great Glen to Kyle of Lochalsh

From Invermoriston or Invergarry, off the A82, two roads join up and go west of the Great Glen to Kyle of Lochalsh, the stepping stone to the Isle of Skye. The A887 from Invermoriston goes 16 miles through Glen Moriston to meet the A87 from Invergarry. Some 12 miles from Invermoriston, look out for the cairn beside the road beyond Achlain. It is in memory of a brave man, Roderick Mackenzie, an Edinburgh lawyer, who had the dubious honour of being a Bonnie Prince Charlie look-alike. Hoping to deflect government troops from their quest for the Prince's head after Culloden, Mackenzie allowed himself to be captured. He lost his life for his gallantry, and his head was presented to Butcher Cumberland in triumph at Fort Augustus.

The A87 runs along the north side of Loch Garry, over high moorland with sweeping views. Five miles west of Invergarry, a narrow single-track road goes out to **Kinloch Hourn**, Loch of Hell. This, despite its name, is a glorious sea loch, snaking out towards the western isles, steep sided and treacherous for sailors in certain winds.

After the two roads join, the A87 runs north of Loch Cluanie, through mountain passes that are a patchwork of heather and scree, with rich wooded glens where the many rivers and burns cascade down from the surrounding hills. The Five Sisters of Kintail dominate Glen Shiel.

Festivals

July: **Highland Games**, Glengarry.

Where to Stay and Eat

Balmacara Hotel, Kyle of Lochalsh, t (01599) 566 283 (*moderate*). Just as nice in a different way, and looks across Loch Alsh.

Conchra House Hotel, Ardelve, t (01599) 555 233, f 555 433, www.conchra.co.uk (*moderate*). Comfortable country house hotel looking across Loch Duich and Eilean Donan Castle. Built in the 1760s as the home of the local constable, it was extended for use as a shooting lodge early in the 20th century. Adjacent farm cottages provide cosy self-catering apartments.

Dornie Hotel, t (01599) 555 205, f 555 429 (*moderate*). Friendly and comfortable.

Duich House, Glenshiel, t/f (01599) 555 259, duich@cwcom.net (*moderate*). Comfortable, friendly and peaceful Wolsey Lodge, dating from 1830, with delicious food.

Lochalsh Hotel, t (01599) 534 202, f 534 881 (*moderate*). Huge hotel on the water at the Kyle of Lochalsh: it's worth every penny for its position, as well as for comfort and good food.

Cluanie Inn, Cluanie, Glenmoriston, t (01320) 340 238, f 340 293 (*cheap*). A beacon of hospitality for the best part of 200 years: the epitome of a wayside inn, with cosy rooms, reasonable food and a Highland welcome.

Loch Duich Hotel, Ardelve, Dornie, t (01599) 555 213, f 555 214, www.lochduich.f9.co.uk (*cheap*). Overlooking Eilean Donan Castle and Skye. Comfortable rooms and good food. Good value.

Marabhaig, Glenelg, t (01599) 522 327 (*cheap*). Mrs Margaret Cameron's extremely comfortable B&B with views across to Kylerhea.

Glenelg Candles, by the barracks in Glenelg. A modern, all-timber Scandinavian-style structure in the garden of Balcraggie House. Good café with excellent home baking. The shop sells books and gifts as well as candles.

The Seafood Restaurant, next to the Kyle Craft and Model Shop in the old station building, Kyle of Lochalsh. Delicious fresh fish, depending on the weather.

Seagreen Restaurant and Bookshop, Plockton Road, in the village school, Kyle of Lochalsh. Licensed restaurant with relaxed atmosphere, a garden and traditional music. The food – seafood and vegetarian, no meat – is made with local ingredients. The shop sells books of local interest, paintings and cards.

Glenelg

At **Shiel Bridge** on Loch Duich, 10 miles west of Cluanie, a narrow, twisting road branches left and climbs over the **Mam Ratagan Pass**. This was the route taken by the drovers bringing cattle and sheep from Skye down to trysts at Falkirk and Crieff. It follows the course of the military road out to **Fort Bernera**, 8 miles west of Shiel Bridge. Johnson and Boswell travelled along this road in 1772, when soldiers were still working on it. The ruins of the Bernera Barracks are north of Glenelg, just before the ferry across to Kylerhea in Skye. They were built in 1722 and used until after 1790. Boswell eyed them as he shepherded an ill-humoured Dr Johnson towards what proved to be very poor lodgings: 'I looked at them wishfully, as soldiers have always everything in the best order.'

Glen Beg runs east off a narrow road 2 miles south of Glenelg, with two splendid examples of the Iron-Age brochs built to provide shelter and refuge for the chiefs and their people: **Dun Telve** and **Dun Troddan**. Their double walls are honeycombed with galleries and pierced by a single small entrance, easily defended. At the end of the road a track leads to Dun Grugaig, an earlier fort, on the brink of a steep gorge.

Not far south of Glen Beg is **Sandaig**. The house where Gavin Maxwell lived with his otters was on the beach below Upper Sandaig – since burnt to the ground. In his books, *Ring of Bright Water*, *The Rocks Remain*, and so on., Maxwell misnames the place Camusfeàrna (bay of the alders), in order to preserve its isolation. There are many other, genuine, Camusfeàrnas in Scotland, causing some confusion.

This narrow road goes right on down to Arnisdale and Glen Corran on Loch Hourn, 10 miles or so to the south. Back on the main road round Loch Duich, stop at **Morvich**, 2 miles beyond Shiel Bridge at the head of the loch. There is a **National Trust for Scotland Visitor Centre** here, with an audiovisual exhibition giving an excellent picture of the surrounding Kintail estate, with its many walks and climbs. They have details of the route out to the spectacular **Falls of Glomach**, about 7 miles on and a good walk. The 370-foot falls are among the highest in Britain, falling in two spectacular cascades over a projecting rock into a breathtakingly deep chasm. The air is full of the sound of water, and the sides of the gorge are hung with lush ferns and foliage.

Eilean Donan Castle (*open Mar–Nov daily 9–5; adm*) is 10 miles northwest of Shiel Bridge, one of the most photographed castles in Scotland and familiar to anyone who saw the film *Highlander*. Standing on a rocky island reached by a causeway, on the edge of Loch Duich, it was built in 1230 on the site of an ancient fort, and was the seat of the MacKenzies, Earls of Seaforth. What you see today is almost entirely Victorian – a loose 19th-century reinterpretation of a medieval castle, not entirely accurate. It was garrisoned by Spanish troops in 1719, supporting one of the Jacobite attempts to regain the throne for the Stuarts; in reprisal it was bombarded by English warships. It is dedicated as a war memorial to the Clan Macrae, who held the castle as Constables to the Earls of Seaforth. Among other things are interesting Jacobite relics.

Kyle of Lochalsh is 7 miles west, terminus for the railway from Inverness and the ferry to Skye. Until 1995 it was a busy little place, its car park crammed with vehicles waiting for the ferry across the Kyle, and holiday-makers hanging about, stocking up in the shops. Now, with the new bridge marching across the narrow channel, not so many people linger here. The bridge has been a bone of contention since its inception: the price of the toll has raised local blood pressure and many are the amusing stories told about the ingenious ways tried to avoid paying it. The elegant bridge has a foot planted firmly on **Eilean Ban**, a tiny island in the Kyle where the writer Gavin Maxwell lived in the lighthouse cottages for the last 18 months of his life. These have been restored as accommodation for the warden. The main room has been preserved as a memorial to Maxwell, with some of his possessions on display. Boat trips run to Eilean Ban from Kyleakin, **t** (01599) 350 040 (*see* p.516). The **Kyle Craft and Model Shop**, in the old station building, is full of railway memorabilia.

The Southwest Corner

The southwestern corner of the Highland Region is Jacobite country and still remains very Catholic. It is an enchanted land, full of beauty as well as history. Cars should be abandoned whenever possible, and sailors should put to sea.

Festivals

July: **Highland Games**, Arisaig.
August: **Mallaig and Morar Highland Games**.
Highland Games, Glenfinnan (on the
Saturday nearest the 19th).

Sports and Activities

Boat cruises run from Arisaig to Rum, Eigg and
Muck. Murdo Grant, **t** (01687) 450 224;
cruises or charter, weather permitting.
Bruce Watt, **t** (01687) 462 320); Mallaig–Inverie
three times a week.
Caledonian MacBrayne ferries from Mallaig to
Ardvasar in Skye, the Small Isles, and
Castlebay/Lochboisdale in the Outer Isles.

Where to Stay and Eat

What hotels might lack in sophistication in
this area, they make up for in hospitality.
Arisaig House, **t** (01687) 450 622, **f** 450 626,
www.arisaighouse.co.uk (*expensive*). Built in
1864 as the new mansion house for the
estate, it became one of the headquarters
for the Special Operations Executive during
the Second World War, where agents trained
in the surrounding area before being
dropped into occupied territory. A dour-
looking country house from the outside, it is
an elegant hotel inside, with good food and
expensive furnishings, enlivened by touches
of Art Deco. It has a walled garden where
they grow their own fruit and veg, terraces
and fine wooded grounds.
The Arisaig Hotel, **t** (01687) 450 210, **f** 450 310,
www.arisaighotel.co.uk (*moderate*).
Delightfully warm, friendly early 19th-
century coaching inn, serving good bar
meals. There's an above-average craft-
and book-shop, called Ginger, in an
extension.

Cuildarroch, near Lochailort, **t** (01687) 470 232,
f 510 238 (*moderate*). A Wolsey Lodge with a
proper family-home atmosphere and
excellent food.
Feorag House, Glenborrodale, **t** (01972) 500
248, **f** 500 285, *www.feorag.demon.co.uk*
(*moderate*). 5-star guesthouse overlooking
the water, with everything you could wish
for in comfort and hospitality.
Garramore House, South Morar, **t/f** (01687)
450 268 (*moderate*). A truly rare treasure: a
rambling, picturesque, cottagey-style
Victorian sporting lodge, used as the main
SOE training centre (where people like
Odette trained) in the war. It overlooks a
lush woodland garden and a family of
peacocks. Julia Moore, the owner, is a great
collector of *objets d'art*, and there are lots of
paintings of Eigg, where she spent her childhood. Her daughter, Sophie, runs an
excellent restaurant (open to non-residents)
with wonderful seafood. *Dinner May–Sept,
or by arrangement. House open all year.*
Kilcamb Lodge, Strontian, **t** (01967) 402 257,
f 402 041, *kilcamblodge@aol.com*
(*moderate*). Idyllic setting overlooking Loch
Sunart to the Morvern Hills and
Ardnamurchan, and a lovely relaxed and
friendly place to stay, with a communal
jigsaw for wet days and excellent food.
Meall Mo Chridhe Country House, Kilchoan,
West Ardnamurchan, **t/f** (01972) 510 238
(*moderate*). An imposing country house
above the village, once an 18th-century
manse and now an upmarket guesthouse,
with very good food and lovely views.
Morar Hotel, Morar, **t** (01687) 462 346, **f** 462 212
(*moderate*). Good family hotel overlooking
the Silver Sands and across to the Inner
Hebrides. Log fires, electric blankets, friendly
staff and local fishing. *Open Mar–Oct.*
Old Library Lodge and Restaurant, Arisaig,
t (01687) 450 651, **f** 450 219,
www.oldlibrary.co.uk (*moderate*). 200-year-

The **Corran Ferry**, southwest of Fort William, crosses Loch Linnhe at the Corran
Narrows, a frequent service taking 5 minutes. Several districts occupy the peninsula to
the west and south, known from time immemorial as The Rough Bounds – *an-Garbh-
chiochan* – Ardgour, Moidart, Sunart, Ardnamurchan, Morvern and Kingairloch. This
was the heartland of the Lords of the Isles, accessed by sea and guarded at every
headland by a fortress. Much of the interior is still reached only by the old hill tracks

old stable with a nice bistro atmosphere, excellent food and outside seating. There are six very cosy bedrooms, with reductions for stays of 3 nights or more.

The Prince's House, Glenfinnan, t (01397) 722 246, f 722 307, *princeshouse@ glenfinnan.co.uk* (*moderate*). An inn in 1658, now small and family-run, with cosy rooms and good food, especially the seafood.

Skiary, Loch Hourn, t (01809) 511 214 (*moderate*). A guesthouse in the wilds, only accessible by boat (with your host at the helm) or on foot. No electricity, but as cosy, comfortable and idyllic as anyone could wish. Daily or weekly terms.

West Highland Hotel, Mallaig, t (01687) 462 210, f 462 130 (*moderate*). Splendid, hospitable family-owned hotel overlooking the islands, with fresh seafood on the menu daily. *Open April–Oct.*

Belmont, Acharacle, t (01967) 431 266 (*cheap*). Very comfortable and friendly B&B, in a former manse.

Camusdarroch, between Arisaig and Morar, t (01687) 450 221 (*cheap*). Mrs Simpson offers B&B in a delightful, spacious old house tucked away in the dunes with its own beach (where some of *Local Hero* was filmed). Great hospitality and good value. Also a discreet, well-equipped campsite.

Clanranald Hotel, Acharacle, t (01967) 431 202 (*cheap*). Homely little hotel, with not too many frills but masses of lively character.

Creageiridh, about a mile out of Inverie, Knoydart, t (01747) 852 289, *www.creageiridh.co.uk* (*cheap*). Comfortable self-catering house on the water (sleeping 11). They meet you off the boat and you can rent their Land Rover.

Doune Stone Lodge, on the western tip, t/f (01687) 462 667, *www.doune-marine.co.uk* (*cheap*), only accessible by sea: they collect you from Mallaig by boat. A custom-built lodge, with not too many frills, but an excellent base for outward bounders.

Glashoille Holidays, Knoydart, t (01333) 360 251 (*cheap*). Another self-catering option on the water, with 6 bedrooms (sleeping 10).

Glenuig Inn, near Lochailort, t (01687) 470 219, *www.glenuig.com* (*cheap*). Dear little inn, on a secluded bay with a sandy beach and freshwater trout lochs nearby. First-class food, especially the seafood. *Open April–Oct.*

Loch Morar House, Beoraid, Loch Morar, t (01687) 462 823 (*cheap*). A new B&B: spotless and spacious, decorated with pine, and with breakfasts to die for. *Open Mar–Oct.*

Pier House Guest House, Inverie, Knoydart, t (01687) 462 347, *www.thepierhouse.co.uk* (*cheap*). Knoydart isn't exactly packed with places to eat and sleep: be grateful to find anywhere. Good seafood.

Salen Hotel, Acharacle, t (01967) 431 661 (*cheap*). Friendly atmosphere and delicious salmon sandwiches for lunch.

The Ariundle Centre, Strontian, t (01967) 402 279. A short distance from the village centre. A craft centre/workshop and coffee shop. Candlelit dinners available. Good food, knitwear and tweeds.

Glenfinnan Dining Car, Glenfinnan Station, t (01397) 722 300/295. Imaginative (unlicensed) restaurant for excellent meals and snacks. Booking advisable. *Open June–Sept.* An adjacent sleeping car has been restored as accommodation. *Open all year.*

Glenfinnan House Hotel, Glenfinnan, t/f (01397) 722 235 (*cheap*). Splendid old mansion overlooking the Glenfinnan Monument, with glorious views of Loch Shiel – and pipe music. *Open April–Nov.*

Sheena's Backpackers' Lodge, overlooking the harbour, Mallaig. Splendid place with a covered timber veranda where you can while away any spare time munching freshly cooked prawns, home-made scones and cakes on comfortable sofas and chairs.

on which intruders were ambushed. Rugged, mountainous and beautiful, deeply cut by lochs and glens, this is one of the most magical corners of Scotland.

The road south from Corran goes down Loch Linnhe, branching left after 7 miles to become the B8043. Keep on southwest through Morvern, cut by lush green glens alive with the sound of water and bird song. **Lochaline**, on the southern shore of the peninsula, means 'the beautiful loch'. It faces across the Sound of Mull to Fishnish

Point, linked by a fairly frequent car ferry taking 15 minutes. Silica sand is mined at Lochaline, used for making optical glass. The Church of St Columba has an extremely important collection of carved medieval gravestones.

Ardtornish House (*open April–Oct daily 10–6*) is a striking landmark at the head of Lochaline, a Victorian mansion designed by Alexander Ross in the late 19th century and described as 'a suburban villa afflicted with elephantiasis'. It stands in a woodland garden full of unusual and exotic plants, shrubs and trees. Among the outbuildings are some of Scotland's earliest concrete estate buildings.

There is no road to **Ardtornish Castle**, on a point a couple of miles east of Lochaline. Built in 1340, it was for many years a stronghold of the Lords of the Isles. The ruined keep and ramparts are custodians of a stirring past when proud, independent chiefs ruled over this territory with a total disregard for the authority of the Crown. The 4th Lord Macdonald of the Isles received ambassadors from Edward IV of England here in 1462 and signed the Treaty of Ardtornish, a somewhat futile agreement promising the Lords of the Isles lands which they already dominated, in return for an English pension and allegiance to Edward.

Fiunary is 5 miles west of Lochaline along the coast, the home of George Macleod, the left-wing Presbyterian who re-established a community on Iona in 1938 and took the name Lord Macleod of Fiunary when he was made a life peer in 1967. He was one of six Moderators of the Church of Scotland descended from the original Rev. Norman Macleod of Fiunary, who came to the Fiunary Manse in 1775. There are lovely views across the sound from this road, which peters out after 8 or 9 miles.

Strontian, north of Lochaline on the A884, is at the head of Loch Sunart. From the Strontian Lead Mines, opened in 1722, came the discovery of the element strontium, named after the place. These mines, manned by French prisoners of war, provided bullets for the Napoleonic Wars. There is a well-stocked yacht chandler here, and an inn where groups of holiday-makers often create their own spontaneous ceilidhs in the summer months. The heart of Strontian is characterized by a 1960s development of houses, pleasantly sited around a central green.

Loch Sunart is a perfect, safe anchorage for boats. For sailors, there can be few more enjoyable experiences than to sail out of Loch Sunart early on a fine morning, the wind on your quarter, the sun on your back, watching the whole of the island-studded Minch open up ahead. The **Natural History Centre** (*open April–Oct Mon–Sat 11.30–5.30, Sun 12–5.30*), at Glenmore on the north side of Loch Sunart, has good wildlife exhibitions, as well as home baking, books and gifts.

Ardnamurchan

Halfway along the north shore of Loch Sunart, the B8007 is a cul-de-sac branching west to Ardnamurchan, a rugged, windlashed peninsula, familiar to west-coast yachtsmen as the most westerly point on the mainland of the British Isles. The ruin of **Mingary Castle**, about 16 miles along, was once the stronghold of the MacIans of Ardnamurchan. It stands on a rock cliff, its walls rising sheer with the cliff on the seaward side, guarding the entrance to Loch Sunart and to the Sound of Mull. James VI came to Mingary to receive the homage of the Lords of the Isles, and was

> ## The Floating Church
> It was just off Strontian, in Loch Sunart, that the 'Floating Church' was anchored in 1843, during the 'Disruption', when the Free Church broke away from the Church of Scotland. The local laird refused members of the breakaway church land on which to build their kirk, so they bought an old ship on the Clyde, fitted it up as a church and towed it to Loch Sunart; the congregation rowed out to worship in it.

disappointed by their lack of enthusiasm for his sovereignty. The castle was taken by Montrose's men in 1644 and garrisoned in 1745 by government soldiers, who built a barracks within the walls.

Ardnamurchan Point, about 22 miles from Salen, is wild, heather-clad rock with a lighthouse at its tip (*open April–Oct daily 10–5.30*), a good 5-mile walk from the road. The lighthouse, designed by Alan Stevenson in 1848, is a listed building. The Ardnamurchan Lighthouse Trust opened an interactive display in the principal keeper's house in 1997, with relevant historical artefacts and a 'time capsule' showing a keeper's living quarters in the 1940s. The assistant keepers' cottages have been converted to holiday lets, with a small café and gift shop in stables nearby. This dramatic headland takes the full force of westerly gales and can present quite a challenge to small boats, even in lighter winds.

Moidart

Moidart, north from Salen, has a Jacobite legend in every glen, hill and loch. **Acharacle** (the 'ch' is guttural) is a scattered village at the western end of **Loch Shiel**, 3 miles north of Salen. With plenty of kit houses, this is a very typical 20th-century Highland community. From here, **Ardtoe** is another 3 miles west on **Kentra Bay**. This sheltered, sandy haven has been turned into a vast seawater reserve for white-fish farming. Ardtoe is a delightful place, popular with artists.

Just north of Acharacle, an unmarked lane to the left twists and turns out to the south channel of Loch Moidart, and one of the most stirring, romantic ruins in Scotland. **Castle Tioram**, pronounced 'chiram' and meaning 'dry land' in Gaelic, stands high on a rocky promontory overlooking Eilean Shona, reached on foot by causeway at low tide. This 13th- to 14th-century castle was the seat of the Macdonalds of Clanranald. It was burnt in 1715 by the staunchly Jacobite chief, to prevent it from falling into government hands while he was away fighting at Sheriffmuir. The tower dates from 1600; the walls enclose an inner courtyard, with several chambers.

In 1984 these ancient walls became the fine setting for an international gathering of Clanranald Macdonalds. They were entertained by their chief in the roofless banqueting hall, roasting whole lambs in the old hearth, and for a few hours the castle lived again, vibrant with pipe music and laughter. The next day an open-air Mass was celebrated in the courtyard to rededicate the Clanranald banner, said to have survived from Culloden. The ruins have since been bought by a well-meaning businessman, Lex Brown, who planned a sympathetic restoration, with a dwelling for himself and a centre for Clanranald Macdonalds. He spent vast sums of money in research and had almost total support from local people. However, the Ministry of

Interference has recently turned down his application for planning permission on the grounds that it is much more authentic to have a useless pretty ruin than a rich man's home generating employment and stability in an area where jobs are scarce.

Kinlochmoidart, 5 miles north of Acharacle, is where Prince Charles stayed after landing at Arisaig in August 1745, before going on to raise his father's standard at Glenfinnan. The present house (1882) stands close to the site of the one in which the prince stayed, which was burnt down in 1746. Here he waited while the clans were rallied to his cause, and it was here that his charm began to work on the chiefs who were reluctant to take part in the Rising. Traditionally, he sailed in through the north channel of Loch Moidart between Eilean Shona and the mainland and landed on the flat stretch of its northern shore. The **Seven Men of Moidart** mark this spot – five large beech trees, plus two saplings planted to replace the two blown down in gales.

The road twists up through Moidart and follows the zigzag of **Loch Ailort** to its head where you turn left on the A830 (another cul-de-sac) for about 6 miles to **Loch nan Uamh** (Loch of the Caves; pronounced 'naan ooa'). Here, on 25 July 1745, Prince Charles landed from Eriskay, with only seven companions, at the start of his campaign to restore the Crown to the Stuarts. A cairn on a crag overlooking the loch beside the road commemorates the event. A year later, broken and defeated, the Prince embarked from this same place to return to France, effectively ending what became known as *Bliadhna Teàrlach* (Charles' Year). You can still see the cave he hid in.

The knobbly hills of South Morar, to the northeast, mottled sepia-greyish, are rather gloomy, but the view across to Eigg and Rum is splendid.

Arisaig

Arisaig, about 7 miles west of the cairn, has a sheltered anchorage and is a peaceful holiday village from which boat cruises run to Rum, Eigg and Muck (*see* above).

Around the bay attractive houses cling to the hillside. The prominent tower of the Catholic church was erected in memory of Alasdair MacMhaigstir Alasdair, one of the greatest of the Gaelic poets, who took the Jacobite side in 1745 and was tutor/bard to the prince. The tower is a landmark for boats.

Borrodale House is a large, restored farmhouse, the core of which dates back to about 1745. It had strong Jacobite connections and was burnt down in 1746. It was possibly the home of the Macdonald of Borrodale who entertained Prince Charles.

Morar

Morar, about 7 miles north of Arisaig, stands on a sheltered bay with glorious silver sands. **Loch Morar** runs 9 miles eastwards, the deepest inland loch in Europe at over 1,000ft. North Morar, on its far shore, and Knoydart, beyond Loch Nevis to the north, are wild and roadless, accessible only by boat or on foot.

Mallaig

Mallaig is about 10 miles north of Arisaig on the western tip of North Morar. The road to it from Fort William is one of the most scenic in Scotland and under heavy pressure, being the only route to the rail and ferry terminus. This bustling little fishing port is unspoilt, in spite of being a favourite for holiday-makers. The quays are a jumble of fish-curing sheds and all the clutter of fishing: stacks of creels and fish boxes, piles of netting and gear. If you want to take a box of kippers home with you, this is the place to buy them (if you persevere). Cruises run to many of the islands, and there is a steam train to Fort William. There is a **Marine World**, and a **Heritage Centre** (*open May–Sept daily; adm*), in a new building on the site of the old rail-waymen's hostel. This is above average, covering the fishing tradition and the social history of the Rough Bounds, with videos and some fascinating photographs.

Knoydart

Knoydart is one of Scotland's most remote peninsulas, inaccessible by road, and the northern extent of the Rough Bounds. There is a track across from its only village, Inverie, to Barrisdale on Loch Hourn about 8 miles north, and another 6 miles or so on around the loch to the nearest road at Kinloch Hourn. Knoydart's history is rather gloomy. It was 'cleared' in 1853, its people shipped to Nova Scotia in the wake of the potato famine. The land was sold repeatedly during the 20th century to a succession of buyers with ulterior motives, who came, exploited and departed. The residents (none of whom are descendants of Knoydart people) mounted a successful buy-out bid in the late 1990s, and are now in control of its future.

Glenfinnan

From Mallaig it is necessary to backtrack to Glenfinnan, 14 miles east of Lochailort. The road twists and is very steep, with lovely views between banks of rhododendrons, until it drops into Glenfinnan. A column topped by a Highlander rises from a marshy plain at the head of Loch Shiel, where three glens meet against a backdrop of layers of blue-grey hills. The Glenfinnan Monument, another milestone in *Bliadhna Teàrlach*, was erected in 1815 to commemorate 19 August 1745, when Prince Charles raised his father's standard and the clans rallied to his cause.

It is easier to recall the past if you turn your back on this Victorian folly and look down the loch and up into the hills. This was where the Prince stood on that summer's day, so full of hope, surrounded by those of the clans who had already committed themselves, waiting to see if Cameron of Lochiel would join them, a man whose great influence would sway the decisions of other clans. This powerful chief had not been enthusiastic about the uprising, but he was a brave man and a loyal one. 'I'll share the fate of my Prince', he had said, and now, in the still afternoon, the waiting clans heard the skirl of pipes. They turned to watch Lochiel, at the head of 700 clansmen, marching down from the hills to join Prince Charles' cause. The well-known 'March of the Cameron Men' was composed by Mary Maxwell Campbell in 1829 to commemorate this event.

The excitement must have mounted to feverpitch, for Lochiel's action quickly brought in other clans, and later in the afternoon the great red and white silken banner was unfurled: the Prince's father was proclaimed King James III of Britain, with Prince Charles Edward his Regent. Whatever misguided folly may have influenced this final Jacobite rising, no one with a shred of romance in their veins can stand here, remembering that day, and not feel staunchly Jacobite. However, many wise, clear-sighted chiefs remained neutral, without dishonour, and it was those men, ruled by their heads rather than their hearts, who did more for Scotland's subsequent survival than the impetuous Jacobites.

The **National Trust Visitor Centre** (*open April–Oct daily 10–5; mid-May–Aug daily 9.30–6; adm*) is across the road from the monument. It provides excellent maps showing the progress of the Prince's army, and traces his wanderings after Culloden out to the islands and finally back to Loch nan Uamh.

Trains still stop at **Glenfinnan Station**, including the tourists' steam train from Fort William. The building has been rescued from disuse by conversion to a museum (*open June–Sept daily 9.30–4.30*), with a 'diner' in a carriage in the siding (*see* above).

The **Glenfinnan Viaduct**, carrying the railway across the glen, is an impressive land-mark and a considerable engineering feat. When built between 1897 and 1900 it was the longest, and first mass concrete, viaduct in Britain. If you want a leg-stretch, a track under the viaduct leads through Glen Finnan and up the river into the hills.

The Gothic-style Catholic church above Loch Shiel must be the most beautifully sited Catholic church in Scotland, overlooking the loch with the hills behind. Inside there is another monument to the Prince.

West of Inverness and the Northwest Coast

Kyle of Lochalsh to Inverness via the West Coast

The coastal route back to Inverness opens up more wonderful scenery. Take the narrow road to the left in Kyle of Lochalsh and follow the coast (and the railway) round for about 7 miles to Plockton. (The railway journey between Kyle and Inverness is well worth doing; you can sit back and enjoy unsurpassed scenery without distraction.) The views are across to Applecross and Torridon in the north and west to Skye.

Plockton, in a sheltered appendix off the southwest of Loch Carron, was laid out as a planned Highland village in 1794 and was then a working fishing village. It is now a picturesque tourist trap, its neat stone cottages, craft shops and cafés all painted and trim, with velvet lawns and palm trees, lush shrubs, birches and pines, grouped attractively around a sheltered bay dotted with pleasure boats. This is an artist's haven.

From Plockton the road follows the southern shore of Loch Carron to the narrows at Stromeferry (no ferry now), and up to Strathcarron at the head of the loch.

It is interesting to reflect that there were virtually no roads in this area until General Wade's military roads were constructed in the first half of the 18th century. When the Highlands were devastated by the potato famine in the middle of the 19th century, Destitution Committees were set up to send supplies of meal and provisions to the starving Highlanders. Some of the 'Destitution Funds' collected were used to build access roads to remote communities, making it easier to send help and providing work for the people. Some of these roads became known as 'destitution roads'.

West of Inverness and the Northwest Coast

Cape Wrath
Durness
Laid
Loch Eriboll
A838
Kinlochbervie
Loch Inchard
Rhiconich
Laxford Bridge
Handa Island
Scourie
Loch More
A836
Kylesku
Loch Merkland
Unapool
Loch Glencoul
Loch Assynt
Lochinver
Ardvreck Castle
Glencanisp Forest
Inchnadamph
Suilven
Canisp
Loch Shin
Rubha Coigeach
Ledmore
Stac Pollaidh
Cul Mor
A838
Cul Beag
Achiltibuie
Drumrunie
Summer Isles
Coigeach
Lairg
Strath Oykel
A836
A835
Stornoway
Ullapool
Mellon Udrigle
Gruinard Island
Loch Broom
Cove
Laide
Gruinard Bay
Little Loch Broom
Loch Ewe
Dundonnell
Inverewe Gardens
Poolewe
Beinn Dearg
Gairloch
Corrieshalloch Gorge
Badachro
Shieldaig
H I G H L A N D S
Redpoint
A835
Ben Wyvis
Loch Maree
Slioch
Cromarty Firth
Loch Torridon
Kinlochewe
Lower Diabaig
Beinn Eighe
Garve
Black Isle
Achnasheen
Strath Bran
Loch Luichart
Upper Loch Torridon
Torridon
Strathpeffer
Shieldaig
Ben-damph Forest
Contin
Applecross
Beauly
Beauly Firth
Tornapress
Kilmorack
Inverness
Lochcarron
Strathcarron
Loch Monar
Glen Strathfarrar
Kiltarity
Struy
Loch Carron
Plockton
Stromeferry
Achmore
Glassburn
Strathglass
A82
Erbusaig
Kyle of Lochalsh
Glen Cannich
Cannich
Glen Urquhart
Loch Ness
Affric Lodge
Glen Affric

N
20 km
10 miles

The Minch

Tourist Information

Gairloch: Achtercairn, t (01445) 712 130, f 712 071; *open all year*.

Shopping

West Highland Dairy, Achmore, near Stromeferry. Speciality cheese and dairy products from cows, goats and sheep – delicious ice creams, yogurt and cheese.

Where to Stay and Eat

Gairloch Hotel, Gairloch, t (01445) 712 001, f 712 293 (*moderate*). A huge Victorian pile overlooking the sea. Reasonably modern and comfortable, and all 66 rooms are en suite. *Open Feb–Nov*.

Little Lodge, by Gairloch, t (01445) 771 237 (*moderate*). A very special little guesthouse with a marvellous atmosphere, great hospitality and a lovely position.

Loch Maree Hotel, t (01445) 760 288, f 760 241, *www.lochmareehotel.co.uk* (*moderate, see below*). Splendidly unspoilt, and seems to be still living in the age when Queen Victoria stayed here, apart from the mod cons.

Loch Torridon Hotel, t (01445) 791 242, f 791 296, *www.lochtorridonhotel.com* (*moderate*). Victorian baronial red sandstone mansion in 56 acres, with lovely views across the loch. Tasteful rooms and the ambience of a shooting lodge, which it was.

The Old Mill Highland Lodge, Loch Maree, t (01445) 760 271 (*moderate*). Comfortable and peaceful in nice grounds. Good food.

The Old Smiddy, Laide, t (01445) 731 425, f 731 696, *oldsmiddy@aol.com* (*moderate*). A delightful old crofthouse overlooking the sea, with comfortable B&B and dinner on request. Charming, thoughtful hostess.

Plockton Inn, Plockton, t (01599) 544 222, f 544 487, *plocktoninn@plocktoninn.freeserve.co.uk* (*moderate*). A hundred yards from the seafront, comfortable, with a good blackboard menu – try their *moules marinières*.

Plockton Hotel, t (01599) 544 274, f 544 475 (*moderate*). Village inn overlooking the water, with excellent food.

Pool House Hotel, Poolewe, t (01445) 781 272, f 781 403, *www.inverewe.co.uk* (*moderate*). Family-run hotel in a lovely position by the bridge where Loch Maree pours out into Loch Ewe, and very near Inverewe Garden.

Shieldaig Lodge Hotel, near Gairloch, t (01445) 741 250, f 741 305,

Applecross Peninsula, around the head of Loch Carron and west from Lochcarron village, is another area of striking Highland scenery. There are no orchards – the name comes from Aber-Crossan, the estuary of the Crossan, now the River Applecross. Spectacular *Bealach-nam-Bo*, Pass of the Cattle, is a steep, narrow road across the southern end of the peninsula, with hairpin bends that make the adrenalin flow. The scenery is almost alpine, fringed by cliffs and rock spurs, dotted with glinting lochans and burns, with the distant hills of Skye ever present to the west. Cattle were driven over this pass from Applecross en route for the lucrative markets on the east coast. Records in 1794 tell of 3,000 cattle leaving the district.

Don't miss the excellent **Lochcarron Weavers** at Lochcarron.

There is a sandy beach at Applecross, on the west coast of the peninsula, in a sheltered bay. An Irish monk, Maelrubha, founded a monastery north of the village in 673. It became an important centre of Christianity until it was destroyed by Norsemen. A cul-de-sac runs to the south of the peninsula. It is possible to drive right around the north coast from Applecross beach, along the southern shore of Loch Torridon, Loch Shieldaig and Upper Loch Torridon to Torridon village.

The 26,000-acre **Torridon Estate** was acquired by the National Trust for Scotland in 1967. There is a visitor centre at the road junction at the head of Upper Loch Torridon, with an audiovisual presentation on the area. There is also a deer museum set up by a *www.shieldaiglodgehotel.com* (*moderate*). A Victorian country house, right by the water and backed by trees. Good food.

Applecross Inn, t (01520) 744 262, **f** 744 400 (*cheap*). Truly remarkable inn with comfortable rooms and celestial food from a local chef trained by Marco Pierre White and the Roux Brothers. Traditional music in the bar.

Aultbea Hotel, t (01445) 731 201, **f** 731 201, *aultbeahotel@btconnect.com* (*cheap*). Small hotel on the eastern shore of Loch Ewe. Quiet and comfortable with good food.

Badachro Inn, t (01445) 741 255, **f** 741 319, *www.badachroinn.com* (*cheap*). Small whitewashed inn with splendid atmosphere and a small garden on the edge of the bay.

Drumchork Lodge Hotel, near Aultbea, **t** (01445) 731 242, **f** 731 246, *www.drumchork.com* (*cheap*). Slightly bigger, slightly more expensive, with the same stunning views.

Kinlochewe Hotel, t 01445 760 253, **f** 760 253, *kinlochewehotel@tinyworld.co.uk* (*cheap*). Cheap and reasonably comfortable.

Ocean View/Sand Hotel, Sand, **t** (01445) 731 385 (*cheap*). Plenty of sea and sand, and a marvellously jolly, friendly atmosphere.

Rua Reidh Lighthouse, t/f (01445) 771 263, *ruareidh@netcomuk.co.uk* (*cheap*). 10 miles along a single-track road from Gairloch. Cheap holiday accommodation in converted lighthouse with fairly spartan bunk rooms and a handful of bedrooms, some en suite. Not too many frills, but an unsurpassed cliff-top position above deserted beaches. For those more interested in location and outdoor activity than luxury. Walking programmes and rock climbing courses.

Applecross Flower Tunnel and Campsite, t (01520) 744 268/284. An idyllic spot to camp above the village, with good facilities and a grocers. *Open Easter–Oct*. The Flower Tunnel is a licensed restaurant amidst myriad flowers, with good home cooking.

Kishorn Seafood Bar, Kishorn, **t** (01520) 733 240. Mouthwatering seafood sea-to-plate, eat in or take away. You can sit in, or outside on a fine summer day enjoying the glorious west-coast air.

Off the Rails, Plockton Station. Imaginative café/restaurant in the timber-lined station waiting room.

The Old Schoolhouse, Erbusaig. Good candlelit dinners to the strains of Beethoven, in a small crofting hamlet just before Plockton.

The Torridon Youth Hostel, t (01445) 791 284. In a lovely position on the coast.

local man who certainly knows his deer and spares you no details, both about the damage they do and the way they suffer at the hands of man. The 750-million-year-old red sandstone mountains dominate the whole of this part of the region with their distinctive white quartzite peaks.

The **Beinn Eighe National Nature Reserve** (pronounced Ben Ay) is northeast of Torridon on the A896, and was the first in Britain established for the preservation and study of the remains of the Caledonian Forest. The wildlife in the area includes deer, wild mountain goat, wild cat, pine marten and eagles. For those who like leaflets, posters and illustrated information, there is a visitor centre at **Aultroy Cottage**, just northwest of **Kinlochewe**, with advice on walks, an illuminated model of the district, and details about the work done on the reserve.

The drive west along the northern shore of Loch Torridon goes through scattered crofting townships, with sea views backed by massive hills, as far as Lower Diabaig, about 8 miles. A track goes further around the coast to a youth hostel. From here it is a lovely walk up the rocky coast to Redpoint. The A832 goes northwest from Kinlochewe along the south shore of beautiful **Loch Maree**, dominated by **Slioch** on the opposite side. Loch Maree is 12 miles long, its name derived from St Maelrubha, the monk who founded the monastery at Applecross. He spent some time as a hermit on one of the islands on the loch and, according to tradition, he is buried there.

About 8 miles on is the **Loch Maree Hotel**. Nothing seems to have changed here since Queen Victoria visited it in 1877 and stayed for six days. A rock on a bank in front of the hotel, inscribed in Gaelic, commemorates the queen's visit. This is a fishing hotel, with an impressive log of catches on the hall table. Some locals can still remember the day, in the mid-1920s, when a fishing party from the hotel ate sandwiches made from paste that had seen better days. Several of them died from botulism – others were dreadfully ill.

The A832 leaves Loch Maree soon after the hotel and goes west towards Gairloch. At **Kerrysdale**, about 10 miles beyond the hotel, the River Kerry dashes towards the sea through mossy glades and silver birches, with a few gnarled oaks and feathery rowans. Carpeting the dappled turf is a profusion of wild flowers: lousewort, milkwort, primroses, bluebells, wood anemones, orchids, and many more.

Take the very minor cul-de-sac left from Kerrysdale, past the sheltered anchorage of **Shieldaig**, and the attractive bay at **Badachro**. This was once a large fishing station where curers bought herring, cod, ling, etc., from local fishermen. Now the community life is centred on a tiny, friendly shop-cum-post office. The road, built with money from the Destitution Fund, goes on to **Redpoint**. Heather-carpeted moorland runs down to rocky cliffs and crescents of red-gold sand. The views are across to Rona and Raasay, with the island of Skye beyond. An otter swims in the sea and builds its cone of fish remains on the turf. Wheatears, ringed plovers, linnets and skylarks fill the air with song. Colonies of sea birds mass on the rocks: cormorants, shags, gulls, terns, fulmars, gannets. An old man with piercing blue eyes sits on a rock, sucking his pipe: 'You could never be bored here,' he says. 'If you run out of things to do, you can just watch the weather.'

Back at Kerrysdale, turn left to **Gairloch**, a well-developed holiday resort with excellent sandy beaches and several hotels. The hub of this community seems to be the Wild Cat Stores, purveyors of fresh milk, fresh baps and local chat. Opposite is the award-winning **Gairloch Heritage Museum** (*open April–Oct Mon–Sat 10–5; adm*), easy to miss and well worth a visit. In only a few rooms one can learn a great deal about life in the western Highlands. The exhibits range from Pictish stones and relics to Victoriana. There is a portable pulpit for outdoor preachers of the Free Church; an old ice-making machine; stuffed birds and wild animals; an illicit still; spinning wheels with the various wools and natural dyes; a wash house; a school room, with Gaelic on the blackboard; a village store; and a fisherman and his gear. The highlight is the replica of the inside of a croft house. This is imaginatively set up with press buttons to illuminate it, set the spinning wheel in motion, and animate the old woman in front of the peat fire. She sings a haunting Gaelic lullaby to the baby, rocking in a cradle. An annex contains interesting history displays and old photographs of the area.

Poolewe is 7 or 8 miles northeast of Gairloch. Stop on the bridge to watch the mighty force of water from Loch Maree thrusting its way out into Loch Ewe, forming the pool that gave the place its name.

Inverewe Garden (*open mid-Mar–Oct daily 9.30am–9pm; Nov–mid-Mar daily 9.30–5; adm; shop and restaurant open Mar–Oct; no dogs allowed in garden and no shade in car park; t (01445) 781 200*), at Inverewe half a mile from Poolewe, is owned by the

National Trust for Scotland, and famous to horticulturists all over the world. It was created by Osgood Mackenzie, a Victorian who had spent much of his early life on the Continent. If you can find a copy of his book *A Hundred Years in the Highlands* you will never regret it. Son of the Laird of Gairloch, he was given the estate at the head of Loch Ewe in 1862: a peninsula of red Torridonian sandstone, pocked by peat-hags and bare of vegetation except for heather, crowberry and dwarf willows. It is hard to believe, now, what this enterprising man achieved from such unpromising beginnings in an era when there were few roads and soil was carried in wicker creels. He planted an outer windbreak of Corsican and Scots pine, behind deer- and rabbit-proof fences. Plants were introduced from all over the world. Now, there are some 2,500 species in 50 acres of woodland, covering a steep hillside that juts into the loch, sheltered by hills behind. This exotic, subtropical paradise lies only a little to the south of the latitude that runs through Cape Farewell in Greenland. The proximity of the Gulf Stream is responsible for making this garden so fertile. Palm trees, rock gardens, peat-banks and ornamental ponds all display a profusion of blooms from Japan, Chile, South Africa, the Pacific, and many other places.

An attractive cul-de-sac drive down the west side of Loch Ewe goes as far as **Cove**. Cove Cave is so deep and sheltered it was once used as a place of worship.

Gruinard Bay, about 11 miles north of Poolewe, has sandy beaches surrounded by hills, and views out to the Summer Isles. It is a magnificent spot, with a campsite right on the beach at **Mellon Udrigle**. Gruinard Island, in the bay, was infected with anthrax during the last war and was forbidden territory for years. It was pronounced 'decontaminated' in 1987 (although it is said that anthrax spores can live on for a thousand years) and has been restored to its original owner.

Laide

A small sign beside the road, not far east of **Laide** on the bay, points the way down a cliff path to two caves. The largest was a meeting place for hundreds of years, and was used as a church for Presbyterians as late as 1843. The smaller cave was lived in by an old woman and her girl companion in 1885. Families evicted from their crofts during the Clearances used to take shelter here. It is a magic place: at the entrance to the larger cave, with its protective wall in front, it is intriguing to picture it when perhaps several families were huddled together inside, with what they had saved of their possessions and livestock. The fire would be burning, children and dogs playing, and people making do with whatever fish and game they had managed to catch. Picture it when the wind blew in from the north, rolling the great boulders on the shore. Picture it, too, in summer, with thrift and honeysuckle growing down the rocks, and the sea as calm and clear as a Pacific lagoon.

The A832 skirts Little Loch Broom (stop and look at the spectacular **Ardessie Falls** about two-thirds of the way along), and cuts across the moors. The part of the road from Dundonnell, by Feithean, to Braemore Junction, was another built with funds raised during the potato famine and hence called the 'Destitution Road' (*see* p.470). The name could not be more misleading: it's lovely.

Braemore Junction is where the A832 meets the A835 to Ullapool, about 28 miles from Gruinard. It is also at the confluence of the rivers Broom, Cuileig and Droma, known locally as 'The Valley of The Broom'. Stop at the large observation car park just before the A835. It is a staggering view down into the junction of the three valleys, the steep wooded banks ablaze with colour in the autumn. Less than a mile further on, a sign on the left marks the Corrieshalloch Gorge and the Falls of Measach. It is only a short walk from the road, and there is an alternative approach from around the corner, where there is another car park and signs, on the A835.

Corrieshalloch

Corrieshalloch is unforgettable: a mile-long box canyon, 200ft deep, its sheer rock sides festooned with ferns and mosses, saxifrage, sorrel, tufts of grasses and wood-millet. Miraculously rooted wych elm, birch, hazel, sycamore, Norway maple and beech trees cling to the sides, with goat-willow, bird-cherry and guelder-rose. There is an observation platform from which to look back at the Falls of Measach, a single cascade of 150ft that seems to hang in the air like smoke. There is an even better view from the suspension bridge that spans the gorge, but this is not for vertigo sufferers. The deep pools below are rich in trout, and, above the roar of the falls, the angry 'pruk' of the ravens can be heard, as they nest on a ledge opposite the viewing platform.

Inverness to Durness

The first part of the drive to Durness goes through farmland backed by hills, rapidly turning to moor and rugged mountain as the road crosses to the west. From Loch Broom north it is all mountains and vistas of loch, mountain and sea.

Beauly and Around

Beauly is 10 miles west of Inverness at the head of the Beauly Firth. This is Lovat country. The Lovat family came to Britain with the Normans and it was their French influence that inspired the name Beauly, *Beau Lieu*. (Romantics attribute the name to Mary, Queen of Scots, fresh from France, exclaiming, '*Ah, quelle beau lieu!*')

The centre of Beauly is a widening of the main road, making an attractive rectangular market place with the ruin of **Beauly Priory** (*open daily 10–5*) at the north end, beyond the old cross. Founded in 1230 for Valliscaulian monks, the priory is now a roofless shell. In the south wall are three fine triangular windows embellished with trefoils dating from the original building. It fell into ruin after the Reformation. The town was developed in 1840 by Thomas Fraser of Strichen, Lord Lovat. The monument in the centre of the square commemorates the Lovat Scouts, a special unit raised in 1900 by Simon Joseph, 16th Lord Lovat, to serve in the Boer War. They became famous for their service in harsh conditions, being Highlanders born and bred to survive and work in tough surroundings – men who had been stalkers, keepers, or ghillies, in harmony with nature. The imposing Victorian Catholic church just beyond the square is well attended, the Catholic Lovats having attracted a large local Catholic retinue.

The Old Fox of the '45

Perhaps the most colourful member of the family was Simon, Lord Lovat, born in about 1667. His many notorious escapades included the attempted abduction of a nine-year-old heiress and his subsequent marriage by force to her mother, a deed that left him convicted of high treason and outlawed. Having come into the title by devious means, he became a Jacobite agent, involved in conveying false information to the enemy. Outlawed once more, he turned government man and received a full pardon. Swearing loyalty to the Crown, he sent his son to fight for Prince Charles in 1745. He was beheaded, finally, in London, meeting his end with humorous dignity. 'You'll get that nasty head of yours chopped off, you ugly old Scotch dog,' taunted a Cockney woman in the crowd. 'I believe I shall, you ugly old English bitch,' he replied. Hogarth painted a portrait of him in hideous old age, just before he was helped up the steps to the scaffold – bloated, villainous, with satanic eyebrows and a cruel mouth, racked by gout. Known as 'The Old Fox of the '45', he was indisputably a rogue, traitor and hypocrite. Alternative, more kindly, reports also credit him with intelligence, charm and sly Celtic wit.

Before continuing north, it is worth making a detour to visit the glens of Farrar, Glass, Beauly, Cannich and Affric. From Beauly, take the A831 southwest down Strathglass to **Glen Affric**, through wooded glens following the River Beauly and then the River Glass. The remains of two Iron-Age forts lie off to the right from **Kilmorack**, two miles from Beauly. Here, and at **Aigas**, three miles further on, are hydroelectric dams where visitors can watch salmon being 'lifted' on their way upstream to breed. The old church has been converted into an art gallery. **Tomich** is an attractive estate village built in the late 19th century. The home farm up on the hill has been converted as a holiday centre, *see* below.

There are lovely walks in this area, where the three glens of the Farrar, Glass and Beauly meet; the scenery is gentler than that of the western Highlands but just as magnificent, enhanced rather than spoiled by the hydroelectric developments that have changed the landscape. Steep, pine-clad rocks rise from peaty lochs in broad, green valleys.

At **Glassburn**, look out for the **Holy Well of St Ignatius**, beside the road: an intriguing old headstone in a modern cairn, with engravings that include references to saints Columba (563), Bean (1015) and Margaret (1070), as well as Pope Leo XIII. There is also a poem which could be the marching song of the Temperance League:

Water bright water, pure water for me,
the drink of the wise, the wine of the free...

Stop off at the chapel of St Mary's, in **Eskadale**, a mile beyond Aigas. The pretty, early Victorian church was once the main Catholic centre for this area. In the graveyard is a memorial to an almost-forgotten episode in Scotland's history: the graves of the 'Sobieski Stuarts'. These two brothers, John Sobieski Stolberg Stuart (1795–1872) and Charles Edward Stuart (1799–1880), conned Victorian society into accepting them as grandsons of Prince Charles Edward Stuart. They claimed that their father, Lieutenant

Tourist Information

Strathpeffer: The Square, t (01997) 421 415; *open April–Sept.*
Ullapool: Argyle Street, t (01854) 612 135, f 613 031; *open all year.*

Festivals

July: Highland Gathering, Durness.
Early August: Highland Games, Strathpeffer; in the grounds of Castle Leod, with all the traditional events such as tossing the caber, putting the shot, piping and dancing.

Shopping

Achiltibuie Smokehouse, Altandhu, northwest of Achiltibuie t (01854) 622 353. Watch the process of curing and smoking, then visit the shop. *Open May–Sept Mon–Sat 9.30–5; Oct–April Mon–Fri 9.30–5.*
Balnakeil Craft Village, along the track that runs west from Durness. Rather depressing 'community co-operative of crafts' selling predictable, not always home-made wares in an atmosphere of apathy – but there are a couple of coffee shops and you might find bargains if you persevere. *Shops mostly open Easter–end Oct; some closed Sun.*
Campbells of Beauly, the Square, Beauly. Internationally known treasure-trove of tweeds, woollens, tartans and all possible Highland accessories.

Highland Wineries, Moniack Castle, southeast of Beauly, t (01463) 831 283. Home-produced country wines, meads and a variety of delicious jellies. Also tours and free tastings. *Open Mar–Oct daily 10–5; Nov–Feb daily 11–4.*
West Highland Stoneware Potteries, Lochinver, t (01571) 844 376. A working pottery, with a shop; some true bargains.

Where to Stay and Eat

Altnaharrie Inn, t (01854) 633 230 (*expensive*). An old drover's inn on the shores of Loch Broom, reached by private launch from Ullapool. Small and very select, its bedrooms are pretty, and the food is sublime. This is the only place in Scotland to have been awarded two Michelin stars – well deserved.
Inver Lodge, Lochinver, t (01571) 884 496, f 844 395, *stay@inverlodge.com* (*expensive*). Modern and characterless, but in a lovely position with every possible comfort, and excellent food.
Summer Isles Hotel, Achiltibuie, t (01854) 622 282, f 622 251, *summerisleshotel@aol.com* (*expensive*). Has been in the Irvine family since the 1960s, in a spectacular setting overlooking the Summer Isles and beyond to the Hebrides. The rooms are country-house style and comfortable, and there is a 'trust bar'. A log-cabin annexe has rooms on to a veranda. There is everything here for lovers of solitude and beauty, and it's worth every penny. *Open Easter–Nov.*

Thomas Allen, Royal Navy, was Prince Charles' son. They called themselves Comtes d'Albanie and there is a splendid book, *The Sobieski Stuarts* by H. Beveridge, about them. They lived at Eskadale House, further down the valley, and at Eilan Aigas House, where they kept deer hounds and invented several tartans with which to impress their gullible friends.

More lovely scenery is at **Cannich**, 17 miles southwest of Beauly, where the River Glass meets up with the rivers Affric and Cannich. There is a youth hostel here (*see* below). About 3 miles southeast, the **Corrimony Cairn** is a Stone- and Bronze-Age burial cairn, its passage still roofed and surrounded by a stone circle.

Although it is far nicer to walk, it is possible to drive the 12 miles up **Glen Farrar** to **Loch Monar**; it is a private road so permission must be obtained (ask at the house, or enquire locally). A road runs 8 miles up **Glen Cannich** to Cozac Lodge, and another up **Glen Affric** (one of the most beautiful glens in Scotland) to a car park, two miles short of Affric Lodge. Each glen has its own charm, with tumbling burns, lichen-hung trees,

Aigas Field Centre, Beauly, t (01463) 782 443, f 782 097, www.aigas.co.uk (moderate). Victorian-Gothic mansion on a working estate in a magnificent setting. Very friendly and ancestral. Optional field study programmes. Open April–Oct.

The Albannach, Lochinver, t (01571) 844 497, f 844 285 (moderate). A friendly place with imaginative furnishings and flagstones, wood-lined ceilings in the older bedrooms, four-posters and Victoriana. Good food in a cosy restaurant. Open Mar–Dec.

Cape Wrath Hotel, Durness, t (01971) 511 212, f 511 313, www.capewrathhotel.com (moderate). Easy-going, comfortable hotel on this far northern coast. Built in 1820 as a sporting lodge, it hasn't been spoilt by modernization, although it is well equipped. Can arrange fishing. Closed Feb.

Coul House Hotel, Contin, t (01997) 421 487, f 421 945 (moderate). Secluded 19th-century country mansion looking across to the Strathconon hills. Elegant rooms and candle-lit dinners. Very comfortable. Dogs welcome.

Eddrachilles Hotel, Badcall Bay, Scourie, t (01971) 502 080, f 502 477, eddrachilles@compuserve.com (moderate). In a beautiful position overlooking the bay and islands, with quite good food. Open Mar–Oct.

Four Seasons Travel Lodge, Garve Road, Ullapool, t (01854) 612 905, f 612 674 (moderate). Friendly modern monster on the shores of Loch Broom, with good seafood.

Inchnadamph Hotel, Loch Assynt, t (01571) 822 202, f 822 203, inchnadamphhotel@assynt99.freeserve.co.uk (moderate). Known as the 'Anglers' Retreat'. This is another genuine Highland establishment where homely comfort is important. There is free fishing for salmon, grilse and brown trout, and excellent home cooking.

Kinlochbervie Hotel, Kinlochbervie, t (01971) 521 275, f 521 438, www.kinlochberviehotel.com (moderate). Friendly family hotel overlooking Kinlochbervie harbour and Loch Clash. Excellent food. Ask the proprietor about the Sandwood Bay ghost (see below).

Mullardoch House Hotel, in Glen Cannich, t/f (01456) 415 460, www.mullhouse1.demon.co.uk (moderate). Sporting lodge in a peaceful Highland setting with 11 Munros on the doorstep: an unexpected oasis in the middle of nowhere. Top-class food, including fresh seafood from the west coast, excellent service, very comfortable rooms and every other sort of extra.

Old School, Kinlochbervie, t/f (01971) 521 383 (moderate). Restaurant with rooms in the old school house, looking out across Inshegra. The schoolroom is the dining room with school memorabilia as décor. Good plain food with plenty of fresh seafood. The bedrooms are in an annexe at the back beside a burn, cheerfully furnished and cosy.

Scourie Hotel, Scourie, t (01971) 502 396, f 502 423, www.scourie-hotel.co.uk (moderate). Comfortable and very friendly, with good home cooking. Popular with fishermen. Open April–Oct.

glinting sheets of water, all sheltered by hills. From Affric Lodge there is a good hike, 10 miles west, to the youth hostel at Aultbeath (see below). Another 10 miles or so reaches Loch Duich. It cannot be emphasized too often that anyone walking and climbing here, and anywhere else in the Highlands, should be fit, sensibly equipped, and should carry and know how to use a map and compass. They should also make sure it isn't the stalking season.

Contin, 11 miles north of Beauly, has an old coaching inn, on the west side of the River Blackwater, from which passengers used to depart on the tortuous journey west to Poolewe and Ullapool, after the roads were built in the 18th century. Telford built the first bridge here, later swept away by flood water. Dealers used to come up from England to the Contin Horse Fair to buy sturdy Highland ponies for work in the coal mines. Fair days were festive occasions, drawing people in from far afield, to jostle and gossip over the braziers, among the peddlers' stalls and animal pens.

Tanglewood House, Ullapool, t/f (01854) 612 059, *www.tanglewoodhouse.co.uk* (*moderate*). Comfort, hospitable Wolsey Lodge in a modern house with antique furniture on a headland above Loch Broom, with panoramic views from every room.

The Céilidh Place, West Argyle Street, Ullapool, t (01854) 612 103, f 612 886, *www. theceilidhplace.com* (*moderate–cheap*). Highly popular, extremely good, rather unexpected sort of arts centre where you can stay, eat wonderful seafood, and listen to live jazz, classical and folk music in the clubhouse opposite. The accommodation ranges from cosy bedrooms to a bunkhouse. There is a large, comfortable residents' sitting room with a 'trust bar', lots of books and an annexe kitchen for tea and coffee.

Kylesku Hotel, Kylesku, t (01971) 502 231, f 502 313, *kylesku.hotel@excite.co.uk* (*moderate–cheap*). Delightful little place in lovely surroundings overlooking the old ferry jetty at Kylesku, with good seafood caught in their own boat. *Open Mar–Oct.*

Culag Hotel, Lochinver, t (01571) 844 270 (*cheap*). An excellent place on the shore of Loch Inver, with glorious views.

Ferry Boat Inn, Shore Street, Ullapool, t (01854) 612 366 (*cheap*). Cosy, family-run inn looking across Loch Broom. Rather noisy.

Inchnadamph Lodge, t (01571) 822 218 (*cheap*). Splendid 'budget' hostel with dormitories and private rooms, self-catering facilities, and an on-site shop for snacks and stores.

Morefield Motel and Mariners Restaurant, Ullapool, t (01854) 612 161, f 612 171 (*cheap*). Purpose-built in the middle of a housing estate, and not what you would expect from its appearance. Its seafood is acclaimed – and it's well worth a journey to eat here.

Parkhill Hotel, Durness, t (01971) 511 202, f 511 321 (*cheap*). Friendly hotel.

Struy Inn and Glass Restaurant, Strathglass, t (01463) 761 219 (*cheap*). Great atmosphere and delicious food, with cosy rooms if you want to stay. Dougie Brown is your host.

Aultbeath Youth Hostel, t 0870 155 3255.

Cannich Youth Hostel, t (01456) 415 244.

Gillies Fine Foods, Strathpeffer. New tearoom with home-made soups and savoury snacks, shortbreads and cakes, and delicious aromas in the background.

Glen Affric Chalet Park, Tomich, t (01456) 415 369. Holiday centre with chalet accommodation and a swimming pool.

Inchbae Lodge, Garve, t (01997) 455 269, f 455 207, *inchbae@globalnet.co.uk.* Victorian hunting lodge in attractive setting, with good food in a conservatory dining room.

Ledgowan Hotel, Achnasheen, t (01445) 720 252, f 720 240, *info@ledgowanlodge.co.uk.* Originally built as a private shooting lodge, now a comfortable country-house-style hotel. *Open Easter–Dec.*

Lily Pond Café, the Hydroponicum, Achiltibuie. Unlicensed café in an attractive covered water garden, serving produce from the Hydroponicum, *see below. Open daily 10–6; May–Aug Thurs–Sun also open for dinner.*

Strathpeffer

Strathpeffer, a couple of miles northeast of Contin, was a famous spa town until the First World War. People came from overseas, including foreign royalty, to the sulphur and chalybeate springs. The springs were used as early as 1770, but it was not until the first pump room was built that Strathpeffer's fame spread over the border. It has recently been restored and is now open to the public with free tasting of the waters – hold your nose! Lying in a sheltered hollow among wooded hills, the town is a popular holiday centre, with plenty to do, including climbing Ben Wyvis, the great bulk a few miles to the north with a signed path to the top. Houses and hotels rise in neat terraces from the heart of the town, whose gently refined atmosphere has won it the title 'Harrogate of the North'. The Spa Pavilion is to be restored as a centre for performing arts, and the gardens by the pump room are in the process of restoration.

The **Eagle Stone** stands 3ft high on a hillock to the east of Strathpeffer, reached by a lane near Eaglestone House. It is a Pictish symbol stone with an engraved eagle and a horseshoe, and was the subject of one of the Brahan Seer's prophecies. If the stone should fall three times, he said, then ships would tie up to it. Setting aside a tidal wave, this seems improbable. However, the seer had an uncanny eye and it is said that the stone has already fallen twice (hence its having been cemented into place and surrounded by wire), and that on the second occasion the Cromarty Firth flooded up to the old county buildings in Dingwall. The stone is only 4 miles to the west and the River Peffery runs very close by.

Strathpeffer Craft Centre (*open April–Oct*) has craftsmen at work in what was the Victorian station. The **Highland Museum of Childhood**, also in the old station (*open April–Oct Mon–Sat 10–5, Sun 2–5; July and Aug Mon–Sat 10–7, Sun 2–5*), is a splendid celebration of childhood past, with customs, traditions and folklore, dolls, toys, games and activities, as well as a café and gift shop.

To the south, on a ridge called **Druim Chat** ('cat's back'), there is a well-preserved vitrified fort, **Knockfarrel**, one in a line of three great Pictish defence sites (the other two are at Craig Phadrig in Inverness and Ord Hill in Kessock). You can see the foundations clearly – a vast place, extending to some 810ft. This is believed to have been a stronghold of Fingal and his warriors, and many are the legends told about it.

A terrible clan battle took place in 1429 to the southwest, at **Kinellan**, between the Macdonalds and the Mackenzies. The Macdonalds, seeking vengeance after an alleged insult, lost the fight and were later punished by James IV who deposed them as Lords of the Isles.

Rogie Falls are just over 2 miles northwest of Contin, well signposted and only a short walk from the car park. This is a popular picnic spot, but it is usually possible to find a reasonably secluded spot amongst the birches, rowans and gnarled old oaks, carpeted in heather, bracken and mossy crags. There is a suspension bridge over the river where you can, with luck, watch salmon trying to leap the falls; they often achieve astonishing heights.

Five miles on, the road divides, beyond **Garve**. The A832 to the left goes southwest along attractive Strath Bran, past Loch Luichart (where there is an excellent knitwear shop) and out to **Achnasheen**, a lonely, scattered hamlet where the railway widens to provide a passing place for trains. Here the road divides again, southwest to Loch Carron and Applecross (*see* p.472) or northwest to Loch Maree (*see* p.473).

Ullapool

Ullapool is 32 miles northwest of Garve, a pleasant drive through moorland and river-filled glens, backed by hills including massive Beinn Dearg, 3,547ft, to the north. The **Lael Forest Garden Trail** is further on, with over 150 different species of trees and shrubs, all labelled. There are good views across Loch Broom, fringed with beaches and nice picnic spots.

The town was the first of a number of new fishing settlements in the Highlands and Islands, founded in 1788 in the hope of bringing a measure of prosperity to a depressed area. But by 1830 herring stocks were dwindling and the industry was in decline. The railway never got this far, the enterprise was considered a 'dismal failure' and its carefully designed grid-plan town was downgraded to a 'dreary fishing village'. Then the road improved and, when east-coast trawlers discovered Ullapool's excellent deep-water anchorage and sheltered harbour in the 1920s, the town was regenerated. It is now a popular holiday resort as well as an important fishing port and the ferry terminus for boats to Stornoway in Lewis. Freshly painted houses line the sea front in an original, curving terrace, their upper windows sharply gabled, some looking down on the jumble of quays and slipways, cluttered with small boats and fishing gear, creels, spars, nets and fish boxes. There are often east European and Russian fishing boats at anchor in the bay in the anchorage, usually scruffy-looking tubs, bringing a gabble of foreign languages to the streets. It is not unknown to find a female skipper in Soviet boats. Locals will tell intriguing tales of shady people coming and going from the boats with very little interference: splendid material for a spy thriller. The town has a good range of shops, boutiques, restaurants, cafés, bars and every sort of accommodation. Some of the street names are written in Gaelic.

Ullapool Museum and Visitor Centre (*open Mon–Sat 10–5; adm*) is in West Argyle Street in a converted church designed by Telford in 1829. It charts the development of the fishing industry and tells the life of the community over the past 200 years, including crofting, fishing, education, religion and emigration. 'The People of the Loch' is a good audiovisual presentation which you can watch from the old kirk pews.

The tourist information office will give information on sea fishing, boating, pony trekking and cruises. There is a youth hostel and the surrounding countryside is perfect for walking.

Around Ullapool

Drumrunie is about 8 miles beyond Ullapool on the A835. Turn left here on to a minor road that skirts the **Coigeach** peninsula, winding through land and sea lochs in some of Scotland's loveliest and wildest scenery. **Achiltibuie**, about 13 miles round, is a honeymooners' paradise and a perfect holiday base. Boats run to the Summer Isles, scattered a few miles off the Coigeach Peninsula.

Horticulturists should visit the **Hydroponicum**, in Achiltibuie (*open Easter–30 Sept daily 10–6 for 60-minute tours every hour on the hour; Oct Mon–Fri tours at 12 and 2; adm; t (01854) 622 202; www.thehydroponicum.com*). When its creator, Robert Irvine, took over the Summer Isles Hotel, he found that the harsh climate and poor soil, together with difficult access to distant markets, made the supply of fresh vegetables, salads and fruit to his guests almost impossible. Hence these hi-tech soilless growing houses made out of gale-proof bubble wrap, with three distinct climates: Hampshire, Bordeaux and the Canaries. Strawberries are picked fresh every day from April to October and bananas flourish. Figs, lemons, passion fruit, vines, vegetables, flowers and herbs all grow luxuriantly without soil; it is all done with liquid feed. The tour is well worth doing and includes information on the use of solar energy. There is a shop, and the Lily Pond Café, *see* above.

Back on the A835, the road runs northwards through the **Inverpolly National Nature Reserve**, a remote, lonely stretch of moorland dotted with lochs, burns and great jagged red sandstone peaks. These include Stac Pollaidh (2,009ft), Cul Beag (2,523ft) and Sul Mor (2,786ft), all very popular with climbers. There is a Nature Conservancy Council visitor centre at Knockan, less than 5 miles up the road, with full information about this area.

Ledmore is less than 8 miles beyond Drumrunie. Here, an alternative route southeast runs 30 miles through Strath Oykel to Bonar Bridge through moorland and attractive wooded valleys.

North to Cape Wrath

Ardvreck Castle (*always accessible*), about 6 miles north of Ledmore, is a jagged fang of a ruin, three storeys high, on **Loch Assynt**. Dating from 1597, it was one of the few castles to be built in this area where lack of roads in the old days made it difficult to maintain large establishments. The Community Council is hoping to consolidate the ruin. It was a Macleod stronghold, and carries in its stones a poignant echo of the last days of Montrose. There are several conflicting stories, but it is certain that gallant Montrose, fighting for Charles II, fled to Assynt in 1650 after his final defeat at Carbisdale, near Bonar Bridge. Some say he threw himself on the mercy of the Macleod laird of the time, who responded by selling him to the government for £25,000. Others say Macleod found him and took him prisoner honourably. Whatever the story, Montrose was imprisoned in this grim fortress on its rocky peninsula jutting into the loch. From here he was taken ignominiously to Edinburgh, tied back to front on his horse, and abandoned by the king to whom he had given his loyalty.

Inchnadamph Caves, south of Ardvreck, yielded evidence of occupation by early man and also bones of late Pleistocene animals, going back at least 10,000 years.

Lochinver is 10 miles to the west on the A837, along the north shore of Loch Assynt, a large-ish village and the only place of any size between Scourie and Ullapool. It is a delightful place on one of the most beautiful stretches of coastline in Scotland, with heart-stopping views all around. Two-hour wildlife cruises run from Lochinver in summer, with a chance to see some of the many birds and the colonies of seals basking on the rocks.

Dramatic sugar-loaf **Suilven** (2,399ft) is five miles to the south in **Glencanisp Forest**, with **Canisp** (2,779ft) two miles beyond to the east. Both are well worth climbing on a clear day. The coast road from Lochinver is another stunner, about 35 miles in all, joining the A894 near **Kylesku**, where a bridge replaces the small ferry that used to hold up traffic for hours in the holiday season. Boats run from Ullapool down Loch Glencoul to the southeast to see Britain's highest waterfall, **Eas-Coul-Aulin**, a fantastic sight, 658ft high, in a wild, melancholy setting that seems appropriate for such a giddy cascade, almost four times the height of the Niagara Falls.

Yet another beautiful drive of nearly 10 miles reaches **Scourie**, a popular holiday village in a sheltered bay with a sandy beach and rocky pools, slightly spoiled by a camping ground. Several varieties of orchid thrive in the mild climate here; boats run from Tarbet to the nature reserve on **Handa Island**, a mile off the sandy beach north of Scourie (*call t (01971) 502 340, for details*). Here you will see a great variety of sea birds, including razorbills, guillemots, puffins, kittiwakes and skua.

The road north goes inland a few miles to **Laxford Bridge**. An alternative route goes southeast from here to Lairg (*see* p.495), through rocky mountains that tower threateningly over the road, with sharp turns and terrifying blind summits. On a sunny day, with the sparkling waters of Loch More, Loch Merkland, and Loch Shin, it can be beautiful, but on a grey, sullen day of mist and rain, it is an awe-inspiring route.

Four miles north of Laxford Bridge, at Rhiconich, a good new road goes 4 miles west to **Kinlochbervie**, on Loch Inchard, an important west-coast fishing port. Strong currents around the northern headland make swimming here very dangerous. For one of the most beautiful beachs in Scotland, drive 5 miles on past Kinlochbervie to Sheigra, almost at the end of the road. A signpost marks the start of the 4-mile walk on a stony and in some places boggy track over rugged moorland to **Sandwood Bay**. Entirely remote, it is outstandingly beautiful, with sand, cliffs and columns of rock rising from the sea. It has a ghost – ask the proprietor of the Kinlochbervie Hotel – and some people say they experience an aura of oppression and doom here.

The drive north from Rhiconich is through a bleak wilderness of rock-strewn glens, forbidding mountains and dark, sombre lochs.

Durness

Durness is about 15 miles northeast of Rhiconich, perched on the north coast, built to withstand the fury of the elements. It is a good base for exploring this north-western corner and has plenty of places to stay. **Durness Old Church**, on a lovely sandy bay not far along the road, dates from 1619, an ivy-clad, roofless shell on the site of an older church. Just inside the entrance on the left is a recessed tomb dated 1623 and well preserved. Look for the skull and crossbone carving. It is thought to mark the site of the grave of a notorious highwayman, Donald MacMurchov, who hoped to buy his way into the afterlife by making substantial contributions to the church building. The previous church on this site appears in records in the Vatican as having contributed to one of the Crusades in the 12th century. There was a summer palace for the Bishops of Caithness where the substantial farmhouse now stands, opposite the church.

Smoo Cave is signposted from the road as you leave Durness. You must climb down a steep, stepped path where a grassy slope opposite is festooned with the names of visitors of all nationalities, picked out in pebbles on the turf. The vast limestone cavern has three compartments, formed and still being formed by continuous erosion. The main chamber is 200ft long and 120ft high, with holes in the roof and access to the inner chamber over a bridge. Here the Alt Smoo River thunders down from the cliffs into the cave in an awe-inspiring 70ft waterfall, filling the cave with spray. You can only reach the third chamber by boat, when there isn't too much water.

Cape Wrath

A passenger boat runs across the Kyle of Durness in summer (*weather and conditions permitting; t (01971) 511 376*). It connects with a minibus that goes out to the Cape 10 miles northwest (*t (01971) 511 287/343*). Officially the boat runs from 9.30, making about eight 2-hour trips a day but, as it can't cross at low tide, the timetable is flexible. It is MOD territory and you are not allowed to walk.

Cape Wrath (pronounced 'Raath') got its name from the Viking word *hvarf* meaning 'turning place', not from the furious sea which pounds at the 523-foot-high cliffs. The Clo Mor Cliffs are the highest in Britain, with veins of rich pink pegmatite running through the gneiss; the lighthouse was built by Robert Louis Stevenson's father. It is an outlandish place, compelling in its end-of-the-world, wild loneliness and a paradise for ornithologists. On a clear day you can see the Orkney Islands to the east, some 60 miles away, 45 miles west to the Butt of Lewis, and 80 miles southwest to Harris. To the north lies the island of North Rona, with Stack Skerry and Skule Skerry further east. Turn your back on the neat fort-like lighthouse and look across the bleak moor – **The Parbh**. Wolves once roamed here in great numbers; an eerie thought as the mist comes creeping in over the desolate wasteland and you look around to make sure the minibus hasn't left without you.

It is possible to walk on around the coast to Sandwood Bay, only 6 miles as the crow flies but over difficult, slow terrain with several rivers to be forded, with no track. It can take as much as 7 hours if you aren't too good with a map, and it is then another 4½ miles on down to the road at Kinlochbervie. It is much better to walk from the south as described above.

The Northeast Highlands

Inverness to John o' Groats

The A9 north from Inverness crosses the **Kessock Bridge**, where the Beauly Firth meets the Moray Firth, in the lee of the Black Isle. Until 1982 this narrow neck of water was crossed in a small car ferry, known to side-slip in violent currents. The bridge, opened by the Queen Mother, won a design award. This east-coast route to the top righthand corner of Scotland crosses the fertile Black Isle and then hugs the coast almost all the way. The worst of the Highland Clearances took place in Sutherland and Caithness, and the scattered ruins of abandoned croft houses can be found in deserted glens. Long straths run inland through vast tracts of moor and fen, linking the east with the north and west coasts. This, in Caithness, is the Flow Country, the biggest blanket bog in the world, coveted by forestry kings. Conservationists are struggling to stem the huge plantations already eating up this amazing concentration of wildlife. It is a fragile living surface of floating peat, with heather and sedges over a carpet of sphagnum mosses. Among the threatened victims are 55 species of birds related to Arctic tundra, including 70 per cent of Britain's greenshanks, meadow pipits, red-throated divers with their primitive whale-like cries, peregrines and merlins. Among the many plants threatened is the rare insect-eating sundew. Dubh lochans, black from peat, speckle the land.

The Black Isle

Although not actually an island, being securely joined to the mainland by the 5-mile isthmus between Beauly and Dingwall, the Black Isle is sufficiently sea-girt to feel like

The Northeast Highlands

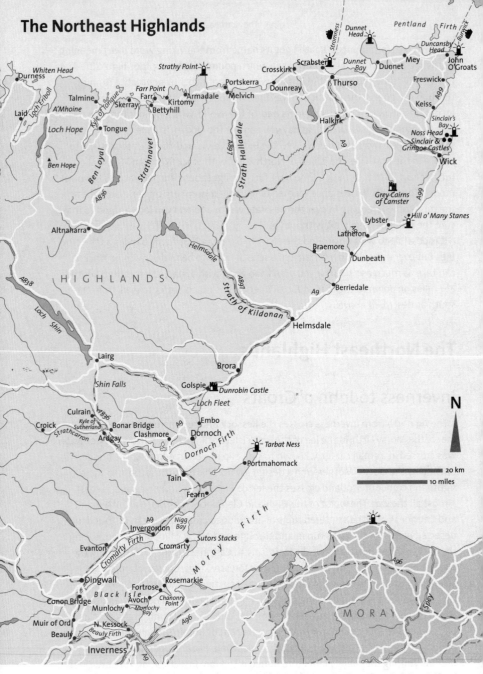

one, and has its own, soft, singsong dialect. It is made up of rolling farmland, wildfowl beaches and attractive fishing villages. The Moray Firth coast is one of the best places in Europe from which to spot dolphins, porpoises and whales. The new main road seems to rip through it in a few moments, showing little of its charms. It would be a pity to dash past it without noticing. Take the first turning right after the bridge to

Tourist Information

There are a number of seasonal information offices (*usually open Easter–end Sept/Oct*).

North Kessock: Black Isle, t (01463) 731 505, f 731 701; *open Easter–Oct.* With a Red Kite Viewing TV link-up, with live pictures of the birds on their nests (*May–Aug*); and a visitor centre in the car park, t (01463) 731 866, where you can listen to sound recordings of dolphins and seals (*April–Oct*).

Dornoch: The Square, t (01862) 810 400, f 810 644; *open all year.*

Wick: Whitechapel Road, t (01955) 602 596, f 604 940; *open all year.*

John o' Groats: t (01955) 611 373.

Festivals

July: Highland Gathering, Dingwall.
August: The Black Isle Show, Muir of Ord.

Shopping

Anta Pottery, Fearn, t (01862) 832 477. Excellent factory outlet with amazing bargains, seconds, etc. *Open Mon–Sat 9–5.*

Hunter's of Brora. Renowned woollen mills, with a factory shop on the outskirts of Brora. *Open Mon–Fri 9–5.30, Sat 9–5.*

North Shore Pottery, Mill of Forse, near Latheron, t (01593) 741 700. Working pottery, with a shop in the restored mill.

Sports and Activities

Dolphin Ecosse, Cromarty, t (01381) 600 323. Boat trips to spot dolphins, porpoises and whales.

Fortrose and Rosemarkie Golf Course. Golfers can enjoy an invigorating game in spitting distance of the sea on this 18-hole course.

Lyth Arts Centre, about 4 miles inland from Wick, t (01955) 641 270. Unexpected venture in a Victorian village school in the middle of nowhere. Permanent collection of Scottish work, plus, for two months a year, international art exhibitions. Also live performances of theatre, dance, jazz, folk and innovative music (*April–Sept*). Snack bar during gallery hours and on performance evenings. *Gallery open July and Aug daily 10–6.*

Majestic Cruises, c/o North Kessock Hotel, t (01463) 731 661. Cruises looking for dolphins, seals and wildlife on the Moray Firth. *Daily in summer.*

Wildlife Cruises, John O'Groats, t (01955) 611 353. Cruises to see puffins, arctic skuas, storm petrels and lots more. They also run tours to Orkney. *Late June–end Aug daily at 2.30, lasting about 1½ hours.*

Where to Stay and Eat

Links Hotel, Brora, t (01408) 621 252, f 621 181, highlandescape@btinternet.com (*expensive*). Next to the sea and the 18th hole, with all

explore properly – a hidden turning, easy to miss. **Munlochy Bay**, about 3 miles up this twisting minor road, is vibrant with the cackle of geese in winter, targets for sportsmen who like to see their wildfowl at the end of a gun, and a menace to farmland on which they are voracious grazers. Ask in the village for the 'Clootie Well'. This one is not so well known as one near Culloden but over the years petitioners have turned the hedgerow into an extraordinary collage of filthy rags and all materials including plastic. The origins are pagan, the superstition still strong: no one dares to remove the offerings for fear of reprisals.

The **Black Isle Wildlife and Country Park**, at Drumsmittal (*open Mar–Nov*), is good for children. In spring you can be lucky and see chicks pecking their way out of their eggs.

Avoch (pronounced 'Auch') is a picturesque fishing village with a small harbour. There are miles of bracing walks on the tidal sand flats, with views across the firth. Surnames such as Patience and Skinner are common here, dating back to Cromwell's soldiers. The **Avoch Heritage Centre** (*open June–Sept Mon–Sat*) is worth a visit.

mod cons, including a heated swimming pool, sauna and leisure facilities.

Mansfield House, Tain, **t** (01862) 092 052, **f** 892 260, *www.mansfield-house.co.uk* (*expensive*). Baronial Victorian country mansion in nice grounds. The food is excellent, the rooms very elegant with antiques, and it has a scattering of en-suite jacuzzi baths.

Royal Golf Hotel, Dornoch, **t** (01862) 810 283, **f** 810 923 (*expensive–moderate*). Large, comfortable hotel on the golf course, with reasonable food.

Burghfield House Hotel, Dornoch, **t** (01862) 810 212, **f** 810 404 (*moderate*). Turreted baronial mansion, run by the same family since 1946. It is known for its good food; there is a hairdressing salon, sauna and solarium – and they welcome dogs.

Cadboll Cottage, Fearn, **t** (01862) 871 572, **f** 871 520 (*moderate*). Attractive Victorian farmhouse with spectacular views. A comfortable Wolsey Lodge, with delicious dinners.

Dornoch Castle, **t** (01862) 810 261, **f** 810 981, *www.dornochcastlehotel.com* (*moderate*). Very special. This 400-year-old castle was formerly the Bishop's Palace and reeks of history. Its restaurant is one of the best in the area and the cellar is good. There is a sunny terrace and formal garden, a 16th-century panelled bar overlooking the Square, and nice bedrooms.

Dornoch Hotel, Dornoch, **t** (01862) 810 351, **f** 810 675 (*moderate*). Imposing seaside hotel overlooking the golf course: solid, old-fashioned and comfortable.

The Dower House, Highfield, a mile out of Muir of Ord, **t/f** (01463) 870 090, *info@thedowerhouse.co.uk* (*moderate*). More a private house than an hotel: a marvellous guesthouse where you can lounge about in front of log fires and feel at home. People travel some distance for the food.

The Factor's House, Berriedale, **t** (01593) 751 280, **f** 751 251, *robert@welbeck2. freeserve.co.uk* (*moderate*). About 10 miles north of Helmsdale, a proper family house, 300ft above the sea with wonderful views, in a sporting estate, and run to Wolsey Lodge standards by very friendly hosts.

Instore Guest House, Castle Street, Dornoch, **t** (01862) 811 263, *www.instore.co.uk* (*moderate*). Cosy bedrooms in a Victorian town house above the **2 Quail Restaurant**, **t** (01862) 811 811, *www.2quail.com*. An up-market restaurant run by a friendly husband and wife team. Just the place for a special night out. Booking essential.

Morangie Hotel, Tain, **t** (01862) 892 281, **f** 892 872 (*moderate*). More secluded hotel, with a good reputation for comfort.

Navidale House Hotel, Helmsdale, **t** (01431) 821 258, **f** 821 531 (*moderate*). Splendid fishing hotel overlooking the sea. Good seafood.

Ord House Hotel, Muir of Ord, **t/f** (01463) 870 492 (*moderate*). Delightful 17th-century laird's house in 50 acres of garden and woodland. Hospitable, comfortable and friendly.

Oykel Bridge Hotel, Rosehall, near Lairg, **t** (01549) 441 218, **f** 441 384 (*moderate*). Charming place by the river, catering mainly

Fortrose is a pleasant, no-nonsense resort town, sheltered by Chanonry Point and excellent for small boat sailing. **Fortrose Cathedral** is a mere fragment of the great church founded by King David I in the 12th century. All that remains are the south aisle of the nave and the sacristy. There are memorials here to Lord Seaforth and his family – an interesting confirmation of the Brahan Seer's prophecy about the downfall of the House of Seaforth (*see* p.56). In 1880 a hoard of silver coins dating from the reign of Robert III was dug up from the green. Cromwell recycled much of the fabric of the cathedral to build a fort in Inverness. Look out for a memorial stone on **Chanonry Point**, east of Fortrose. It marks where the Brahan Seer was burned in a barrel of tar.

Rosemarkie is a popular beach, with sand and rock pools at the far end. St Moluag founded a school and a church here in the 6th century, and tradition holds that he is buried below the Pictish stone in the churchyard. The east end of the point beyond the lighthouse is a good place for spotting dolphins, porpoises and whales.

for fishermen. There's a secluded, colourful garden, the rooms are comfortable, and the food is delicious.

Royal Hotel, Tain, **t** (01862) 892 013 *(moderate)*. Right in the middle of town and quite comfortable, although some of the decor is a bit overpowering. Reasonable food.

St Callan's Manse, Rogart, **t** (01408) 641 363, **f** 641 313 *(moderate)*. Splendidly friendly, hospitable and cosy guesthouse.

Tulloch Castle Hotel, Dingwall, **t** (01349) 861 325, **f** 863 993 *(moderate)*. Comfortable, friendly and dependable.

Castle Hotel, Portmahomack, **t** (01862) 871 263 *(cheap)*. Small, friendly and cosy with panoramic views over the Dornoch Firth.

Conon Hotel, Conon Bridge, **t** (01349) 861 500, **f** 861 879, *thecononhotel@talk21.com* *(cheap)*. Attractive inn by the River Conon, renowned for its fishing. The staff are helpful and the food isn't bad.

Fannyfield House, Evanton, **t** (01349) 830 520, **f** 830 493 *(cheap)*. A terrace of 4 cottages converted into a cosy family home above the River Skiach. B&B, with dinner on request, in relaxed friendly atmosphere.

Golf Links Hotel, Golspie, **t** (01408) 633 408, **f** 634 184, *www.golflinkshotel.co.uk (cheap)*. Right on the golf course, and only 300 yards from the beach.

John o' Groats Hotel, **t** (01955) 611 203, **f** 611 408 *(cheap)*. Recently done up. Its position on the edge of the world is dramatic.

North Kessock Hotel, **t/f** (01463) 731 208 *(cheap)*. Proper old-fashioned inn over-looking the old ferry terminal, with views across the Beauly Firth to Inverness. A listed building, it is small and cosy with a genuine Highland atmosphere and good bar lunches. The late James Robertson Justice was an enthusiastic customer here.

Portland Arms Hotel, Lybster, **t** (01593) 721 208, **f** 721 722, *www.portlandarms.co.uk (cheap)*. Early 19th-century, attractive and comfortable hotel, with friendly staff and good food.

Royal Hotel, Fortrose, **t/f** (01381) 620 236, *royal-fortrose@cali.co.uk (cheap)*. Central hotel on the corner of Union Street, with reasonable food and friendly staff.

Brambles Tearoom, Tain. Tempting home baking and a small gift shop.

Carbisdale Castle, Invershin, *see below*, **t** (01549) 421 232. Very upmarket, remarkable youth hostel, where you are expected to earn your keep.

Florence's Tearoom, Church Street, Cromarty. Excellent teas and light lunches, with home baking and delicious cakes and biscuits. *Open Thurs and Sat–Mon.*

The Tea Cosy/Chanonry Restaurant, Fortrose. Tearoom with delicious home baking by day. New name, memorable seafood and mouth-watering puddings by night.

Capaldi's Ice Cream Shop, Brora. Delicious family-made ice cream since the 1920s.

La Mirage, opposite the turning to Timespan, Helmsdale. Café, all decked out in pink with acres of photographs of celebrities, run by a great fan of Barbara Cartland (who had a holiday house in the area). The food isn't remarkable, but it's worth a visit.

Groam House Museum *(open May–Sept daily 10–5; Oct–April Sat and Sun 2–4, or by appointment t (01381) 260 961/261 730; adm)*, in Rosemarkie, has remarkable local and archaeological exhibits, all well displayed: carved stones found in the vicinity of the church, indicating the importance of Rosemarkie in early-Christian times; fragments of cross-slabs, and grave stones and a fine Pictish slab. You can make rubbings of the Pictish stones and play a reconstructed Pictish harp. There is an audiovisual show about the Picts and the Brahan Seer, and the curator is extremely knowledgeable.

Cromarty

Cromarty, on the northeastern tip of the Black Isle, about 23 miles northeast of the Kessock Bridge, is an 18th-century fishing town and port, a Royal Burgh for seven centuries. Some of its old merchants' houses are important examples of domestic architecture of the period. Sheltered by the great headland of the South Sutor at the mouth of the Cromarty Firth, rows of terraced cottages stand gable-end-on to the street, hunched against the wind, forming rope walks where the fisherwomen used to stretch out the new ropes from the rope factory.

The town was bought in 1772 by George Ross, some of whose descendants still live here. He built the harbour, founded a cloth factory, the rope factory, a nail and spade factory, a brewery and a lace industry, and built a Gaelic chapel for the Highlanders who came flocking to the town for employment in 1783. You can see the poignant ruins on the hill above the town, where an imposing monument to Hugh Miller serves as a landmark for mariners. Cromarty has been skilfully and imaginatively restored. The old brewery is now a small conference centre and can be hired by groups for seminars and residential courses. Part of the old ropeworks is now housing and a restaurant. The sheltered bay was used as an anchorage for destroyer flotillas in the First World War.

Cromarty Courthouse (*open April–Oct daily 10–5; Nov, Dec and Mar daily 12–4; Jan and Feb by appointment; adm; t (01381) 600 418; www.cromarty-courthouse.org.uk*) is another of the town's successful restorations of an old building, and has won several deserved awards. It is an '18th-century experience', with a court-room scene and animated models. There is a visitor centre and museum, and a shop where you can hire a 'walkman tour of Cromarty' narrated in English, French and German, written by Hugh Miller himself (*see* below), included in your entry ticket.

Hugh Miller's Cottage (*open May–Sept daily 12–4, or by appointment; adm; t (01381) 600 245*), in Church Street, offers a nostalgic journey into the past. This long, low, thatched cottage with crow-stepped gables, its tiny upper windows half-buried in the eaves, was built *c.* 1711 by the great-grandfather of Hugh Miller (1802–56). He rose from simple beginnings to become a famous geologist, stonemason, naturalist, theologian and writer. (Among other things, he wrote about the Brahan Seer in *Scenes and Legends of the North of Scotland*.) A radical theologian, torn apart by religious doubt and fear of impending insanity, he shot himself on Christmas Eve 1856 having recorded 'a fearful dream'. He was in great pain, which may have contributed to his suicide.

Restored by the National Trust for Scotland, the cottage contains a museum devoted to collections of his writings, personal belongings, geological specimens, and such endearing memorabilia as the wooden chair in which his mother sat to nurse him. A Hugh Miller Centre, to mark the bicentenary of his birth, will adjoin the cottage and include a study centre, a state-of-the-art geological exhibition with Miller's fossils on display, a re-created family drawing room, and lots more.

In four restored cottages near the seafront, the work of resident craftsmen and women are displayed and sold: pottery, silver, printed hangings, jewellery, etc. There is also a small art gallery with exhibitions of local paintings.

The **North and South Sutors**, who guard the entrance to the Firth like two massive sentinels, were once two giant cobblers (souter is the Scots word for shoemaker) who protected the Black Isle from pirates. For some reason – perhaps they slept on duty – they were turned to stone. A nice woodland walk from the village to the top of the South Souter (where you will see the remains of First and Second World War gun emplacements) gives fantastic views of the Dornoch Firth, Nairn and the Cromarty

Firth. It's a good spot to see the oil rigs, when they are there. There are foreshore walks and long expanses of sand lining Cromarty Bay. Charles II landed here on his way to be crowned at Scone in 1650. A car ferry runs between Cromarty and Nigg (*May–Sept daily, t (01862) 871 255*).

Continuing around the Black Isle, the B9163 runs down the coastal plain south of the firth 17 miles to **Conon Bridge** and across the neck of land that joins the Black Isle to the mainland, about 4 miles to **Muir of Ord**.

To complete a circular tour of this attractive peninsula, a one-track road skirts the northern shore of the Beauly Firth for 10 miles back to the Kessock Bridge. It hugs the shore for the last stretch, where the tidal flats are rich in wildfowl, backed by blue-grey hills to the north. The rose-red shell of a ruined castle (*private but clearly visible*) behind an ivy-clad wall at the western end of the firth is Redcastle, originally built by William the Lion in 1178 and reputed to have been one of the oldest continuously inhabited strongholds in Scotland. The original castle, Edradour, passed through several hands before it was annexed by the Crown after the fall from power of the notorious Douglas family. The Mackenzies held it for 200 years from 1570. According to stories, they resorted to sorcery and human sacrifices in an attempt to save the land from a cattle plague. This illicit activity backfired, and the family was henceforth under a curse.

Until it was abandoned in the 1950s it was a splendid lived-in castle with well-tended gardens; now it is an architectural tragedy, its present owners having resisted all attempts to save it: its final death-throes are imminent, but there is still pressure to find a buyer who would restore it.

North Kessock, an attractive village straggling along the shore of the Beauly Firth, merging with Charlestown to the west, its core of attractive fishermen's cottages now somewhat swamped by new housing, used to be the ferry terminal. Locals are fiercely fighting plans by a speculator to develop the land to the west of the village with many more houses, industrial buildings and a golf course with hotel and club house.

Dingwall

Dingwall, at the southwestern corner of the Cromarty Firth, is at the junction of several main routes. It is a busy little market town, its curious name being derived from the Norse words *thing* (parliament or council) and *volle* (place). Macbeth may have been born in the castle that once stood in Castle Street, of which only a few old stones remain. Robert the Bruce's wife was held prisoner here during part of his exile. It is hard to believe that Dingwall was a thriving port, before the waterway at the mouth of the River Peffery silted up. The canal at the end of Ferry Road was built by Telford in an attempt to cut through the encroaching mudflats.

Dingwall has always been an important cattle and livestock market, and even today it is just possible to hear a few exchanges in Gaelic around the market square any Wednesday.

The **Town House** (*open Easter–Sept; adm*), dating from 1730, is a museum. A special exhibition relates to General Sir Hector Macdonald (1853–1903), popularly known as 'Fighting Mac' – a local man who rose from the ranks to become a distinguished soldier. He served in the Second Afghan War, the Egyptian Police and the Egyptian Army, and was given command of troops in Ceylon in 1902. He surpassed himself at the Battle of Omdurman in 1898 and was greatly revered. Subsequently 'grave charges' that were almost certainly totally unfounded, were laid against him and he committed suicide. Deeply shocked by this appalling smear against their beloved hero, the locals erected the impressive monument to him on Mitchell Hill, a battlemented tower that is a landmark for miles around.

The surprising **Indian temple** on the hill above Evanton, known as Fyrish Monument, was a folly erected by General Sir Hector Munro (1726–1805) as a philanthropic gesture, giving work to the unemployed in the area. It is modelled on the gateway to Negapatam, an Indian town captured by Sir Hector in 1781. It is clearly visible from the road, but much more fun close to and not an exacting climb.

The Tain Peninsula

Although the exploitation of North Sea oil fields has inevitably changed the character of the hammerhead peninsula jutting eastwards between Nigg Bay and Tain, there are plenty of attractions to tempt the traveller to make a detour from the journey north.

Invergordon

The A9 bypasses Invergordon, a busy industrial centre on the western tip of Nigg Bay, dominated by all the surrealistic constructions built for the oil industry. The Cromarty Firth is one of the finest deep-water anchorages in the world and is now one of the most important European centres for the repair and maintenance of the exploration rigs. There is something curiously beautiful about some of these giant skeletons whose fragile-looking girders are built to withstand the full force of a North Sea gale. Inland, here and there, a lane or wood or farm is as peaceful as it was before the oil men came.

Fearn

Don't let the A9 sweep you past the B9165 turning to Fearn, 11 miles northeast of Invergordon and the hub of the peninsula, with cottages and pretty gardens grouped around a green. In the restored 13th-century **Fearn Abbey**, the nave and choir are still used as the parish church. Fearn Abbey was the seat of the first martyr of the Scottish Reformation, Abbot Patrick Hamilton, who was burned at St Andrews for heresy in 1528 (see St Andrews, p.340). The Reformation was responsible for the decay of the original abbey. In 1742, after it had been partly rebuilt to accommodate the parish church, the soaring voices of the parishioners had a disastrous effect on the stone-vaulted roof, which crashed down and killed 44 of them.

Tarbat Ness, about 9 miles beyond Fearn on the northern tip of the peninsula, has one of the highest lighthouses in Britain, warning ships of the dangerous sandbanks threatening the entrance to the Dornoch Firth. The Norsemen called them Gizzen

Briggs and were no doubt among their earliest victims. The views are stupendous, and there are sometimes seals basking on the rocks below.

Portmahomack, a couple of miles south of the lighthouse, is a popular resort sprawling upwards around a sheltered harbour that once supported a fishing fleet. There is a nine-hole golf course, and the **Tarbat Discovery Centre** (*open Mar–Dec*), in an historic old church, which focuses on local archaeology and a major current dig.

Shandwick is halfway down the east coast, 8 miles south of the lighthouse. Fossil hunters may be rewarded if they search below the red sandstone cliffs and in the caves here. The 9-foot-tall stone cross slab above the village was erected in memory of one of three Norse princes who were shipwrecked on one of the reefs.

Tain

Tain – like Dingwall derived from the Norse word *thing*, a meeting place or parliament – stands on the south side of the Dornoch Firth. It is a holiday resort and market centre for the surrounding area and is of more historic than aesthetic interest, though it has a pleasant, east-coast sturdiness.

St Duthus was born here in about 1000, and his bones were brought back here after his death in Ireland to be interred in **St Duthus Chapel** (*always accessible*), now an overgrown ruin in the cemetery between the town and the 18-hole golf course. It was built on the site of his birthplace as a 'prayer cell', with the resident hermit guarding the sacred relics, which were believed to work miracles and attracted hundreds of pilgrims.

Elizabeth de Burgh, wife of Robert the Bruce, and her children, took refuge here when fleeing to Orkney, relying on its status as a sanctuary for fugitives. This was violated by the Earl of Ross, who ignored the safety zone and captured her in 1307 – an act Scotland did not forget. The chapel was burnt down in 1427 by a smuggler, McNeill of Creich, to destroy an enemy he had chased inside.

St Duthus Collegiate Church was built in 1360 on the site of an earlier church, traces of which can be seen in the chapter house. It is now a memorial, no longer used for worship. After the chapel (*see* above) was burnt down, the relics of St Duthus were brought here, becoming the focus for pilgrims until they disappeared in 1560.

Among the visitors to the church and reliquary was James IV, seeking absolution for having been instrumental in his father's death. He came every year for 20 years, but not entirely for religious reasons. He liked to keep in touch with his people all over Scotland and had established his favourite mistress, Janet Kennedy, in Darnaway Castle in Morayshire, giving him a friendly staging post.

Look for the stained-glass windows showing Malcolm Canmore and Queen Margaret bestowing a royal charter on the town; and an assembly of the Scottish parliament adopting John Knox's Confessions of Faith in 1560.

Tain Through Time (*open mid-Mar–Oct daily 10–6; Nov–mid-Mar Sat only 12–4; adm, includes a tour of the church and the museum; t (01862) 894 089*) has a sound and light show, guides in costume, an audiovisual show, live acting, artefacts and documents, all giving an imaginative interpretation of Tain and its history. You can also hire a personal CD player for a tour of the historic sites.

Tain Museum (*open as above*), in Castle Brae off the High Street, was founded as an exhibition for the visit of the Queen Mother in 1966 and became permanent. It has relics, manuscripts, photographs, and archaeological remains. It includes details of St Duthus and of the patronage of James IV – though not of Flaming Janet – and good displays showing what life was like in the 18th and 19th centuries in a thriving market town. This is also the Clan Ross Centre.

The **Tolbooth** is a fine example of many built in the 16th and 17th centuries: a tall, castellated keep with angle turrets and the original curfew bell of 1616.

The **Highland Fine Cheeses Factory** shows how cheeses are made and allows sampling. North of the town is the **Glenmorangie Distillery** (*open all year, with a new visitor centre; for guided tours* **t** *(01862) 892 477*), founded in 1843, where whisky is produced using water from the burn. **Aldie Watermill** (*open 10–5; ring* **t** *(01862) 893 786, to check seasons*) is a working pottery in a restored watermill, with an above-average shop. **Grants**, the baker, still use the original bread ovens, over 100 years old.

The A9 now sweeps across the **Dornoch Firth** on a grand causeway-bridge, cutting the journey north considerably. The drive along the southern shore of the Firth to **Struie** is attractive, but by far the most scenic approach from the south is on the B9176 due north, 3 miles beyond Evanton. This road goes up over the moors and down to the Firth.

Stop at Struie, at the **Stone Viewpoint**, about 10 miles up the road, for panoramic views over the **Kyles of Sutherland**. There is a view indicator, and a board explaining about the glacial action that created this beautiful spot. Windswept heather and pines fringe a road that zigzags down through dramatic ravines.

Croick Church

Turn left at Ardgay (pronounced Ardguy as in Guy Fawkes), 14 miles west of Tain, at the head of the Firth. Drive 10 miles up Strath Carron, along a burn bordered by lichen, bracken and birches. Little Croick Church lies in a walled churchyard, surrounded by a few wind-bent trees in a pocket of desolate moorland, one of the most poignant places in Scotland. In the spring of 1845 families who had been evicted from their crofts in Glencalvie and who had nowhere to go camped here in the churchyard in an improvised shelter made of tarpaulin, rugs and plaids stretched over poles. They scratched memorials on the diamond panes of this simple kirk, which can still be read today: 'Glencalvie people was in the church here May 24 1845 ...' 'Glencalvie people the wicked generation...'.

Inside, it is plain with unadorned walls, an iron stove, benches and table and a big pulpit. There is an interesting display board with contemporary newspaper cuttings from *The Times*.

Around Bonar Bridge

Bonar Bridge, a mile north of Ardgay, is so called after the bridge that spans the Kyle of Sutherland. Once a staging post on the A9, when this was the only way north, it is now a backwater, hoping to lure tourists to its excellent fishing, walking and boating.

Carbisdale Castle, high above the river at **Invershin**, a couple of miles northwest, is near the site of Montrose's final disastrous battle, from which he fled to Assynt. The massive neo-Gothic pile had nothing to do with Montrose, but was a 20th-century peace-offering to the dowager Duchess of Sutherland after family squabbles over her husband's will. It is now a remarkable youth hostel, *see* above. There is a pleasant detour, up the River Shin, to Lairg. The **Falls of Shin**, on the way, are a popular beauty spot, complete with attendant café, gift shop and car park.

Lairg, at the southern end of Loch Shin, is a fisherman's haven and a good base from which to explore the rugged hinterland of Sutherland. For those who don't want to spend their holiday on the end of a fishing rod, there are lovely walks.

Returning along the northern shore of the Dornoch Firth, the A949 passes several prehistoric remains: Dun Creich, a vitrified fort on the promontory 3 miles out of Bonar Bridge; traces of a chambered cairn at Clashmore, west of the school; another cairn at Evelix; and a standing stone on the outskirts of Dornoch, 10 miles east of Bonar Bridge. These remains indicate what a large number of Pictish and Norse settlers populated this area.

Dornoch

Dornoch, isolated enough to retain its old-world dignity, though more accessible with the new bridge, remains unspoiled by its popularity as a holiday resort, a charming, higgledy-piggledy town, full of character. Its dignity was briefly threatened not long ago when the pop star, Madonna, chose it as the theatre for the production of her wedding. The cathedral was the stage for the baptism of her child, and Skibo Castle (an exclusive sports club and hotel) was chosen for the festivities surrounding the flamboyant pageant, including the marriage cerermony. Long famous as a golfing centre, Dornoch's links have been played on since at least 1616. On the same latitude as Hudson Bay and Alaska, it is the most northerly first-class golf course in the world. Excavations have dated settlements here at least as far back as 1000 BC.

Dornoch Cathedral dates from 1224 when the town became a bishopric. It must be the cosiest cathedral in the country: small and cruciform, with colourful windows illuminating its warm, mellow walls. It was burnt in a clan dispute between Murrays and Mackays in 1570, when only the tower and spire survived. Restored in 1616, it was then further, and tastelessly, restored in Victorian times. Mercifully it was restored in 1924 to celebrate its 700th anniversary and much of the awful Victorian work was stripped away to reveal the original 13th-century stonework. It is now the parish church.

Andrew Carnegie, the humble lad from Dunfermline who made a fortune in America and spent his latter years spending it on good causes, bought nearby Skibo Estate and Castle as a holiday home, and endowed the stained-glass windows in the north wall of the cathedral.

Dornoch is flanked by miles of clean sand, ideal for holiday-makers but not so good for the evicted crofters who, during the Highland Clearances, were expected to settle here and farm the infertile dune land. Small wonder so many of them emigrated.

History Links, in the Meadows (*open June–Sept daily*, *t* *(01862) 810 339*), is an exhibition of Dornoch's history.

Embo, about 3 miles north along the sands, was one of the villages set up during the Clearances to house crofters who had been displaced from their homes. The cottages of the original hamlet were mostly built in 1830, gable-ends facing the sea. The whole area is now a gigantic caravan park and holiday resort with yachting and water-skiing facilities.

At the entrance are the remains of two Stone-Age burial chambers dating from 2000 BC. When these were excavated it was discovered that two later cist tombs had been built into the original ones.

On the shore of **Loch Fleet,** a couple of miles further north, there is the scant ruin of 14th-century **Skelbo Castle** on a grassy mound. It was here, in an earlier, wooden castle in 1290 that emissaries of Edward I waited to greet the little Princess Margaret, Maid of Norway, whose marriage to Edward's son was to solve the problem of sovereignty in Scotland. Whether it would have done so or not was never to be known, for it was here that they heard of the child's death caused by sea sickness on the voyage. This triggered off the Scottish Wars of Independence and Edward's ruthless hammering of the Scots.

Golspie, 9 miles north of Dornoch, is the farming centre for the area. There is an 18-hole golf course. 17th-century St Andrew's Church has a splendid old canopied pulpit, some fine panelled walls and carvings. The great statue on Ben Vraggie, behind Golspie, is to the first Duke of Sutherland, a man who was on the one hand blamed for his harshness to crofters during the Clearances and, on the other, praised for sponsoring many social improvements in the area.

Dunrobin Castle

Open April–Oct Mon–Sat 10.30–4.30, Sun 1–4.30;
June–Sept Sun 1–5.30; adm; **t** *(01480) 633 177.*

Dunrobin Castle stands high on a natural terrace overlooking the sea, a mile north of Golspie. Built in the 13th century on the site of an ancient broch, this seat of the Dukes of Sutherland was considerably restored in Victorian times. The huge extravaganza, standing on a massive plinth, is more like a château than a castle. Its towers and turrets are a flamboyant pastiche of French and Scottish architecture. Formal gardens below the castle, bordering a long terrace, are a riot of colour in summer. Many of the rooms reflect the hand of the architect Sir Robert Lorimer, who made many improvements during the First World War. There are some fine paintings, including two Canalettos, as well as magnificent furniture, tapestries and family heirlooms. There is also a museum in a summerhouse in the park, with archaeological exhibits, Victoriana, crafts and natural history, including a zoo-ful of stuffed animals. There is a café-restaurant in the castle.

Dornoch to Wick

Brora

Brora, 5 miles up the coast from Golspie, is a small tourist resort with good salmon fishing and an 18-hole golf course. The harbour, once used by fishing boats, is now silted up. In the middle of the 19th century crofters sailed from here to New Zealand to start fresh lives away from the threat of eviction during the Clearances. **Brora Heritage Centre** (*open June–Sept*) is a particularly good one, though small, and gives an informative account of the local history, including Brora's importance as a brick-making town in the past.

There are two brochs, one either end of Brora, the better about 3 miles north between the road and the sea, with domed chambers in the walls and outworkings. Two headless skeletons were excavated from the site in 1880. There is hardly a hill or hummock in this area that is not crowned by some sort of fort or broch. As you go north, you will find fewer Gaelic-derived names and more with Nordic origins.

Helmsdale

Helmsdale, 10 miles north of Brora, is a fishing and holiday town where the main road and railway part company. You must search for the remains of 15th-century **Helmsdale Castle** on a plateau above the harbour. It was within these innocent-looking walls in 1567 that Isobel Sinclair poisoned the Earl and Countess of Sutherland so that her son might inherit the earldom. This somewhat drastic solution failed, however, because her son drank the poison and died with them. The castle was rebuilt in the early 19th century by the Duke of Sutherland who, having evicted the crofters from his lands, tried to make amends by resettling them. Helmsdale was devised as a fishing/farming community, the streets laid out in neat geometric parallels, named after the Duke's estates.

Timespan Heritage Centre (*open Easter–mid-Oct Mon–Sat 9.30–5, Sun 2–5; July and Aug Mon–Sat 9.30–6, Sun 2–6; adm*) is just off the main road in the village and is a gem. It traces the history of man in the Kildonan area from the stone circles, cairns and brochs of prehistory, through Norse invasion, the Clearances, herring fishing, gold rush and crofting to the present. The **River Helmsdale** is one of the most renowned salmon rivers in Scotland and there is a nine-hole golf course.

Strath of Kildonan

An alternative route north from Helmsdale goes inland on the A897, 38 miles up to Melvich on the north coast, through Strath of Kildonan: a windswept, treeless moorland, broken by delightful river valleys. **Suisgill**, 10 miles from Helmsdale, was the centre of a mini gold rush towards the end of the 19th century, when a considerable amount of gold was panned from the rivers. Kildonan lost four-fifths of its population in the first half of the 19th century, during the Highland Clearances. Now it is sparsely populated with shooting lodges and sheep farms along the Helmsdale – one of Scotland's top fishing rivers. Several years ago, there was a bout of 'lodge burnings', thought to be the work of drunks or Scottish Nationalists, which left a number of smoking shells. Suisgill Lodge was one of the victims: all that is left is one end of the house; a complete wilderness replaces what was once a beautiful garden. **Strath Halladale**, running north from Strath Kildonan on this road, is green and fertile, fed by rivers and burns – attractive farmland for the invading Vikings so many years ago.

Ord of Caithness

Going on up the A9 from Helmsdale, the scenery becomes more dramatic, with ravines and steep cliffs as the road climbs to a high plateau with spectacular views from the Ord of Caithness about 4 miles beyond Helmsdale. No superstitious Sinclair will cross the Ord on a Monday since that Monday in 1513 when the men of the clan passed this way to fight with James IV at Flodden, from which not one of them returned. There are often red deer up here, especially in the early morning or at dusk.

There is a broch at Ousdale, a couple of miles beyond the Ord, where the main road runs inland for a while. Take the track out to the old hamlet of Badbea on the cliffs. Crofters took refuge here during the Clearances and stories are told of the beasts and the children having to be tethered to prevent them being blown into the sea.

The 15th-century castle (*private*), visible from the road at **Dunbeath**, was captured by Montrose in 1650. Neil Gunn, the well-known Scots writer who depicted the herring industry so brilliantly in *Silver Darlings*, was born here in 1891, and **Dunbeath Heritage Centre**, in the Old School (*open April–Oct daily 10–5*), will tell you more about him. His book *Highland River* portrays life around Dunbeath Water, and *Morning Tide* mirrors his upbringing here. Six miles to the west, at **Braemore**, a monument was erected after the air crash here that killed the Duke of Kent in 1942. The Dunbeath Highland Games are held in July.

Laidhay Croft Museum (*open Easter–Sept daily 10–5; adm*), 2 miles north of Dunbeath, shows a typical Victorian croft house, looking cosier, perhaps, than it was in reality. These interiors are excellent for displaying domestic detail, but not so good at conveying the damp, cold, smoky atmosphere, when rats ran around the floor and animals shared the living space. There is also a collection of farm implements in an outhouse, some of which, like the peat-cutters, are still used today.

The **Clan Gunn Museum and Heritage Centre** (*open June–Sept Mon–Sat 11–1 and 2–4; July and Aug also Sun 2–4; adm*) is in the old parish church, a couple of miles further north beyond Latheron with its picturesque harbour.

Turn off the broad thoroughfare, flanked by sturdy, dignified houses, in **Lybster**, 4 miles north of Latheron. Dip down to the harbour, scooped out of rock to provide a perfect haven for the large fishing fleet that once plied from here in the 19th century. The fleet is reduced now to a few lobster boats and a number of pleasure craft, but the atmosphere is still very much that of a fishing community, with piles of creels and fishing gear, and the salty tang of the sea.

Lybster Harbour Visitor Centre (*open April–Oct daily 10–8*) focuses on local birdlife, the history of the herring industry, boat building, etc. There is a coffee shop and yacht facilities. The **art gallery** (*open June–Sept*) shows local arts and crafts.

Inland from Lybster a minor road joins the A895 north to Thurso. A few miles further on is the **Achavanich Standing Stone Circle**. This ritual site, in the form of an unusual truncated oval, may once have contained as many as 60 stones. Less than a mile west of here, on the main road up from Latheron, is Rangag Broch, dating from 150 BC, once 40 or 50ft high.

About a mile east of Lybster on the A99, take the minor road north up the Clyth Burn, signed to **Grey Cairns of Camster**, about 5 dead straight miles over the moor. In this remote spot, and easy to miss in the mist if there aren't cars already parked there, are two truly spectacular restored Neolithic monuments, including what has been described as the most outstanding long (200ft), horned cairn in the country, dating back to around 3800 BC. You approach on duckboards over the bog and can crawl inside the cairns – not for the claustrophobic. There are detailed explanation boards. Both animal and human remains were excavated from this site.

A couple of miles to the east, reached up a short road signed off the A99, the **Hill o' Many Stanes** is an early Bronze-Age site which has puzzled archaeologists for years. This fan of small standing stones has ribs, each containing about eight or more stones, numbering some 200 in all – thought to have originally been about 600. It looks random now, and could have been a ritual site for burials, like other henges, or some form of astronomical calculator, lined up with the stars. Whatever its purpose, it is eerie to stand on this lonely, windswept moor and try to picture how it must have been for those early settlers, once so numerous in this northern corner.

About 7 miles from Lybster, past a church on a sharp bend, is the unsigned hamlet of **Whaligoe**. A staggered crossroads has a turn left marked to an Alpine nursery. Almost opposite, a small road goes past a row of terraced cottages to a house with a high stone wall, where you can park. A flight of 365 stone steps twists steeply down the cliff to where the old harbour used to be. Now disused and overgrown, it was once used by fishing fleets to moor and unload their catches, among the cheerful bustle and raucous banter of the fishermen and the teams of women working at the gutting. The steps are only for the sure-footed: they can be extremely slippery.

Wick

Wick, so called from the Viking word *vik* meaning 'bay or creek', is a substantially built seaport and tourist centre, stretching around the sweep of Wick Bay. There is a harbour, airport and railway terminal. Norse pirates were drawn to Wick by the shelter of its bay at the mouth of the river and by the magnet of the rich farmland that beckoned from the west. Created a Royal Burgh in 1140, it was only properly developed in the 19th century, by the British Fisheries Society, who commissioned Telford to design a model village for them at Pulteneytown. It is difficult to believe, now, that 1,122 herring boats once plied from the complex of three harbour basins, before the decline of the herring stock and the development of vast refrigerated factory ships. On the morning of 19 August 1848 a gale from the southeast struck Wick just as the fleet was heading homewards. Forty-one boats were lost, most of them within sight of the harbour, still used today by white-fish trawlers.

The **Heritage Museum** (*open June–Sept Mon–Sat; adm*), near the harbour, tells the story of fishing in Wick. Its collections include a fishing boat, working lighthouse, kippering kilns, blacksmith shop, coopering shop and fishing gear.

Carnegie Library has a small museum displaying the history of the area, with its domestic and farming life.

At **Caithness Glass Factory** (*open daily 9–5, exc Sun in Jan and Feb*), on the north side of town, you can watch craftsmen shaping and engraving molten glass. This factory was established in the slump of the herring industry to offer alternative employment for the fishermen. It is interesting to notice that in this land so full of echoes of the Norse occupation, the designs of the glass are distinctively Scandinavian.

Also south of the town is the shell of **Old Wick Castle** (*always accessible*), three storeys high on a rock promontory, and known to seamen as the 'Auld Man o' Wick'. Without its own water supply, the castle was unable to withstand lengthy sieges and was abandoned in the 16th century.

Look out for the **Brig o' Trams** nearby, a spectacular natural rock arch formed by the erosion of sea and weather. There are more spectacularly shaped rocks 3 miles to the north along the cliffs, at **Noss Head**. It is possible to drive, but it is also a glorious walk, buffeted by the wind.

From the point it isn't far to **Sinclair and Girnigoe Castles** (*always accessible; quite dangerous – so watch your children*). These two dramatic ruins extend from a keep and were lived in as one dwelling by the Sinclairs, Earls of Caithness, for 200 years. The eastern part is 15th-century, the western, 17th-century. The jagged ruin seems to grow up out of horizontally layered rock on a cliff above a sheltered cove. Ghosts lurk in these history-soaked walls: in 1570 the 4th Earl of Caithness, suspecting his son of plotting to kill him, imprisoned him in the dungeons for seven years till he died of 'famine and vermine'.

The great sandy sweep of **Sinclair's Bay** leads north along coastland believed to be among the earliest inhabited in Scotland. Excavations revealed that middle Stone-Age man existed here in large numbers, on the fertile hinterland.

The tall, slender tower on top of the cliff at **Keiss**, 8 miles north of Wick, is all that remains of Keiss Castle, home of William Sinclair, founder of the first Baptist church in Scotland. The ruin of 12th-century **Bucholie Castle**, a mile north, was the stronghold of Sweyn Aslefson, a Norse pirate whose name features often in the old Norse sagas. A 10th-century Viking settlement is in the process of excavation, a mile further north at **Freswick**. **Northlands Viking Centre**, at Auckengill (*open June–Sept daily*), tells the Norse story.

John o' Groats

Although it is neither the most northerly nor the most easterly tip of Britain, John o' Groats is loosely accepted as the northeastern extremity, linked diagonally to Land's End, 876 miles away in the southwest, which, in turn, is neither the most southerly, nor the most westerly tip of the country.

Stop on the summit of the final curve of the moor and look down. It is a bleak, scattered village, washed by the Pentland Firth whose islands sometimes appear so close you could almost jump the gap. It is an awe-inspiring vista – the edge of the world. But John o' Groats itself is often a disappointment to tourists – little more than an uninspiring coach park, a few ugly buildings containing souvenirs, snacks and woollens, an overpriced 'craft-community' complex and a flat, dreary landscape.

Much of John o' Groats has recently been bought by a rich Englishman with ambitious plans for improvement, including a grand new hotel, yet to be built. He could hardly make it any worse.

The small settlement, given over to supplying the needs of the dozens of tourists who come here, got its curious name from a Dutchman, Jan de Groot, who established a ferry link with the newly acquired Orkney in 1496, under the rule of James IV. There are several explanations for the octagonal house he built, with eight doors, no longer standing but represented by the octagonal tower on the hotel which is believed to stand on the site of de Groot's house. One explanation is that he wanted to provide shelter from every point of the fierce wind for his waiting passengers. A nicer theory is that when his eight sons squabbled over who should take precedence at the dinner table, he decided to settle the dispute by having an octagonal table and eight doors, so that each son had his own entrance and no one, or everyone, sat at the head of the table. There is a **Last House Museum** (*open all year*), with local history and photographs of local shipwrecks, and a **Journey's End Exhibition** (*open Easter–Oct*), with an audio-visual presentation.

Duncansby Head

Duncansby Head is Scotland's true 'top righthand corner', where many different species of sea birds throng the dramatic cliffs. A road runs out to the lighthouse on the cliffs, from which the only limit to the view over the Pentland Firth, in clear weather, is the keenness of your eye. Walk round from the lighthouse to see dramatic stacks and rock formations. The 12-knot tide rip here is a notorious hazard to shipping: over 400 wrecks have been recorded in only the last 150 years. Once you get away from the blemishes of tourism, this coastline is perfect for those who like wild and lonely places and extremes of weather.

The North Coast: John o' Groats to Durness

This is an edge-of-the-world highway, with detours into tracts of barren wasteland to the south, and side-tracks to the north with endless vistas over the Pentland Firth, from cliff-tops and sandy beaches, sheltered bays and gale-lashed headlands. Spare a thought for the Roman fleet of Agricola, which battled round from the east coast and triumphantly reported back to the boss that Britain was, indeed, an island.

The **Castle of Mey**, 7 miles west of John o' Groats, was built around the middle of the 16th century for the 4th Earl of Caithness and remained in his family until 1889. It was bought and restored in 1956 by one of Britain's best-loved public figures, Queen Elizabeth, the late Queen Mother, who died in March 2002 aged nearly 102. Turrets of the castle can be glimpsed from the road, sheltered by trees. Until the future of the castle is decided, the gardens will open on certain days in the summer in aid of charity. Check locally or with the tourist office.

Dunnet Head, 9 miles further on, is the most northerly point of Scotland's mainland. Walk out – if you don't get blown away – to the tip on a carpet of pink thrift, laced with tormentil, trefoils, wild thyme, yellow saxifrage, purple butterwort and many other wild flowers. You might be lucky enough to see puffins burrowing in the turf. The view from Dunnet Head is memorable, especially at sunrise or sunset. The village is a scattering of houses near the vast sweep of Dunnet Bay.

Tourist Information

Thurso: Riverside, **t** (01847) 892 371, **f** 893 155.
Durness: Durine, **t** (01971) 511 259, **f** 511 368.

Where to Stay and Eat

Forss Country House Hotel, near Thurso,
t (01847) 861 201, **f** 861 301, *jamie@ forsshouse.freeserve.co.uk* (*expensive*).
Very special. Built as a private house in 1810 in 20 acres of woodland, only 100 yards from the River Forss. The garden is pretty, and when conditions are right you can sit and watch salmon leaping in the river. The hotel is well run, with comfortable, elegant rooms, a welcoming feel and first-class food. There are well over 100 malt whiskies to sample. There are lodges in the garden with five more rooms, for more privacy and flexibility.

Altnaharra Hotel, **t/f** (01549) 411 222, *www.altnaharra.com* (*moderate*). 17 miles south of Tongue away from the coast, a real Highland hotel in a sheltered spot on the river. It has been catering for fishermen since 1800, and is also known as The Sportsman's Retreat. Excellent food and atmosphere.

Ben Loyal Hotel, Tongue, **t** (01847) 611 216, **f** 611 212, *thebenloyalhotel@btinternet.com* (*moderate*). Comfortable and pretty, with a range of accommodation from 'superior' to 'bungalow annexe'. The hosts are genial, the food good, and there are views of the Kyle of Tongue.

Borgie Lodge Hotel, Skerray, **t/f** (01641) 521 332, *www.borgielodgehotel.co.uk* (*moderate*).
Fishing hotel, in a charming old family house in secluded grounds. The owners have managed to retain the 19th-century character of the house, with original panelled rooms, stag's antlers, tartan carpets, sporting prints and log fires. They will arrange fishing, tackle and tuition.

Castle Arms Hotel, Mey, **t/f** (01847) 851 244 (*moderate*). Attractive 19th-century coaching inn near the Queen Mother's castle. They are proud of their royal neighbour and have a Royal Gallery with a unique collection of photographs of her and her family, copies of which can be bought. One of the very comfortable bedrooms looks across at the castle and the local shop is round the back.

Northern Sands Hotel, Dunnet, **t** (01847) 851 270, **f** 851 626 (*moderate*). Friendly hotel on the coast, 5 minutes from the sandy beach.

Royal Hotel, Traill Street, Thurso, **t** (01847) 893 191, **f** 895 338 (*moderate*). In the town centre, and not over-endowed with style. However, it offers game and sea fishing, and the staff are obliging and very friendly.

Tongue Hotel, Tongue, **t** (01847) 611 206/7, **f** 611 345 (*moderate*). Victorian hotel with its original character and style. Built in 1880 as a hunting lodge for the Duke of Sutherland, it overlooks the Kyle of Tongue. Ask about the ghost.

Ulbster Arms Hotel, Halkirk, **t** (01847) 831 641, **f** 831 206 (*moderate*). On the River Thurso, 5 miles south of Thurso in Flow Country. Amiable staff and nice atmosphere.

Signed on the way out to the point is **Mary Ann's Cottage** (*open June–Sept Tues–Sun 2–4.30; adm; t (01847) 851 383*). Mary Ann Calder lived here until she moved to a nursing home in 1990 at the age of 93, and the cottage and croft have been preserved as they were when worked by Mary Ann and her husband James, and by their predecessors 150 years ago. The tower of the white church behind the hotel, with its saddle-backed roof, dates from the 14th century, a pre-Reformation survivor adding continuity to a place where nothing seems to have changed much over the years. The fishing is good, from sea, river and loch. A halibut weighing 210lbs was caught here with rod and line in 1975. **Castlehill Harbour**, 6 miles south of Dunnet Point, was the centre of the Caithness flagstone industry. Some stone is still produced today. There is a **Flagstone Trail**, at Castletown (*open all year*), which covers the industry's history.

Thurso

Thurso, 20 miles west of John o' Groats, is a large, thriving holiday resort and an important fishing port, built on the River Thurso. Elegant 18th-century houses built of brown sandstone surround a central square, with a long, narrow harbour.

The name stems from the Norse *Thorsa* – meaning 'river of the God Thor'. This important Viking stronghold reached its zenith in the 11th century under Thorfinn, who defeated King Duncan's nephew in 1040 in a mighty battle here. The town was the chief trading port between Scotland and Scandinavia in the Middle Ages.

Thurso Folk Museum (*open June–Sept Mon–Sat; adm*), in the High Street, has a good collection of exhibits of local interest, including a reconstruction of a traditional croft house kitchen, whose homely equipment was often just as efficient as its modern, electric counterparts. The Pictish 'Ulbster Stone' is in the museum, with intricate carved symbols. **St Peter's Church**, near the harbour, dates from the 12th or 13th century. It was restored in the 17th century and used for worship until 1862. Some of the original stone can be seen in the curious choir – a semicircular apse within a square end. **Harald Tower**, just over a mile's walk along the coast to the northeast, was built in the early 19th century as a burial place for the Sinclairs. It stands on the grave of Harald, Earl of Caithness, a mighty war lord who ruled over half Caithness and Orkney and was killed in battle nearby in 1196. There are good shops in the town, plenty of places to stay, an 18-hole golf course, and splendid walks all around.

Scrabster Harbour, not far round the bay, is the terminal for the car ferry, St Ola, to Stromness in Orkney. It is an invigorating two-hour trip and on Mondays and Thursdays in the summer it links with special bus tours to make a pleasant day excursion, returning to Scrabster in the evening.

St Mary's Chapel, at **Crosskirk**, 6 miles to the west, is signed from the main road, with a half-mile walk across turf on low cliffs. This simple little roofless kirk dates from the 12th century, its chancel containing three Gunn memorials, linked to the nave by a small doorway. Remote and peaceful in a walled churchyard, it has a timeless serenity.

Dounreay

The **Dounreay Nuclear Power Station** was established in 1954 and brought tempo-rary prosperity to Thurso, with a workforce of 2,000. Its closure in 1994 brought hardship to many who had settled within commuting distance of the works, and relief to the antinuclear activists. Work is now in progress to 'decommission' the three reactors and associated plant, a £500-million, 10-year operation ensuring local employment for the duration. Non-nuclear projects are being investigated for the future. An **exhibition** (*open May–Oct daily; t (01847) 802 233/572*) gives an insight into Dounreay's role in British science.

About 6 miles west, the A897 branches off south back to Helmsdale through Strath Halladale and Strath of Kildonan.

Just outside **Melvich**, a couple of miles on round the coast, is the **Split Stone of Melvich**. An old woman was returning from a shopping trip when she was chased by the devil. She ran round and round this stone and escaped: the devil was so furious he split it in two. Parts of **Portskerra Fort**, a mile or so beyond Melvich on the point, rise 80ft sheer from the shore.

At **Strathy Point**, 12 miles west of Dounreay, the sea has carved fabulous arches and caverns in the cliffs. The variety of the coastal scenery is amazing; there are many types of rock, sandy beaches, sheltered bays and the restless sea, licking the feet of the cliffs. There is good bird-watching here and lots of wild flowers.

To the west is **Armadale Bay**, with a lovely sandy beach, and between the next two points, **Ardmore** and **Kirtomy**, the sea has carved out a natural tunnel from the cliffs. On **Farr Point**, 3 miles west, **Borve Castle** was a stronghold of the Clan Mackay in medieval times. It was destroyed by the Earl of Sutherland's army in 1515.

Bettyhill

Bettyhill, 10 miles on, is said to have been named after a local woman, Betty Cnocan who kept an inn at the top of the hill, not after Elizabeth, first Duchess of Sutherland, who was responsible for much of the anguish this village commemorates.

Strath Naver Museum (*open April–Oct Mon–Sat, and by arrangement, t (01641) 521 330; adm*) is in a large converted church, once the parish church of Farr. The story of the Clearances is poignantly told by local schoolchildren in the extremely well laid out museum, giving a fascinating insight into Strath Naver's chapter of that period (*see* **Topics**, 'Highland Clearances', p.52). It is likely that the minister may have read out eviction notices from his pulpit here. There is much else to see, and a well-informed, helpful curator. Next to the museum, the **Old Nick Tearoom** can be a welcome if unsophisticated place for a snack. There is a craft shop upstairs and a small Tourist Information office in the building.

After the museum, go through the village and take the little road south signed to **Achanlochy** by the bridge over the River Naver, to get some idea of how the people of Strath Naver suffered when they were cleared to Bettyhill and told to rebuild their lives by cultivating wind-torn land on the infertile coast. About a mile along there is a cairn in a gravel pit with Achanlochy written on it. Walk up the slope to the site of one of the cleared hamlets, well explained on an information board. From here you can picture what sort of lives those people lived before 1819, in this lush, green, sheltered strath. Further along this road, up on the left, is a Neolithic chambered burial cairn, a great mound of tumbled stones 75 yards long with its entrance running in from the north. One of the three chambers, now unroofed, is fairly easy to get into, and you can see the method of construction with huge stone slabs set vertically with flat-laid drystone walling. The B871 to the south runs through **Strath Naver**, where many croft houses went up in flames during those troubled times and where people died of exposure, huddled against the ruins of their homes.

Invernaver National Nature Reserve, 2 miles south of Bettyhill, is a gold mine for nature lovers. It is situated around the mouth of the River Naver, with the finest collection of mountain and coastal plants in the north. Among the rarer birds that breed here are greenshank, ring ouzel and twite. On the edge of the reserve is **Baile Marghait**, once a Neolithic community, with graves, hut circles and a broch.

Tongue

Tongue is on the eastern shore of the Kyle of Tongue, with Ben Hope and Ben Loyal to the south. When Borve Castle, along the coast, was destroyed by the Gordons of Sutherland in 1554, the Mackays adopted Tongue as their stronghold.

The name Tongue is Norse and the ruin of **Castle Varrich** which stares down on the village from a rocky hill was a Norse stronghold in the 11th century. Nothing much is known about it, but it is a nice walk out from the village with a profusion of wild flowers including gentians in August, and good views. On the way you pass a series of reed beds, with information boards explaining how these are a 'green' way of purifying sewage.

The **Kyle of Tongue**, crossed by a causeway, is a long, shallow inlet from the wild sea outside, so shallow that at low tide it almost seems to dry out. The lane up the west side winds among sandy bays, cliffs, weirdly shaped rocks and islands, remote and lovely. **Port Vasgo**, at the northern end, is one of the few places where you will find the exquisite and rare *primula scotica*, nestling in the turf on the cliff-top.

From Tongue, the A836 goes south through the heart of the Flow Country, past Loch Loyal, 38 miles to Lairg.

There are good walks out along the coast to **Whiten Head** – or Kennageal – at the tip of the peninsula between Tongue and Loch Eriboll, with caves under the cliffs and Atlantic grey seals. This peninsula – **A 'Mhoine** – is a wilderness of moor, rock and hill, beautiful in sunshine but awesome in storm.

A couple of miles before Loch Eriboll on the A838 a road runs south down **Loch Hope**, with more picture-postcard views, to Altnaharra and the road southwards. About 10 miles along, on the River Hope, there is a well-preserved broch, **Dun Dornadilla**, well placed to guard the glen and provide shelter in times of attack.

Loch Eriboll, 10 miles west of Tongue, is a sea loch running 10 miles inland, very deep and beautiful. This was one of the subjects of a prophecy by the Brahan Seer early in the 17th century. He named Loch Eriboll as a place where a war would end one day. In 1945 German submarines came into the loch to surrender, at the end of the Second World War. Servicemen stationed here during the war to protect convoys passing through the Pentland Firth, nicknamed it Loch 'Orrible.

After the First World War, land on the west side of the loch was allocated to the repatriated heroes to give them a chance to start a new life. One look at the inhospitable landscape will explain why they were less than delighted with this munificent gesture.

There are the remains of several ancient settlements around here. About a mile north of Laid School on the west side of the loch, there is a souterrain, complete and untouched, with curved steps leading down to a round chamber. Look out for two cairns in a bracken-infested lay-by on the right just past a fish farm in a bay; the souterrain is towards the loch from here. You need a torch for this earth house, which floods after heavy rain.

Smoo Cave (*see* p.484) is signposted just before Durness, down a steep, stepped path to a vast limestone cavern with three compartments. The Alt Smoo River thunders down into the inner chamber in an awesome 70-ft cascade that fills the air with spray. You can only get into the third chamber by boat, when the water is low.

Durness is the gateway to Cape Wrath and the top lefthand corner (*see* pp.483–5). It is a useful provisioning base, with a good little supermarket and tourist information centre. Once a Pictish settlement, it has been a farming area ever since. Some of the local crofters protested so vehemently against attempts to 'clear' them in 1841 that they were reprieved, and gave heart and inspiration to others.

Durness Old Church is a roofless shell dating from 1619, with some interesting tombs, including one of a pirate, and a monument to Rob Donn (1715), one of the greatest Gaelic poets. The large farmhouse opposite was the Summer Palace for the bishops of Caithness before the Reformation. One of the best walks in the area is along the beach and out to the cliffs through swathes of wild flowers.

The
Western Isles

20

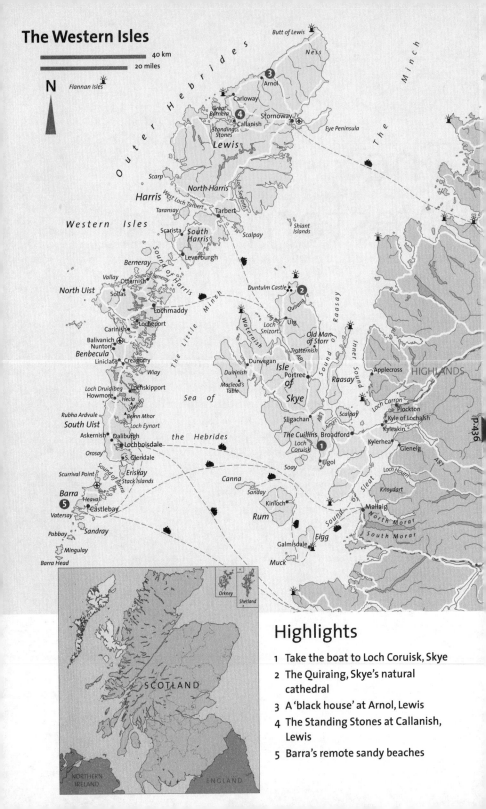

The Western Isles

40 km
20 miles

N

Flannan Isles

Outer Hebrides

Butt of Lewis

Ness

3 Arnol

Great Bernera **4** Carloway

Stornoway

Callanish *Standing Stones*

Lewis

Eye Peninsula

The Minch

Scarp

North Harris

Harris *West Loch Tarbert* *Loch Seaforth*

Taransay Tarbert

Western Isles

Scarista *South Harris*

Leverburgh

Shiant Islands

Scalpay

Berneray

Sound of Bernera Otternish *Vallay*

Sollas

North Uist

Lochmaddy

Locheport

Carinish

Balivanich Nunton

Benbecula Liniclate Creagorry

Wiay

Loch Druidibeg Torlum Howmore *Hecla*

Ushnish

Benn Mhor

Rubha Ardvule *Loch Eynort*

South Uist Daliburgh

Askernish Lochboisdale

Orosay S. Glendale

Scurrival Point *Sound of Barra*

Eriskay *Stack Islands*

Barra **5** *Heaval*

Vatersay Castlebay

Pabbay

Sandray

Mingulay

Barra Head

Duntulm Castle **2**

Quiraing

Uig Bay *Ulg*

Loch Snizort

Old Man of Storr

Trotternish

Dunvegan

Duirinish

Macleod's Table

Isle of Skye Portree

Waternish

Sea of the Hebrides

Raasay

Sound of Raasay

Inner Sound

Applecross

HIGHLANDS

Loch Carron Plockton

Sligachan

The Cuillins Broadford **1**

Loch Coruisk

Soay Elgol

Scalpay

Kyle of Lochalsh

Kyleakin

Kylerhea

Glenelg

A87

Loch Hourn

Knoydart

Loch Alsh

Canna

Sanday

Rum KinToch

Eigg

Galmisdale

Muck

Sound of Sleat

Mallaig

North Morar

South Morar

p.436

Orkney

Shetland

SCOTLAND

NORTHERN IRELAND

ENGLAND

Highlights

1 Take the boat to Loch Coruisk, Skye
2 The Quiraing, Skye's natural cathedral
3 A 'black house' at Arnol, Lewis
4 The Standing Stones at Callanish, Lewis
5 Barra's remote sandy beaches

From the lone shieling on the misty island
Mountains divide us, and a waste of seas
Yet still the blood is strong, the heart is Highland
And we, in dreams, behold the Hebrides.

Canadian Boat Song

Skye and the Small Isles lie close to the west coast between Ardnamurchan Point and Gairloch. They are separated from the Outer Hebrides by the Sea of the Hebrides and the Minch, a notoriously capricious channel.

First known to be populated around 3800 BC, the Hebrides are rich in archaeological sites, many of which are yet to be dug. Mesolithic man gave way to Neolithic, who came in boats made of animal hide, bringing skills and culture and leaving burial cairns as evidence of his existence. Gaelic immigrants from Europe arrived with Celtic arts, building brochs and stone circles, practising a Druid religion and worshipping nature gods, until the first Christian missionaries arrived from Ireland early in the 6th century. The Norsemen arrived at the end of the 8th century and remained until the defeat of King Haakon by Alexander III at Largs in 1263. After this the islands were ceded to the Scottish Crown. But stronger than the authority of the Crown was the Lordship of the Isles. Chiefs as powerful as kings paid no heed to a government which ruled from the east of mainland Scotland.

A succession of Stewart kings tried to whip in the arrogant clans of the Western Isles, but they clung to their own traditions. A patriarchal clan system existed, with every member of the clan family being independent and equal in status, looking to their chief for guidance and justice but not for oppression. This was the foundation of that proud independence that still endures in Hebrideans today, a truly classless pride that endured even the suppression of the clans after Culloden and, in the 19th century, the appalling depopulation of the Highland Clearances.

The islands to the south of Benbecula rejected the Reformation in favour of the Gaelic-speaking monks who came over from Ireland and who kept the faith alive. They reconverted, with the help of the Clanranalds, Macneils and Macleods of Skye, who had political influence (the Macleods later defaulted). These islands are almost entirely Catholic. North Uist, Harris and Lewis, and Skye embraced the Reformed Church with such enthusiasm that even today visitors must be careful not to offend their strong Sabbatarianism.

Most island families have their own croft, or smallholding, their tenancy carefully controlled by the Crofters Commission, brought about in 1886 as a result of public indignation after the Highland Clearances. But crofting is a hard life in the islands. With only a few acres, poor markets and expensive freight, few can exist solely on its returns. The crofting way of life has always been one of doing many jobs and getting work where you can. It is therefore usually an auxiliary occupation, during weekends and days off from more lucrative employment such as building, fishing and public works. Fish farming and the public sector are the main employers, with information technology and tourism becoming important. A number of craft centres, visitor centres and art galleries are springing up, with related workshops.

The old thatched croft houses have mostly been replaced by modern ones, but some are still occupied. In the old 'black houses' the byre was usually part of the dwelling, with the peat fire on a raised platform in the middle of the room, its smoke escaping through a hole in the roof. True black houses are only seen now as folk museums, restored and probably misleadingly cosy. No museum can duplicate the reality: the vermin, the pervading damp, the smell from the byre and heavy pall of smoke.

Electricity transformed living conditions, but it brought with it the television, which has effectively killed the ceilidh tradition. In the old days, when a crofting township was totally communal, the day's work was done on a cooperative basis and in the evenings communities gathered together around the fire in one of the black houses to listen to music and poetry and to tell the old sagas. Attempts have been made to capture some of this ancient folklore and imprison it on paper, but it was a living thing, passed orally from generation to generation, embroidered and altered year by year; its true spirit cannot be appreciated except by ear.

Gaelic is still the first language for most people in the Outer Hebrides, but an influx of non-Gaelic speakers means that the children of today are choosing to speak English as their first language.

Those who go to the islands for their holidays enjoy the outdoor life: walking, climbing, bird-watching, wild flowers, boating, fishing. Whatever the weather, and it is often good, each day is an adventure. Walk 5 miles to an isolated beach, collect driftwood and make a fire using dried heather twigs as kindling. Cook sausages on the stones and wash them down with peat-coloured water from a burn. Collect mussels from rocks below the high tide and rake cockles out of the white sand. Have a quick swim, diving into deep water as clear as glass (whatever people may say about the proximity of the Gulf Stream, the waters of the Minch are icy). Pick wild mushrooms from the grassy hillsides.

Except in Portree in Skye and Stornoway in Lewis there aren't many shops in the outer isles, and these are mainly general foodstores and co-op supermarkets which stock most things from boots to butter. There are a few craft/souvenir shops, weavers, and a post office here and there. Because of deeply held religious beliefs, most of the shops and petrol stations are closed on Sundays and there is no scheduled public transport in Harris and Lewis. In the Presbyterian islands most hotel bars, pubs and restaurants are also closed, though some hotels are open to non-residents for meals. Some landladies prefer it if guests don't arrive or depart on Sundays so it is worth checking to avoid giving offence.

For public entertainment, there may be a local ceilidh or concert in the village hall to mark a particular occasion, and there are Games in the summer on most of the larger islands. Otherwise, evenings are spent in front of a peat fire with a good book, or the television if there is one; or listening to the tales of local people, who can still tell much of the old folklore, and who will often make music for you; or in the pub. Skye, like Mull, being more accessible, has a much more modern culture.

The Small Isles: Rum, Eigg, Canna and Muck

Rum

Rum is a squashed diamond-shaped island, rising to a series of peaks; an unmistakable landmark for sailors, 8 miles west of Sleat in Skye. The Rum Cuillins reach 2,000ft and contain some semiprecious stones and rocks similar to those found on the moon. Inhabited almost continuously since the Mesolithic Age (about 6000 BC), its population of over 400 was reduced to one family in 1826, to make way for one sheep farm of 8,000 sheep. Deer were then introduced and it became a private sporting estate until the Nature Conservancy acquired it in 1957. It is now an 'outdoor laboratory', trying to discover how the Hebrides can best support wildlife and human beings.

The name Rum is thought to come from the Greek *rhombos*, referring to the rhomboid shape. The 'h' that sometimes creeps into the spelling of Rum was added by the Bulloughs, *see* below, who hoped to give a Gaelic flavour to the name, not realizing that in Gaelic 'r' is never aspirated. (Some say that the reason for the 'h' was George Bullough's wish to disassociate his island from alcohol, but this is unlikely as he was a dedicated bon viveur and no stranger to the demon drink.) Rum's chief interest is its geology: special permission must be obtained from the Scottish Natural Heritage warden to visit some places. Coastal names are Gaelic, but the hills have Norse names – the seafaring Vikings using the prominent peaks as important landmarks.

The half-wild golden-brown ponies are said to be descended from the survivors of a Spanish galleon which was part of the Armada wrecked off these coasts in 1588. There are also wild goats, golden eagles and plenty of red deer.

The red sandstone castle that looks across the bay is **Kinloch Castle**, built in 1901 by the then owners of the estate, the Bulloughs of Lancashire. So bitten by the Scottish bug were the Bulloughs that it is said they offered extra wages to employees who would work in kilts, despite the fact that Rum is notorious for its midges. Until recently it was an hotel and most of the original furnishings survive intact, if a little jaded. One of the features is the extremely rare electric 'orchestrarian', a Heath Robinson contraption whose parts represent a full orchestra, activated by a vast library of pre-set cylinders, each programmed with a well-known tune. All the working components can be seen in action in a huge glass chamber in the hall. George Bullough's widow, Monica, an aristocratic French Catholic, sold Rum to the Nature Conservancy for less than £1 an acre on condition it was used as a Nature Reserve in perpetuity; she gave the castle to the nation.

Although the castle is no longer run as an hotel, you can still stay there (*see* below), and there are conducted tours of this amazing time-warp, embellished with amusing and mostly apocryphal gossip about past visitors, including Edward VII in amorous pursuit of the mistress of the house. The only inhabitants on Rum today are employees of Scottish Natural Heritage.

Eigg

Eigg is about 7 miles off the mainland, 4 miles southeast of Rum, and is 7 miles by 5 in dimension. Shaped like an upturned boat, or a crouching lion, dominated by the huge black hump of the Sgurr, surrounded by clear, sparkling water, it is a magic place. Settled since prehistoric times, it has Iron-Age forts, a 6th-century Christian church, Viking burial mounds and the site of a Macdonald burial ground. This was a base for the Lords of the Isles and their Clanranald descendants, who were not above acts of piracy in the seas around here. Debt forced them to sell up in 1828 and there followed a succession of industrial tycoons, one of whom created an Italianate lodge and garden in the late 1920s. In recent years it has evolved into a joke soap-opera island, largely inhabited by 'white settlers' and escapers from the mainland, very different from the gentle, courteous, intelligent islanders who are heavily outnumbered. The 'community' decided to become masters of their own destiny. Fundraising, much publicity, generous donations and the pledge of considerable sums of public money, enabled them to buy the island. At present public subsidies support a couple of basket makers, someone whittling sticks, a few artists and tillers of soil, and some rather prickly drawers of the dole. One thing is sure: Eigg has no place in *Gaidhealtachd* – Gaeldom – today.

Walk up from the little harbour in the southeast, east around the bay to the ancient burial ground at **Kildonan Church**. This is the resting place of the Macdonalds who once held the island. A broken Celtic cross, a scattering of grave stones and a roofless ruin are all that remain. An aura of tragedy still hangs over *Uamh Fhraing*, a cave southwest of the pier, easily reached by a path from Galmisdale – torch advised. In 1577 some Macleods were forced to shelter from storm on Eigg. Owing to constant feuding over disputed land, the Macdonalds were not hospitable. The Macleods left and returned later to take revenge. The Macdonalds took shelter in this cave and the landing party found one old woman, whose life they spared. But as they were putting out to sea they saw a scout, sent from the cave to see if they had gone. They rushed back, found the cave and lit a fire in the mouth of it, suffocating the 398 inhabitants. Sir Walter Scott is said to have found bones here in 1814 and taken a souvenir away with him. Several people have seen ghosts here.

Palm trees and flame trees thrive in the garden surrounding the lodge, and there are lovely walks. Go up to the northwest corner, the glorious **Bay of Laig**, with 'Singing Sands'. The sands make a curious keening sort of song in certain conditions. Cattle wander on the beach and the views across to Rum are magnificent on a clear day.

Canna

Canna is charming – serene and lonely, with a good harbour. Sometimes called 'the Garden of the Hebrides', it lies less than 5 miles off the west coast of Rum and is actually two islands, joined to Sanday in the southeast by a causeway. Together, they are shaped like a hand gun, measuring 5 miles by 1, with a grassy plateau sloping in

Getting There

Caledonian MacBrayne runs a service to all four islands (*not daily and not Sun*). Ring for schedules, t (01475) 650 100.

Murdo Grant, t (01687) 450 224, runs regular cruises from Arisaig at Easter and from May to September, less frequently out of season. His boat, MV *Shearwater*, is fast and comfortable (with a bar), and takes 130 people. He will also charter.

Tourist Information

Local knowledge is best, or consult the Highlands of Scotland Tourist Board, t (01997) 421 160, *www.highlandfreedom.com*.

Where to Stay and Eat

The **Glebe Barn**, Cleadale, Eigg, t (01687) 482 417, *glebebarneigg@compuserve.com* (*cheap*). 24 beds at £9.50 per night.

Kinloch Castle, Rum, *see* below, t (01687) 462 026/037. Has a sort of hostel where you can stay in somewhat spartan but quite adequate accommodation (*cheap*), and a canteen-type restaurant. There is also accommodation in the peculiar sandstone castle itself.

Kildonan House, Eigg, t (01687) 482 446. Farmhouse accommodation.

For details of other guesthouses and self-catering, call Marie Kirk on t (01687) 482 416.

An Laimhrig, Eigg, t (01687) 482 468. A tearoom/craft shop serving light lunches and evening meals.

The **Estate Office** on Muck, t (01687) 462 365, can arrange self-catering cottages and camping.

National Trust for Scotland, 5 Charlotte Square, Edinburgh EH2 4DU, t (0131) 226 5922. The Trust has a guesthouse on the island of Canna; members take priority.

Tearoom/craft shop, Muck, t (01687) 462 362/990. With excellent home baking and craft courses.

---

stepped terraces to the sea, sliced off by cliffs to the north. The highest point of this long thin island is only 690ft above sea level. Compass Hill (458ft), in the north, is so called because of its magnetic rock that can distort the readings of a ship's compass.

Canna was an early-Christian settlement and the remains of a Celtic nunnery can still be seen, with one of the three oldest Celtic church structures identified in Scotland. The ruined tower near the harbour was owned by a Lord of the Isles, who is reputed to have imprisoned his beautiful wife in it, suspecting her of infidelity. Once held by the Clanranald Macdonalds, whose debts forced them to sell it in the 1820s, Canna was another victim of the Clearances, with 200 islanders evicted. In 1938 it was bought by the late John Lorne Campbell and his wife Margaret Fay Shaw, learned scholars of Gaelic music and literature. They gave the island to the National Trust for Scotland in 1981. Since John Lorne Campbell's death in 1992 the island has become a centre for Gaelic culture and learning, with Dr Fay Shaw, a tiny nonogenarian, still holding court at Canna House. The library incorporates the largest collection of Gaelic folk songs and tales ever made, and complete sets of all the relevant reference books. Meanwhile, a tiny, fragile Hebridean community survives here – just.

Muck

Muck, 7 miles south of Rum, is the smallest of the Small Isles, its strange name being derived from the Gaelic *muc mara* – a sea-pig or porpoise, of which there are many around. It is a green, pretty little island with lovely sandy beaches.

Skye

Speed bonny boat, like a bird on the wing,
'Onward' the sailors cry;
Carry the lad that's born to be king
Over the sea to Skye.
            from the 'Skye Boat Song' by Sir H. E. Boulton

Skye is *An t-Eilean Sgiatheanach* – The Winged Island – *sgiath* being 'wing' in Gaelic, referring to the flying 'winged' promontories of Trotternish in the northeast and Duirinish and Vaternish in the northwest. On the map it looks like a great, misshapen lobster claw, its pincers lumpy peninsulas separated by fiord-like inlets, surrounded by many islands. From the distance its silhouette is dominated by the Cuillins in the middle, a massive range of pointed peaks – training ground for international climbers – and by Macleod's Tables, two distinctive, flat-topped hills further north. The Cuillins act as a magnet for the clouds which, drawn to the peaks, tend to release their moisture rather frequently. The island contains unique geographical features such as the Quiraing and the Old Man of Storr.

Prince Charles hid in Skye for a while during his escape back to France after Culloden, having been escorted there from the Outer Isles by brave Flora Macdonald. The island is dotted with caves he is said to have hidden in, rocks he sat on, huts he sheltered in and places where he bid his faithful followers goodbye. (The outer isles are dotted with them, too, but they don't make such a to-do about them, being less tourist-orientated.)

The Clearances took their toll in Skye: 30,000 people are thought to have emigrated between 1840 and 1888. Protest by the people in the townships of Braes, south of Portree, against their landlord Lord Macdonald who was depriving them of essential grazing land, resulted in the Battle of Braes, the catalyst for the Crofters Act of 1886, establishing security of tenure at a fair, controlled rent and still effective today.

Skye is the most touristy of the Western Isles because of its accessibility, but tourism has not yet spoiled it. However, in 1991 the Scottish Office approved a long-disputed plan to build a half-mile toll bridge between Kyle of Lochalsh and Kyleakin – the longest single-span bridge outside Australia. This government-sponsored and privately funded road bridge opened in 1996 and has improved communications dramatically for the locals. Whether they will appreciate this in a few years' time, when Skye has become a Bonnie Prince Charlie Theme Park, remains to be seen.

Off the main road there are still rural communities quite untouched by the influx of knapsacks and campers. Gaelic is no longer the first language, though it is still spoken, and road signs are bilingual. Attempts are made in certain parts to revive the old language, with Gaelic teaching, a Gaelic College – *Sabhal mor Ostaig* – in Sleat, and Gaelic playgroups opening all over the island.

Portree is the only town on the island, a lively little place, busy in summer. The island now has arts centres, theatre shows, opera, traditional music and even reasonable restaurants.

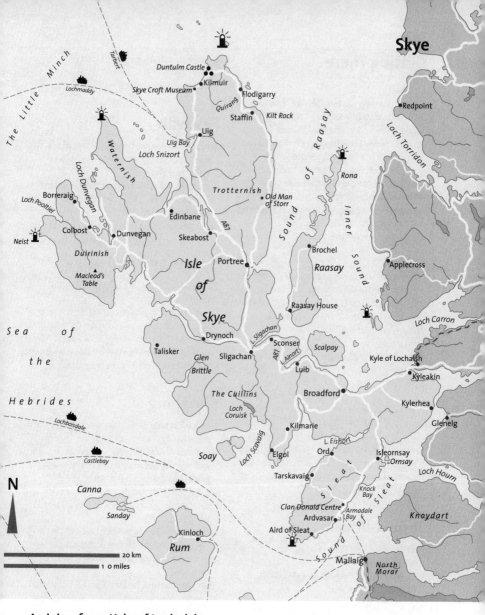

Arriving from Kyle of Lochalsh

Kyleakin, until recently a busy ferry terminus, stands around a small bay overlooked by a fragment of a ruin on a knoll; a jagged double tooth, familiar from postcards. The 12th-century relic was once a Mackinnon stronghold: **Castle Maol** or Moil, or Dunnakyne. (Kyleakin and Dunakin are said to be so named from King Haakon, who passed through on his way to Largs.) A story is told of one of the castle's earliest inmates, Saucy Mary, a Norwegian princess, who somehow managed to stretch a barrier across the Kyle in order to levy tolls from passing ships.

Getting There

By Sea

There is a daily car ferry service from Mallaig to Armadale (*Mar–mid-Oct*), taking half an hour, for which it is essential to book (*passengers only Nov–Mar, when there is no need to book*). There is a frequent service for the 5-minute, picturesque crossing from Glenelg to Kylerhea – the old drovers' route (*April–Oct*). (This is a private car ferry with turntable access.) Ferries run from Uig to the Outer Isles and from Sconser to Raasay.
Caledonian MacBrayne, t (01475) 650 100.

By Train

Trains run from Inverness to Kyle of Lochalsh – the Kyle Line, one of the most beautiful in Britain. Just as scenic is the West Highland Line, from Glasgow to Mallaig, via Fort William, connecting with the ferry to Armadale.
Scotrail, t 08457 484 950.

By Road

Coaches run from Glasgow and Inverness.
Citylink/National Express, t (0141) 332 9191.
Skyeways, t (01599) 534 238.
The new road bridge crosses from Kyle of Lochalsh to Kyleakin. Once on the island, there is a limited bus service and you can hire cars at Broadford and Portree. Broadford has a 24-hour petrol station.

Tourist Information

Broadford: t (01471) 822 361, **f** 822 141; *open May–Sept.*
Portree: Bayfield House, **t** (01478) 612 137, **f** 612 141; *open all year.*
Uig: t/f (01470) 542 404; *open May–Sept.*

Dunvegan: t (01470) 521 581, **f** 521 582; *open May–Sept.*
Or visit *www.highlandfreedom.com.*

Festivals

June: Skye Week, Portree; every sort of Scottish entertainment both indoors and out.
July: Portree Show.
August: Portree Folk Festival. Skye Highland Games, Portree. **Gala Day**, Dunvegan. **Dunvegan Show.**
September: Portree Fiddlers Rally.

Sports and Activities

Sabhal Mór Ostaig (big barn of Ostaig), a couple of miles from Isleornsay in Sleat, **t** (01471) 844 373. Gaelic college in a former Macdonald home farm, so popular and successful that they have built a great new extension. It runs courses on Gaelic music and culture as well as the language.

Shopping

North West Fishermen, Portree. Down by the pier. Fishing tackle, flies and fishing permits.
Ragamuffin, Armadale Pier. Unprepossessing-looking hut, but an Aladdin's Cave of very pricey knitted woollen garments.
Sleat Trading, Armadale Pier. Very superior tourist trap with an excellend second-hand book selection.
Skye Silver, in the old school, Colbost. Large range of original sterling silver and gold jewellery, and bargains if you are lucky. *Open daily 10–6.*
Skye Woollen Mill, Portree. Excellent cashmere and lambswool products at reduced prices, as well as a coffee lounge.

The **Brightwater Visitor Centre** on the pier (*open May–Nov*) tells the story of the Vikings and lighthouses, and lets you pry into the private lives of the otters on Eilean Ban (*see* p.463) and of seals and birds. Boat trips run to Eilean Ban from Kyleakin, **t** (01599) 350 040.

The new bridge whips you away westward along the coast. About 4 miles along, a very minor road leads southeast across moorland to **Kylerhea** (pronounced 'Kile-ray') and the ferry back to Glenelg.

Where to Stay and Eat

A rapidly expanding tourist industry means that there are literally hundreds of places to stay in all categories. These are but a few.

Flodigarry Country House Hotel, Staffin, beneath the Quiraing, t (01470) 552 203, f 552 301, www.flodigarry.co.uk (*expensive*). Has historic connections (*see* p.522), fine views across to the Ross-shire coast, and surprising Moorish-style décor in the converted billiard room. The food in its **Water Horse Restaurant** is usually excellent, apart from a tendency to disguise ingredients with unusual and not always enhancing sauces. Flora Macdonald's Cottage is an annexe next door. The hotel has collected up a commendable clutch of awards.

Hotel Eilean Iarmain, Isleornsay, t (01471) 833 332, f 833 275, www.eileaniarmain.co.uk (*expensive*). Traditional 'Highland' hotel with sporting trophies, tartan galore and suitable prints, right on the water with views over the Sound of Sleat. It is owned by Sir Iain Noble, the Gaelic-speaking white settler and entrepreneur who has done much to foster the revival of Gaelic – he founded the Gaelic college up the road – and who encourages his staff and guests to speak Gaelic. The food is excellent, both in the restaurant and the bar, and the bedrooms are tastefully decorated. It is a lively place and has art exhibitions in the adjoining Ceilidh Hall.

Kinloch Lodge, Sleat, t (01471) 833 214, f 833 277, www.kinloch-lodge.co.uk (*expensive*). On the northeast corner of the Sleat peninsula overlooking Loch na Dal. A former tacksman's house, it was converted into a Macdonald lodge in the 1870s and is now the home of Lord and Lady Macdonald and their family. Lord Macdonald is High Chief of Clan Macdonald, and Lady Macdonald is well known in her own right as Claire Macdonald, the cookery writer. The hotel feels lived-in and homely, with family portraits and antiques to add an ancestral touch and, needless to say, the food is first class. *Open Mar–Nov.*

Three Chimneys and House Over-By, Colbost, near Dunvegan, t (01470) 511 258, f 511 358, www.threechimneys.co.uk (*expensive*). First-class restaurant with six luxurious rooms. Highly recommended.

Ardvasar Hotel, Ardvasar, t (01471) 844 223 (*moderate*). Simple and friendly, near the pier at Armadale. *Open Mar–Oct.*

Corry Lodge, Liveras, Broadford, t (01471) 822 235, f 822 318, www.corrylodge.co.uk (*moderate*). Very upmarket guesthouse/B&B (dinner by arrangement) in a charming 18th-century house with sea views, nice grounds, a warm welcome and excellent food. Very comfortable.

Cuillin Hills Hotel, t (01478) 612 003, f 613 092, www.cuillinhills.demon.co.uk (*moderate*). Overlooks Portree Bay from attractive grounds, and has a highly recommended restaurant.

Dunollie Hotel, Broadford, t (01471) 822 253, f 822 060 (*moderate*). On the main road in Broadford, and has been extended into a large, predictable but reliable base with all mod cons. Has sadly lost much of its former atmosphere.

Isle of Raasay Hotel, t/f (01478) 660 222 (*moderate*). Overlooks the Sound of Raasay. Comfortable.

Kinlochfollart, by Dunvegan, t (01470) 521 470, f 521 740 (*moderate*). Restored former manse on the shore of Loch Dunvegan, run with the informal atmosphere of a Wolsey Lodge, with good home cooking. No smoking.

Lyndale House, Edinbane, t (01470) 582 329, linda@lyndale.free-online.co.uk (*moderate*).

Sleat

A couple of miles on past the turning to Kylerhea, the A851 leads south to the Sleat Peninsula (pronounced 'slate'), Macdonald territory. Isleornsay is an attractive hamlet on the east coast of the peninsula, 9 miles across heather-carpeted moor, looking across the Sound of Sleat into the mouth of Loch Hourn. Once the commercial centre for the island, called Eilean Iarmain, this attractive group of buildings includes a hotel,

Very comfortable B&B in a 300-year-old ex-tacksman's house, in a lovely setting with charming hosts.

Portree Hotel, Somerled Square, Portree, t (01478) 612 511, f 613 093 (*moderate*). Good old-fashioned hotel looking on to the square, with a seafood restaurant, bistro and carvery. Central, with a good atmosphere.

Rosedale Hotel, Portree, t (01478) 613 131, f 612 531 (*moderate*). On the waterfront overlooking the harbour; ask for a room with a sea view.

Royal Hotel, Portree, t (01478) 612 525, f 613 198, *info@royal-hotel.demon.co.uk* (*moderate*). Not quite as it was the day Prince Charles took his leave of Flora Macdonald in one of its parlours, but the older part has plenty of character.

Skeabost Hotel, near Portree, t (01470) 532 202, f 532 454, *skeabost@sol.co.uk* (*moderate*). Large Victorian lodge, built in 1870, very comfortable and old fashioned. They offer salmon fishing and serve good lunches.

Sligachan Hotel, t (01478) 650 204, f 650 207, *www.sligachan.co.uk* (*moderate*). Easy-going, ideally placed for the Cuillins, and still has the same port-in-a-storm feeling that H.V. Morton was so delighted with (*see* p.520).

Uig Hotel, Uig, t (01470) 542 205 (*moderate*). Wonderful old coaching inn overlooking Uig Bay, only a couple of minutes from the ferry. Cosy, friendly and highly recommended – especially for its breakfasts.

Viewfield House Hotel, t (01478) 612 217, f 613 517, *www.skye.co.uk/viewfield* (*moderate*). Set in 20 acres of garden and woodland on the outskirts of Portree as you come in from the south. Run by the family for whom it has always been home, it still retains the atmosphere of a relaxing, comfortable family establishment, surrounded by pictures, furniture and heirlooms that have

been there since the house was built. You'll feel you have been invited to stay with old friends. *Open April–Oct.*

Sconser Lodge Hotel, t (01478) 650 333 (*moderate–cheap*). Once a Victorian shooting lodge, at the mouth of Loch Sligachan, looking across to Raasay, small and welcoming, and the sea view is worth paying for.

Mrs B. La Trobe's House, Fiordhem, Ord, t (01471) 855 226, *www.fiordhem.co.uk* (*cheap*). The sea laps below the dining room, whose picture windows look west to the setting sun. B&B, with dinner by prior arrangement; take your own wine.

Braes, high above the Narrows of Raasay, south of Portree, t (01395) 597 214 (*cheap*). One of the nicest self-catering houses: a cosy, converted croft house (sleeping 6–7), looking across the Isle of Raasay to the mainland. Because it is also the much-loved home of the owners, it contains all the comfortable extras of family life.

Duntulm Castle Hotel, t (01470) 552 213, f 552 292, *www.duntulmcastle.co.uk* (*cheap*). High above Score Bay looking across to the Outer Isles, a view worth paying a bit extra for, with the castle close by. They also have five self-catering cottages, all with sea views, sleeping from 4 to 8 people, ranging in price and quality from cosy chalet to luxury bungalow. *Open Easter–Oct.*

Eilean Dubh, Edinbane, t (01470) 582 218 (*cheap*). Flora Cumming offers such welcoming and hospitable B&B, it's like going to stay with an old friend.

Ferry Inn Hotel, Uig, t (01470) 542 242 (*cheap*). Great atmosphere and not too many frills.

Neist Point lighthouse, t (01470) 511 200. The lighthouse keepers' cottages are available as holiday lets.

shop, small art gallery, ceilidh hall and whisky centre, as well as the old sea-flushing lavatory – now a dovecote. The Isle of Ornsay is just offshore from the hotel, with a lighthouse and a ruined chapel dedicated to the Columban monk, Oran.

At **Knock Bay**, Castle Camus or **Knock Castle** (*always accessible*), an overgrown ruin on a rocky peninsula, was held by the Macdonalds on condition they were always ready to receive the king or one of his representatives. Watch out for the *glaisrig* who haunts this ruin – a female sprite who graciously accepts libations of milk.

Armadale Castle was built by Gillespie Graham in 1815, incorporating an earlier mansion, with additions by David Bryce in 1856. Gutted, partly demolished and left as a 'sculptured ruin', it stands as a centrepiece to the restored gardens. A brand new **Museum of the Isles** has just opened, incorporating the Clan Donald Centre and the history of the Lords of the Isles (*open end Mar–end Oct daily 9–5.30; adm;* **t** *(01471) 844 305/227; grounds open all year*). The museum is excellent – worth crossing the Skye bridge for – the gardens are beautiful, and the former coach house/stable block has won prestigious awards for its restoration and conversion to a well-stocked book and gift shop, and a restaurant.

Armadale Pier, the terminal for the ferry to Mallaig, is unexpectedly well served for such an end-of-the-road place. There is a seafood takeaway and a few excellent shops. The road goes on another 5 miles to **Aird of Sleat**, with glorious views across the sound. A couple of miles' walk reaches the lighthouse on the southern tip of the peninsula where there is a sandy beach and more good views. Returning on the same road, take the narrow, twisting lane to the west, a mile north of Armadale. It runs for 5 miles through woodland and moor, past lochans and mossy glades among silver birches, out to the west coast of Sleat.

Tiny settlements cluster around coves and sandy beaches. The road goes north from **Tarskavaig** about 2 miles to **Dunsgaith Castle** (*always accessible*). This is one of the oldest fortified headlands in the Hebrides, home of the Macdonalds until the late 16th century. Little remains now but stacks of stones on a rock 40ft high, overlooking Loch Eishort. Celtic legend tells of Scathac the Wise, Queen of Skye in the Dark Ages, who held court here and preached the arts of peace and war to Cuchullin, an Ossianic hero. Cuchullin went off to a foreign land to practise his newly learned arts, leaving his beautiful wife, Bragela, weeping in vain at Dunsgaith, on 'The Isle of Mist'. He never returned.

The views at **Ord**, particularly of the Cuillins across Loch Eishort, and southwest to Rum, are magnificent, especially at sunset.

From here it is 15 miles or so to **Broadford**, rejoining the A851 a couple of miles short of Isleornsay. Broadford, a straggling settlement, is a busy place on a crossroads. It has hotels, shops and, inevitably, groups of people bowed under knapsacks. A new baker attached to the General Store makes delicious bread and cakes. Other shops include Skye Jewellers, a candlemaker and several craft shops. **Skye Serpentarium** (*open Easter–Oct daily; adm*) has a collection of the smaller reptiles such as snakes, lizards, frogs and tortoises; they also give homes to abandoned or illegally imported reptiles, and there are handling sessions, should you feel the urge.

Take the narrow, cul-de-sac road 14 miles southwest to **Elgol**, a scattered village with more splendid views. Here you can take the *Bella Jane* across Loch Scavaig to **Loch Coruisk** (*all year; essential to book:* **t**/**f** *(01471) 866 244,* **t** *0800 731 3089, 7.30–10am or 7.30–10pm*). This was a popular destination for Victorian tourist steamers, and was painted by Turner. The round trip takes over an hour, and you have time to walk across ice-smooth rocks to the inland loch, long, deep and dark, reaching northwestwards into the foothills of the Cuillins which fence it round with steep, uncompromising security. In the evening the sun goes down behind the hills, sending up great shafts of colour refracted by their proximity. For the energetic, another way is out along the Camasunary track from **Kilmarie**, about 3 miles before Elgol. It is an easy walk over stony ground through bracken and heather, with just one tricky bit – The Bad Step – where care is needed.

Anyone fortunate enough to be exploring by boat should put into the perfect natural harbour on the island of **Soay**, off the entrance to Loch Scavaig. The remains of a shark factory can be seen on the quay, established after the Second World War by the author Gavin Maxwell. His subsequent book, *Harpoon at a Venture*, is a compelling read, telling about these waters in the days when sharks and whales were so plentiful in the Minch that at times the water was literally black with them.

Continuing around the island from Broadford, the road follows the coast, looping around long inlets, zigzagging up the hills. In a thatched cottage at **Luib**, on Loch Ainort, there is is a **Folk Museum** (*open Easter–Sept Mon–Sat; adm*) furnished in the style of a croft house 100 years ago, with an 'on the trail of Bonnie Prince Charlie' exhibition and some interesting newspaper clippings about the Battle of Braes and other incidents at that time. From Luib there is an easy 4-mile walk due south following the river along Strath Mor, between the rounded paps of the red Cuillins and mighty Blaven, an isolated black Cuillin.

Continuing north, the main hazard for golfers on the nine-hole course at **Sconser** is sheep. The ferry for **Raasay** sails from here (*five times daily*).

The Cuillins

Beyond the lochs of the blood of the children of men,
beyond the frailty of plain and the labour of the mountain,
beyond poverty, consumption, fever, agony,
beyond hardship, wrong, tyranny, distress,
beyond misery, despair, hatred, treachery,
beyond guilt and defilement; watchful
heroic, the Cuillin is seen
rising on the other side of sorrow.

> The final lyric from 'The Cuillin', by the late Somhairle Macgill-Eain (Sorley MacLean), Skye's greatest poet

The Sligachan Hotel is a landmark at the head of **Loch Sligachan**, 5 miles west of Sconser on the junction of the east and west routes to the north, and is popular with fishermen and anyone planning to climb in the Cuillins. H.V. Morton visited it in the late 1920s in a raging storm: 'in spite of its hot baths, its aquatints and its garage, it was spiritually a mountain hut: the only place of warmth and shelter in the abomination of desolation'. Here, surrounded by the sound of falling water, the Cuillins reign supreme. Whether capped with snow, their lower slopes mottled and smeared like camouflage jackets; or elusive and eerie in mist; or shrouded by swirling cloud; or brilliant against a postcard-blue sky, they always present a challenge. Only experienced climbers with proper equipment should attempt to conquer these mountains, which have claimed many lives over the years.

The road up the east coast from Sligachan to Portree runs through valleys, pine woods and moorland past fast-flowing rivers and burns. Just south of Portree, a minor road goes out to Braes overlooking the Sound of Raasay, with lovely views and sheltered bays below the cliffs. This was the scene of the Battle of Braes in 1882, and home of the late Sorley MacLean whose evocative poetry lives on to prove that Gaeldom has not yet been completely smothered.

Portree

Portree is a busy little tourist resort, lively and attractive, built around a natural harbour with bright, neatly painted houses rising steeply from the water's edge. The name Portree is derived from the Gaelic *Port righ* – King's Port – after a visit by James V in 1540 when he came to subdue the islanders. During the summer, bus excursions run from here to many of the island's beauty spots.

Coming into Portree from the south you will see the **Aros Experience** (*open Mar–Oct daily 9am–9pm; Nov–Feb daily 9–6; adm*), one of the best of these many ventures, with an excellent exhibition which starts with an audiovisual show and takes you through graphic representations of the Jacobite rising with life-like tableaux. There is a good restaurant and a shop, and also Gaelic concerts on Thursdays in summer – ask at the desk. You can follow signed forest walks from the car park.

It was in a room in what is now the Royal Hotel that Prince Charles took his leave of Flora Macdonald. He repaid her the half-a-crown she had lent him, gave her a miniature of himself, and said: 'For all that has happened, I hope, Madam, we shall meet in St James yet.' He bowed and kissed her hand – a fugitive with a bundle of clean shirts, a chicken, a bottle of whisky and a bottle of brandy tied at his waist, and a £30,000 reward on his head. Such is the romance of Scotland.

An Tuireann Arts Centre and Café (*open daily 10–5; t (01478) 613 306*), in Struan Road, is a go-ahead place in the former fever hospital, with a gallery that has monthly exhibitions, live performances, workshops, and a new café with delicious home-made food.

Trotternish

Going northeast from Portree, up the Trotternish Peninsula, Prince Charles' Cave is about 3 miles north, out on the coast – one of the more doubtful of the Prince's alleged hiding places.

There is good trout fishing in the stocked **Storr Lochs**, from bank or boat.

The road twists and turns up the east coast, with views across the islands of Rona and Raasay, to Dundonnell, Torridon and Applecross on the mainland, south to the Cuillins and west to the Quiraing ridge. Stop at the car park at **Loch Mealt**, 7 miles north of the Old Man of Storr where the road comes to the brink of the cliff. The loch

The Old Man of Storr

Geographically part of the Quiraing, or Trotternish ridge, The Old Man of Storr, about 7 miles north of Portree, to the west of the road, is another of those landmarks made familiar by cameras. The easiest approach is through the forestry woods along maintained paths, rather than up the steep, southerly grass slopes. At over 180ft high and 40ft in diameter, The Old Man is the tallest of a group of mighty towers and pinnacles of basaltic rock, a great weathered stack, undercut and pointed at the top, like a giant fir cone.

In 1891, on the shore below the Old Man of Storr, a hoard of treasure was unearthed – a remarkable collection of silver neck rings, brooches, bracelets and beaten ingots, together with many 10th-century coins, some from Samarkand. It is believed they must have been left there by a Norseman, who never returned to claim them. These treasures are now in the Royal Museum of Scotland in Edinburgh.

drains in a sheer 300ft white cascade, plummeting into the cobalt sea. Extreme care should be taken here and vertigo sufferers should not think of approaching the edge, even though it is fenced. **Kilt Rock**, on the north side of Loch Mealt, has vertical columns of basalt over horizontal strips of grey and white oolite, like the pleats and pattern of a kilt.

The **Quiraing** is 2 miles west of Staffin. Park by the burial ground or in the lay-by at the top of the hill and approach it across the moor – a well-trodden path, you can't miss it. The last bit is quite a scramble up scree, through a steep, narrow gorge flanked by great pillars of basaltic rock like a surreal Gothic cathedral. At the top there is a plateau of emerald-green grass, as big as a football pitch: a magical place with panoramic views. Cattle used to be driven up here for safety during raids in the old days – they must have been as nimble as mountain goats.

Flodigarry, about 3 miles north of Staffin, is where Flora Macdonald lived for eight years after her marriage to Captain Allan Macdonald of Kingsburgh in 1751. Six of her seven children were born in **Flora Macdonald's Cottage**, which is now an annexe to the hotel, remodelled in a late 20th-century interpretation of 'traditional'.

Duntulm Castle

This is a jagged ruin, less than 5 miles to the west. The castle, with a water gate, stands in an easily defended position on a precipitous cliff on the northwest coast. Built on the site of an earlier fortress, it was a stronghold of the Macdonalds of Sleat, under the authority of James VI during his attempts to discipline the Hebridean chiefs at the turn of the 16th century. Sir Donald Gorme Macdonald was ordered to maintain his fortress in good condition, to restrict his household to six gentlemen, to limit his consumption of wine to four tuns (1,008 gallons) a year, and to produce three of his kinsmen annually as surety for his good behaviour. The family left the castle after a nursemaid dropped the laird's infant son out of a window into the sea. The luckless nursemaid was punished for her carelessness by being cast adrift in an open boat full of holes.

Kilmuir

One of Scotland's most endearing heroines, Flora Macdonald, is buried below a large white Celtic cross in the windswept churchyard at Kilmuir, a couple of miles further south. The cross is a replacement of the original which was a victim of souvenir-hunters. They say her shroud is a sheet on which Prince Charles slept when he was hidden at Kingsburgh House. Flora smuggled the Prince, disguised as her maid Betty Burke, from Loch Uskavagh in Benbecula to Skye. For this act of courage she was briefly imprisoned. She lived with her family in North Carolina for some years, but returned to Skye for the last decade of her life, dying at the age of 68. A portrait by Allan Ramsay shows a classic Scottish beauty with large eyes and a calm, fine-boned face. Dr Johnson, who was a guest at Kingsburgh in 1773, wrote of her:

> Flora Macdonald, a name that will be mentioned in history, and if courage and fidelity be virtues, mentioned with honour. She is a woman of middle stature, soft features, gentle manners and elegant presence.

From the churchyard you can look westwards across the entrance to Loch Snizort, to where Flora and the Prince came on their daring voyage.

The **Skye Museum of Island Life** (*open April–Oct Mon–Sat; adm*), close to the church-yard, is much the best of its ilk. Two thatched cottages (one unusually large) and a byre have been restored, and a number of new buildings constructed in recent years, to show life in a mid-19th-century crofting township, complete with the usual domestic artefacts and some interesting documents and photographs. The land stretching away to the south is known as the Granary of Skye, and was once a loch until drained by the Macdonalds.

Monkstadt House

Monkstadt House, 4 miles south of Kilmuir, now virtually a ruin, succeeded Duntulm as the Macdonald seat before they built Armadale Castle. This was the home of Sir Alexander Macdonald of Sleat who supported the Hanoverian cause. Flora and Prince Charles landed here while the house was occupied by Hanoverian troops. Fortunately Macdonald was away ingratiating himself with the Duke of Cumberland at Fort Augustus and his wife, Lady Margaret, was a staunch Jacobite. The Prince hid in the grounds where he was served by Macdonald of Kingsburgh who brought him food and wine under the noses of the soldiers.

Uig Bay

Uig Bay lies below a green amphitheatre of hills, its long pier cutting across it like an outflung arm. The hamlet of Uig is busy with ferry traffic, for this is the terminal for the steamer to the Outer Isles. If you are lucky, one of the fishing boats that use the pier may have berthed with a load of scampi and may agree to sell a bagful, scooped up off a great pile on deck. Anyone with a portable camping stove should boil these for just a few moments and eat them while still warm, accompanied by a slice of locally baked brown bread from the village shop.

Vaternish

At Borve, 11 miles south of Uig, take the right turn (west) and stop in **Skeabost**, a pretty hamlet at the head of **Loch Snizort Beag**. Below the stone bridge the river branches around an island, now reached by a bridge. (Take the road to the village hall; by the stone bridge on the right, a path leads to the new bridge.) This was the site of an ancient Christian settlement, probably founded by St Columba, whose name it bears, with the ruin of a Celtic chapel and a collection of old gravestones carved with effigies. It was a burial ground for the Bishops of the Isles, certainly from 1079 (except for about 60 years when it was transferred to St Germain's on the Isle of Man) until the bishopric moved to the Benedictine Monastery of Iona in 1498 after the eclipse of its patrons, the Lords of the Isles. The small church dates from the 13th century; the 16th-century mortuary chapel is said to contain the remains of 28 Nicolson chiefs.

Annait is the site of the oldest Christian settlement in these parts. The wall and foundations of a small chapel and the monks' cells are scattered across a green promontory between two deep gulleys. In this wild and lonely place the only sounds are the piping of skylarks, the chatter of running water and the wind.

At **Trumpan** is the consolidated ruin of Cille Chonain, a church with an unholy history. In 1579 the Macleods were attending a service in the church when they were attacked by their bitter enemies, the Clanranald Macdonalds from South Uist, who massacred them, setting fire to the church and burning the congregation. One woman, cutting off a breast in order to escape through a window, managed to get away and warn the remainder of the Macleod clan. When the Macdonalds returned to their boats they were massacred by the alerted Macleods.

Dunvegan

From the road south towards Dunvegan, the outline of Macleod's Tables dominates the horizon 10 miles away to the southwest. It is said that when Alasdair Macleod went to the court of King James V at Holyrood in Edinburgh in the 16th century, he was asked somewhat patronizingly whether he was impressed by the grandeur of the palace. He replied that he saw nothing to compare for grandeur with his own domain in Skye. When James V then visited Skye, trying to rally support from the Hebridean clans, Macleod gave an open-air banquet for him on the lower of the two 'tables', lit by his kilted clansmen, each holding aloft a flaming torch. 'My family candlesticks', he told the king, with a sweep of his hand. One can only hope it was a fine day and that the monarch was supplied with a good horse or some stout walking shoes.

Dunvegan Castle (*open Mon–Sat 10–5.30, Sun 1–5.30; facilities open Mar–Oct; in winter castle open 11–4; adm*), seat of the Macleods since at least 1200, is a massive castle on a rock, with Georgian sash windows and Victorian embellishments which do little to soften its fortress-like appearance. Today it is approached by a bridge over a ravine which once formed a dry moat. In the old days the only way in was from the sea through a watergate on to the rocks.

Boat cruises run from the jetty below the castle to the little islands where seals bask on the rocks. Look out for the excellent craft shop in the former factor's house just

The Fairy Flag

The castle contains family heirlooms, pictures, arms, original furnishings, documents and relics. The history of the Macleods can be traced back 30 generations to their Norse ancestry. The *pièce de résistance* is the Fairy Flag, a frail scrap of faded and worn silk, shot with gold thread and marked with crimson 'elf spots'. Legend tells of the Macleod who fell in love with a fairy, hundreds of years ago. The lovers were forced to part (at Fairy Bridge, to the north) and the fairy left the flag as a coverlet for their child. This flag had the power to save the Macleod clan from destruction three times, but only if waved in a genuine crisis. It has been used twice: once at Trumpan (*see above*), helping the Macleods to massacre the marauding Macdonalds of South Uist, and once during a famine, caused by cattle plague. It was unromantically subjected to modern tests that dated it to between AD 400 and 700 and gave it Middle Eastern origins. Perhaps an early Macleod went on one of the Crusades.

outside Dunvegan on the Portree road. Drive a few miles on past the castle to see seal colonies and swan lochs. At Claigan, follow the path to the coral beaches – don't be put off by the Aberdeen Angus bull who rarely bothers people.

Duirinish

The Duirinish Peninsula, topped by Macleod's Tables, stretches away west of Loch Dunvegan. Macleod's Maidens, only visible if you walk or go by sea, are off the southern tip 8 miles south of Dunvegan. These three basalt stacks are called after the wife and daughters of a Macleod, who drowned here in a shipwreck.

Colbost Folk Museum (*open Easter–Sept Mon–Sat; adm*) is a thatched black house with a peat fire in the middle of the room and all the implements and furnishings of the 19th century. There is also a replica illicit whisky still, once common all over the Highlands. The museum includes a watermill, 3 miles to the west at Glendale.

The **MacCrimmon Piping Heritage Centre** (*open April, May and Sept Tues–Sun; June–Aug daily; for information t (01470) 511 316/369*) at Borreraig, 2 miles north of Colbost, is a must for piping enthusiasts. It is a tribute to the MacCrimmons, hereditary pipers to the Macleods of Dunvegan and leading pipers and pipe teachers through the 17th and 18th centuries. One of them, Padruig Og, founded a piping school here which closed in about 1770, its scant remains marked by a cairn on the headland. The Piping Museum, in the old school, offers an opportunity to hear wonderful recordings of *piobaireachd*.

The **Toy Museum** at Glendale (*open Mon–Sat 10–6*) has a good collection of old toys.

Carry on west to Loch Pooltiel, with its sheltered anchorage, and then on to **Neist Point**, the most westerly point in Skye. Park at the top and walk down to the lighthouse, unmanned these days, its cottages available as holiday lets (*see above*).

Going south on the main road from Dunvegan, after about 8 miles look carefully up to the left as you drop down into Bracadale. **Dun Beag** (*always accessible*), one of the best brochs in Skye, seems to grow out of the hillside and would be easy to miss. It is only a few minutes' climb over springy turf and stones to this 2,000-year-old relic, which once stood 40 or 50ft high. This refuge, once used by farmers and herdsmen, has double walls braced by a honeycomb of chambers and galleries, with cells, passages and stairways and traces of outbuildings.

A detour west from Drynoch takes you to **Talisker**, home of Skye's only malt whisky distillery (*open for tours April–Oct Mon–Fri 9–4.30; July and Aug Sat also 9–4.30; Nov–Mar Mon–Fri 2–4.30; adm*). Johnson and Boswell stayed at Talisker House, at the foot of Preshal Mor, and Johnson found it rather gloomy. To the south are glorious sands and coastal and hill walks at **Glen Brittle**. This is a base for exploring the Cuillins and there is a campsite and a hostel here.

To complete a circular tour of Skye, take the road that runs southeast along the northern edge of the Cuillins, dappled with brown, tan, grey, blue and ochre, 14 miles back to Sligachan and the route to the mainland.

Raasay

The island of Raasay can be reached by ferry from Sconser (*Mon–Sat 10 crossings (15mins) from 8.30am*). It is about 13 miles long and about 3 at its widest, with the smaller island of Rona just off its northern shore and the fat lump of Scalpay to the south. Within the lee of the Skye and Applecross hills, it is sheltered and relatively fertile, and was once the hiding place of the fugitive Prince Charles, who spent a couple of nights in a shepherd's hut. The island suffered severe retribution for the loyalty of its Jacobite men, a hundred of whom fought in the prince's army. Dr Johnson visited the island during his tour of the Hebrides with Boswell and was lavishly entertained at Raasay House, rebuilt by the Macleods in 1746 to replace the one that had been gutted in the reprisals. The house and land were badly neglected by an absentee landlord in the 1970s, giving rise to much publicity and local outrage. It now houses the **Raasay Outdoor Centre** (*open April–Oct; courses from 1 day to week-long residential, covering most outdoor pursuits; also a good licensed café/restaurant*).

Castle Brochel

Castle Brochel – *Caisteal Bhrochail* – is a ruin on a rock on the eastern shore overlooking a bay, with the hills of Torridon massing on the eastern horizon. The danger notices are justified. Boswell, exploring this ruin, discovered that it contained a privy – a convenience that was sadly lacking in Raasay House where they were staying. He pointed this out to their host: 'You take very good care of one end of a man, but not of the other.'

There are two carved Celtic crosses within easy walking distance of Kilmaluag, and a ruined medieval chapel dedicated to St Moluag of Lismore, standing beside an 18th-century chapel in an enclosed burial ground. Dun Borodale has the scant remains of a broch. A pleasant walk up the Inverarish Burn reaches the flat-topped, volcano-like Dun Caan, upon which Boswell and his companions danced a Highland fling while he was being shown the island on a 24-mile hike.

The Outer Hebrides

Of all Scotland's islands, the Outer Hebrides seem to evoke the deepest nostalgia, its exiles suffering the strongest pangs of homesickness. There is no specific explanation. The distinctive tang of peat smoke, the Gaelic, the wild flowers on the machair, the cry of the curlew, the fundamental faith, the humour: these and many other things cast an unbreakable spell.

The Outer Isles run about 130 miles from the Butt of Lewis in the north, down to Barra Head in the south. The main islands include Lewis and Harris, Berneray, North Uist, Benbecula, South Uist, Eriskay, Barra, Scalpay, Vatersay and Mingulay.

Each is unique, with dialects that differ even between the moorlands of Lewis and the mountains of Harris. Gaelic still lives, the first language for many and fighting to remain so. North of Benbecula the islanders are almost entirely Presbyterian, and south almost entirely Catholic. The islanders are famous for the warm hospitality and friendliness they offer to strangers.

The scenery is made up of miles of white sand; acres of machair, rich in wild flowers; rugged hills and moorland carpeted with heather. The east coast is indented by long

Getting There

By Sea

Caledonian MacBrayne no longer hold the monopoly for ferries to the Outer Isles. Taygram, from Aberdeen, is setting up a rival service from Ullapool to Stornoway.

Roll-on/roll-off car ferries run from Ullapool to Stornoway in Lewis (2hrs 40mins); from Uig in Skye to Tarbert in Harris and Lochmaddy in North Uist (both 1½hrs); from Oban to Castlebay in Barra and Lochboisdale in South Uist (5hrs Oban–Castlebay, 3½hrs Mallaig–Castlebay, 1½hrs Castlebay–Lochboisdale). There is also a ferry between Otternish (Newton Ferry, North Uist) and Leverburgh, Harris (1hr). The timetable varies from day to day and for winter and summer. Apply to Caledonian Macbrayne, t 08705 650 000, www.calmac.co.uk. Local boats run between the smaller islands. Their timetables are sometimes subject to tides and sometimes they do extra runs to connect with other services. Details of these times are available from the Comhairle, t (01851) 703 773, locally, and tourist information centres.

By Air

British Airways fly to Stornoway from Glasgow and Inverness (Mon–Sat up to 3 times daily). They fly to Barra and Benbecula from Glasgow (Mon–Sat; also Sun to Barra in high summer). Highland Airways run inter-island flights between Stornoway, Benbecula and Barra, and also a competitive service between Inverness and Stornoway.
British Airway Express, t 0845 773 3377, www.britishairways.com.
Highland Airways, t (01851) 701 282, www.highlandairways.co.uk.

By Rail

Trains go to Oban, Mallaig and Kyle of Lochalsh. For Ullapool go to Inverness by train and link with a bus.
National Rail Enquiries, t 08457 484 950.

By Road

Buses to Ullapool, Uig, Oban and Mallaig all connect where possible with ferries:
Scottish Citylink Coaches, t 08705 505 050, www.citylink.co.uk.
Skyeways Express Coaches, t (01599) 534 238.
Public transport in the islands is operated through local garages, supplemented by the Post Bus Service, which is excellent: it is now possible to travel by bus from the Butt of Lewis to Barra, seamlessly in one day. For visitors wanting to explore at random, a car is essential. Cars can be hired locally; consult the tourist office for more information.

sea lochs that provide shelter for boats in bad weather. An aerial photograph reveals a land broken up by a vast number of lochs and lochans, which once provided waterways throughout the islands. The climate is unpredictable.

Tourists should note that some road signs are only in Gaelic, and are often difficult for strangers to pronounce and to translate into the more familiar Anglicized version. For example, if you saw *Taobh a Deas Loch Aineort*, you might not realize you had reached South Locheynort. In this guide, the Gaelic translation is given where it differs from the Anglicized name. The Western Isles Tourist Board have published an excellent leaflet with all the names in both English and Gaelic.

Lewis (Eilean Leodhas) and Harris (Hearadh)

Lewis and Harris are joined to form one island, the largest and most northerly land mass in the Outer Hebrides – Siamese twins with two separate identities.

Lewis, the northern two-thirds, has mountains in the southwest, undulating moor in the middle, thousands of lochs, especially in the southeast, green fertile croftland and many fine beaches. Aline Lodge, at the head of Loch Seaforth, marks the boundary between the two lands.

Harris is divided into north and south by a narrow isthmus at Tarbert (Taibeart), between East and West Loch Tarbert. North Harris has outstanding mountain scenery and the west coast of South Harris has machair and vast white sandy beaches. The east coast of South Harris is a complete contrast, with a rugged, rocky landscape cut by numerous inlets studded with rocks and islands. Although geographically one island, Lewis and Harris are effectively divided by the high range of hills along their border, the moors of Lewis giving way to the hills of Harris, dominated by Clisham, the highest mountain in the Western Isles (2,600ft).

The two lands share an early history. The first settlers were thought to be a Mediterranean race, megalithic Stone Age or early Bronze Age, who colonized the west of Britain by sea and built the Callanish Standing Stones in Lewis in the second millennium BC. Then came migrating Celts from central Europe in about 500 BC who built brochs, such as Carloway.

Norse invaders in the 9th century are thought to have married into island families and given their blood to the original clans: the Morrisons, Nicolsons and MacAulays. But it was the Macleods who dominated much of Lewis' history, also reputed to have

Harris Tweed

There is still a flourishing network of tweed weavers throughout both Lewis and Harris. Under the Harris Tweed Act, the cloth is only pure Harris tweed if it has been handwoven from local wool in the home of an islander, and finished in the islands; and it must comply with the quality requirements in the regulations which apply to the famous Orb trade mark. Visitors can stop off at the houses where it is still made and can usually buy the products.

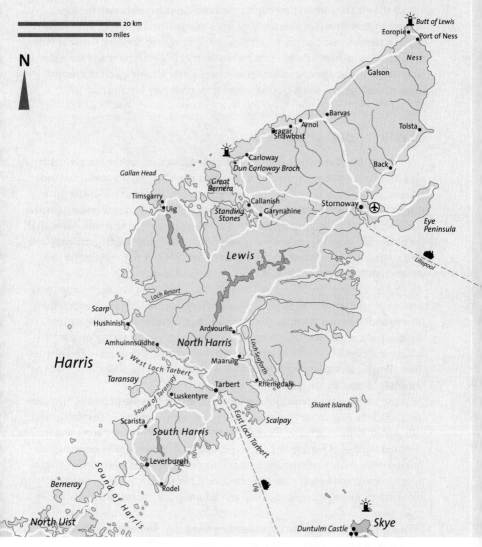

20 km
10 miles

N

Butt of Lewis
Eoropie • • Port of Ness

Ness

Galson •

Barvas •

Arnol •
Bragar • Tolsta
Shawbost •

Carloway •
Dun Carloway Broch

Back •

Great
Bernera
Gallan Head

Timsgarry •
Callanish •
• Uig Standing Garynahine •
Stones Stornoway

Eye
Peninsula

Lewis

Ullapool

Loch Resort

Scarp
Hushinish •
Ardvourlie •
North Harris

Amhuinnsuidhe •
Maaruig •

Harris West Loch Tarbert

Taransay Tarbert • • Rhenigdale

Sound of Taransay • Luskentyre
Shiant Islands

Loch Seaforth

Scarista •
Scalpay •
South Harris

East Loch Tarbert

• Leverburgh

Berneray
• Rodel
Uig

North Uist
Duntulm Castle • Skye

Sound of Harris

been of Norse descent, and it was between two Macleod brothers that Lewis and Harris were divided at an unknown date.

The economy of the two islands is based on crofting, fishing and Harris tweed, supplemented by increasing investment in tourism. The biggest employers are fish farming and the public sector, with tourism and information technology catching up.

Controversial plans to open huge quarries in the hills of Harris, for rock infill, have been refused permission, but an appeal is likely. They could provide much-needed employment but could also bring less welcome developments: a rash of unattractive housing estates, a severe threat to fragile road networks, damage to the environment, and shattering of the tranquillity.

Since the 1843 Disruption the people have been staunch members of the Free Church, and nowhere else have the 'Wee Frees' exerted more influence. The islanders speak different Gaelic dialects. Local children are brought up speaking Gaelic at home, but a growing number of 'white settlers' means that English is more and more the language of the playground and at social events. Gaelic is having a bit of a renaissance at the moment, and is playing a more important part in education.

Lewis (Eilean Leodhas)

After centuries of dispute over its ownership, Lewis was sold by the Mackenzies in 1844 to Sir James Matheson, who built Lews Castle overlooking Stornoway and tried to create a viable economy for his new island, including an unsuccessful attempt to extract tar from peat. He did much good, including afforestation, new houses, gas and water works and an improved harbour in Stornoway. He tried to help his tenants after the potato famine in 1845 by providing work on road and quay building, drainage and land improvement. He established a regular shipping service to the mainland and was responsible for the building of about 150 miles of roads.

In 1918 Lord Leverhulme, founder of Lever Brothers and Sunlight Soap, bought Lewis (and Harris) and spent close to a million pounds trying to redeem the islanders from poverty and create wealth through enterprise and the exploitation of the natural resources of the sea. He financed fishing boats, a cannery and ice factory, roads, bridges and even a light railway. He created a chain of retail fish shops – MacFisheries – with the ambition of controlling the fishing industry from the time the fish left the sea until it arrived on the table.

But the islanders are a proud, independent people and they like to control their own lands. After the First World War, when there was a certain amount of land settlement taking place elsewhere, those who had survived the horrors returned home and preferred the idea of possessing their own crofts to Lord Leverhulme's expensive 'improvements'. Both national and local politics finally defeated Leverhulme's philanthropic dreams and he was forced to withdraw his interests from Lewis, bringing about drastic unemployment, hardship and the emigration of over a thousand men to America.

Lewis is about to take off as a major surfing resort. An international festival, attracting world champions, has brought it up in line with Tiree.

Stornoway (Steòrnabhagh)

Stornoway, administrative centre for the Western Isles, and the only town in the islands apart from Portree which is more than a large village, is on the east coast. In the 16th century it was an historic burgh and flourishing trading centre, but the 20th century did it few architectural favours. It forms a sturdy metropolis built around a picturesque harbour busy with fishing boats and all the clutter of the waterfront, surrounded by brightly painted houses, reasonable shops and plenty of amenities including the **An Lanntair** arts centre, a swimming pool, golf course (*www.stornowaygolfclub.co.uk*) and a college.

For such a small town, Stornoway has a surprising range of restaurants, including Thai, Indian and Chinese, as well as excellent restaurants in the hotels.

When economic recession caused failure of the herring markets and Lord Leverhulme was forced to abandon his dreams, he offered to give Lewis to the people, but, much as they valued land ownership, pride drove them to refuse to accept his gift. Stornoway Town Council, however, accepted the land of the Stornoway Parish, including croftland, the town itself, **Lews Castle** and grounds. The Stornoway Trust was formed, an innovation for land ownership in the Highlands. It is administered by elected trustees so that the crofters are at the same time their own landlords and tenants of the Stornoway Trust, which is democratically administered by themselves. So far, their track record in land management has not been remarkable, particularly in respect of Lews Castle. They have recently invested considerable sums in the grounds, however, which are now well kept, with walks and viewpoints, and a woodland inter-pretation centre (*all open to the public*). The future of the castle is in the melting pot – meanwhile it stares gloomily down on the town, empty and reproachful, awaiting a sympathetic investor. The original Lews Castle, near the present ferry terminal, was the stronghold of the Macleods and was destroyed by Cromwell.

On New Year's Day 1919 a troop ship, the *Iolaire*, hit Holm Rock on the other side of the harbour in a gale, and sank, drowning 205 men returning from the war. Almost every family on the island was affected. Most of the 79 survivors owed their lives to John Macleod who swam ashore with a heaving line attached to a hawser, giving a handhold along which they could pull themselves.

Museum nan Eilean – Western Isles Museum (*open July and Aug Mon–Sat 10–1 and 2–5; Sept–June Mon–Fri 10–1 and 2–5*) is at the top end of Francis Street, with good local history displays, though you must allow time for reading a large number of wall hangings to get the full benefit, well displayed but indigestible if you are in a hurry.

Award-winning **An Lanntair Gallery**, in South Beach Street (*open Mon–Sat; t (01851) 703 307; www.lanntair.com*), is lively and popular, with local, national and interna-tional exhibitions, programme of events, a café and small book/craft/souvenir shop. The exhibitions are changed every month; the events range from traditional and clas-sical to jazz and rock, with plenty of emphasis on Gaelic culture.

Lewis Loom Centre (*open Mon–Sat 10–5; adm; t (01851) 703 117; www.lewisloom centre.co.uk*), in an old grainstore overlooking the inner harbour in Bayhead beyond Cromwell Street, is an excellent place to learn about the Harris tweed industry. A 30- to 40-minute guided tour leads you through the traditional methods of carding, spin-ning, warping, waulking and weaving by hand with plant-dyed wools. There is a shop.

About 3 miles south of the castle, on the edge of Arnish Moor, a cairn commemo-rates the night Prince Charles spent here while trying to negotiate for a boat during his fugitive days after Culloden. (Such was rumour in those days that when one of his three companions, Donald Macleod, went ahead of him into Stornoway to make arrangements, he found large numbers of armed Mackenzies preparing to fight off the Prince and an estimated army of 500 Highlanders.)

Tourist Information

Lewis: Western Isles Tourist Board,
26 Cromwell Street, Stornoway, t (01851) 703
088, f 705 224, www.witb.co.uk,
www.visitscotland.com; open all year.
Harris: Pier Road, Tarbert, t/f (01859) 502 011;
open all year.

Festivals

July: Hebridean Celtic Festival, Stornoway,
www.hebceltfest.co.uk; international music
festival with world-famous performers,
concerts and fringe events.

Where to Stay and Eat

Lewis t (01851–)
Baile-Na-Cille, Timsgarry, Uig, t 672 242, f 672
241 (moderate–cheap). Converted 18th-
century manse in a superb position
overlooking Uig Sands; probably the nicest
place to stay in Lewis. Its delightful hosts
offer easy, friendly hospitality, with delicious
set-menu dinners served at a communal
table. Open Mar–Oct.
Galson Farm, South Galson, Ness, t/f 850 492,
www.galsonfarm.freeserve.co.uk
(moderate–cheap). Restored 18th-century
farmhouse for marvellous B&B, with dinner
by arrangement. Delightful hosts, and the
sea on the doorstep.
Hebridean Guest House, Stornoway, t 702 268,
f 701 791, hebgh@sol.co.uk (moderate–cheap).
If you have to stay in Stornoway, try to stay
here. Overlooking the golf course at
Bayhead, it is easily the nicest place in town:
comfortable and friendly.
Royal Hotel, Cromwell Street, Stornoway, t 702
109, f 703 900 (moderate–cheap). Your best

alternative in Stornoway, fairly traditional
and very central.
Scaliscro Lodge, Uig, t 672 325, f 672 393
(moderate–cheap). Comfortable, family-run,
remote and secluded, with outstanding
views and salmon fishing. Open April–Dec.
Eshcol Guest House, Callanish, t/f 621 357,
www.eshcol.com (cheap). With wonderful
views, with the stones in the background.
Very comfortable and hospitable.
Gearrannan Blackhouse Village, Carloway,
t 643 416, f 643 488, www.gearrannan.com
(cheap). Two bedrooms (sleeping 5).
Delightful and cosy, though not particularly
peaceful, on the beach.
Seaside Villa, Back, t/f 820 208 (cheap). Try
Margaret Fraser for a recommended B&B,
with wonderful views and welcome.
Bonaventure, Aird, t 672 474. A most unexpected French–Scottish restaurant run by
Richard, the chef, who is French, and Joanne,
his wife, a Scottish artist. The food is
fantastic, the views stunning and the
atmosphere great. Closed Sun and Mon.
The Copper Kettle, overlooking Loch Dalbeg,
signed off the main road, t 710 592. Part
tea room, with home-baked goodies; part
restaurant – an unexpected haven with
excellent food. Book for evening meals.

Harris t (01859–)
Abhainnsuidhe Castle, t 560 268, www.
castlecook.com (expensive). Residential
cookery and painting school with the
celebrity chef Rosemary Shrager. Also runs
up-market fishing and stalking holidays.
Ardvourlie Castle, t 502 307, f 502 348
(moderate). Splendid, rather gaunt house
overlooking Loch Seaforth not far from
where Prince Charles landed after his
narrow escape from the avaricious minister,
Macaulay, on Scalpay. Once a Victorian
shooting lodge, the forbidding exterior hides

Around the Island

East of Stornoway, past the airport, a narrow neck of land connects **Point** (an Rubha)
to the rest of Lewis. It is also called the Eye (or Ui) Peninsula, after a Norse word
meaning narrow ford or isthmus. The 14th-century **St Columba's Church**, at the
western end of Point, is the burial ground of the Macleod chiefs. There is some fine
carving in the church, which was last used in 1828 and is now seriously threatened by
erosion from the sea.

a delightfully comfortable guesthouse with marvellous ancestral bathrooms and beds. Run by a brother and sister team, the atmosphere is relaxing and people come back. The dining room is lit by gas and oil lamps. There's a well-supplied 'honesty bar' in the sitting room and a grand piano in the library. An unusual place and very friendly.

Harris Hotel, Tarbert, t 502 154, f 502 281, *cameronharris@btinternet.com* (*moderate*). Large by island standards, sprawling, easygoing and comfortable. Not all the 24 bedrooms are en suite, but the staff are helpful and accommodating.

Leachin House, just along the north shore of West Loch Tarbert, t/f 502 157, *www.leachin-house.com* (*moderate*). The best place to stay around here, a comfortable Victorian house – formerly a tweed merchant's – run as a family home. It is very friendly, the food is excellent and you might see otters from your bedroom window.

Rodel Hotel, Rodel, t 520 210, *www.rodelhotel.co.uk* (*moderate*). Recently restored to its former excellent standard of comfort and Highland hospitality.

Scarista House, Scarista, t 550 238, f 550 277, *www.scaristahouse.com* (*moderate*). Guesthouse in a listed Georgian manse above the road at Scarista, with a reputation endorsed by those who go back for more. It is comfortable, with peat fires, antique furniture and a good library, overlooking 3 miles of glorious sandy beach. Non-residents can eat here (although you must book) and the set-menu dinner is excellent, with an extensive wine list. There are two self-catering cottages in the grounds (sleeping 6, and sleeping 4).

Am Bothan, Leverburgh, t/f 520 251, *www.ambothan.com* (*cheap; from £10 a night*). Timber bunkhouse for self-catering, built by Ruaridh Beaton, an enterprising boat designer, builder and yachtsman. You

can't miss it on the crest of the brae, and there is no other place quite like it for atmosphere and Hebridean hospitality. Beautifully designed and equipped, with full facilities for people with disabilities.

St Kilda House, Leverburgh, t 520 419 (*cheap*). Small guesthouse in a school teacher's house, cosy and friendly. Good food.

Scaladale Centre, Ardvourlie, t/f 502 502, *www.scaladale.co.uk* (*cheap*). Newly built self-catering complex (sleeping up to 28). For group activities. *Open all year*.

Tigh na Mara, East Tarbert, t 502 270, *www.tarbert-harris.freeserve.co.uk* (*cheap*). A really good B&B. A modern house with lovely views, 5 minutes' walk from the ferry. Mrs Flora Morrison gives her guests every attention and is proud of her home baking and hearty meals (dinner on request).

The Anchorage, Leverburgh. A new wooden building by the pier serving meals; also lively themed evenings.

Carminish House, t 520 400, f 520 307 (*cheap*). Overlooking the Carminish Islands and the Sound of Harris just south of Leverburgh. A good base for this area: friendly, modern and comfortable.

First Fruits Tearoom, Pier Road Cottage, Tarbert. Delicious meals or snacks in traditional surroundings.

Berneray t (01876–)

Berneray Hostel, Gatliff Hebridean Hostels Trust, *www.gatliff.org.uk*. Two converted black houses (sleeping 16). No booking.

Donald MacKillip, t/f 540 235 (*cheap*). Does B&B and will share his crofting activities.

Mrs MacAskill, t 540 230. A modern, well-equipped croft house overlooking the sea, for self-catering (sleeping 8).

Mrs Mairi MacInnes, t (01876) 540 253 (*cheap*). B&B.

Mrs Peggy MacLeod, t 540 254 (*cheap*). B&B.

North of Stornoway, **Back** (Am Bac) and **North Tolsta** (Tolastadh) have fertile croft land, steep cliffs and large white beaches, unique on the east coast of the Western Isles. At the end of the road is Lord Leverhulme's 'bridge to nowhere', the beginning of the road he hoped to build between Tolsta and Ness to complete the coastal road.

The **Butt of Lewis** (Rubha Robhanais) is a bleak headland on the northern tip of the island, 27 miles from Stornoway by road, and topped by a lighthouse. This is a birdwatcher's dreamland: shags, cormorants, puffins, razorbills, guillemots, terns, kittiwakes, fulmars, gulls, oystercatchers, plovers, redshanks and greenshanks are just a few of the birds whose calls echo among the cliffs.

The 'Ness' (Nis) district just to the south has a good museum, the **Ness Heritage Centre**, at Habost (*open summer only; for times call* **t** *(01851) 810 377*), which serves tea, coffee and home-baked cakes. The **Harbour View Gallery**, at Port of Ness, has contemporary watercolours, prints and cards featuring local scenes. **Taigh Dhonnachaidh** is a new arts centre in Ness, which also boasts an active football and social club. There are good beaches here, particularly the one near the harbour at Port of Ness. On the road out to the lighthouse the old *feannagan*, or inappropriately named lazy beds, can be seen clearly, characteristic of the old type of agriculture practised throughout the islands. There was nothing lazy about the hard work that went into digging these strips and fertilizing them with seaweed carted from the shore in heavy creels.

At **Eoropie** (Eoropaidh), the hamlet southwest of the lighthouse, is the restored 12th-century **St Moluag's Chapel**, known as Teamphull Mholuidh and built on the site of an early Christian chapel. The key for this charming little place is in the shop. Episcopal services are held occasionally, and there is a strong feeling of the simple, uncomplicated faith that keeps such a remote church alive.

About 10 miles down the A857, the 20ft monolith, the **Thrushel Stone** (Clach an Truiseil), is the largest single stone in Scotland, a relic from prehistoric settlers. This and the burial cairn within a stone circle surrounded by bleak moorland at **Steinacleit**, about a mile or so away, have a marvellously primal atmosphere.

Arnol Black House Museum (*open Mon–Sat; adm; for times call* **t** *(01851) 710 395*), about 8 miles further on, is an authentic restored black house dating from 1870 and inhabited until 1964, perhaps the best example of its kind, particularly if you can persuade the curator to turn off the electric lighting. A peat fire burns all day on the floor in the middle of the main room, surrounded by original furniture made mostly from driftwood. The house is much larger than those seen on other islands, with a large enclosure for animals at one end, a sizeable bedroom with box beds, and several store rooms. Without artificial lighting, with the wind howling outside and the rain lashing the sod- and reed-thatched roof, you can really feel how it might have been.

At **Bragar**, little more than a mile beyond Arnol, look for a gateway set back and at right angles to the road, topped by the massive jaw bone of an 85ft blue whale that came ashore in the bay here in 1920. It had been harpooned and the harpoon remains embedded in the bone.

Shawbost (Siabost) Folk Museum (*open April–Sept Mon–Sat; donation box*), in a converted kirk, is a couple of miles further on and easy to miss. It stands beside the school in front of a factory-type building; the windows are covered in corrugated sheeting and a blue sign on the wall looks like a church notice board until you are close enough to read 'Museum'. Started by local schoolchildren, the museum is a splendidly random collection of artefacts mostly donated by members of the local community. Exhibits are laid out on tables like contributions to the white elephant stall at the village fête, with delightful hand-written labels. To the provenance of a miner's lamp, remarkably similar to those sold by Habitat in the 1970s, is added the comment that the owner 'had no idea where it came from'.

L for Leather, just beyond the museum on the same side of the road, is a small cottage identified by piles of netting and buoys in the garden, and the name painted on the gable end. Inside you will find Kenny Stephen perched in a dentist's chair in a trim, flower-bedecked workshop, surrounded by bags, belts and luggage he created from leather collected with hair-raising stories from all over the world. Even if no longer in production, he still welcomes visitors for a yarn.

Shawbost Norse Mill and Kiln (*always accessible*) is signed not far beyond Shawbost to the right, with a car park and a short walk over the brae. These two small thatched buildings illustrate how barley was processed into meal at a time when this was a crucial part of crofting life. They were restored with assistance from the school-children who helped set up the museum.

Between Shawbost and Carloway (Carlabhagh), there are beautiful sheltered beaches at **Dalbeg** (Dail Beag) and **Dalmore** (Dail Mor), down turnings off the A857.

The Gearrannan Black House Village

In **Carloway**, 5 miles southwest of Shawbost, drive out to the parking place at the end of the Gearrannan road. Just around the corner a cobbled road twists down to a cluster of traditional black houses – the fishing settlement of Gearrannan. One is the Gatliff Trust Hostel, pretty basic but with a very cosy living room. The rest of the houses have been well restored by the Gearrannan Trust (*www.gearrannan.com*) and are a great attraction. One is available for self-catering.

Carloway Broch (*always accessible*), on a small hill signed to the right a couple of miles beyond the village, is the best-preserved broch in the Hebrides, second only in quality of preservation to Mousa Broch in Shetland. Part of its double-thickness, dry-stone wall rises to about 30ft, close to its original height, with a honeycomb of galleries and stairs in the cavity, many of which can still be explored. A good informa-tion board illustrates the probable construction of less durable accommodation inside the enclosure. These 2,000-year-old brochs that litter the coastline of Scotland are thought to have been built to shelter communities and their animals from invaders. The one small entrance to the tapered tower would have been easy to defend. There is a good little visitor centre (*open May–Sept Mon–Sat 10–5*).

Callanish (Calanais) Standing Stones

The Callanish Standing Stones (*always accessible*) are well signed, about 6 miles south of Carloway along the northern shore of East Loch Roag. A path leads up from the car park to the stones and, unlike Stonehenge with which they rank in impor-tance, there are no restrictions to access, though visitors are encouraged to use an encircling path. Erected about 4,000 years ago, they form one of the most complete prehistoric sites in Britain. The 47 surviving stones are said to depict a Celtic wheel-cross, not easy to make out, with a burial cairn at the centre, approached from north and south by avenues of pillars. Traces of cremated bones were found in the cairn. The central pillar casts its shadow along the entrance passage into the grave only at sunset on the days of the equinox. It is a dramatic place, primal and mysterious, conjuring up the burial of some priest-king with the elaborate ritual practised in the centuries before Christianity. Engineers from the Hydro Electric, laying power lines near the site, unearthed numerous drinking vessels with traces of potent heather beer, honey mead and a crude form of whisky. These have led archaeologists to believe that the people who erected the stones indulged in the 'ritualistic and habitual use of alcohol' – *plus ça change.*

Beyond the car park a **museum/visitor centre** (*open April–Sept Mon–Sat 10–7; Oct–Mar 10–4; adm to museum and audiovisual show*) is carefully designed to be out of sight of the stones. There is a scant, predictable souvenir shop and a café where you can get filling meals and excellent home-made soup.

Far more atmospheric, and easy to miss because the tourist signs all point you to the Historic Scotland-owned visitor centre, is a converted **Black House Café** and gift shop, diagonally opposite the stones (you can drive round to it on a badly signed road about half a mile north of the main turning). Inside this authentic-looking building there is a cosy tearoom with home baking, and quite expensive tweedy and wollen garments and craft-type souvenirs.

On a clear day the **Flannan Islands Lighthouse** can be seen, 15 miles to the west. In 1900 a gale raged at Christmas and all three of the lighthouse-keepers vanished without trace, leaving a meal on the table and an overturned chair: a famous unsolved mystery.

South from Callanish

After Callanish, the B8011 branches south at **Garynahine** (Gearraidh Na H-Aibhne) for **Bernera** (Bearnaraigh) and **Uig**. The island of Bernera is reached by a 'bridge over the Atlantic', built in 1953. The men of Bernera were agitators in the period leading up to the 1886 crofters' revolt, when they marched with their grievances to the landlord, Sir James Matheson, in his castle in Stornoway. **Bost Iron-Age House**, at Bernera (*for opening times call t (01851) 612 331*), is a replica Iron-Age house and museum built close to where archaeologists excavated the real thing. The community centres at both Bernera and Uig are open for tea, coffee and home-baked cakes. **Bosta Beach**, on the northern tip, is well worth a visit. Continue down the B8011 and explore the district around Uig, which has some of the most beautiful scenery in the islands. At Valtos, there is an outdoor centre, for rock climbing, abseiling, archery, etc.

The famous **Lewis Chessmen**, made of walrus ivory, were discovered in 1831 (dug up by a cow) in the sands of **Ardroil** (Eadar Dha Fhadhail), a few miles south of Gallan Head. Of Norse origin, they are thought to have been buried here to save them from plunder by nuns living in a Benedictine convent at Brenish at the end of the road. Replicas can be bought all over the islands. The original chessmen are divided between the British Museum and the National Museum of Scotland.

This is grand walking country – along the coast to the Uig Hills and south to the hills of Harris. Going south from Stornoway, the road goes through the 'Lochs' area and a detour east on the B8060 leads down to **Lemreway** (Leumrabhagh). The land is split by deep sea lochs and masses of little lochans, surrounded by heathery hills, and not very beautiful.

Harris (Na Hearadh)

The boundary between Harris and Lewis runs between lochs Resort and Seaforth with Harris itself being further split into north and south by the narrow isthmus at Tarbert, between West and East Loch Tarbert. This relatively small 'island' contains a kaleidoscope of scenic variety: mountains, moorland, lunaresque rockscapes, sandy beaches and, on the southeast coast, myriad rocky/sandy inlets backed by heather-strewn crags.

The early history of Harris is similar to that of Lewis, until it was given a separate identity in Norse times when the one land mass was divided between two Macleod sons. The Macleods held Harris for 500 years, subservient to the Lords of the Isles, with fewer battles for supremacy than were fought in Lewis. Captain Alexander Macleod of Berneray, who bought the property from a kinsman in 1779, was an enlightened landlord who had made a fortune in India. He promoted the fishing industry, improving existing facilities and building more; he imported east coast fish-ermen to teach the islanders, lent money for boats and equipment, and provided cottages and land, rent free. He established a spinning factory, built a school and an inn, and constructed roads. In 1834 his grandson sold Harris to the Earl of Dunmore, who later sold North Harris to the Scotts.

When Lord Leverhulme, who had bought Lewis and Harris (*see* above) in 1918, pulled out of Lewis in 1923, he concentrated his energies on Harris. He started to develop Obbe as a fishing station, renaming it Leverburgh, bought a Norwegian whaling station at Bunavoneadar, built a spinning mill, and started on an ambitious road-building programme. Although his schemes had more support than they had had in Lewis, none flourished, for a variety of reasons, and they died with him in 1925. The estates and developments were subsequently sold for a fraction of the sum Leverhulme had invested in them. Today, as in Lewis, the economy is based on fishing, tweed and, increasingly, tourism and information technology.

Tarbert (An Tairbeart)

Tarbert, Harris' main village, at the head of East Loch Tarbert on the east coast, is an attractive, down-to-earth place with a good tourist information centre, a few shops (*mostly souvenirs*), and the ferry terminal for Skye. It is a good base for fishermen, for salmon, sea trout and trout, and for sea fishing.

Scalpay and Shiant Islands

Scalpay (Scalpaigh), at the entrance to East Loch Tarbert and accessible by causeway, was where the fugitive Prince Charles stayed whilst trying to arrange a boat from Stornoway. He and his three companions spent four nights here as guests of the tenant, Donald Campbell. It was here that the only recorded attempt to betray the Prince for the £30,000 reward offered for his capture was made. John Macaulay (grandfather of the historian Lord Macaulay) was the Presbyterian minister in South Uist. A zealous Whig on a Catholic island, he sent word to his father, Aulay Macaulay, who was minister in Harris. He warned him of the Prince's arrival and urged him to contact Colin Mackenzie, the minister in Stornoway, and arrange to have the fugitive arrested. A boatload of armed men led by Aulay duly landed on Scalpay 'with a determined resolution to seize the Chevalier and secure the bribe offered by the Government'. They reckoned without Donald Campbell who, although not a Jacobite, was deeply aware of his obligations as a Highlander and a host. He refused the offered bribe and dismissed the invaders with bitter scorn; they slunk away, ashamed. Donald Campbell's house is now the Free Church Manse.

The footpath east from Tarbert to Scalpay was until now the only access by land to the little village of **Rhenigadale** (Reinigeadal). The new road down from Maraig makes life a lot easier for this small community, which includes a Youth Hostel (Gatliffe Hebridean Trust).

When weather permits, boat cruises run from Tarbert to the **Shiant Islands**, 12 miles to the east, a wild cliff-land with a natural sea arch and a huge colony of puffins and other sea birds. Compton Mackenzie owned them for a while, and wrote some of his books here.

Around the Island

North of Tarbert is **Ardvourlie Castle**, once a shooting lodge and now a guesthouse (*see* above) on the west side of the loch. It was near here that Prince Charles landed to walk the rest of the way to Arnish. There is a newly built activity centre, the **Scaladale Centre**, at Ardvourlie, *see* above.

The B887 goes west off the A859 to **Bunavoneadar** (Bun Abhainn Eadarra), where the Norwegian whaling station was built in 1912 when whales were plentiful, and which Lord Leverhulme tried unsuccessfully to regenerate. All that is left is the tall, red chimney from the oil-extraction plant and a few desolate ruins.

About 8 miles further on, salmon jostle in the sea, waiting to jump the falls where Loch Leosaidh disgorges down a series of rock slabs into the sea below **Abhainnsuidhe Castle** (difficult to pronounce – approximately, Avensoyr). If you are lucky you will see the fish making their heroic leaps from pool to pool, against seemingly impossible odds, on their journey to the spawning grounds. There is a lay-by but you are not encouraged to linger. The road runs right past the front door of the castle, literally through the front garden. It was a Victorian shooting lodge built in 1867 for the Earl of Dunmore; today it is a private house, run as a cookery and painting school (*see* above). James Barrie began his novel *Mary Rose* here.

The beaches at **Hushinish** (Huisinis), another 5 miles on at the end of the road, are magnificent. **Scarp**, the island off the tip at Hushinish, is best known because in 1934 it was to be the recipient of a very advanced method of postal delivery: mail was to be sent by rocket. A special stamp was issued, and the first rocket was fired. Unfortunately it exploded, as rockets tend to, destroying the mail and the project. A film has been made about this Rocket Project (scheduled for release in 2002).

Familiar to TV fans is the island of **Taransay**, inhabited until 1974 and the stage for *Castaway 2000*, when a handful of volunteers were dumped on the island and supposed to be self-sufficient for a year. It wasn't exactly pioneering, with living 'pods' and livestock provided, and rescue every time anyone felt a sniffle coming on, but it provided great amusement for the TV viewers and for those who sneaked in by boat with contraband supplies and listened to the less-publicised stories. The schoolhouse is available for holidays (*contact the tourist information office*). The Rocket Project film was shot on Taransay.

The east coast route down South Harris, called the Golden Road, is a tortuous single track through a bleak, stony landscape enhanced by wonderful remote rocky inlets and the clustered cottages of small communities. The tiny cultivated patches were painstakingly nurtured by people evicted from the fertile west coast and forced to live here and try to make a living from fishing. Many of their descendants are now weavers, and around **Plocrapool** (Plocrabol) there are several places where you can watch them weaving Harris tweed on looms in their houses. A good one to visit and buy reasonably priced tweed and woollens is run by the Campbell family, signed off the road in Plocrapool. They usually have a good stock of sweaters, socks and stockings and tweeds. There is little hand-spinning to be seen these days, but you can see the whole process in an unlikely looking, tiny corrugated shack at **Clo Mor**, signed off the road at **Likisto**. There is a Youth Hostel at Stockinish (Stocinis) (*open summer only*).

At **Rodel** (Roghadal), on the northern headland of Loch Rodel, **St Clement's Church** is the finest pre-Reformation church in the Western Isles, its cruciform design thought to have been influenced by that of Iona Abbey. The present building, probably built on the site of a former church, dates from the mid-16th century. With the coming of the Reformation soon after its completion, it was hardly used for worship before it became redundant. Frequently restored, and recently repaired by Historic Scotland, some of the walls and the greater part of the tower are original. You can climb to the top of the tower on a series of stairs and ladders. Of the two medieval tombs inside, the most magnificent is that of Alasdair Crottach, the Macleod chief from Dunvegan who entertained James V on Macleod's Tables (*see* p.524) and died in 1548.

Walk around the outside to the east face of the tower and look for the *sheila-na-gig* – a 'fallen angel' with flowing hair and skirts lifted to display her private parts – a common device originating from Ireland, thought to distract evil spirits that followed worshippers into church. Most unfortunately, some completely hideous public lavatories have slipped past the watchful eye of conservationists and landed up just below this otherwise sublime building.

The attractive, secluded 18th-century harbour at Rodel is overlooked by the **Rodel Hotel** (recently restored and rescued from dereliction, *see* above), with a plaque on the wall recording a visit by Queen Elizabeth II in 1956. The house was built by Captain Alexander Macleod (*see* above) in 1785 when he returned rich from India and bought Harris. He built the harbour and established a fishing station here with ancillary buildings as part of his plan to develop the potential of the island.

Leverburgh (An T-ob/Tob), on the south coast about 3 miles northwest of Rodel, was developed from the small settlement of Obbe by Lord Leverhulme after his plans for Stornoway had collapsed. He put a great deal of money into improving the harbour, building a large pier, houses, kippering sheds, roads and lighthouses. But he died a year after the local fishing industry began to flourish, and with him died the drive and energy needed to keep things going as he had planned. It isn't much of a place to linger in; a few rather dismal souvenir and book shops, a café above the General Store and, somewhat surprisingly, a smart beautician. A car ferry runs from here to North Uist; it only has vending machines for beverages and snacks.

At Northton (Taobh Tuath), to the northwest, **Seallam** is a new genealogy research and visitor centre (*for times call* **t** *(01859) 520 258, www.seallam.com*), with a fascinating exhibition on the Story of the Western Isles, a café and shop. Nearby in the old schoolhouse, Bill Lawson has genealogy and history books, photographs, illustrated talks and lectures, and runs guided walks (**t** *(01859) 520 488*). The **MacGillivray Centre**, at the end of the road in Northton, is an unmanned interpretation centre telling of the ornithologist W. MacGillivray, and the flora and fauna of the area.

Wonderful sandy beaches fringe the west coast, including the huge **Luskintyre Beach** (Losgaintir) – one of the most beautiful you could ever hope for, sheltered and empty against a backdrop of hills. It looks westwards to the island of Taransay. Park at the end of the road and walk on around the dunes to the north.

Berneray (Eilean Bhearnaraigh)

This small, peaceful island (pronounced Bernera) lies to the south of Harris, just off the northern shore of North Uist, and is accessible by causeway. About 8 miles in circumference, with a population of about 130 – engaged mainly in crofting, lobster fishing and knitting – it is low-lying with 3 miles of sandy beach on the west coast. The name comes from the Norse: *Bjorn's Isle*. At Ruisgarry, Laimrig and Baile, groups of surviving thatched houses still have their roofs on, albeit abandoned. There are plans for restoration. Meanwhile two have been converted into a hostel. For some time Berneray was the favoured retreat of the Prince of Wales, who came here to play at being a crofter.

North Uist (Uibhist a Tuath)

The island of North Uist, between Harris and Benbecula to which it is linked by causeway, is about 17 miles long and 13 miles wide and a great deal of it is water. Wild peat moors cover the eastern side and the centre, with gentler green farmland to the west and glorious sandy beaches. Loch Eport almost cuts the island in two from the east. Of the few, insignificant hills, Eaval is the highest (1,138ft), a wedge shape dominant over its low-lying surroundings.

As with the other islands, prehistoric remains tell of ancient settlers, and Nordic colonists bequeathed many Norse place names – Uist is derived from the Norse *I-vist*, an abode or in-dwelling. The Macdonalds of Sleat, descendants of Somerled, held the island from 1495 until 1855. The early 19th-century kelp boom encouraged more settlers than the poor land could support, so that by the time the market slumped the population had risen to 5,000. This slump and the subsequent clearance of the land by Lord Macdonald – to make way for more lucrative sheep – forced over 1,000 islanders from their lands and caused violent confrontation between crofters and the police. The island is now owned by the Granville family.

The present population is about 1,800, with an economy based on crofting and fishing – mainly for shell fish – fish farming, tweed, knitwear and tourism. The island is as fervently Presbyterian as its northern neighbours, in contrast to the strong Catholicism of the south.

Lochmaddy

Lochmaddy (Loch Na Madadh) is the island port, a sprawling place with a sheltered harbour. Some say the three rocks at the harbour entrance look like crouching dogs and, indeed, the port's name comes from the Gaelic for dog – *madadh*. It has a court house, hospital, church, several shops, a bank, hotel and guesthouses.

The excellent museum and arts centre in the former inn, **Taigh Chearsabhagh** (*open Mon–Sat; adm; www.taigh-chearsabhagh.org*), near the pier, has exhibitions of local history, activity workshops, a shop and café. The tourist information centre is beside the harbour too.

Around the Island

A road circles the island, an attractive drive through a series of crofting and fishing communities. Peat bogs flank the road with rows of neatly stacked peat bricks waiting to be transported to the houses. Almost all the outer isles use this free fuel, each croft having its own 'hag', supplemented by gas and, in recent years, electricity. The peat is cut in spring and stacked on the site until dry enough to cart. It is then built into piles beside the houses and used on open fires and in stoves for the rest of the year.

There are several prehistoric remains to look at around the island. About 3 miles west of Lochmaddy, going anticlockwise, there are three standing stones on the slope of **Blashaval** (Blathaisbhal). These are known as the Three False Men, said to be three men from Skye who were turned to stone by a witch as punishment for deserting their wives.

Five miles west of Lochmaddy, a small road goes 4 miles north to **Otternish/Newton Ferry** (Port Nan Long) and the ferry to Leverburgh. In a loch on the right of this road, just before its end, is a well-preserved fortress, **Dun-an-Sticir**, reached by a causeway and occupied as late as 1601.

Back on the circular road, **Eilean-an-Tighe**, a rocky islet in Loch-nan-Geireann, 2 miles west, was the site of a Neolithic potters' workshop, the oldest to be excavated in western Europe. The pottery found was of a very high quality, better than that of later times, and there was so much of it that the factory must have supplied a large area.

In **Sollas** (Solas), 3 miles west, a medieval settlement is being excavated. This district was the scene of one of the episodes of the Highland Clearances. In 1849 Lord Macdonald, 4th Baron of the Isles, was faced with debts of around £200,000, due mainly to the decline of the kelp industry. Among other schemes to find money to pay off his creditors, he decided to evict some 600 people from the overcrowded, uneconomic area around Sollas and rent the land to sheep farmers. Since the potato famine in 1846, the people had been living well below subsistence level. However, they loved their land and resisted eviction physically during some extremely unfortunate skirmishes with the Sheriff's officers and police. Eventually they were forced to give in, but for various reasons there was a three-year delay before they were shipped off to Canada – in a frigate carrying smallpox germs below decks.

Vallay (Bhalaigh), pronounced Varlie, is an island at the entrance to a wide, shallow bay running north and west from Sollas. Here stands a big Edwardian house sadly dying of neglect, inhabited only by birds and the occasional dead sheep, but once the home of Erskine Beveridge, the famous naturalist and archaeologist. There are also the remains of the earlier house and outbuildings, built in 1727, and home of the Macdonalds of Vallay, one of whom became senator for British Columbia. You can walk out to Vallay at low tide, but watch out: it is very easy to get cut off.

Follow the road about 4 miles around the coast westwards to **Hosta**. Here, a footpath goes 2 miles east across the moor, to a chambered cairn on **Clettraval**. This was built before peat covered the land, in the days when birchwood copses grew here. A fort was built over it in the Iron Age, from which pottery was excavated and found to be the same as that made in the factory at Eilean-an-Tighe.

At **Balranald** (Baile Raghaill), stretching out to the most westerly tip of the island at **Aird an Runair**, there is an important RSPB reserve supporting one of the highest densities of breeding waders in Britain. Altogether, 183 species of bird have been recorded on the reserve. Visitors are asked to report to the RSPB cottage on arrival.

Unival is a hill north of the road, 6 miles southeast of Huna. Walk across the moor, up its eastern flank on the west side of Loch Huna to another chambered burial cairn with a small cist.

A couple of miles further down, the road forks, south to the right and northeast to the left. The left-hand road completes the circuit of the island and takes in two of its greatest treasures.

Two miles along this road back to Lochmaddy, a track to the right is signposted to Langlass Lodge Hotel, less than a mile away. Park at the hotel and take the footpath up behind it, a 10-minute climb through heather, bracken and bog-myrtle. On the hillside is an oval of standing stones called **Pobull Fhinn** (Finn's People), a prehistoric site deeply overlaid with mysticism. It is believed this may have been one of the sites where, hundreds of years before Christ, an annual ritual included the ceremonial sacrifice of the king.

Back on the road, continue less than a mile northeast. On the shoulder of *Ben Langass* on the right there is a grey lump, obviously man-made, shaped like a squashed beehive. This is **Barpa Langass** – a truly magnificent and amazingly well-preserved burial cairn, the tomb of a chieftain, thought to date from about 1000 BC. Visitors are asked not to crawl through the tunnel into the cairn, both for their own safety and for the preservation of the site. Great stone slabs line the interior and there are traces of where other cells may have led off the main chamber.

From here it is about 6 miles on to Lochmaddy, to complete the circuit of the island. Return southwest to the fork, and turn left. **Carinish** (Cairinis) is 2 miles down the road, with some of the most interesting, though by no means the oldest, remains in North Uist.

Tourist Information

Lochmaddy: Pier Road, t (01876) 500 321.

Getting There and Around

Lochmaddy is the terminal for car ferries from Uig in Skye and Tarbert in Harris. A car ferry also runs from Newton Ferry (Otternish) to Leverburgh in Harris. Balivanich Airport, across the causeway in Benbecula, provides an air link with Glasgow, Stornoway and Barra.

Sports and Activities

Uist Outdoor Centre, on the outskirts of Lochmaddy, t (01876) 500 480. Adventure training establishment for sub-aqua diving, watersports of all kinds, climbing, walking, wildlife watching, environmental and field studies – and a lot more.

Where to Stay and Eat

North Uist t (01876–)

Langlass Lodge Hotel, Locheport, t 580 285, f 580 385, *langlass@btinternet.com* (*moderate*). Converted shooting lodge overlooking Loch Langlass, cosy, remote and peaceful. The food is first class, especially the seafood. Prices vary considerably. *Open Mar–Jan.*

Lochmaddy Hotel, t 500 331/2, f 500 210 (*moderate*). Wonderfully traditional sporting hotel. Old-established, friendly and comfortable, and convenient for the ferry terminal.

Mrs Clarke, Balemore, t (020) 8888 2449 (*moderate*). Traditional croft house (sleeping 6).

Mrs Kathy Simpson, Hougharry, t 510 312, *sqeirruadh@aol.com* (*moderate*). B&B on the Balranald Bird Reserve, with a deserted beach on the doorstep.

Mrs MacDonald, Balemore, t 510 342 (*moderate*). A modern house beside the loch (sleeping 15).

Mrs MacLeod, Grimsay, t (01870) 602 029, *glendale@ecoss.net* (*moderate*). B&B in a comfortable modern house overlooking the harbour.

Mrs Mary-Ann Macdonald, Daisy Bank, Sollas, t 560 208 (*moderate*). Wonderful B&B with hospitable hostess, a great knitter of socks.

Mrs Norma Shepherd, Sollas, t 560 282 (*moderate*). B&B in a modern house with lovely views and 4-star treatment.

Mr Seale, Lochportan, t (0131) 447 9911 (*moderate*). A modern, well-equipped self-catering cottage (sleeping 6–7).

Mrs Sandra MacIntosh, Sollas, t 560 288 (*moderate*). B&B ten minutes from the Otternish ferry, amidst miles of sandy beaches with glorious sea views.

Uist Outdoor Centre, on the outskirts of Lochmaddy, *see above*, t 500 480. Good accommodation.

Teampull-na-Trionaid (Trinity Temple) is a ruin on the top of a knoll on the Carinish promontory at the southern end of the island. A large building, with a detached side chapel reached by a vaulted passage, this early 13th-century church was regarded as an important seat of learning for the training of priests, similar to the one on Iona.

The last battle to be fought in Scotland using just swords and bows and arrows was the Battle of Carinish in 1601, between the Macdonalds of North Uist and the Macleods of Harris. The cause of the battle appears to have been the insulting behaviour of one of the Macdonalds, who divorced his Macleod wife and sent her home. The Macleods descended on Carinish in a wild frenzy, but in the furious battle that ensued all but two of them were killed. **Feith-na-Fala** (The Field of Blood) marks the site of the battle, just north of the Carinish Inn.

Ben Lee (896ft), southeast of Lochmaddy, gives a marvellous view of the island with its mass of lochs and great expanses of moorland, peat and hill.

Benbecula (Beinn Na Faoghla)

Benbecula is linked to the south of North Uist by over 3 miles of causeway. The low-tide route across North Ford by foot, once the only way, is extremely dangerous for those who don't know the path. Locals tell hair-raising stories of lost travellers and quicksands. Rocky bays and inlets surround the causeway, washed by the ever-changing tides.

The Gaelic name means 'the mountain of the fords'. The only mountain is Rueval in the east, a small round hillock only 409ft high, but with good views from the top. The island is flat and waterlogged, with a fertile strip on the west side. The main road cuts through the middle with minor roads off to the east and a circular road around the west coast to the airport at **Balivanich**, with links to Glasgow, Stornoway and Barra.

Benbecula has an army base which runs the rocket range to the south. In the north-west corner there is a large army camp – a rash of utility buildings not designed to please the eye. The airport is just beside the army camp at Balivanich. In contrast to the ugly military buildings, there are white beaches, spectacular views and a landscape dotted with old stone houses. Near the airfield are the remains of St Columba's Chapel, dating from early Christian times. There is a well close by, now marked by a cairn, where people came to drink the holy water.

The history of the island is that of its neighbours, recorded in a few prehistoric remains and predominantly Norse place names. It was part of the patrimony of the Macdonalds of Clanranald from the 13th to 19th centuries, when the lands were sold off to pay impatient creditors. Most of the ruins are of Clanranald origin, and the island is owned by the South Uist Estates.

Shopping

D. MacGillivray and Co., opposite the high cone-shaped water tank at the airport in Balivanich. Unpretentious building concealing an Aladdin's Cave of tweed and woollen products, including some fantastic bargains, and new and second-hand books.

Where to Stay and Eat

Benbecula t (01870–)

Creagorry Hotel, Creagorry, t 602 024, f 603 108 (*cheap*). An old inn with a newish extension, known for its convivial bar.

Dark Island Hotel, Liniclate, t 603 030, f 602 347, *darkislandhotel@msn.com* (*cheap*). Modern hotel.

Inchyra Guest House, Liniclate, t 602 176 (*cheap*).

Mrs Emma MacDonald, Muir of Aird, t 602 965 (*cheap*). B&B.

Mrs Gretta Campbell, t 602 685, f 603 235, *campbell.m3@talk21.com* (*cheap*). B&B on a croft, with the remains of Borve Castle.

Macleans of Benbecula, Balivanich. Bakery well known for its shortbread and cookies, sold in gift boxes under the Scottish Parliament brand name.

Mrs Esther MacDonald, Bramsdale, t 602 536. For self-catering, a traditional thatched croft house (sleeping 2–4).

Mrs Margaret Shepherd, Liniclate, t 602 235. Modern bungalow (sleeping 6–7).

Mrs Morag MacIntosh, t 602 239. Well-equipped, modernized house overlooking South Ford (sleeping 6).

Stepping Stones, Balivanich. Restaurant/café, with good seafood.

At **Nunton**, 2 miles south of Balivanich, there is a ruined chapel which belonged to a nunnery whose nuns were brutally massacred when the building was destroyed during the Reformation. The stones of a large-ish farmhouse by the road came from the nunnery. This is Nunton House, L-plan with a pavilion on each side of the entrance to a courtyard, the 18th-century home of the Macdonalds of Clanranald. The steadings have been restored and are used as offices, with a small history section (*open to the public Sun pm*).

Borve Castle, a gaunt ruined keep near the road 4 miles south of Balivanich, was a Clanranald stronghold and scene of many a bloody skirmish.

In 1988 a new community school was built at **Liniclate** at the southern end of the island. It is a huge place with a swimming pool, superb sports facilities, restaurant, library and museum, serving children throughout the islands, some of whom previously had to board on the mainland for their education. It is also open to the public, and has been the cause of a rare dispute between Presbyterians and Catholics over Sunday opening.

Wiay, an island off the southeast tip of Benbecula, is a bird sanctuary supporting snipe, duck, geese and swans.

It was from **Rossinish**, on the northeast corner, that Prince Charlie sailed 'over the sea to Skye' disguised as gawky Betty Burke, the servant of Flora Macdonald.

South Uist (Uibhist a Deas)

A straight causeway links Benbecula with South Uist, less than half a mile across South Ford, a white strand that yields an abundant harvest of cockles at low tide. When the tide is out there is usually at least one stooped figure scooping the molluscs into a bucket.

South Uist is about 20 miles long and 7 miles wide at its widest point, with mountains and long sea lochs to the east and silvery shell-sand and machair to the west. The peat bog and moorland in between are studded with more than 190 freshwater lochs with excellent trout and sea-trout fishing. Beinn Mhor, less than halfway down in the east, is the highest peak (2,034ft).

The island suffered badly from the Clearances in the 19th century at the hands of Colonel Gordon of Cluny. He bought it in 1838, along with Benbecula, Eriskay and Barra, from the Macdonalds of Clanranald. Between 1841 and 1861 the population fell from 7,300 to 5,300 as townships were cleared for sheep; many islanders emigrated to North America and Canada.

The present population of about 2,200 occupies crofting townships scattered throughout the island, linked by a network of one-track lanes radiating from the main north–south road which varies from single track to short stretches of EU-funded double-track carriageway. These random lengths of fast highway terminate abruptly, often without obvious warning, and can be extremely dangerous.

Since the second half of the 20th century the economy has been dominated by the army missile range on the northwestern corner of the island, the closure of which is discussed periodically. Other scources of income are crofting, fishing (mainly for shell-fish), fish-farming and seaweed, as well as maintenance of public services.

A roadside shrine to the Virgin Mary, just south of the causeway, seems to be a gentle reminder that you have left the Presbyterian north and are on the threshold of the Catholic south.

The first road to the east, a mile south of the causeway, goes out 2 miles to **Loch Carnan**, a beautiful fiord-like sea loch with a pier for large boats.

Three miles to the south, the main road becomes a causeway and crosses **Loch Bee**, one of the largest swan reserves in Britain. The area of marshland to the east is a nature reserve, the breeding ground of many wildfowl, including greylag geese. The hill on the left, just south of Loch Bee, is another **Rueval**, crested by a futuristic contraption which is an army range head. Rocket targets can often be seen off the west coast, and you will hear the muffled bang of firing.

On the western slope of Rueval, clearly seen from the road, there is a classically beautiful statue by Hew Lorimer of **Our Lady of the Isles**. Carved from white granite, it stands high on the hillside, the Child held up on His mother's shoulder. The clean-cut simplicity of the statue seems to embody the deep faith that exists in these islands.

The next road east, a mile south, runs 4 miles out to **Loch Skipport** (Loch Sgioport), another fiord-like sea loch where there is a deep-water anchorage, a salmon farm and a skeleton pier which used to be the main one for the island.

The **Loch Druidibeg National Nature Reserve**, just to the south, provides an ideal habitat for may species of waterfowl.

Less than 2 miles further south on the main road, beyond the road west to **Drimisdale** (Dreumasdal), there is a small loch with an island and a ruined castle. A submerged causeway runs out to the island. Beware! Some of its wobbly stones have been known to topple the unwary into the dark peaty water of the loch. The ruined castle is **Caisteal Bheagram**, a 15th- or 16th-century keep that was once a mighty Clanranald stronghold. Some years ago the present Captain of Clanranald tried to map out the original layout of the castle and discovered when the nettles were cleared that ruins cover almost all the island.

A mile south, the side road runs west a mile to **Howmore** (Tobha Mor), the most important religious site in the Outer Hebrides, with a history that goes back over a thousand years to the dawn of Christianity in the Western Isles. There are substantial fragments of two churches and three chapels, as well as a number of grave stones and wheel-cross monuments. Several members of the ruling family of Clanranald were buried here between 1500 and 1700. In 1990 the 16th-century **Clanranald Stone**, a heavy armorial panel from one of the chapels, vanished. It was discovered five years later in the flat of one of the two young men who had stolen it and was returned to South Uist amidst much rejoicing. The young man had come to an untimely end, fuelling the belief that a curse was attached to anyone removing the stone. It is now in the small museum at Kildonan.

A network of one-track roads and tracks west of the main road meander through the machair, linking small townships and isolated dwellings. Some lead across dunes to the beach.

Tourist Information

Lochboisdale: Pier Road, **t** (01878) 700 286; *open Easter–Sept.*

Festivals

July: **South Uist Games**, on the golf course at Askernish (Aisgernis); piping, dancing and all the traditional sports, usually followed by a dance or a concert in the church hall.

Sports and Activities

There's a nine-hole **golf course** on the machair at Askernish (Aisgernis), where players must dodge sheep and plovers' nests among the dunes.

Shopping

Jewellery workshop/gift shop, Iochdar. Wrought-silver craft work, pottery, books and the usual range of gifts. Should you have an urgent need for a passport photograph, they also provide this service.

Where to Stay and Eat

South Uist

Lochboisdale Hotel, **t** (01878) 700 332, **f** 700 376, *www.lochboisdale.com* (*expensive–cheap*). Splendid Victorian dowager overlooking Loch Boisdale by the ferry terminal. It has exclusive rights to most of the best fishing lochs and has long been popular with anglers. The food is generally first class and the rooms are comfortable.

Borrodale Hotel, Daliburgh, **t** (01878) 700 444, **f** 700 446 (*moderate*). At the crossroads in Daliburgh. Busy and cheerful, one of the centres of island social life. It is comfortable, friendly, the food is good and there may be live music from local or visiting musicians.

Orasay Inn, Lochcarnan, **t** (01870) 610 298, **f** 610 390, *orosayinn@btinternet.com* (*moderate*). At the north end of the island, a small, family-run hotel with good food. Special rates for longer stays.

Pollachar Inn, on the southern shore, **t** (01878) 700 215, **f** 700 768 (*moderate*). 17th-century inn with one of the best views in Scotland, and a convivial bar. It is comfortable and very friendly.

Anglers Retreat, Iochdar, **t/f** (01870) 610 325 (*cheap*). Small, modern hotel on a croft, catering especially for fishermen, bird-watchers and hill walkers. *Open Mar–Dec.*

Clan Ranald, Garryhallie, **t** (01878) 700 263, *clanran@dialstart.net* (*cheap*). Guesthouse just north of Daliburgh, not far from the golf course. It is comfortable and well run with good food and a kind welcome.

The Shieling, almost next door, **t** (01878) 700504 (*cheap*). Run by Mrs Katie Pereranna, a bit cheaper and equally friendly and cosy.

Mrs Flora MacInnes, South Lochboisdale, **t** (01878) 700 580 (*cheap*). By far the nicest B&B on the island, it looks down over the loch, is supremely comfortable, and exudes warm island hospitality and kindness.

Tobha Mor, Howmore, *www.gatliff.org.uk*. Newly renovated black house, run by SYHA (Gatliff Trust). No telephone, no bookings: just turn up.

Eriskay

Mrs Marion Campbell, Eriskay, **t** (01878) 720 274 (*cheap*). Self-catering chalet (sleeps 4).

Ormaclete Castle (Ormacleit) (*always accessible*), a couple of miles or so to the south of Howmore between the main road and the sea, is a roofless shell attached to a late 18th-century farmhouse, the latter recently restored. The castle, finished in 1707, was built for Allan Macdonald of Clanranald whose wife Penelope refused to live there until a new house was built, since 'even her father's hens were better housed'. Only eight years after its completion it was accidentally burnt down, on the day of the Battle of Sheriffmuir in which the chief was killed. (*See* also 'Castle Tioram', p.467.)

Hecla (1,988ft) and **Beinn Mhor** (2,034ft) rise to the east of the road, from which they can be approached over a wasteland of bog. The summits are dangerous in high winds, especially the sharp serrated edge of Beinn Mhor, with dizzying drops off the east side.

To the south a road runs east to **Loch Eynort** (Loch Aineort), another sea loch, cutting deep into the east coast and a starting point for good walks over the remote moorland between it and Loch Skipport. Beinn Mhor can also be reached from here, as can **Glen Corodale**, about 4 miles northeast of the end of the road. This wild country north of Loch Eynort, among the hills and glens surrounding Beinn Mhor and Hecla, was where Prince Charles took refuge for a while in a forester's hut in a shieling, hiding in a cave when discovery seemed likely. The cave is not the one marked on the map, by a group of ruined houses by a burn. The real one is difficult to find, up on the rock face. This whole area is only accessible on foot or by boat. In the summer of 1980 Hercules the bear, star of several television advertisements, went for a swim with his owner off this coast. Freedom went to his head and he escaped. He was missing for three weeks, during which time frantic bear-hunting went on. He was finally recaptured, weighing a mere fraction of his normal weight, having been too domesticated to cope with life in the wild. The death of Hercules, from old age, was recently announced in the newspapers.

Bornish, west of the main road about a mile south of the Loch Eynort turning, is a straggle of dwellings and a church. Gaunt and rectangular on the outside, this charming church has a raw, unfaced stone interior with a large crucifix against a rich red cloth behind the altar as the focal point. A homely Lady Chapel with a lace backdrop, simple stations of the cross and the steady, ruby glow of the sanctuary lamp give this church a remarkable, warm feeling of 'The Real Presence'.

This road runs out west to **Rubha Ardvule**, surrounded by slabs of flat rocks – a good viewpoint, particularly during Atlantic gales. Archaeologists from Sheffield University have excavated a broch at **Dun Vulan**, on this narrow peninsula, and have made interesting and important discoveries. It is the dun you can see on the left.

Kildonan Museum (*open June–Sept; adm*), beside the main road a couple of miles to the south, has been restored and extended, with a Lottery grant and public funding. Incorporating part of the old Kildonan school, the museum contains displays of archaeological finds, crafts, local artefacts, photographs and history. A café and attractive landscaping enhance this imaginative project, still in its infancy. Members of the archaeological department of Sheffield University have been working on the island for many years and the fascinating results of their research are a frequently updated feature in the museum.

Three miles south of the turning to Loch Eynort, a road runs west, signposted to **Milton** (Gearraidh Bhailteas) where a cairn marks Flora Macdonald's birthplace (she was born here in 1722). Flora's father was a tacksman. She was tending her brother's cattle in the shieling about 3 miles from here when the Prince was brought to her in need of her help.

Daliburgh (Dalabrog) is a village on the crossroads west of Lochboisdale. There are three shops and a post office, a small hospital and an old people's home. The road to the west leads to the Catholic parish church of **St Peter's**, a large, simple building dating from the 1860s, weathered and unadorned. This is the living heart of the island, filled to capacity at every Sunday Mass and well attended throughout the week, as indeed are the other churches that support it to the north and south. The Church of Scotland kirk and manse stand prominently on the crossroads. Northwest of St Peter's is what must be one of the most beautiful, lonely burial grounds in the country, on the edge of the machair, overlooking the wild Atlantic.

The road east from Daliburgh goes 3 miles to the port of **Lochboisdale** (Loch Baghasdail), with a hotel, bank, police station, harbour and a row of newly constructed shops. The village is at its busiest when the Caledonian MacBrayne ferries are arriving or departing, turning the quay into a bustling place, with a babble of Gaelic voices. A few visiting yachts anchor in the small bay in summer, and the hotel overlooking the harbour, with its reputation for fishing and for food, attracts many visitors. The harbour is currently the focus of a Harbour Improvement Scheme. Towering over the northern shore of Loch Boisdale is **Beinn Ruigh Choinnich**. There is a challenging race to its summit every year for the young men of the area, who may take whatever route they choose to the top. It has been known for competitors to start by diving off the pier – taking the shortest route 'as the crow flies'.

South Uist is littered with places where Prince Charles is said to have sheltered. He certainly hid for a time in the jagged, ruined castle on **Calvay Island** at the entrance to Loch Boisdale, clearly seen from the ferry.

A mile south of Daliburgh a small road runs about 2 miles west to **Kilpheder** (Cille Pheadair), from where a track leads out on to the machair to an Iron Age–Pictish wheel house. This is a communal dwelling with a central hearth, with cells radiating from it like the spokes of a wheel, elaborate drainage systems and storage places sunk into the floor.

Two miles south of Daliburgh, a road runs east for 2 miles, through **South Lochboisdale** (Taobh A Deas Loch Baghasdail) to a parking bay. From here a map is needed to follow a faint track over hills and moor, along lochs Kerrsinish, Marulaig and Moreef, a total of 5 miles southwest to the coast. **Bun Sruth** is a loch joined to the sea by a narrow passage of sheer rock, surrounded by hills. It is inaccessible except by boat or on foot, peopled only by sheep and birds and the ghosts of the people who once lived in the now-ruined croft houses that lie scattered over the valley. When the tide is out the loch is higher than the sea, draining over a shelf of rock in the entrance passage and marooning boats until the next tide, which comes in through the passage fast and hard. Golden eagles can be seen, gliding on the wind above the hills north of Loch Marulaig.

All this southeastern foot of the island is good walking country, and the views from the summits of the hills are spectacular. On a clear day you can see Ardnamurchan Point on the mainland. The road out to the west, opposite that to South Lochboisdale, leads to a white beach with the gloomy remains of a once-flourishing seaweed factory, a ghostly shell of flapping corrugated iron and scrap. A few years ago any islander could cut seaweed – a laborious job – and sell it to this factory, where it was processed into alginates for use in a large number of products ranging from soap to cosmetics. Now, any seaweed that is harvested is collected in lorries and shipped to factories on the mainland. The white beach runs for miles in great sweeps of sand where keen eyes will spot tiny pink cowrie shells. The wide fringe of machair is famous for its carpet of wild flowers in the summer. Opposite the seaweed factory there is a small conical island called **Orosay**, accessible at low tide, with lovely views. In westerly gales, spray has been known to break over its top.

The road south climbs to the modernist wedge-shaped church at **Garrynamonie** (Gearraidh Na Monadh), built in 1963 and rather bizarre in its setting. It has an enam-elled mosaic behind the side altar and Stations of the Cross designed by a priest from Barra, Father Calum McNeil. Here, as in the other churches, you can hear Mass in Gaelic, with a haunting chant from the choir.

At the end of the road, 5 miles south of Daliburgh, is the **Pollachar Inn** (Pol A Charra) – the old ferry inn (*see* above) – overlooking one of the most beautiful views in Scotland, across the sound to Barra and east to Eriskay. Sit outside and enjoy your drink overlooking a standing stone and the Sound of Eriskay, across to the heart-shaped hills of Barra.

Ludag is a couple of miles east along the south coast, and ferries run from the pier here to Barra (*passengers only*). Since the new causeway was built, there are no ferries to Eriskay. A lovely sandy bay beyond at **South Glendale** dries out at low tide and makes an excellent picnic spot and cockle-source, sheltered all around by turf-covered rocks. East of the bay, along the rocky shore and below the water, lies part of the wreck of the *Politician*, immortalized as the *Cabinet Minister* by Compton Mackenzie in his book, *Whisky Galore*. The true story was only slightly embroidered in the novel. The ship was carrying 20,000 cases of whisky to America in 1941, at a time when whisky was scarce in the islands. Magnetic minerals in the rocks distorted the compass read-ings and she went off course, riding over Hartamul, the rock at the entrance to the Sound of Eriskay, and finishing up against the cliff. The islanders made a valiant attempt to 'rescue' the whisky, thwarted by the bureaucracy of the customs and excise department, and not a few families still own a much-valued 'Polly bottle'. Stories are still told, with a twinkle and a knowing shake of the head, of animals reeling down the road, and of bottles dug up on the machair that had been buried for years. Not so long ago the last of the bottles went up for auction and fetched nearly £100 each.

Eriskay (Eiriosgaigh)

For some, the island of Eriskay is the jewel of them all. A new causeway links it with Ludag in South Uist.

When Colonel Gordon of Cluny bought it in 1838 he offered some of the Uist crofters holdings in Eriskay where the land was too poor even for sheep and so of no use to him. With the choice between this meagre allotment and emigration many of them chose the former and managed to subsist on scant crops and potatoes grown in lazybeds.

The causeway crosses the mile-wide sound to **Haun** (Haunn), a smiling village of freshly painted white cottages with roofs of bright blue, pink, green and red, sheltered by hills. St Michael's Church, perched high above the harbour, is the heart of the community. It was built in 1903 by Father Allan MacDonald, who wrote down the folklore and many of the songs of the Hebrides, and was a distinguished poet. The altar is shaped like the prow of a ship, worshipped at by a community whose existence has always been shaped by the sea. The ship's bell outside, beyond the church, was rescued from the *Derflinger*, one of the German ships that sank in Scapa Flow in 1919.

Just beyond the village on the western shore there is a crescent of sand called Prince Charlie's Bay. This was where the prince landed from France on 23 July 1745 and where he spent his first night on Scottish soil. The black house he stayed in was only pulled down in 1902. Its smoky interior drove him out into the fresh air several times during the night, drawing reproofs from his host. It was a simple place like all the others of its kind, with cupboard beds, hens running over the earth floor and wooden trunks holding the family possessions. The pink convolvulus called Prince Charlie's rose, in the machair around Prince Charlie's Bay, is said to have been introduced here from a seed dropped from his shoe.

The **Stack Islands** lie just off the southern tip of Eriskay. There is a rock creek on the main island where boats can moor in calm weather. It is then a scramble to climb the precipitous cliff to the Weaver's Castle at the top. Here a notorious Macneil lived, a much-feared wrecker and pirate. He built the castle as a hideout, and stole a girl from a shieling in South Uist to be his wife and the mother of a large number of sure-footed children.

Barra (Barraigh)

Barra, 4 miles south of South Uist at the nearest point, is partly fringed by a number of smaller islands, known as the Bishop's Isles (including Vatersay – still inhabited – Sandray, Parbay and Mingulay to its south). Eight miles long by 4–5 miles wide, Barra is encircled by a 12-mile road with an arm running north to the airport and Scurrival Point. It has a mainly Catholic population of about 1,300.

Beaches and machair, croftland and a hilly interior make up this compact haven which took its name from St Barr of Cork, who converted its people to Christianity. Barra has seascapes and landscapes that have inspired many artists, writers and musicians. The history of the island echoes that of the other islands, with prehistoric remains, Norse names and a medieval castle to show for it. When it was bought by Colonel Gordon of Cluny in 1838, he offered to sell it to the government as a penal colony. His offer was turned down. Later the Clearances led to massive emigration.

No one arriving in the ferry forgets their first sight of **Castlebay** (Bagh A Chaisteil). **Kisimul Castle** (*open Easter–Oct; adm; for opening times and boat access ring* **t** *(01871) 810 449*) stands on a rock in the middle of the harbour. Some people claim that it originates from 1060 and is one of Scotland's oldest castles, but there is no firm evidence that it existed before the 15th century. It is a splendid sight in any weather, but most romantic when silhouetted against a half-dark sky on a summer night. The Macneils acquired the castle as a reward for fighting for Robert the Bruce at Bannockburn. This clan was famous for its lawlessness, piracy and arrogance: a clansman from Barra is said to have declared, 'The reason there was no Macneil on Noah's Ark is that the Macneil had a boat of his own.' Kisimul was virtually destroyed by fire at the end of the 18th century. It remained in ruins until the 45th chief of the Macneil clan, returning from his adopted homeland in America in 1937, restored it to its present 20th-century interpretation of the original. Recently in need of attention, it was taken over from the present Macneil, who lives abroad, by Historic Scotland – for the price of a bottle of his favourite whisky.

Neat shops and houses line the road that climbs from the harbour in Castlebay, overlooked by **Heaval**, Barra's highest hill (1,260ft). High on Heaval's southern shoulder stands a statue of the Blessed Virgin, her Child on her shoulder holding a star. The statue, carved from Carrara marble, was erected in 1954 to celebrate the Marian Year and in memory of the 58 men from Barra who died in the Second World War, mostly in the Atlantic convoys. This and the large, well-attended Catholic church, Our Lady, Star of the Sea, which overlooks Castlebay, are symbols of the deep faith that governs the lives of these islands. Dualchas is the excellent **heritage and culture centre** in Castlebay (**t** *(01871) 810 413*), with high-quality exhibitions, a genealogy research service, and a good café.

Isle of Vatersay (Bhatarsaigh), just off the south coast of Barra, has a population of about 70. Until 1990 cattle destined for the market had to swim across the sound of Vatersay to meet the ferry in Barra but, when a prize bull, Bernie, was drowned in 1986, the ensuing outcry forced the Government's hand and a long-awaited causeway was built. The other islands here, now uninhabited, are only accessible by private boat.

Going clockwise, 2 miles west from Castlebay, the standing stones beside the road past the Isle of Barra Hotel are said to mark the grave of a Norse pirate. **Dun Bharpa** is a large chambered cairn surrounded by standing stones on the eastern side of Beinn Mhartainn, reached from the end of the road through Craigston.

On the eastern side of the peninsula at the north end of the island, are the 2 square miles of dazzling cockle-shell strand, **Tràigh Mhór**, where the plane comes droning in like a bumble-bee, to touch down on the firm sand when the tide permits.

Suidheachan, the house overlooking this unique aerodrome, was built in 1935 for Compton Mackenzie, the writer who settled in Barra in 1928 and so perceptively caught the spirit of the Hebrides. A cockle factory for many years, it has recently been restored as a private house again. He attracted a lively community of writers and Gaelic scholars when he lived here. He is buried in the graveyard at **Eoligarry** (Eolaigearraidh), just to the north. Here in the roofed-over ruins of a chapel are burial slabs said to have arrived from Iona as ballast in an ancient galley. This is Barra's most important historic site, **Cille Bharra** (St Barr's), founded in the 7th century but with ruins of three medieval buildings, probably 12th century and later. The stones in the chapel include the cast of one from the 10th or 11th century, with Christian carvings on one side and Runic (Norse) on the other. (The original, discovered in 1865, is in the National Museum of Scotland in Edinburgh.)

Another well-known name can be seen in the cemetery: that of John Macpherson, better known to lovers of Gaeldom as 'The Coddy', who died here on his native island in 1955. *Tales from Barra*, recorded in both Gaelic and English and recently republished, is a large collection of folk tales told by the Coddy in his inimitable voice – a delight for exiled Scots all over the world.

A grassy mound is all that remains of Eoligarry House, a three-storey house built by the Macneils after Kisimul Castle burned down in 1795. It was a substantial ruin for years, until it was demolished.

St Kilda

St Kilda, consisting of four islands and a few great rock stacks, is the most westerly of the British Isles apart from Rockall. This lonely archipelago is owned by the National Trust for Scotland, partly occupied by a small detachment of gunners who man a missile-tracking station, and with a nature reserve managed by Scottish Natural Heritage.

There are cruises to St Kilda, but passengers are only able to land when weather permits, which isn't very often. The best approach is via the NTS, who may be able to arrange for you to join a working party (*May–Aug, 14-day trips from Oban; t (0131) 226 5922*). Private yachts are frequently unable to find safe shelter for long enough to anchor and go ashore. Ask at the Stornoway, Castlebay or Lochboisdale Tourist Centres for information about locally organized cruises, or see *www.kilda.org.uk*.

The main island on which the people used to live is called **Hirta**, possibly derived from the old Norse for shepherd – *hirt*. The origin of the name St Kilda is disputed: there was no saint of that name. Kilda may have come from Hirta, which the islanders pronounced Hilta.

Essential reading for anyone attempting a visit is *The Life and Death of St Kilda* by Tom Steel, and *An Island called Hirta* by Mary Harman. The islands' history is one of decline brought about by isolation in a world increasingly obsessed by centralization and conformity. There is evidence of human occupation as far back as the Iron Age, with the remains of a pottery and earth house. A small, patriarchal, strongly Presbyterian society subsisted here, paying its rent with meat, feathers and oil from seabirds. They were often cut off by storms. The population of about 200 in the 18th and 19th centuries remained fairly constant, except for a smallpox epidemic in 1727, kept in check by puerperal fever. The introduction of money and visitors from the mainland reduced their self-reliance and many of the younger ones left. In 1930 the few remaining able members of the community, attracted by the lure of the outside world and dragged down by hardship, persuaded the older ones they should move to the mainland, and a mass emigration took place.

Some of the houses at Village Bay on Hirta have been preserved, with their cleits – beehive-shaped cells of rough stone that served as larders and storerooms. The careful design of these cleits allowed air and wind to circulate inside and preserve the meat of the sea birds. It also kept clothes and gear dry.

A visit to this gale-torn outpost is a curiously melancholy experience, contemplating the community that existed here for so long, beset by such hardship, finally forced to sail away and abandon their roots for ever.

The
Northern Isles

The Northern Isles

40 km
20 miles

N

Atlantic

Ocean

Muckle Flugga
Haroldswick
Baltasound
Unst
Yell
Fetlar
Ronas Hill
Esha Ness
Hillswick
Sullom
Brae
Toft
Out Skerrie
Whalsay
Papa Stour
Sandness
Mainland
Walls
Whiteness
Scalloway
Shetland
Lerwick
Isle of Noss
Bressay
Foula
Sandwick
St Ninian's Isle
Mousa Broch
3
Jarlshof
Sumburgh
Sumburgh Head

4
Fair Isle

North Sea

Papa Westray
North Ronaldsay
Westray
Rousay
Eday
Sanday
Egilsay
Stronsay
Brough of Birsay
Birsay
Gurness Broch
Wyre
Skara Brae
Dounby
Balfour
Shapinsay
Mainland
2 Maeshowe
Ring of Brodgar
Stenness
Kirkwall
Orkney
Stromness
1
Lamb Holm
Old Man of Hoy
Rackwick
Scapa Flow
Burray
Hoy
St Margaret's Hope
South Ronaldsay
Pentland Firth
Burwick
p.436
Scrabster
Dunnet Head
Duncansby Head
John O'Groats

Orkney
Shetland
SCOTLAND
NORTHERN IRELAND
ENGLAND

Highlights

1 Wreck-diving at Scapa Flow, Orkney
2 Stone-Age cairn at Maeshowe, Orkney
3 Mousa Broch, Shetland
4 Bird-watching on Fair Isle

Although separated by 60 miles or so of ocean and very different in character, Orkney and Shetland have a common history and tend to be bracketed together. Norsemen called them the 'Nordereys'.

Both groups – about 70 Orkney islands, and 100 Shetland islands – were inhabited in the Stone Age. The Picts colonized them in the 1st century AD and were subjected to continual harassment from the Vikings for centuries until the Norse King Harald Harfagri annexed them in 875. When Harald succeeded to the throne of Norway in about 860, large parts of his kingdom didn't recognize the authority of the Crown – like the Lords of the Scottish Isles. Harald was in love with a Princess Gyda, daughter of one of the rebel 'kings', and she refused to marry him until he had conquered all Norway. He vowed that he would not cut his hair or his beard until he'd done this. He claimed his bride 10 years later. All the dispossessed *jarls*, or minor kings, took refuge in Orkney and Shetland and from here proceeded to harass Norway with wild Viking raids. Harald, exasperated, collected up a fleet and sailed down to put an end to their antics. He landed at what is now Haroldswick in Unst, Shetland, and declared all the islands to be a 'Jarldom'. The Norse occupation of these islands is recorded in stirring sagas, handed down over the years. *The Orkneyinga Saga* is one of the best known.

By the 13th century, although still under Norse rule, the islands were presided over by Scots earls. When Princess Margaret of Norway and Denmark became betrothed to James III of Scotland in 1468, her father, King Christian I, pledged the islands to Scotland as part of her dowry. They were formally annexed in 1472 and since then they have been part of Scotland.

Norse place names still predominate, and the people of these northern islands are a blend of Norse and Scots, very different in character from the dreamy Celts of the Hebrides. They are extremely friendly, extrovert and stolid, industrious and mainly Presbyterian. Their accent is singsong; the old 'Norn' language disappeared during the 18th century, although some phrases have remained, and when the islanders talk among themselves they use many words more akin to Norwegian than English.

The coming of the oil boom struck hard at established roots, bringing innovations that were not always popular and making Shetland relatively rich compared with the rest of Scotland. However, on the whole the islanders managed to retain their old way of life.

Orkney

Orkney's 70 or so islands are 6 miles off the north coast of Scotland on a level with Leningrad. They extend 53 miles from north to south and about 23 from west to east: Oslo is closer than London. Nineteen of them are inhabited, and when an Orcadian talks of the Mainland, he means Mainland Orkney – the big island. (The Mainland of Scotland is 'the sooth'.) Orkney means 'seal islands', the *ey* being Norse for islands: no one talks of the Orkneys, just Orkney.

First impressions are of emerald-green plateaux of turf above sheer rock cliffs and sandy beaches, fertile farmland and a sparkling sea. Apart from Hoy, nothing is higher than 900ft. A great dome of clear sky seems to shed an ethereal greenish light. Sunsets in May and June are fantastic. At midsummer the sun is above the horizon for 18 hours, and it is possible to read a book outside all night. This Midsummer Twilight is called 'Grimlins', from the Norse word *Grimla*, to glimmer or twinkle.

Mainland Orkney

Kirkwall

Kirkwall is the capital of Orkney and one of the earliest established Norse trading towns. It is referred to in *The Orkneyinga Saga* as Kirkjuvagr, 'Church-bay-of-the-Vikings', indicating that the Norsemen found an early Christian church here when they arrived. It is an ideal centre from which to explore these fascinating islands.

St Magnus Cathedral (*open daily exc Sun, when it is only open for worship*) dominates the town, though it is not in fact as large as its clever proportions suggest. This cruciform building founded in 1137 was built up of alterating stripes of local red sandstone and yellow stone and looks more continental than British. St Magnus, who was murdered in 1116 and whose canonization may have been more political than spiritual, was the uncle of Jarl Rognvald Kilson, the founder of the cathedral. The bones of both these men now lie below the columns of the central bay of the choir. They were discovered, hidden in chests, during repair work in the 20th century. The cathedral has been carefully restored; the rose window is modern but the east window dates from 1511. Although it is still called a cathedral, the services are Church of Scotland.

The old part of the town clusters round the cathedral, with the ruin of the 12th-century **Bishop's Palace** next door (*open April–Sept daily 9.30–6.30; adm*). It was here that poor old King Haakon of Norway died, having struggled back this far from his defeat by Alexander III at Largs in 1263. It was rebuilt in the late 15th century and restored in the mid-16th century. Further work was done by Earl Patrick Stewart who saw it as his own fortified residence.

Across the road from the Bishop's Palace is the ruin of the **Earl's Palace** (*open same hours as the Bishop's Palace; adm*), built by forced labour for a much-loathed tyrant, Earl Patrick Stewart, at the beginning of the 17th century. The palace is L-shaped, with attractive angle-turrets, once described as 'the most mature and accomplished piece of Renaissance architecture in Scotland'. Earl Patrick was Steward of Orkney and Shetland and entirely corrupt. He was finally executed for his awful crimes against humanity, having been granted a week's reprieve to learn the Lord's Prayer.

The Ba' Game

Kirkwall has its own unique 'Ba' Game', loosely described as football. It is played on Christmas and New Year's Day, between the 'trsuppies' and 'trsdoonies', and often involves as many as 150 men from either end of the town. If the ball finishes up in the harbour, it is victory for the 'trsuppies'; if it reaches the goal at the old castle, then the 'trsdoonies' win. The game can last all day and dates from Norse times.

Shapinsay's Famous Son

In 1760 a family called Irving emigrated to America from Quholm in the northeast corner of the island. They sided with the rebels in the Revolution and made their fortune. Washington Irving, born to this family in 1783, became America's first internationally successful writer. He came back to Britain, struck up a friendship with, among other literary lions, Sir Walter Scott, and with Scott's encouragement returned to America and wrote a number of best-selling essays and tales, including adaptations of Rip Van Winkle and The Legend of Sleepy Hollow. His most prodigious work was a 5-volume biography of George Washington, after whom he was named.

Tankerness House Museum (*open Mon–Sat 9.30–6; May–Sept also Sun 2–6; gardens always open*) is in a very well-restored 16th-century merchant's town house, with an attractive courtyard and garden. Over 4,000 years of Orkney history is displayed here.

Orkney Library (*open Mon–Sat*), founded in 1683, is the oldest public library in Scotland and has an excellent Orkney Room for anyone wanting to delve more deeply into the history of the island.

The **Mercat Cross**, on Kirk Green by the cathedral, dates from 1621, though it was only moved here in 1762. It is a replica of the one inside the cathedral. This is where the 'Ba' is thrown up, to start the Christmas and New Year 'Ba Game'. Public proclamations were always made from the Cross, and it was also used as the town pillory. Kirk Green is the venue for the annual St Magnus Fair in August.

Among the other things to visit in the town are the **Silver Works** and the **Highland Park Distillery**, which welcome visitors (*open Mon–Fri*).

Shapinsay

The island of Shapinsay guards the entrance to Kirkwall harbour, and it was from Elwick Bay that King Haakon sailed south in 1263 to his ignominious defeat at Largs. And earlier still, in AD 84, they say that one of Agricola's galleys was wrecked at Grucula on the west coast. **Balfour Castle**, in the southwest corner, was designed by David Bryce in 1848 for a Colonel Balfour and his son, who did much to improve the farming methods of the island. You get a good view of this imposing pile, with its turrets and towers and battlements, from the ferry from Kirkwall. It is now run as a private hotel (*see* above), and you can also arrange guided tours of the castle and Victorian gardens through the tourist board (*Wed and Sun*). Much of the interior is unchanged from when it was created by 30 Italian craftsmen 150 years ago.

There is a reconstructed broch at **Burroughston**, with illustrated explanations of its features. Shapinsay's Lairobell Farm goat's cheese is particularly tasty, in spite of its makers having to struggle with the bureaucracy of the EU.

Stromness

Stromness, about 17 miles west of Kirkwall, is the only other proper town in Orkney. Delightful and full of character, it is reminiscent of a Norwegian fishing village with a sheltered harbour and steep, winding cobbled streets lined with early 18th-century houses, many with their own jetties, which seem to jostle each other to get the best position along the mile of waterfront. It was once a principal port on the sailing route around the north of Scotland and base for the Hudson's Bay Company ships. Many local men went to do contract work in Canada. Stromness is the terminal for the car ferry from Scrabster.

The **Pier Arts Centre** (*open Tues–Sun*) is housed in well-restored 18th-century buildings and has an excellent modern collection including work by Ben Nicolson and Barbara Hepworth. There is also a variety of exhibitions throughout the year and a children's workroom.

Stromness Natural History Museum (*open April–Sept daily; reduced opening hours in winter; adm*) has collections of birds, fossils, shells and butterflies. There are also exhibitions covering whaling, fishing, the Hudson's Bay Company, Scapa Flow and the German fleet.

Scapa Flow

Scapa Flow is a great inlet to the south of Mainland, surrounded by protective islands. This perfect deep-water anchorage, up to 10 miles wide, was adopted as the main base of the Grand Fleet in 1912. At the end of the First World War the German Navy sailed their fleet into Scapa, having surrendered. Then, on 21 June 1919, on the order of Rear Admiral Ludwig von Reuter, the whole fleet of 74 warships was scuttled, a dramatic event that was witnessed by, among others, a party of schoolchildren on a trip around the Flow. At the beginning of the Second World War a German U-boat crept through the defences and sank the *Royal Oak*, after which the Churchill Barriers were erected, making the anchorage almost impregnable. Today sculptural wrecks break the water in violent contrast to the peaceful scenery. Most of the wrecks have been salvaged; seven warships and four destroyers remain on the bottom giving great scope for wreck diving. Good supplies of air are obtainable locally.

Birsay

Birsay Brough is a tidal island in the north of Mainland, reached by a causeway which is open for about 2 hours at low tide. Here are the remains of a Viking village, and St Magnus, a Romanesque church built in 1064 and rebuilt in 1664 and 1760. St Magnus' body was taken here after his murder in 1116, to be interred in the cathedral in Kirkwall later. Back across the causeway to the village of Birsay, there is a huge palace built by Earl Patrick Stewart, with fine stonework. At the farmhouse close by there is a double water mill with both over- and under-shot wheels, still intact but urgently in need of restoration.

Walk northeast along the footpath to **Skipi Geo**, a former fisherman's cove with a restored turf-roofed hut and two of the cleets they used for hauling up the boats in winter. A few hundred yards on there is a huge whalebone like a gigantic sculptured bird. Yet further on, **Longaglebe Geo** is a wonderful gorge eroded 650ft inwards by the sea. In early summer the cliffs are covered in colourful wild flowers and nesting birds.

The Principal Prehistoric Sites

Maeshowe

*Open April–Sept daily 9.30–6; Oct–Mar Mon–Sat
9.30–4, Sun 2–4; adm.*

Maeshowe is 10 miles west of Kirkwall, just off the main road to Stromness. It is a huge Stone-Age burial cairn, unquestionably the most outstanding in Britain. The passage into the cairn, made of huge single slabs of stone, is so aligned that a shaft of sunlight pierces its 36ft length into the chamber on only one day of the year, that of the winter solstice. Burial cells lead off the main chamber, which has massive stone buttresses in each corner.

When Maeshowe was first excavated in 1861 the cells were found to be empty, and this fact, together with runic Viking inscriptions on the walls, misled archaeologists into thinking the tomb was Norse. Then it became obvious that the structure dates back many centuries before that and probably to around 3500 BC. The Vikings came much later, sacking the tombs and leaving their graffiti on the walls.

In fact the graffiti are just as fascinating as the much older cairn. There are references to treasure and to the Crusades, and a collection of sex slogans that are as modern as any today: 'Thorny was bedded, Helgi says so', reads one; 'Ingigerd is the best of them all', says another. There is an excellent guidebook on sale at the site. Beside the car park is **Tormiston Mill**, a restored 19th-century water mill with a restaurant and a craft centre.

The Ring of Brodgar

The Ring of Brodgar (*always accessible*) is on the narrow neck of land between Harray and Stenness Lochs, 4 miles northwest of Maeshowe. From the original 60 stones, 36 remain. They are precisely set, being 6° apart, with a surrounding ditch cut from bedrock, as much as 9ft deep and 27ft wide, crossed by two causeways. These stones date from about 1560 BC and are believed to be some sort of lunar observatory, a splendid reminder that those Stone-Age men may have been primitive but they certainly weren't stupid.

The Stones of Stenness

The Stones of Stenness (*always accessible*) date from around the 3rd millennium BC, and only four stones remain of the original circle. Excavations uncovered an almost square setting of horizontal stones, scattered with fragments of cremated bones, charcoal and shards of pottery, indicating that this must have been some sort of cremation and burial site. The two outlying stones, the Barnhouse and the Watch Stone, were probably associated with this circle, as must have been the many cists and cairns that have been unearthed in this area.

Skara Brae

Open April–Sept daily 9.30–6.30; Oct–Mar Mon–Sat
9.30–4.30, Sun 2–4.30; adm.

Skara Brae is 5 miles northwest of the Stones of Stenness, on the west coast and on the southern arm of the sandy **Bay of Skaill**. This was a Stone-Age settlement, hit by a massive storm that buried it in sand for about 4,000 years. Another storm then blew away some of the sand to reveal the village to archaeologists. It is unique, giving an insight into the whole way of life of those prehistoric tribes, rather than just revealing a burial cairn, which only tells a fraction of their story.

Careful excavation has uncovered about six of the original 10 one-roomed houses, and a workshop, with covered passages from one to another and a communal paved courtyard. Lack of wood meant that these Stone-Age people used stone for their furniture, and the old bed platforms, cupboards, hearths, fish tanks and tables can still be seen, as well as a fascinating collection of tools and implements. Recent progress in carbon-dating means that more and more information is coming to light about those mysterious settlers, and there is an excellent guidebook with up-to-date findings. Midden (rubbish heap) excavations have revealed that the inhabitants of this earliest fishing village in Scotland were also farmers.

Skaill House

Skaill House, at Sandwick (*open April–Sept Mon–Sat 9.30–6.30, Sun 11.30–6.30; adm*), overlooks the lovely Bay of Skaill, 300 yards from Skara Brae. This is one of the most complete 17th-century mansion houses in Orkney, surrounded by lawns and gardens. It was built in the 1620s and has been added to by successive lairds ever since, culminating in the north tower and wing which give it such a distinctive profile.

Inside the beautifully restored rooms, including the rather cosy bedroom of Bishop George Graham for whom the house was built, you can see such things as Captain Cook's dinner service and other endearing memorabilia collected up by the house's various owners.

Orkney's only surviving **Click Mill** is beyond Dounby, about 8 miles northeast of Skara Brae. It is a horizontal water wheel, built in about 1800 from an earlier design, and so called from the noise it makes as it turns. It is preserved in working order, although the pond has been drained.

Gurness

On the wild, windswept headland at Gurness, 5 miles northeast of the Click Mill, there is one of the best brochs in Orkney (*open daily; adm*). A booklet describes the very complicated layout of the site. It was built as a broch and then added to over the centuries by the Norsemen, and includes many domestic buildings, Norse long-houses, partitioned chambers and a well.

Islands South of Mainland

Lamb Holm

Lamb Holm, linked by a mile of causeway south of Mainland, has the heart-stirring little **Italian Chapel** which was created out of two Nissen huts, corrugated iron, plasterboard, paint and cement by Italian prisoners of war, nostalgic for their warm, Catholic homeland during the Second World War. They were building the Churchill Barrier after the sinking of the *Royal Oak* and made the chapel in their spare time. It is a miracle of faith, with delicate wrought-iron tracery and frescoes. The artist, Dominico Chiocchetti, returned in 1960 to restore the original work.

Burray

At Burray, linked to Lamb Holm by a causeway to the south, there is a **Fossil Centre** (*check with tourist office for opening times; adm*), with a collection of fossil fish over 300 million years old – and a convenient coffee shop.

South Ronaldsay

South Ronaldsay, joined to Burray by a causeway, has a picturesque village with a poignant memory – **St Margaret's Hope**. In 1290 the seven-year-old Princess Margaret, Maid of Norway, died of sea sickness in the ship bringing her from Norway to marry Prince Edward of England. (The marriage had been planned as a way of uniting Britain with Norway.) The ship, bearing the wasted body of the little princess, put in to St Margaret's Hope.

The **Tomb of the Eagles** (*open April–Oct daily 10–8; Nov–Mar daily 10–12; or by arrangement, t (01856) 831 339; call at Liddle Farm first*), on the southeast toe of South Ronaldsay, is so named because of the many sea-eagle claws found in the Stone-Age chambered tomb which you can crawl into. Mr Simison, the farmer who found and excavated the tomb, will usher you along a wonderful cliff-top walk to see it, and will tell you all about it. He will also show you, on a different site in the same field, an equally fascinating Stone-Age house complete with oven and cooking facilities. Back in the delightfully amateur 'museum' in the farm house, his daughter will let you hold 5,000-year-old tools, skulls and claws.

Hoy

Hoy, the largest island apart from Mainland, about 3 miles south of Stromness, is the only one that is not flat and has scenery much more like Shetland. Its hills provide a good backdrop to views over the flat green farmland wherever you are in these islands. Ward Hill rises to 1,500 ft. The **Old Man of Hoy** is a rock stack, 450ft high, on a promontory above the sea. This is a favourite challenge to serious rock climbers, a towering pinnacle of horizontally layered rock. The first recorded successful climb was in 1966, done by a three-man team led by Chris Bonnington. A marked footpath takes you out to the Old Man from Rackwick, with one or two quite steep bits, taking about 90 minutes. **St John's Head**, on northwest Hoy, is part of a 1,140ft vertical cliff,

Getting There

By Air

British Airways Express fly to Kirkwall (*daily exc Sun*) from Aberdeen, Glasgow, Edinburgh and Inverness with connections from London, Birmingham and Manchester. There is a Loganair 'Airbridge' flight from Wick to Kirkwall and inter-island services. (The shortest flight, between Westray and Papa Westray, takes a minute in good conditions.)
British Airways Express, t 0845 773 3377, **t** (01856) 873 611, *www.britishairways.com*. **Loganair, t** (01856) 872 494.

By Sea

P&O Scottish Ferries run from Aberdeen to Stromness (*8hrs; book in advance*), and from Scrabster to Stromness (*1hr 45mins; book in advance*). Ferries run from Stromness on to Shetland. In October 2002 Northlink Orkney and Shetland Ferries will take this over. John o' Groats Ferries operate daily (*May–Sept; c. 45mins*), passengers and bicycles only. Pentland Ferries run from Gills Bay to St Margaret's Hope for cars and passengers, with reduced winter rates.
P&O Scottish Ferries, t (01856) 850 655.
Northlink Orkney and Shetland Ferries, t (01856) 851 444, *www.northlinkferries.co.uk*.
John o' Groats Ferries, t (01955) 611 353, *www.jogferry.co.uk*.
Pentland Ferries, t (01856) 831 226.

By Rail

There are national rail links to Thurso to connect with ferries; or to Aberdeen or Wick to connect with flights/ferries.
National Rail Enquiries: t 08457 484 950.

By Road

Scottish Citylink coaches run to the various ferries and airports from all major UK cities, sometimes with overnight stops in Glasgow, Edinburgh or Inverness.
Scottish Citylink, t 08705 505 050, *www.citylink.co.uk*.

Orkney Bus links Inverness and Kirkwall via the John o' Groats ferry (*1 May–7 Sept daily*).
Orkney Bus, t (01955) 611 353.
It is easy to hire cars on Orkney, and there are causeways to some of the islands.

Tourist Information

Kirkwall: Orkney Tourist Board Information Centre, Broad Street, **t** (01856) 872 856, **f** 875 056.
Stromness: Ferry Terminal, **t** (01856) 850 716, **f** 850 777. *Limited opening hours, Oct–April.* Or visit the website, *www.visitorkney.com*.

Festivals

May: **Folk Festival**, Stromness.
June: **St Magnus Festival**, Kirkwall; a week of music, drama and art, rapidly growing in popularity and attracting companies from many countries. The standard is high.
July: **Craftsmen's Guild**, Kirkwall; two weeks of demonstrations of local craftwork. **Shopping Week**, Stromness.
Christmas Day and New Year's Day: 'Ba' Game', Kirkwall, *see* p.558.

Sports and Activities

Bird-watching is almost compulsive. One in six of all sea birds breeding in Britain nests in Orkney. The long-eared owl is an endearing resident; its 'ears' are elongated head feathers. Its low, moaning hoot is an eerie sound at night. There are short-eared owls, which hunt by day over the moors; red-throated divers, so graceful until they come in to land; razorbills, with their fascinating courtship displays and refusal to build nests; puffins, whose brightly coloured bills are a weapon and a spade with which to dig burrows in the turf.

For **botanists** the wild flowers are a joy: tiny *Primula scotica*, a survivor from the last Ice Age; grass of Parnassus, whose honey-scented white flowers litter the marshland; bog

teeming with sea birds and many rare plants. Just off the main road south, clearly visible, is a whitewashed gravestone – **Betty Corrigall's Grave**. Left pregnant and deserted by a visiting sailor in the 19th century, this young girl from Lyness committed pimpernel, oysterplant, bog asphodel, and many more. For **naturalists** there is the Orkney vole to look out for, a sweet little round ball of fur. There are otters – Kirkwall must be about the only town to display a red triangular road sign reading: 'Otters Crossing 100 yds'.

Fishermen leave Orkney with enough fishing stories to keep them happy till they return. The brown trout are the best in Britain and fishing is free, thanks to Norse law. Sea angling is also good. **Water-sports** enthusiasts will find perfect waters for sub-aqua diving, especially wreck diving around Scapa Flow.

Archaeologists will find more prehistoric remains than anwhere else in Scotland, some in a remarkable state of preservation: brochs, standing stones, burial cairns – an average of three sites per square mile. The tourist information office in Kirkwall has a first-class free booklet on what to see.

Where to Stay and Eat

Orkney t (01856–)

Ayre Hotel, Ayre Road, Kirkwall, t 873 001, f 876 289, *www.ayrehotel.co.uk* (*moderate*). On the waterfront, overlooking Kirkwall Bay. Some 200 years old, it is comfortable and friendly. Ask for a room overlooking the sea.

Balfour Castle, Shapinsay, *see below*, t 711 282, f 711 283, *www.balfourcastle.co.uk* (*moderate*). Great informal hospitality in a family home with traditional elegant surroundings (sleeping up to 12). Good value.

Cleaton House, Westray, t (01857) 677 508, f 677 442, *cleaton@orkney.com* (*moderate*). Attractive Victorian manse, now a small, comfortable hotel with lovely views, friendly staff, and a great atmosphere.

Creel Inn and Restaurant, Front Road, St Margaret's Hope, South Ronaldsay, t 831 311, *www.thecreel.co.uk* (*moderate*). Probably the best food in Orkney – the seafood in particular. The bedrooms are lovely and cosy.

Foveran Hotel, St Ola, t 872 389, f 876 430, *www.foveranhotel.co.uk* (*moderate*). Only

2 miles out of Kirkwall with stunning views over Scapa Flow. Peaceful and not too big, built in Scandinavian style in 34 acres. Excellent seafood and helpful hosts.

Kirkwall Hotel, Harbour Street, Kirkwall, t 872 232, f 872 812, *enquiries@kirkwallhotel.co.uk* (*moderate*). Large, French-roofed stone building (1890), overlooking the harbour. Nice, old-fashioned atmosphere. Good food.

Standing Stones Hotel, Stenness, t 850 449, f 851 262, *standingstones@sol.co.uk* (*moderate*). Congenial and comfortable fishing hotel on the shore of the loch, with modern décor. They have boats and ghillies, and the brownies are a good size.

Stromness Hotel, t 850 298, f 850 610, *www.stromnesshotel.com* (*moderate*). Traditional stone-built hotel overlooking the harbour and Scapa Flow, with the usual island hospitality and very reasonable food.

West End Hotel, Main Street, Kirkwall, t 872 368, f 876 181, *westendhotel@orkney.com* (*moderate*). Smaller hotel with more character, lively lounge bar and friendly staff.

Barony Hotel, Birsay, t 721 327, f 721 302 (*cheap*). On the shores of Boardhouse Loch, with views of the village and the Brough. Good food and free trout fishing. *Open May–Sept.*

Beltane House Hotel, Papa Westray, t (01857) 664 267, f 644 282 (*cheap*). In a terrace of recently converted cottages, small, cosy, very friendly, and they will collect you from the boat or plane. The food is homely.

Eviedale Bothies, Evie, t 751 270/254, f 751 270 (*cheap*). Good self-catering in two flats and three cottages in a converted farm steading.

Mrs Gray, the Auld Smokehouse, in the heart of Kirkwall, t/f 874 590, *www.orkney holidays.com* (*cheap*). Two excellent apartments (sleeping 4), newly converted. They'll arrange airport transport and car hire.

Mr Work, in Kirkwall, t/f 873 235, *david_work@tinyonline.co.uk* (*cheap*). Two cottages (sleeping 4).

Hamnave Restaurant, Graham Street, Stromness. Delicious, imaginative food, especially the seafood, reasonably priced.

suicide. Such were the laws of the time that she was not allowed to be buried in hallowed ground and her body was taken to this lonely spot on the parish boundary.

Melsetter House (*not open to the public but visible from the road*) was built on to an older house in 1898 by W. R. Lethaby for Thomas Middlemore, who inherited a fortune from a Birmingham leather business. New and old are kept distinct but the scale and materials used blend nicely into the Orkney landscape

Islands North of Mainland

Rousay

Rousay, a couple of miles northeast of Mainland, has a burial cairn at **Midhowe**. This cairn has a long chamber, 76ft by 7ft, with 24 burial cells leading off it, in which the remains of 25 human bodies were found. Another tomb on Rousay, **Taversoe Tuick**, is unusual because it is two-storied. One tomb sits on top of the other, each with its own entrance passage. Rousay also has a well-preserved broch, with a complex of cells, cubicles, passages, stairs, doorways and outbuildings.

Wyre

Wyre, a mile southeast of Rousay, has the ruin of a 12th-century stone castle, one of the oldest in Scotland, known as **Cubbie Roo's Castle** and probably the stronghold of a Norse robber baron. There is also a ruined 12th-century chapel, St Mary's.

Egilsay is 2 miles east of Rousay. **St Magnus' Church** marks the site of the murder of Jarl Magnus in 1116, after whom the cathedral in Kirkwall is named. The ruined church dominates this small, low-lying island, with a tall, tapering round tower at the west end. This design is of Irish origin, indicating close contact between Ireland and Orkney during Viking times. It was probably built in the 12th century, and its walls still stand to their full height. The tower, nearly 50ft high, was once taller still, and it seems to beckon from all around. Magnus was killed on the order of his rival, Earl Haakon, who wanted sole power over Orkney. Egilsay has a large proportion of southerners in its small population.

Eday

On Eday, 4 miles to the east of Egilsay, there are chambered tombs and an Iron-Age dwelling that was once a roundhouse with radial divisions inside, dating from several centuries BC.

Westray

Westray, 7 miles north of Rousay, is one of the most authentically Orcadian in character, having fewer resident incomers. The formidable ruin of **Noltland Castle** at its north end was built in 1560 by Gilbert Balfour who was implicated in the murder of Cardinal Beaton and served on a French galley beside John Knox in punishment. He was later Master of the Household for Mary, Queen of Scots. Its design is Z-plan, with all-round visibility and an extravagant provision of gun loops. It was burned by Covenanters in 1650.

Papa Westray

Papa Westray, 2 miles off the northeast tip of Westray, is so called from the hermits who lived in the cells here. This island was part of an important Norse family estate in the 11th and 12th centuries, and archaeologists have discovered the remains of Neolithic settlements which have provided valuable clues to the lifestyle of those ancient inhabitants.

North Ronaldsay

North Ronaldsay is the most northern island of Orkney, 15 miles east of Papa Westray and 32 miles northeast of Kirkwall. It is surrounded by a sea dyke designed to keep the unique breed of sheep off the grass, so that they feed from the rich seaweed on the shore. The meat of these small, sturdy animals has a distinctive flavour.

Shetland

According to Tacitus, when the Romans sailed around the north coast of Scotland and found Britain was an island, they 'discovered and subdued' Orkney but they left Shetland alone because of the wild seas that lay between them. He called Shetland *Thule*, that mythical island which the ancients believed lay on the edge of the world.

Sixty miles north of Orkney and halfway to Norway, the character of Shetland is very different to that of Orkney although they share much of their history. In spite of being on the same latitude as Greenland, Shetland's climate is mild, because of the Gulf Stream, with plenty of sunshine in early summer and less rain than the Western Isles. Of the 100 islands in the archipelago, only 15 are continuously inhabited. Like Orkney, Shetland has long summer nights, the 'simmer dim' twilight of midsummer adding a touch of timelessness to holidays. The name Shetland is derived from the Norse word *hjaltland*, meaning Highland. Locals talk about Shetland, never the Shetlands. As in Orkney, when they talk about the Mainland, they are referring to the principal island. Much of the terrain is peat bog and rough highland hillside, carpeted with heather and turf and dotted with small lochs – not so green and fertile as it is in Orkney. Ronas Hill, to the northwest of Mainland, is the highest point at 1,475ft, and nowhere is more than 3 miles from the sea.

There is wonderful cliff scenery with long winding inlets, called 'voes', battered into arches, fissures and jagged stacks. Few trees survive the gale-force winds that lash the islands. There is a fair bit of agriculture: dairy farming and vegetable crops thrive in the south and central Mainland, and sheep farming is important, including the black and brown Shetland sheep. The Shetland cabbage is salt resistant and grown as a fodder crop. Shetland knitwear is world famous. In the old days the wool was plucked or 'roo'ed' from the sheep's neck by hand, being too fine for shears, but this is no longer common except for some show animals. A true Shetland shawl should be so fine it can be pulled through a wedding ring.

Shetland ponies roam over the hills, originally mini draught horses on the crofts and then bred for work in coal mines, with 'as much strength as possible and as near the ground as can be got'. The skeleton of one found in the middle of Jarlshof Broch was smaller than the modern breed. They are not strictly wild as they are all owned. They feed on common grazing, and efforts are made to improve the breed by introducing good Shetland stallions to run with them. Their tail hair was used as fishing line, and it used to be illegal to steal hair from another man's horse.

The old life of crofting, fishing and knitting was greatly changed when the oil boom hit Shetland, but the oil depots are well confined to the Sullom Voe area on the Mainland, where the installations don't even break the skyline. They have not spoiled the rest of the islands and have brought a new prosperity that must make life a lot easier for many. The poet Hugh MacDiarmid said:

> It is indeed impossible to eke out a decent living in Shetland by crofting alone. That is the difference between Orkney and Shetland: the Orcadian is a farmer with a boat, the Shetlander is a fisherman with a croft.

Because they were such good seamen, Shetlanders were vulnerable to press gangs. It was not unknown for a whole community of able-bodied young men to be snatched away in a furtive raid from the sea. The fiddle tune 'Jack is yet alive' was composed for a Shetlander who had been press-ganged, served his time and returned to a family who had written him off long ago. Fiddle music is still very popular throughout the islands. Fiddling and dancing at Islesburgh Community Centre in Lerwick on Wednesday evenings in summer provide lively entertainment (*t* (01595) 692 114 for details). Simmer'n Sessions are sessions of traditional Shetland music in several different places during the summer (*t* (01950) 620 201, for details).

The seascapes are unforgettable: sudden glimpses of an island-dotted sea with dramatic rocks, cliffs and beaches, suffused by an extraordinary clarity of light. The colours must have influenced the natural shades used in the knitwear, particularly those in the Fair Isle designs.

Mainland

Lerwick

Mainland is by far the biggest of the islands, its chief town being Lerwick, Britain's most northerly town, so called from the Norse *leir-vik* meaning 'clay creek'. Overlooking sheltered Bressay Sound, Lerwick has always been a refuge for seafarers. In spite of its geographical isolation, it is a lot more up to date and cosmopolitan than many of the towns in the Highland region of Scotland. It was a stopping-off port for Norsemen: King Haakon reprovisioned his fleet here on the way to defeat at Largs in 1263.

Lerwick has always been important for fishing: the home waters are productive and it lies on the edge of the valuable northern fishing fields. Dutch fishing fleets were based here in the 17th century, and by the 18th century the export of salt fish was thriving. In the 17th century the town became important as a base for the British Navy. Fort Charlotte was built in 1665 to protect the Sound of Bressay from the Dutch.

Nowadays the Sound is sometimes busy with vessels of all kinds and nationalities, the crews of which amble around the town adding a cosmopolitan touch with their different languages. It is said that some Norwegians come here for bargain shopping, away from their own exorbitant prices.

The buildings that grew up around the port were sturdy and compact, designed to withstand violent storms. Many of them were the town houses of Scottish lairds who succeeded the Norsemen and found winter conditions rather bleak in the outlying countryside. Now the older houses are interspersed with a sprawl of characterless modern buildings.

The *Dim Riv* is a replica Norse longship, over 40ft long, which takes visitors on trips round the harbour in summer. The harbour is a lively, bustling place, with a pictur-esque waterfront and the charmingly haphazard, flagstoned Commercial Street straggling up behind. This is the main shopping centre, and the steep, narrow lanes around it are said to cover a network of secret tunnels and passages used by smug-glers in the past. Boat trips run from Victoria Pier, to cruise around the coast in summer. Look out for the distinctive Shetland sailing dinghy, a local design with the elegant double-prow effect of the Viking longboats. They can be seen in most of the harbours around Shetland and are raced in local regattas.

Fort Charlotte (*open June–Sept daily 9am–10pm; Oct–May daily 10–4*), built by Cromwellian troops and the only Cromwellian military building still intact in Scotland, was named after Queen Charlotte, wife of George III. It was partly burned by the Dutch in 1673, repaired and restored in 1781, and garrisoned during the Napoleonic wars. There being no garrison in the 19th century, it was first used as comfortable digs for bachelors and, later, became the prison.

The **Town Hall**, above Commercial Street in Hillhead, is a Victorian-Gothic building built from local stone in 1884. Partly resembling a church, it has a tower and rose window, four corner turrets, a central oriel window and stained-glass windows on the upper floor. These enclose the main hall and depict the history of Shetland, beginning with the Scandinavian conquest in 870. There are full-length figures of Norway's King Harald Harfagri, the conqueror of the islands, and Rognvald, Jarl of More, to whom Harald offered the first earldom. The windows cover all the main events in Shetland's story, including one of the Maid of Norway, who died at sea nearby. This is an inter-esting building and you can climb the tower for magnificent views of the town.

The **Shetland Museum** (*open Mon–Sat; www.shetlandmuseum.org.uk*) is opposite the town hall. It has four galleries devoted to the history of man in Shetland, from prehistoric times to the present. Look for the **Papil Stone**, dating from the 7th century, showing a procession of papas, or priests, one of whom is on a horse. Other exhibits include the history of Shetland knitting and the history of the islands' marine and fishing past. There are also replicas of the treasure found on St Ninian's Isle.

The **Islesburgh Exhibition**, King Harald Street, in the Islesburgh Community Centre (*open mid-May–mid-Sept Wed and Fri evenings*), is an excellent display of island crafts and culture – knitting, weaving, arts and crafts, croft house culture, singing, dancing and fiddle music.

Getting There

By Air

British Airways fly from Aberdeen (*4 flights a day weekdays, a reduced service at weekends*), Glasgow, Edinburgh, Inverness, Orkney and other major UK airports. Sumburgh Airport is 25 miles from Lerwick, and there is a connecting bus service as well as taxis. Cars can be hired at the airport.
British Airways, t 0845 773 3377.

By Sea

P&O Scottish Services operate almost daily between Aberdeen and Lerwick, twice-weekly during the summer via Orkney *(boats usually depart 6pm, and arrive at 8am the next day)*. This will be run by Northlink Service from October 2002. Smyril Line run a summer service from Shetland to Norway, Iceland and Faroe. P&O have their brochures.
P&O Scottish Ferries, PO Box 5, Jamieson's Quay, Aberdeen AB9 8DL, **t** (01224) 572 615.
Northlink Service, t (01856) 851 444, *www.northlinkferries.co.uk.*

Getting Around

By Air

Loganair run a regular inter-island service from Tingwall Airport, Lerwick, to the islands of Foula, Fair Isle, Papa Stour and Out Skerries.

By Sea

A frequent passenger and drive-on/drive-off car ferry links most of the islands with Shetland Mainland. Fares are very cheap but booking is recommended. Full details available from the tourist office in Lerwick.

By Road

Private transport is the best way of exploring Shetland, either in your own car or a hired one. Bicycles can also be hired. Shetland roads are generally good.
John Leask, t (01595) 693 162. Coach tours.

Tourist Information

Lerwick: Shetland Islands Tourism Information Centre, **t** (01595) 693 434, **f** 695 807, *www.visitshetland.com.*
Cycharters, t (01595) 696 598. Sightseeing and sea angling trips.
Boat trips, t (01595) 693 434. Seal- and bird-spotting cruises from Lerwick in summer.

Festivals

Last Tuesday in January: Up-Helly-Aa, Lerwick; Viking fire festival to mark the end of Yuletide and symbolize the desire for the sun to appear again after the long winter nights. A Viking galley is carried to a park in the centre of town, amidst a forest of blazing torches, and set alight while 'The Norseman's Home' is sung as a funeral dirge.
April: Shetland Folk Festival.
October: Shetland Accordion and Fiddle Festival.

Sports and Activities

For **ornithologists**, there are vast colonies of sea birds, both northern and migrant. Among the many hundred species to be seen is the Shetland wren, 'stinkie', even smaller than her more common cousin. As if to make up for her stature, her formal name is *Troglodytes troglodytes shetlandicus*. Fair Isle, halfway to Orkney, has an observation station and is famous as a staging post for migrants.

For **naturalists** there are vast quantities of seals, known locally as 'selkies'. Otters can be seen around small rocks and skerries in the remoter coastal areas. Whales, killer whales, sharks, dolphins and porpoises can all be seen off the coast.

For **botanists** the wild flowers are marvellous, with around 500 species of plants to discover. Because much of the pasture is untreated, many that have become rare elsewhere have survived, including the rather hideous large Australian daisy. There are Arctic

The **Bod of Gremista Museum** (*open June–mid-Sept Wed–Sun; adm*) is an 18th-century fishing cottage with good displays on fishing and the sea. The **Up Helly Aa Exhibition** (*open mid-May–mid-Sept Tues, Fri and Sat; adm*) has a replica gallery and flowers, the American mondey flower, and the tiny blue caucasus from Asia Minor.

Trout **fishing** is excellent in the lochs, of which there are more than 300, with brownies weighing as much as 8lbs, and there are some salmon – including a few escapees from salmon farms. Char can be caught on the Loch of Girlsta. Fishing permits can be bought from the Tourist Office in Lerwick, where you can also get details about boats and local associations. **Sea angling** is first class, for cod, halibut, tusk and many other white fish. Porbeagle shark of up to 450lbs have been caught in local waters and the current European record of a 226.5 lb skate is held by Shetland.

There is a wealth of prehistoric remains for **archaeologists**, and some of the most satisfying **walking** in Scotland. Ask at the Tourist Office for the series of books on walking in Shetland by Peter Guy.

Where to Stay and Eat

Burrastow House, overlooking Vaila Sound on the most westerly point, t (01595) 809 307, f 809 213, *burr.hs.hotel@zetnet.co.uk* (*expensive*). Idyllic 18th-century 'Haa' house, small and extremely comfortable, with gourmet food. Wonderful views: from the terrace you can see seals and otters. A ghillie and boat are available for fishermen.

Busta House, Busta, t (01806) 522 506, f 522 588, *www.bustahouse.com* (*expensive*). Gorgeous old country house overlooking Busta Voe, serving good food and wine and a selection of 120 malt whiskies.

Grand Hotel, Commercial Street, Lerwick, t (01595) 692 826, f 694 048 (*expensive*). In the town centre, with an imposing castellated tower and Shetland's only nightclub.

Kveldsro House Hotel, Lerwick, t (01595) 692 195, f 696 595 (*expensive*). Luxury hotel overlooking the harbour, with excellent food.

Lerwick Hotel, t (01595) 692 166, f 694 419, *reception@lerwickhotel.co.uk* (*expensive*). 10 minutes' walk from the town centre, a comfortable modern building with a

glorious view over Breiwick Bay and Bressay Island. Good service.

Queens Hotel, Commercial Street, Lerwick t (01595) 692 826, f 694 048 (*expensive*). Picturesque, old-fashioned and comfortable hotel right on the water.

St Magnus Hotel, Hillswick, North Mainland, t (01806) 503 372 (*moderate*). An historic Norwegian hotel overlooking St Magnus Bay, with a good reputation for food.

Shetland Hotel, Holmsgarth Road, Lerwick, t (01595) 695 515, f 695 828, *reception@shet-landhotel.co.uk* (*expensive*). Comfortable, modern hotel, opposite the ferry terminal. Well run with friendly staff.

Sumburgh Hotel, close to the airport, t (01950) 460 201, f 460 394, *www.sumburgh-hotel. zetnet.co.uk* (*expensive*). An old laird's house. Lots of character and very friendly.

Baltasound Hotel, Unst, t (01957) 711 334, f 711 358 (*moderate*). Britain's most northerly hotel, with comfortable rooms in a modern timber annexe. Good for outdoor pursuits.

Buness House, Baltasound, Unst, t (01957) 711 315, f 711 815 (*moderate*). Listed 17th-century house with great sea views, owning the Hermaness Nature Reserve. The food is excellent and the hosts hospitable.

Greystones Guest House, on the water's edge at Brae, t (01806) 522 322/634 (*moderate*). Homely, friendly atmosphere and good food.

Hildasay Guest House, Upper Scalloway, t (01595) 880 822 (*cheap*). Warm welcome, and disabled facilities. Can arrange fishing.

Mrs Brown, Weisdale, West Mainland, t (01595) 830 443 (eves; *cheap*). Dear little self-catering cottage on a working croft overlooking Weisdale Voe (sleeping 6).

Mrs Gifford, 12 Burgh Road, Lerwick, t (01595) 693 554 (*cheap*). Quiet and central.

Mrs Grains, Vidlin, North Mainland, t (01806) 577 219 (*cheap*). Traditional house, with lovely views of Vidlin Voe (sleeping 6).

Mrs M. Hunter, Vermentry, Aith, Bixter (West Mainland), t (01595) 810 239 (evenings) or 810 439 (daytime) (*cheap*). Exceptionally nice self-catering cottage in outstanding scenery, and well equipped (sleeping 5).

exhibits related to the festival, with a video. **Clickhimin Broch** (*always accessible*) is on the western outskirts of town, on an island in a loch, reached by a causeway. It is 65ft in diameter, its walls 18ft thick and 15ft high, on a massive stone platform. Excavations on this site suggest that it may have been a late-Bronze-Age settlement. A frequent car ferry crosses to the island of **Bressay**, east of Lerwick, and from here a boat crosses the 200 yards to the bird sanctuary on **Noss** (*open to the public mid-May–end Aug*).

Scalloway

Scalloway is Mainland's other town, in an attractive bay 7 miles west of Lerwick. It was the capital until 200 years ago and is still an important fishing port. It is much older than Lerwick and retains a quiet, old-fashioned atmosphere. There is a small local **museum** in the middle of town, which has, among other things, a detailed history of the Shetland Bus. During the Second World War small Norwegian fishing boats crossed to Nazi-occupied Norway to carry out sabotage or to land secret agents and bring back refugees. 'To take the Shetland Bus' meant to escape from Norway. Lunna House (*see* p.574), in northeast Mainland, now a guesthouse, was the original headquarters of this Norwegian Resistance Movement, before it was transferred to Scalloway where more facilities were available. *The Shetland Bus* by David Howarth gives a good account of the operation.

Scalloway Castle (*always accessible*) dominates the town, a forbidding ruin built by Earl Patrick Stewart in 1600. Stewart was the notorious despot who tyrannized Orkney and Shetland until his death by execution. Built in medieval style, the roofless shell, with corner turrets and gables, stands on a narrow promontory by the water. The Earl is said to have hung his victims from an iron ring in one of the chimneys. The castle was, not surprisingly, left to rot after the Earl's death.

There are bridges across to the islands of **Tronda** and **Burra** just to the south.

Scalloway is at the southern end of the agricultural valley of **Tingwall**, so called after the site of the old Norse parliament, or thing, at the north end of **Tingwall Loch**, reached by stepping stones.

Not far north, at Weisdale, **Shetland Jewellery** make high-quality Celtic- and Viking-design jewellery.

South of Lerwick

Mousa Broch, on Mousa Island (*open daily; adm for 15min ferry; booking essential: contact Tom Jamieson, t (01950) 431 367; www.mousaboattrips.co.uk; mid-April–mid-Sept, weather permitting, a 3hr trip leaving Sandwick at 2pm (Fri and Sun 12.30 and 2). Also evening trips late May–July on Sat and Wed at 11pm to see storm petrels which nest in the broch; no dogs allowed on the island*), is one of Shetland's main archaeological treasures. Mousa Island, a mile offshore, is inhabited only by sheep and ponies and its broch is the best preserved in existence. It is a thrilling experience to climb its steps, walking in the footsteps of its Pictish builders 2,000 years ago. Built from local sandstone, over 49ft in diameter, over 42ft high, with walls that taper from 12ft to 7ft in thickness, this was one of the smallest of the brochs and probably one of the latest. Galleries honeycomb its double walls, and stairways lead to a parapet around the top. This broch illustrates clearly how the builders tapered the walls inwards to within about 10ft of the top and then sloped them outwards, making it almost impossible for invaders to climb.

Mousa appears romantically in two of the old sagas. In 1150 the Norwegian Prince Erland abducted a famous beauty and held her in the broch until her son, a Jarl, unable to storm the impregnable fortress, had to consent to their marriage. Another saga tells of a young man called Bjorn, who brought Thora, whom he had seduced, to Mousa in 900 and here they set up home together.

St Ninian's Isle is 4 miles southwest of Sandwick, off the west coast of Mainland. You can walk to it along a white crescent of sand, called a 'tombolo', that forms a causeway. Here are the foundations of a 12th-century chapel, buried by sand for many hundreds of years. In 1958 Aberdeen University began excavating the site and discovered not only the foundations of the chapel, but also a Bronze-Age burial ground and the remains of a pre-Norse church.

Under a stone slab in the chapel nave they found a hoard of 8th-century Celtic silver, now in the Royal Museum of Scotland in Edinburgh, with a replica collection in the museum in Lerwick. It is believed that this wonderful hoard was buried by the monks who lived here, probably during an invasion threat from Vikings. The treasure includes silver bowls, delicate brooches and a Communion spoon. Lengthy litigation followed the finding, it being disputed whether the Crown could claim treasure in a land where Udal law still applies.

The **Shetland Croft Museum** (*open May–Sept daily; adm*), at Boddam on the east coast of Mainland south of Sandwick, is a restored croft house, typical of the mid-19th century. Inside the cottage is the original driftwood furniture and all the domestic utensils, giving a picture of how crofters used to live. There is also the old water mill, down the hill by the burn. **Quendale Mill** (*open May–Sept daily 10–5; adm*) gives the history of a working 19th-century water mill, with tours, a video and shop.

Sumburgh, with the airport, is at the southern tip of Mainland, 27 miles south of Lerwick. The modern, clean-cut buildings at the airport present a remarkable contrast to the antiquity of Jarlshof, nearby.

Jarlshof (*open April–Sept Mon–Sat 9.30–6.30, Sun 2–6.30; adm; grounds open at all times*) was a name invented by Sir Walter Scott in *The Pirate*. He visited the island in 1814, was impressed by the laird's hall and wrote his story around it. It was not until 1905 that a violent storm revealed that this was a site that had been occupied for over 3,000 years by seven civilizations, of which the Norse Jarls were the most recent.

Unless you are with an expert, buy the guide book to benefit fully from this remarkable site which contains the remains of village settlements from the Bronze Age to Viking times, sprawled over a low green promontory by the sea. The first house dates from the early or middle part of the 2nd millennium BC. The Bronze-Age huts include cattle stalls and a metal workshop; the Iron-Age settlement has two earth houses and a broch. The three 8th-century wheelhouses are thought to be family dwellings consisting of a number of individual recesses separated as if by the spokes of a wheel, all around a central hearth. A confusion of longhouses is all that is left of the Norse occupation. It was the now-ruined medieval farmhouse that Sir Walter used as his setting. A museum exhibits some of the artefacts that have been found on the site, as well as a good ground plan and interpretative display showing the history of Jarlshof.

Old Scatness Broch (*open July and Aug daily exc Fri 10–5.30 for guided tours; adm*) is one of the best-preserved Iron-Age villages in the world, and is still being excavated.

Sumburgh Head is a solid mass of birds – and twitchers on their trail. Hundreds of thousands of guillemots, puffins, gulls, razor-bills and terns crowd the cliffs and stacks below the lighthouse, despite the expansion of the airport into one of the busiest in Scotland. There are also excellent views of Fair Isle from here. The RSPB run guided tours in summer (*t (01950) 860 800*).

North of Lerwick

Sandness is about 25 miles northwest of Lerwick; boats run from West Burrafirth, nearby, to **Papa Stour**, a couple of miles off the coast (*four times a week; day trips possible Fri and Sat*). The sea caves are believed to be the finest in Britain, but you will need to hire a boat locally to see them properly. The scent from the wild flowers on Papa Stour was said to be so strong that fishermen could fix their position from it if caught in fog out at sea.

Lunna is about 18 miles north of Lerwick as the crow flies, out on the east coast. When Lunna House, now a small hotel, was the original headquarters of the Norwegian Resistance, the barns and outhouses were used as an arsenal. **Lunna Kirk** (1753), one of the oldest Shetland churches still in use, is a charming old building with a leper squint, through which lepers could follow the service and receive Communion.

At **Brae**, about 23 miles north of Lerwick, a narrow neck of land called **Mavis Grind** prevents the northwest corner of Mainland from being an island.

Sullom Voe Oil Terminal (pronounced Soolem), with its complex of buildings and jetties, is on the peninsula of **Calback Ness**, northeast of Brae, joined to Mainland by reclaimed land. The terminal is tucked away so discreetly that you are hardly aware of it, though you cannot miss the incongruous, ugly buildings that house the oil workers. **Firth**, nearby, was built to house the oilmen. **Toft** is 4 miles east of Sullom Voe and from here the car ferry crosses to **Yell**, 3 miles northeast.

This northern part of Mainland is dominated by **Ronas Hill**, Shetland's highest point, 1,475ft high, 10 miles north of Brae, and well worth climbing for marvellous views.

Eshaness, on the coast of Mainland 15 miles northwest of Brae, has precipitous cliffs and breathtaking views of the **Drongs**, a collection of weird stacks carved by the force of the ocean. These stacks include a huge natural arch called the **Dore Holm**.

Tangwick Haa Museum, at Eshaness (*open May–Sept Mon–Fri 1–5, Sat and Sun 11–7*), is a former laird's house, renovated with authentic interiors from the past. Microfilm census records are available.

Yell and Unst

The island of **Yell**, to the north, is mostly peat moor. It was described by Eric Linklater as 'dull and dark and one large peat bog'. Although the second-largest of the Shetland islands, it has suffered from depopulation and can be rather depressing. It is one of the best places in Britain to see otters.

The **Old Haa of Burravoe**, on the south end of Yell (*open late April–Sept Tues–Thurs and Sat 10–4, Sun 2–5*) is a 1700s laird's house with local and natural history, an art gallery, tearoom and shop, and great atmosphere.

A Minister of the Kirk once said: 'Yell is Hell, but Unst – Oh! Unst!' **Unst** is Britain's most northern island, with the **Muckle Flugga** lighthouse on a rock just off its northern tip. The lighthouse was built by Thomas Stevenson, Robert Louis Stevenson's father and, while he was designing and building it, his son stayed on Unst, dreaming up *Treasure Island*. Unst supports a number of Shetland ponies and it has wonderful cliff scenery. **Haroldswick**, in northeast Unst, is where Harald Harfagri landed from Norway to subdue the troublesome Viking jarls. There is a nice little **heritage centre** (*open May–Sept daily 2–5*), with the history of the island families and way of life. Also in Haroldswick is the **Unst Boat Haven** (*open May–Sept daily 2–4*), with a collection of sailing and fishing boats and maritime artefacts. **Valhalla Brewery**, at Baltasound (*visitors welcome by appointment, t (01957) 711 348*), is Britain's most northern brewery. The **Hermaness Visitor Centre** (*open April–mid-Sept daily 9–5*) is for birdspotters.

Fetlar

Fetlar, east of Yell and much smaller, derives its name from the Norn name for 'fat land', and is the most fertile of the islands, with a large number of birds. Snowy owls bred on Fetlar until 1975, when the resident male died. Now, although they no longer breed there, visiting females can still be seen. They have a buzzard-like flight and distinctive white plumage. Another of Fetlar's rare visitors is the red-necked phalarope with a long, needle-like beak, which spins round on the water to stir up insects. The whimbrel, rather like a smaller curlew, usually a coastal migrant, nests on Fetlar and can be seen combing the shore for molluscs and worms with its long curved beak.

Whalsay

Whalsay, a couple of miles off northeast Mainland, is important for fishing and fish processing. On the pier there is a 17th-century Hanseatic trading booth. The Hanseatic League merchants came from northern Germany to Shetland to trade, buying fish and salting it for export, until salt tax was introduced in 1712. The traders set up booths like this one, from which they offered fine cloth, fishing tackle, exotic foods, tobacco, fruit and gin at a farthing a pint, in exchange for fish, butter, wool and fish oil. It is intriguing to look at this quiet, peaceful place and picture what it was like when the merchants haggled and bartered from their booths.

Whalsay has two prehistoric sites: the **Standing Stones** at Yoxie, and the **Benie Hoose**, thought to have been the dwelling for the Druid priests who were responsible for the ceremonies performed around the standing stones.

Foula

Foula is an island 27 miles west of Mainland, with dramatic cliff scenery and a colony of skuas. Still inhabited, it is often cut off in bad weather. This was the last place where Norn was spoken, in the 19th century.

Fair Isle

Fair Isle, the 'Far Isle' of the Vikings, halfway between Orkney and Shetland, is a buffer between the Atlantic and the North Sea. It must be the most gale-battered island in Britain, presenting a tough challenge to the 60-odd people who live there. The bird population is enormous, preserved by the warden of the **Observatory** where data is collected and analysed. Over 300 species have been recorded on Fair Isle; as well as resident colonies, it is a regular staging post for many migratory birds. Although bleak, this is a magnificent place, with needle-sharp rocks pounded by ferocious seas and sheer cliffs topped by green turf and wild flowers.

In 1588 *El Gran Grifon*, flagship of the transport squadron of the Spanish Armada, was wrecked on Fair Isle. The 17 households, already barely subsisting, took in, housed and fed the 300 survivors who stayed for 6 weeks. In 1984 a delegation of Spaniards in full conquistador regalia dedicated an iron cross in the island's kirkyard to the 50 men who died.

Legend has it that it was these Spaniards who taught the islanders how to knit their intricate patterns; though this is hotly denied, it is easy to see that there could have been some Moorish influence on designs that actually date back to Viking times. Fair Isle knitting is internationally renowned. There is an island cooperative of men and women who work machines and hand-finish 200 orders of Fair Isle jumpers, scarves, hats and gloves a year, each jersey taking seven hours to finish by hand.

Getting There

Fair Isle is 24 miles southwest of Sumburgh on Mainland, and boats run to it from Grutness Pier, on Sumburgh Head (*Tues, Thurs and Sat, taking 2hrs, for a 3-day stay on the island before the next boat back*). For bookings, ring J. Stout, **t** (01595) 760 222. Alternatively you can fly from Tingwall (*Mon, Wed and Fri; May–Oct also Sat; taking 25mins*). There is also a flight from Sumburgh (*May–Oct Sat*).

Where to Stay

Observatory Lodge, details and bookings **t/f** (01595) 760 258 (*moderate–cheap*). Paying guests can stay at this fairly basic place, which has a friendly crofting community atmosphere. Warm and cosy inside, it provides a range of accommodation (very cheap if you opt for a dormitory), with 15–20% reductions if you stay 7 or more days. It's a great place to stay if you enjoy the company of nature lovers and outdoor enthusiasts, and an excellent base for an invigorating holiday.

Mrs Coull, t (01595) 760 248, *kathleen.coull@lineone.net*. Also B&B.

Mrs Riddiford, t (01595) 760 250. Nice place for cosy B&B.

The Puffin Hostel, t (01595) 760 248. An alternative to the lodge. *Open April–Sept.*

Biographical Notes

The names in this section are mentioned in the text but are not necessarily explained.

Adam, William and his four sons, John, Robert, James and William. Renowned Scottish-born architects, Robert, 1728–92 being the best known.

Adamnan, Saint. *c.* 624–704. Ninth Abbot of Iona and biographer of St Columba.

Barrie, Sir James. 1860–1937. Novelist and playwright. Born in Kirriemuir which he renamed Thrums in a series of novels. *Peter Pan* is one of his best-known works. Part of the Kailyard school of writers who sentimentalized small-town life in Scotland.

Bean, Sawney. Apocryphal 17th-century cannibal who lived with his incestuously bred family in a cave in Ayrshire, existing on the flesh and gold of unwary travellers.

Beaton, David. (?)1494–1546. Cardinal and Archbishop of St Andrews. Notorious for persecution of Reformers. Burned George Wishart for heresy and was murdered in revenge in St Andrews Castle.

Beaton, James. 1470–1539. Uncle of the above. Archbishop of Glasgow, then St Andrews. Opponent of the Reformation and responsible for death of Patrick Hamilton.

Boswell, James. 1740–95. Scottish lawyer, writer and admirer of prominent people. Met Dr Johnson in 1763 and toured Hebrides with him in 1773. Wrote *Life of Samuel Johnson*. A volatile, promiscuous man given to fits of depression. His *Journal of a Tour of the Hebrides* should be read in conjunction with Dr Johnson's account.

Bothwell, James Hepburn, Earl of. *c.* 1535–78. Powerful and ambitious. Closely involved in murder of Mary, Queen of Scots' husband, Darnley. Abducted Mary, and married her after quick divorce from his wife. Escaped when Mary was deposed. Imprisoned in Denmark where he died insane.

Brahan Seer. Coinneach Odhar. 17th century. Given gift of second sight after falling asleep on a fairy hill. Made astonishing prophecies, many of which have been fulfilled. Murdered by Countess of Seaforth having told her of her husband's infidelity.

Bridie, James. 1888–1951. Pseudonym of Osborne Henry Mavor, dramatist. Born in Glasgow, qualified as a doctor and served in RAMC in both world wars. His plays include *The Anatomist*, *Dr Angelus* and *A Sleeping Clergyman*. Amusing, extravagant, thought-provoking and entertaining.

Bryce, David. 1803–76. Edinburgh architect whose speciality was Scottish Baronial, most evident in Fettes College.

Burns, Robert. 1759–96. Scotland's greatest vernacular poet, born at Alloway in Ayrshire of humble parents. Renowned almost as much for his enthusiastic love life and 'joie de vivre' as for his verse. Among the many classics he wrote were 'Tam o' Shanter', 'My Love is like a Red, Red Rose', 'A Man's a Man, for a' That' and 'Auld Lang Syne'.

Columba, Saint. *c.* 521–97. Of royal Irish blood, he was exiled from Ireland for ecclesiastical plagiarism, settled in Iona in 563 and founded a religious community, launching-pad for missionaries who then converted Scotland to Christianity.

Cromwell, Oliver. 1599–1658. Led Parliamentarians in England's civil war and was responsible for execution of Charles I.

Cromwell, Thomas. 1485–1540. Malleus mona-chorum, Hammer of the Monks. Rose from humble beginnings with help from Cardinal Wolsey. Ingratiated himself with Henry VIII, encouraging his first divorce and promising to make him rich. Very active in dissolution of monasteries; served in many high offices before losing favour by encouraging marriage to Anne of Cleves whom Henry disliked. Sent to the tower and beheaded.

Cumberland, William Augustus, Duke of. 1721–65. Fat son of George II, defeated Prince Charles at Culloden 1746, winning nickname of Butcher Cumberland for his brutality.

Douglas. Ancient Scottish family, often so powerful that they were a threat to the Crown. Divided into the Black Douglases and the Red Douglases. The Black Douglases were finally subdued by James II. The Red Douglases, who 'rose upon the ruins of the Black', held considerable power until deposed by James V.

Duns Scotus, Johannes. c. 1265–1308. One of the greatest of the medieval scholars, joined Franciscans, studied and lectured on philosophy and theology in Oxford, Paris, Cologne.

Fingal, or Fionn MacCumhail. c. 3rd century. Legendary Irish warrior and hunter, dominating Gaelic sagas. His band of men were the original Fenians, defending Ireland. Traditionally father of Ossian.

Graham of Claverhouse, John, Viscount ('Bonnie Dundee'). 1648–89. Royalist and notorious persecutor of Covenanters. Led early Jacobite rebellion after James VII/II was deposed, and was killed at Killiecrankie.

Hamilton, Patrick. 1502–28. Proto-martyr of Scottish Reformation, influenced by Erasmus and Luther. He returned to his native Scotland and was burned for heresy by Archbishop James Beaton at St Andrews.

Hertford, Edward Seymour, Earl of. 1506–52. Leading aggressor in Henry VIII's 'Rough Wooing' of Scotland, to punish them for cancelling marriage between Mary, Queen of Scots, and Henry's son, Edward. He was responsible for appalling destruction to many of Scotland's finest Lowland buildings, including the Border abbeys.

Hogg, James. 1770–1835. Protégé of Sir Walter Scott, known as the 'Ettrick Shepherd'. Prolific poet and novelist.

Johnson, Samuel. 1709–84. English lexicographer, critic and poet, whose reputation as a man and a conversationalist is as great as his literary fame. Dogmatic, unreasonable, humble, pious and loveable, his account of his tour of the Hebrides with James Boswell, in 1773, makes marvellous reading.

Jones, John Paul. 1747–92. Born in Kirkcudbrightshire, son of a gardener. He received commission in American Navy and returned to harass the English, but always with honour. Stories are told of his chivalrous treatment of his victims.

Knox, John. c. 1502–72. Leading Scottish reformer. Spent 19 months as French galley-slave, returning to preach fiery iconoclastic sermons in Perth and St Andrews in 1559 which led to destruction of monasteries. Minister of St Giles in Edinburgh, during which time he tangled with Mary, Queen of Scots. The phrase 'monstrous regiment of women' was coined from his pamphlet called: 'The First Blast of the Trumpet Against the Monstrous Regiment of Women'. Although dogmatic, he had a keen sense of humour. As a 51-year-old-widower, he married a girl of 16.

Lauder, Sir Harry. 1870–1950. Mill boy and miner who became a much-loved writer and interpreter of Scottish songs, including 'The Road to the Isles'.

Leslie, David. 1601–82. Scottish Covenanter and General. Defeated Montrose at Battle of Philiphaugh. Supported Charles II in 1650 and was defeated by Cromwell at Dunbar. Imprisoned in Tower of London till Restoration of Monarchy, and then made Lord Newark.

Lorimer, Sir Robert. 1864–1929. Architect responsible for Thistle Chapel in St Giles Cathedral, Scottish War Memorial in Edinburgh Castle, and restoration of many castles and abbeys as well as important houses and buildings.

Macdonald, Flora. 1722–90. Born in South Uist. Tacksman father died when she was two. Adopted at 13 by Lady Clanranald, wife of chief of clan, and brought up in Skye. She smuggled Prince Charles from Benbecula to Skye, disguised as her maid, Betty Burke, thus helping to save his life. Was imprisoned for a year on a troopship. Married son of Macdonald of Kingsburgh and entertained Dr Johnson during his tour of Hebrides in 1773. Emigrated with family to North Carolina where her husband became a brigadier-general in American War of Independence. Returned to Scotland in 1779 and died at Kingsburgh.

MacGregor, Rob Roy. 1671–1734. Known as Rob Roy (Red Robert) from colour of his hair. Cattle-raider and smuggler, romanticized by Walter Scott as philanthropic Robin Hood. Died peacefully, having been imprisoned in London and pardoned.

Mackintosh, Charles Rennie. 1868–1928. Architect, born in Glasgow. He made the 'Glasgow style' famous and exercised considerable influence on European design. His style was simple and uncluttered. The best example of his work is the Glasgow School of Art.

Macpherson, James. 1736–96. Scottish poet who 'translated' the Ossianic poems. Many believed that these works were genuine and they were certainly of great value, but others, including Dr Johnson, doubted their authenticity and it is now believed that Macpherson collected a quantity of Gaelic material and composed his own poems from them. In their own right, whatever the source, they are a valuable and beautiful contribution to Gaelic past.

Monk, George. 1608–69. Parliamentary General in Scotland, fighting for Cromwell at Dunbar and then Governor of Scotland in 1653–8. When Cromwell died he saw that the only way to heal the turmoil in Britain was to restore the Monarchy and he was instrumental in bringing Charles II back to the throne.

Monmouth, Duke of. 1649–85. Bastard son of Charles II by Lucy Waters, he claimed that his parents had been married and raised a revolt against James VII/II, for which he was executed.

Moray, James Stewart. Regent. 1531–70. Bastard son of James V, half-brother to Mary, Queen of Scots. Sided with Lords of the Congregation and became Regent on Mary's abdication. Shot while riding through Linlithgow.

Ossian. 3rd-century Gaelic bard, possibly son of Fingal, chief of the Fenians, semi-mythical military body said to have been raised for defence of Ireland against Norse. Countless tales told. (*See* Macpherson, above.)

Queensberry 'Old Q', 4th Duke of. 1724–1810. Notorious gambler, despoiled many tree plantations in Scotland, to pay his debts.

Ramsay, Allan. 1686–1758. Scottish poet, best known for 'The Gentle Shepherd'.

Ramsay, Allan. 1713–84. Son of above. Famous portrait painter.

Scott, Sir Walter. 1771–1832. Prolific poet and novelist. Remarkable for his efforts to pay off debts of £130,000 after collapse of his publisher, hence the amazing volume of his work. He also did much for Scotland after the despair that followed Culloden. It was he who organized the search for the Scottish Regalia, and he who organized the State Visit of George IV.

Stevenson, Robert. 1772–1850. Scottish engineer responsible for many important lighthouses, including Bell Rock.

Stevenson, Robert Louis. 1850–94. Grandson of above and son of another engineer. Prolific writer, best known for *Treasure Island*, *Kidnapped*, *The Master of Ballantrae* and *Dr Jekyll and Mr Hyde*.

Telford, Thomas. 1757–1834. Scottish engineer famous for his bridges, many of which still exist, his roads and his canals, including the Caledonian Canal.

Thomas the Rhymer. *c.* 1220–97. Thomas Learmont of Erceldoune (Earlston), Scottish seer and poet, many of whose prophecies were fulfilled. Said to have lived with the Fairy Queen for three years in the Eildon Hills. He foretold the death of Alexander III at his wedding feast.

Wade, George. 1673–1748. British general, Irish by birth, sent to Scotland in 1724 to try to bring the Highlands under control. Built a system of metalled roads and bridges that opened up the north.

Warbeck, Perkin. *c.* 1474–99. Claimed to be one of the Princes in the Tower. Put forward by English Yorkists as rightful king. Made three futile 'invasions', was caught and executed. He was in fact the son of a Flemish boatman.

Wishart, George. *c.* 1513–46. Scottish reformer, burned by Cardinal David Beaton in St Andrews.

Wolf of Badenoch. died 1394. Bastard son of Robert II, Alexander Stewart, Earl of Buchan. Also known as 'Big Alastair, Son of the King'. Brutal and merciless, terrorizing the countryside from his castles of Ruthven and Lochindorb. Excommunicated by Bishop of Elgin in 1390, for which he destroyed Elgin Cathedral and much else.

Chronology

AD **83** Defeat of Picts at battle of Mons Graupius by Roman Agricola.

141–2 Building of Antonine Wall.

397 Founding of Christian church at Whithorn by St Ninian.

410 Departure of Romans from Britain.

500 Invasion of Scotland by Irish Scots, settlement of Dalriada.

563 Landing of St Columba in Iona, conversion of Picts to Christianity begins.

794 Invasion of Hebrides by Norsemen.

844–60 Kenneth Macalpine unites Picts and Scots.

1034 Whole of Scotland united into one kingdom under Duncan I.

1040 Duncan I murdered by Macbeth who is in turn murdered by Malcolm Canmore.

1057–93 Anglicizing of Scotland under Queen Margaret.

1102 Western Isles granted to Magnus of Orkney.

1124–53 David I founds many abbeys and burghs, grants land to Normans.

1174 William the Lion forced to acknowledge supremacy of Henry II.

1214 Alexander II, Golden Age of Scottish history.

1263 Battle of Largs, defeat by Alexander III of King Haakon of Norway. Annexation of the Hebrides.

1286 Death of Alexander III, succeeded by Margaret of Norway.

1290 Death of Maid of Norway at sea on her way to Scotland.

1291 Edward I arbitrates between Robert the Bruce and John Balliol. Balliol gets crown.

1296 Balliol renounces his crown in favour of Edward I. Scottish nobility agree to treaty of mutual assistance with Philip IV of France – the beginning of the Auld Alliance.

1297–8 William Wallace stirs up resistance, defeats Edward at Stirling Bridge, and is defeated at Falkirk. Goes into hiding.

1305 Capture and execution of William Wallace.

1306 Robert the Bruce slays John Comyn and is crowned at Scone.

1307 Edward I dies.

1314 Battle of Bannockburn, Bruce defeats English.

1320 Declaration of Arbroath.

1326 First Scottish Parliament at Cambuskenneth.

1328 By Treaty of Edinburgh England recognizes Robert the Bruce as king of independent Scotland.

1346 Battle of Neville's Cross. David II taken prisoner by English.

1371 Robert Stewart crowned Robert II, first Stewart king.

1406 James I captured, Duke of Albany becomes guardian of Scotland.

1414 Foundation of St Andrews, Scotland's first university.

1450–5 Struggle for supremacy between Stewarts and Douglases. Douglases crushed by James II.

1469 Orkney and Shetland pledged to James III as part of dowry of his wife, Margaret of Denmark.

1476 Overthrow of Lords of the Isles.

1488 James III defeated and killed by rebels at Sauchieburn.

1491 Perkin Warbeck claims English throne, encouraged by James IV.

1503 James IV marries Margaret Tudor, daughter of Henry VII.

1513 Battle of Flodden, death of James IV.

1528 Burning of Patrick Hamilton, proto-martyr of Reformation.

1538 Marriage of James V to Marie de Guise-Lorraine.

1542 Defeat of Scots at Solway Moss, death of James V, accession of his infant daughter, Mary.

1544 Rough Wooing, devastation of Lowland Scotland by Henry VIII.

1546 Burning of George Wishart, murder of Cardinal Beaton.

1554 Regency of Marie de Guise.

1557 Signing of first Protestant Covenant.

1558 Marriage of Mary to Dauphin of France, later Francis II.

1559 John Knox returns to Scotland. Reformers destroy the abbey church at Scone.

1561 Mary, Queen of Scots returns to Scotland.

1565 Marriage of Mary to Darnley. Moray's rebellion is suppressed.

1566 Murder of Rizzio. Birth of James VI.

1567 Murder of Darnley, marriage of Mary to Bothwell, defeat, imprisonment and abdication.

1568 Mary escapes to England and is imprisoned by Elizabeth.

1570 Moray is assassinated and Lennox becomes regent of Scotland.

1582 James VI is abducted in the Ruthven raid.

1587 Mary, Queen of Scots is executed.

1603 Accession of James VI to English throne making him James VI/I (VI of Scotland, I of England). Establishment of Episcopacy in Scotland.

1637 Riots of Edinburgh against Charles I's new prayer book.

1638 Signing of National Covenant to uphold Presbyterian worship.

1643 Signing of Solemn League and Covenant recognized by English Parliament.

1645 Battle of Philiphaugh. Defeat of Royalist Montrose by Covenanters under Leslie.

1646 Charles surrenders to the Scots.

1647 The Scots give Charles to the English.

1649 Execution of Charles I, Charles II proclaimed King in Scotland.

1650 Signing of Covenants by Charles II. Invasion of Scotland by Cromwell.

1660 Restoration of monarchy.

1662 Renunciation of Covenants by Charles II and re-establishment of Episcopacy.

1666 Start of the Killing Times, persecution of Covenanters.

1688 James VII/II tries to restore Catholicism. He is deposed in favour of William and Mary.

1689 Highlanders, under Claverhouse, Bonnie Dundee, defeat King's army at Killiecrankie.

1692 Massacre of Glencoe.

1695 Bank of Scotland founded and Company of Scotland established to colonize Darien coast.

1699 Darien colony evacuated.

c.1700–c.1800 The Age of Enlightenment

1707 Union of Parliaments.

1715 Rebellion in favour of the Old Pretender.

1736 The Porteous Riots, Scots rebel against English domination.

1745/6 Final Jacobite rebellion. Defeat of Prince Charles Edward Stuart at Battle of Culloden. Repression of Highlands. Soon followed by the beginning of the Highland Clearances which lasted for over 100 years and depopulated the Highlands.

1760 Carron Ironworks starts production.

1845/6 Irish potato famine spreads to Scotland causing starvation and terrible hardship.

1947 Founding of Edinburgh International Festival, putting Scotland back on the cultural map.

1970s North Sea oil industry developed.

1979 Scotland rejects devolution in a referendum.

1997 Referendum again. Scots vote by 74% for a Scottish Parliament.

1999 First Edinburgh Parliament.

Monarchs

Kenneth Macalpine AD 843–58
Donald 858–62
Constantine I 862–77
Aed 877–8
Eochaid and Giric (joint kingship) 878–89
Donald II 889–900
Constantine II 900–43
Malcolm I 943–54
Indulf 954–62
Dubh 962–6
Culen 966–71
Kenneth II 971–95
Constantine III 995–7
Kenneth III 997–1005
Malcolm II 1005–34
Duncan I 1034–40
Macbeth 1040–57
Lulach 1058
Malcolm III, Canmore 1058–93
Donald III Bane 1093–4 (six months)
Duncan II 1094 (six months)
Donald III Bane 1094–7
Edgar 1097–1107
Alexander I 1107–24
David I 1124–53
Malcolm IV, the Maiden 1153–65
William I, the Lion 1165–1214
Alexander II 1214–49
Alexander III 1249–86
Margaret, Maid of Norway 1286–90
John Balliol 1292–6
Interregnum 1296–1306
Robert I (the Bruce) 1306–29
David II 1329–71

Stewarts

Robert II 1371–90
Robert III 1390–1406
James I 1406–37
James II 1437–60
James III 1460–88
James IV 1488–1513
James V 1513–42
Mary 1542–67
James VI / I 1567–1625
Charles I 1625–49
The Commonwealth 1649–60
Charles II 1660–85
James VII/II 1685–8
William and Mary 1689–94
William (alone) 1694–1702
Anne 1702–14

Hanoverians

George I 1714–27
George II 1727–60
George III 1760–1820
George IV 1820–30
William II/IV 1830–7

Saxe-Coburg-Gotha

Victoria 1837–1901
Edward I/VII 1901–10

Windsors

George V 1910–36
Edward II/VIII 1936
George VI 1936–52
Elizabeth II 1952–

Glossary

aber mouth of: confluence of (rivers)
advocate barrister
aird point, promontory
allt stream
an of the
aros dwelling
athole brose a delicious drink made from whisky, honey, oatmeal and cream, left to soak and squeezed through a cloth: once tasted, never forgotten
auch a field
auld old
aye yes
bairn child
bal town, home
ban fair
bannock oatmeal pancake-ish scone-ish cake
bap bread roll
bard poet
barr crest
beag small
bealach, balloch mountain pass
bean woman
ben, beinn mountain
bhlair plain
blether talk nonsense
bogle frightening ghost
bothy rough hut, temporary accommodation
brae hill
bramble blackberry
branks bridle, halter
braw fine
breeks trousers
bridie pie made with circle of pastry folded over filling of meat, onions, vegetables, etc.
brig bridge
broch prehistoric round stone tower with hollow walls, enclosing cell-like galleries and stairs, often built round a well, purpose only guessed at, probably dwelling for chief and refuge for clan in times of danger

burn stream
byre barn
cadger pedlar
cailleach old woman
cairn stone monument
callan(t) youth
cam crooked
canny prudent
caolas firth
capercailie wood-grouse
car curve
ceann head
ceilidh informal social gathering among neighbours, often with spontaneous singing, music, story telling, etc.
chanter double-reeded pipe on which bagpipe tune is played
cil church
clach stone
cladach beach
clarty dirty
claymore sword
cleg horsefly
close shared entry to tenement, enclosure, courtyard
cnoc hillock
collie sheepdog, wood
corbie crow
corrie hollow
crack conversation
craig rock
crannog small man-made island dating from Iron Age. Stones piled on wooden base with easily defended single dwelling on top, often reached by a sunken causeway
creel pannier-type basket, also lobster pot
croft smallholding
crowdie soft cheese
cuddy donkey
cul recess

cutty short (cutty sark, short petticoat; cutty stool, stool of repentance)
dal field
dalr valley
damph deer, steer
daunder saunter
ding knock, beat
dominie schoolmaster
doo dove
doo'cot dovecote
dour dry, humourless
douse sweet, gentle
dram officially one-eighth fluid ounce: commonly generous tot of whisky
dreich dreary, boring
drochit bridge
dross coal dust
drove road tracks used for herding (droving) cattle or sheep to market, often long distances
druim, drum ridge
dubh dark, black
dun hillfort
dux best pupil
dyke wall of stones or turf
dysart hermit's retreat, desert
eaglais church
eas waterfall, gorge
eilean island
ey island
factor land agent, usually of private estate
fada long
fail rock
fank sheepfold
fash trouble, upset, 'dinna fash yersel' – don't trouble yourself
fear man
feu feudal tenure of land with rent paid in kind or money
fey susceptible to supernatural influence
fillebeg kilt
fionn gleaming, white
firth wide mouth of river, estuary
flit remove, move house
fou full (of drink)
fraoch heather
gearr short
geodha chasm
gil ravine
girdle iron baking tray
glass grey
glen valley
gleo mist

gobha blacksmith
gorm blue, green
gowk fool
greet cry
grieve farm manager
harling rough-cast facing to walls
haver talk nonsense
heugh hillock
hog unshorn lamb
Hogmanay New Year's Eve
holm low ground by river, islet in river
hope bay
how burial mound
howe low-lying ground, hollow
howff meeting place, refuge, burial ground
howk dig
ilk same, of that ilk – surname and name of property the same
inch island
inver mouth of river
jougs iron neck collar used as instrument of public punishment
kail cabbage
kailyard cabbage patch, back yard
keek peep
kelpie water-sprite, water-horse
ken know
kenspeckle easily recognizable, conspicuous
kil burial place, church
kin head (of loch, river)
kirk church
knock, knowe knoll, hillock
kye cattle
kyle strait, narrow channel between two points of land
lag, laggan hollow, dip
laird owner of estate
land tenement
larach site of ruin
larig, learg mountain pass
law round hill
leac flagstone
leana plain
liath grey
links dunes
linn, linne pool
lis garden on site of fortress
loan lane
loch, lochan lake, small lake
lug ear
lum chimney
machair sand-peat lowland bordering seashore

manse minister's house (ecclesiastical)
maol bare headland
march boundary
meikle large
mon moor
mor great
moy plain
muc, muic sow
muckle large
mull promontory
neeps of the turnips (bashed neeps – mashed turnips); turnips in Scotland refer to English swedes
neuk nose
ob, oba, oban bay
ochter high
pit dip
plenishing furniture, domestic equipment
ploy activity
poke bag
policies grounds within an estate
poll pool
provost mayor
puddock frog
quaich shallow, two-handled drinking bowl
rath fort
reek smoke
reidh smooth
rig ridge
ross peninsula
roup auction
ru, rhu, row, rubha point
sark shift, shirt
saugh willow
scunner dislike
selkie seal
sgeir, skerry sea, rock
sgor, scuir, sgurr sharp rock
sheiling hut for summer pasture
sherrif county court judge
shinty hockey
siccar certain
siller silver (money)

slochd hollow, grave
sonsie bonnie
soutar cobbler
spittal hospice
stob stake, point
strath broad valley
strone nose, promontory
struan, struth stream
swither vacillate
syne ago
tarbert, tarbet isthmus
tassie up
thing parliament, council
thole endure
thrang thronged
thrawn awkward
tigh house
tir land
tobar well
tocher dowry
tod fox
tom hillock
toom empty
torr hill
tow rope
tulloch, tilly, tully knoll
uachdar upper, high
uamh cave
uig sheltered bay
uisge, esk water
uisge beatha water of life (whisky)
unco strange, very
usquebaugh whisky
vennel alley
voe narrow bay, fiord
wean child
weems caves
whaup curlew
whinn gorse
wick, vik bay
wight strong
wynd alley
yett gate

Further Reading

Non-fiction

Beveridge, H., *The Sobieski Stuarts.*

Black, David, *All the First Minister's Men.*

Boswell, James, *Journal of a Tour to the Hebrides. See also* Samuel Johnson, below.

Bray, Elizabeth, *The Discovery of the Hebrides.*

Daiches, David (editor), *Edinburgh: A Travellers' Companion.* Excellent new anthology of historical accounts of the city, its life and customs; also, *A Companion to Scottish Culture.*

Duff, David (editor), *Queen Victoria's Highland Journal.*

Fraser, Antonia, *Mary, Queen of Scots.*

Geoffrey of Monmouth, Lewis Thorpe (translator), *The History of the Kings of Britain.*

Grant, Elizabeth, *Memoires of a Highland Lady.*

Grant, I. F., *Highland Folk Ways.*

Haldane, A. R. B., *The Drove Roads of Scotland.*

Harris, Paul, *Scotland: An Anthology.* Delightful, idiosyncratic literary collection covering all aspects of Scotland.

Haswell-Smith, Hamish, *Scottish Islands.*

Johnson, Samuel, *A Journey to the Western Islands.* This and Boswell's *Journal of a Tour to the Hebrides* can be obtained in one volume, and they should be read together. They are fascinating to read as you visit the places they went to.

Keay, John, *Highland Drove.* An account of droving cattle today using the old methods and routes. Good descriptions.

Linklater, Eric, *The Prince in the Heather.* Prince Charlie's escape after Culloden.

Mackenzie, Alexander, *The Prophecies of the Brahan Seer.*

Mackenzie, Osgood, *A Hundred Years in the Highlands.*

Maclean, Alasdair, *A Macdonald for the Prince.* The story of Neil MacEachen, native of Uist and father of Napoleon's Marshal Macdonald.

Maclean, Calum I., *The Highlands.* Charming reminiscences, recently reprinted to include an introduction by his brother Sorley, the poet, with outstanding photographs by his nephew, Cailean.

MacLean, Charles, *The Fringe of Gold.* Wonderful collection of anecdotes about the fishing villages of the east coast.

Maclean, Fitzroy, *A Concise History of Scotland* and *Bonnie Prince Charlie.* Beautifully written and entirely unbiased.

Martin, M., *A Description of the Western Islands of Scotland.* James Thin have reprinted a facsimile of this 1716 gem.

Maxwell, Gavin, *The House of Elrig.* About his childhood in Galloway; also *Harpoon at a Venture; Ring of Bright Water; The Rocks Remain; Raven Seek Thy Brother.* All describe Maxwell's fascinating life in the Western Highlands.

Mitchell, Ian, *Isles of the West*, a truly balanced, up-to-date, no-nonsense view of the Western Isles and their people. Mitchell sails from Islay north through the islands to Harris and back via the Shiants and Summer Isles, Skye and Mull. On the way he examines all the contemporary problems that beset the modern crofter whose way of life is more and more influenced by the different bodies of conservationists with their various acronyms. Essential reading.

Moncreiffe of that Ilk, Sir Iain, *The Highland Clans.* Not particularly readable, but an erudite book of great value.

Morton, H. V., *In Search of Scotland* and *In Scotland Again.* These two were written in 1929 and 1933 and are as fresh and readable today as then.

Murray, W. H., *The Islands of Western Scotland.*

Prebble, John, *The Lion in the North.*

Rea, F. C., *A School in South Uist* (recently reprinted).

Scott, Walter, *Tales of a Grandfather*. The history of Scotland as told by Walter Scott to his young grandson. Delightful.

Smout, T. C., *A History of the Scottish People 1560–1830* and *A Century of the Scottish People, 1830–1950*.

Steel, Tom, *Scotland's Story* and *The Life and Death of St Kilda*.

Wallace, Ian, *Reflections on Scotland*. A traveller's scrap-book, by the well-known Scottish singer.

Wigan, Michael, *Scottish Highland Estate: Preserving an Environment*.

Novels

Banks, Iain, *The Crow Road*.

Buchan, John, *John Macnab, The Thirty-Nine Steps*, etc.

Crichton Smith, Iain, *Consider the Lilies*. Charming, sad story about the Clearances.

Dunnet, Dorothy, *King Hereafter*.

Ellis, Alice Thomas, *The Inn at the Edge of the World*.

Gibbon, Lewis Grassic, *A Scots Quair*.

Gray, Alasdair, *Lanark*.

Gunn, Neil, *The Silver Darlings*.

Howarth, David, *Shetland Bus*.

MacArthur, A., *No Mean City*. Brilliant description of slum life in the Gorbals.

Mackay, Colin, *The Song of the Forest*. A beautiful piece of contemporary writing, giving a picture of life in the Dark Ages. Also *The Sound of the Sea* – equally well written.

Mackenzie, Compton, *Whisky Galore*, and anything else by him.

Profumo, David, *Sea Music*.

Scott, Walter. His vast output includes: *Waverley*, his first novel, about Jacobites; *Redgauntlet*, about how Prince Charlie returned to Scotland to try his luck once more; *Fair Maid of Perth*, set in Perth at the end of the 14th century; *Old Mortality*, about Covenanters; and *Rob Roy*.

Stevenson, Robert Louis, *Kidnapped* and *Catriona*, based on the story of the Appin murder.

Poetry

Barke, James (edited and introduced by), *Poems and Songs of Robert Burns*.

MacDiarmid, Hugh. Anything by him.

Maclean, Sorley, *From Wood to Ridge*. Haunting poems, in Gaelic and English.

McCaig, Norman, *Anthology of Poetry*.

William McGonagall, Poet and Tragedian, *Poetic Gems Selected From the Works of William McGonagall, Poet and Tragedian*. Scotland's worst poet – compulsive reading.

Light Relief

HRH The Prince of Wales, *The Old Man of Lochnagar*.

Author's acknowledgements

The author would like to thank members of the Scottish Tourist Board for their valuable help in updating this edition, especially: Karen Leithhead, Karen Wilson, Judith Mair, Annique Adamson, Elaine Dickie, Griselda Cowen, Sandra Hadden, Allyson Kennedy, Angela McCallum, Mary Kettle, Fiona Meikle, Fiona Jack, Gillian Dykes, Elaine Tulloch, Maurice Mullay, Angela Shaw. She is also indebted to the following experts: David Murray, on piping; Michael Wigan, on fishing; Bruce Critchley, on golf; Chris Hines, on surfing. She would like to thank her editor, Catherine Charles, for her patience and hard work. As always, her greatest debt is to her daughter, Mary, without whose knowledge of Scotland and painstaking red pen these books could not be written.

Index

Main page references are in **bold**; Page references to maps are in *italics*.

Scotland touring atlas

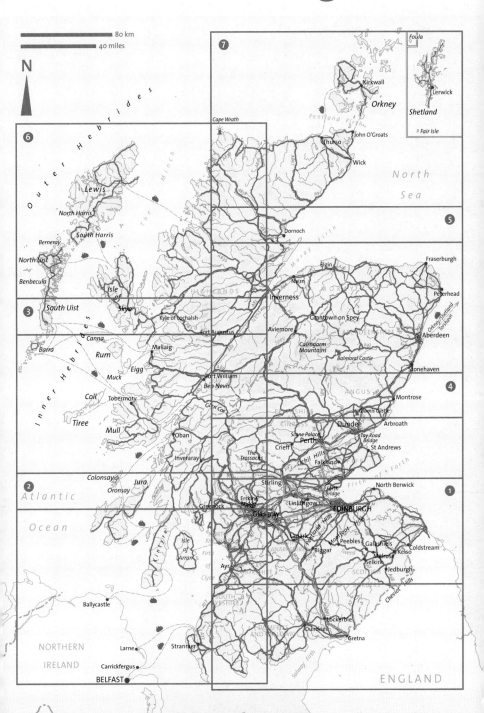

80 km
40 miles

N

Foula

⑦

Kirkwall
Orkney

Pentland Firth

Lerwick

Shetland

John O'Groats

Thurso

Fair Isle

Wick

⑥

Outer Hebrides

The Minch

Lewis

North *Sea*

North Harris

South Harris

Berneray

⑤

Dornoch

North Uist

Moray Firth

Fraserburgh

Benbecula

Elgin

Nairn

Peterhead

Isle of Skye

Inverness

Grantown on Spey

Aberdeen

③ South Uist

Inner Hebrides

Kyle of Lochalsh

Aviemore

DEESIDE

Fort Augustus

Stonehaven

Canna

Mallaig

Cairngorm Mountains

Balmoral Castle

Barra

Rum

Eigg

Fort William

Muck

Ben Nevis

ANGUS

Coll

Tobermory

Glen Coe

Montrose

Tiree

Glamis Castle

④

Mull

Oban

Dundee

Arbroath

The Trossachs

Scone Palace

Perth

Inveraray

Crieff

Tay Road Bridge

St Andrews

Colonsay

Jura

Ochil Hills

Falkland

Oronsay

Stirling

Firth of Forth

②

Forth Bridge

North Berwick

Atlantic

Erskine Bridge

Linlithgow

①

EDINBURGH

Greenock

Glasgow

Ocean

Lanark

Pentland Hills

Peebles

Galashiels

Isle of Arran

Biggar

Moorfoot Hills

Coldstream

Melrose

Kelso

Kintyre

Ayr

Selkirk

Jedburgh

Firth of Clyde

Cheviot Hills

Ballycastle

Lockerbie

Dumfries

Gretna

NORTHERN
IRELAND

Larne

Stranraer

Solway Firth

ENGLAND

Carrickfergus

BELFAST

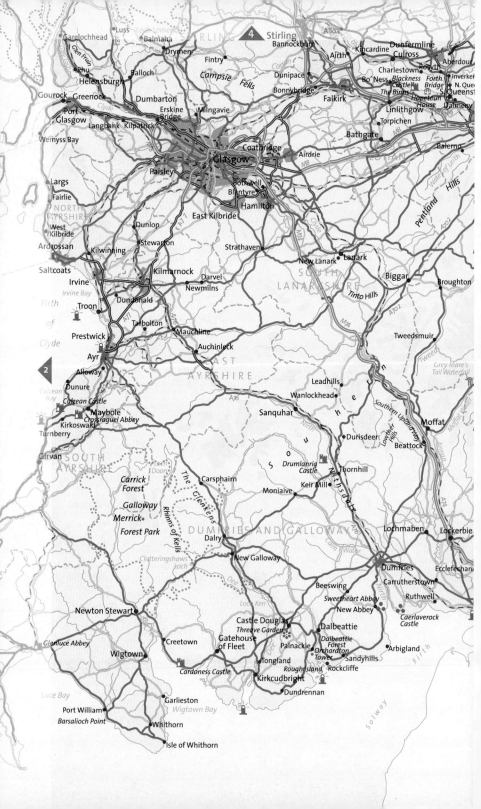

Kirkcaldy

Kinghorn
Burntisland
Inchcolm
thing
Firth of Forth
ensferry
ferry
Inchkeith
Aberlady Bay
Dirleton
North Berwick
Bass Rock
Tantallon Castle
Gullane
EDINBURGH
Leith Port Seton
Cramond
Portobello
Musselburgh
Prestonpans
Aberlady Whitekirk
Athelstaneford
East
Linton
Dunbar
Barns Ness
Traprain
Law
Stenton
Fast
Castle
St Abb's Head
St Abbs
Haddington
Oldhamstocks
Garvald
Coldingham
Gifford
Dalkeith
Scottish Mining Museum
Crichton
Roslin
Penicuik
Gorebridge
Howgate
Temple
Moorfoot Hills
Chirnside
Duns
Manderston
Foulden
Paxton
Eyemouth
Ayton
Berwick-upon-Tweed
Lammermuir Hills
Southern Upland Way
Thirlestane
Lauder
Greenlaw
Ladykirk
Neidpath
Castle
Peebles
Upland
SCOTTISH BORDERS
Coldstream
Innerleithen
Galashiels
Mellerstain
Earlston
Floors Castle
Kelso
Tweed
Traquair
House
Abbotsford
House
Melrose
Smailholm
Tower
Bowhill
Selkirk
Dryburgh
Abbey
Kirk Yetholm
St Mary's
Loch
Jedburgh
The Cheviot
Hawick
Denholm
Hills
Eskdalemuir
Forest
Teviothead
Cheviot
Eskdale
Eskdalemuir
Newcastleton
Langholm
Canonbie
Kirtlebridge
Kirkpatrick Fleming
Annan
Gretna

E N G L A N D

N

40 km
20 miles

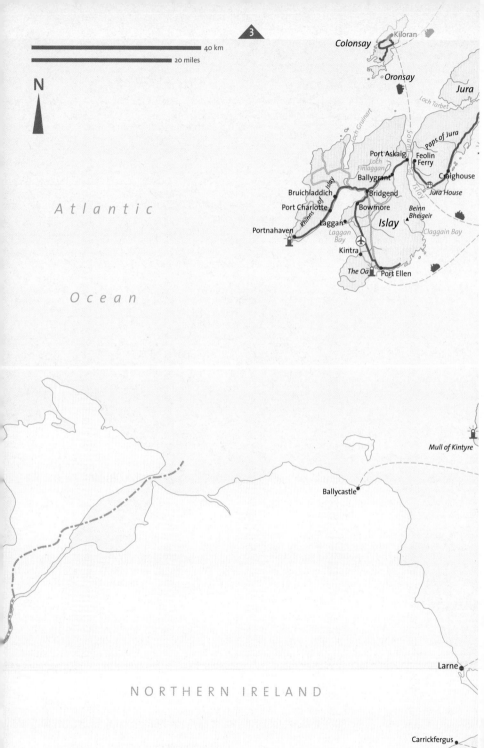

N

40 km

20 miles

3

Atlantic

Ocean

Colonsay

Kiloran

Oronsay

Jura

Loch Tarbet

Pops of Jura

Port Askaig

Loch Finlaggan

Loch Gruinart

Feolin Ferry

Craighouse

Ballygrant

Jura House

Bruichladdich

Bridgend

Port Charlotte

Bowmore

Beinn Bheigeir

Islay

Portnahaven

Laggan

Laggan Bay

Rhinns of Islay

Claggain Bay

Kintra

The Oa

Port Ellen

Mull of Kintyre

Ballycastle

Larne

NORTHERN IRELAND

Carrickfergus

BELFAST

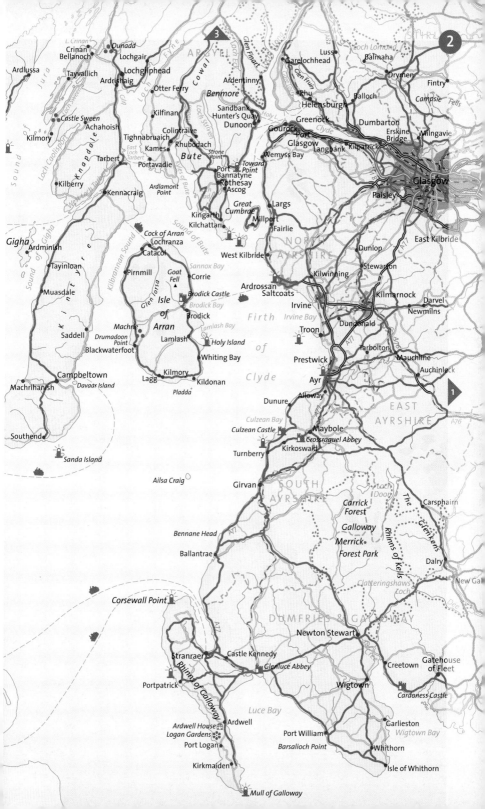

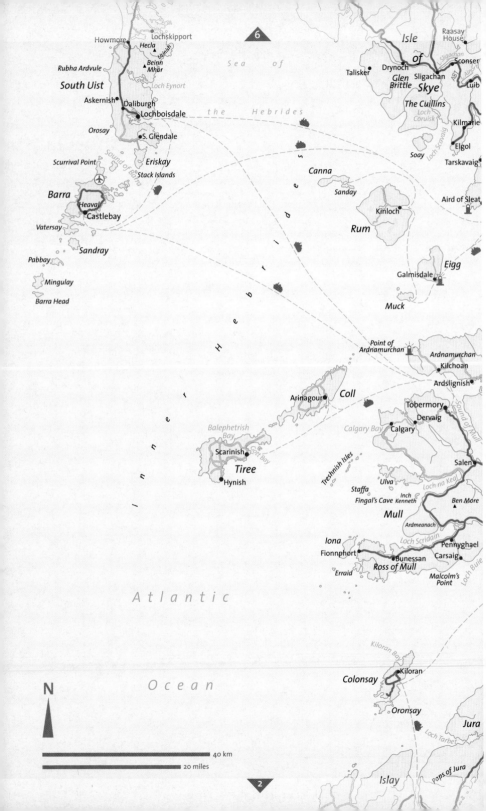

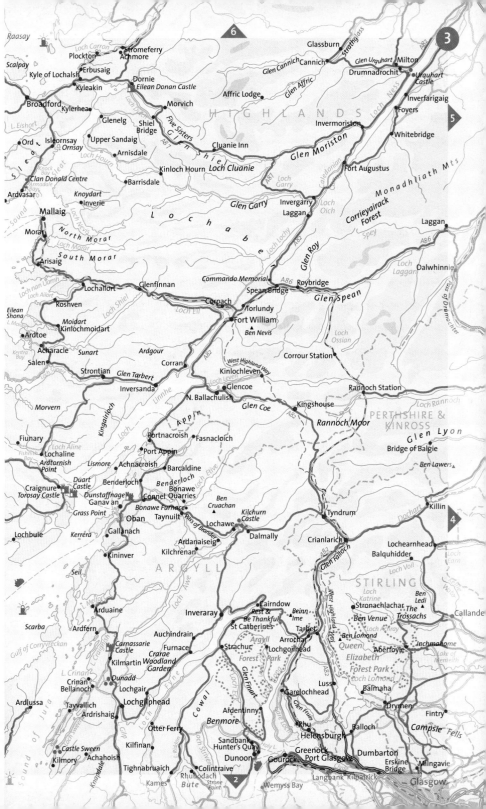

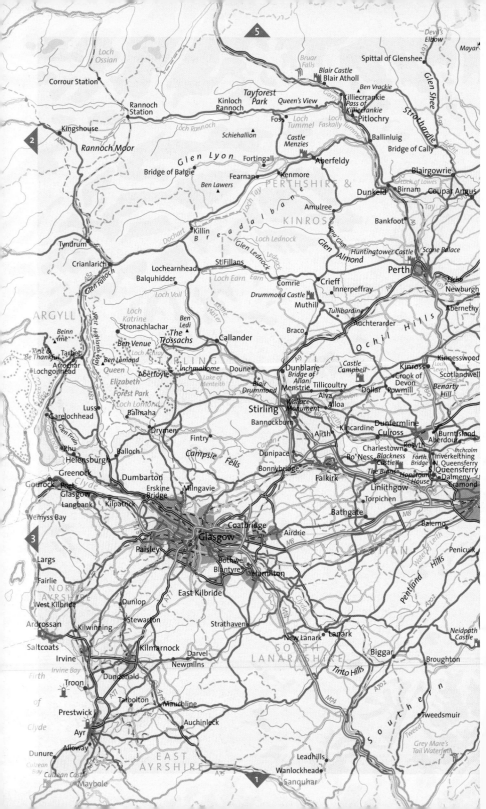

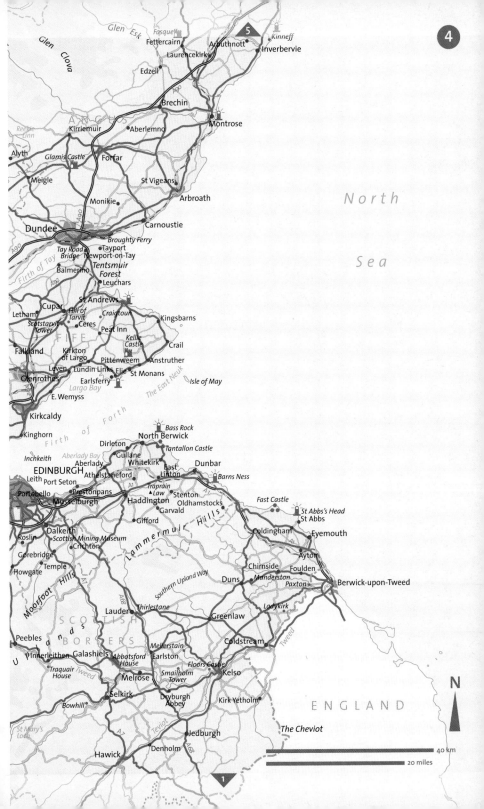

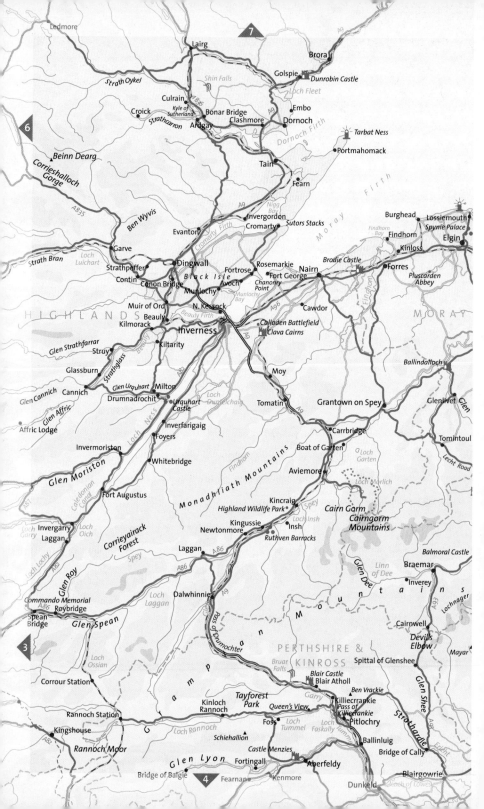

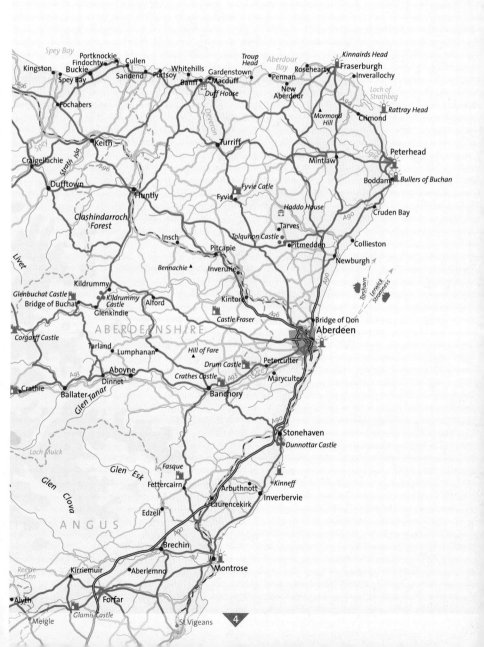

40 km
20 miles

N

Spey Bay
Kingston
Portknockie
Buckie
Findochty
Spey Bay
Fochabers

Cullen
Sandend
Portsoy
Whitehills
Banff
Macduff
Duff House
Gardenstown
Troup Head
Pennan
New Aberdour
Aberdour Bay

Rosehearty
Fraserburgh
Kinnairds Head
Inverallochy
Loch of Strathbeg

Craigellachie
Keith

Dufftown

Huntly
Clashindarroch Forest

Turriff

Mintlaw
Mormond Hill
Crimond
Rattray Head

Peterhead
Boddam
Bullers of Buchan
Cruden Bay

Livet

Kildrummy
Glenbuchat Castle
Bridge of Buchat
Kildrummy Castle
Glenkindle

Insch
Pitcapie
Bennachie
Inverurie
Alford

Fyvie
Fyvie Castle
Haddo House
Tarves
Tolquhon Castle
Pitmedden
Colliestoun
Newburgh

Corgarff Castle
Kintore
Castle Fraser

Torbain
Lerwick
Stromness

ABERDEENSHIRE
Tarland
Lumphanan
Hill of Fare
Drum Castle
Crathes Castle
Peterculter
Maryculter
Bridge of Don
Aberdeen

Crathie
Aboyne
Dinnet
Ballater
Glen Tanar
Banchory

Loch Muick
Glen Esk
Fasque
Fettercairn
Arbuthnott
Kinneff
Inverbervie
Laurencekirk

Stonehaven
Dunnottar Castle

Glen
Glen Clova
ANGUS
Edzell

Reekie Linn
Alyth
Meigle
Kirriemuir
Aberlemno
Forfar
Glamis Castle
Brechin
Montrose
St Vigeans

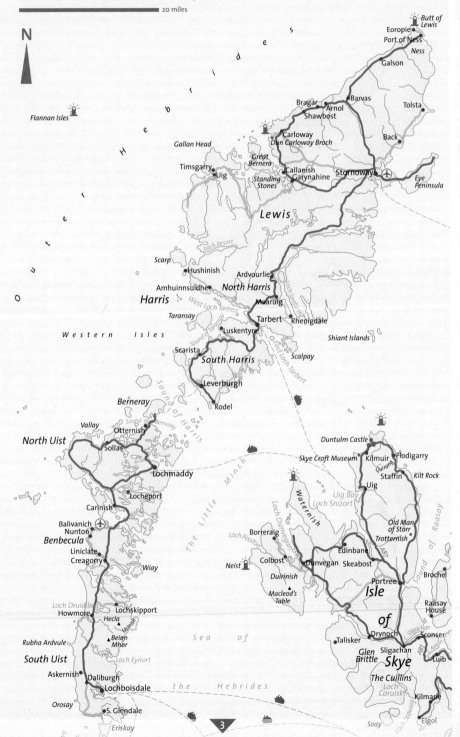

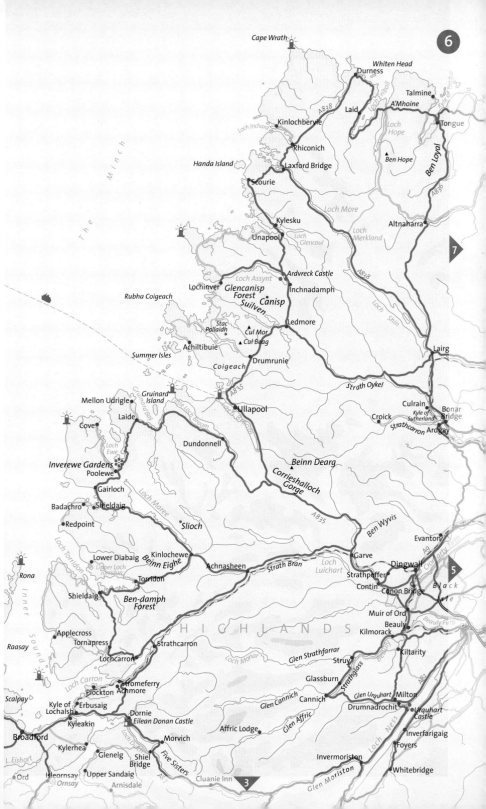

40 km
20 miles

N

Brough of Birsay

Skara Brae

Ring of B

Stromness

Old Man of Hoy
Rackwick

Stromness

Dunnet Head

Cape Wrath

Whiten Head
Durness
Strathy Point
Crosskirk   Scrabster
Dunnet
Dunnet Bay
Portskerra   Dounreay   Thurso
Talmine   Farr Point   Farr
A'Mhoine   Skerray   Kirtomy   Armadale   Melvich
Laid   Bettyhill   Halkirk
Loch Hope
Kinlochbervie   Tongue
Loch Eriboll
Loch Hope
Rhiconich
Ben Hope   Ben Loyal   Strathnaver   Strath Halladale   A9
Laxford Bridge   A836   A897

Loch More

2

Kylesku   Altnaharra   Latheron
Braemore
Unapool   Loch Glencoul   Loch Merkland
Dunbeath
Ardvreck Castle   Berriedale
Loch Assynt   Inchnadamph   A9
Canisp   A838   HIGHLANDS   Strath of Kildonan   A897
Ledmore   Loch Shin   Helmsdale

Helmsdale

Lairg

Strath Oykel   Brora

Shin Falls   Golspie
Culrain   Dunrobin Castle
Croick   Kyle of Sutherland   Loch Fleet
A836   Bonar Bridge   Embo
Strathcarron   Glashmore   Dornoch
Ardgay   A9
Tarbat Ness
Dornoch Firth
Portmahomack

5

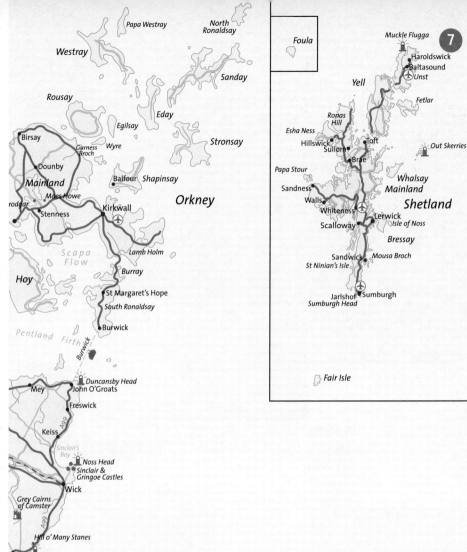

PARIS
Dana Facaros & Michael Pauls

LONDON
Andrew Gumbel

EDINBURGH
Charles Godfrey-Faussett

CADOGANguides

Cadogan City Guides...
the life and soul
of the city

Also available
Amsterdam
Barcelona
Bruges
Brussels
Florence
Madrid
Prague
Rome

CADOGANguides
well travelled well read